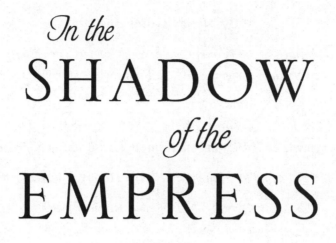

In the
SHADOW
of the
EMPRESS

By Nancy Goldstone

*Daughters of the Winter Queen: Four Remarkable Sisters,
the Crown of Bohemia, and the Enduring Legacy of Mary,
Queen of Scots*

*The Rival Queens: Catherine de' Medici, Her Daughter
Marguerite de Valois, and the Betrayal That Ignited a Kingdom*

The Maid and the Queen: The Secret History of Joan of Arc

*The Lady Queen: The Notorious Reign of Joanna I,
Queen of Naples, Jerusalem, and Sicily*

Four Queens: The Provençal Sisters Who Ruled Europe

Trading Up: Surviving Success as a Woman Trader on Wall Street

By Nancy Goldstone and Lawrence Goldstone

*The Friar and the Cipher: Roger Bacon and the Unsolved Mystery
of the Most Unusual Manuscript in the World*

*Out of the Flames: The Remarkable Story of a Fearless Scholar,
a Fatal Heresy, and One of the Rarest Books in the World*

Warmly Inscribed: The New England Forger and Other Book Tales

Slightly Chipped: Footnotes in Booklore

Used and Rare: Travels in the Book World

Deconstructing Penguins: Parents, Kids, and the Bond of Reading

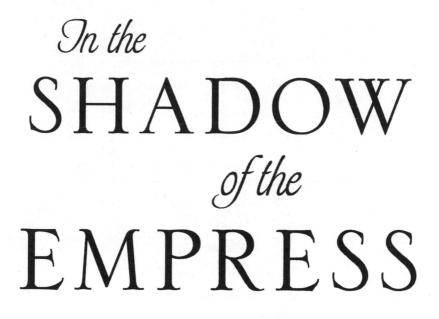

In the SHADOW of the EMPRESS

The Defiant Lives of Maria Theresa,
Mother of Marie Antoinette, and Her Daughters

NANCY GOLDSTONE

Little, Brown and Company
New York • Boston • London

Little, Brown and Company
Hachette Book Group
1290 Avenue of the Americas, New York, NY 10104
littlebrown.com

First Edition: September 2021

Little, Brown and Company is a division of Hachette Book Group, Inc. The Little, Brown name and logo are trademarks of Hachette Book Group, Inc.

The publisher is not responsible for websites (or their content)
that are not owned by the publisher.

The Hachette Speakers Bureau provides a wide range of authors for speaking events. To find out more, go to hachettespeakersbureau.com or call (866) 376-6591.

Illustration credits begin on page 593.

Maps © 2021 by Jeffrey L. Ward

ISBN 978-0-316-44933-5
LCCN 2021930547

Printing 1, 2021

LSC-C

Printed in the United States of America

For Larry, Lee, and Tyler, without whom none of this would matter

Contents

❧

Contents

PART III
In the Shadow of the Empress

I would rather seem weak than unjust, from which God save me.

—Maria Theresa, 1765

You do not know me. I am not a woman like the others, fearful and discouraged.

—Maria Christina, 1789

I leave my justification to time and to Heaven.

—Maria Carolina, 1806

Of all the daughters of Maria Theresa, am I not that one whom fortune has most highly favored?

—Marie Antoinette, 1792

AUSTRIA-HUNGARY
and its Neighbors to the North and West
circa 1750

KINGDOM
OF NORWAY

SCOTLAND

North Sea

IRELAND

KINGDOM OF
DENMARK

KINGDOM OF
GREAT BRITAIN
AND IRELAND

THE AUSTRIAN
NETHERLANDS

ELECTORATE
OF HANOVER

London

The Hague   Leyden
HOLLAND
FLANDERS   BRABANT

English Channel

Antwerp   Turnhout
Ghent   Brussels
Fontenoy   Maastricht   Cologne
HAINAUT   Bonn
Mons Liège Aachen
Jemappes   (Aix-la-Chapelle)

Cherbourg

H O L Y

Compiègne   Sommevesle   Montmédy   Frankfurt   Dettingen
NORMANDY   Reims   Longwy Luxembourg Aschaffenburg
Paris   Valmy   Trèves
St. Cloud Meaux   Varennes   Zweibrücken   Ansbach
Versailles   Chaintrix   Verdun   Metz   Heidelberg
Rambouillet   Châlons   ELECTORATE OF
Fontainebleu   Nancy   ALSACE   BAVARIA
Sens   Stuttgart
DUCHY OF LORRAINE   Strasbourg

Atlantic Ocean

K I N G D O M   O F   F R A N C E

Rhine R.

Rhône R.

SWITZERLAND

SAVOY

PIEDMONT   MILAN

PROVENCE

© 2021 Jeffrey L. Ward

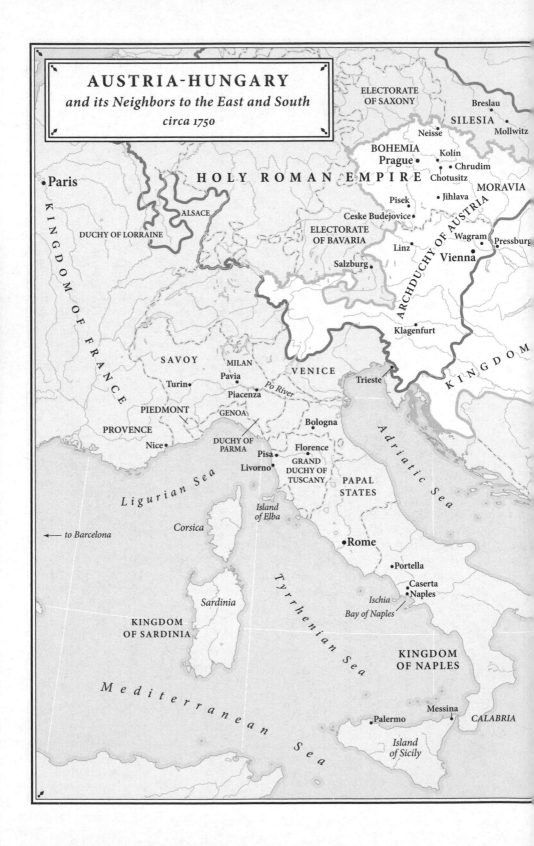

AUSTRIA-HUNGARY
and its Neighbors to the East and South
circa 1750

ELECTORATE
OF SAXONY

Breslau

SILESIA

Neisse · Mollwitz

BOHEMIA · Kolín
Prague · · Chrudim
· Chotusitz
MORAVIA

Pisek · Jihlava

HOLY ROMAN EMPIRE

Paris

ALSACE

Ceske Budejovice ·

DUCHY OF LORRAINE

ELECTORATE
OF BAVARIA

ARCHDUCHY OF AUSTRIA

Wagram · Pressburg

Linz · Vienna

Salzburg ·

KINGDOM OF FRANCE

Klagenfurt ·

KINGDOM

SAVOY

MILAN

VENICE

Trieste

Turin · Pavia ·
Po River
Piacenza ·

PIEDMONT

GENOA

Bologna ·

PROVENCE

Adriatic Sea

DUCHY OF
PARMA

Florence ·

Nice ·

Pisa · Livorno ·

GRAND
DUCHY OF
TUSCANY

PAPAL
STATES

Ligurian Sea

Island
of Elba

Corsica

← to Barcelona

Rome

· Portella

· Caserta
Ischia · Naples
Bay of Naples

Tyrrhenian Sea

Sardinia

KINGDOM
OF SARDINIA

KINGDOM
OF NAPLES

Mediterranean Sea

Messina

· Palermo · · CALABRIA

*Island
of Sicily*

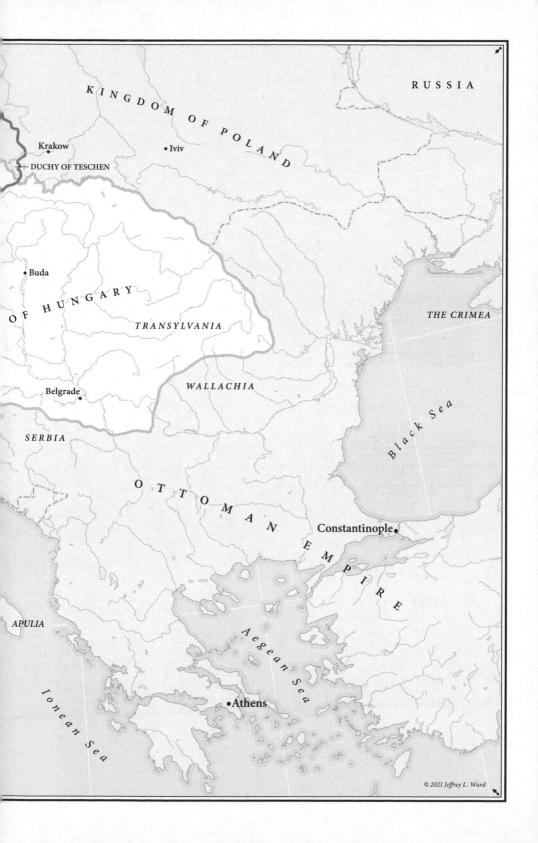

RUSSIA

KINGDOM OF POLAND

• Krakow

• Iviv

DUCHY OF TESCHEN

• Buda

OF HUNGARY

TRANSYLVANIA

THE CRIMEA

WALLACHIA

• Belgrade

Black Sea

SERBIA

O T T O M A N   E M P I R E

Constantinople•

APULIA

Aegean Sea

Ionean Sea

•Athens

© 2021 Jeffrey L. Ward

Selected Genealogy

AUSTRIA

Leopold I (b. 1640–d. 1705), Holy Roman Emperor, King of Hungary and Bohemia, married Eleonore Magdalene of Neuburg (b. 1655–d. 1720), Holy Roman Empress. The couple had two sons.
1. **Joseph I** (b. 1678–d. 1711), Holy Roman Emperor, King of Hungary and Bohemia
2. **Charles VI** (b. 1685–d. 1740), Holy Roman Emperor, King of Hungary and Bohemia

Joseph I married **Wilhelmine of Brunswick** (b. 1673–d. 1742). The couple had two daughters.
1. Maria Josepha (b. 1699–d. 1757) married Augustus III (b. 1696–d. 1763), King of Poland, Elector of Saxony.
2. Maria Amalia (b. 1701–d. 1756) married Charles VII (b. 1697–d. 1745), Elector of Bavaria, Holy Roman Emperor.

Charles VI married Elizabeth Christina of Brunswick-Wolfenbüttel (b. 1691–d. 1750). The couple had two daughters.
1. **Maria Theresa** (b. 1717–d. 1780), Holy Roman Empress, Queen of Hungary and Bohemia, married **Francis I of Lorraine** (b. 1708–d. 1765), Holy Roman Emperor.

2. **Maria Anna** (b. 1718–d. 1744), Governor-General of the Austrian Netherlands, married **Charles of Lorraine** (b. 1712–d. 1780), Governor-General of the Austrian Netherlands.

Children of **Maria Theresa** and **Francis of Lorraine**:
1. A daughter (b. 1737–d. 1740)
2. Marianne (b. 1738–d. 1789), Abbess
3. A daughter (b. 1740–d. 1741)
4. **Joseph II** (b. 1741–d. 1790), Holy Roman Emperor, King of Hungary and Bohemia, married first **Isabella of Parma** (b. 1741–d. 1763 of smallpox) and second Maria Josepha of Bavaria (b. 1739–d. 1767 of smallpox).
5. **Maria Christina ("Mimi")** (b. 1742–d. 1798), Duchess of Teschen, Governor-General of the Austrian Netherlands, married **Albert of Saxony** (b. 1738–d. 1822), Duke of Teschen, Governor-General of the Austrian Netherlands.
6. Maria Elisabeth (b. 1743–d. 1808), Abbess
7. Charles (b. 1745–d. 1761 of smallpox)
8. **Maria Amalia** (b. 1746–d. 1804), Duchess of Parma, married Ferdinand (b. 1751–d. 1802), Duke of Parma.
9. **Leopold II** (b. 1747–d. 1792), Grand Duke of Tuscany, Holy Roman Emperor, married Maria Luisa of Spain (b. 1745–d. 1792).
10. A daughter (b. 1748, lived only one hour)
11. Maria Johanna (b. 1750–d. 1762 of smallpox)
12. Maria Josepha (b. 1751–d. 1767 of smallpox)
13. **Maria Carolina ("Charlotte")** (b. 1752–d. 1814), Queen of Naples, married **Ferdinand IV** (b. 1751–d. 1825), King of Naples.
14. Ferdinand (b. 1754–d. 1806), Governor of Milan
15. **Marie Antoinette** (b. 1755–d. 1793), Queen of France, married **Louis XVI** (b. 1754–d. 1793), King of France.
16. Maximilian (b. 1756–d. 1801), Elector of Cologne

GERMANY

Saxony

Augustus II the Strong (b. 1670–d. 1733), Elector of Saxony, King of Poland, married Christine Eberhardine of Bayreuth. The couple had one son, **Augustus III,** Elector of Saxony and King of Poland.

Augustus III (b. 1696–d. 1763) married Wilhelmine's fertile elder daughter, Maria Josepha. The couple had sixteen children; the following are relevant to this story:

1. Frederick Christian (b. 1722–d. 1763) succeeded his father as Elector of Saxony.
2. Maria Amalia (b. 1724–d. 1760) married **Don Carlos,** King of Naples; mother of **Ferdinand IV,** King of Naples.
3. Franz Xavier (b. 1730–d. 1806) became Regent of Saxony on Frederick Christian's death.
4. Maria Josepha (b. 1731–d. 1767) married **Louis the Fat,** Dauphin of France.
5. **Albert** (b. 1738–d. 1822), Duke of Teschen, Governor-General of the Austrian Netherlands, married **Maria Christina.**

Bavaria

Charles VII (b. 1697–d. 1745), Elector of Bavaria and hapless Holy Roman Emperor, married Wilhelmine's younger daughter, Maria Amalia. This couple had seven children. Here are those relevant to this narrative:

1. Maximilian III (b. 1727–d. 1777) succeeded his father as Elector of Bavaria. It was Maximilian's death that prompted **Joseph** to send troops to Bavaria, causing war with Frederick the Great.
2. Maria Josepha (b. 1739–d. 1767 of smallpox), **Joseph's** unloved second wife

SPAIN

Philip V (b. 1683–d. 1746), King of Spain, married **Elizabeth Farnese** (b. 1692–d. 1766), Duchess of Parma, Queen of Spain, his second wife. The couple had two sons.

1. **Don Carlos** (b. 1716–d. 1788), King of Naples, later Charles III, King of Spain
2. **Don Philip** (b. 1720–d. 1765), Duke of Parma

ITALY

Naples

Selected children of **Don Carlos,** King of Naples (Charles III, King of Spain), and his wife, Maria Amalia of Saxony (b. 1724–d. 1760), Queen of Naples:

1. Maria Luisa of Spain (b. 1745–d. 1792) married **Leopold II,** Holy Roman Emperor, Grand Duke of Tuscany.
2. Charles IV (b. 1748–d. 1819), King of Spain, married Maria Luisa of Parma.
3. **Ferdinand IV** (b. 1751–d. 1825), King of Naples, married **Maria Carolina,** Queen of Naples.

Children of **Maria Carolina,** Queen of Naples, and her husband, **Ferdinand IV:**

1. Maria Teresa (b. 1772–d. 1807) married Leopold's eldest son, **Francis II,** Holy Roman Emperor.
2. Maria Luisa (b. 1773–d. 1802) married Leopold's second son, Ferdinand III, Grand Duke of Tuscany.
3. Carlos (b. 1775–d. 1778 of smallpox)
4. Maria Anna (b. 1775–d. 1780 of smallpox)
5. Francesco (b. 1777–d. 1830), Crown Prince of Naples, married Leopold's daughter Maria Clementina and then Maria Isabella of Spain (b. 1789–d. 1848).

6. Maria Christina (b. 1779–d. 1849) married the brother of the King of Sardinia.
7. Gennaro (b. 1780–d. 1789 of smallpox)
8. Giuseppe (b. 1781–d. 1783 of smallpox)
9. Maria Amalia (b. 1782–d. 1866), Queen of France, married Louis Philippe I, Duc d'Orléans, King of France (b. 1773–d. 1850).
10. A daughter (b. 1783, stillborn)
11. Maria Antoinetta (b. 1784–d. 1806) married Ferdinand VII of Spain (b. 1784–d. 1833).
12. Maria Clotilde (b. 1786–d. 1792 of smallpox)
13. Maria Enricheta (b. 1787–d. 1792 of smallpox)
14. Carlo (b. 1788–d. 1789 of smallpox)
15. Leopold (b. 1790–d. 1851)
16. Alberto (b. 1792–d. 1798 of dehydration on board the *Vanguard*)
17. Maria Isabella (b. 1793–d. 1801)

Parma

Selected children of **Don Philip,** Duke of Parma, and his wife, Louise Élisabeth (b. 1727–d. 1759), eldest daughter of **Louis XV:**
1. **Isabella of Parma** (b. 1741–d. 1763 of smallpox) married **Joseph II,** Holy Roman Emperor.
2. Ferdinand (b. 1751–d. 1802), Duke of Parma, married **Maria Amalia,** Duchess of Parma.
3. Maria Luisa (b. 1751–d. 1819), Queen of Spain, married Charles IV, King of Spain.

Tuscany

Leopold II, Holy Roman Emperor and Grand Duke of Tuscany, and his wife, Maria Luisa of Spain (daughter of Don Carlos, sister of Ferdinand IV, King of Naples), had sixteen children of whom a whopping twelve were sons. Only a handful of these offspring figure prominently in this story. These are:

1. **Francis II** (b. 1768–d. 1835), Holy Roman Emperor, first married briefly a relation of Catherine the Great and afterward Maria Carolina's eldest daughter, Maria Teresa of Naples. Francis's eldest daughter, **Marie Louise** (b. 1791–d. 1847), married **Napoleon.**

2. Ferdinand III (b. 1769–d. 1824), Grand Duke of Tuscany, married Maria Carolina's second daughter, Maria Luisa of Naples.

3. **Archduke Charles** (b. 1771–d. 1847) was adopted by **Maria Christina** and **Albert.**

4. Maria Clementina (b. 1777–d. 1801) married Maria Carolina's eldest son, Francesco, Crown Prince of Naples.

FRANCE

Louis XV (b. 1710–d. 1774 of smallpox), King of France, married Marie Leczinska (b. 1703–d. 1768), daughter of Stanislas, King of Poland.

Selected children of **Louis XV** and Marie Leczinska:
1. Louise Élisabeth (b. 1727–d. 1759) married **Don Philip,** Duke of Parma; mother of **Isabella of Parma.**

2. **Louis the Fat** (b. 1729–d. 1765), Dauphin of France, married Maria Josepha of Saxony.

3. Madame Adélaïde (b. 1732–d. 1800)

4. Madame Victoire (b. 1733–d. 1799)

5. Madame Sophie (b. 1734–d. 1782)

6. Madame Louise (b. 1737–d. 1787). These last four are Louis XVI's unmarried aunts.

Selected children of **Louis the Fat** and Maria Josepha of Saxony:
1. **Louis XVI** (b. 1754–d. 1793), King of France, married **Marie Antoinette.**

2. The Comte de Provence (b. 1755–d. 1824), later **Louis XVIII,** King of France

3. The Comte d'Artois (b. 1757–d. 1836), later **Charles X,** King of France
4. Madame Élisabeth (b. 1764–d. 1794)

Children of **Marie Antoinette** by **Louis XVI:**
1. Marie-Thérèse (b. 1778–d. 1851)
2. Louis-Joseph (b. 1781–d. 1789), Dauphin of France

Children of **Marie Antoinette** by **Count Axel von Fersen:**
1. Louis-Charles (b. 1785–d. 1795), Dauphin of France after the death of his older brother, later **Louis XVII**
2. Madame Sophie (b. 1786–d. 1787)

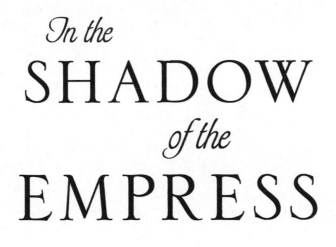

In the

SHADOW

of the

EMPRESS

Introduction

*Paris, the palace of the Tuileries, in the waning hours
of June 20, 1791—*

IT WAS A LITTLE AFTER ten o'clock and darkness had only just fallen
on this, the evening before the longest day of the year. Marie Antoinette, queen of France, had already retired for the night. Earlier that
afternoon, she had taken her twelve-year-old daughter, Marie-Thérèse,
and her six-year-old son, Louis, the dauphin, for a drive to a private
garden renowned for its beauty, about a quarter mile away, to give
the children some fresh air. They had returned from this excursion
at about seven o'clock, after which the siblings were sent to their
separate rooms to be fed and put to bed. Marie Antoinette herself
had dined quietly at nine, as was customary, with her husband, Louis
XVI, and his sister, Madame Élisabeth. After dinner, upon entering
her private apartment, the queen was undressed by her first
lady-in-waiting, to whom she gave the order, as she routinely did, as
to what time she should be awakened the next morning. This command was duly relayed to the soldier who stood guard outside her
door, also as usual. The queen then lay down in bed.

But she did not fall asleep. For at last had come the hour for which
Marie Antoinette had hoped, prayed, and prepared for months: the
moment of the royal family's escape from Paris and the revolution.

The certainty that it would come to this—that she, her husband,
and her children would be reduced to terrified, ignoble, clandestine
flight in the dead of night—had grown within the queen ever since
the day two years earlier when a mob of enraged Parisians had

attacked and successfully overrun the Bastille, a mighty fortress that until that moment the royal court, and indeed all of France, had assumed to be impregnable. As soon as she learned what had happened, the queen had urged her husband to remove himself and his family immediately from the Palace of Versailles, where they were then living, and go east to the more secure location of Metz, next door to the lands ruled by her brother, the Holy Roman Emperor. Once safely away, the king could then recruit enough troops to return at the head of an army sufficiently powerful to impose order on the capital. So convinced was Marie Antoinette of the necessity of this course of action that she began packing hurriedly. "She made me take all her jewels out of their cases, to collect them in one small box, which she might carry off in her own carriage," her lady-in-waiting, an eyewitness to these events, reported.

But Louis XVI had vacillated. As was his habit, he summoned his councillors to ask for their advice. Marie Antoinette was present at this meeting but despite an impassioned appeal was unable to influence the collective judgment. "The affair was decided: the army was to go away without the King," the queen despaired to her servants upon returning to her quarters. "He did not choose this course for himself; there were long debates on the question; at last the King put an end to them by rising and saying, 'Well, gentlemen, we must decide; am I to go or to stay? I am ready to do either.' The majority were for the King staying; time will show whether the right choice has been made." But it was clear that Marie Antoinette knew it to be a serious error.

She who was not able to save herself or her family in this time of crisis yet had the power to rescue others. The lives of all who were closely associated with the queen of France were in danger. Chief among these was Marie Antoinette's dearest companion, the charming duchesse de Polignac. The queen called the duchess to her side on the evening of July 16, 1789, just two days after the fall of the Bastille, and implored her to flee. "I fear the worst; for the sake of our friendship leave," she begged. The queen even enlisted her husband in her entreaty, and Louis XVI did not hesitate to echo her appeal. "I have just commanded the Comte d'Artois [Louis's youngest brother] to take his departure; I give you the same order," the king exhorted the duchess. "Do not lose a single instant; take your family with you."

And so the duchesse de Polignac, with her husband, daughter, and two attendants, fled the palace at midnight that very evening in a heavy, oversized carriage called a berline, the duchess outfitted as a chambermaid to disguise herself. The deception worked: when the berline stopped at Sens for fresh horses, its occupants were questioned as to "whether the Polignacs were still with the Queen," their interrogators obviously having no idea that these well-to-do travelers *were* the Polignacs. They were thus able to answer "in the firmest tone, and with the most cavalier air, that they [the Polignacs] were far enough from Versailles, and that we had got rid of all such bad people," and so were allowed to pass safely out of France. They went first to Switzerland and from there to Italy, to seek aid from Marie Antoinette's family, including her spirited, resolute sister Maria Carolina, the influential queen of Naples, to whose court Élisabeth Vigée Le Brun, Marie Antoinette's favorite portrait painter, also fled for protection.

But it would not be Maria Carolina, the sister closest to her in age and affection, to whom Marie Antoinette would run when her time finally came, no matter how much she might have wished to. Southern Italy was simply too far away to be a practical outpost from which to organize an effective counteroffensive. Her husband, she knew, would need foreign loans and soldiers as well as a place closer to home from which to rally the many loyal countrymen who could still be counted on to fight for the Crown. This meant a flight to her brother the emperor—and with it, somewhat less happily, to one of his closest advisers, her eldest surviving sister, Maria Christina, governor-general of the Austrian Netherlands.

Marie Antoinette's history with this sister, thirteen years her senior and given to dispensing unsolicited advice, was checkered.

They had never been close. The queen of France openly resented what she considered to be Maria Christina's meddling and on more than one occasion had suspected her of tattling on her to their august mother, Maria Theresa, the powerful empress. But then her mother had died, and Maria Christina had stepped into the void created by her death to hold the family together. As the situation in Paris worsened, whatever lingering doubts Marie Antoinette might have had as to her elder sister's value and allegiance were overcome by her sibling's generosity and her own pressing need. For suddenly, on May 29, 1790, less than a year after the Polignacs' escape, in an unprecedented outpouring of affection and gratitude clearly precipitated by an overture of aid, the queen of France wrote to Maria Christina from her summer palace at Saint-Cloud, "You are so good, my dear sister! Your letter brought me to tears." When the decision to flee was finally made, it would be the highly competent Maria Christina who helped make the escape possible.

But there is a great deal of difference between intending to go and actually leaving. All that summer, the king and queen, along with their children and his sister, were at liberty to hunt and wander the spacious grounds of their château at Saint-Cloud. It would have been a relatively easy matter to slip away and get a head start on any potential pursuers in a dash to the border. That this did not happen prompted Madame Élisabeth to confide despondently to a friend in a coded letter of October 24, 1790, that "My patient [Louis XVI] still has stiffness of the legs, and I am afraid it will attack the joints and there will be no cure for it." But in fact, on the very day his sister sent her letter, Louis XVI dispatched a secret messenger to a loyal general of the French army stationed at Metz, about 200 miles east of Paris, announcing the royal family's determination to flee soon after their return to their winter quarters at the palace of the Tuileries, and requesting that troops be mustered to defend their route. It took until the summer of the following year to organize the intrigue, but at last the hour of Marie Antoinette's deliverance had come.

Encouraged by the success of the Polignacs' ploy, the queen of

France had modeled her own escape on the pattern of her former favorite's departure. The royal family, disguised as servants, planned to roll quietly out of Paris just after midnight in the comfort of a spacious, well-appointed berline. The children's governess would play the part of a fictitious baroness with two daughters (the dauphin was to be dressed as a girl) on her way to visit relatives; Madame Élisabeth, attired as her maid, would be her pretended companion on the journey. Louis XVI, in a brown coat, round hat, and wig, had agreed to impersonate the baroness's valet, while Marie Antoinette, in a plain dress and short black cape, her telltale hair and face obscured by a hat, would act the role of the children's governess.

And so, approximately fifteen minutes after she had been undressed and put to bed in the darkness of that late June evening in 1791, the queen of France rose silently from her pillows and made her way by secret passage to the rooms where her children slept. Her daughter was easily roused but the dauphin was deep in slumber. To prevent his crying out at the shock of being woken abruptly, his mother knelt at his bedside. "We are off," she murmured. "We are going to the wars, where there will be ever so many soldiers."

She knew her son; he opened his eyes at once. "Quick, quick, let us hurry, let us be off," he said.

ALL THE WORLD KNOWS the outcome of this journey, and the terrible fate of Marie Antoinette and her family. Hers is one of those sagas that, because of its riveting nature, can be told over and over again without ever losing its immediacy; it has seared itself into the popular consciousness, transcending history and approaching myth.

And yet, even after so many recountings, a persistent undertone of mystery still clings to these events. How was it that this escape failed so spectacularly, when every other member of the French royal family, including both of Louis XVI's brothers, with their wives and children, and even the king's elderly aunts, managed to elude the guards and slip quietly and swiftly across the border to freedom? Why did the king send the duchesse de Polignac and her family away for their safety but not his own wife and children? What was Marie Antoinette's influence in all of this? How much responsibility does she, whose name today is synonymous with the culture of haughty privilege that so inflamed her subjects that they exploded in revolution, bear for that cataclysmic episode?

These questions have so far remained unanswered, not because the puzzle cannot be solved but because the pieces are part of a larger narrative. It is the story of a family of immensely strong women, beginning with Marie Antoinette's formidable mother, the empress Maria Theresa, one of the most remarkable leaders Europe has ever produced, and three of her daughters, of whom the notorious queen of France was but the youngest. Her talented older sister, Maria Christina, governor-general of the Austrian Netherlands, too, fought the dangers and intrigues unleashed by the revolutionary frenzy in France, while Maria Carolina, the astoundingly courageous queen of Naples, survived the first wave of terror only to then be forced to face the cyclone of Napoleon. Their reigns, like Marie Antoinette's, were packed with splendor and suspense; their adventures informed each other's stories and today illuminate the extraordinary century in which they lived.

Defying tradition and stereotype, Marie Antoinette and her sisters forged their own paths. But it was their august mother, the first woman in history to inherit the vast Habsburg Empire in her own right, who set them on the road.

PART I

Maria Theresa

...in her early twenties

1

An Imperial Decree

It is manifest that for one country to gain, another must lose.

—Voltaire, *The Philosophical Dictionary*

MARIA THERESA WAS BORN a little after seven o'clock in the morning on May 13, 1717, at the majestic Hofburg palace in Vienna, venerable seat of the imperial government. Her father was Charles VI, Holy Roman Emperor and king of Hungary and Bohemia, one of the most powerful men in Europe; her mother, the empress Elizabeth Christina, was renowned for "a beauty that has been the admiration of so many nations," as Lady Mary Wortley Montagu, the wife of an English envoy, reported. "She has a vast quantity of fine fair hair...The Graces move with her; the famous statue of Medecis [*sic*] was not formed with more delicate proportions." Lady Mary's enthusiasm was genuine; she was not the sort of correspondent ordinarily given to excessive praise. Of the other highborn women of her acquaintance in Vienna, for example, Lady Mary complained that their hairstyles and fashions were "monstrous and contrary to all common sense and reason...You may easily suppose how much this extraordinary dress sets off and improves the natural ugliness with which God Almighty has been pleased to endow them all," she observed.

The birth of a daughter to a ruling household was never a source of unqualified joy, but Maria Theresa's arrival was viewed, especially by her father, as even more depressingly problematic than usual. Of course Charles VI had wished for a son—all emperors desired sons, so as to solidify the line of succession. Elizabeth Christina's first child, born the previous April, had in fact been a boy, but to the devastation of his parents and their subjects the baby died before the year was out; and now this second infant was a daughter. And having a daughter before a son forced the emperor to deal with an issue that he would have much preferred to avoid—the terms of a secret pact imposed upon him that dictated the standing of his dead brother's children relative to his own.

On the surface, Charles's dilemma stemmed from both his position as a younger son and the noticeable lack of healthy male heirs in the family. But his real problem was that Charles was a Habsburg, and to be a Habsburg at the start of the eighteenth century was a little like standing guard over a vast, ancient castle full of treasures that had all the doors and windows thrown wide open, and the drawbridge let down. No matter how diligent the sentinel, someone was always sneaking in and making off with the silver.

The principal thief, from the imperial point of view, was Louis XIV, the Sun King. Prior to Louis's reign, it had been understood that one member of the preeminent Habsburg dynasty would govern as Holy Roman Emperor, overseeing Germany, Austria, Bohemia, Silesia, Hungary, and northern Italy, while a second Habsburg family relation would rule the kingdom of Spain, which included the Spanish Netherlands (modern-day Belgium and Flanders), and additional territories in southern and central Italy, plus holdings in the New World. This staggeringly far-reaching expanse of wealth and property the Habsburgs considered theirs not simply through birthright but also legally, according to centuries-long precedent.

That is, until Louis XIV ascended the throne of France. Demonstrating a singular disregard for tradition, Louis made it the business of his seemingly endless reign (he held the crown for seventy-two years) to challenge the Habsburgs' authority at every turn. He wrested territory from them on France's northern and eastern borders. He coaxed important German barons, who owed at least nominal allegiance to the emperor, into the French camp, and made them his allies. He invaded the Palatinate, an important province in central Germany, and claimed it in the name of his brother's wife.

But Louis XIV's most audacious act came on November 1, 1700, when the Habsburg king of Spain (not the most incisive ruler) died without siring an heir, and it was revealed that just before he expired he had been convinced by the pope to leave his realm to the Sun King's sixteen-year-old grandson, rather than to one of his own imperial relations. The emperor at the time, Leopold I (Charles's father), naturally protested this inheritance, claiming it for his second son (Charles) instead. By way of response, Louis XIV's armies invaded Belgium, Germany, Italy, and Spain, touching off the War of the Spanish Succession, an international crisis that embroiled all of the major European powers for the next twelve years.

In 1705, early into this conflict, Leopold died, and Charles's elder brother Joseph succeeded his father as emperor. Charles, only twenty years old at the time, was in Spain doing his best to wrest the kingdom away from his French counterpart. But where Joseph, aided by Britain, Holland, and Savoy, racked up impressive victories against Louis XIV's armies at Blenheim and Turin, Charles, who had only a small force with him, never managed to get farther inland than Barcelona, and even this conquest was regularly besieged by Louis XIV's grandson, who had successfully consolidated his hold on the rest of the realm and was consequently recognized throughout Europe as Philip V, king of Spain.

Still, Charles, who quite liked warm, sunny Barcelona—who wouldn't?—remained where he was for the next several years, prepared to hunker down indefinitely and fight it out to the bitter end. And then something entirely unexpected happened. His thirty-two-year-old brother, Joseph, despite his physicians' best efforts, which involved shuttering all the windows in his overheated sickroom and rolling him up in 20 suffocating yards of flannel, was carried off by smallpox in 1711. As Joseph left behind a wife and two daughters but no son, twenty-six-year-old Charles suddenly found himself promoted to the lofty position of Holy Roman Emperor.

Trying to run an enterprise as sprawling and complex as the empire from a besieged outpost in southern Spain was obviously out of the question, so Charles left balmy Barcelona and returned to Vienna, only to find that his deceased brother's allies, having already achieved their military and political aims, were tired of fighting. Bowing to necessity—Charles could not continue to prosecute the war without Britain and Holland—the new emperor reluctantly signed a series of peace treaties that officially transferred the formerly Habsburg territories of Spain, southern and central Italy, and the New World into the hands of the victorious Philip V. Although by these agreements Charles retained the Spanish Netherlands (in addition to Germany, Austria, Silesia, Hungary, Bohemia, and northern Italy), there was no escaping the fact that this time the thief had gotten away with far more than just the silver—he now occupied almost half the castle.

And as if it was not degrading enough to be the first member of his family to begin his reign by *losing* territory that had been held for centuries, because his firstborn son had died and this new baby, Maria Theresa, was a daughter, Charles had now to contend with the conditions imposed by the *pactum mutuae successionis,* the clandestine agreement he had signed in September 1703, right at the beginning of the War of the Spanish Succession. Drawn up at the behest of Leopold I, this secret document dictated that if both Charles and his elder brother, Joseph, died without siring a male heir, Joseph's daughters would take precedence over Charles's when it came to inheriting the empire. At the time, his father's reasoning had been clear. Leopold had naturally expected that Charles would oust the French usurper from Spain and reclaim the kingdom and all of its territories for the Habsburgs, so he ordered the succession to reflect this assumption. In the absence of a male heir, Joseph's eldest daughter would rule the empire. Left unstipulated was the implication that Charles's family would be compensated with the throne of Spain.

It might seem odd that Leopold had the prescience to anticipate such a specific turn of events, but Joseph's dying without siring a male heir had not been a difficult scenario to forecast. Joseph had been an open and energetic philanderer. There were rumors that he had contracted syphilis and had generously shared the condition with his wife, causing her to become sterile. If true, this might have accounted for the prematurely truncated state of their physical relations. "I have heard that the Emperor [Joseph] no longer lives with his wife. If this is so, she will not have a son," observed Louis XIV's sister-in-law Liselotte, the duchess of Orléans, a relative of the empress. "It often happens that men of debauched life have few children. A doctor here who was asked why the Queen's children were never healthy, replied, 'That is because the King only brings the rinsings of the glasses to the Queen.'"

Although he had acceded to his father's wishes while Joseph was still alive, soon after becoming emperor himself, Charles came to question the terms of this irksome pact. Obviously, the circumstances under which he had signed it had changed. He had in fact lost Spain and all the other Habsburg territories that went along with it, and so could no longer leave them to his daughter. Of course, he expected to have a son eventually, and that would take care of the problem. Unlike Joseph, Charles was very happy with his beautiful wife. "Well now, I never dreamed you were so pretty!" he had exclaimed upon meeting Elizabeth Christina, and he apparently worked diligently to produce a male heir. He "loves his Queen so tenderly that he cannot bear to allow her out of his sight; whenever he has a moment of leisure, he rushes to spend it with her," a courtier noted.*

But of course no one could predict the future. If (God forbid) it did come down to a female heir, why should one of his brother's

---

* So taken was Charles with his bride that he even wrote a formal thank-you note to her grandfather, who had engineered the match. "I shall be eternally grateful to you for making it possible that this angel should become my queen," Charles enthused.

daughters succeed to the empire, and not one of his own? It did not seem quite fair.

But what to do about it? Charles had made a binding commitment to his father, the emperor. And then, in a flash of inspiration, he realized that *he* was now emperor. And an emperor could decree whatever he wanted, even if it meant reversing the policies of a previous emperor.

And so that is what he did. On September 19, 1713, before his first child was even born, he called his government together and, to the intense displeasure and eternal enmity of his sister-in-law, Wilhelmine, Joseph's widow—the *pactum mutuae successionis* turned out to be not quite as secret as Charles had believed it to be—issued an imperial edict whereby his nieces were unceremoniously demoted, and his own daughters substituted in their place. This decree was awarded the lofty title of the Pragmatic Sanction. Wilhelmine fought back, marshaling allies to support her position, and at first Charles pretended to accommodate her, hoping that the birth of a son would settle the dispute amicably. But the appearance of Maria Theresa in the spring of 1717 forced the issue once more to the forefront—if he did not take a firm stand now in favor of his own daughter, she would likely forever lose the chance to inherit his property.

The Pragmatic Sanction was reinstated, and to underscore that this time the emperor's decision was final, Charles commanded that his nieces walk behind his infant daughter as she was carried to her baptism on the evening of the day she was born. The ceremony was so well attended that it had to be held in the great hall of the palace, which was lit up with hundreds of candles for the event. There, to the accompaniment of trumpets, a grand procession composed of the elite society of Vienna made its solemn entrance: members of the imperial council, generals, distinguished government functionaries, the papal nuncio and other ambassadors, as well as, of course, the emperor himself, followed by the rest of the imperial family. Everyone was already in place when the Lord High Chamberlain carried the infant archduchess, nestled on an ornate pillow, to the baptismal font. As directed, Joseph's two daughters trailed after them, a highly public humiliation carried out "right before the eyes of Joseph's widow," as a witness reported.

The baby was christened Maria Theresa Walburga Amalia Christina. She had not been alive twenty-four hours and her succession was already under threat.

As MIGHT BE EXPECTED from someone boasting so attractive a mother, Maria Theresa, with her blond curls, pink-and-white complexion, and large, expressive eyes, was enchanting, even as a child. Even better, her temperament matched her appearance. She was sunny and sweet-tempered, qualities that were only enhanced by the warmth and stability of her home life. She saw her parents regularly and adored them. Her governess was loving and kind and became almost a second mother to her. On September 14, 1718, just sixteen months after Maria Theresa was born, the empress was delivered of another child (also, disappointingly, a daughter), named Maria Anna, so Maria Theresa even had a devoted little sister and playmate for company. Consequently, she experienced as close to an idyllic childhood as it was possible to achieve at an imperial court.

Her education, too, was pleasant. Despite the issuance of the Pragmatic Sanction and her father's insistence that his daughters take precedence in terms of the succession, no one, including Charles himself, seriously believed that a woman would govern the empire. A healthy son would one day be born or, failing that, whoever married Maria Theresa would be crowned and rule as emperor. Maria Theresa's job would be to ornament the court. And so she was given the same not particularly taxing schooling she would have received had she been born the daughter of any high aristocrat. This meant a focus on the graceful arts.* There was a heavy emphasis on music —

---

* While her curriculum did include some history, it was limited to the distant classical past and so was not particularly useful. She was required to answer, among other pressing questions, "Which of the ten patriarchs lived before the Flood, which ones after it?"

all the imperial court, but especially her father, loved Italian opera—and she learned to play the clavier and to sing arias. Special attention was paid to her dancing, in anticipation of the many grand balls that she would later host or attend, so the chief choreographer of ballet at the Vienna State Opera House was hired to teach her to glide and hop. She studied drawing and painting with a leading Austrian draftsman. She excelled in linguistics, mastering French, German, and even Latin, which was the dialect the imperial government used to communicate with its Hungarian subjects. Maria Theresa's easy fluency in these languages suggests that she was highly intelligent.

But while Charles VI afforded his eldest daughter no formal instruction in statecraft, bright little Maria Theresa had only to witness the singular methods employed by her father to ensure her unchallenged succession to his property to acquire a first-class, if backhanded, training in the art of geopolitics. And as she grew up, Maria Theresa had every reason to pay attention.

It was brought home to Charles very quickly that simply issuing the Pragmatic Sanction was perhaps not going to be enough to ensure that his daughter actually inherited the empire after his death. Maria Theresa was still a toddler when on August 20, 1719, the resentful Wilhelmine struck back by marrying her eldest daughter to the son and heir of Augustus the Strong, elector of Saxony and king of Poland. Augustus was one of the most opportunistic and ambitious barons in Germany. He had achieved the Polish throne through a judicious blend of policies that included converting to Catholicism, allying with Russia, and outright bribery. Three years later, on October 5, 1722, Wilhelmine followed up this coup by wedding her younger daughter to the son of the elector of Bavaria, another German prince who openly hankered after a crown. Although Charles insisted that both bridegrooms sign lengthy documents renouncing any right to his property or the imperial succession, there was of course no way to guarantee that they would abide by these agreements after his death. Wilhelmine had thrown down the gauntlet.

Although his most experienced general, Prince Eugene of Savoy, warned him that "the Pragmatic Sanction could only be guaranteed by a full treasury and two hundred thousand fighting men," Charles chose to ignore this helpful bit of practical wisdom. Rather, he decided to employ a more nuanced strategy of his own devising. He sought to gain international adherence to the Pragmatic Sanction through the time-honored medium of payoffs.

He began with the kingdom of Hungary. The Hungarians made for difficult subjects. A proud, independent people, they rebelled frequently. They were considered savage, unreliable allies who would just as soon turn against their sovereign as fight for him. But keeping the Hungarian throne was vital to Austrian and imperial interests. Hungary was all that stood between Vienna and the menacing Ottoman Empire.

So, in the winter of 1722, just after the marriage of his second niece to the heir to Bavaria, Charles called a meeting of the Hungarian representative assembly, the Diet, in the nearby capital city of Pressburg, which was located only about 35 miles east of Vienna. There, over the next several months, the Hungarians were offered a series of extremely generous political and economic concessions, including but not limited to the ability to make their own laws; a guarantee that the nobility would be exempt from taxes in perpetuity; and the creation of a standing army financed and manned entirely by the (conveniently unrepresented) lower classes. In light of these happy inducements, in the spring of 1723, the kingdom of Hungary officially accepted the Pragmatic Sanction.

Buoyed by this success, Charles turned his attention to the problem of choosing an appropriate husband for his eldest daughter. There was plenty of time—she was only six—but already Eugene of Savoy was urging the emperor to affiance Maria Theresa to the eldest son of the duke of Lorraine. The duke was an old army comrade whom Eugene knew to be an exemplary warrior. Moreover, the duchy was coveted by the French—Louis XIV had occupied it at one point but his soldiers had ultimately been beaten back by imperial forces—and a marriage alliance would reward the duke for his loyalty, and help keep Lorraine for the empire. The emperor agreed to extend an invitation to the prospective suitor to come to Vienna, ostensibly to complete his education but actually as a sort of trial run, to see how well he fit in with the family. It seemed like an easy way to satisfy his general, who was getting on in years, without actually having to commit himself to the match.

Alas, the eldest son died before he could take advantage of this kind overture. Fortunately, the duke of Lorraine had a second son who could take the place of his deceased brother. Charles accepted the substitution, and so the invitation was renewed, this time to the surviving heir to the duchy of Lorraine. He arrived in Vienna in the fall of 1723.

By that time, Charles was somewhat less concerned about his elder daughter's marriage, as Empress Elizabeth Christina was pregnant again. If she gave birth to a boy, then all his worries would be over. His son would inherit his lands and thrones and there would be no need for the Pragmatic Sanction to take effect. It was in this optimistic frame of mind that he and the rest of the imperial family welcomed fourteen-year-old Francis Stephen of Lorraine to the Hofburg palace.

2

Archduchess of Austria

The motto . . . Kingdoms given away, was indeed very applicable to this period.

— Voltaire, *Sequel of the Age of Louis XIV*

NATURE COULD NOT HAVE PROVIDED a suitor more destined to please than Francis of Lorraine. Curly-haired and slender, he boasted the sort of puppy-dog good looks that have caused legions of adolescent girls to swoon through the ages. To this undeniable advantage he combined an easy athleticism and an agreeably mild, winning personality. What he lacked in concentration—under no circumstances could Francis be called a scholar—he more than made up for with his instinctive talents for dancing and riding. He was passionate about hunting, which made him an excellent companion for Charles, who shared the teenager's enthusiasm for the sport. The emperor invited Francis to stay on indefinitely in Vienna, which of course gave everyone (including his elder daughter) the impression that this golden boy would be her husband. To Charles, fun-loving, personable Francis was the son he craved but had so far been denied. To elementary school–aged Maria Theresa, in awe of this high school heartthrob, he was a god.

Yet as much as the emperor enjoyed Francis's company, he would not publicly commit to the marriage. In fact, within a year of the young man's arrival at the Hofburg palace, Charles, forced once again

Francis of Lorraine as a boy

into a defensive posture by the actions of his still-indignant sister-in-law, was already wavering.

The obstacles to Francis's suit began in the spring of 1724, when, to the by now customary general despair, the empress's much-heralded pregnancy resulted in the birth of yet another unwanted daughter.★ Emboldened by this latest failure to produce a male heir, Wilhelmine struck again. Using connections from her side of the family, she arranged an alliance between France and her new sons-in-law's principalities of Saxony and Bavaria, an agreement designed specifically to upend the Pragmatic Sanction and return her daughters to their place of prominence in the imperial succession. Charles knew that Wilhelmine was in a strong position, as his elder niece, the one married to the crown prince of Saxony, was

★ This child, born on April 5, would die at the age of six.

turning out to be unfairly fertile. In a most unsportsmanlike fashion, she had already produced *three* sons (one had died, true, but the other two were reported to be healthy), and Charles noted glumly that she was pregnant again.

Although Louis XIV had passed away nearly a decade earlier, and his great-grandson, Louis XV, had only just turned fourteen, Charles knew to take this threat to the Pragmatic Sanction seriously. If, after his death, mighty France sent an army to support one of his nieces' claims to the imperial throne, his daughter was going to need strong allies of her own to help her defend her inheritance. It stood to reason that she might have to marry into the family of one of the other great powers in order to induce them to help her. Hence the emperor's reluctance to commit to Francis, no matter how much everybody liked him.

And so, for the next ten years, all through Maria Theresa's childhood and adolescence (during which time the young Adonis from Lorraine continued to live with them and she progressed from hero worship to infatuation to trembling, full-on first love), her father did his best to sidestep the question of when she and Francis would be married. It wasn't that the engagement was ever called off completely. It was just that Charles needed to keep his options open while he pursued the one goal that overrode every other imperial consideration: to get the other prominent European kingdoms to agree to uphold the terms of the Pragmatic Sanction after his death.

NEVER DID A MAN try so industriously to implement a course of action. The emperor was willing to bribe, cajole, or bully his way to success. No scheme that resulted in the desired objective was deemed too far-fetched. It is difficult, however, to play a winning hand when everyone who comes to the table already knows what cards you are holding.

The first monarch to take Charles up on his offer of material advantage in exchange for recognition of his daughter's rights was none other than his old antagonist, Philip V of Spain. Philip was in something of a bind himself. He had married a new young wife, Elizabeth Farnese, formerly duchess of Parma. In 1721, the couple's three-year-old daughter was engaged to her cousin Louis XV and sent to Versailles to accustom herself to her future realm until she grew old enough to consummate the marriage. But then, three years after she arrived, a new French minister came to power and it was decided to wed the fourteen-year-old king to a twenty-one-year-old princess from Poland instead. When Elizabeth Farnese discovered that her six-year-old daughter was going to be returned like a pair of defective gloves, she was so furious that she wrenched off the miniature of Louis XV she wore in a jeweled band around her wrist and stomped on it.

In retaliation, she and Philip V dispatched a clandestine envoy, the duke of Ripperda (who, to disguise his mission, adopted the suitably droll cover name of "Baron Pfaffenberg"), to Vienna. What the phony baron lacked in experience, common sense, and overall intelligence, he more than made up for with bravado and bluster. In a series of meetings made possible by 400,000 florins' worth of bribes, Ripperda painted the picture of a future made glorious by Spanish-imperial cooperation. They would wage war on their mutual enemies together; why, just the announcement of the alliance would make France and England cower in fear, the duke predicted! To ensure victory on all fronts, Ripperda promised that Philip would send Charles 3 million in gold annually to improve the imperial army, which was in a woeful state of decay due to insufficient funds. In return, Charles would send Philip 30,000 soldiers to help Spain recover Gibraltar from Britain. Most importantly, the Spanish would agree to uphold the emperor's precious Pragmatic Sanction in exchange for Charles's agreeing to wed Maria Theresa to Philip and Elizabeth Farnese's eldest son, Don Carlos. Since a marriage alliance with a major power like Spain was obviously more desirable than one with a small duchy like Lorraine, in May of 1725, the emperor secretly agreed to everything.

This happy plan fell apart almost immediately. Ripperda's imagination far exceeded his authority; Philip had expected the 400,000 florins to cover the entire cost of the arrangement with Austria, not simply serve as a down payment on the alliance. The duke remembered this fact only after his return to Madrid, however, so while he bragged loudly to Philip V and Elizabeth Farnese about his prowess as a negotiator, he failed to mention the additional 3 million in annual payments. Charles consequently pressed fruitlessly for the promised mountains of Spanish gold so as to be able to expand his army, while Philip V grew increasingly annoyed when the imperial troops he had been assured were on the way did not arrive. Eventually, the Spanish king caught on and ordered Ripperda to be arrested. To save himself, the visionary dealmaker hid in the house of the British ambassador in Madrid, where he spilled the entire scheme to his startled host in exchange for protection from his irate sovereign.

The British ambassador told London, and London told France. Rather than cower in fear as Charles had been led to believe, the two kingdoms decided instead to go to war together against Spain and Austria. England went even further, and brought Prussia, its traditional ally, into the mix. As soon as these powers began marshaling troops—the Prussian king had a formidable army of 70,000 very tall soldiers at his disposal—Philip V prudently switched sides and *also* turned on Austria. By 1731, Charles had gone from the glorious future promised by Ripperda to the prospect of being invaded by Britain, France, Spain, and Prussia all at the same time.

As it was obvious that he could not fight all of these kingdoms at once, the emperor was forced to sue for peace. But of course it wasn't enough just to go back to the old alliances; Charles needed each of these hostile powers to sign off on the Pragmatic Sanction. This resulted in the innovative strategy of the emperor's protecting his daughter's future inheritance by giving large portions of it away. Britain was assigned Austrian shipping rights and two German duchies in exchange for its assent to the document; Spain received Parma and Tuscany. To deflect the threat from nearby Prussia, Charles strove to bring the monarchy into the imperial family, and even went so far as to offer to marry Maria Theresa to the crown prince. When this offer was reluctantly declined on the basis of religion (Prussia was Calvinist, Austria Catholic) the emperor substituted one of his wife's Protestant relations. Thus was Prussian acceptance of the Pragmatic Sanction secured.

BY THIS TIME, Maria Theresa was fourteen years old and maturing quickly into a lovely young woman who was looking forward to the formal announcement of her engagement to her beloved. Francis was twenty-two and on the recent death of his father had come into his inheritance as the new duke of Lorraine; he was also expecting a public declaration. Belatedly realizing just how attached his eldest daughter had become to this extended houseguest (and not just Maria Theresa; her younger sister, Maria Anna, wanted to marry Francis, too), Charles thought it might be a good idea to remove the object of her affection from the immediate vicinity, just in case the secret nuptial agreement with Spain actually came to pass. So he sent Francis on a tour of Europe as part of a charm offensive to smooth over any lingering hard feelings caused by the ill-fated Spanish alliance, a role for which the amiable young man was ideally suited.

The outside world naturally interpreted this diplomatic initiative as a way for the new duke of Lorraine to develop the sort of personal relationships with foreign courts that would prove useful to him after he became Maria Theresa's husband. Francis was consequently welcomed wherever he went as an imperial representative of the highest order. He went first to England, arriving on October 14, 1731, where he spent the next ten weeks having a wonderful time hunting, dancing, and paying social calls on all the most fashionable people at court. He observed a chemical experiment at the famous Royal Society, and they were so pleased by his interest that they made him a member on the spot. He was such good company that when he left, the king, George II, sent him off with a letter of recommendation. He was equally successful at his next stop, The Hague, where he spent a month before it was on to Prussia. He arrived in Berlin at the end of February 1732, having dutifully visited a series of German duchies along the way, and immediately made friends with the twenty-year-old crown prince, Frederick.

And just at this moment Frederick was sorely in need of a friend. Although nothing would have given him more pleasure than to see the great courts of Europe, as Francis was doing, his father had forbidden him to travel. Instead, he was being made to marry the empress's relative as part of the new alliance with Austria. The unhappy bridegroom wrote a letter to his sister on March 6, 1732, in which he described his future wife as "neither beautiful nor ugly... very ill brought up...and totally behind in manners and social behavior." Francis arrived just as the betrothal ceremony was taking place. As the ranking dignitary present, he stood beside the Prussian royal family at the service, where a despondent Frederick and his despised fiancée exchanged rings, and attended the gala ball afterward. But what he really did was help the crown prince get through this difficult event by showing him so much warmth, affection, and sympathy that Frederick kept up a correspondence with Francis after he left and even sent him a gift of salmon in gratitude.

It was all going so well. Back home in Austria, Maria Theresa heard the reports of Francis's success with pride. "She sighs and pines all night for her Duke of Lorraine," Sir Thomas Robinson, the long-standing British ambassador stationed in Vienna, observed bluntly to his government. "If she sleep, it is only to dream of him; if she wake, it is but to talk of him to her lady-in-waiting."

But still Charles fretted. A number of important monarchies (including France) had not yet accepted the terms of the Pragmatic Sanction. And then a piece of luck fell his way. The king of Poland died and his eldest son, Augustus III of Saxony, who also happened to be Wilhelmine's son-in-law (the one married to her exceptionally fertile elder daughter), claimed the Polish crown as his inheritance. As Charles had made no secret of his desperation to secure Maria Theresa's succession, Augustus offered to give up his wife's claim to the imperial estate if the emperor would help him take the throne.

Of course Charles leapt at the chance to get his elder niece's husband, who was such a threat to his daughter, to sign off on the Pragmatic Sanction. He fell over himself promising to do everything in his power to help, and immediately sent imperial troops to the Polish border in an effort to encourage the native citizenry to accept Augustus as their new sovereign.

Regrettably, Louis XV had married a Polish princess and she wanted her father, Stanislas, to be king. Louis allied with Elizabeth Farnese of Spain, who had taken umbrage at Francis's European tour, complaining that Charles had reneged on his original agreement to marry Maria Theresa to her eldest son, Don Carlos. In the late fall of 1733, Charles reeled from the one-two punch of a French army invading and occupying Lorraine while a Spanish force led by seventeen-year-old Don Carlos swarmed over Naples.

Sixteen-year-old Maria Theresa, still unmarried, swallowed up the news of these defeats as though her life depended on it, as indeed, from her perspective, it did. Although deliberately excluded from her father's council, she nonetheless made her views known, and these were that she would not give up Francis under any circumstances, and especially not to marry Don Carlos, no matter what the pressure from Spain. The archduchess, Sir Thomas observed, "was a princess of the highest spirit. She reasons already. Her father's losses are her own. She admires his virtues but condemns his mismanagement."

So again Charles, whose one thought throughout these machinations had been to save his daughter's inheritance, had to give large parts of it away. By a treaty signed on October 5, 1735, Spain got the kingdom of Naples, which represented the entire southern boot of Italy, everything south of Rome, plus the island of Sicily, and all the ports in Tuscany. France was willing to cede Poland to Augustus but only if Stanislas got Lorraine (conveniently being held for him by the occupying French soldiers), after which it would revert to Louis XV. Charles's only recompense for this considerable outlay of booty was an agreement by both kingdoms to uphold the Pragmatic Sanction after his death.

The emperor did not have the courage to tell Francis to his face that he had traded away his home duchy of Lorraine, which had been in Francis's family for generations, without even bothering to consult him. He sent one of his ministers to do the dirty work instead. Francis could not believe that he had been sold out in this manner. His mother was incensed and begged him not to agree to it. She and Francis's younger brother and sisters would lose everything: their wealth, their home, their friends, their peaceful and prosperous subjects, their beautiful ancestral palace, the fertile countryside, the cultivated gardens. To sign the proffered renunciation papers meant shouldering a burden of emasculation, regret, and guilt for the rest of his life. Francis's was not a strong spirit, but even he rebelled at the magnitude of the betrayal. Three times, the minister put the quill in his hand and three times twenty-seven-year-old Francis threw it on the floor. But the imperial councillor remained unmoved. "No abdication, no Archduchess," he threatened crudely. On the fourth try, Francis signed.

The long-awaited wedding took place in Vienna on February 12, 1736, at the Church of the Augustinian Friars, which neighbored the Hofburg palace. All the grandeur of the empire was on display, as befitted this momentous occasion. Francis was splendid in a silver cloak over his ivory coat and breeches. A thoroughly bejeweled Maria Theresa, who was walked down the aisle by both her mother and her aunt Wilhelmine, was also in white. "What was most remarkable about the bride's dress was that besides the other incumbrances of great loads of diamonds upon her head and neck, the very robe itself was embroidered, to use that expression, with diamonds," reported the obviously impressed Sir Thomas. "Few persons of their high rank have had the advantage of founding their mutual desires and sentiments upon a personal acquaintance for so long a time before their marriage," he added thoughtfully. The wedding ceremony was followed, as was customary, by a magnificent banquet at the palace.

Maria Theresa had won, but at what a price! She was acutely

aware of what Francis had given up to marry her; it was as if he had endured an amputation for her sake. And all the diamonds in the world could not mask the cracks in the alliance. The groom's mother refused to attend, choosing instead to lash out at her eldest son and Charles for agreeing to such bitter and dishonorable terms. "I greatly love Lorraine and the Lorrainers," Maria Theresa's new mother-in-law wrote, in lieu of the customary congratulations. "They do not dislike me, and so I will remain with them until the end of my days. As for the Emperor, I would rather die at this moment than come under his domination!" Charles was forced to agree to marry Maria Theresa's sister, Maria Anna, to Francis's younger brother at some time in the unspecified future in order to placate her.* And although Wilhelmine had condescended to participate in the wedding, and had even helped give the bride away, significant in their absence were her younger daughter and her husband, the elector of Bavaria, who still refused to confirm the Pragmatic Sanction.

Even the radiant joy of Maria Theresa, one of a handful of princesses in history who succeeded in marrying for love, was tinged by sadness for her new husband's plight, especially after his mother's written tirade. Although Charles had succeeded in convincing the Spanish to compensate his son-in-law for the loss of Lorraine by ceding him the much less desirable grand duchy of Tuscany in its place (basically Florence and the surrounding countryside), this compromise in no way made up for his sacrifice. Francis made every effort to hide the shame he felt at having failed his family and subjects from her, but Maria Theresa knew it was there, gnawing away at his self-respect. She would spend the rest of her life trying to make it up to him.

NOTWITHSTANDING THE LOSS OF LORRAINE, Maria Theresa's first year of marriage seems to have been everything she could have hoped

---

* Francis eventually prevailed upon the French court to allow his mother to keep a small residence in Commercy, 33 miles west of Nancy, for her lifetime, as she absolutely refused to move to the establishment in Brussels that Charles offered her.

for. After so long a time apart, she was finally united with her adored Francis, could see him every day if she wanted to (and she did), as well as sleep with him at night. Much to the joy of everyone in Vienna, this delightful state of intimacy resulted in the archduchess conceiving within three months of the wedding, a development that only added to her contentment. Maria Theresa knew that it was her job to deliver the heir her parents had been unable to provide, and becoming pregnant so quickly seemed like a good omen.

This blissful interlude was cut short, however, by the deliverance on February 3, 1737, of a daughter. This all too potent reminder of Elizabeth Christina's dismal record at procreation naturally brought up fears that Maria Theresa, too, would be unable to provide her husband with a son. The birth also coincided with the advent of a fresh anxiety — her father's decision to join with Russia to launch a war against the Ottoman Empire.

Charles, still smarting from having lost Naples, Sicily, and Lorraine, reasoned that fighting the Turks would be an easy way to recoup his prestige and add territory. The Russians had already invaded the Crimea, so the enemy's forces would have to be divided; he could swoop down from Belgrade, open up a second front, and score a quick victory or two. Looking around for a commander, he lit on Francis as the best man for the job. Recognizing that his son-in-law had never directed an army before, he assigned a more seasoned warrior to work under him to provide whatever combat knowledge Francis might be lacking.

The new grand duke of Tuscany and his more experienced subordinate went off to Belgrade in the late spring of 1738. Soon after they arrived, they and their troops were involved in a skirmish with the enemy. To the collective joy of Vienna, but especially Maria Theresa, who was pregnant again, the imperial side WON. Even better, Francis covered himself with glory in the encounter. "The important and singular success of our grand duke gives a high opinion of him in the minds of the people," Sir Thomas observed enthusiastically to London on July 16, 1738. "A letter from the field of battle says 'his royal highness, perceiving that the enemy had pierced the line, exposed himself greatly, and gave his orders with a coolness and wisdom which would have done honor to an old soldier.'"

Unfortunately, it turned out that the Ottoman battalion faced by the imperial troops represented only an advance guard of the main divisions, a grim reality Francis discovered soon after he pushed on and ran headlong into the full strength of the enemy army. Although in the resulting action he again behaved bravely, this time it was in the service of a desperate retreat. He and his soldiers were forced back even farther behind their own lines, and once camped were beset by disease, including plague. Like the majority of his army, Francis fell ill. Concluding that he would recover more quickly at home, he left Belgrade to return to Vienna.* Once reunited with Maria Theresa, he improved so markedly that he was soon up and hunting again, a recreation Francis much preferred to his martial duties. It was *so* much pleasanter to shoot at something that didn't shoot back.

Maria Theresa was of course very relieved to see him return to health so quickly. Having him in Vienna also helped her to bear the disappointment of delivering yet *another* daughter, on October 6, 1738. The couple named the baby Maria Anna, after the archduchess's younger sister, but everyone called her Marianne.

Meanwhile, back in Belgrade, the defeats piled up. The Austrian citizenry, frustrated by the dismal performance of the imperial army, turned on Francis. It was felt that the duke had shamefully abandoned his post in order to amuse himself with hunting, and perhaps had even deliberately sabotaged the war effort because as a foreigner he was more loyal to Lorraine than Vienna. And it certainly didn't help that he seemed unable to father a son. There were riots and calls for Maria Theresa to be replaced in the order of succession by her

---

* Sadly, the men under his command, many of whom undoubtedly felt that they, too, would recover more quickly at home, did not have this option.

younger sister. It got so bad that on December 17, 1738, Charles sent his elder daughter and her husband off to Francis's new grand duchy of Tuscany just to get them out of town.

So, Maria Theresa very reluctantly left her newborn and not yet two-year-old daughter, both of whom were obviously still too young to undertake an arduous journey, in the care of nurses and traveled to Florence with her husband. The two of them arrived on January 20, 1739, and were apparently surprised to discover that Francis's new duchy was a place of great natural beauty. A British tourist ran into them on the road to Siena and was impressed enough to record the encounter. "The whole country of Tuscany is very pleasant, abounding with fine hills and fruitful vales, rivers, and fountains, and many delightful prospects, in a serene and healthful air," he enthused. "It might make a happy country if the present Grand Duke can keep it in peaceable possession."

But this was not to be. Back home in Vienna, the city was bombarded with bad news from the front lines. The Austrian population panicked, believing that Turkish soldiers would overrun the imperial army and appear at any moment outside the capital. "Everything in this Court is running into the last confusion and ruin," Sir Thomas recorded bluntly. The emperor fell into depression and, fearful that the succession would be compromised if he should die while his heir was out of the country, recalled his daughter and her husband from Tuscany almost as soon as they had arrived.

A once again pregnant Maria Theresa returned home in June 1739 to every mother's nightmare. Her younger daughter, Marianne, had become sickly in her absence, and would remain so for the rest of her life. Maria Theresa blamed herself for leaving her child with servants at such a susceptible age. Additionally, her father was beside himself: facing what he had believed to be the annihilation of his army, the emperor had enlisted the French to act as mediator to end the conflict, and they had slyly used their influence to weaken the empire. In September 1739 the articles of the peace treaty they had helped to negotiate were published, and to Charles's shame, he was forced to surrender Belgrade, northern Serbia, and Wallachia, which ignited public fury. A heavy gloom settled over the capital. "Our only hope rests on the birth of a prince," a member of the imperial court declared flatly.

As terrible a year as it was, the next was even worse. In January 1740, the scenario the archduchess most dreaded came to pass when she was delivered of her third child—yet another girl.* "Will it never be granted to me to see a male heir of my race?" Charles groaned. Then, on June 8, Maria Theresa's eldest daughter, a lively, adorable three-year-old, the delight of the family but especially of her grandfather, died in acute pain from a stomach infection. The illness had come on so suddenly that the entire court was taken by surprise and went into shocked mourning. Maria Theresa was devastated.

Thoroughly miserable, Charles insisted later that fall on going hunting in Hungary, as was his habit. The weather was atrocious. A driving rain, often turning to sleet or snow, fell nearly every day, but the emperor, needing distraction, pushed himself and went out anyway, with the inevitable result that he came down with a bad cold. On October 10 he felt a little better and ate a large bowl of locally harvested mushrooms stewed in oil, one of his favorite dishes. Alas, this delectable concoction disagreed with him so violently that he spent the rest of the night throwing up. He was rushed back to Vienna the following morning, where his condition worsened by the day until it became clear to his doctors that he would not recover. For fear of infection, a fourth-time pregnant Maria Theresa was at first not allowed to see him. He did manage to hold a long interview with Francis, however. "It is my greatest comfort to know that my daughter is in such good hands," the emperor told his son-in-law.

Charles VI died on the morning of October 20, 1740, surrounded by his family. He was fifty-five years old and had been emperor for nearly three decades. He left behind a ruined army, an empty

---

* This baby lived only a year.

treasury, a rebellious populace, a vastly reduced territory, and a series of paper promises from ambitious, land-hungry monarchs guaranteeing the right of succession to his twenty-three-year-old, untrained, four-months-pregnant daughter, the first woman ever to inherit the empire.

"A pot of mushrooms changed the history of Europe," noted Voltaire.

3

Queen of Hungary

I am going to play for a high stake, and if I turn up aces, we will go shares.
— Frederick the Great to the French ambassador,
December 13, 1740

Though I am only a queen, yet have I the heart of a king.
— Maria Theresa to her ministers, October 20, 1740

THE PROTOCOL FOLLOWING THE DEATH of the emperor was mercifully understated. As it was above all imperative that the public be assured of a stable government and an orderly transition of power, just a few hours after Charles's passing, Maria Theresa appeared in the throne room before the handful of senior ministers who had constituted her father's inner circle. She had Francis with her, but it was she who stood alone on the steps leading up to the throne. She was dressed in mourning, pale and shaken from having just witnessed her father's final agony. Her grief was obvious but she knew her duty. Fighting back tears, she thanked each official for his past loyalty and asked the group as a whole to continue in their posts. Then one by one, the councillors mounted the steps, kissed her hand, and bowed to her as the new monarch. "An accession in these countries [is] attended with no very pompous circumstances," Sir Thomas explained, in a report of these proceedings sent to London.

"The Queen of Hungary and Bohemia takes upon herself the government in the very same manner that a new king would."*

But what a government to inherit! The councillors whom she had just reconfirmed in their posts were the very same men who for decades had unctuously encouraged her father to undertake one disastrous enterprise after another. All but one were over seventy (and this at a time when the average life expectancy fell significantly under fifty), with the infirmities and cautious outlooks that accompany old age. "The Turks seemed to them already in Hungary; the Hungarians themselves in arms; the Saxons in Bohemia; the Bavarians at the gates of Vienna; and France the soul of the whole," Sir Thomas observed of these ministers. "I saw them in despair."†

Just how poorly this administration had functioned under the previous emperor was no doubt brought home to Maria Theresa the very next day, when she held her first council meeting and her advisers enlightened her as to the true state of the realm's finances and military preparedness. It appeared that the imperial treasury was down to its last 100,000 florins, and the ability to obtain future credit was seriously compromised by the uncertainty associated with the ascension of an untested, young, pregnant monarch. The army, if anything, was in even worse shape, with only some 30,000 soldiers who could reliably be mustered in the event of an emergency. Add to this that the weather had turned frigid early that year, which exacerbated the woes of an already impoverished, fearful population. "The murmur of tumultuous voices says that the kingdom should not be ruled by a woman, and that public interest requires

---

* Hungary and Bohemia were the realms she inherited outright from her father. Although it was customary that whoever ruled these countries also ruled the empire, Maria Theresa (or, rather, her husband, Francis, for Germany would insist on a male sovereign) still had to be voted emperor (and, by extension, she empress) at a formal meeting of the German electors. Until this ballot took place, Maria Theresa could officially claim only the title of queen of Hungary and Bohemia.

† Consider that when Elizabeth I ascended the throne, she had the invaluable William Cecil to guide her; Queen Victoria had the advice of the equally skillful Lord Melbourne; Elizabeth II had the indomitable Winston Churchill. By contrast, Maria Theresa had the eighteenth-century equivalent of the regulars at Wednesday night bingo at the senior center.

that a German prince should be chosen," the Venetian ambassador informed his government. As if on cue, Wilhelmine's younger daughter's husband, the elector of Bavaria, announced his determination to oust Maria Theresa and succeed to Charles's lands by right of a former claim.

But from the moment she set foot in that throne room, Maria Theresa never wavered. She assumed the full mantle of leadership. She made every decision. Ever mindful of her husband's dignity and the need to make him feel that his sacrifice of Lorraine had been worth it, she named Francis co-regent and put him in charge of the defense of the realm. She did this against the advice of her ministers, who pointed out that Francis was still despised by her subjects and that the appointment would work against her own popularity and serve the elector of Bavaria's interests. To relieve the suffering of her subjects, she ordered that trees be cut down for fuel, that the previously protected game that had stocked the imperial hunting grounds be reduced, and poachers forgiven, to help assuage the hunger of the most needy. Still, the magnitude of the poverty was such that these measures proved insufficient, and a riot had to be put down in the capital in early November. What the situation really called for were funds to import supplies and improve the economy, and these Maria Theresa did not have, and could not obtain on credit, until she was formally recognized by the great powers as her father's legitimate heir.

And so the most important order of business after Charles's death became to reaffirm the guarantees of the Pragmatic Sanction that he had worked so diligently to obtain. A formal statement announcing the untimely decease of the emperor and Maria Theresa's ascension to his lands and titles was accordingly drawn up and sent out to all the sovereign courts of Europe. How each monarch responded to this communication would, her aged ministers hoped, "distinguish between the countenances of her friends and those of her pretended friends but real enemies," as Sir Thomas clarified bluntly.

The first replies to dribble in were encouraging. Francis's goodwill tour had clearly reaped benefits. The old king of Prussia had died just a few months before the emperor, and his eldest son, Frederick, the same prince whom Francis had befriended during the trying period of that young man's forced engagement, had ascended to the throne. King Frederick now generously expressed his appreciation by being one of the first to confirm the Pragmatic Sanction and pledge Prussian support for Maria Theresa's rule. "You are aware of the great esteem in which I hold you and the deep friendship I have always felt for you," Frederick wrote to Francis. "In accord with these sentiments, I beg your Royal Highness to look upon me as your good and tender cousin." In fact, Frederick went even further and used his influence with the king of Poland (Augustus III of Saxony, the one married to Wilhelmine's elder daughter) to secure *his* endorsement and backing as well, which was a big relief, as it was feared that family feeling might have led the Polish king to support his brother-in-law of Bavaria's claim to the inheritance. "Really, the King [Frederick] is behaving like a father to the Queen and myself and we shall never be able to repay our obligations to him," Francis gushed in gratitude to the Prussian ambassador. Similarly, England's king George II, who also remembered and admired Francis, indicated that he had every intention "of fulfilling his engagements with regard to the Pragmatic Sanction." Other sovereigns—Russia, Sardinia (Savoy), the papacy—while neatly dodging the main issue, nonetheless also sent expressions of friendship. Sir Thomas noted the relieved pleasure of Maria Theresa's aged council with "every letter they receive from one neighboring power or other, with the title of Queen, Sister, Majesty. It is not, I tell them, the acknowledging of the Queen, it is the acknowledgment of the Pragmatic Sanction and of the indivisibility of the late Emperor's possessions that is the present object," the ambassador observed in frustration.

He was right, of course. And as if to underscore his concern, powerful France, whose acceptance of Maria Theresa's undisputed claim to the inheritance was vital, remained disquietingly reticent on the subject of the Pragmatic Sanction. Their silence was especially disappointing as the cardinal in charge of French foreign policy had reiterated Louis XV's commitment on this issue just a few months before the emperor's death. "Your Majesty [Charles] may rest assured that the King [Louis XV] will observe the engagements he has entered into with the most exact and inviolable fidelity," the cardinal had written on January 26, 1740. When pressed, the French ambassador excused the delay in communicating formal recognition on the grounds that it was necessary for his government to research the proper etiquette to use in the letter.

All during the month of November Maria Theresa waited for the French to make up their minds. During this time, acutely conscious of the threat (for if France decided to support the elector of Bavaria's claim it might mean armed conflict), she threw herself into her work with such attention to detail that she barely slept. "The Queen gains the hearts of everybody," Sir Thomas reported with admiration. "She shows an uncommon quickness in taking, a like judgment in digesting, and no less resolution in supporting the weightiest affairs of State. The Grand Duke is indefatigable in business." Even better, because of Marie Theresa's energy and commitment, the Austrians were persuaded of her goodwill and the unrest died down. By the end of November there existed in Vienna "perfect tranquility and submission to the new government, and most lively zeal for the service of the Queen," the British ambassador concluded.

And then suddenly and without warning, Frederick of Prussia attacked. "He dropped the mask," a French statesman observed astutely.

FREDERICK THE GREAT—for this was in fact he—is one of the most celebrated figures in history. Much admired for his success in battle, over the centuries this Prussian king has come to embody the German ideal of discipline, efficiency, tactical superiority, and elite militarism. Frederick is, if anything, equally revered for his cultured appreciation of music and literature, and is perhaps best known for his famous friendship (for a while, anyway) with the immortal

Voltaire, the preeminent wit and philosopher–playwright of Europe, with whom he traded verses and sardonic one–liners. This is the Frederick the Great of the history books, the master strategist who later inspired a fractured Germany to rise up and shake off centuries of foreign domination, to unite finally as one nation.

But the truth is that Frederick the Great was the battered son of a horrifically abusive, alcoholic father, a boy who suffered physically, mentally, and spiritually at the hands of his parent as no child ever should, and the world has been contending with the results of their malignant relationship ever since.

Frederick was born on January 24, 1712, which made him just five years older than Maria Theresa. He was his parents' second surviving child. (An elder sister, Wilhelmina, with whom he grew to be very close, was born in 1709.★) The kingdom was jubilant over the birth of a son and heir, and as a measure of the high hopes his father had for him, the king of Prussia even solicited Maria Theresa's father, Charles, to stand as godfather to the crown prince.

But as early as the age of six, when Frederick's personality began to develop and show itself, he became the object of his father's wrath. The king of Prussia had on his ascension to the throne imposed an atmosphere of bullying austerity (except for copious quantities of beer) unusual for a royal court. He loathed spending money and kept his household on such a tight budget that his family often went hungry. He despised culture, frivolity, or ostentation in any form and dressed more like a soldier than a sovereign. Equally out of the ordinary, almost alone among his peers, the king of Prussia did not keep a mistress. This was not out of love for his wife, whom he treated despicably, but rather a preference for the company of men, particularly soldiers. In fact, Frederick's father was fixated on assembling an army of exceptionally tall warriors. "His principal occupation was to drill a regiment...which was composed of colossal men six feet

---

★ Wilhelmina is not to be confused with Wilhelmine, Charles's irate sister-in-law. Luckily, Frederick's sister spelled her name with an *a* at the end, so it shouldn't be too difficult to tell them apart.

in height," Frederick's sister Wilhelmina reported in her memoirs. "All the monarchs of Europe eagerly sent recruits for it. This regiment might justly be styled 'the channel of royal favor,' for to give or procure tall men for the King was sufficient to obtain anything of him."*

It was Frederick's misfortune, with a cruel, rigid, alcoholic father like this, to have been born gay, with an irresistible, flamboyant love of color, beauty, music, poetry, literature, and extravagant, sumptuous clothing. As a result, everything his father wanted him to be, he wasn't, and everything he wanted to be, his father scorned and tried

Frederick the Great as a child

---

* The king did not limit himself simply to accepting exceptionally tall men for favors but actively sent agents out into other realms to "recruit"—i.e., kidnap—this sort of soldier for Prussia. He also ordered tall women to marry these men, so as to produce future tall combatants for his service. Anyone wondering where Adolf Hitler came up with the notion of a German super-race need look no further.

to beat or intimidate out of him. The king of Prussia demanded that his eldest boy (he would eventually sire three younger sons as well as five more daughters) spend his free time hunting and practicing military drills, and gave him weapons and his own regiment of 300 noblemen's sons to command when he was nine, but Frederick preferred to stay home and play the flute. "My brother was odious to him, and never appeared before him but to be ill-used," Wilhelmina reported sorrowfully. "This inspired the prince royal with an invincible fear of his father, which grew up with him even to the age of maturity."

To change his son's nature, in addition to verbal humiliation, physical abuse, and the denial of love, the king put the boy on a grueling academic schedule. Frederick was awakened at 6:00 every morning and given fifteen minutes to wash his hands and throw on the required drab, constricting Prussian military uniform (Frederick called this army tunic his "shroud, *Sterbe-kittel,* or death-clothes"). Every hour of his day was accounted for, with a heavy emphasis on religion, geography, maps (for military purposes), morality, and German. "The poor prince had not the smallest relaxation," noted Wilhelmina. "Music, reading, sciences, and arts were prohibited as crimes."

But one of his tutors had been forced to flee France as a child, and against the king's wishes he instilled a love of French culture in his pupil, to the point where at sixteen Frederick grew his hair long and secretly purchased a crimson dressing gown trimmed in gold after the fashion in Paris. In this outfit he was one day surprised while surreptitiously playing music with another young man by his father, who had made an impromptu visit to his heir's quarters. The king's fury was profound. The beautiful robe went into the fire and Frederick's hair was summarily cut off. Soon thereafter the king whipped his son viciously with a cane and tried to strangle him with the cord used to tie back the curtains. Frederick was only saved by the timely intervention of a servant who heard his screams. "Thy obstinate perverse disposition which does not love thy Father—for when one...really loves one's Father, one does what the Father requires, not while he is there to see it, but when his back is turned too. For the rest, thou know'st very well that I can endure no effeminate fellow...who puts himself to shame, cannot ride nor shoot...frizzles his hair like a fool, and does not cut it off," the king wrote coldly in response to Frederick's pleas for forgiveness. "I am in the utmost despair," Frederick wrote to his mother in a letter of December 1729, after this incident. "What I had always dreaded has at length happened. The king has entirely forgotten that I am his son and treated me like the meanest of men...I am driven to extremes; I have too much honor to submit to such treatment, and I am determined to put an end to it one way or another."*

Frederick did not mean by this to take his own life but rather to liberate himself from his father's control by fleeing the kingdom. Together with his most intimate confidant, Lieutenant Katte, the crown prince planned an elaborate escape that involved a secret midnight dash across the border on horseback. In the blackness of the early morning hours of August 5, 1730, Frederick awoke and, according to plan, dressed silently so as not to disturb his sleeping valet. Significantly, as this was the hour of his emancipation, he put aside his detested Prussian uniform in favor of a French nobleman's costume. Then he slipped outside and made his way to the site where he had previously arranged to have horses waiting.

But alas for Frederick, his scheme had days before been betrayed to his father, and his valet was only feigning sleep. His departure was reported instantly to the authorities, and both he and Katte were shadowed, apprehended, and thrown into prison. What followed is

---

* There is reason to believe that Frederick's father was also homosexual but repressed it. The elector of Saxony once tempted the king of Prussia with a naked woman "more beautiful than they paint Venus and the Graces" while hosting him on a visit to Dresden, but much to the elector's and his guests' amusement the king fled the woman's presence in a panic. If so, this might account for the king's lack of mistresses, his obsession with men, particularly soldiers, his abusive behavior toward his family, his drunkenness, and his extreme reaction to his eldest son. It's possible he felt the need to distance himself from Frederick's homosexuality for fear it would reflect on him and that others would then discern his secret.

one of the most terrible acts of vengeance ever perpetrated on a child by a parent. On November 1, a court-martial was held at which both Frederick and Katte were found guilty of treason and sentenced to death. On November 6, eighteen-year-old Frederick was informed that one of the executions had been scheduled. He was removed from his cell believing his life to be over. Instead, he was forced to watch as Katte, his dearest companion and most likely his lover, was dragged to the block. Frederick did everything he could to save him. He frantically pleaded to renounce the throne, to substitute himself for his friend, anything, anything. "How wretched I am, dear Katte! I am the cause of your death. Would to Heaven I were in your place!" Frederick cried out. "Ah!" replied Katte, "if I had a thousand lives, I would sacrifice them all for your royal highness." The axe fell; Katte's bloody severed head rolled toward Frederick; the prince fainted at the sight.

This was by no means the end of Frederick's suffering. His father was adamant that the sentence of execution imposed by the court-martial be carried out against his eldest son. The king of Prussia saw a chance to rid himself of his disappointing scion and substitute Frederick's younger brother, whose conduct he found more to his liking, as heir to the throne. It was only through the intervention of his godfather, Charles, who took pity on the teenager, that Frederick's life was spared. The emperor sternly reminded the king of Prussia that the crown prince was a subject of the empire and could not therefore be executed without imperial permission. Charles even kindly sent Frederick some money to live on, as his father was denying him sustenance.

No one lives through an ordeal like this unscathed. Frederick's father kept him in prison for a full year before deigning to see his eldest son again. The person he met on August 15, 1731, was a different Frederick. This Frederick was a model of obedience. This Frederick acted to perfection the part of the penitent, servile son, groveling at his father's feet as he begged for forgiveness. This Frederick pledged, if the king of Prussia would but free him from his cell, to do instantly whatever was demanded of him in the future. This Frederick's first act, upon gaining his smug parent's release from prison, was voluntarily to go hunting, as a symbol of his complete submission to his father's preferences.

This was the Frederick whom Francis had met on his goodwill tour: the Frederick of the mask. The cowed prince who dutifully married a woman he loathed ("Thank God that's over!" he wrote to Wilhelmina after his wedding night) and who appeared touchingly grateful for the (then) duke of Lorraine's friendship. The Frederick who never again donned colorful French finery but instead embraced his somber Prussian uniform, and who so threw himself into his military training and regiment that he actually won his father's approval sufficiently to be promoted from colonel to major general. The Frederick who prudently affected no interest or ambition in government (so as not to arouse his father's jealousy) and instead lived quietly in the countryside north of Berlin, privately diverting himself with music, literature, and writing fan letters to Voltaire, these activities being no longer prohibited now that he was a married man and suitably groveling son.

But all the while, behind this docile facade lay another Frederick. This Frederick hurt, and therefore became intent on hurting. This Frederick, having been preyed upon when weak, perceived strength as preying upon the weak. This Frederick had learned to despise the time-honored chivalric values of love, honor, truth, and loyalty as empty words and to substitute in their place an ethos of sneering cynicism, opportunism, and treachery. This Frederick, having been bullied and beaten down by his father, schemed to have his revenge, and in so doing became his father, only on a far more consequential and dangerous scale.

It was this Frederick who assumed the throne upon the death of his father on May 31, 1740. It is a great irony that Charles, who loved and cherished his daughter, and did everything he could think of to protect her after his death, left her a ruined army and no money, while Frederick's father, who despised his son and had done all he could to destroy his spirit, left him the largest military force in Europe—80,000 well-trained soldiers, more than Spain, Britain, or France could summon—as well as, from decades of penny-pinching, the financial means to support it. But where the father had been content merely to hoard these assets, from the moment he took over, Frederick intended to use them. It was simply a matter of finding a suitably vulnerable target.

And then his godfather the emperor, the man who had intervened to save Frederick's life when his own father had wanted to kill him, died and left all of his property to an untried and imperiled young woman.

FREDERICK'S PLAN WAS SIMPLE. He would expand his own kingdom by invading and annexing neighboring Silesia, which belonged to Maria Theresa, on the grounds that it was his by an ancient claim, although even Frederick knew this to be a pretext. "When one is in a good position, should one take advantage of it or not?" he explained blithely in his instructions to his ambassador to the court of Vienna. "My troops and I are quite ready for anything; if I do not make use of this good fortune, I fail to use an instrument which is actually in my hand."* Once he had occupied the province, Frederick continued, the ambassador might then be permitted to pay Maria Theresa "a couple of millions," if she put up too much of a fuss about it.

This course of action necessarily depended upon speed and deception, so as to leave the court of Vienna no time to prepare an adequate defense. Charles VI died on October 20, 1740; the news was communicated to Frederick by messenger on the twenty-sixth; and by October 29, Frederick's chief ministers had already outlined a precise method of attack. In November, Prussia's most experienced

---

* Voltaire claimed that Frederick was even more explicit in the manuscript he later wrote chronicling these events, which the king of Prussia sent to his literary friend for comments before publication. "Troops always ready to act, my well-filled treasury, and the vivacity of my disposition—these were my reasons for making war upon Maria Theresa," he had boasted. This was a little too much candor even for Voltaire, and he made Frederick take that sentence out.

general was called up from retirement, and by the end of the month the kingdom was clearly on a war footing, with artillery, ammunition, and some 20,000 soldiers converging on the southern border. So, all the time that Frederick was warmly assuring Francis of his support, he was actually mobilizing his forces for an invasion.

But even in an age before electronic communication, it was very difficult to move that many men and large guns without *somebody* noticing, and by the beginning of December reports were filtering into Vienna of uncommon military traffic along the border with Prussia. Although Maria Theresa, questioning Frederick's ominous buildup of soldiers to her circle of white-haired councillors, was told, "Do not be afraid; he will be just like his father, who all his life kept his gun loaded, and never once fired it," she nonetheless sent an emissary to Berlin the first week in December to confront the Prussian king as to his intentions. The envoy, who had to struggle through roads clogged with Frederick's battalions and arsenal just to get to the capital, could see instantly that Silesia was the target. His suspicions were confirmed in a private audience on December 10, when Frederick, clearly reveling in his own duplicity, confessed his military intentions but insisted that he was undertaking this campaign for only the most thoughtful of motives. "I am going to Silesia, but, you understand, as a good friend, not so much to establish any rights I may have, as to defend the hereditary rights of the Queen against all her enemies," the would-be savior assured the envoy.

The imperial emissary dispatched his report of this disquieting conversation to Vienna by messenger as quickly as he could; it arrived on December 20. But by that time Frederick had already joined his troops and crossed the border into Silesia. Maria Theresa just had time to process the extent of the threat before the Prussian ambassador appeared and demanded an audience. She refused to see him personally and instead sent her husband to represent her government. "I bear in one hand the salvation of the House of Austria, and in the other the Imperial Crown for your Highness," the ambassador announced dramatically upon meeting Francis, adopting the same high-minded manner Frederick had employed in Berlin. "The treasury of the King my master is at the service of the Queen; he will also secure to her the assistance of his allies, England, Holland, and Russia." Then, abruptly dropping the pose, he continued in a far more menacing tone: "In return for these offers, and to compensate for the peril he incurs by making them, he demands the whole of Silesia, but nothing less. The King's determination is immovable; he will, he can take Silesia, and if it be not offered to him with a good grace, he will give his troops and his money to Saxony and Bavaria." But Maria Theresa had already formulated her response, and her husband delivered it word for word. "The Queen," returned Francis firmly, "is not reduced to such despair that she must throw herself into the arms of a prince who enters her States as an enemy…Return then to your master, and tell him that, so long as he leaves one man upon the territory of that province, we will perish rather than treat with him."

Determined to fight, Maria Theresa called up one of her father's veteran commanders and over the next three months managed to raise a force of some 20,000 men. The imperial soldiers were recruited mostly from next-door Moravia (which, being on the border with Silesia, had every incentive to hold the line against the invader), augmented by a regiment of seasoned Austrian cavalry.

Even before her army had a chance to move into Silesia, however, Maria Theresa achieved a signal victory that had been denied the empire for nearly half a century. On March 13, 1741, she gave birth to her fourth child—*and it was a boy.*

It is impossible to overstate the importance of this event. Maria Theresa was a deeply religious woman, and there is little doubt that she took the birth of her son as a sign from God of the legitimacy of her rule. She named the child Joseph, after the saint to whom she had prayed during her delivery and who she was convinced had intervened in her favor. "I cannot remember that I ever desired anything by his [Saint Joseph's] means which he hath failed to obtain for me," she later wrote. The citizens of Vienna were just as ecstatic to have the curse of successive daughters lifted, and public celebrations continued for a full week after the christening. "Her Majesty's subjects had now a precious pledge and hope of their future security," reported a local gazette.

The birth of the prince could not have been more fortuitous. For less than a month later came the news of the defeat of the imperial army at Mollwitz.

MOLLWITZ, THE SITE OF THE BATTLE, was a small village in Silesia located about 40 miles south of the capital city of Breslau. Although the Austrian general sent to dislodge the Prussian forces knew that they were in the vicinity, he did not expect them to march as quickly as they did, and so was taken by surprise. Still, the imperial commander was able to recover quickly, and immediately sent in his most experienced troops, the cavalry, as his opening salvo. A ferocious wave consisting of 4,500 dragoons, sabers drawn and supported by cannon fire, thundered on horseback into the enemy soldiers, scattering the opposing cavalry and demolishing the Prussian forward line of defense.

This was Frederick's first battle. He had all those years of drilling that his father had insisted upon, of course, but unlike his general (who was second-in-command after the king), Frederick had never experienced actual combat before. It must be admitted that his reaction to being under fire was not encouraging. No sooner did he witness the violent charge of the Austrian cavalry than he turned tail and fled. As his horse was acknowledged to be the fastest in the Prussian cavalry, he shouted back over his shoulder at the men for whom he was responsible, and whom he was deserting in their hour of need, "Farewell friends, I am better mounted than you are!"

By rights, that should have been the end of any future dreams of glory the Prussian king was harboring, but fortunately for Frederick, his soldiers did not have the same option. His general knew quite well that if *he* abandoned his post as his sovereign had, he would be executed for treason. Also, he had faith in his infantry. The Prussian military had developed a new tactic in the art of warfare. And so, literarily within minutes of its initial success, the imperial army found itself facing line after line of disciplined Prussian foot soldiers armed with high-performance muskets that each unit had been trained to shoot in concert. It took less than an hour for the relentlessly advancing, methodical barrage of bullets fired by the Prussian infantry to convince Maria Theresa's general to sound a retreat. The brave king of these exceptional warriors did not find out he had won the battle until the next morning, when the messenger sent with news of the victory discovered Frederick hiding out in a mill 30 miles away and brought him back to his men "all covered with fame and flour," as one of his contemporaries quipped.

But it didn't matter that he'd fled; all that mattered was he'd won. The ability to deliver on the battlefield was a potent lure in the eighteenth century. In the wake of the victory, envoys from all over Europe flocked to Frederick's command headquarters in Silesia with offers of alliance.

The pressure on Maria Theresa to sue for peace was enormous. The 15,000 or so imperial troops who had survived the battle were in full retreat, and she was heavily in debt. Her only hope was that England would intervene, George II having formerly promised to send soldiers to Austria's aid. But the English king took fright after Frederick threatened to turn his army against George's home province of Hanover if he meddled in the conflict. So, instead of honoring his commitment, George II instructed Sir Thomas to insist that Maria Theresa meet Prussian demands and surrender Silesia to Frederick. "The security of Hanover . . . was always put foremost," admitted an English diplomat stationed at The Hague, who was involved in these negotiations.

But no matter how hard she was pressed by England to yield, or how dire the situation presented to her by her quaking councillors, Maria Theresa remained unbowed. "Not only for political reasons, but from conscience and honor, I will not consent to part with much in Silesia," she burst out heatedly when informed of the humiliating terms proposed by Sir Thomas. "For no sooner is one enemy satisfied than another starts up; another, and then another must be appeased, and all at my expense."

Determined to resist, Maria Theresa knew she needed to act quickly to rebuild her army. If she could not get additional troops from England she would recruit them from within her own borders. Without bothering to consult her ministers, she announced that in June she would travel to Hungary to be crowned queen, after which she would personally appeal to her Hungarian subjects for soldiers to fight Frederick.

Her elderly advisers were aghast and fell over themselves counseling against such a risky and potentially lethal course of action. The Hungarians, they explained, were a notoriously vicious and untrustworthy people, a source of continual rebellion, who in the past had even been known to ally with the Turks against the Austrians. It was much too dangerous for her to put herself in their hands!*

But Maria Theresa ignored them and continued with preparations for the journey. The Hungarian coronation ceremony, heavy on symbolism, was somewhat arduous, particularly for a woman who had just given birth. As part of the ritual, the incoming sovereign (exclusively male in the past) was required to don the traditional robe of Saint Stephen (king of Hungary in the eleventh century, later canonized), a garment rather the worse for its extreme age and wear, mount a large horse, charge up an embankment, and wave a heavy sword (also a relic of the aforementioned saint) to the north, south, east, and west, as a sign of the new monarch's resolve to protect against all enemies. Faced with this daunting test of physical fitness, Maria Theresa, who had never been particularly athletic, prudently opted for additional riding lessons.

But she didn't need any help at all in mastering her vows, as she

---

* Of these timorous, white-haired officials Maria Theresa would later observe: "If God Himself had not arranged for the death of them all I should never have come through."

was fluent in Latin, the official language of the Hungarian government. Even more importantly, she was extremely sensitive to the underlying distrust this volatile realm had for its previous imperial overlords. The Hungarians were used to being treated as inferior by the Austrians. Maria Theresa was determined to show them that she was different by orchestrating an overt display of deference and respect.

And so, when the embattled queen, accompanied by a sizable entourage that included her husband and Sir Thomas, left Vienna for the Hungarian capital of Pressburg on June 19, 1741, the riverboats carrying the royal party flaunted flags and pennants emblazoned with Hungarian coats of arms; the crew, even to the oarsmen, were arrayed in the Hungarian national colors of red, white, and green; and Maria Theresa herself wore a gown specifically designed to emulate traditional Hungarian finery.

They arrived in Pressburg the next evening and were greeted by cheering crowds and an imposing cannon salute. It had been a very long time since the city had hosted a coronation, and the excitement was palpable. The ceremony was scheduled for June 25 and was to be conducted at the venerable Saint Martin's Cathedral, founded in the fifteenth century, traditional site of Hungarian coronations. Maria Theresa's father had been crowned in this same church three decades earlier.

She knew what the people wanted, and she gave it to them. On the appointed morning, the hordes of spectators lining the streets straining for a glimpse of her were treated to the sight of their new sovereign arriving at the cathedral by carriage at the end of a long and satisfyingly regal procession. Her magnificent coronation robe, richly embroidered in gold and precious jewels, blazed in the sunlight and testified to the solemn grandeur of the occasion. Once inside the church, she followed tradition to the letter. She knelt to receive the crown and swore to protect "the old laws, rights, and liberties of the land." When she rose, she slipped the decrepit mantle of Saint Stephen on over her coronation dress and pulled the iron sword handed to her out of its ceremonial sheath. She lifted it high and used it to make the sign of the cross. Afterward, she sat on her throne with her orb and scepter to receive the homage of her barons.

The religious ceremony over, it was time for the final test. A carriage brought the new queen of Hungary to a hillock by the river, where in full view of her subjects she climbed up into the saddle of the powerful black stallion that had been chosen for her to ride. Grasping the heavy sword of Saint Stephen, she once again raised it high as she charged up the hill, "her long, loose, yellow locks, like golden wire," flowing behind her. Sir Thomas, who recorded these events for his government, was thunderstruck by her performance. "The queen was all charm; she rode gallantly up the royal mount, and defied the four corners of the world with the drawn saber, in a manner to show she had no occasion [no need] for that weapon to conquer all who saw her," he raved.

She had done it. "Long live our Lady the King!" came the roar from the assembled crowds.

Four days later came word that Louis XV of France had signed a secret military agreement with Frederick the Great of Prussia to provide men and arms to place the elector of Bavaria on the imperial throne, and to divide up Austrian territory as they saw fit. Maria Theresa was now facing a two-front war.

4

Queen of Bohemia

We shall only need to take a map, and trace with a pencil upon it what he [Louis XV] would like to have, and . . . he shall have it.

—Frederick the Great to the French ambassador,
March 18, 1741

Although a woman, I do not lack courage . . . and I have many subjects who will sustain my rights, and rather than see me abased, will risk all.

—Maria Theresa to Cardinal Fleury,
chief minister of France, September 27, 1741

THE SECRET ALLIANCE BETWEEN Protestant Prussia and Catholic France, signed on June 5, 1741, was as unlikely as it was unexpected. Since the accession of Louis XIV the century before, Prussia had been a stalwart member of the military alliance between Great Britain, Holland, and the empire dedicated to *opposing* French expansion in Europe. Additionally, since George II was Frederick's uncle, and the two shared the same religion, it was more or less assumed that Prussia and Great Britain would maintain friendly relations, which by default meant working together against France. The British were always suspicious of the French.

But Frederick cared only to make the best possible deal for himself, and Louis XV's ambassador (who was also commander of the French army) was keen to reprise past military glories, particularly against so weak an opponent as Maria Theresa. Impressed by the size and professionalism of Frederick's soldiers—"Nothing can equal the excellence and the discipline of the Prussian troops," the ambassador exclaimed upon observing them in action—he at once gave in to all of the king of Prussia's demands. These involved sending not just one French army against the queen of Hungary but *two*. The first battalion, composed of some 40,000 warriors, was to cross the Rhine in August and meet up with a force of similar size mustered by the elector of Bavaria (who was also in on the scheme) for the purpose of invading Austria. At the same time, *another* 40,000 French soldiers were to be dispatched to march on Hanover as a means of intimidating George II (and hence Great Britain), to keep him from coming to Maria Theresa's defense. Frederick himself planned to have over 100,000 Prussian troops available by September to secure all of Silesia. The strategy was clearly to wrest as much territory as could be had from the queen of Hungary through the use of speed and overwhelming force. "You can understand the necessity of fulfilling your engagements without delay," Frederick rallied his French counterpart in a letter of July 18, 1741. "France may at this moment strike the greatest blow she has ever struck in her life. Instead of creeping up to power, she can reach it in an Homeric stride, and you have before you the fairest harvest of laurels that ever a general in France has reaped," he cajoled shamelessly. And with this, the plan was launched into action.

So confident were the conspirators of victory that not much emphasis was placed on keeping the signing of this agreement a secret, with the result that the general outline of the intrigue, if not all of the specifics, was leaked pretty quickly to the British. Consequently, it fell once more to Sir Thomas to be the bearer of bad tidings to Maria Theresa's senior citizen advisers in Vienna. "On hearing, beyond possibility of doubt, that Prussia, France, and Bavaria had combined, the whole...Council fell back into their chairs like dead men," Sir Thomas reported.

Faced with so dire a predicament, the British envoy again urgently pressed Maria Theresa to concede defeat, accept Prussia's usurpation of at least some of Silesia, and attempt to salvage what remained by bribing Frederick to abandon his new allies and be content with the spoils he'd already appropriated. The queen of Hungary resisted at first, but Sir Thomas kept after her so insistently that she at last very reluctantly agreed to offer Frederick the sum of 2 million guilders (approximately £200,000, to be provided by Britain), as well as a considerable portion of her property in the Austrian Netherlands, as compensation for Frederick's willingness to cease hostilities. But she was wretched about it. "I hope very much that you will not succeed," she told the ambassador bluntly on August 3, when he left to present these terms to Frederick, and as soon as he had ridden off, she sent the same offer by private messenger to the elector of Bavaria. In fact, she was stalling for time. "I deceive my ministers," she wrote. "My firm resolution is never to give up anything in Silesia, still less all the lower part."

She needn't have worried that Frederick would take the bait; the king of Prussia, holding every card (including having been leaked the details of this overture in advance), had no intention of accepting Maria Theresa's terms. Instead, Frederick decided to have a little fun with the British by using the mediation process to ensure that France had sufficient opportunity to muster its armies and commence the invasion on schedule. "This proposal is a snare to embroil me with you," he explained to the French ambassador on July 28, 1741, a week before Sir Thomas's arrival. "But I will secure full time for the King [Louis XV] to act, by asking for leisure to reflect, and then I will make such big proposals that they cannot accept them... Is it my fault they are such fools?" he chortled.

And that is exactly what happened. On July 31, the elector of Bavaria, with 30,000 men, invaded Austria, took the city of Passau, about 175 miles west of Vienna, and announced his intention to forcibly seize all of Maria Theresa's inheritance, which he considered his by virtue of his wife's earlier claim. Then, over the course of the next week, two separate armies, each consisting of approximately 40,000 soldiers, left France, one on its way to threaten Hanover, the other to rendezvous with the Bavarians at Passau. By August 9, Frederick was able to drop the act, look the startled Sir Thomas in the eye, and close off all hope of mediation. "I am at the head of an invincible army, already master of a country which I will have, which I must have," he threatened imperiously. "Return with this answer to Vienna; they who want peace will give me what I want"—which was nothing less than to cede all of Silesia to Prussia.

By the time Sir Thomas returned with this disheartening result, news of the invasion of Austria by Bavaria, and the taking of Passau, had made its way to Maria Theresa and her government. She appealed for help to George II, but the king of England, menaced at Hanover by the second French army, behaved exactly as Frederick had predicted and elected to stay out of the coming conflict rather than risk losing his beloved home territory. This in turn allowed the elector of Bavaria, freed of the worry that he might be attacked from behind by soldiers paid for or recruited by Britain, to continue *his* assault. The promised 40,000 French troops assigned to him having arrived at the end of August, on September 10, 1741, he easily took the undefended city of Linz and publicly proclaimed himself archduke of Austria.

The capital city of Vienna, only 115 miles to the east, suddenly facing a possible onslaught by 70,000 enemy soldiers, went into a panic. Noble families packed up what they could and fled to the perceived safety of their country houses; there was hoarding in the event of a siege; those inhabitants who could not afford to leave believed devastation and death to be hourly imminent, particularly as Maria Theresa, too, had departed, apparently leaving the city to its fate.

It is true that she had left her Viennese subjects, but she had not abandoned them. She had known what she was going to do from the day she was crowned queen of Hungary. At eleven o'clock on the morning of September 11, the day after the taking of Linz, she was in Pressburg, addressing the Hungarian Diet. She stood before the assembled representatives, all of them men. She was dressed in black and wore her crown and ceremonial sword. "The misfortune of our situation renders it a duty to inform our faithful States of the illustrious kingdom of Hungary, of the invasions in arms of our hereditary province of Austria, and of the danger which threatens the kingdom itself, and also to propose the means of remedying these ills," she began, speaking in Latin so they would understand. "The existence of those two kingdoms, that of our own person, our children, and our crown is at stake. Forsaken by all, we have no resource but the fidelity of these illustrious States and the ever-renowned valor of the Hungarians. We earnestly entreat the different orders of these faithful States not to lose a moment in decreeing and putting into execution such measures as are rendered necessary by this extreme danger... As for what depends upon us, our faithful States may rest assured that our royal affection will be careful to do all that may secure the maintenance, integrity, felicity, and honor of this kingdom," she promised fervently in conclusion.

The emotional effect of this plea upon the assembled delegates, communicated so fluently and with such obvious respect and sincerity in their own language, was profound. No sooner had Maria Theresa finished speaking than the Hungarian Diet voted unanimously to provide her with an army of 30,000 infantry, to be marshaled immediately. Further, many of those present pledged to recruit and personally lead an additional 25,000 in cavalry, and to call upon their allies in Croatia and Transylvania to join the struggle against the invaders. Together with the regiments of the Austrian army that had survived the battle of Mollwitz, this meant the queen of Hungary could now rely on a force of potentially as many as 100,000 soldiers.

Ten days later, on September 21, as a further gesture of solidarity, the Diet offered Francis, as the husband of their queen, the co-regency of the kingdom. Maria Theresa knew that Francis, who could not

speak Latin and was perceived of as arrogant by her Hungarian subjects, was not popular, and that this was a concession on the part of
the representatives to please her. And so she returned the favor as
only she could. The day before, she had had her son, Joseph, not
quite six months old, brought to Pressburg. Now she had the baby
carried into the audience chamber and in a moment of high drama
took him in her arms and held him up high for the assembled company to see. This infant, her heir, was the visible sign of her faith in
her subjects and her commitment to them; he represented the promise of continuity, the king they would one day have. "At the sight of
him the deputies made great acclamation," testified Sir Thomas,
who was there.

She had her soldiers, and the loyalty of the Hungarians. Now to
use them.

NEWS OF MARIA THERESA's gambit in Pressburg, and the successful
outcome of her appeal, had an immediate effect on her opponents'
strategy. The elector of Bavaria, who had been perfectly happy to
make plans to swoop down and seize Vienna while it lay unprotected, was rather less enthusiastic when he discovered that it was
now to be defended by 30,000 able-bodied, bloodthirsty (by reputation) Hungarians. Serious fighting, where he might get captured or
hurt—or even killed, perish the thought—was definitely not what
he had signed on for, particularly when there were so many other,
tantalizingly easy targets among Maria Theresa's extensive possessions to invade. And of these, Prague, the capital city of Bohemia,
stood out. Prague, defended by a standing garrison of only about
3,000 soldiers, had the additional advantage of being over 200 miles
away from Pressburg, so if he hurried he could get there without
running into any Hungarians. The French commander having
agreed with this assessment, in October the elector of Bavaria, leaving 20,000 men at Linz to defend his conquests in Austria, bravely
set out for Prague with an army of some 50,000 soldiers. Thus was
Vienna saved from violent occupation.

But now Prague was in serious jeopardy, and even worse, Augustus III of Saxony (whom Maria Theresa's father had helped make king of Poland), worried that his brother-in-law would eclipse him in fame and spoils, had abruptly switched sides and thrown in with France and Bavaria. In exchange for providing 20,000 men toward the capture of Prague, Augustus had been promised the Austrian territory of Moravia by his new allies.

Even with the full support of the Hungarians, Maria Theresa understood that it was impossible to defend against attacks in Silesia, Bohemia, and Austria all at the same time. If she didn't find some way to break up the coalition against her, she would be stripped of most of her inheritance. She needed to coax at least one member of the opposing alliance to betray the others and settle separately with her.

So she secretly sought to bribe each of the principals to suspend hostilities against her. To France, she offered to cede Luxembourg; to Bavaria, Milan or the Netherlands; to Prussia, Lower Silesia. It was the equivalent of testing different spots on a shoddily constructed fence for a loose board.

France and Bavaria each instantly turned her down coldly, and made haste to apprise the others of this insidious attempt to sabotage their coalition. Frederick, too, was transparent with his allies, reporting that he had scornfully rejected an English mediator who had approached him with a similar offer from Maria Theresa. "Either they think me a rogue or the stupidest of men," Frederick snorted to a French envoy, who duly conveyed these sentiments to his superiors. "No one can be more touched than I am, by the solicitude with which your Majesty has deigned to inform me of the fruitless negotiation of the English," declared the French commander in a letter to Frederick on October 2, 1741. The elector of Bavaria, who had received his own communication from Frederick on this subject, agreed. "We must certainly, my dear Marshal, render justice to the King of Prussia. It would be impossible...to act with more straightforwardness and honesty than he does," the elector observed to the French commander on October 9.

Except Frederick *hadn't* turned it down. On October 9, the very day the elector of Bavaria was singing his praises, the king of Prussia slipped away from his camp and met in secret with the Austrian general he'd recently fought against at Mollwitz. There, Frederick gave his word to cease hostilities in exchange for Silesia. But as he also wished to keep this deal hidden from his former allies, an elaborate deception had to be staged to cover his treachery. Frederick, who loved nothing better than to playact, gleefully suggested that he *pretend* to besiege Neisse, an important town in Lower Silesia, while the Austrians pretended to defend it. "We want to put an end to the war, but we do not want to appear to have done so," the Prussian ambassador charged with communicating this unusual arrangement to Vienna later explained helpfully.

And so it was agreed. Frederick, having gotten what he wanted, then grew expansive. "Nothing could exceed his [Frederick's] satisfaction that the Queen and the Grand Duke [Francis], whom he had always loved, had at length abandoned their obstinate attitude… Now he was much moved by their misfortunes, and asked no better than to do them every possible service. Was the Queen in need of money? He could put fifty thousand crowns at her disposal to help her to get through the winter," dryly reported an eyewitness to these negotiations.

Frederick's motivations for abandoning his former alliance were threefold. First, he was furious that the elector of Bavaria had not kept to the original plan and advanced on Vienna. By instead veering off toward Prague, the French and the Bavarians freed Maria Theresa to use her Hungarian soldiers to defend Silesia, making Frederick's conquest there much more difficult. This way, he got Silesia without having to fight for it. Second, he was also extremely put out that his former allies had ceded Moravia to Augustus—if they were so intent on giving property away, why reward Saxony, which after all had come very late to the party, and not Prussia? Finally, Frederick was convinced that he could conclude a secret separate peace with Maria Theresa at no risk to himself because he could always just deny he'd done it, a position he expressed with uncharacteristic candor at the October 9 negotiation. "Be fortunate [in battle], and I am with you; but, if you are beaten, I shall think of myself [and return to the alliance with France and Bavaria]," he told the Austrian commander. Everyone on Maria Theresa's side understood this. "If you have him to-day, he will be at the service of France to-morrow, if France has him to-day, we may have him to-morrow," Francis sniffed. But with Prague in danger they had no choice.

Freed for the moment from the necessity to protect against Prussian advancement, Maria Theresa was finally able to deploy her forces wholeheartedly against the French and Bavarian offensive. Holding back approximately 12,000 men under the command of her most experienced cavalry officer, Marshal Khevenhüller, so as not to leave Austria completely unprotected, she mobilized everything else she had—the surviving portion of the army that had fought against Frederick at Mollwitz and the majority of the guard stationed in Vienna, supplemented by 20,000 of her newly levied Hungarians, for a combined force of some 60,000 soldiers—under her husband's command and beseeched him to hurry and save Prague.

Francis's martial abilities, however, had not improved with age. Unaccustomed to the rigors of active duty, he moved slowly, rested often, and spent much time complaining of privation and hardship in his reports home. As a result, it took the force he was leading until November 26, 1741, to reach the outskirts of Prague. He arrived only to discover that the city had fallen to the enemy the day before, its garrison taken by surprise in a sneak attack. The elector of Bavaria had already entered the capital in state, and he and the victorious army he commanded were safely behind its walls. So secure did the elector feel that he had himself crowned king of Bohemia on December 19 and then left immediately afterward for Frankfurt, where the Imperial Diet was based, to claim the empire.

After all her efforts—including the voluntary surrender of Silesia to Frederick, which was like giving up one of her own children to the enemy—to have Prague taken was a terrible blow to Maria Theresa. It must have seemed as if her cause was doomed, and yet she did not give up hope or let others surrender to it. "Here is Prague lost and the consequences will be very bad," she wrote to her Bohemian chancellor, who had accompanied Francis and the army. "Now...is the time when courage is needed, when the territory and the Queen must be preserved, for I am a poor princess without that. For my part, my resolution is taken, everything must be risked and lost to sustain Bohemia, and on that basis you may work and arrange everything...I must have territory and for that all my troops, and all the Hungarians would have to be killed before I could yield anything. In short, this is the critical moment...You will say that I am cruel, and it is true; but I know well that all these cruelties which *I may cause to be done* now to sustain the country, I shall be hereafter enabled to repair a hundredfold and I will do so, but at this moment I close my heart to pity," she finished passionately. And to underscore her commitment to success she recalled Francis to Vienna (a humiliation that she tried to disguise by announcing she couldn't bear to have him away from her, a pretense that fooled no one) and replaced him as commander of the army with his younger brother, Charles of Lorraine, who had demonstrated significantly more initiative.

Charles listened to his more experienced officers and, keeping the army together, fell back south of Prague in order to coordinate a daring new two-pronged plan of attack with Vienna, which, at Maria Theresa's urging, was put into action with uncharacteristic energy. On December 22, 1741, while both the elector of Bavaria and the commanding general in charge of the French forces were in Frankfurt lobbying in preparation for the imperial election, the 12,000 dragoons who had been left behind to protect the capital, augmented by an additional 4,000 Hungarians, left Vienna and raced north toward Linz under the direction of Marshal Khevenhüller, Maria Theresa's most adept warrior. Simultaneously, the main Austrian army under Charles spread itself out in a ring around

Prague, cutting off the enemy's ability to send reinforcements in defense of its prior conquests. Consequently, on January 24, 1742, just as the delegates in Frankfurt, pressured and bribed by the French commanding general, cast their ballots unanimously in favor of the elector of Bavaria as the new Holy Roman Emperor, the French garrison at Linz, which through illness and desertion had been whittled down to only about 10,000 men, surrendered to Khevenhüller's superior force and was retaken by Maria Theresa. Thrilled at this victory, she sent Khevenhüller a letter promising him "her whole power and resources—everything in fact that her kingdom contains or can effect...Fare well and fight well," and backed it up with a further 10,000 soldiers, which he used to push on to the west. And so, on February 12, 1742, the very same day that the new emperor was being crowned in an opulent ceremony in Frankfurt, came the news that Maria Theresa's forces had not only reclaimed all of her territory in Austria but, not bothering to stop at the border, had also invaded and overrun the new emperor's home duchy of Bavaria (left inadequately defended as his army was off being pinned down in Prague) and were occupying his capital city of Munich.

IT WAS A MASTERSTROKE. Nothing depicted sham and impotency so much as an emperor who could not go home to his own château. It made the elector of Bavaria and his French ally look ridiculous, and with that perception momentum abruptly shifted from the pursuers to the pursued.

As had happened to Frederick after the battle of Mollwitz, Maria Theresa's success in battle bred allies, the most important of which was Britain. Impressed by her initiative, and always delighted to see the ambitions of its hated rival France checked, the British government now declared itself ready to drop its former neutrality and enter the war on the side of plucky Austria. The result was an immediate (and much-needed) cash infusion of £300,000, as well as the deployment of a force of 16,000 men bound for Germany.

Unfortunately, Britain wasn't the only realm to reevaluate its position in the light of Maria Theresa's victories. In a turnaround that surprised no one, Frederick, evidently regretting his earlier inclination to ally himself with her only if she won, instead used her conquests as an excuse to renege on his truce with her and return to the battlefield. Still miffed that Moravia had not been awarded to Prussia, Frederick, to ensure that he was not cut out of this important spoil, suddenly approached his former allies as though he'd never left them and suggested that he lead an invasion of that province while the Austrian army was conveniently away in Bavaria and Bohemia. The French, who by this time knew he was not to be trusted, and in any event wanted him to come to their aid in Prague, turned him down, but he managed to convince Augustus III (somewhat reluctantly) to support the plot.* And so, no sooner did Maria Theresa receive word that her army had taken Munich than she also learned that Frederick had marched an advance force into Moravia and easily overrun the undefended border town of Jihlava, which lay approximately halfway between Vienna and Prague.

The queen of Hungary, six months pregnant with her fifth child, and coming off her resounding victory in Bavaria, with the promise of British money and troops to aid her, was in no mood to dally with Frederick. Without hesitation, she sent a contingent of Hungarians flying across the border who turned the king of Prussia and his Saxon warriors out of Jihlava like a band of itinerant squatters. By March 8 Frederick had relinquished not simply the town but also his hopes of Moravia, and retreated hastily back to the main force of his army, which had been brought over from Silesia and was now stationed in Bohemia at Chrudim, about 80 miles east of Prague.

---

* The French were aware that Frederick had made a side deal with Maria Theresa to secure Silesia even before they took Prague. The French ambassador confronted the king of Prussia with the intelligence in a meeting on November 11, 1741, at which Frederick denied everything. "What can I do about it? Can I prevent mischief-makers from spreading lying reports, and fools from believing them?" the king of Prussia had demanded in an injured tone. "But, Sire, they come from Marshal Neipperg [the Austrian general] himself," protested the envoy. The commander of the French army soon came to the same conclusion about Frederick that Francis had. "He comes to our aid when we no longer want him," he observed wearily.

This failure, the first of Frederick's experience since he had started the aggression against Maria Theresa, was to have a profound effect on the war. The French ambassador noted nervously that the king of Prussia returned to camp from his Moravian escapade in a particularly foul temper. It seems to have finally dawned on Frederick that, should he continue to push Maria Theresa in this way, there was a possibility he might end up losing Silesia, the territory he had already gained, and which was of primary importance to him. He, who having begun his reign with a full treasury two years previously, was already running out of money; worse, he was continually beseeched by his worthless Bavarian ally, the new emperor, for loans and other handouts. His Saxon partner was equally useless; the troops supplied by Augustus III were poorly trained, and Frederick foresaw that Prussian soldiers would be doing the brunt of the fighting, and therefore the majority of the dying, in any future joint campaign. France he didn't trust at all, suspecting that, given the chance, Louis XV would turn on him (as Frederick himself had already turned on the French). All these thoughts he jotted down in a paper entitled "A Statement of the Reasons which I may have for remaining in Alliance with France" and "A Statement of the Reasons which I may have for making a Peace with the Queen of Hungary," a canny document of which a later historian noted dryly, "had it emanated from any other person...might be called an examination of conscience."

The result of this agonizingly heartfelt assessment of which of his allies would ultimately be the most useful to double-cross this time was made manifest two weeks later when on March 22, 1742, Frederick reached out secretly to the British and asked for aid in arranging a permanent peace treaty. As usual, his first demands were outrageous. In exchange for withdrawing from the conflict, the king of Prussia now asked not only for all of Silesia but also for territory in Bohemia (currently occupied by his *other* allies, France and Bavaria) that Maria Theresa would award to him after she had reconquered them without his help. Sir Thomas, none too pleased to be the emissary chosen to break these terms to the queen of

Hungary, waited until the end of April to make Frederick's overture known to her. Maria Theresa, nearing her time of confinement, refused even to discuss a peace agreement unless Prussia first officially agreed to turn on its former consortium and fight side by side with Austria and Britain against the French and Bavarians, a demand that she knew her nemesis would reject. When Francis, more willing to leave the diplomatic channel open than she, offered to communicate directly with Frederick, she answered warmly, "My dear heart, you shall write if it pleases you to do so; but he is not worthy of it, and he will make a bad use of it. Do not degrade yourself" — and she instead instructed Francis's brother, Charles of Lorraine, still commanding the army in Bohemia, to march on Frederick's military camp at Chrudim as a more pointed demonstration of what she thought of his peace plan.

The queen's position was conveyed to Frederick on May 10, 1742, along with the intelligence that a division of the Austrian army was breaking off from its former position in order to target him. Recognizing that if he let her run him out of town this time it would only encourage her to try to take back Silesia as well, the king of Prussia decided to turn the tables by launching a preemptive strike, in the hopes of finding her army unprepared as he had at Mollwitz. "I am going to advance upon the Austrians, and I will not let them make another step with their Hungarian rabble," he announced dramatically to the rather startled French ambassador (who of course had no idea that Frederick had been treating secretly for the last two months with the queen of Hungary). "I want it to be myself alone who shall beat them and have the pleasure of humbling them."

And so, on May 13, just as Maria Theresa was giving birth to her fourth daughter, whom she and Francis named Maria Christina, Frederick mobilized his army and marched out of camp with the intention of taking up a superior position and catching the Austrian army by surprise. Four days later these two opposing forces met up at the village of Chotusitz, about 20 miles west of Chrudim, and fell upon each other.

The ensuing battle was short—it lasted only four hours, from eight in the morning until noon—but exceptionally fierce. On the whole, the two armies were equally matched. This time, Frederick did not gallop away at the first charge but remained with his troops to direct the operation. Again, the Austrian cavalry distinguished itself; again, it fell to the Prussian infantry to hold the line. This they did despite devastating losses, prompting the Austrians to retreat, and affording Frederick the intense satisfaction, while still on the battlefield, of dashing off a gloating bulletin to Louis XV—"Sire, Prince Charles has attacked me, and I have beaten him."

He had won the battle, yes—but at a terrible cost. Although he would later inflate the number of Austrian casualties and minimize his own in order to aggrandize his achievement, Frederick in fact witnessed the death or wounding of nearly 5,000 of his soldiers in a single morning. Austria lost a little over 6,000 men, but the preponderance of these had been taken captive. More than this, Charles of Lorraine, who had other troops in Bohemia that he could call upon, had salvaged enough of his battalion to come back again under more advantageous conditions in the future, an eventuality that Frederick clearly understood. So while publicly he crowed loudly, privately the Prussian king reached out the very next week to the British and tried again to secure a separate, permanent peace with Austria.

Her army's inferior performance at Chotusitz, coming on the heels of her other victories, was a cruel disappointment to Maria Theresa. She had believed she had Frederick on the run, that this engagement would be the preliminary to ultimately taking back Silesia. Now she was advised by Sir Thomas to conclude a separate peace with Prussia on the grounds that it would deprive the occupying French army of the only power in Bohemia that could effectively come to their aid, and so this was clearly her best chance of liberating Prague. Although she recognized the logic of his argument, she still could not bring herself to approve this expedient until the ambassador assured her that the treaty could always be repudiated in the future, as it was understood "that these concessions are wrung from her by violence, and a double perfidy," and that consequently "no power in heaven or upon earth can blame the House of Austria in the future, if it uses reprisals hereafter, and on the first opportunity retakes by force that which is taken from it today." Even then, she absolutely refused to grant Frederick an inch of territory in Bohemia, and her defiance is indicative of the depth of her bitterness. "I will not let it be touched even though the King of England should ask it of me at the head of his parliament. I would rather bury myself under the ruins of Vienna," she burst out passionately.

But while these negotiations continued, her commander in Bohemia was busy redeeming himself. Upon being informed that the king of Prussia was treating for a separate peace and so was unlikely to march to his ally's aid, Charles of Lorraine moved quickly to confront the forward arm of the French army, consisting of some 25,000 troops stationed at Pisek, about 60 miles south of Prague, with the full complement of the Austrian forces, which at this point totaled an impressive 60,000 men. The French, surprised and outnumbered, hastily abandoned the outpost and fell back on Prague, leaving Pisek in Austrian hands.

This routing, in addition to providing a much-needed boost to Austrian morale, had a discernible effect on negotiations with Prussia. Fearful that the victory would embolden Maria Theresa to withdraw her consent from the peace process altogether, on June 11 Frederick abruptly agreed to abide by the terms of their original agreement, which guaranteed him Silesia. A formal contract, known as the Treaty of Berlin, was signed on July 28, 1742.

And with the announcement of this pact, Prussia was stunningly, publicly, out of the war. Within two months, Augustus of Saxony, none too pleased at his odds, and under pressure from Britain, prudently followed suit, renouncing his former allies. As Bavaria, represented by the hapless emperor, was in reality more of a liability than an asset, this meant that the remnants of the French army stationed in Bohemia were suddenly completely isolated.

★   ★   ★

THE PRUSSIAN WITHDRAWAL from the war dropped like an iron can-
nonball shot from Berlin on the heads of the French government.
Although Louis XV and his ministers had of course been aware that
Frederick was unreliable, they were unprepared for the full extent of
his treachery. They had been counting on Prussia to come to their
relief in Prague, or at the very least to keep pressure on the Austrian
forces in Bohemia so that the combined strength of Maria Theresa's
army might not be used against them. By the time they were disabused of this fantasy, the French regiments trapped in Prague, who
were down to some 30,000 men due to casualties, defections, and
disease, had already been surrounded by Charles of Lorraine's 60,000
troops. Food and other supplies were running out; the soldiers could
not survive long without armed intervention. The French battalion
positioned at Hanover to threaten George II's property was hastily
sent to break the siege but, confronted by the obstacle of the Austrian army, failed to give battle. Worse, their redeployment allowed
the British division stationed in Flanders to march uncontested into
Germany, and at this point it became clear to everyone involved that
France had lost the war.

It was now a question, on the French side, of salvaging what could
be had from the situation. The commanding general of the besieged
warriors at Prague offered to quit the city without a fight if he could
take his men and artillery with him. The venerable Cardinal Fleury,
at ninety still Louis XV's chief minister, swallowed his pride and
wrote pleadingly to an intermediary in the Austrian army, asking
him to approach Maria Theresa on France's behalf to arrange for an
honorable withdrawal.

But the days when the queen of Hungary could be imposed upon
were long over. She was not about to let French soldiers and French
artillery, which might then be summoned against her again in the
future, slip out of her grasp. So that there would be no confusion as
to her position, in response to the overtures from France, she brought
all of her ministers together and addressed them in state. "I will

71

grant no capitulation to the French army," she declared firmly. "I desire no proposition nor project from the Cardinal; let him address himself to my allies. I am astonished that he should make any advances; he who, by money and promises, incited all the German princes to crush me. I have acted with too much condescension toward the court of France," she continued hotly. "Compelled by actual necessity, I debased my royal dignity, by writing to the Cardinal in terms which would have softened the most obdurate rocks; he insolently rejected my entreaties...I can prove, by documents in my possession, that the French endeavored to start sedition in the very heart of my dominions; that they sought to put aside the fundamental laws of the empire and set fire to the four corners of Germany; and I will transmit these proofs to posterity, as a warning to the empire against France," she avowed fiercely in conclusion. She would admit to no solution but the capture or unconditional surrender of the French army.

This she would be denied. Winter came early that year and the icy temperatures, mounds of snow, and fierce winds so worsened conditions within Prague that it seemed to the Austrian soldiers ensconced outside the city that the enemy pinned inside had no alternative but to capitulate. Expecting daily for this to happen (and freezing themselves), they relaxed their guard. Their failure to remain vigilant afforded the French commanding general the opportunity to adopt a daring maneuver. On December 16, 1742, leaving behind those too weak or wounded to travel, he crept out of Prague just before nightfall with 11,000 infantry and 3,000 cavalry, dragging behind them all the French artillery. For twelve days this remnant of the once-mighty French army struggled through a forced march under horrific conditions. There was no rest, no warmth, nor cover from storm or snow; as a result, it was possible to trace the progress of the retreat simply by noting the piles of corpses that littered the sides of the roads they had traveled. In this fashion, they reached the comparative safety of the western border of Bohemia, over 100 miles away, with every cannon intact but 1,200 men sacrificed along the way to exposure, frostbite, and fever. Of those who made it, nearly a third were fatally ill, so in the end only 8,000 or so eventually found their way back to France; the general himself only survived because he was carried throughout on a stretcher. Maria Theresa was so frustrated when she heard the news that the French had eluded the siege and gotten away that the Prussian ambassador reported to Frederick that she threatened to "take the command of her Armies on herself."

She may not have had her captives, but she had Prague. To prevent their deliberately destroying the capital in retaliation, the 4,000 or so French wounded who had been left behind were given safe passage out of the city, and Austria officially reclaimed the kingdom.

The joy in Vienna was profound. On January 2, 1743, to celebrate the victory, the royal court arranged to hold a grand spectacle, known as a carousel, in which magnificently dressed riders competed on horseback or in a chariot race for prizes. But in a twist, this time, to emphasize the benefits of female sovereignty, all the contestants were women. Both Maria Theresa and her sister, Maria Anna, participated enthusiastically. The queen, splendid in red velvet, was mounted on a white stallion; she and her sister also paired up to compete in the four-wheeled chariot race. The event was held indoors, in the riding ring of the royal stables, but afterward, in a complete departure from past protocol, Maria Theresa led the entire company out into the streets of the city so that the ordinary citizens of Vienna could share in the pageantry of the occasion. Her father had never made himself accessible to his subjects in this way, and the gesture was greeted by cheering crowds.

But the queen's elation at the recovery of Prague was tempered by her resentment at what she considered to be the kingdom's too-quick embrace of the elector of Bavaria as sovereign. The Bohemians had to fear her as they had feared the Bavarians and the French, or it would never end. With this objective in mind, she ordered an investigation into those who she suspected had aided the usurper. She was evidently trying to be just, as on the whole she protected the common people, who were exempted from reprisals on the grounds that they had been helpless in the face of an armed assault. (The only exceptions to this rule were the Jews, who were initially banished for having enabled the elector of Bavaria by loaning him money, but who were eventually allowed to remain after being forced to pay a substantial cash donation. Maria Theresa, a devout Catholic, was openly and shamefully anti-Semitic.) Those noblemen found guilty were subjected to penalties ranging from forfeiture of property to imprisonment. There were even instances in which death was recommended, although these she later overruled as too severe. There is a line between punishment and brutality that in almost all cases Maria Theresa declined to cross.

It must have worked, because that spring, five months pregnant again, she entered Prague in state to the noisy celebration of the populace, who lined the streets in gratifyingly large, demonstrably appreciative crowds. On May 12, 1743, Maria Theresa was officially crowned queen of Bohemia at the traditional venue of Saint Vitus Cathedral. Even before the ceremony itself took place, "Whoever thought himself entitled to do so, stepped into the apartments of the queen, while a huge crowd flooded the gardens and gave themselves up to unbridled outbursts of jubilation," reported the Venetian ambassador, who witnessed the coronation.* The festivities were so exuberant that they naturally carried over to the next day, May 13, Maria Theresa's birthday.

She was twenty-six years old.

---

* Nonetheless, she prudently took the crown, which was ordinarily housed at the cathedral in Prague, home with her to Vienna. No sense tempting fate a second time.

5

Holy Roman Empress

⟨✦⟩

If you want to get the mouse, don't shut the trap; leave the trap open.
— Frederick the Great to the French ambassador

The King of Prussia only wishes to lull me to sleep, and to attack me again when I least dream of it.
— Maria Theresa to the Venetian ambassador

TWENTY-SIX IS NOT VERY OLD. Despite everything she had been through in the less than three years since her father had died, Maria Theresa had lost neither her desire for fun nor her youthful energy. She had put on some weight—five pregnancies will do that to a person—but she was still a spirited young woman who relished music, parties, and riding, and who could enthusiastically stay up to all hours of the night dancing with the husband she adored. "Her countenance is beautiful...her expression is fresh...Her demeanor is sprightly and happy, and her greeting always warm and pleasant; there is no denying that Maria Theresa is a most charming and delightful woman," even the Prussian ambassador to Vienna was forced to admit, in a report to Frederick.

But she also took her responsibilities as a ruler very seriously, and recognized that she had much to learn. By the time of her Bohemian coronation, two of the elderly councillors she had inherited from her father had already passed away, and it was clear that those remaining would soon follow suit. To fill their places, she had begun to seek out and promote new administrators and advisers whose intellects and abilities she trusted.

It was during this first, tentative period of reorganizing her government that Maria Theresa took a step that was highly unusual for a monarch at any age, and that was certainly unique among her contemporaries. Clearly remembering the predicament her father had fallen into, and determined to stay out of it herself, the queen of Hungary and Bohemia surprised everyone by appointing an official whose sole task consisted of critiquing her behavior and job performance with brutal honesty, "this being most necessary for a ruler, since there are few or none at all who will do this, commonly refraining out of awe or self-interest," as she herself observed.

The official's name was Count Emanuel da Silva-Tarouca. Maria Theresa had known him since childhood. He was a Portuguese nobleman almost twice her age who had immigrated to Vienna as a young man during her father's reign. Count Tarouca, as may well be imagined, was not especially gratified to have been singled out for this employment. Having to inform his august sovereign, however gently, that she had behaved badly, or even in a misguided fashion, could under no circumstances be considered an optimal method by which to secure advancement at court. In fact, it generally ensured the opposite.

But Maria Theresa insisted. She even wrote out a formal decree outlining his duties, in which she referred to herself in the third person. "From now on, without intermission," this interesting document read, "you are to tell Her where she errs, and to explain with perfect openness Her faults of character."

And so he did. Among his other criticisms, Count Tarouca told her she was too impatient with people, and needed to moderate her language. "Every human being has some imperfection, some weakness, some streak of smallness," he wrote. "If he does not tolerate these in others, how can he flatter himself that others will make allowance for them in him?" There were perhaps other, more productive methods, the count urged tactfully, "for a Queen to convey a strong sense of disapprobation without calling a Minister 'a fool,' or a general 'a coward.'" Similarly, she was sometimes too hasty in her decision-making, giving in to the passion of the moment rather than taking time to pause and reflect. Emotional responses, in particular, the count noticed, tended to be set off or exaggerated by fatigue. She was attending too many parties and staying up too late in the evening, he told her flatly. It was cutting into her time for sleep.

To break her of these habits, Count Tarouca devised a rigid schedule that accounted for every hour of Maria Theresa's day. How steadfastly the queen of Hungary and Bohemia held to this methodical time management system is underscored by the testimony of the Prussian ambassador, who was once again forced to report with grudging admiration to Frederick (famous himself for the discipline of his daily routine) of the firmness of her purpose. Maria Theresa, he observed, "loves pleasure, but never allows it to interfere in the least with her work. Formerly she danced most passionately, and was very fond of attending masked balls, but now she dances rarely and attends but few balls... In the winter she rises at six, but in the summer at four, or never later than five, and works the whole forenoon at reading dispatches, signing documents, and attending meetings of her ministers. She lunches at one, after which she rests, but generally not longer than a half hour... In both summer and winter she frequently takes her meals in solitude, and after them hurries for short walks; during all the time thus spent she is constantly glancing at important papers and dispatches. From seven to half past eight in the evening, she amuses herself; then eats a light supper—often only a bowl of broth—takes another short walk and goes to bed," he continued.* As her children grew older, more time was eventually made

---

* Contrast this report of Maria Theresa's work ethic with that of her thirty-three-year-old French counterpart, Louis XV, as observed by one of his ministers: "Nothing affects him [Louis XV] in council. He appears to be absolutely indifferent... He signs

for them, but throughout her reign Maria Theresa made almost no concession to her many pregnancies. "Sometimes only a few hours before the birth of a child, the Queen may be seen in the opera, and the people scarcely hear that she has been confined before she is racing through the streets in her carriage, or sitting at her desk at work," the Prussian ambassador marveled.

The compulsion Maria Theresa felt to improve herself, to master the art of sovereignty in all its myriad military, political, diplomatic, economic, cultural, and social complexities, was born of the hard lessons inflicted by Frederick (just as Frederick's craving for aggrandizement at any cost was the result of the emotional wounds his father had inflicted upon him). She identified the king of Prussia as her mortal enemy and was keenly aware that he would take advantage of any misstep, any lapse in vigilance or downturn in fortune, to strike again. She was determined to thwart him and reclaim Silesia.

But first she had a war to finish.

BY 1743, FREDERICK'S CHARMING new philosophy of military opportunism—basically, that those sovereigns quick and strong enough to act could ignore international treaties, legal precedent, and fundamental morality to grab what they wanted from those weaker than themselves—had already caught on and sparked imitation. Maria Theresa, with so much territory to protect, much of it noncontiguous, was once again the favored mark of these would-be conquerors. No sooner did the queen of Hungary and Bohemia send her army to reclaim one province than a new interloper, taking advantage of the deployment, would emerge to threaten her from an entirely different direction. The most recent entrant into this eighteenth-century version of when-the-cat's-away was Spain, still ostensibly led by an increasingly unsound Philip V but whose gov-

---

unread whatever is presented to him. One is paralyzed by the little interest the king takes, and by the profound silence he observes," the French minister wrote in despair in the summer of 1743.

ernment was actually controlled by his far more enterprising second wife, Elizabeth Farnese.

Elizabeth Farnese had followed the course of combat in Austria and Bohemia with interest, and it had occurred to her that she might make use of Vienna's preoccupation with recovering Prague to launch her own attack. After all, if a two-bit player like that upstart king of Prussia could successfully appropriate the rich province of Silesia, surely mighty Spain, a genuine world power, could rifle among the rest of Maria Theresa's inheritance to seize its own fair share of the spoils. She had already secured the kingdom of Naples for her eldest son, Don Carlos, from Maria Theresa's father, but she also had a second son, Don Philip, whom she had just married to one of Louis XV's daughters. Since Don Philip had no independent establishment of his own, as a fond parent, the queen of Spain thought to provide him with one by invading what remained of Maria Theresa's possessions in Italy, which had been more or less left defenseless when the majority of the guard had been summoned to help fight in Bavaria.

And so that is what Elizabeth Farnese did. While Maria Theresa was busy managing the war in Bohemia, Spain landed approximately 25,000 soldiers in Italy. They were joined by an additional 12,000 men supplied by Don Carlos, king of Naples, who had been ordered by his mother to help. The crown had barely settled on Maria Theresa's head at Prague when France jumped into the Italian conflict as well, Louis XV pledging to aid his son-in-law, Don Philip, to acquire the duchy of Parma. Suddenly, the queen of Hungary and Bohemia faced as powerful an alliance against her in the south as she had in the north.

And her allies were nearly as destructive as her enemies. England had finally put an army into the field and won a battle against the French at Dettingen, about 23 miles southeast of Frankfurt, on June 27, 1743. George II had personally accompanied his troops, and almost gotten himself captured. (That was the last time *he* took the field.) This victory, in combination with the large cash subsidies dispensed by Parliament to

Vienna, put the British in a very strong negotiating position with Austria, and their policy was aimed at containing France, denying it Parma, and getting out of the war in Italy as quickly as possible. To do this, the English needed the aid of the king of Sardinia, who controlled the critical territory of Piedmont at the foot of the Alps on the border with France.

Problem was, the king of Sardinia refused to fight against the French unless he was compensated for his efforts by an enlargement of his domain. As everything near Piedmont was owned by Austria, this meant that Maria Theresa would have to bribe the Sardinian monarch by voluntarily ceding him territory in order to ensure his aid in the upcoming struggle for Parma. The British were perfectly happy to sacrifice Maria Theresa's interests in pursuit of this objective, and Sir Thomas was instructed to insist that she accept the Sardinian ultimatum.

Maria Theresa, who had just returned to work after giving birth to a fifth daughter, Maria Elisabeth, on August 13, considered the king of Sardinia's demands to be little more than blackmail (which they were). "If I am to be robbed, it may as well be by my enemies as by my friends. I had better make terms with my opponents than pay what is demanded of me by my defenders," she retorted. But she could not afford to have the British withdraw their subsidies, and a month later, on September 13, 1743, Austria signed the Treaty of Worms, whereby Maria Theresa gave the king of Sardinia Piacenza, Pavia, and Po in exchange for a military alliance against Spain and France. The best the queen of Hungary and Bohemia could get out of this transaction was a secret promise by George II, also a signatory to this pact, that to compensate her for her concessions to Sardinia, Britain would do everything it could to help her to regain the kingdom of Naples from Spain.

But it was not lost on Maria Theresa that, when it came to the dispersal of properties, it seemed that *she* was always the person required to give up something immediately on the vague assurance of a proportionate gain at some point in the future. Already, George II had strongly recommended that she return Bavaria to the helpless emperor in exchange for his pledge to refrain from causing any more trouble. She had countered by proposing instead to give Bavaria to her husband, and recompense the emperor with the faraway duchy of Tuscany (cleverly mimicking the deal the French had imposed on Francis before her marriage, when they had invaded and annexed Lorraine). The British declined to support these terms, but they could not force her to give back Bavaria, as her soldiers still held Munich, and this too taught Maria Theresa a valuable lesson: occupy first, negotiate later.

There was no denying, however, that despite these challenges, the queen of Hungary and Bohemia was in a far superior position than she had been at the beginning of her reign, and this was cause for celebration. And so she opened the new year, 1744, with a gala, weeks-long extravaganza whose centerpiece was the January 7 wedding of her younger sister, Maria Anna, to Francis's younger brother, Charles of Lorraine, a ceremony that had until this point been delayed due to lack of funds, the existential threat to the succession, and the bridegroom's being continually called away to command the army.

It was an adroit bit of theater, a gift to her subjects as much as to her cherished sister. After so much worry and fear, it signaled a return to normalcy, and the enduring stability of the monarchy. All of Vienna was reminded of the splendor and artistry of the Habsburgs. The wedding, held at the Church of the Augustinian Friars, was a lavish affair: "The Queen and her sister in their robes of state had the appearances of goddesses in the likeness of women," an onlooker rhapsodized. It was followed by a series of magnificent fêtes, including a costume ball, with Maria Theresa and Francis dressed up as innkeepers, as well as musical evenings and concerts (always the favorite entertainment of the Viennese). The merrymaking went on for so long that Count Tarouca, not daring to object in person, sent a memo remonstrating with Maria Theresa over her lack of sleep and inattention to her duties. She returned it to him with a good-humored note: "Tell me all this again at the beginning of Lent."

To ensure that the newlyweds had sufficient rank and income, Maria Theresa appointed Charles and Maria Anna as governors-general of the Austrian Netherlands, headquartered at Brussels. As the majority of the executive duties would inevitably fall to her sister (Charles continuing in his position as commander general of the army and therefore likely to be unavailable), the queen assigned one of her most talented up-and-coming officials, thirty-three-year-old Count Wenzel Kaunitz, to advise Maria Anna and act as administrator.

Then, at the end of February, she bade her sister a tearful goodbye and sent her off to Belgium; allotted Charles an army of 70,000 soldiers to lead across the Rhine into Alsace; and commanded him to wrest her husband's beloved home duchy of Lorraine back from Stanislas and the French. At the same time, she sent a force of 25,000 men into Italy and ordered the general in charge of the battalion to attack Don Carlos at Naples and conquer the Spanish kingdom for Austria.

MARIA THERESA WAS NOT the only monarch to begin 1744 with an aggressive war plan. That spring, Louis XV, after first failing to invade England by sea, instead turned his ambitions north and marched an army of some 87,000 men into Flanders. Prodded by his current paramour, who wanted him to mimic Louis XIV and bring glory to France (and consequently to herself), Louis even managed to rouse himself sufficiently from his customary torpor to accompany his troops on this expedition. "The King has his master of ceremonies, his chamberlain, his cooks, and his scullions. Nothing is left behind but the mistress," noted a French chronicler on May 3, 1744. As Louis's divisions overwhelmingly outnumbered the defending garrisons, within a matter of weeks the French had taken most of Flanders and were threatening to attack both Holland to the north and Brussels to the south.

But for once Maria Theresa had the jump on her opponents. On June 30, while Louis and his army were busy marching north, the battalions of the newly married Charles were crossing the Rhine, and by July 3 *her* 70,000 soldiers, having met little resistance, were at the border of Lorraine. "At last we are in Alsace," Charles crowed in his report to his brother Francis. "You may expect to hear from me next in Paris," he added confidently.

Louis hastily divided his troops and, leaving approximately half of his soldiers behind to protect his conquests in Flanders, accompanied the rest of the French army southeast to meet the new threat. But finally, it was Maria Theresa who was the recipient of a piece of good luck. Louis and his men arrived at Metz, about 30 miles north of Nancy, the capital city of Lorraine, on August 4. Having not seen his mistress in some time, the king arranged to have her meet him there, and to celebrate their reunion organized a great feast in her honor. Louis must have overdone it at the party, because the next day he woke up with such a high fever that it was feared he would die. This immobilized the bulk of the French army, leaving only a small force to defend against the Austrian invasion. Charles knew that if he moved quickly he could complete his mission and retrieve Lorraine for his family.* Maria Theresa's gamble was about to pay off.

And it was at this critical juncture, when Maria Theresa was on the brink of realizing the sort of military triumph that would have finally inspired the fear and respect necessary to secure her position and allow her to dictate terms, that Frederick abruptly chose to reenter the fray. On August 15 the king of Prussia officially declared war on Austria and marched an invasion force of some 80,000 soldiers into Bohemia, with the intent of capturing Prague.

NOTHING BESPOKE MARIA THERESA's rising credibility as a major European power more than Frederick's willful decision to renege on his peace treaty and attack Bohemia in August of 1744. Four years previously, the king of Prussia had struck at the archduchess of Austria

---

* Stanislas certainly thought so. He and his entire court packed up and fled so ignobly that the servants and the horses bearing the luggage ran wild, overtaking their aristocratic betters and scattering their masters' belongings, including their wigs, along the way for Charles's soldiers to find. That must have been satisfying.

and grabbed Silesia because he judged her too weak to resist. This time, he set about ambushing her because he feared she was about to become too strong.

Frederick had monitored Maria Theresa's progress in the war from his home base in Berlin with mounting alarm. He had noted with chagrin Britain's entrance into the European theater as her ally the year before; the large subsidies they provided, which allowed her to feed and supply her armies; their diplomatic efforts on her behalf. He was especially annoyed to observe his uncle, George II, with whom he was extremely competitive, personally leading an army into the field and defeating the French forces at Dettingen. "The victory of Dettingen by no means gave so much pleasure to the King of Prussia as it had done to the King of England," he later wrote sourly in his memoir of this period.

But mostly what he was worried about was keeping Silesia. He knew that, even though she had acquiesced to a peace treaty accepting the loss of the province, Maria Theresa was not resigned to it, and would come after him again as soon as she felt herself in a position to do so. "She detests Your Majesty," the Prussian ambassador to the court at Vienna informed Frederick flatly. "She cannot forget the loss of Silesia, nor her grief over the soldiers she lost in wars with you."

And so, to prevent the queen of Hungary and Bohemia's armies from conquering so much territory that she became unstoppable, he double-crossed her again. He pretended to sit idly in Berlin, hosting Voltaire, writing pretentious verses, and arranging the marriage of one of his sisters to the king of Sweden, but all the while he was quietly building up his army, restocking his treasury, and entering into secret negotiations with both France and the displaced Bavarian emperor, to renew their original military alliance. On June 5, 1744, they came to terms, and a clandestine pact between the former conspirators was signed. France agreed to unite once again because a Prussian advance in the east would divert Austrian attention from the Netherlands and Lorraine; the emperor agreed because Frederick promised to hold the capital city of Prague in his name; and Frederick agreed because he was to be compensated for his initiative with the bulk of Bohemia. It was just like old times!

Maria Theresa, however, was experienced enough by now to know to keep a sharp eye on the king of Prussia. The movement of so many men and arms was again difficult to keep secret, and she had reports of military activity in Berlin at the beginning of August. This time she did not send an envoy to ascertain the enemy's intentions but instead acted instantly. On August 8, a full week before Frederick's official declaration of war, Charles received the order to turn his 70,000 soldiers around and race back to meet the threat.* It meant forgoing the opportunity to seize her husband's homeland, but Prussia, by breaking the treaty, was giving her the chance to reclaim Silesia, and, given the option, Maria Theresa did not hesitate to choose Silesia. Francis concurred. "We must crush this devil [Frederick] so he can never again be an object to fear," he declared.

Of course Frederick's 80,000 troops had a head start and so easily overwhelmed the regiment Maria Theresa had left behind to defend Bohemia. Prague fell to him on September 16, 1744. From there, relying once again on speed and surprise, he continued to advance south, assigning garrisons to protect his various conquests and extending his occupation. In this fashion he succeeded in capturing territory all the way to the town of Ceske Budejovice, only about 100 miles from Vienna, by the beginning of October.

But by that time, Maria Theresa had already appeared once again before the Hungarian Diet in Pressburg to appeal for help against Frederick while she awaited the return of Charles and the bulk of her army. The Hungarians, who had no love of Prussia, and who were thrilled to be on the winning side for a change, responded enthusiastically to her

---

* Naturally, it wouldn't do to advertise that he had gone to war in order to annex Bohemia, so Frederick opted for a somewhat loftier tone in his public pronouncement. "The King asks for nothing and with him there is no question whatever of personal interests," he observed airily in his war manifesto. "His Majesty has recourse to arms only to restore liberty to the Empire, the scepter to the Emperor, and peace to Europe."

summons and immediately promised an additional 70,000 warriors; approximately 40,000 were mustered immediately. Charles, too, made excellent time, as the French army, which Frederick had been counting on to strike down Maria Theresa's soldiers while they were exposed recrossing the Rhine, instead stood by passively, allowing the Austrian force to slip away unharmed. "What can I expect from France? Or can I expect nothing at all?" Frederick railed in a letter to Louis XV when he discovered the betrayal (conveniently forgetting that he had done exactly the same thing to his French ally when they had so gravely needed his help in Prague two years earlier). By the second week in October, Charles and approximately 55,000 of his men had made it to the western border of Bohemia. They were soon joined by a battalion of some 20,000 Saxons, also eager to fight against Frederick as payback for the insults heaped on them by the king of Prussia at the time of his disastrous Moravian campaign.

And the Austrians, Saxons, and Hungarians were not the only people harboring a grudge against Frederick. The Bohemians were none too fond of him, either. The first thing he'd done after taking Prague was to shake down the local population for taxes and impose forced conscription into the Prussian army. Also, after the last time, the citizenry, including the aristocracy, knew Maria Theresa would be back. Overwhelmingly, they stayed loyal to her. Consequently, at the approach of Frederick's men, the Bohemians buried their food to keep it safe, hid in the woods, and informed on troop movements to the roving bands of Hungarian irregulars who preyed incessantly on the increasingly cold and hungry Prussians, to devastating effect.

By November, the weight of the opposition allied against him, in combination with the frigid weather, forced Frederick to sound a retreat that in a very short time turned into a rout. Charles did not even have to engage Frederick's soldiers in battle—in fact, he was encouraged not to by his second-in-command, who understood that cold, starvation, and illness would do the work of driving the Prussians out of Bohemia far more safely and effectively than a military encounter. He was right: Frederick's much-admired troops left their posts in droves; it was reported that, during one ten-day period alone, 9,000 Prussians deserted to the Austrian side. On November 26, bowing to reality, Frederick gave up Prague, and the 17,000 Prussian soldiers who had been left there to hold the city were advised to get away as best they could; in a chilling reprise of the infamous French retreat two years earlier, only 2,000 of the garrison made it back to Berlin. By mid-December, the king of Prussia had lost an estimated 30,000 men to death or desertion, and what was left of his army was forced to fall back to Silesia. There is no question that Maria Theresa had him on the run. Determined to deliver a decisive blow, she commanded Charles to follow the crippled Prussian army into Silesia and liberate the province, even though it was unusual to order an attack in winter due to the difficult conditions.

But whatever joy she may have taken in having rescued Bohemia so quickly was soon tempered by personal tragedy. In October, her sister, Maria Anna, still in Brussels, had given birth to a stillborn child after an extremely difficult delivery—so difficult that it was feared that she, too, would succumb. Maria Anna had rallied but two weeks later had fallen ill again. A specialist from Leyden had been summoned, and Maria Theresa, despite being pregnant again herself, had dispatched her own physician to tend to her sister. But neither doctor could arrest the progress of her ailment, which was most likely bacterial. On December 27, 1744, came word to Vienna that twenty-six-year-old Maria Anna, who had been Maria Theresa's constant companion nearly all her life, had died on the sixteenth of the month. Neither her husband nor any of her loved ones were at her bedside; she who before her promotion to governor-general of the Austrian Netherlands had never left the familiar confines of home, unless it was to travel with her sister and the rest of the Viennese court, ended her days in the loneliness of a foreign city. She did not even live long enough to celebrate her first wedding anniversary. "God could have permitted no more terrible trial to befall me than the death of my sister," Maria Theresa mourned in a letter at the beginning of January 1745. "Time, they say, heals griefs of this kind. Time will only make me feel more keenly the greatness of my loss."

Charles, too, was bereft. He had lost both his wife and child while he was far away fighting in Bohemia. Although he continued to hold the position of commanding general, he was never quite the same afterward.

Nonetheless, throughout December and into the new year he pursued the fleeing Prussian soldiers into Silesia. Frederick was not there—the brave king of Prussia, who had started this whole mess, had escaped back to the comfort and safety of Berlin. He left to his general the responsibility for regrouping what was left of his wretched, demoralized army and defending Silesia amid the bitter cold of winter. Although any major offensive would have to wait until spring, Maria Theresa's chances of recovering the province had never looked better.

And then, out of the blue, came news that the forlorn emperor, worn down by regret and humiliation, had died on January 20, 1745, leaving the imperial dignity once again vacant and provoking yet another succession crisis. "This was the only event wanting to complete the confusion and embroilment which already existed in the political relations of the European powers," Frederick observed glumly.

CONFUSION MAY BE DESTRUCTIVE but it also creates opportunity. From her palace in Vienna, Maria Theresa understood instantly that the death of the emperor gave her the chance to reclaim the remaining component of her father's legacy that had been stolen from her at the time of her ascension. Just before she gave birth, on February 1, 1745, to her seventh child (triumphantly a boy, named Charles, thus proving that his elder brother Joseph had not been a fluke), she offered to return Bavaria to the deceased emperor's seventeen-year-old son and heir, Maximilian Joseph, if he would stop contesting her legitimacy and give up all claims to the empire. These terms were extremely generous; Maria Theresa was in effect willing to overlook the father's treason if the son remained loyal to her. This leniency was not simply fairness on her part but also because they were members of the same family, as she took pains to remind him. "Everything that is harmful originates in the division of our two houses, and only through unity can it again be set right," she coaxed in the letter she sent outlining her proposal.

But of course nothing was ever easy. Max Joseph was urged to decline this tempting overture by the French and Prussian ambassadors attached to his father's court, who still exerted a dominating influence. So Maria Theresa had to pull troops away from Charles in Silesia to send an army into Bavaria. She made her point: reflecting that it might be better after all to hold on to what he had rather than to further emulate his father's failed career, Max Joseph speedily capitulated and sued for peace. On April 22, 1745, he signed the Treaty of Füssen, in which he withdrew all claim to the empire or any of Maria Theresa's other lands in exchange for the peaceful return of Bavaria to his family. The path was now clear for Francis to win the imperial election.

To see her husband crowned emperor was, along with the recovery of Silesia, Maria Theresa's most heartfelt desire. She did not covet the imperial throne for herself. Both tradition and political reality dictated that only a man could hold the office of emperor. The title of empress was a mere politeness, a way of referring to the reigning potentate's wife. But the office had been her father's, and it was only right that Francis should have it. He had given up his patrimony for her, and this way his sacrifice would not have been in vain. She couldn't retrieve Lorraine for her husband—that dream had vanished the moment Frederick set foot in Bohemia—but she could do this for him.

Maria Theresa knew she had the votes—she had already launched a diplomatic offensive—but experience taught that it was helpful to remind the various delegates of whom they had committed themselves to in the days leading up to the election itself. Historically, the best way to do this was to plant a large, imposing army just outside the imperial city of Frankfurt, where the voting took place. This tended to ensure the fidelity of the electors.

So, as soon as Max Joseph signed the peace treaty relinquishing all claim to the empire, Maria Theresa again siphoned soldiers away from Charles's divisions in Silesia in order to put together an appropriately impressive force for her husband to lead to Frankfurt in anticipation of his coronation. Although Francis was nominally the commander of this army, Maria Theresa, conceding her husband's general lack of military ability and concerned for his safety (the French could easily send a battalion or two to contest the election), also took Charles's clever second-in-command and made him the de facto head of her husband's Frankfurt troops. This in turn deprived Charles of the advice and experience of the one man most responsible for defeating Prussia so decisively in the first place. But it couldn't be helped; ensuring Francis's election took priority. Besides, she had every reason to believe that Charles, who had proved his worth fighting against the French in both Bohemia and Lorraine, could finish off the weakened Frederick on his own.

By this time, the king of Prussia was back in Silesia. Frederick had used the three months he had spent in Berlin to raise as much cash as possible. He had raided the royal treasury, begged for loans, sold the dining room silver. He had even gone so far as to pawn the family chandeliers, smuggling them out in the dark of night so as not to alert the neighbors. Consequently, he had brought back with him both supplies and healthy, badly needed reinforcements to those remnants of his Bohemian regiments who had survived the winter. These troops he drilled mercilessly throughout the spring. "My determination is taken," he wrote home to Berlin on April 20, 1745. "If we must fight, we will do it like men driven desperate. Never was there a greater peril than that I am now in . . . The game I play is so high, one cannot contemplate the issue with cold blood. Pray for the return of my good luck," he concluded grimly.

Charles was apprised of Frederick's return but he was not

concerned—on the contrary, he was aware that the Austrians had the advantage in terms of numbers and morale, and so was eager to give battle. His knowledge was based on information coming directly from a spy within the enemy camp who had close ties to the Prussian inner command circle. As a result, Charles not only knew how many men Frederick had deployed throughout Silesia but also the various locations at which the Prussian battalions were stationed. He had reports of enemy troop movements and from this intelligence could extrapolate his opponent's most likely targets. He was thus able to choose the time and place for an attack that would catch the king of Prussia unprepared, and he made haste to do so. "There can be no God in heaven if we do not win this battle," he assured Maria Theresa at the beginning of June 1745.

There was just one small problem, however: his informant had actually been planted by Frederick to provide disinformation. So instead of the 40,000 troops that Charles was told he was going up against, the Prussian military in Silesia actually numbered closer to 85,000, and these soldiers were not where Charles thought they were. Accordingly, it was instead the Austrian army that was taken by surprise by the Prussians, who made a daring march in the darkness of the early morning hours of June 4 while their opponents slept carelessly in the open. Charles's forces were routed by 8:00 a.m.; worse, although in this battle the Prussian and Austrian sides were equally matched at about 55,000 soldiers each, Charles lost three times as many men as did Frederick. It was a decisive and humiliating defeat. "In war artifice often succeeds better than force," Frederick noted succinctly to the French ambassador.

And just like that, he was back on top.

AGAIN, FREDERICK'S PLAN WAS to use this victory to secure ownership of Silesia by forcing Maria Theresa to accept peace terms favorable to Prussia, and again, he cleverly used her own ally, Great Britain, against her. He knew that England's greatest concern was to keep France in check and that the British were in danger of failing in this objective. The French had an outstanding new general who a month earlier had won a decisive victory against the allied English, Dutch, and Austrian armies at Fontenoy, about 60 miles west of Brussels. Suddenly, it looked like France was invincible in Flanders and the Netherlands; if Prussia also started winning, the allied cause was lost. Frederick, playing on his uncle's fears, opened a clandestine diplomatic channel to George II, offering to abandon his military alliance with France if Britain would intercede on his behalf and arrange a peace treaty with Austria that allowed him to retain Silesia.

To George II, Maria Theresa's ambition to reclaim her lost territory was a sideshow the British could not afford. Her campaign to invade Naples had also failed; her armies were being pushed back in Italy and the Netherlands; and now her general had been defeated in Silesia. Without bothering to inform the Austrians, George II leapt at Frederick's offer, agreeing to all of his terms. Maria Theresa was only made aware of her ally's stance when Sir Thomas confronted her on August 3, 1745. "England has this year furnished £1,078,753 [to Vienna], not to mention the three-fourths expected by the electors of Cologne and Bavaria," the envoy lectured her sternly.* "The nation is not in a condition...to maintain the necessary superiority in the most essential parts, and, by endeavoring to provide for so many services, will fail in all. The force of the enemy must therefore be diminished; and as France cannot be detached from Prussia, Prussia must be detached from France. This return the English nation expect for all their exertions in favor of the house of Austria," he finished firmly. And he threatened to withdraw support for Francis's election if she did not cede Silesia to Frederick.

But for Maria Theresa, Prussian aggression was no sideshow. If she allowed Frederick to keep Silesia, she gave him an entrenched military base from which to launch future attacks against her in

---

* The payments to Cologne and Bavaria referred to by the ambassador were bribes furnished by the British to help get Francis elected emperor.

Bohemia and even Vienna, acts of treachery that, a settled peace treaty notwithstanding, he had already proven himself more than capable of committing. It was as dangerous for her to cede this province to an incorrigibly unscrupulous enemy like Frederick as it would have been for England to allow France to annex Scotland. Even the goal of enthroning Francis paled before this threat. "The imperial dignity!" she exclaimed. "Is it compatible with the fatal deprivation of Silesia? Good God!" Then, believing that she was dealing in good faith with an ally who just needed to be reminded that her armies could provide victories as well as defeats, she stalled for time. "Give me only till the month of October," she pressed Sir Thomas. "I shall then, at least, have better conditions."

But George II was not acting in good faith, a fact that was brought home to Maria Theresa when, less than a month later, on August 26, Great Britain signed a separate peace treaty with Prussia, guaranteeing Frederick's right to Silesia. She was enlightened still further as to the extent of British subterfuge when soon thereafter her army surprised the king of Prussia in his camp and captured his private papers, which he was forced to leave behind in his rush to escape. It was reported that when she read Frederick's secret correspondence with England and knew herself to have been sold out by her ally, she was so incensed that she cried with rage. Her future mistrust of Britain, and her determination to seek other allies, may be dated from this moment.

For the time being, however, there was nothing to be done but ignore the betrayal and concentrate on the task at hand, which was to secure her husband's ascension to the imperial throne. And here, at least, she achieved a brilliant political success. Through a combination of diplomacy, the customary liberal dispersion of cash and favors, and the daunting presence of an army of nearly 50,000 of her soldiers camped at nearby Heidelberg, Francis was elected Holy Roman Emperor by a majority vote in Frankfurt on September 13, 1745. Only the king of Prussia and one other elector signified their displeasure to his candidacy by abstaining.

The coronation was scheduled for early October. Francis had assumed that Maria Theresa would be crowned alongside him, but to his surprise, she refused. She had already been installed as queen at two formal rituals, in Hungary and Bohemia, in which her husband had performed no function beyond that of fond witness; this time it would be she who played the jubilant spectator.

Having defined her role, a four-months-pregnant Maria Theresa set out for Frankfurt. She traveled by land to Aschaffenburg, where she had arranged to take the last stage of the journey by barge, arriving on September 24. "Francis, from Heidelberg, thinks to meet his wife, but comes too late," reported the famous German writer Johann Wolfgang von Goethe, who had the story from his aged neighbors, who were present at the coronation and upon whom the appearance of the imperial couple had clearly made a lasting impression. "Unknown, he throws himself into a little boat, hastens after her, reaches her ship, and the loving pair is delighted at this surprising meeting...all the world sympathizes with this tender pair, so richly blessed with their children, who have been so inseparable since their union," Goethe noted.

The next day they reached Frankfurt and Maria Theresa, "welcomed in the city with rejoicings," immediately repaired to a local inn, appropriately named the Roman Emperor, to watch Francis make his first solemn entrance into the imperial city. The coronation itself was held a little over a week later, on October 4. By this time, the invited dignitaries had arrived and the ceremony unfolded with all due pomp and magnificence. Inside the cathedral, Francis donned the traditional imperial robe (a little old and moth-eaten, like those Maria Theresa had worn in Hungary and Bohemia) and was crowned according to ancient religious rite; his wife made a point of removing her gloves so he could better hear her clapping. Afterward, as the imperial procession wound through the crowded streets, "older persons, who were present...related that Maria Theresa, beautiful beyond measure, had looked on this solemnity from a balcony window," again reported Goethe. "As her consort returned from the cathedral in his strange costume, and seemed to her, so to speak, like a ghost of Charlemagne, he had, as if in jest, raised both his hands, and shown her the imperial globe, the scepter, and the curious gloves, at which she had broken out into immoderate laughter, which served for the great delight and edification of the crowd, which was thus honored with a sight of the good and natural matrimonial under-standing between the most exalted couple of Christendom. But when the Empress, to greet her consort, waved her handkerchief, and even shouted a loud *vivat* to him, the enthusiasm and exultation of the people was raised to the highest, so that there was no end to the cheers of joy," he concluded.

It's a tender image of a husband and wife publicly sharing a light-hearted moment, and of a woman's great pride in her spouse's career. But despite every step she had taken to ensure that the spotlight fell on Francis alone, there was not a person present in Frankfurt that day, or in all of Europe for that matter, who did not understand that it was in fact Maria Theresa, and not her husband, who wielded and embodied the power of the imperial office.* On his own, Francis was nothing more than a minor figure; without her, he could no more have aspired to be crowned emperor than he could have wished to be enthroned king of England. It was Maria Theresa who ruled, it was her subjects who fought, who paid their taxes, who fol-lowed her commands. For the first time in the thousand-year history of the empire, a woman was acknowledged to have placed a candi-date of her choosing on the imperial throne, and the significance of this achievement should not be underestimated.

It was well that she had this interlude of gaiety, and the quiet sat-isfaction of knowing herself to have succeeded against pernicious odds in compelling the sovereigns of the great European powers to accept and recognize her right, and that of her husband, to rule among them. For although the political victory was Maria Theresa's,

---

* When Francis had first arrived in Frankfurt, the local citizenry, on sight of their future emperor, called out: "Look! It's the Queen of Hungary's husband!"

in the critical struggle for Silesia it would be Frederick who ultimately prevailed.

WAR IS NOT ABOUT crowns and scepters, or stately processions, or even unfailing, valiant resolution in the face of adversity. War is about winning battles. And to win battles requires not simply soldiers and supplies but also generals who possess the elusive qualities of martial leadership: an innate grasp of the fundamentals of combat; lightning-quick reflexes in the face of changing conditions or a sudden attack; and, most importantly, the ability to inspire the conscripts under their command to fight and endure, or to die in the attempt.

There was no one within the Austrian military who fulfilled these requirements. In Italy, Maria Theresa's commander was hopeless. By the time of Francis's coronation, her army had given up so much territory to the Spanish and French that Elizabeth Farnese's second son, Don Philip, had already exultantly proclaimed himself king of Lombardy. Gone was the dream of retaking Naples; if something were not done to reverse the trend, the empress would have no southern territory left at all. "My circumstances in Italy grow daily worse; and I fear that they will soon have reached a point where no salvation is possible," Maria Theresa confessed to the Venetian ambassador.

Her real problem, however, was Charles of Lorraine. For all of his experience, Charles had not grown into his job. If anything, he had become slower and more cautious over the past year, to the point of incompetence. No matter how many men and arms she gave him—and Charles regularly had the advantage of numerical superiority when starting out on a campaign—he simply could not convert these assets into solid territorial gains. He might have blundered through, winning some and losing some, if he had been up against a mediocre general like himself, but that was not the case. He was up against Frederick, and unlike Charles, Frederick had developed into a brilliant commander. Even Maria Theresa recognized this. "Nobody can deny that he [Frederick] is a prince of great perspicacity and far-ranging talents," she conceded to the Venetian ambassador. "It must be admitted that he devotes himself without respite to his duties as a ruler; and on the battlefield these qualities are joined by that never-slackening alertness that is indispensable in the leader of an army."

Still, as she had no outstanding candidate to take his place, Maria Theresa left her husband's brother as commander of her army and instead devised what she believed to be a foolproof strategy to carry her cause to victory. In the late fall of 1745, hoping to use her nemesis's own tactics against him, she ordered Charles to mount a clandestine operation with Saxony and catch Frederick unawares by launching a two-pronged sneak attack on Berlin. But even here, the king of Prussia, forewarned by spies of the coming assault, instead turned the tables and invaded Saxony. The Saxons, taken by surprise, folded; Charles, moving with his customary lethargy, failed to arrive in time to help them and then, accosted by the Prussians on his own, was as usual defeated; and by December 18, Frederick had marched smartly into Dresden at the head of his troops and occupied the Saxon capital city. "Henceforth it will not be advisable to entrust Prince Charles with the command of an army that has to fight the King of Prussia who, so help me God, is just too smart for him," the Austrian minister sent to Dresden to deal with the ensuing fallout recommended candidly.

And it was at this point that Maria Theresa, recognizing the futility of continuing to risk lives and resources in the face of so many losses, capitulated, and agreed to a peace. The Treaty of Dresden, between Prussia and Austria, was signed on December 25, 1745. In it, Maria Theresa affirmed the cessation of Silesia to Prussia, and Frederick recognized Francis as the legitimate emperor. The war between Austria and Prussia was over. "However remote the thought of signing so calamitous a treaty may have been from my mind, and no matter how little I imagined, at the start of the campaign, that things would ever come to this pass, I nevertheless am resolved, as is my wont, to live up to this agreement as a hallowed obligation," Maria Theresa avowed.

After the terms of the peace treaty were announced, Frederick rode back into Berlin to wild acclaim. He had started a world war, and wrested Silesia from the empress; he had taken Prussia, a minor kingdom, and turned it into a regional power. No one remembered or cared that he had done it through brutal, unprovoked aggression against a friendly neighbor, by cynically repudiating international treaties of long standing, and by cheerfully double-crossing every ally he'd ever had. He had won, and that was all that mattered. From this time on, he would be known as Frederick the Great.

THE SIGNING OF the Treaty of Dresden brought peace—for Frederick. Everybody else—those he had brought into the war originally, or who had jumped in later hoping to siphon off some spoils—was still fighting.* For Maria Theresa, this meant two more years of hostilities in Italy and the Austrian Netherlands, fending off Spain and France and sometimes both at the same time.

It wasn't all ruinous; during that period, the empress managed to secure some significant victories. Not having to contend with Prussia meant that at least she could now send more troops to help defend her possessions in Italy. In the spring of 1746, soon after she had given birth, on February 26, to her eighth child, Maria Amalia, Maria Theresa recalled her inept southern general, replaced him with a slightly better one, and sent an additional 30,000 soldiers into Italy to see if they could do better against the Spanish this time. She was extremely gratified to discover that they could. In April, she recovered Parma; by June, her army had retaken Piacenza and Don Philip was in full flight. "I hope that this event will make my enemies drop the idea of driving me out of Italy," she murmured pointedly to the Venetian ambassador.

Also in June of 1746, she achieved a major diplomatic triumph by signing a defensive alliance against Prussia with Empress Elizabeth

---

* Combat had by this time spread beyond Europe and into the New World, where loyal, enterprising English colonists had taken it upon themselves to seize the important French fortress of Louisbourg on Cape Breton Island, off the coast of Canada.

of Russia. Maria Theresa had been unsuccessfully trying for years to isolate Frederick by coaxing Russia to her side. It wasn't until the king of Prussia occupied Dresden that Elizabeth woke up to the danger he represented to Poland and, by extension, her domain. She told the Austrian ambassador in Russia that she was ready to attack Frederick immediately. (If only the tsarina had mentioned this the year before, when Charles was campaigning against the Prussian army! It might have made all the difference.) But Maria Theresa had already signed the Treaty of Dresden and she refused to be the one to break the peace. Besides, she knew that someday Frederick would—that he would not be able to resist coming at her again. The treaty of the two empresses, signed on June 2, 1746, which committed Austria to fight on Russia's side and Russia to fight on Austria's in the event of a Prussian attack, was for that future day.

But these gains were offset by Maria Theresa's losses in the Austrian Netherlands, where the French had taken Brussels as well as Flanders, forcing the acting governor, Count Kaunitz, her most talented official, to flee to Antwerp. By the spring of the following year, as she gave birth, on May 5, 1747, to her ninth child and third son, Leopold, Maria Theresa was actively looking for a way out of the war that would leave her with enough Italian territory to compensate for the dispossession of Silesia. "May the Almighty bring about the end soon," she prayed to one of her ministers. "The situation will not be better in two months, and not even so good."

She was not the only head of state to feel this way. The war had been raging for seven years with no clear victor. Every participant felt the pain of scarcity and death; every government struggled with debt and stood on the brink of economic ruin. Even Louis XV, surveying a battlefield in the aftermath of a narrowly won victory in July 1747, was sufficiently jolted by the carnage out of his habitual indifference to express an opinion. "Is it not better to think seriously about peace than to be killing so many brave men?" he asked his general.

By the fall of 1747, it was so clear that the conflict would end through negotiation rather than aggression that the various warring parties had already chosen the town of Aix-la-Chapelle, on the border between Germany and Belgium, as the site for a general diplomatic parley to be held in the spring of the following year. Of course, nobody waited for the official congress to convene. Instead, secret emissaries were immediately dispatched with instructions to begin haggling for advantageous terms. Maria Theresa, suspecting that George II would sell her out again as he had with Frederick, chose Count Kaunitz to represent her in these talks, charging him with getting the best deal he could from the French. "The English system appears clearly," she wrote in her instructions to him. "It consists in increasing the greatness of Prussia and Sardinia at our expense... France must see that England and Prussia are working to weaken the great Catholic powers, and that our common interests require measures to defeat their projects."

She was right: that was exactly what the English were doing. In fairness, they saw themselves as having little choice. Although England had triumphed at sea, France had definitively won the land war. If there were no cessation of hostilities, Holland would surely fall to the French. In a letter of August 14, 1747, the prime minister of England noted, "It is too late to look back. We might have had, last year, a better peace than we shall be able to obtain this; and this, a better than we shall get the next. We fight all; and we pay all, it is true; but we are beaten, and shall be broke," he admitted.

Because of its recent conquests in the Netherlands, of all the combatants, France was in the strongest position going into the peace talks. But the price it had paid for those victories was very high. England had more or less destroyed its navy; debt, inflation, and scarcity had impoverished the kingdom; the death toll and casualty rate were horrific. Louis XV, tired of it all, wanted an immediate peace, and he was willing to make serious concessions to get it.

There was never really any question but that the interests of France and England, the two greatest powers in the war, would set the terms of the final treaty. The English wanted Belgium and Flanders returned to Austria to once again create a buffer state around Holland. This France was willing to do if the English returned Fort Louisbourg in Canada and—this was the tricky part—if their ally Don Philip was given his own state somewhere in Italy. This meant that either Maria Theresa or the king of Sardinia was going to have to give up territory to the Spanish prince. Without consulting the empress, England surreptitiously volunteered to give Don Philip the Austrian duchy of Parma (only recently won back). Equally surreptitiously, France agreed and the peace was made. It was only on May 1, 1748, well after these terms were settled, that this forfeiture of her property was duly communicated to Maria Theresa by Sir Thomas.

Her wrath was monumental. She understood instantly that George II had had a choice, and that he had once again betrayed her by promoting the king of Sardinia's interests over hers. "You sir, who had such a share in the sacrifice of Silesia," Maria Theresa lashed out at the unfortunate Sir Thomas, tasked with convincing Austria to agree to the compromise, "you who contributed more than any person in procuring the additional cession made to the King of Sardinia; do you still think to persuade me? No; I am neither a child nor a fool!... If you will have an instant peace, make it; I can accede, can negotiate for myself. And why am I always to be excluded from transacting my own business?" she continued indignantly. "My enemies will give me better conditions than my friends... YOUR KING OF SARDINIA must have all without one thought or care for me! The treaty of Worms was not made for me, but for him singly! Good God! how I have been used by that Court!... Indeed, indeed, all these circumstances at once, rip up too many old and make new wounds."

But in the end there was nothing she could do about it; she could not continue to prosecute the war alone. More importantly, she did not want to—her subjects were suffering, and she craved peace as much as England and France did. In October of 1748, Count Kaunitz conceded this reality and agreed to the Treaty of Aix-la-Chapelle on behalf of the empress. The War of the Austrian Succession, as this seven-year conflict would eventually be dubbed, was over.

Although it is doubtful that it provided her any consolation, Maria Theresa was by no means the only person dissatisfied with the terms of the peace. The French nation, as one, was dumbfounded to learn that Louis XV had elected to surrender *all* of the conquered territory in Flanders and Belgium in exchange for one Canadian fort and the establishment of Don Philip as the duke of Parma. For this had they sacrificed the lives of so many husbands, fathers, and sons? The French general responsible for the victories in the Netherlands could not help voicing his incredulity. "It is worthwhile to be at some trouble to acquire a province like this, which furnishes a magnificent port, millions of inhabitants, and an impregnable barrier," he pointed out dryly in a letter to Paris protesting the return of Flanders. "Such are my views. I don't understand your infernal politics, but I know that the King of Prussia took Silesia and kept it, and I wish we might imitate him." Frederick himself was withering when the terms of the treaty were published. "The men who govern France are idiots and ignoramuses not to know better how to profit by the situation," he observed.

And so the Treaty of Aix-la-Chapelle, although it brought a halt to the bloodshed, in no way resolved the conflict. In fact, the resentment it engendered almost ensured that fighting would start up again as soon as everyone's armies and treasuries had recovered. Frederick understood this instantly. "This pacification resembled rather a truce, in which all the parties profited by a moment of repose to seek new alliances, in order to be in better condition again to take up arms," he noted later in his memoirs.

For Maria Theresa, bitter as the outcome of the settlement was, the official end of hostilities brought great relief. For the first time since ascending to monarchy, she did not have to fight for her very existence, did not have to worry about battle plans and generals, or about conjuring the immense sums and soldiers necessary to put an army into the field. She could focus instead on what she considered her primary, her most profound, responsibility: improving the lives of her subjects. "I forthwith turned my thoughts to a different channel," she affirmed. "The internal condition of my realm absorbed my whole attention."

But she, too, perceived the inevitability of future combat—and knew further that the first blow, when it fell, would again come from Frederick. Maria Theresa had no crystal ball; she did not know how long she had before he would try again. But however long it was, this time, she would be ready for him.

6

Imperial Affairs

‿

Thus were two powers during peace preparing for war; like two gladiators who impatiently burn to employ the swords they are sharpening.

—Frederick the Great

Even in the distant future, posterity will acknowledge that Maria Theresa was one of the great woman rulers of history. Surely the House of Habsburg has never had her like.

—A Prussian envoy to the court of Vienna

NOTHING TEACHES LIKE FAILURE.

By the winter of 1748, after the Treaty of Aix-la-Chapelle, the lessons of the past eight years were obvious to Maria Theresa. She recognized that she had lost Silesia because she had been forced to try to defend her lands and subjects "without an army, without money, without credit, without experience or knowledge of her own, and even without counsel, because every minister gave his first attention to observe how the matter in consideration would affect himself," she acknowledged ruefully. "I believe that nobody will deny that it will not be easy to find a parallel in history, or that a crowned head ever began to reign under more unpropitious circumstances than I," she added.

She knew also that, while she had been fortunate to be able to obtain sizable English subsidies for most of the war, these handouts had been offset by a disturbing loss of prestige and bargaining power at the peace negotiations. This could not be allowed to happen again. "Better to rely on our strength alone, and not go begging for money abroad," she forcefully directed one of her ministers in the wake of the treaty. So the demands of the treasury must be her first priority. But how to go about raising the vast sums of money that she would need in order to be self-sufficient? And then, one man intervened. "By the extraordinary Providence of God I had come to know Count Haugwitz, and this was the saving of the monarchy," she would later report simply.

Count Frederick William Haugwitz made for an unlikely redeemer. A minor Silesian nobleman who had fled to Vienna when Frederick's troops rolled in, Haugwitz was impoverished, homeless, lacking aristocratic manners, and unattractive to the point of outright ugliness. To these traits was apparently added an unfortunate facial tic that did nothing to enhance his overall presentation. He was quaintly described by a colleague as "a wise man who looked uncommonly like a fool."

But both Francis and Count Tarouca recommended him as a person of sound financial judgment, so Maria Theresa gave him an audience and asked him, as she had asked the members of her council, for suggestions as to what could be done to improve her income sufficiently to provide for a standing army. But where the others had vacillated, Haugwitz astonished her by providing a detailed memorandum, supported by extensive research and hard data, outlining her present economic position, her projected needs over a ten-year period, and the reforms that would be necessary to fill the gap between the two. She hired him on the spot.*

Haugwitz, having been a victim of Prussian opportunism himself, wholeheartedly agreed with Maria Theresa's assessment that Frederick would attack her again as soon as he felt able to do so. In his new post as Minister of the Interior (a position the empress created

---

* Although all but one of the councillors she had inherited from her father had passed away, in general the entrenched high nobility promoted to take their places were not impressive. Maria Theresa, rather than simply accepting the situation, was resourceful enough to listen to an outsider like Haugwitz.

especially for him), Haugwitz estimated that she would need a standing army of over 100,000 highly trained soldiers to meet the inevitable threat to her borders, and that the cost of maintaining such a force would require the generation of an income stream of many millions more than she currently obtained from her subjects. Fortunately, he had come up with a visionary new plan for raising the necessary sums without having to resort to borrowing or the acceptance of foreign stipends: tax the nobles and the Church.

The radical nature of Haugwitz's proposal cannot be overstated. For as long as anyone could remember—certainly for at least the last five or six hundred years—the landed aristocracy and the priesthood had been exempted from paying taxes. Peasants, although they represented the least wealthy segment of the population, were nonetheless primarily responsible for satisfying the demands of the royal tithe collector. My goodness, that's what peasants were *for*.

It does not take much imagination to conjure up the howl of protest and the correspondingly deep degree of resistance that greeted the announcement of Haugwitz's new program. "All the ministers condemn the project most fiercely," the Venetian ambassador acknowledged. But Maria Theresa, who appreciated the intrinsic fairness of spreading the tax burden more equitably among her subjects, held firm. Charged by the members of her own council (among many, many others) with violating her God-given responsibility to maintain "the good and ancient privileges of the nobility and clergy," she returned tartly that "Good privileges were safe enough so far as she was concerned, but immunity from taxation was not good, it was wholly evil." Despite the public outcry, the delaying tactics of the regional authorities, and even, in some places, civil unrest, by May of 1749 she and Haugwitz had begun to implement the new tax system throughout Austria and Bohemia.*

---

* She tried to impose taxation of the nobility in Hungary as well, but this time the Hungarians lived up to their reputation for truculence. They absolutely refused to consider the measure and voted her only half the revenues she asked for despite another personal appeal to the Diet.

Having taken this step to materially improve her finances, Maria Theresa turned her attention to her greatest concern: the defense of her realm. Based on the recent woeful performance of her troops, it clearly wouldn't do to continue staffing and recruiting in the old haphazard way. "Who would believe," she would later write, "that no sort of rule was in force among my troops? Each unit had a different order of marching, a different drill... one practiced rapid fire, another slow. The same words of command were differently interpreted in each unit. It is really no wonder that ten years before my accession the Emperor was defeated every time!" she exclaimed. What Austria needed was a state-of-the-art army, and that meant employing modern, cutting-edge methods. In this, the empress did not have to look far for inspiration. What Frederick did, she would do.

The structure, operations, and recruitment of the military were entirely reformed from the bottom up. Consolidation and consistency were introduced wherever possible—in uniforms, in wages, in training. Weaponry and heavy artillery were upgraded, and classes convened to educate gunmen in mechanics and maintenance. Officers were schooled in geography, history, fortification, and battle tactics, and regional camps were established for the purpose of drilling the infantry according to the Prussian example. Maria Theresa made a point of visiting these camps herself, to encourage her soldiers.

But she didn't stop there. She went after education as well, which had stagnated under her father's rule, largely owing to the prevalence of Jesuit teaching. Although a devout Catholic herself, Maria Theresa was under no illusions as to the general bankruptcy of the Jesuit approach; she had experienced firsthand the lack of practical knowledge among her father's advisers. Both the University of Vienna—"whose lectures surely are of little worth," she sniffed—and Prague University were put under new management, and leading professors from all over Europe coaxed onto the faculties by the promise of large salaries. The medical school, in particular, was completely reorganized. Maria Theresa even installed her personal court physician as provost after he brought to her attention the horrifying mortality rate among infants whose mothers had the misfortune to give birth at the Vienna hospital—of 600 babies delivered annually, only 20 survived. Finally, to ensure a steady stream of qualified students, in 1749 the empress opened a boarding school that for the first time was available not simply to the children of wealthy patricians but also to those of the lesser gentry. "Nothing will be more conducive to the welfare of my dominions than my offering to the nobility…the opportunity to give their sons the kind of education…that will enable them to render useful service to the commonweal, and to me and my successors," she declared.

This combined approach to finance, education, and military reform was unprecedented and very soon began to show results so tangible that even her enemies were forced to acknowledge her achievement. Her annual revenues rose to 36 million florins, a substantial increase over her father's income stream, even though she did not have the benefit of tax receipts from wealthy Silesia and Naples, as he had had. Even more significantly, the money was being used much more efficiently to better the lives of her subjects and especially to shore up the national defense. "By these various cures, the army acquired a degree of perfection before unknown under the emperors of the house of Austria; and a woman executed plans worthy of a man of genius," Frederick would later admit.

BUT AS FARSIGHTED, JUST, and courageous as these policies were—and make no mistake, they were; if France had implemented a similar program there would have been no need for a revolution—it must be confessed that Maria Theresa was not a perfect ruler. The years of struggle and disappointment had taken their toll. She was plagued by anxiety and depression. The more she learned about governing, the more she felt the terrible burden of her responsibility. The job began to consume her.

It didn't help that she continued to bear children at the same relentless pace as she had when she was a decade younger. On September 18, 1748, tragedy struck when she delivered her tenth baby, a daughter who died within an hour of birth. Her eleventh, Maria Johanna, was born on February 4, 1750, and was followed by Maria Josepha on March 19, 1751, and Maria Carolina on August 13, 1752. A little less than two years later, on June 1, 1754, the empress produced her fourth son, Ferdinand; Ferdinand was soon followed by Maria Antonia on November 2, 1755; and, finally, a fifth son, Maximilian Francis, on December 8, 1756.

The physical price Maria Theresa paid for having brought to term sixteen pregnancies in twenty years was severe. Her weight gain was significant—her subjects openly called her "the fat one," which hurt. The excess pounds combined with the demands of office made it difficult for her to exercise as she had formerly; she tired much more easily. Even the hours spent riding horseback, which she had loved, were sharply curtailed until they dwindled away altogether. It was an unhealthy cycle, often compounded by postpartum depression. In the fall of 1752, she was so unlike herself that Count Tarouca intervened, advising her to make time for the entertainments and pleasures she had thrown herself into with such gaiety in the past. Her reply was chilling. "I am no longer the same person," she told him. "Amusements no longer exist for me. I must not think of them." She was thirty-five years old.

Overshadowing all of this was her complicated relationship with her husband. She loved Francis as passionately as ever, but she had long since concluded that he did not have the focus or temperament for governance. He was emperor in name only, trotted out to perform the numerous tedious ceremonial duties associated with the office (which he loathed), while Maria Theresa and her advisers handled the real business of the empire.* She went through the motions of asking his opinion but rarely listened to it. The Prussian ambassador gleefully recounted an incident in a report to Berlin in

---

* The one exception to this was finance; Francis had a solid understanding of investment and credit, and Maria Theresa generally deferred to him in this area.

which the empress, "who had been defending with ardor her own opinion against the ministers', asked him [Francis] sharply to keep his own counsel, implying that he ought not to mix in affairs about which he knew nothing." She was fortunate that her spouse, who in any case much preferred the pleasures of hunting and society to long hours spent reading memoranda or arguing policy, did not openly rebel against this diminution of the traditional male role. Still, it must have rankled at least a little. "Don't mind me," he once tellingly observed to visitors to the court. "I am only a husband."

It should come as no surprise, then, that Francis's attentions had begun to wander. He had always enjoyed the company of pretty women, and although his wife's frequent pregnancies testified to his continued sharing of the conjugal bedchamber, it's pretty clear that hers was not the only boudoir with which he was familiar. "He used to dine with them in secret," the Prussian ambassador smirked of Francis's illicit lovers. "But the jealousy of the empress has compelled him to restrict this sort of thing...He is still said to have his little escapades, pretending to go hunting miles away."

The knowledge that her husband was physically attracted to younger, slenderer, more vivacious beauties, combined with the forlorn sensation that her own charms were fast fading away, caused Maria Theresa no end of torment. With so much work to do, she could allot only half an hour to her morning toilet, and it was reported that her ladies-in-waiting feared this interval more than any other as their mistress's expectation of what could be achieved in so short a time inevitably exceeded the results as reflected in the looking glass. Her hair, in particular, was a problem. Maria Theresa's blond curls had always been a source of admiration, and she wanted them arranged just so—it was remarked that if she was unhappy with the way her hair looked in the morning, the rest of her day would be ruined.* The poor young woman responsible for the empress's coiffure, who had to rise before the break of dawn to

---

* She has my total sympathy here.

fulfill her duties and be on call the rest of the day, would later refer to her employment at the royal court as "glorious slavery."

Keeping the emperor's affections from straying was, of course, yet another battle she could not win. As an aggrieved wife, there was very little Maria Theresa could do beyond the usual tears, guilt-inducing recriminations, and stony silences (all of which Francis, who had no wish to hurt her, would respond to, at least temporarily), but as a sovereign she had other options. To reduce the temptation that the emperor (and other similarly misguided Austrian husbands) felt to cheat, she decided to legislate the morality of her subjects and established a special unit of undercover operatives to clamp down on philandering and licentious behavior in the general populace. Labeled the chastity commission, her agents wandered the streets of Vienna arresting adulterous wives and deporting unescorted women who had the misfortune to be mistaken for prostitutes; following and informing on army officers who frequented houses of ill repute and who were subsequently denied promotions; and conducting raids on parties in private homes to ensure that the dinner guests did not engage in prohibited dalliances. (By sheer coincidence, Casanova happened to be passing through Vienna just as these new regulations hit. He found them most uncongenial and cut his visit short.) Although the outcry against this invasion of privacy was so pronounced that the program was scrapped within six months, Maria Theresa remained convinced of its efficacy and would later mobilize these same operatives to inaugurate a new department of law enforcement commonly known as the secret police.

But her worst transgression was her horrifically bigoted attitude regarding religion. Her subjects' beliefs were minutely scrutinized and regulated. Only practicing Catholics could hold a position in Maria Theresa's government. Protestantism was considered by the empress to be heresy, and she believed that members of dissenting sects, for their own good and the salvation of their souls, should be forced to recant. Faced with this reality, most Protestants chose, or were pressured, to convert.* But where Maria Theresa's virulent adherence to Catholicism truly betrayed her realm was in her policies toward Jews, whom she had loathed and feared since childhood. She tried to banish them outright from Bohemia, Moravia, and Austria, but the economic impact of this was so detrimental that the regional authorities protested and she had to back down, although not before extorting a contribution of 300,000 florins in "voluntary gifts" from the Jewish community at large. Although she never condoned violence against them, her intractable anti-Semitism, which even her closest councillors could not modulate, would persist throughout her reign.

As BURDENED AS MARIA THERESA WAS by her misguided attempts to meddle in her subjects' personal lives (not to mention the implementation of her sweeping administrative reforms and the demands of her enormous, ever-expanding family), she never for a moment took her eyes off Frederick. Any future threat to her realm, she knew, would come from him, and there was only so much she could do on her own. She was going to need strong allies who also recognized the danger posed by the belligerent king of Prussia, and who were willing to work with her to thwart him. Again, she asked her council for suggestions as to what might be done; again, the majority hemmed and hawed; and again, one man's reasoning stood out as so clearly superior to the others' that to Maria Theresa it was like coming across the clear, true, powerful voice of a world-famous opera singer after spending her whole life listening to the music of organ-grinders.

---

* Although Maria Theresa's intolerance was extreme, her policies were not dissimilar to those of other realms. For example, in terms of homogeneity of religion, England was a mirror image of Austria; there, only Anglicans were eligible for official employment, while Catholics and other dissenting sects were relegated to second-class citizenry. Voltaire, who spent three years in London, noted, "No person can possess an employment either in England or Ireland unless he be ranked among the faithful, that is, professes himself a member of the Church of England. This reason... has converted such numbers...that not a twentieth part of the nation is out of the pale of the Established Church."

This was Count Wenzel Anton von Kaunitz, the same young nobleman the empress had sent to Brussels to help her sister, Maria Anna, before her untimely death, and the official Maria Theresa had named to negotiate the terms of the Treaty of Aix-la-Chapelle on her behalf. Like Haugwitz, Count Kaunitz did not, on first impression, give off an air of any particular competence, unless the subject under consideration happened to be the latest styles in upscale menswear. He was so notoriously vain that it was reported that he dressed surrounded by four mirrors every day, to ensure that there were no unsightly wrinkles or hanging threads from any angle. "I should have supposed he was more occupied with caring for his hair, his dress, and his complexion, than for the interests of his country," remarked one of his associates. "But the error of such an opinion was conceded by all," he admitted. Kaunitz was also conspicuous for his frequent ill health and general hypochondria, which he took pains to pamper by doing as much of his work as he could lying in bed until noon and by rejecting invitations to dinner unless his servants were allowed to bring him his food from home. He had such a

Count Kaunitz

horror of drafts that he refused to enter a room if it contained an open window, an eccentricity that put him into direct conflict with Maria Theresa, who, perpetually overheated by pregnancy, insisted on fresh air indoors even in the coldest weather. But such was her admiration for the count that the empress surrendered to his whim and worked out an early-warning system to alert the household to Kaunitz's presence and the need to close the windows. "He's coming! He's coming!" she would scream as soon as his carriage pulled up outside the palace.

In a lengthy memorandum notable for its rigorous, step-by-step, almost mathematical logic, Kaunitz laid out the case for a complete realignment of historical imperial alliances and foreign policy objectives. The amoral, opportunistic militarism of Frederick the Great, he argued, "had changed the old system of Europe." For centuries, France had been Austria's greatest threat to security, and it had made sense to combine with England and Holland to keep Louis XIV's terrible ambitions in check. But now Frederick had usurped the role of enemy-in-chief. In keeping Silesia, the king of Prussia had gotten a taste for conquest, and it was clear that he would not stop until he had expanded his territory still farther at the empress's expense. All of Maria Theresa's energies must now be channeled into reducing Frederick's capabilities, destroying his army, and reclaiming what was rightfully hers, or she would never be safe. The alliance with Empress Elizabeth of Russia was a good first step toward achieving this goal, but it was not enough. Maria Theresa *must* lure another great European power to her side. It was apparent from the last war that in this respect England would be uncooperative; that left France.

To propose the jaw-droppingly radical solution that Vienna seek out an alliance with Paris was the foreign policy equivalent of Haugwitz's recommending that the empress tax the nobles. Her other councillors again fell over backward arguing against such a dangerous strategy. But Kaunitz was without question the smartest person in the room—he was always the smartest person in the room—and

Maria Theresa could not help but be swayed by his arguments. Frederick wasn't the only one getting reports on his adversaries. The empress had spies, too, and these warned her that Prussia was stockpiling weapons and supplies and had upgraded its artillery. Alone among the European nations, Frederick maintained a peacetime draft, with one out of every thirty of his subjects conscripted into the military. She knew these soldiers were not there for defense but to be used—against her. In October 1750 she sent Kaunitz to France as her ambassador and authorized him to propose a defensive alliance with Louis XV.

To send an envoy so interested in fashion and high living to Paris was a stroke of brilliance. Not that he made any headway with his official counterparts—these ignored him. But he was perfect for the *un*official center of French power: Louis XV's new mistress, Madame de Pompadour.

Madame de Pompadour had been born Jeanne Antoinette Poisson on December 29, 1721. She was the daughter of a very pretty mother who had cheated on her husband, a midlevel banking employee, who had in turn cheated on his banking house, resulting in his having to flee the authorities.* His wife and daughter were rescued from destitution and obscurity by Jeanne's real father, a wealthy financier who paid the bills, saw to it that his illegitimate offspring had a first-rate education, and married her at twenty to his dullard of a nephew, by which time she had grown up to be even prettier than her mother. "She was rather above the middle height, slender, supple, and graceful," reported an admirer who knew her. "Her hair was luxuriant, of a light chestnut shade rather than fair, and the eyebrows which crowned her magnificent eyes were of the same hue. She had a perfectly-formed nose, a ravishing smile, while the most exquisite skin one could wish to behold put the finishing touch to all her beauty."

---

* He was eventually pardoned and allowed to return after an absence of fifteen years "thanks to the tears and smiles of a daughter whom no one could refuse, and of a wife who could refuse no one," a French wit observed.

Madame de Pompadour

Egged on by her ambitious parent, she had Louis XV in her sights from the beginning. With her husband's money she entered Parisian society in style. Luminaries like Voltaire and Montesquieu attended her parties, and her country house was right next door to the king's favorite hunting château at Choisy. It was inevitable that they should meet, and when Louis XV's former mistress died, in December 1744, Jeanne naturally took over. Since it wouldn't do to have a bourgeois nobody as the king's lover, very soon afterward Jeanne Antoinette Poisson was raised to the high aristocracy and became Madame de Pompadour.

It was no easy business being a king's mistress, especially when the sovereign in question was as jaded as Louis XV. Physical attraction was not enough; passion dwindled with familiarity. She had to make herself necessary in other ways. Very quickly, she understood that the surest means of holding her place was to keep the king amused at all times.

No social director ever worked harder than Madame de Pompadour. She was equal parts court jester, stage manager, diva, snake charmer, and tour guide. To entertain her royal charge she started her own small theater, putting on light comedies and musicals (serious dramas being too taxing for the French monarch's notoriously limited attention span), in which she often played the leading role. Attendance became all the rage, and the nobility competed for parts. The king and queen were usually present, seated in the front row, the better for Louis to make the comparison. Madame de Pompadour made sure that her costumes and performance showed off her considerable assets to advantage. It clearly worked: "You are the most charming woman in France," the king pronounced after one of these theatrical evenings.

It wasn't just his nights she had to fill but his days as well. Louis required amusement whenever he was bored, and just about everything bored him. So she organized spontaneous trips to the best hunting grounds; kept his ministers away from him (nothing put Louis in a fouler mood than having to listen to council reports or make policy decisions); spent 4 million livres of the royal treasury's money on brilliant festivities to keep him occupied; and spent another 3.5 million on an expert chef, pastry maker, and wine steward, among other kitchen staff, to turn out culinary masterpieces delectable enough to tempt even Louis's coddled palate. Through it all, she had no illusions as to the tenuousness of her position, how easily she could be replaced. "My life is a perpetual contest," she admitted candidly. "If the King found someone else with whom he could talk about his hunting and his affairs, at the end of three days he would not know the difference if I were gone."

It didn't take Count Kaunitz long to figure out that the best way to approach the French monarch was to play up to Madame de Pompadour. "The more I see of this court, and the interior administration of this monarchy, the more I discover its defects," he wrote home to Maria Theresa in 1752. "Most things are done by intrigue and cabal." So Kaunitz, too, threw lavish parties to please the king's mistress and by degrees insinuated himself into her circle. Once there, he flattered her shamelessly, making her feel as though she was an integral component of the balance of power in Europe. And although by the time he left in April 1753 he was still unable to convince the king or his ministers formally to reject their alliance with Frederick in favor of one with Austria, he had succeeded in planting the seeds of the idea and establishing a clandestine channel for future communication.

And then, the very next year, Kaunitz's proposal suddenly got a very big boost when, some 4,000 miles away across the Atlantic, in the untamed wilderness of a territory called "Ohio," a callow twenty-two-year-old colonial militiaman brazenly exceeded his orders and reignited the war in Europe.

ALTHOUGH ACCORDING TO THE TERMS of the Treaty of Aix-la-Chapelle the British had agreed to return property conquered in Canada to its French owners, this had not resolved the growing problem of the rivalry between France and England for control of America. There was simply too much wealth to be had for either side to step aside and let the other take what it wanted, and the issue of who owned what was further complicated by disagreements over boundaries. For example, the French had a compelling argument for insisting that *they* owned the Ohio River. A Frenchman had discovered it; they had long-established trading posts on it; and it had been in continuous, uninterrupted use and accepted as the link to their property in Louisiana since France had first landed in North America. Still, this had not stopped the British from sending traders into the area to try to undercut them commercially and establish a foothold. So, in the spring of 1753, France sent an army of some 2,000 men down from Canada to build a couple of forts to the east of Lake Erie, in order to discourage further trespassing.

This escalation did not sit well with the British governor of Virginia, who had just invested a significant sum of money in a land development company operating within what was known in England as the Ohio Territory, which *also* claimed the lands to the east of Lake Erie.★ Naturally unhappy with the idea of losing his stake, the governor sent a party of some fifty men to erect a competing fort in the area. They arrived in February 1754 (not the best time of year for building, what with the frigid temperatures, driving snow, fierce winds, and such) and managed to hammer together a small enclosure.

Of course, almost from the moment they arrived, the opposition knew from spies and reconnaissance that they were there. And so when the weather improved, the French commander marched 600 men plus artillery out to surround the building. The soldiers arrived on April 16, 1754, and as it was clearly no contest, the British troop surrendered more or less immediately. There was no bloodshed; in fact, the victors couldn't have been nicer. They let everybody go home, and gave them food and supplies for the trip back in exchange for leaving the tools they'd used to construct the makeshift fort in the first place. The French commander even invited the British commander to dinner before they left.

Unfortunately, the Virginia governor, unaware that the skeleton stronghold had been taken, had already dispatched a new troop of about 180 colonials under the direction of a keen young officer by the name of George Washington. Washington's orders were very clear; he was to take his men "to the Fork of Ohio [and there] finish and compleat the Fort…already begun by the Ohio Company."

On May 23, the French were informed that a new British force was in the area. Since the trespassers' numbers were again insignificant, the regional commander did not even bother to confront them militarily but instead sent a squad of about thirty-five men to find the intruders and advise them to be on their way. Four days later this group still had not found Washington's company, so when evening fell they stopped to make camp. As it was raining hard that night, they put their muskets away to keep them dry before they went to

---

★ They called it the Ohio Territory, but actually all of this transpired in what is today Pennsylvania, just to make it as confusing as possible.

sleep. Because they had been sent only to communicate a message, they did not even bother to post sentries.

They may not have found Washington, but Washington had found them. Although he had no authority to attack, and by doing so was in violation of the Treaty of Aix-la-Chapelle (not to mention his own orders), he could not resist the temptation to score an easy victory against the French. Aided by Iroquois warriors, he made a night march through the rain, surrounded the camp, and began firing at dawn. Some of those surprised contrived to retrieve their weapons and got off a few rounds before being forced to surrender, and one soldier, who had risen early to relieve himself in the woods, managed to escape, but ten were killed that morning and the rest captured. Washington, clearly moved by the bravery he and his men had displayed by shooting at the sleeping French, was poetic in his report home to Virginia. "I heard the bullets whistle, and believe me there is something charming in the sound," he enthused.

The result of this ill-considered foray was an immediate escalation of hostilities. The French scathingly referred to Washington's action as "assassination," and on June 28, the regional commander sent a regiment of 500 men to intercept the perpetrators. Washington, deprived of the edifice he had been sent to work on, had instead fallen back about 60 miles in order to build his own bulwark, Fort Necessity, a modest enclosure that resembled a stronghold in name only. On July 3, he and his regiment were discovered and surrounded. They took fire all day before agreeing to surrender. Once again, the French demonstrated restraint and allowed everyone to go home, and even agreed to hold their belongings for them until suitable transport could be arranged to carry them back. Their one condition was that Washington sign a confession admitting to murder, which, not understanding the language of the document, he did, an act of humiliating contrition that saved him and, ultimately by extension, the United States.

But the damage was done. George II, fearing to lose the Ohio Territory altogether if he did not move quickly enough, used the loss of

Fort Necessity as a pretext to send a new army, supplemented by naval power, to America. Louis XV naturally followed suit, and by 1755 it was clear to everyone in Europe that the heedless action of one inexperienced, overeager colonial officer was about to precipitate yet another conflagration between England and France. And since everyone also recognized that this was not a new war but merely a resumption of the old one, they understood that the battleground would not be limited to America, but would play out once again on the Continent. This in turn meant that anyone who had been disappointed with the outcome of the previous altercation was going to get another crack at it. Like children participating in a schoolyard game, the rest of Europe obediently lined up to choose sides. The question was, whose team would Prussia decide to play on this time around?

BY THE SUMMER OF 1755, Frederick, who had used the years of peace productively, could congratulate himself on his foresight and the superiority of his methods. He had revived the Prussian economy, encouraged industry and agriculture, and successfully yoked his ill-gotten gains to his administration. ("We have drawn upon ourselves the envy of Europe by the acquisition of Silesia," the king noted modestly in 1752.) To celebrate, he had built himself a brand-new palace and a large, very grand opera house in Berlin, to which he lured a number of Italian singers and French actresses with the promise of large salaries.* After numerous flattering and pressing invitations, he had even succeeded in coaxing the eminent Voltaire to his court, only to then fall out with him. When the French philosopher finally contrived to escape his uncongenial host, Frederick had him pursued, arrested, and thrown into prison in Frankfurt.

But most importantly, Frederick had managed, through a forced draft that basically covered every healthy male in the kingdom, to raise a standing army of over 150,000 soldiers with supplies to feed

---

* Those virtuosos who took him up on it would find out only afterward that they could not leave without the king's permission, and as he rarely gave his permission, they were stuck there.

them for a year and a half, in addition to the guns, bullets, bayonets, and artillery necessary for a full two years' worth of military operations. Not to mention the more than 16 million thalers he had saved up in the royal treasury for contingencies.

Additionally during this period of peace, Frederick made a habit of sitting down to long, leisurely meals with anyone of importance who happened to be visiting Berlin, during which he wittily skewered his fellow crowned heads of Europe and their companions. Maria Theresa, as well as her ally Empress Elizabeth of Russia, and Madame de Pompadour, whom he particularly scorned, were favorite subjects of his ribaldry.* He referred to this group contemptuously as "the three petticoats." Maria Theresa was "Empress Petticoat I," and Madame de Pompadour was "Queen Petticoat II." To abase Empress Petticoat I, he tsk-tsked publicly at Francis's humiliating infidelities and chortled over her foolish chastity commission. As for Louis XV's mistress, "My dogs destroy my chairs," he explained to his guests in mock innocence, "but how can I help it! If I were to have them mended to-day, they would be as bad again to-morrow . . . [and] after all, a marquise de Pompadour would cost me a great deal more, and would not be either so fond or so faithful." About the tsarina, although Frederick knew that she commanded immense resources— "I fear Russia more than God," he once confessed—he could not resist smirking about her overindulgence in wine, her questionable personal hygiene, and especially her propensity for taking young, attractive male lovers and heaping gifts and favors on them. (He was one to talk. It was well known that Frederick had a series of special— and especially handsome—young men whom he invited into his bedchamber, and who were subsequently given high positions at court, titles, estates, large bank accounts, jeweled snuff boxes, and other tokens of their monarch's esteem.)

---

* Frederick had a low opinion of women in general. Once, at a dinner in honor of his wife's birthday (the only time he saw her all year), he complained that the ladies attached to his court were ugly "and you can smell these horrible cows ten miles away."

Although malicious gossip of this sort was of course no reason to alter foreign policy, it did not recommend the king of Prussia to the courts of France, Russia, and Austria. "The King [Louis XV] disliked the King of Prussia because he knew that the latter was in the habit of jesting about his mistress, and the kind of life he led," volunteered Madame de Pompadour's private maid in her memoirs. "It was Frederick's fault...that the King was not his most steadfast ally and friend...but the jestings of Frederick stung him."

Then came the conflict over America, which was exactly the opportunity Frederick had been looking for to annex more territory. As early as 1752, he had already decided who his next victim would be and had laid out an acquisition plan. "Saxony would be the most useful...What would facilitate this conquest would be...a pretext to march into Saxony, disarm its troops, and establish oneself in force in the country," he proposed in a document intended for his successors.* A war between England and France was just the excuse he needed to make his move. England would need him to help fight off French incursions into Germany, and France would need him to help keep Austrian ambitions in check, so he reasoned that, just like the last time, neither would mind if he helped himself to a property next door. In fact, he was counting on both of them, but especially France, to stop Maria Theresa from using this new conflict to try again for Silesia. "France...cannot suffer Austria to recover Silesia," he argued smugly, "because that would weaken too greatly an ally [Prussia], which is useful to her for the affairs of the North and of the Empire."

And so, as soon as it became clear that there would be a resumption of European hostilities, Frederick did what he always did: prepared to double-cross his allies. In this case, to obtain the best deal

---

* Note that Maria Theresa's property was no longer at the top of Frederick's most wanted list. That's not because he didn't desire it—he clearly coveted Bohemia—but because she had strengthened her military sufficiently that he could no longer count on an easy victory. Frederick's entire philosophy was based on attacking far weaker opponents. Thus his interest in Saxony. He *knew* he could take them.

for himself, he entered into covert negotiations with England, all the while pretending to be unshakably attached to France.

Maria Theresa, who had been expecting something like this, recognized her opportunity. On August 31, 1755, the new Austrian ambassador to France, acting on orders from Count Kaunitz (now raised to chancellor of state in Vienna), approached Madame de Pompadour with a request. Would she be willing to act as a personal intermediary and present a secret proposal to Louis XV on behalf of the empress?

This appeal, the groundwork for which had been laid several years earlier, was too flattering to be denied. It vaulted Madame de Pompadour, who had begun life as the dubious daughter of a bourgeois nonentity, and a disgraced one at that, into the accepted ranks of the great power brokers of Europe. For a woman who, despite her title and access, was routinely sneered at by the ministers and aristocracy of France, this was sweet revenge indeed. She quickly agreed, and in September, she and a trusted adviser met quietly with the Austrian ambassador at her country house in Meudon. The ambassador explained that Maria Theresa was once again seeking an alliance with France against Prussia. The empress desired to avoid regular channels of communication and work directly with Louis XV. As a token of her goodwill, Maria Theresa wished to warn the king that her spies had evidence that Frederick was secretly negotiating to betray France by signing an alliance with England.

Through her adviser, Madame de Pompadour made haste to pass along this intelligence in confidence to her royal lover. Without bothering to mention the Austrian offer, Louis XV queried his ministers as to the state of the French alliance with Prussia. He was apprised that renewal of the long-standing treaty between the two realms was expected daily but in any event the signed document was merely a formality, as Frederick had already assured them of his loyalty. Upon hearing this report, Louis XV, who whatever his other faults was a man of his word, rejected Maria Theresa's proposal on the grounds that he had already committed himself to Prussia.

Then, on January 16, 1756, Frederick blindsided his French allies by signing the Treaty of Westminster, a defensive agreement whereby Prussia and Britain agreed to aid each other in the event that either was attacked. Although this arrangement did not convert Frederick into an active enemy, it was nonetheless clearly intended to limit French strategic options by preventing France from launching an invasion of George II's property at Hanover for fear of having to fight Prussia as well. "Now surely the King of France will renounce the faithless ally who has once more deserted him, and seek the trusty friendship of Maria Theresa," said Kaunitz.

He was right: that did it. Six months later, on May 1, 1756, France and Austria signed the Treaty of Versailles, in which Louis XV and the empress, in a complete reversal of their previous policies, pledged to come to the material aid of the other should either be attacked in the future. "Never during all my reign, have I signed a treaty with so cheerful a heart!" Maria Theresa exclaimed.

And not a moment too soon. On May 17, 1756, England officially declared war on France. On June 16, France returned the favor and proclaimed war on England. Two months later, Frederick attacked Saxony.

But this time, Maria Theresa was ready for him. This time it was *she* who had left the door to the trap open. And the king of Prussia walked right into it.

7

The Sisterhood of the
Three Petticoats

∾

I have not abandoned the old system, but Great Britain has abandoned me . . . by concluding the Prussian treaty, the first intelligence of which struck me like a fit of apoplexy.

—Maria Theresa

I am always a long time making up my mind, but when once I have decided what ought to be done, I stick to my opinion. I mean to continue this war . . . even if I am compelled to sell all my diamonds and half my clothes.

—Elizabeth of Russia

I hate the King of Prussia. I hate him more than ever . . . Let us demolish this Attila of the North, then I shall be as contented as I am at present ill-humored.

—Madame de Pompadour

THE SNARE MARIA THERESA HAD SET was complex. Like a grand master executing a series of precision moves in chess, it had required painstaking coordination, not simply with France, but with Russia as well. Empress Elizabeth's participation was, if anything, even more critical to Austrian success than Louis XV's. Russian troops

Empress Elizabeth of Russia

had not been a factor in the previous war. The tsarina's soldiers were not as disciplined as their Prussian counterparts, it was true, but what they lacked in professionalism they more than made up for in quantity and sheer endurance. Elizabeth's entrance into the revived conflict would thus mean the introduction of a new and potentially game-changing alliance.

Maria Theresa was in no way the only sovereign to understand this, and for this reason the tsarina's favor was courted assiduously by all the major powers. Frederick, understanding that he might not be particularly welcome at Elizabeth's court after all he'd said about her at his dining room table, had put up his new British allies to intercede for him. Their idea had been to buy the tsarina's friendship, or at least her neutrality, by offering to pay hefty stipends. As this method had always worked in the past, they assured Frederick that Russia would not pose a threat in the coming campaign. But unbeknownst to the English ambassadors, Maria Theresa, who had been in covert negotiations with Elizabeth since the end of the last war, had already received the tsarina's pledge to reject the British stipends and instead send an army of 80,000 to help Austria recover Silesia.

It was imperative to Maria Theresa's plot that this agreement with Russia be kept a secret. She had signed a treaty with Frederick at the end of the previous war that prohibited each from initiating an attack on the other, and she intended to honor that commitment. The only way she could legitimately call upon the promised Russian troops was if she could goad Prussia into striking her first. Fortunately, long experience with Frederick had demonstrated that he was already prepared to do this, so all that was needed was a little push.

Her first move had been to raise the king of Prussia's suspicions by adopting an air of innocent indifference with the British ambassador at Vienna (it was a new one, Sir Thomas having been replaced), knowing that anything she said would be instantly passed along to Frederick. The English, who had taken it for granted that Austria would fight on their side in any struggle against the French, were taken aback by Maria Theresa's defensive pact with Louis XV, which had been made public. At a hastily convened interview, the ambassador protested strongly against this untoward change in foreign policy. Maria Theresa, whose interests had so often been trampled on by this very same ally, and who understandably enjoyed being on the other side of the negotiation for a change, listened to him with indulgent good humor. "Why should you be surprised if, following your example in concluding a treaty with Prussia, I should enter into an engagement with France?" she countered sweetly.

She let that sink in for a bit before leaking hints about her arrangement with Russia to Frederick's spies in Saint Petersburg. She followed this up at the end of May 1756 by moving a large number of Austrian troops into Bohemia.

She had him cold. It took Frederick less than a month to take the bait. On June 23 he wrote to his general, "You know already how... the Austrian court, from hatred of my successful convention with England, took the course of allying itself with France. It is true that Russia has concluded a subsidy-treaty with England, but I have every reason to believe that it will be broken by Russia and that she has joined the Austrian party and concerted with her a threatening plan." And he began calling up troops in preparation for a surprise attack. "In a fortnight's time he will be ready to act," the British ambassador attached to the Prussian court assured his government in his report home to London.

During this period, Maria Theresa continued to play her part in the game. When the Prussian ambassador, under instructions from Frederick, demanded an audience to ascertain Austrian military intentions, she neatly dodged him by reading from a prepared statement—she, who never relied on written documents to make her points—that was carefully worded to say absolutely nothing. "The critical state of affairs has led me to think those measures necessary which I am taking for my safety and for the defence of my allies, and which have no object beyond this, and are intended to injure no one," she intoned evenly.* The king of Prussia, it turned out, did not appreciate having his own evasive methods employed against him. "I must know whether we are at peace or at war," he raged at his envoy.

Soon after this, just as Maria Theresa had predicted, Frederick attacked. On August 29, in one of his lightning-quick sneak campaigns, he led an army of 70,000 soldiers into Saxony (he was always going to invade wealthy Saxony—it made for such a tempting target) and within two weeks had occupied the capital city of Dresden. Emboldened by the ease with which he had succeeded, he continued his high-speed onslaught, ordering several Prussian divisions into Bohemia with the aim of annexing as much of Maria Theresa's territory as possible. So confident was he of success that he threw away all caution and on September 13, 1756, boldly declared war on Austria.

And with this single stroke, he freed the empress from the pesky encumbrances of her treaty obligations. As the king of Prussia had

---

* You can see how much fun she was having.

just revealed himself to the world to be the aggressor, she could now legitimately call upon her new French and Russian allies, and with their aid take back Silesia and defeat her nemesis once and for all.

Frederick had walked voluntarily into Maria Theresa's trap. Now all she had to do was bang the door shut behind him.

SO BEGAN A CONTEST for which Maria Theresa had been preparing for eleven long years, ever since she had been compelled to cede Silesia to Prussia. Although its ostensible aim was the recovery of that province, it was actually about something much deeper. At issue were two distinct theories of rule. Frederick's naked territorial ambitions and overriding emphasis on militarism—Prussia was "not a country with an army but an army with a country," as one wit had quipped—contrasted sharply with Maria Theresa's belief in the intrinsic rights of property and her overriding feeling of responsibility to her subjects. The years of peace had shown her just how much work she still had to do to achieve her domestic aims. If Frederick was not beaten decisively, and his opportunism discredited, at the very least she would spend the rest of her reign in a perpetual arms race, with an ever-increasing proportion of state revenues siphoned off for defense; and then there was always the threat that no matter how valiantly she fought, bit by bit she might lose all. Either way, there would never be enough left over to promote agriculture and commerce, or to make the critically needed improvements to education and health that her people deserved. Although the king of Prussia also aspired to a strong economy, this goal served chiefly as a further inducement to conquest: the more he took, the more he had; the more he had, the wealthier the realm. For Frederick, this war was a game of glory, fortune, and skill. For Maria Theresa, it was a crossroads.

With so much at stake, she kept a close watch on every aspect of the conflict. She read volumes of reports from the front lines and notated extensively in the margins of council memoranda, asking questions, raising potential difficulties, and offering solutions. No issue, no matter how small, escaped her notice. When requisitions for horses fell short, she immediately provided mounts from her own stable, inspiring other members of the nobility to do the same. She worried whether her soldiers had enough blankets to ward off the cold; reprimanded her ministers for not transporting combat equipment quickly enough to the locations that needed it most; and pored over maps to ensure that supplies were delivered by the surest route.

But there was much she could not control. Empress Elizabeth, for example, was enraged to discover that the troops she had pledged to Maria Theresa would not be combat-ready until the following year. "You it was who magnified my forces before we declared war," she thundered at the quaking Russian minister in charge of military preparedness. "Do you not fear God that you so deceive me?" Similarly, Louis XV, already in conflict with Britain, needed time to raise the promised funds and soldiers. This meant that, at least for the foreseeable future, Maria Theresa was going to have to confront Frederick alone.

And by taking Saxony first, the king of Prussia had significantly augmented his strategic position. Not only had he seized all of the duchy's gold and other valuables and transferred them to his own war chest, but he also insisted that the entire Saxon army be compelled to fight for the rest of their lives on behalf of Prussia. His obvious intention was that these troops would bear the brunt of any future combat so as to spare casualties among his own countrymen. "Good heavens, no one on earth ever heard of such a demand!" sputtered the poor Saxon envoy charged with negotiating the terms of the province's surrender. "I think it is not without precedent," Frederick had allowed modestly. "But you know, I do pride myself on being original."★

★ The Prussian occupation was absolutely brutal. "His [Frederick's] treatment of the Saxons...scarcely admits of any justification," reported a scandalized chronicler. "Hundreds of Saxon young women, carried off by violence from their paternal cottages, were sent to the remotest provinces of the Prussian monarchy, and there matched with husbands provided for them by the state...numbers of the Saxon youth, either taken in arms, or dragged from the domestic occupations of husbandry, were

Still, Maria Theresa had faith in her own forces, which she had worked so diligently to improve, and this confidence had been justified in their very first encounter with Prussia. When, soon after occupying Dresden, Frederick had pushed on and invaded Bohemia, her divisions, under the command of one of her best new field marshals, and equipped with modernized artillery, had been there to meet him on October 1, 1756. The king, despite having paid lip service to the progress made by the empress in reforming her military over the past few years, still did not have a very high opinion of Austrian capabilities. Accordingly, he had attacked on an extremely foggy morning without even bothering to figure out the strength of the opposing force—and gotten a big surprise. His most fearsome unit, the Prussian cavalry, was so pelted by strangely accurate artillery fire that they came hurtling back (he had them shot for cowardice); his infantry did no better. When the mist finally cleared and he saw that he was significantly outnumbered, for the second time in his career Frederick turned tail and ran, leaving the fighting to his general, who this time prudently called a retreat.

But although she had pushed him out of Bohemia for the winter, Maria Theresa knew that Frederick would try again in the spring, and she was determined to be ready for him. She had everything in place when Charles of Lorraine, who had been ushered into discreet retirement in Brussels after his previously disastrous tenure as head of the military, turned up in Vienna begging for a second chance.

SHE DIDN'T WANT TO DO IT but she felt she had no choice. Francis had interceded directly with her on behalf of his younger brother and she could not say no to him. To her profound unhappiness, her husband was drifting away from her, and she knew that at least some of this was her fault. Francis, who hated Louis XV for appropriating Lorraine, had spoken out against the alliance with France. In her

---

obliged to enter into Prussian service, and to carry destruction into the bosom of their native country." You really did not want to be conquered by Frederick.

anxiety over the coming war, she had lost her temper and sharply overruled him, humiliating him in front of everyone in her council. His warnings that she was overburdening her financial resources also went unheeded. Bored by the endless meetings in which he had no say, he spent his time hunting and in the company of friends, particularly one glamorous young woman his eldest daughter's age who was so radiantly good-looking that she was universally known simply as "*la belle princesse.*"

Fearful of losing him completely, Maria Theresa let her love for her husband overwhelm her good judgment. Charles was appointed commander general and sent to Bohemia to prepare for the spring campaign, with predictable results. On May 6, 1757, Frederick, moving with his trademark speed at the head of an enormous army of some 116,000 soldiers, caught the Austrian forces by surprise. Charles took one look at the vast enemy host and passed out cold from heart palpitations. He had to be carried off the field in a litter. As this was not an encouraging sign, what remained of his divisions scurried back to Prague to take shelter behind the strong walls of the capital. Now Maria Theresa was required not only to try to hold off Frederick but also to rescue her brother-in-law and the approximately 48,000 Austrian servicemen who were trapped in the city and under siege by the Prussians.

She didn't hesitate for a moment. At once, she ordered the mustering of an additional 54,000 warriors under the command of Field Marshal Daun, yet another of her new, significantly more energetic senior officers. At the same time, to keep up her soldiers' spirits (and prevent Charles from capitulating prematurely to the besieging army) she found a way to get a stirring personal message smuggled into Bohemia. "I am concerned that...so considerable a force, must remain besieged in Prague; but I augur favorably for the event," her letter began. "The honor of the whole nation, as well as of the imperial arms...the security of Bohemia, of my other hereditary dominions, and of the German empire itself, depends on a gallant defence, and the preservation of Prague. The army under the command of

Marshal Daun is daily strengthening, and will soon be in a condition to raise the siege...and in a short space of time, affairs will, under the divine Providence, wear a better aspect," she calmly reassured the troops.

But for all her outward confidence, privately Maria Theresa trembled in suspense while awaiting word from Daun, who set off with his men for Prague in June. At last, a messenger arrived with news. The field marshal had caught up with the enemy at Kolín, 45 miles east of Prague, and, in a daring night operation, had outflanked and gained a superior tactical position on his Prussian opponents while they slept. Battle had been joined the next morning. It was a rout. Frederick lost 14,000 men, fully a third of his force, along with 45 heavy guns. Three of the Saxon cavalry units that had been forced into Frederick's service began shooting at the Prussian infantry from within its own ranks, causing a panicked confusion that contributed greatly to the death toll. The triumph was so complete that even Charles had felt safe enough to lead his men out of Prague to chase after the hurriedly retreating Prussian soldiers, leading the empress mistakenly to believe that he had had a hand in the operation.

Maria Theresa's relief at this victory, the news of which arrived at seven in the morning, was such that she was almost giddy. She did not even sit still long enough to finish having her hair done before running to hug each of her ladies-in-waiting. She ordered the bells rung; the official announcement of the glad tidings was heralded by the blare of 24 trumpets; a *Te Deum* was hastily organized; and a grand celebration, complete with banquet and fireworks, was ordered. The empress drove out of the palace that very afternoon to call on Field Marshal Daun's family to express her extreme gratitude for his achievement. To Daun himself she wrote fervently, "The monarchy thanks you for its preservation, I for my existence. God preserve you long, for me, in the service of the State, the army, and my person, as my best, truest, and good friend." For the rest of her life, Maria Theresa would refer to June 18, the anniversary of the battle, as simply "The Birthday of the Monarchy."

She had done it—held off her nemesis long enough for her allies to enter the campaign. For the victory at Kolín coincided with the signing of a *second* Treaty of Versailles, this one much more aggressively dedicated to defeating Prussia, which had again been coordinated through the good offices of Madame de Pompadour. By this agreement, Louis XV pledged 100,000 men, available immediately, and 12 million guilders a year, to help Maria Theresa recover Silesia.* Empress Elizabeth, too, had made good on her commitment. France and Russia were finally ready to put troops in the field.

"Can you conceive of anything more extraordinary?" an aggrieved Frederick demanded when the details of this formidable alliance were made public. "The first three whores in Europe unite together to provoke, beyond the bounds of endurance, the man who of all the world should be the most indifferent to them."

A MONTH LATER, 60,000 French soldiers opened up a western front, rolled over their far weaker British opponents, and by the beginning of September 1757 controlled nearly 100 miles of German territory, including George II's ancestral duchy of Hanover. To Frederick's fury, the English king made haste to abandon his Prussian alliance in exchange for the return of his property and agreed to remain neutral for the rest of the war, thus leaving the French army free to attack Prussia with impunity. "This neutrality is infamous...the *canaille* [scoundrels] *of Hanover* have done this!" the king of Prussia fumed when informed of the terms of this treaty.

At almost exactly the same time, Prussia was menaced to the east when the promised Russian army began resolutely trudging its way toward the strategically vital port of Kaliningrad on the Baltic coast. The battle that took place on August 30, which Frederick had to leave to a subordinate (being still with his main force fleeing the

---

* Maria Theresa was so overjoyed with the terms of this second treaty that she made Madame de Pompadour a present of an exquisite lacquered writing table, complete with a miniature portrait of the empress surrounded by precious jewels. The frame alone cost 80,000 livres.

Austrians in Bohemia), was notable for the magnitude of its carnage. Although the Russian infantry certainly did not aim with the deliberate precision of their Prussian counterparts, there were a lot more of them firing and bayoneting, and they seemed to have an unlimited capacity for suffering. In the end, the invaders held the field, littered though it was with the corpses of their companions, and the demoralized remnants of the Prussian garrison retreated, leaving Kaliningrad open to enemy occupation. "What is wanting to place me completely in the situation of tormented Job?" railed Frederick, upon being informed of this latest defeat.

As for Maria Theresa, she felt herself at last to be on the verge of redress. On September 7, 1757, her army won a further engagement that resulted in the Prussians abandoning Bohemia completely in favor of Silesia, which is just where she wanted them. In October, one of her captains even led a small, one-day raiding party into Frederick's home capital of Berlin, which the king of Prussia had been forced to leave unprotected. In directive after directive she urged Charles, still commander general, to hurry up and finish off the weakened Prussian army and liberate Silesia.

She had Frederick on the run. It was only a matter of time.

PART II

Three Imperial Princesses

*Maria Christina, Maria Carolina, and
Marie Antoinette*

Mozart is introduced to Maria Theresa.

Maria Christina

"Mimi"

...at eight years old

8

The Favorite

There are so many kinds of love, that in order to define it,
we scarcely know which to direct our attention to.

—Voltaire, *The Philosophical Dictionary*

MARIA CHRISTINA WAS BORN on her mother's twenty-fifth birthday, May 13, 1742, during that interval in the first war with Frederick when Maria Theresa had secured the Hungarian throne but had not yet been crowned queen of Bohemia. Although Maria Christina was her parents' fourth daughter and fifth child, two of her siblings had already died, so at the time of her birth she had only one older sister, three-year-old Marianne, and her elder brother, Joseph (the long-sought, much-heralded male heir), just over a year old. This relatively compact and manageable family unit was, however, short-lived. By the time she was six, Maria Christina, or Mimi, as everybody called her, had four additional siblings: Maria Elisabeth, a year younger, born on August 13, 1743; another brother, Charles Joseph, born on February 1, 1745; Maria Amalia, three years younger, born on February 26, 1746; and, finally, a third brother, Leopold, who came into the world on May 5, 1747. Maria Theresa would go on to have six more children, but they came too late to be companions to Mimi in her early years. Rather, it would be these three brothers (Joseph, Charles, and Leopold) and three sisters (Marianne, Maria

Elisabeth, and Maria Amalia) who would form the nucleus of her world during childhood and young adulthood.

Mimi was a winning little girl, possessed of a sunny disposition and mild temperament. Although perhaps not quite as handsome as her younger sister Maria Elisabeth, the acknowledged family beauty, Maria Christina, with her halo of blond curls like her mother's, long neck, and graceful figure, was certainly a very attractive child. She had a quick intelligence, too, and was good at her lessons, particularly (again like her mother) at languages. By the time she had reached her teens she was fluent in French and Italian, and could even speak English.* As musical entertainments played a large role in the cultural life of the court—"If the Queen [Maria Theresa] has any pleasure in life it is in music," Sir Thomas had observed—Mimi was encouraged, as were all the empress's children, to sing and play instruments, in her case, the clavier and the viol. What she really loved, however, and manifested a demonstrable talent for, was art. Mimi began drawing early and soon graduated to painting.

But while Vienna was entering its Golden Age for music, witnessing the rise of such peerless composers as Christoph Willibald Gluck, Joseph Haydn, and Wolfgang Amadeus Mozart, all of whom performed for Mimi and her family, the empress's taste in art tended toward the safely conservative, and this set the tone.† Her court painter was Martin van Meytens, the Swedish-born son of a Dutch artist. As part of his studies, Van Meytens had made a tour of Paris and Italy before finally settling in Vienna. He was extremely accom-

---

* As Francis had never been able to master German, the family primarily communicated in French. All of Maria Theresa's letters to her children were in French, and as adults the siblings also used this language when writing to each other.

† In truth, Maria Theresa's musical aesthetic was none too progressive either, but it was overwhelmed by the sheer magnitude of the brilliance surrounding her. Like many people, she had the strongest feelings for the melodies of her youth. "As for dramatic music," she wrote, "I confess that I would rather have the slightest Italian thing than all the works of our composers, Gaisman, Gluck, and others. For instrumental music, we have a certain Haydn who has good ideas, but he is just beginning to be known." As a teenager, Haydn performed in a school choir for the empress; she was not impressed. "Joseph Haydn sang like a crow," she observed to the choirmaster after the performance.

plished at rendering large, highly detailed crowd scenes as well as intimate chamber interiors, but in Austria he found an immediate niche painting impressively sumptuous aristocratic portraits in a style known as rococo (he was especially good at depicting luxurious ball gowns). He was so popular that within two years Maria Theresa had taken him on as her court painter, and commissioned him to paint likenesses of her family; in 1759 she appointed him director of the Vienna Academy of Fine Arts.

To instruct her talented daughter, the empress selected Friedrich August Brand to be master of drawing at court. Brand, himself a graduate of the Vienna Academy, specialized in landscape painting. He was also known for his skill at intricate techniques such as etching. Under his tutelage, Mimi learned to work with pastels and gouache (a pigment similar to watercolors, only thicker), much admired in France and Vienna for the richness of the hue they produced. The favored method of teaching during this period was to have the student copy the pictures of celebrated artists, and it is clear from her later drawings and paintings that Mimi was exposed in this way to Dutch, French, and Italian influences.

Her days, like her mother's, were diligently ordered. All of the children were awakened every morning at 7:30 and obliged immediately to turn their thoughts toward piety and submission. "The day is always to be begun with prayer," Maria Theresa firmly directed the nobleman responsible for Joseph's education. "The first result of his devotion...is to be reverence and love towards his parents, which is always to be impressed on him, and set before him as a pleasant and unavoidable duty." After prayers, from 8:30 to 10:00, Mimi and her sisters were instructed in handwriting and grammar; at 10:00 they attended Mass; then came French until the midday meal. Afterward, they saw their mother for an hour or so, and from 2:00 on they were taught religion, followed by embroidery, music, or art lessons. At 5:00 they were back in church for devotions and a walk outside for exercise. Only in the evening did they have unstructured time. This was often devoted to putting on concerts, operas, or musical comedies for a private audience consisting of their parents, visiting dignitaries, and trusted friends. "A person of great distinction, who had been present, told me that they [Mimi and her sisters] were extremely beautiful, sung and acted very well for princesses, and the Archduke Leopold danced in the character of Cupid," volunteered a noted music critic after one such imperial family production.

Despite the ever-present notes of war that hummed insistently in the background like an offstage orchestra warming up to play a particularly somber arrangement, Mimi's was a very happy childhood and adolescence. She saw her parents daily and knew herself to be loved, and so loved in return. There were often holidays from the school schedule, like sledding parties when it snowed, and picnics in the summer. Maria Theresa believed in fresh air for her children, so in the warm weather they moved to Schönbrunn Palace, their mother's magnificent country estate, from their winter quarters at the Hofburg. There were also grand occasions, like the time when twelve-year-old Mimi, as well as Marianne and Charles, were invited with their parents to the home of an immensely wealthy Hungarian nobleman (the Hungarian aristocracy having successfully resisted taxation), and spent a series of days being fêted with theater, opera, fireworks, and other, similarly spectacular entertainments. And, although her school days were ordered, her studies were far from taxing. Sadly, Maria Theresa, with so many sons in reserve, saw no reason to train her daughters for rule. Rather, she chose to educate them as she herself had been instructed—that is to say, to be charming and ornamental, in order to please their husbands. Subjects like math, philosophy, and science were reserved for the boys.*

But the relative ease of her studies was not the primary reason for Maria Christina's general contentment. There was a strict, if unspoken, hierarchy among the older progeny. Joseph, as heir to his mother's many thrones and properties, was naturally at the pinnacle of

---

* It is actually physically painful for me to write this.

this group, but Mimi unquestionably occupied second place as head girl. Her older sister, Marianne, was sickly and often bedridden; she was more an object of sympathy than of parental pride. Maria Elisabeth was prettier, but Maria Theresa thought her vain, an unattractive trait. "It mattered not if the look of admiration came from a prince or a Swiss guard, as long as someone was doing homage to her beauty, Elisabeth was satisfied," the empress sniffed. Maria Amalia was perfectly good-looking but had not Maria Christina's graceful motions, nor her sweet, yielding disposition. It was not difficult for Mimi to excel at her lessons, to be accommodating, to obey instructions—in short, to behave as Maria Theresa herself had behaved as a child.

The same could not be said of the empress's other children, especially Joseph. Joseph was a handful. Hailed from birth as a gift from God, he (not unreasonably) had grown up believing himself to be one. He was cutting and arrogant, lording it over the other children, his adult servants, and even senior government officials. He threw temper tantrums if he did not get his way, and preferred punishment to admitting that he might be wrong. Although intelligent, Joseph refused to apply himself to his lessons. Maria Theresa, who expected her children to behave rather like her soldiers, gratefully and unfailingly obeying her instructions as a matter of course, was flummoxed at how best to deal with so contrary an heir. "As my son has been tended from the cradle up with great tenderness and love, it is certain that his wishes and desires were too much yielded to in many points, and...that his attendants misled him, not only through open flattery, but also several untimely representations of his exalted rank, to love seeing himself obeyed and honored, to find, on the other hand, opposition unpleasant and almost unsupportable, to deny himself nothing, but to act towards others lightly, without kindness, and roughly," the empress admitted regretfully when Joseph was ten and Mimi was nine. "One of the tendencies which must be most contested, and which it must be attempted to prevent, is the desire... to watch in everyone the outward and even inward faults, to let himself be prejudiced by them, to mock at them, which so sorely hinders not only the love of our neighbors, but also a sensible judgment," she sighed.

And the older he got, the more challenging he became. By the time he was a teenager and had begun to sit in on council meetings, Joseph was publicly second-guessing Maria Theresa's policies. Was she "safe in trusting France, who had so frequently deceived her?" he queried her skeptically in front of her ministers when the alliance with Louis XV was discussed. Worse, like Empress Elizabeth's heir, Peter of Russia, Joseph looked up to Frederick the Great, although he made an attempt to keep his admiration a secret, which Peter did not. Peter of Russia openly called Frederick the Great "the King my Master."*

Joseph's willfulness reflected more than ordinary teenage rebellion or the natural desire to separate from a powerful parent and so achieve independence (although of course these impulses also likely influenced his behavior). There was something deeper at work within him: a determination precipitated by a thrilling new school of thought that was reaching its kindling temperature at exactly the moment when this all-important firstborn son was making the transition from late adolescence to young adulthood. For the heroes of the mid-eighteenth century were not in fact the brave field marshals and generals who clashed for glory on the battlefield, but rather a small band of harassed and impoverished writers living hand to mouth in the garrets of Paris. These were the architects of the Enlightenment, one of the most powerful intellectual movements ever to sweep across the soul of Europe. Their leader was a man named Denis Diderot, and it was under his direction that these daring if somewhat threadbare scholars and philosophers toiled away at a new, incendiary, and dangerously subversive weapon called an "encyclopedia."

---

* Young men, in particular, seemed to be vulnerable to the image of the enlightened, ironic warrior-statesman that Frederick did all he could to promote.

As pernicious threats go, an attempt to communicate a general knowledge of the natural world through the commission of scholarly articles published collectively in a set of volumes in alphabetical order might not be regarded as high on the list of terrifying evils against which the population must be guarded assiduously. But Diderot and his colleagues, influenced by a wave of discoveries in physics, mathematics, and chemistry, as well as new theories on the nature of man mostly emanating from London's Royal Society, were taking an innovative approach to the material. They insisted on applying secular reasoning to subjects like nature, history, government, and, most importantly, theology. This put them in direct conflict with the Catholic Church and in particular the Jesuits, an entrenched and powerful faction in education and at the French royal court. The result was that no sooner did each succeeding volume of the Encyclopédie come out—from 1752 to 1757 seven were published and they had only gotten up to the G's—than it was almost immediately banned.

Alas, the Jesuits did not understand how publishing works. From the dawn of time, there has been no surer way to promote a book than to try to suppress it. Sales took off immediately. The encyclopedists' ideas—that knowledge was secular and observed, rather than revealed by Scripture; that the human condition could be improved by utilizing the tools of science rather than relying on ignorance and superstition; and, most importantly, that theological doctrines and divisions should be tempered by reason and toleration—spread quickly through France and into Germany and Austria. "I know nothing so indecent and nothing so injurious to religion as these vague declamations of theologians against reason," Diderot wrote. "One would suppose, to hear them, that men could only enter into the bosom of Christianity as a herd of cattle enter into a stable; and that we must renounce our common sense either to embrace our religion or to remain in it…Such principles…are made to frighten small souls; everything alarms them…they spy danger in any method of arguing which is strange to them; they float at hazard between truths and prejudices which they never distinguish, and to which they are equally attached, and all their life is passed in crying out either miracle or impiety," he concluded in frustration. Voltaire, a writer not generally known for lavishing praise on rival authors, understood instantly what Diderot was attempting to accomplish with his Encyclopédie. "Men are on the eve of a great revolution in the human mind, and it is you to whom they are most of all indebted for it," he told him simply.

Maria Theresa, intensely religious herself, also perceived the work of these enlightened authors (whom she never read) as a threat to the Catholic Church and society in general, and so had the books banned throughout her realm—to the same effect. The encyclopedists' arguments quickly made their way to the imperial court at just the time when Joseph was most receptive to them. "It would be easy to prove that, despite the existing vigor, every prohibited book is available at Vienna, and everyone, attracted by the veto, can buy it at double the price," he noted. To his mother's great distress, Joseph embraced the new philosophy, including the notion of religious tolerance.

But from the first, in stark contrast to her brother, Mimi followed Maria Theresa's lead. Mimi, although as clever and talented as Joseph, never questioned authority. She did not read banned books. She was devout in worship. She detested Frederick the Great. As she grew older and became more and more aware of the world outside the court, of the approach of war and the threat to her homeland, she was acutely conscious of the strain the empress was under and did her best to strengthen and comfort her. Maria Theresa, forced to deal with the hurtful rebellion of her sarcastic eldest son, and the heartbreak and humiliation of her husband's visibly deepening infatuation with a younger woman (not to mention the mind-numbing chatter, energy, scuffles, demands, and emotions of ten younger children), by degrees came to regard Maria Christina as more than a daughter. Mimi was her confidante, her best friend, her refuge. The other children all jealously recognized her as their mother's favorite.

★   ★   ★

MARIA CHRISTINA WAS FIFTEEN at the time of the Austrian triumph at Kolín. The year had not begun auspiciously for her. In the spring of 1757, while her uncle, Charles of Lorraine, and a good chunk of the empress's army were still trapped in Prague, first Joseph, then she, had fallen ill with smallpox. Terror gripped the court when the disease showed itself. The pox was a merciless killer. It could destroy an entire family. Even those who survived were to be pitied, being frequently disfigured by scarring. In England, they advocated a preventative called inoculation, but because physicians had not yet learned to inject pustules from the less virulent strain of cowpox, people often died from the treatment. Consequently, the procedure did not overly recommend itself as a remedy, and her mother was afraid to try it.

Mimi was lucky; she was not as sick as her brother, and her spotting appears to have been minimal. It took longer for Joseph to recuperate but he, too, made a full recovery. Most importantly, the disease did not spread to the rest of the family. Her mother, crediting her children's survival to God and the "care, devotion, and skill" of her court physician, poured out her heart to the conscientious doctor in a letter. "I have been your debtor for many a long day," she wrote humbly. "You must judge for yourself the extent of my gratitude for this new benefit. I have no words to express it. I only feel how glad I am." And, as though it were a sign, her children's recovery was followed almost immediately by news of Austria's comprehensive victory at Kolín.

But within a mere six months, the euphoria in Vienna over the prospect of thoroughly trouncing Frederick had vanished abruptly. In a turn of events that should have surprised absolutely no one, Charles, despite the benefit once again of significant numerical superiority—an army of some 55,000 compared to the king of Prussia's 40,000 warriors—was completely outmaneuvered and outfought by his counterpart, with the result that on December 5, 1757, he suffered a crushing defeat, losing some 9,000 soldiers to death and injury, with another 12,000 captured—more than a third of the men under his command. Worse, this fiasco came just a month after a similarly dispiriting engagement in Saxony by the French (whose commander, sad to say, was so inept that he made Charles look good), whereby a scant 22,000 of Frederick's soldiers routed some 50,000 of Louis XV's troops in a battle so one-sided that it lasted barely an hour. These two astonishing underdog victories, coming one after the other like rapid cannon fire, not only cemented Frederick's reputation as a once-in-a-lifetime leader but, more importantly, shifted the momentum of the war back in his favor.

And so a contest that should have been over in 1757 instead dragged on with no end in sight. Maria Theresa knew that she had only herself to blame for having left Charles in a position for which he was unsuited. This time, she acted swiftly and without sentimentality. In 1758, her brother-in-law was summarily retired once again to Brussels, and Field Marshal Daun was promoted in his place. Daun would deliver a major victory for her against Frederick at the Saxon town of Hochkirch that year, keeping her hopes alive for a successful outcome to the war.

But she couldn't control her allies' behavior, and this worried her. The French were doing terribly against both Frederick in Germany and the English in America.★ Louis XV's minister of state, seeing the defeats and the commensurate casualties and expenses pile up, strongly advised the king of France to make a separate peace with Frederick. But paying attention to the administration and financing of the war bored Louis. He left these details instead to Madame de Pompadour, and Madame de Pompadour held firm to the Austrian alliance. "Never before did anyone play at so great stakes with the unconcern that he would show at a game of cards!" the frustrated French minister complained of his sovereign.

★ The Russians also failed to follow up on their initial success, and in August 1758 Frederick managed to hand *them* a major defeat as well. But Empress Elizabeth, like Maria Theresa, refused to back down. Consequently, the war played out rather like an interminable match point in the finals of a championship tennis tournament—no sooner would one side score an advantage than the other side would rally and bring it back to deuce.

The result of all of this was that in March 1759 a *third* Treaty of Versailles was signed between France and Austria. Owing to Madame de Pompadour's getting the old minister of state out, and putting in a fresh one (handpicked by Count Kaunitz; that little ornate writing desk certainly served its purpose), this new compact was even more favorable to Vienna than its previous incarnation. By this third treaty, Louis XV agreed to commit yet another 100,000 soldiers to the war against Frederick. All the king of France asked for in return was that the empress's heir, Joseph, take a bride—his granddaughter Isabella of Parma, daughter of Don Philip (younger son of Elizabeth Farnese). As by this marriage Maria Theresa not only secured the French-Austrian alliance without having to give up any additional territory, but also put her family one step closer to reclaiming the property in Italy that the British had forced her to surrender after the last war, the empress wholeheartedly endorsed the arrangement. "The advantages of this treaty are decidedly on our side, and we have good reason to be content with it," Count Kaunitz, employing considerable understatement, comfortably assured Maria Theresa.

LIKE ALMOST EVERYONE ELSE in Vienna, Maria Christina was excited about Joseph's impending wedding. It had been three long years since the capital had had anything to celebrate. The demands of the war had reversed many of the accomplishments of her mother's reign. No one had envisioned so prolonged a conflict; even with the broadened tax base, the income flow to the Crown was insufficient to cover the needs of the military, and the court had been forced to borrow. With the economy once again facing a crushing burden of debt, it had been necessary to exercise austerity. To lead by example, Maria Theresa had pawned her jewels.

But the marriage of the heir to the throne—or thrones, in this case—with its promise of a continued line of succession, was too significant an event to quibble over costs. No expense was spared. A magnificent solid-gold dining service, for use by those seated at the head table at the wedding banquet, was ordered from the capital's leading goldsmith; 300 horses were pressed into service to transport the imposing diplomatic escort charged with fetching the bride from Parma; and Van Meytens was commissioned to document the cycle of festivities in a series of oversized paintings scaled to emphasize the heady splendor of the occasion. Just about the only person in Vienna not looking forward to the joyous event was the prospective bridegroom. Joseph was resigned to doing his duty, but he wasn't happy about it (although he did perk up a little when he saw Isabella's portrait). "I shall do everything to win her respect and her confidence. But love? No, you know that it is impossible for me to be agreeable to pose as a lover. That is against my nature," he confided dolefully to a friend.

Maria Christina's interest in her brother's marriage went beyond the simple anticipation of welcoming a new sister-in-law into the family and enjoying a round of parties. Mimi was now seventeen, and it would soon be her turn to marry. As the charming daughter of so desirable and exalted a mother and father, she was already in some demand: the handsome younger son of the duke of Württemberg, whose home was located near Stuttgart, aspired to her hand. She was very much inclined to give it to him, but Francis wished her instead to marry his nephew, the only son of the king of Sardinia. Mimi knew that her father's choice represented a far more prestigious match, as the nephew would inherit the Sardinian throne and Mimi would consequently become queen of this strategically vital (if very small) kingdom. Besides, Francis's younger sister had tragically died giving birth to the nephew, and the emperor wanted to honor and maintain the family connection. Mimi couldn't even try to get around him by entreating the empress to intervene, as her mother almost always acceded to her father's wishes in any matter not directly related to government. Reduced to hoping that her father would change his mind, Maria Christina continued to sigh over the dashing prince of Württemberg, just as Maria Theresa had once dreamed of Francis of Lorraine.

But with such a large, noisy family surrounding her, vivacious Mimi had little time to brood over romance. "In spite of the war, there was much in the way of entertainment and merrymaking, both at Court and in the residences of the nobility," reported one of her many cousins, who popped in to Vienna for a visit at this time. "The Emperor's love of social pleasure, the Empress's desire to please her husband, a young household with its natural propensity to enjoyment, all combined to keep things lively," he observed cheerfully.

The cousin's name was Albert, and he knew something about large families. He was the fourth son of the eleven surviving children of Augustus III of Saxony (which made his mother Wilhelmine's elder, highly fertile daughter). Until just recently, owing to Frederick's army having barreled into his home city of Dresden, Albert had been trapped in his parents' palace with three of his sisters. It was only after General Daun wrested Dresden back from Prussia in September 1759 that twenty-one-year-old Albert managed to escape the nightmare of close confinement with so many unmarried females. (He later complained that he had felt rather like he was living in a harem. In his desperation to get out, he even announced to his father that he intended to devote himself to the Church.) The very first thing he did after securing his freedom, however, was not to take his religious vows but rather to join the Austrian army to continue the fight against Frederick, a step that pleased the empress very much. Consequently, Albert was invited to participate in all the court festivities when he arrived in Vienna in January 1760 in advance of the spring campaign.

Her cousin's desire to flee female company seems to have been limited to his sisters, as Albert left a memorable description of Maria Christina's numerous charms during the time he spent with her family. "All the princesses were beautiful," he confessed, "but the second had such a graceful figure, such a noble, intellectual countenance that I was in love with her from the very first moment. During our visit to Vienna [Albert was accompanied by his younger brother], there was a great deal of snow. One day the Court made an excursion to Schönbrunn in sleds. The ladies and gentlemen drew lots for partners. As luck would have it, my lot was to be the companion of the Archduchess, whose engaging qualities had already made so profound an impression upon me. Thus I was able to spend several hours in her society. Her conversation was as delightful as her appearance, yet I dared not tell her what I felt. A princess of her standing was far above a portionless younger son," poor Albert, fourth in line to an inheritance currently under occupation by a hostile power, concluded miserably. (He did, however, make haste to inform his father that he no longer wished to enter the priesthood.)

Mimi's affections were in no way engaged to the same degree. Albert was a nice young man, of course, but she had her beau. If anything, her mother seemed to like Albert more than Maria Christina did. Not as a suitor for one of her daughters—with no money, no title, no realm, and no prospects of acquiring any of these necessary assets, that was of course completely out of the question—but he did have such a pleasant demeanor and such winning manners. And he reminded the empress that, without her and her army, this respectful young cousin would still be in Frederick's clutches. So she made a point of treating him with kindness, appointed him a captain in the army, and even graciously invited him back at the end of the summer to spend a short holiday with the rest of the imperial family.

Albert gladly took Maria Theresa up on her offer and spent an enjoyable week with his cousins, mooning after Mimi, befriending her brothers, hunting with the emperor, and generally making himself agreeable to all concerned. It didn't get him any closer to being considered a romantic interest, but at least everyone liked him. Even Joseph, who ordinarily preferred solitude and sarcasm to sociability, warmed to Albert. But then Joseph respected military service. He had wished to join the army himself, but his mother wouldn't hear of it. With the finality of his compulsory wedding looming ever closer, the imperial heir was particularly gloomy that summer. "I am more afraid of marriage than of battle," he groaned when the holiday at last came to an end and it was time for Albert to rejoin his troops and for Joseph, Mimi, and the rest of the family to return to Vienna, there to await the bride.

Isabella of Parma's entrance into Vienna

And that's where they all were on October 1, 1760, when an immense procession of some 200 carriages clattered into the capital and snaked its way through the streets of the city to the Hofburg palace. Isabella of Parma had arrived.

SHE WAS EXOTIC and slender and fascinating. Possessed of a restless intelligence and intense eyes, she stood out among the imperial family like a vivid wild rose amid a bed of domesticated daisies. Having been brought up by her mother, Louis XV's eldest daughter, to be familiar with court customs at both Versailles and Madrid, her manners were flawless. In addition to this, Isabella was exceedingly well-read, with a command of subjects ranging from literature to history and philosophy. "Her attainments would have been thought remarkable in an able young man," the Austrian ambassador to Parma remarked approvingly.

Supercilious Joseph, whose previous experience with passionately complex women seems to have been extremely limited, was mesmerized. He fell for Isabella like a starving man suddenly presented with a divinely rich, imported chocolate soufflé. They were married with all due pomp and ceremony on October 6. The empress, noting his ardor, could not suppress her satisfaction. "We have gained a charming daughter-in-law in every respect, and I am on the tip-top of happiness," Maria Theresa exulted. "The weather, the festivities, everything, in short, was all that could be desired. I quite forgot that I was a King in my gladness as a mother."

Mimi, too, was delighted with this bewitching new family member. Isabella was just her age—eighteen—so it was really more like making an interesting new friend than gaining a sister. They shared a love of music and art, so naturally they gravitated toward each other. Isabella was definitely more introspective than Maria Christina, more given to brooding over serious subjects, but that made a nice foil for Mimi's blithe gaiety.

Yes, especially for an arranged marriage, it could not have worked out better. The family could breathe a sigh of relief: snide Joseph, so difficult to please, had actually fallen in love with his wife! Isabella, too, as these things happen, had conceived a grand passion. It was not for her husband, however, but for his sister Mimi.

Ordinarily, it is very difficult to pinpoint the initiation and progress of an extramarital affair, as the participants know to be discreet. And Isabella *was* careful. On the surface, she was never anything but the perfect wife and daughter-in-law. Joseph never had a hint that the woman he held in his arms every night was not wholly devoted to him; indeed, probably could not bear his touch. His mother, too, was never given any cause to complain: Isabella performed both the public and private duties of her office with a convincing obedience. She did whatever was asked of her, whether it be attending her mother-in-law for hours at church during religious holidays or participating in impromptu musical evenings with the rest of the family. True, she spent as much of her free time as possible with Maria

Christina, but this, too, was to be expected. Isabella was new to the court and possibly a little homesick; it was natural that she should seek out the sister closest to her own age for company and guidance. So far was any hint of passion or sexual impropriety from Maria Theresa's mind that she laughingly referred to her new daughter-in-law as Mimi's "dear other half."

But Isabella's ardor was not to be denied and demanded an outlet. So, despite living in the same palace as Maria Christina and seeing her nearly every day, she began also to write her letters—uniquely fervid letters, dozens of them, that detailed her innermost thoughts, emotions, and desires. From an initially chaste greeting, during the first days of her marriage in October 1760, of "Bonjour, dear Sister," these progressed rapidly over the next few months to the coy "Bonjour, adorable Sister," "cruel Sister," and "very cruel Sister," until finally coming to an unvarnished declaration: "I adore you and my love grows with each passing moment."

In the beginning, at least, it seems likely that Maria Christina did not grasp the full significance of this outpouring of affection. The year 1761 started off very badly for Mimi. Her younger brother Charles, second after Joseph, fell ill of smallpox, and this time neither God nor the family doctor could save him; to the horror of the court, he died on January 18, just two weeks shy of his sixteenth birthday. Although they were lucky and the infection did not spread to any of the other children, this was the first time that a member of the immediate family had succumbed to the disease. This tragedy was followed soon after by personal grief: in February her mother, in an effort to promote the Sardinian alliance, insisted that Maria Christina break off her relationship with the handsome prince of Württemberg. A crushed Mimi, her romantic hopes dashed, evidently confided in her sister-in-law, asking for advice.* "You desire, dear Sister, that I tell you sincerely what I think," Isabella began

---

* Only one of Maria Christina's letters to Isabella has survived. Still, it is often possible from Isabella's letters to infer what subjects were raised, as is the case here.

gently, in a lengthy missive that was as revealing of her own situation as it was of Mimi's. "I will not hesitate to open my heart to my most tender and dearest friend...What can the daughter of a great prince expect?" she posited philosophically. "She is condemned to give up everything, her family, her country, and for whom? For a stranger whose character she does not know...for a family who may regard her with jealousy...She leaves, abandoning everything that is dear to her, unsure even of pleasing the one to whom she is destined... But does she remain a girl all her life?" spirited Isabella reminded Mimi, before firmly encouraging her to take this disappointment in stride. "Has she nothing better to hope for than what is being offered today?...You are not independent and nothing is so easy as obeying...especially since you will spend your life with someone who loves you," Isabella finished warmly, meaning herself.

By the summer of 1761, however, Mimi could not have helped but be aware that her new friend's notions of what constituted a close relationship with another woman were unlike any she had experienced in the past. "You will comfort me, you will give me life, and we will both be reborn into a more beautiful tomorrow," her sister-in-law rhapsodized. "I adore you, I burn for you." Later, in August, Isabella discovered to her unhappiness (hidden from her husband and mother-in-law, of course) that she was pregnant. "I want to kiss you, it's the best way to beguile me," she wrote urgently to Mimi. "But to kiss wisely because you know that my love is angelic," she reassured her quickly, there evidently already having been times when Isabella had not kissed wisely.

Although it is impossible to judge just how far they progressed sexually in these early months of their relationship, it is fair to say, again judging by the outpouring of letters, that Mimi did not discourage her sister-in-law's passion. If anything, the sentiments expressed became more and more desperate, as Isabella clung to Maria Christina almost as to a lifeline against despair. "To be deprived of your presence is a martyrdom I can barely endure," she confessed bleakly in the fall of 1761. "There is no more joy nor pleasure, everything becomes drab, I cannot hope for better than sorrow and pain."

Mimi, her own desires having been thwarted so recently by Maria Theresa's stern termination of the romance with the prince of Württemberg, and fearful of her prospects for amorous fulfillment with the son of the king of Sardinia, for whom she seems to have taken a decided dislike, was also emotionally vulnerable during this period. The unqualified adoration of a woman as intelligent and accomplished as Isabella no doubt flattered and soothed her. It's quite possible her sister-in-law's arguments about taking control of her own happiness as much as possible while appearing to conform outwardly to societal and family expectations made sense to Mimi, or at least encouraged experimentation. For whatever reason, she kept the letters and this aspect of her relationship with Isabella hidden from everyone, including her mother. It was a secret just the two of them shared, a private life within a life that thrilled with the excitement of forbidden kisses.

Maria Theresa was unlikely to have noticed anyway, even if they had not been so guarded. She was naturally elated by Isabella's pregnancy, which promised the continued succession of the monarchy. But even this was secondary to the principal event that autumn. For after five horrifically brutal years of bloodshed, she and Empress Elizabeth, working together, had finally cornered Frederick. She was going to get Silesia back after all.

OVER THE COURSE of the past two campaigns, the Austrian and Prussian armies had basically been reduced to chasing each other back and forth between Saxony and Silesia, with first one side and then the other winning territory, only to be beaten back a few months later or forced to withdraw for lack of supplies. But what appeared on the surface to be a stalemate was in reality a slow, steady grind toward an ultimate Austrian victory. Maria Theresa's government, it was true, once again labored beneath a burden of enormous debt, but she and her allies still had far more soldiers at their command than did Prussia. And although Frederick pushed himself and his men to almost herculean efforts—in one battle alone two horses were shot out from under him—he began to recognize that even he could not be everywhere at once. By October of 1760 his mood, reflecting his dwindling resources and prospects, fluctuated between doleful self-pity and sullen defiance. "The close of my days is poisoned and the evening of my life is as hideous as its morning," he moaned in October of 1760. "I will not endure the moment that must force me to make a dishonorable peace [read: surrender]. No persuasion and no eloquence will be strong enough to make me sign my shame. I will bury myself under the ruins of my fatherland, or if this consolation seems too sweet to the misfortune that persistently pursues me, I will myself put an end to all my woes." And he started to carry around a little pouch of opium pills, so as to be able to commit suicide rather than capitulate.

Maria Theresa, too, was disheartened. Her subjects were suffering, and she did not know how long she could continue to pursue a contest that was draining her of every asset. And then, at the beginning of 1761, she was suddenly given a significant boost in confidence. Empress Elizabeth, who had been seriously ill the previous year, recovered, and, furious with the cautious strategy adopted by the military during her prostration, dramatically stepped up Russian participation against Frederick. "Our allies show signs of weariness and exhaustion; only the hope of terminating the war in another campaign has inspired the Empress-Queen [Maria Theresa] to rally her last resources," the tsarina informed her government. This time, when she fielded her army, she sent it to Austria's aid with explicit instructions to bring the battle to Frederick. "Without wasting any more words, we command you to proceed forthwith to Berlin... [and] occupy it," Elizabeth wrote severely to the general in charge of this new force. "You are to attack at once without any more councils or deliberations," she continued hotly. "There have been so many councils-of-war in this campaign, that the very phrase 'council-of-war' has become an abomination to us. If anybody in future dares to say that our army is not fit for attacking strongholds, he is instantly to be arrested and sent hither in chains."

That did it. On October 1, 1761, in a daring predawn raid, an Austrian battalion, in cooperation with a Russian infantry force, stormed the most secure fortress in Silesia, which had been held since the beginning of the war by the Prussians. The walls were scaled and the defenses overcome in ferocious hand-to-hand combat with bayonets; in an almost superhuman effort, the Russian unit, blocked unexpectedly by water, was reported to have formed a bridge by walking over one another, drowning those of their compatriots who stood heroically beneath. By sunrise the Prussian commander left in charge (Frederick having departed to oversee military operations in Saxony) had surrendered, and the fortress and all of its artillery were captured. This victory, which gave Austria its strongest position in Silesia since Maria Theresa had first ascended to the throne, was followed (after a brutal two-month campaign in the bitter cold) by the Russian seizure of the stronghold of Kolberg in East Prussia on Christmas Day. Thus Frederick, his arms depleted and his men demoralized, not only found himself forced out of Silesia but also saw his own territory under occupation, Berlin threatened, and the Austrian army preparing to drive him out of Saxony completely.

It was at this point that he cracked. There was no more bravado, no more talk of suicide, or fighting to the last man. On January 6, 1762, he matter-of-factly authorized his minister to begin discussing the terms of his surrender. "It seems to me that we ought now to think of preserving...by way of negotiation, whatever fragments of my possessions we can snatch from the avidity of my enemies," Frederick wrote in his instructions. "Be persuaded that if I saw a gleam of hope, even by running the greatest risks, of re-establishing the state on its ancient foundations, I would not use such language, but I am convinced that, morally and physically, it is impossible," he conceded. For once, there was no drama or hyperbole in his assessment; his inevitable defeat was obvious to all. "I have enjoyed the revenge of consoling the King of Prussia, and that satisfies me," Voltaire, still smarting from his previous treatment at Frederick's hands, exulted to a friend. "He beats and is beaten, and will be ruined without a new miracle," he concluded bluntly. The celebrated Frenchman was reporting only what was generally conceded by everyone: Frederick needed an act of wonder to survive.

And then, unbelievably, just in the nick of time, he got one. Although the king of Prussia didn't know it, on January 5, 1762, *the day before* he commanded his minister to begin the process of surrender, Empress Elizabeth, who had relapsed and taken to her bed a short time earlier, abruptly breathed her last, and her nephew, Peter, Frederick's most slavish admirer, ascended to the throne of Russia.

9

An Archduchess in Love

≈

Never marry a man who has nothing to do.

—Maria Theresa

A GRIM FOREBODING DESCENDED ON the court at Vienna when news of the tsarina's death arrived—and with good reason. On February 23, 1762, as one of his first dictates, Peter ordered the immediate withdrawal of the Russian army from the war with Prussia. Within weeks, he had signed an armistice that not only restored to Frederick all territory and prisoners captured during the conflict but also made clear the new tsar's intention to reverse his predecessor's policy completely by entering into an alliance with Prussia *against* Austria. So eager was Peter to curry favor with his hero that he even begged for a position in the Prussian army. "The Tsar of Russia is a divine man; to whom I ought to erect altars," Frederick chuckled, and immediately designated Peter a colonel, complete with his own regimental uniform, in which costume the new tsar paraded proudly around his court at the Winter Palace in Saint Petersburg.

Maria Theresa, who had just released 20,000 of her soldiers from active duty to preserve funds, on General Daun's recommendation that the enemy had no choice but to concede defeat, was reduced to despair by this sudden turnaround of fate. Her worst fears were realized that spring when Peter made good on his promises to Frederick and dispatched a battalion of some 18,000 Russians to fight side by side with the Prussians against her. She knew she had not the resources left to compete against so potent a combination—the French treasury was as exhausted as her own, and Louis XV's army was clearly no match for Frederick's. Now it was she who needed to save whatever territory she could by suing for peace. "Her Imperial Majesty for some time past, spends half her time in praying to the Virgin, and the other half weeping," jeered a friend of Frederick's, on hearing a report from Vienna.

Nor was Francis any help during this wrenching period. With her husband's confidences increasingly devoted to his mistress—"I wager that she is consulted about many things she has no business to meddle with," Isabella observed shrewdly—Maria Theresa turned instead to her favorite daughter for emotional support. "You don't realize what a great influence this woman [*la belle princesse*] has on him [Francis]," Maria Christina reported unhappily to her sister-in-law. "He has absolute faith in her, and he hides nothing from her. The Empress is extremely jealous of this attachment."

Isabella, too, was in great need of Mimi's affection. On March 20, 1762, just a few days after the catastrophic Russian armistice with Frederick was announced, she gave birth to her first child—a girl. Although she and Joseph made haste to christen their daughter Maria Theresa in honor of the empress, the failure to deliver a son could not have helped but raise the age-old specter of a general inability to produce a male heir. The sensitive new mother found little comfort in her husband's company. "His nature is not primarily emotional," Isabella conceded wearily to Maria Christina. Weakened by what was reported to have been an extremely difficult delivery, and understanding that she was expected to conceive again as soon as possible, a morose Isabella remained bedridden for six weeks.

She emerged from this ordeal even more passionately attached to Mimi than before. Her head, Isabella wrote to her sister-in-law, was filled with a jumble of "philosophy, morals, stories, profound reflections, songs, history, physics, logic, metaphysics, and rapture for you." "I am told," she observed to Mimi in another missive, "that one should begin the day with God. I, however, begin the day by thinking of the object of my love and I end it with thoughts of the same." By this time, they were arranging surreptitious meetings. "If the Archduke [Joseph] goes out, I will be at your house," Isabella promised. "Or, if I do not have the strength to ride, I will ask you to come down. In the meantime, I want you with all my soul."

But it is not so easy to live a double life, to obey on the outside and burn within, and Isabella struggled with depression. "Death is a good thing," she wrote to Maria Christina. "I swear to you that in my life I have never thought about it more seriously than at this hour. I have contemplated at length and in great detail all the horrors of perishing and I confess that this, far from dissuading me, has made me wish to die more than ever... If it were permitted by God to take my own life, I would be well tempted to do it."

Responsible Mimi, by nature cheerful and even-tempered, was appalled by this talk. "Allow me to tell you that your longing for death is an out-and-out evil thing," she responded emphatically to Isabella. "It either points to selfishness or a desire to seem heroic, and it is at variance with your own loving disposition. It ought to be repugnant to you to give utterance to sentiments so grievous to people who are absolutely bound up in your existence."

Sensitive to the general atmosphere of gloom surrounding the court, Maria Christina did her best to distract and ease the troubled minds of her mother and sister-in-law. "God having given you so many talents and charms... [has] visibly chosen you out among your numerous family to be the happiness and comfort of your parents," Maria Theresa would later acknowledge gratefully. "Pray for fine weather if you wish to possess me," Isabella wrote urgently that summer. "I kiss everything that you let me kiss."

BUT THERE WAS ONLY SO MUCH a well-meaning and sympathetic twenty-year-old archduchess could do in the face of shattering adversity. By June 1762, Frederick, with the new tsar's help, had regrouped his army and was back in Silesia. He only just made it in time. On July 9 Peter, whose policies of blithely returning territory so recently won at the bitter, bloody cost of thousands of Russian lives had not sat at all well with senior members of his own military, was overthrown with their help by his wife, Catherine, soon to be known as Catherine the Great. Although as one of her first acts as tsarina, Catherine canceled the treaty with Prussia and recalled her soldiers, she did not resume the alliance with Maria Theresa. Rather, she chose to stay out of the war entirely. Frederick, who found out about the coup before the Austrians did, bribed the Russian divisional commander assigned to him to stay in Silesia just long enough for Prussia to secure a victory. By October 8, after a prolonged siege, Frederick had retaken the impregnable fortress he had lost the previous year; by October 29 he once again occupied Dresden. "So dark is the outlook," Maria Theresa mourned, "that we must either have immediate peace, or none," and she, who only months earlier had been so close to defeating Prussia outright, surrendered all hope of gain and instead opened negotiations to end the war, knowing that the terms would be harsh.

It was with this forlorn outlook that the court at Vienna contemplated the holiday season that year. In a gesture perhaps indicative of her desire to brighten the spirits of those around her, Mimi chose this period to paint a group portrait, *The Imperial Family Celebrating Saint Nicholas*. But unlike Martin van Meyten's impressive rococo renderings of the emperor and empress, all grandeur and dignity, Maria Christina instead depicted her parents and siblings in an amusingly chaotic scene around the breakfast table. Francis, in his robe and slippers, a towel wrapped around his head to keep him warm, sits at one end, toasting his feet by the fire and reading a newspaper. Next to him, in a simple blue dress with a white kerchief tied around her neck, is Maria Theresa, serving the coffee. Beside her mother is Marie Antoinette, then seven years old, proudly displaying a new doll, while Maria Christina, also dressed informally in pink with a kerchief, attends to eight-year-old Ferdinand, who, from the attitude of his parents, appears to be causing something of a fuss. Taking advantage of the diversion caused by his older brother is little Maximilian, age six, sprawled out on the floor, a miniature rocking horse beside him, happily devouring a pile of cakes stolen from the table.

Impossible to look at this painting and not smile! It might have been a portrait of the local greengrocer and his family on their day off. And yet there is nothing derisive about the humor. It is witty, not satiric; the effect is warm, sympathetic, and gentle. The painter has put herself into the picture—she is part of the joke, laughing with and not at her subjects. It is charm itself.

This fleeting moment of playfulness was supplanted almost immediately by a fresh tragedy. On December 15, 1762, Mimi's younger sister Maria Johanna, then twelve, so unaffected and sweet that her mother had already chosen her to promote Austrian interests by arranging a marriage alliance with the eldest son of the king of Spain, fell ill. The telltale marks of smallpox appeared; eight days later, she was dead. "She never caused me grief till I grieved for her loss," Maria Theresa wept.★

This heartache, following so unexpectedly upon the death of Maria Christina's brother Charles from the same disease a little less than two years earlier, rekindled Isabella's morbid fascination with oblivion. She became convinced that she, too, would perish imminently from smallpox—so much so that she began composing a long treatise to her sister-in-law, sort of an amateur psychologist's last will and testament that she called "Advice to Marie." Filled with candid family and societal observations as well as general life lessons, this document was clearly intended to help her beloved Mimi navigate the future in the event of Isabella's demise. "The Empress has an exceptionally tender, clinging, sympathetic disposition," Isabella expounded in a passage typical of the overall tone of the manuscript.

★ Maria Johanna, born February 4, 1750, was the eldest of the empress's six younger children. This group included Maria Josepha (age eleven), ten-year-old Maria Carolina, Ferdinand, Marie Antoinette, and Maximilian (he of the cakes under the table).

"Those whom she loves, she loves in very truth. She would sacrifice herself for any member of her family, or even for her friends... through suffering she has learned to know life and the world. Her advice is therefore extremely helpful," Isabella continued forcefully. "If you find yourself in any difficulty, I counsel you to go straight to the Empress and get her opinion then and there. When she has told you what she advises, hasten to thank her, to express conviction of the rightness of her decision and your desire that the matter should remain between herself and you. Then you may feel sure it will go no further," she instructed.

Luckily, there was no need yet for this farsighted, if somewhat macabre, precaution; the pestilence did not spread beyond its initial victim. The new year dawned and everyone remained healthy. Isabella, far from perishing, found herself pregnant again. And there was hope this time not just for a male heir but also for a renewal of life and prosperity. For February 1763 brought with it a blessing that had eluded Vienna, and indeed all of Europe, for seven long years: peace.

UNLIKE ITS PREVIOUS INCARNATION, the War of the Austrian Succession, which had basically ended in a stalemate, this time around the bedlam of global combat had produced a definite, flat-out winner: Britain. The British navy had so trounced its French and Spanish adversaries (Spain having been coaxed into the conflict at the last minute by France, who had called upon the family connection in its desperation to fend off total defeat) that there was a question as to whether the English would even consider terminating a contest so one-sided that it could yet yield further spoils. Luckily for the vanquished, George II had by this time died and been succeeded by his grandson, George III. For the first time in half a century, England had a sovereign who had not been born and raised in Germany and who consequently did not feel the need to defend Hanover. Nor did the new king much care for his cousin Frederick, whom he dismissively referred to as "that *too ambitious Monarch*...that *proud, overbear-*

ing Prince." The storied English naval victories, while undoubtedly a boon to the public spirit, also unfortunately represented a blight upon his majesty's finances. Prolonging the war would mean shouldering the burden of additional debt, and for what? England was already in the enviable position of being able to dictate terms. George III accordingly cut off Prussian subsidies and orchestrated a change in government more amenable to a negotiated peace.

The result was the Treaty of Paris, signed on February 10, 1763. By this merciless document the French ceded Canada and everything else they owned in North America (save Louisiana and a few islands in the Caribbean) as well as all their colonial possessions in India—in effect, *their entire overseas empire*—to Britain. Spain, which had been in the war for barely a year, was forced to surrender Florida and everything it owned east of the Mississippi to the British. Louis XV felt so guilty about this that he offered to compensate the Spanish for their injury. "I wish sincerely that Spain should not suffer from a war which the personal tenderness of your Majesty for me has led her to undertake," he wrote impulsively to Don Carlos, now Charles III, king of Spain. "If New Orleans or Louisiana can be of any use . . . I offer them to you." Charles did indeed find them useful, so Louis gave them to him. Thus France also ceded Louisiana—to the Spanish.

It was not lost upon Louis's subjects that they had suffered through seven years of privation and sacrifice, through scarcity, high prices, and crippling taxes, not to mention the numbers of dead and injured, only to be stripped of the wealth of all of their colonies and, worse, to have their once-feared army, for a century the dominant force in Europe, humiliated. In fact, the only reward the French king had sought and actually achieved was to have his granddaughter Isabella of Parma married to Maria Theresa's eldest son, Joseph, and this was deemed of limited utility to the general public. The majority of the French citizenry had been suspicious of Louis's decision to ally with Austria, their traditional enemy, in the first place, and being bested in so decided a fashion did nothing to allay their misgivings. The hot shame of defeat demanded the identification of a villain responsible for the crushing failure, and an ailing Madame de Pompadour (she would die from tuberculosis the following year), with her championship of the court of Vienna, made for an easy target.

Maria Theresa had her own failings to repent. She and Frederick were not parties to the Treaty of Paris but instead signed a separate peace agreement five days later, on February 15, at the small Saxon town of Hubertusburg. By this treaty, Frederick was induced to return Saxony to its rightful owners, but only at the cost of the empress surrendering all of Silesia to Prussia. So Maria Theresa's subjects, too, had suffered through the hard years of pain and bloodshed, overburdened by debt and taxes, only to find themselves *in exactly the same place* that they had been at the start of the war—not an inch of territory recovered.

For Frederick, who had come so close to ruin, this outcome represented a victory, and he behaved accordingly. True, he gave back Saxony, but only after plundering the duchy of every possible movable asset. As its towns and villages had been the scene of repeated battles, whoever ended up with Saxony was going to have to spend more to rebuild it than it was worth anyway; it would only have been a burden to Prussia, which had its own finances to recoup. Frederick had no problem letting it go.

But what he surrendered in territory he more than gained in reputation. He framed himself as the victor and was universally perceived as such. For seven years, he had withstood a combined assault by the three preeminent powers in Europe and come out on top. By doing so, he put Prussia, formerly a nonentity, on the international stage. For his perseverance and military ability Frederick the Great was now an acknowledged world power; he had earned his sobriquet.

Even more importantly, he had shown up the one person who, despite being long dead, still mattered the most to him, the person with whom fifty-one-year-old Frederick, now a worn-out, peevish veteran plagued by chronic gout and hemorrhoids, was obviously still locked in combat: his abusive parent. "My father wanted me to become a soldier, but he never suspected that one day I should in this respect be what I am," he observed revealingly to one of his closest courtiers toward the end of the conflict. "How astonished he would be if he saw me...amidst an army that is worth a little and a cavalry especially of which he would not have the least idea; he would not believe his eyes," he congratulated himself.

As for Maria Theresa, there is little doubt that she considered the Peace of Hubertusburg to be the culmination of a crippling defeat for which she blamed herself. She had subjected her realm to intense privation and suffering in pursuit of Silesia, a goal she now believed, through the prism of hindsight and much soul-searching, to have been unattainable from the beginning. The only concession she could wring from Frederick during the treaty negotiations was an agreement that he would support Joseph's candidacy as his father's successor to the imperial throne as a means of ensuring the stability of her realm. "There is not a moment to lose," she fretted in a note to one of her ministers. "The Emperor and I are getting on in years. If one of us goes, what would happen? General tranquility is only just restored." But other than this, everything went back to the way it was just before Prussia invaded Saxony.

As a result, unlike Frederick, who gained in stature, Maria Theresa emerged from the Seven Years' War with *less* prestige and standing in Europe than she had had going in. "I, who have suffered so much grief on account of this war, am resolved to live at peace hereafter," she wrote humbly. "I love my family and my people too much to sacrifice them in another war." And, later, "It is better to be a second class power with peace and a happy people, than a first class power and always at war," she observed simply.

As she saw it, she had abjectly failed her people and diminished her family in the eyes of the world. But lost in the fog of guilt and remorse that Maria Theresa felt was the one critical objective that she had in fact achieved. Her primary reason for entering this contest, although she had forgotten it when it seemed she might recover her lost property, had been the fear that, if he wasn't stopped, Frederick would simply keep on invading her lands until he had annexed whatever he could get away with, as he had with Saxony. Bohemia would have been next on his list, and even Vienna might never have been safe from his armies. She would have been forced into a game of continual catch-up, matching him gun for gun, soldier for soldier, with no hope of saving enough money to make the sort of peacetime improvements that she so fervently desired for her subjects.

And in this goal—and make no mistake, it was a big one—she succeeded. She had been every bit as determined as Frederick, every bit as relentless. By persisting to the bitter end, she had given him pause. He played the swaggering conqueror, it is true, but underneath he had learned to respect and even, perhaps, to fear her.

He never attacked her again.

THE TERMS OF THE TREATY might have been depressing, but there was nothing gloomy about the sense of relief that rolled over Vienna at the signing of the peace. At last, the seemingly endless war was over and the court could return to its customary social patterns. There were picnics, family concerts, and other agreeable diversions. Jean-Baptiste Pillement, a noted French artist specializing in quaint scenes of Chinese figures at play, was invited to Vienna. Maria Theresa loved the delicate, Eastern-inspired drawings he produced, known as chinoiserie, which were generally used to adorn tea sets and home furnishings. "All the diamonds of the world are as nothing to me," the empress declared to a friend. "Only objects from the Indies [she meant Asia], such as lacquer work and wallpaper, give me pleasure." To please her mother, Mimi and her father, along with Isabella and occasionally others in the family, began working on a grand project to decorate Maria Theresa's private office by employing a Chinese motif. The famous Pillement was commissioned to create the designs for the undertaking, but he did not execute them himself. Rather, each drawing was copied laboriously by a member of the imperial family. Although the size of the pictures varied, everyone used the same blue ink. Each drawing, when finished, was framed identically in gold and then hung in columns on the walls of the small study. There were 213 of them in all, with artistic Maria Christina contributing by far the most, and the whole made for quite a striking effect. Mimi understood that the long hours spent copying had the additional advantage of keeping Francis pleasantly occupied at home and so away from his mistress, which benefited her mother perhaps more than the ornamental images themselves. "The Emperor is a very good-hearted father; one can always rely upon him as a friend, and we must do what we can to protect him from his weaknesses," she observed tactfully to Isabella.

Also with the arrival of spring and peace came a familiar visitor to Vienna: Mimi's cousin Albert of Saxony. Albert had fought against Prussia and survived the war; by the terms of the Treaty of Hubertusburg, Dresden and the rest of his family's property had been returned and he was free to pay his respects, and to offer his thanks, to his imperial benefactress.

This time around, when he was included in family activities, Mimi looked and saw her cousin's virtues. Albert was slender and assured; his army experience had seasoned rather than hardened him. Intelligent, perceptive, and sensitive, he was charming in company but also had depth. And he still adored her.

Maria Christina was no longer a naive teenager playing at love with a romantic fantasy. Her former suitor, the prince of Württemberg, rather than persisting in the face of adversity, had proved fickle and married someone else barely a year after her mother broke off their relationship. She had an eyewitness view of her brother's marriage, and the helplessness and despondency that would be the likely by-products of wedding a stranger with whom she might prove incompatible. She certainly cared for her sister-in-law, and may have experimented with her sexually, but whatever sensation these guilty trysts produced was clearly nothing like the magnetic desire that swept over her in Albert's presence. Like a character in a novel, Mimi suddenly woke up and realized that her true love had been in front of her the whole time—she just hadn't noticed.

Albert, no slouch, picked up on this fortuitous turn of events and ran with it. He and Mimi began spending more time together. Unsurprisingly (and especially since she was engaged in an extensive drawing project that took up so many hours of her day), he expressed an interest in art. In turn, she took it upon herself to educate him, suggesting he read the essays of a prominent German critic and demonstrating techniques as she worked.

The ever-perceptive Isabella, hypersensitive to her surroundings, caught on right away. She began referring to Albert as her rival. "It's not jealousy...that feeling is too hateful even for me," she wrote unconvincingly. "But may I see you without deigning also to have your lover around, whom you prefer to me, not once but a hundred times?" And, "Believe that from now on my strength will increase [a reference to her pregnancy] and that I will never use it except in opposition to those who contest against a heart that is made only for you...Come strengthen me with your kisses, otherwise I am good for nothing," she pleaded. When Albert's visit was concluded and he went home to Dresden, she did everything she could to intensify her bond with Maria Christina. "I hope it will be sunny tomorrow because otherwise we will not see each other at our ease," she urged on July 15, 1763. "I embrace you a thousand times and a thousand times with all my heart while waiting for tomorrow."

Poor Isabella. As summer blazed into fall, and the time of her confinement drew near, the old demons returned. This time, she did not speak of suicide but rather suffered fearful premonitions of an early grave. "Perhaps we will be separated, perhaps death will end a life that is dear to me only because it is devoted to you," she penned sorrowfully to Maria Christina at the end of October.

And then, on November 19, in the last weeks of her pregnancy, Isabella fell ill. "Do not be afraid," she reassured Mimi. "I'm not worse than I have been. I will perhaps find an opportunity to speak to the Empress but besides that I would like to remain quiet the rest of the time to preserve my energy for what may come [she meant labor], which I cannot do if I see you, as I love you too much not to exert myself to talk to you. Goodbye, sleep well...I will kiss you tomorrow with all of my strength."

Tragically, the baby, born prematurely, caught her parent's illness and would live only a few hours. Isabella just had time to name her daughter Maria Christina before the infant girl died.

Grief over the child turned quickly to terror for the life of the mother. Weakened by the delivery, Isabella developed a high fever. The dreaded spots appeared. Mimi had also fallen ill and could not come to her; the empress, who had never had smallpox, was not allowed in her room; so it was Joseph alone, hoping beyond hope for her recovery, who watched frantically over her that final week. His wife's last letter was to his sister. It was very short. "God is too benevolent not to let me have the pleasure of kissing you again, and too just not to allow you to scold me before my death," she wrote weakly. "Goodbye, be well."

Isabella died, her husband at her side, on November 27, 1763. She was twenty-one years old.

JOSEPH WAS DEVASTATED. It turned out that his wife had been wrong; underneath his carefully constructed facade of cynicism, he *was* emotional, in fact deeply, movingly, almost poetically so. "I have lost everything," he mourned in a letter to his father-in-law written just hours after Isabella's death. "My adored wife, my love, my only friend is gone...You will also grieve for her loss, but think what it means to me. Wounded to the quick, I hardly know if I am still alive. Shall I survive this terrible separation? I fear the answer must be yes; but there can be no more happiness for me while life endures." And two weeks later, again in a letter to Parma, he vividly expressed his agony. "The only thing that comforts me is to be alone in my room, where I can gaze at the portrait of my beloved wife and handle her writings and other possessions," he revealed. "Often I seem to see her so clearly that I speak to her and feel less lonely. When she withdraws herself again and I can perceive nothing, imagine my despair...Our joys and sorrows have been honestly shared, and the days together were full of brightness," he confided poignantly. "No one can take her place...To me this treasure was given; I have lost her, and I am only twenty-two." And he clung to and cherished his surviving daughter, twenty-month-old Maria Theresa, as the sole living remembrance of his vanished joy.

Maria Christina was also profoundly affected by this shocking bereavement, although her grief was complicated by guilt. She had not been there to comfort Isabella, as she knew only she could, in her loved one's extremity. She, too, reached out for Isabella's daughter, whom everyone in the family called Little Theresa. Instinctively, Mimi stepped into her sister-in-law's place and assumed responsibility for the care of her dead friend's child. It was remarked at court that she loved Little Theresa as much as she would have if she had borne her herself.

But where Isabella's death caused Joseph to retreat once more behind a facade of self-pity and caustic bitterness, it served rather as a turning point for Maria Christina. All of her brilliant friend's observations and insights came into sharp focus with her demise. Mimi was the daughter of a great prince, it was true, but, as Isabella had noted, she did not have to remain a girl, and therefore powerless, forever. She could exert some control over her life, make a grab for happiness while there was still time. Mimi could do nothing about natural dangers like war or disease, but, using intelligence and subtlety, she might yet avert the fate of a distant, loveless marriage. When Albert returned to Vienna in the New Year to express his condolences to her family, she secretly promised to marry him, but warned him that he must sit quietly and leave everything to her.

THE MAIN EVENT in the spring of 1764 was Joseph's election and coronation in Frankfurt as imperial heir (he would officially be known as king of the Romans, as his father remained Holy Roman Emperor), a ceremony that Maria Theresa rushed to organize as quickly as possible in order to establish her son's undisputed right to the succession. Francis and Joseph left Vienna in March at the head of a procession that included "the most magnificent state-carriage, furnished even at the back part with an entire window of plate-glass, ornamented with paintings, lacquer, carved work, and gilding, covered with red embroidered velvet on the top and inside," as Goethe, again a chronicler to these festivities, reported somewhat breathlessly. On April 3, 1764, Joseph, like his father before him, was crowned at the Frankfurt cathedral, and afterward he and Francis paraded through the streets of the capital together so that the throngs lining the way could get a glimpse of both their present and future rulers. Required throughout to remain in his ancient coronation costume, the heir to the empire apparently did not cut an imposing figure. "The young King...in his monstrous articles of dress, with the crown-jewels of Charlemagne, dragged himself along as if he had been in disguise, so that he himself, looking at his father from time to time, could not refrain from laughing. The crown, which it had been necessary to line a great deal, stood out from his head like an overhanging roof," Goethe, who was otherwise much impressed by the spectacle, was forced to concede. But Joseph's comical appearance in no way diminished the delight of the crowd at his ascension. "The rejoicings, which resounded in the market-place, now spread likewise over the great square, and a boisterous *vivat* [Long live the King!] burst forth from thousands upon thousands of throats and doubtless from as many hearts. For this grand festival was to be the pledge of a lasting peace, which indeed for many a long year actually blessed Germany," Goethe cheered.

But not even the obviously sincere expressions of approval from his future subjects could lift the new king of the Romans from the depths of his sorrow. "On the 29th [of March], it was four months since I was separated from all of her that was mortal, and that was the date of my public entry [into Frankfurt]," Joseph brooded in a letter to his mother, who had elected to stay at home so as not to distract attention from her son and husband. "The difference it would have made if these ceremonies had been graced by the presence of my Queen!" he exclaimed touchingly. "Forgive me, my very dear mother, if I grieve you by my words. But have pity on a son...who is on the verge of despair."

It's possible, of course, that if he had been allowed to experience the ordinary grieving process, Joseph might have recovered from what he clearly felt was an insupportable loss. But in the eighteenth century, the sons of great princes had to obey, just as the daughters did. Joseph's romantic life was not his own. With his coronation, Maria Theresa had assured the continuation of the imperial dignity to her family; now she needed Joseph to do his part and sire a legitimate male heir. As he could not do this without a wife, it became necessary that he procure one at the earliest opportunity. He no sooner returned to Vienna from Frankfurt than she began flinging the names of eligible princesses at him.

Joseph, appalled at the barbarity of replacing the ethereal creature he had held in his arms every night the same way he would have ordered a pair of new riding boots after his previous footwear had worn out, did his best to wriggle out of it. He did, indeed, ask if he could marry Isabella's younger sister, but she was already spoken for. And besides, his in-laws, having already sacrificed one daughter to smallpox in Vienna, probably did not relish the idea of hazarding another. But when this alternative was denied to him, Joseph made no secret of his disgust at the idea of forming a new attachment. "I laugh with my lips while my soul is in tears," he confessed to Maria Theresa. "Were I not so fond of you...I would remain a widower, or rather be united eternally with an angel in heaven."

Maria Christina, watching her brother's agony, was torn. She saw that Joseph was in danger of idealizing Isabella and the love he believed they had shared to such an extent that it would prohibit him from ever giving another woman a chance at making him happy. She knew that she possessed information about the genuine state of Joseph's marriage of which he had been ignorant. Given that he *must* wed for the sake of the dynasty, and wed soon, might it not help him to know the truth, that Isabella had in fact given her heart and soul, had poured out all of her passion, not to Joseph but to Maria Christina?

But then again, what if she were wrong? Might it not be cruel to undeceive her brother in this brutal way? Unsure of what to do, she turned to Albert, to whom she had pledged herself. This was a risk, as to disclose her sister-in-law's secret infatuation inevitably raised uncomfortable questions as to how Mimi herself had responded to this deluge of illicit affection. Having seen what happened when conjugal bonds were built on duplicity, however, she decided that she wanted more from marriage and was willing to be honest to try to get it. "Let nothing remain hidden between the two of us," she told Albert. "Let us share all feelings, cares, and woes." And she showed him Isabella's letters and asked him if he thought it would help her brother to have a look at them.

There is no record of how Albert reacted to his intended's role in this affair. He seems to have taken the letters merely as proof of a troubled young woman's one-sided yearnings, nothing more. (Well, there were over 200 of them. It is possible he did not bother to read them all.) But he evidently agreed that it was important for Joseph to see them, because he counseled Maria Christina to show them to him. So she did.

Poor Joseph. Although Mimi's action had the desired effect—he acceded to his mother's wishes and reluctantly agreed to remarry—the fact of those letters, the reading of them, must have been like getting stabbed twice in the same unclosed wound. It is clear from his later behavior that he did not hold this well-intentioned, if misguided, shock treatment against his sister. But the revelation of Isabella's true feelings nonetheless had the effect of confirming the sort of misanthropic tendencies to which, before his marriage, he had already demonstrated a marked susceptibility. Whatever his potential capacity for compassion, trust, and generosity of spirit withered and died that day.

And as if this were not bad enough, the damage inflicted by the letters was compounded by his mother's choice of bride. In her anxiety to get him remarried as soon as possible so he could produce a male heir, Maria Theresa skewed her decision toward availability rather than other qualities, such as allure, refinement, or even basic attractiveness, which young men generally consider useful to the maintenance of an until-death-do-us-part relationship. To strengthen family ties, the empress preferred that her son's second wife come from either Saxony or Bavaria, both of which boasted daughters of an appropriate age. When Joseph refused to choose between them, Maria Theresa took matters into her own hands and on Francis's recommendation selected Maria Josepha of Bavaria. Apparently even she was taken aback when the bride-to-be arrived in Vienna in January 1765. "You are to have a sister-in-law, and I a daughter-in-law," she announced to Maria Christina. "Unfortunately it is Princess Josepha. It went against the grain to have anything to do with a settlement without my son's co-operation. But neither to me alone, nor to the Emperor, nor to Kaunitz, would he express any preference. The worst of it is that we must pretend to be pleased and happy. My head and my heart are not as one on this subject, and it is difficult to retain my equanimity."

Thus was Joseph, after three all too brief years of champagne nights, sentenced the second time around to a lifetime of castor oil. His description of his new wife was memorable for its succinct severity. "Her age is six-and-twenty," he reported to his former father-in-law. (Joseph was twenty-three.) "Her figure is short, thick-set, and without a vestige of youthful charm. Her face is covered with spots and pimples, and her teeth are horrible."

The unhappy couple was married at Schönbrunn Palace on January 25, 1765, a mere fourteen months after Isabella's death. To no one's surprise, the union proved to be a disaster. Joseph could not stand his new wife. "I find myself in a very sad plight...Love does not yield to common sense and it is not my nature to pretend," he observed grimly. Maria Josepha was as discontented with her husband as he was with her, and she let it show. Only Francis, who had urged the marriage, was friendly toward her; everyone else in the family, including Maria Theresa, avoided her. "I am willing to believe in her goodness," the empress remarked of her new daughter-in-law, "but she is neither pretty nor very agreeable."

"I believe that if I were his [Joseph's] wife and should be treated thus," Maria Christina confided to Albert, "I should have taken flight and hanged myself from a tree at Schönbrunn."

HER ELDEST SON'S CONNUBIAL MISERY did not discourage Maria Theresa from vigorously pursuing marriage alliances for her other children. She focused next on her second surviving son, Leopold. When Mimi's younger brother Charles had died of smallpox five years earlier, Leopold, then thirteen, had taken his place in the line of succession. With the possibility of Joseph dying without producing a male heir looming larger with each moment he spent shunning his new wife, the empress needed to get Leopold out there and started on a family as soon as possible. This time, she looked farther afield for a bride and succeeded in snaring nineteen-year-old Maria Luisa, the younger daughter of the king of Spain, as the bride-to-be. The wedding was scheduled to take place on August 5, 1765, just three months after Leopold's eighteenth birthday, in the little mountain town of Innsbruck, to take advantage of the cooler air in summer.

The approaching ceremony put Maria Christina in a critical position. Her mother had evidently previously clung to the hope that Mimi's elder sister might somehow be married off, but by this time it was obvious to everyone that Marianne, who had developed a crooked spine, was destined for a convent. Mimi's beautiful younger sister, Maria Elisabeth, was already sought-after, but Mimi knew her parents would want to see her settled first. Francis was still insisting she marry his nephew and, in a none too subtle hint that time was up and she was next, had invited the prospective suitor to the festivities at Innsbruck to meet the family. If she did not do something before Leopold's wedding to alter her circumstances, she knew she would be faced with a stark choice. It would be the son of the king of Sardinia—or the nunnery.

So she did what Isabella, in her "Advice to Marie" last will and testament, had counseled: she went privately to her mother, told her of her love for Albert and their desire to marry, and begged Maria Theresa to save her from the Sardinian alliance.

It was a tremendous risk. If anything, Albert was an even *less* impressive candidate for marriage than he had been when he first showed up in Vienna. His family had been ruined by the war, and with the death of his father, Augustus III, two years earlier, they had also lost the kingship of Poland, which for sixty years had added to the prestige of the ancestral estate. Catherine the Great, who preferred to assign the Polish throne to one of her former lovers rather than keep it in Albert's family, had reached out to Frederick and dangled a defensive alliance with Russia as a reward if he supported her in this initiative. Thrilled to get back in her good graces, Frederick had enthusiastically endorsed her candidate as a man "who has long been known to the Empress of Russia, and whose person is agreeable to her," as he so delicately put it.

There had been nothing Maria Theresa could do about it; it had all been negotiated behind her back. She had not the resources to go to war to help her Saxon cousins even if she had wanted to engage in another conflict (which she did not), and so Albert's family, already on a steep downslide, had become weaker still with the loss of Poland, and he, as a younger son with no income, land, prospects, or influence, was similarly diminished.

It should have been futile. And, in fact, her mother could not give Mimi much hope. Maria Theresa would never overrule Francis if he remained committed to the Sardinian marriage. But the entry of Maria Josepha into the family had changed the equation. It was beginning to dawn on the empress that, unlike Isabella, her new daughter-in-law made a poor substitute for her beloved Mimi. Joseph wasn't even bothering to bring his new wife to Innsbruck for the wedding, and his mother had not argued with his decision. She recognized that everyone was simply happier when Maria Josepha was not around.

The empress, "not without reason," as she herself put it, was in particularly low spirits that summer. "I need a little comforting, for I am weary and depressed," she confessed to a friend just before Leopold's wedding—and she consequently was in no hurry to lose the one member of her numerous offspring who could always be counted on to lift her spirits. So she stalled for time. She told Maria Christina to wait until Francis had met his nephew at Innsbruck—perhaps the young man would fail to make a good impression. In addition, possibly to provide her husband with a means of comparison, Maria Theresa invited Albert to attend the festivities. But that was as far as she would go. Mimi was given to understand that her choice of bridegroom ultimately rested with her father.

And so it was with no little trepidation that Maria Christina traveled with her mother, father, Joseph, and Leopold (the younger children stayed at home) in early July to Innsbruck. When they arrived, the bride's party, which had been delayed by bad weather, was still nowhere to be seen, so Francis and Leopold rode south in search of her; they soon found Maria Luisa and her attendants and escorted the company back to Innsbruck, arriving on July 30. This time, Maria Theresa could congratulate herself on her matchmaking ability. "The Infanta [Maria Luisa] has a dazzling complexion, with a lovely color, clear blue eyes, and the most beautiful hair I have seen in my life," she raved. "She has a very fine figure, in a word, a charming young person, frank, and full of life and good spirits. I am quite taken with her," she pronounced with evident relief.

But relief once again turned quickly to alarm. Leopold had caught cold and developed a fever on the road. By August 5, the day of his wedding, he was so ill that he could barely stand to take his vows. He collapsed immediately after the ceremony and had to be helped back to his rooms. For a week he lay in bed burning with fever.

But thankfully no sinister rash appeared this time, and, after the crisis, Leopold began to improve. Of course, there was no thought of moving him until he had thoroughly recovered, but as long as everyone was stuck in Innsbruck anyway, there seemed no reason not to go ahead with the various balls, feasts, performances, and other merry-making festivities that had been planned to celebrate the wedding.

Francis, who loved socializing, played the host during Leopold's recovery, dashing from party to party. On August 18, 1765, two such engagements were scheduled—a stage-play at the imperial theater followed by a supper party at the adjoining residence. About halfway through the dramatic performance Francis suddenly felt unwell and decided to go back to his rooms to rest before dinner. Joseph, seeing his father somewhat unsteady, followed him out to ensure that he was not seriously ill. The emperor only made it a few steps out of the theater before staggering and then crumpling; Joseph just barely caught him before he hit the floor.

Although help was summoned immediately, it was of no use. Fifty-six-year-old Francis I, Holy Roman Emperor and grand duke of Tuscany, the adored consort of the queen of Hungary and Bohemia, had suffered what appears to have been a massive stroke. He died within moments in his eldest son's arms.

The news paralyzed the court. "Never can I forget that evening," a shaken Albert recorded in a letter home to Saxony soon afterward. "Think of it; the Emperor dead, the Empress supported to her apartments by her brother- and sister-in-law [Charles of Lorraine and a surviving sibling], who were almost as overcome as herself; the Archduke ill in bed, the Archduchesses prostrate with grief, the guests arriving for the supper and bursting into tears till all the palace seemed to echo with sobs and groans." Maria Theresa retired into her rooms and did not come out for days. She spent the time helping to sew her husband's shroud and praying continually for his soul, panicked that he had not had time to confess and receive absolution before dying. "I have lost in him the most affectionate friend, the most dearly beloved companion during a union of thirty years, and the only joy of my life," she grieved. "During the harassing times of the first twenty years of my reign he soothed my cares and my anxieties by sharing them."

When she did come out, she showed what she was made of. The dignitaries and other courtiers surged around her offering their condolences — all except one young woman, dressed in deep mourning, who stood alone in the corner sobbing; no one would speak to her. This was *la belle princesse,* whom Francis had invited along to his son's wedding to keep him company. Maria Theresa went up to her and, in a gesture of shared anguish, clasped her hands. "We have indeed suffered a great loss, my dear," she said.★

But she returned to Vienna a broken woman. She cut her hair and from that time on never appeared in anything but black. She could not bear to sleep alone in the bed she had shared with her husband, so she moved from her rooms on the first floor of the Hofburg palace to a suite on the third floor, where she had all of the furnishings draped in ebony velvet.

Fall came, then winter, and her sorrow was just as strong. "I hardly know myself now, for I have become like an animal with no true life or reasoning power," she wrote despondently to her oldest adviser, Count Tarouca, then in his seventies. "I forget everything. I get up at five. I go to bed late, and the livelong day I seem to do nothing. I do not even think. It is a terrible state to be in."

In her misery, there was only one person who could be reliably counted on to soothe her: her darling Mimi. Prior to her husband's death, Maria Theresa had merely wished not to be parted from her daughter; now she could not bear the thought of it. And in her mother's great need lay Maria Christina's opportunity. Maria Theresa must have given her daughter the necessary encouragement, as, in November 1765, a mere three months after the tragedy at Innsbruck, Albert's oldest brother, in his position as head of the Saxon side of the family, made a formal request for Maria Christina's hand on behalf of the hopeful groom.

But it was not enough to have just her mother's permission —

★ She maintained this magnanimity even when she discovered that Francis had left his mistress 200,000 florins at his death. She paid the sum without protest.

Mimi now also required her eldest brother's approval to wed Albert. Thanks to Maria Theresa's foresight in having pushed for an early coronation in Frankfurt, Joseph had succeeded his father without incident; there had been no protests, no invasions, no rival princes jockeying to challenge his ascension—instead, he was quickly and matter-of-factly recognized as Joseph II, Holy Roman Emperor.★ More to the point, as the eldest male, Joseph had also inherited his father's position as head of the family. And, although Maria Theresa retained her titles, lands, and authority, she had further decided to name her son co-regent of her government, to help prepare him for his duties in the event that she, too, keeled over one day without warning. So, Maria Christina's union, representing as it did an alliance of state, fell doubly under Joseph's authority.

Bitter and unhappy in his own marriage, prone to harbor grudges, Joseph was by no means sure to give his approval. Maria Theresa herself must have been wary of his reaction, because she dispatched Count Kaunitz to apprise her eldest son of the Saxon proposal, rather than approaching him personally.

To her great relief, Joseph agreed to the match with enthusiasm. "You sent my son back to me very quickly and quite decided," an elated Maria Theresa informed her minister on November 11, 1765. "He couldn't wait for the moment when his sister was to be told. I summoned her; it was a touching scene, but the pleasure that I saw my son had in making them happy affected me more even than the satisfaction of arranging this marriage." Joseph made a point of breaking the good news to Albert himself. "It was a long time before he would believe that I was speaking seriously," the new emperor chuckled in a letter to his brother Leopold (who had inherited Francis's Italian estates and, with his new wife, Maria Luisa, taken up residence in Florence as the grand duke and duchess of Tuscany). "When he was convinced beyond doubt, you can imagine the look that came

---

★ This also meant that Maria Theresa was no longer empress—that title now belonged to her son's wife, Maria Josepha.

over his face at the thought of a speedy fulfillment of the cherished hope of the last six years." Then, revealingly, Joseph explained to Leopold the reasoning behind his consent to the marriage. "To me, the philosopher Joseph," he continued, "nothing could be more agreeable than this assurance of congenial society for the rest of my life. As there is no pleasure for me in my own household, I will seek distraction in the new one. I predict that the moments I can devote to relaxation will be spent with my sister and brother-in law."

But this was just the beginning of the couple's good fortune. Because Albert was a landless younger son, lacking the necessary income stream to provide for her daughter in the manner to which she had become accustomed (a fact noted in Mimi's official marriage contract), Maria Theresa, "out of tender love and motherly care," proposed to rectify this deficiency through the mechanism of a special gift. Mimi, like all of her sisters, had been promised a set dowry of 100,000 guilders; to this sum Maria Theresa now added precious jewels, a silver service, two of the wealthiest estates in Hungary, and a tidy nest egg of 666,821 guilders in banking securities.

Joseph, for his part, ceded them the important duchy of Teschen, attached to the Bohemian crown, which had come to him at the death of his father, along with all of its duties, rents, and other income streams. The couple was further promised the future governorship of the Austrian Netherlands, along with all of *its* duties, rents, and income streams, after the death of Charles of Lorraine, its current occupant. Additionally, Albert, in recognition of his much-improved status, was awarded a prestigious medal, generally reserved for the highest nobility, a bejeweled clasp and ring, an ornamental sword, and a belt emblazoned with diamonds.

Finally, to ensure that her daughter's husband's days were filled with gainful employment (and thereby hopefully prevent the sort of extramarital philandering that she associated with idleness), Maria Theresa also threw in the governorship of Hungary, an office that conveniently came with its own imposing palace in nearby Pressburg, to make it easier for her to visit.

The sum total of this fond example of maternal solicitude: a whopping *4 million* guilders. It was such a staggeringly generous bequest, so obviously preferential (no archduchess had ever received anything close to a dowry this size; there were princesses of France, Spain, and Great Britain who could not claim riches like this at the time of their betrothal), that for years Mimi's marriage contract was treated as an official Austrian state secret.★

The wedding of Maria Christina and Albert, who by this ceremony took their place among the wealthiest couples in Europe, was held on April 8, 1766, at the intimate private chapel at Schloss Hof palace, one of Maria Theresa's country estates. As the court was still in mourning for the bride's father, it was a somewhat muted affair. The men, a select group of family, high court officials, and foreign dignitaries, were arrayed respectfully in charcoal gray; the gowns of the women were adorned with black ribbon. Among these, the slender bride, a month short of her twenty-fourth birthday, stood out in a white dress embellished with a generous sprinkling of precious gems and embroidered flowers in silver thread. "The young archduchess, who is endowed with more than ordinary beauty, vivacity, and *esprit,* and with charming and gracious manners, appeared, covered with splendid diamonds...and caused many to envy her husband," one of the guests, a high-ranking representative from Venice, admitted. Albert's younger brother, Clement, a bishop — with no other options, Clement had taken his brother's place in the Church and so presented a visible reminder of what had originally been in store for the lucky bridegroom — officiated. Afterward, there was a traditional wedding feast, which was followed by music, pageantry, balls, and dancing, until five days later, on April 13, the newlyweds made their official entry into Hungary, arriving in state at their magnificent residence in Pressburg. Maria Theresa and

---

★ As for the groom, it was as though he had stepped into a familiar nursery tale — only in this one the gender roles were reversed: Maria Christina played the prince and *Albert* was Cinderella, with Maria Theresa as the fairy godmother.

Joseph lent their prestige to the occasion by attending the reception of the new governor and his wife.

No battle had been fought, no artillery fired, no blood spilled. But a campaign had been waged nonetheless—waged and won. Under the protective cover of obedience but without ever being untrue to herself—for Maria Christina sincerely loved her mother and wished to please her—the daughter of a great prince had quietly defied the odds and gained a measure of control over her life.

Maria Carolina

"Charlotte"

...at sixteen

10

The Understory

A poxe on both your houses.
                                    —Mercutio, *Romeo and Juliet,* Act 3, Scene 1

MARIA CAROLINA, WHOM EVERYONE called Charlotte, was born on August 13, 1752, almost exactly midway through the sliver of peace wedged in between the end of the War of the Austrian Succession and the beginning of the Seven Years' War. She was her parents' thirteenth child and tenth daughter,* which put her squarely among the offspring who constituted Maria Theresa's younger brood. As the members of this group were almost always deemed too infantile to participate in the activities of their older siblings, Maria Carolina found her playmates among the company of her sisters Maria Johanna, born on February 4, 1750, and Maria Josepha, who, with a birthday of March 19, 1751, was only a year older; her brother Ferdinand, who came along on June 1, 1754; Maria Antonia (Marie Antoinette), who appeared on November 2, 1755; and of course the baby, Maximilian, Maria Theresa's final child, born on December 8, 1756.

Number thirteen out of sixteen is almost a guarantee of some degree of parental laxity. Even mothers who do not have to rebuild armies, impose taxes on the nobility, wage war, arrange marriages, forge new international alliances, review mountains of memoranda,

---

* This includes the daughter born in 1748 who survived for only an hour.

and monitor the day-to-day administration of two kingdoms and an archduchy may be excused for letting things slide a little after the first dozen or so. It's not that Maria Theresa didn't try, but inevitably something had to give, if only for lack of space. "Whenever she is tired of working and wishes for relaxation, she sees her children," a courtier noted in 1754, when Charlotte was two years old. "At Vienna she does so three or four times every day without exception. At Schönbrunn and Laxenburg [another of Maria Theresa's country houses] there is not room enough for the whole family; the youngest children, therefore remain in Vienna, and the Empress sees them only once a week." Even when she did visit with the junior archdukes and -duchesses, it could not always be classified as one-on-one quality time. Maria Theresa once excused the incoherence of a letter to a friend on the grounds that she had been obliged to write it "in four installments, with six children in the room, and the emperor, too."

By necessity, then, in lieu of personal attention, Maria Theresa relied even more heavily on instructors and governesses to educate and discipline this younger group than she had with her older offspring. But while her commands were very explicit, and her objectives laudable, many parents will recognize that there was a degree of difficulty involved in achieving them that she perhaps underestimated. For example, "It is my wish," Maria Theresa informed her surrogates when Maria Carolina was about six years old, "that the children are to eat everything before them without making any objections. They are not to make any remarks about preferring this or that, or to discuss their food. They are to eat fish every Friday and Saturday and on every fast-day...All my children seem to have an aversion against fish, but they must all overcome this, there is to be no relenting in this matter."

Additionally, Charlotte, with so many siblings ahead of her, failed to stand out in any way. She was not talented at drawing, like Mimi, or music, like Joseph. She was not as pretty as Maria Elisabeth or as charming as her next-eldest sister, Maria Josepha.★ She was very bright, and could do all of her lessons easily, but failed to apply herself, much preferring to have fun with Marie Antoinette instead. In fact, Charlotte was far cleverer and more spirited than her governess (whom she shared with her younger sister). There were frequent tests of wills over Maria Carolina's poor attitude and general lack of diligence toward her schoolwork, which the governess inevitably lost; as a result, her charge's sharp intelligence went unrecognized. As so often happens in large families, responsible Mimi, as the second-eldest daughter, tried to help by keeping a watch on her younger siblings' behavior, to encourage them to improve their manners and academic performance. For this unenviable and mostly fruitless exercise of authority she was deeply resented by both Charlotte and Marie Antoinette.

With an ineffective governess and so few demands on her (well, except for the fish), Charlotte was allowed to develop at her own pace, which in this case meant a semblance of a normal, happy childhood. This was not to say that she did not experience grief. She was ten when her twelve-year-old sister, Maria Johanna, died of smallpox. This must have been terrifying, as Maria Johanna had been a part of Charlotte's daily routine since birth; they took their lessons and meals together; theirs was a shared childhood. But Maria Carolina does not seem to have been emotionally scarred by this loss, and here her mother's philosophy, which was to approach life's tragedies head-on, might have helped. "As [her youngest children] must not be afraid of illnesses, you will talk to them about any of these quite naturally, even of smallpox," Maria Theresa instructed her daughter's circle of servants. "And of death also, for it is well to familiarize them with the thought of it."

★ Of course it is not difficult enough to have to account for sixteen children, but one of them also had to have the exact same name as Maria Theresa's new daughter-in-law! In an attempt to prevent confusion, from now on I will refer to Joseph's second wife as "Empress Maria Josepha" and to his younger sister simply as "Maria Josepha," and we will see if that works.

But because Charlotte spent almost all of her time with her younger siblings, the majority of the family joys and sorrows appeared to her to occur offstage, as if in another dimension. She was probably aware of the war with Prussia but, as she was only ten when it ended, could not comprehend the significance of its unhappy outcome. Similarly, the death of Isabella, whom she saw only on those rare occasions when the whole court was together, would likely have been viewed as a remote and fleeting phenomenon of the secretive grown-up world. Charlotte did not attend Leopold's wedding in 1765 and so was not present when her father died; the news was broken to her days after the fact by servants. And although she was nearly fourteen when Mimi married Albert in April 1766, Charlotte, to her disappointment, was still deemed too juvenile to witness the celebration.

Perhaps because she was treated as a child, she remained one—romping with Marie Antoinette, who dogged her heels; playing silly games; daydreaming through her studies. At fourteen she inhabited that twilight interval between girlhood and adolescence, sensing the precarious adult currents swirling around her but not fully under-standing them—an unremarked player waiting to be called from the dressing room.

IN THE AFTERMATH of Mimi's wedding, during the fall and winter of 1766, Maria Theresa, having secured her favorite child's happiness, turned her attention to negotiating advantageous futures for her remaining daughters. As expected, twenty-seven-year-old Mari-anne took the veil and made plans to enter a prestigious convent in Prague, where out of deference to her royal birth (and a contribution of 2 million guilders by her mother) she was immediately accepted as abbess.* Of the remaining circle of older children, this left twenty-two-year-old Maria Elisabeth and twenty-year-old Maria

---

* Marianne's fellow nuns would have to make do without their superior as, fearing homesickness, their new abbess ultimately refused to take up residency among them. "You will be surprised to hear that Marianne has lost all inclination to go to Prague, and I prefer to let her do as she likes in the matter," Maria Theresa shrugged to one of her friends. Accordingly, a proviso was executed that allowed Marianne to keep her

Amalia still to be provided for. Each young woman had a declared suitor—the new king of Poland, Catherine the Great's former lover, had come forward and asked for beautiful Maria Elisabeth's hand, while Maria Amalia had fallen in love with a distant cousin, the prince of Zweibrücken.

But Maria Theresa had objections to both these wooers, and she wavered. In Maria Elisabeth's case, she did not wish to condone the recent usurpation of Poland by marrying her daughter into the new dynasty. As for the prince of Zweibrücken, although he was in line for Bavaria should its current elector die without a male heir, the prospect of this actually occurring was so uncertain, and in any event so far in the future, that it could not be weighed in his favor. Without this he had neither the standing nor the income to justify an alliance with an imperial princess (Albert being the great exception to this rule). Moreover, there was still the son of the king of Sardinia, Mimi's jilted beau, to be considered; surely Maria Elisabeth or Maria Amalia should be given to him? Further complicating this juggling of nuptial alliances, the duke of Parma, Isabella's father, had by this time died, leaving a seventeen-year-old son who would soon come into his majority as his heir. A wedding between one of her daughters and her dear Isabella's younger brother was highly desired, as it would help bring Parma back under Austrian influence.*

All of these considerations obviously had to be analyzed, debated, and negotiated with an eye to foreign and domestic interests, and this of course took time; winter turned to spring of 1767 and still no decision on any of these suitors had been made. Instead, Maria Theresa focused on the one union that took precedence over all the others: the fast-approaching wedding of her ninth daughter, sixteen-year-old Maria Josepha, just seventeen months older than Charlotte, to Ferdinand, king of Naples.

---

vocation but avoid the cloister, and so the abbess of Prague stayed in Vienna and lived at home with her mother.

   * Remember, Isabella's father was Don Philip, Elizabeth Farnese's younger son, to whom Maria Theresa had lost Parma at the end of the War of the Austrian Succession.

The recovery of the strategic realm of Naples (which included the island of Sicily), even if only through marriage, was of primary importance to both Maria Theresa and Joseph. Elizabeth Farnese had wrested this valuable asset from the empire and bestowed it upon her eldest son, Don Carlos; as a result, Maria Theresa's armies had been forced to fight Don Carlos's during the War of the Austrian Succession, and this had contributed to the loss of Parma. But then, like some miraculous trick of political alchemy, enmity had been abruptly transmuted into affection when France and Spain had been cajoled into taking Austria's side in the Seven Years' War, and this had meant harmony with Don Carlos as well.

By 1767, Don Carlos was no longer sovereign of Naples; he was now Charles III, king of Spain, having inherited the Spanish crown some years before.* He had transferred his southern Italian dominion to his third son, Ferdinand, who at sixteen was in need of a wife, and so the engagement with Austria was arranged. Maria Theresa, thrilled at so advantageous a match, had originally intended that Maria Johanna wed Ferdinand, but then poor Maria Johanna succumbed to smallpox, so the next in line, Maria Josepha, had gotten the job.

This was not an enviable employment. Ferdinand evidently left much to be desired as a potential lord and master. His parents had decamped from Naples to Madrid when he was only eight years old, leaving him in the care of a council of aged advisers not unlike those with whom Maria Theresa had been saddled upon the death of her father. Except in Ferdinand's case, there had been one ambitious younger minister, a man by the name of Bernardo Tanucci, who had seized power from all the others. Not wishing to invite future competition from his young sovereign, he had instructed Ferdinand's tutor not to bother with the boy's education but instead to distract him with sports, games, and other amusements.

---

* It was Don Carlos's daughter who married Leopold at the disastrous wedding in Innsbruck where Francis died.

Maria Theresa, who had eyewitness accounts of her future son-in-law's behavior, was appalled. "The young King shows no taste for anything but hunting and the theater; he is unusually childish, learns nothing, and knows nothing except bad provincial Italian, and has on several occasions given proof of harshness and arbitrariness. He is accustomed to have his own way, and there is no one with him who can or will give him a good education," she worried. "My mother's heart is very uneasy," she confessed to Maria Josepha's governess. "I look upon poor Josepha as a sacrifice to politics." But of course, the innocent bride-to-be wasn't to be forewarned of her fate. "All this that I indicate must remain for you alone," Maria Theresa warned the governess sternly.

To make up for what had every promise of being a lifetime of marital unhappiness, Maria Theresa went out of her way to indulge Maria Josepha and make her feel special, as a mark of her coming improvement in rank. Her younger sister Charlotte could not have helped but observe with envy the difference that being engaged to the king of Naples meant to her sibling's daily routine. "Breakfast is to be changed daily, according to her [Maria Josepha's] wishes," her mother further instructed her sister's governess. "She is also to be allowed to eat bread with it, as much as she likes, except on established fast-days, when she shall always take chocolate with four pieces of bread, but never a croissant... Normally, at midday and evening, she is to be given enough to eat, what and as much as she likes, without quibbling about it." (No fish for Maria Josepha! Maria Theresa must really have felt guilty about her role in arranging this marriage.) "She is to go out as often as may be, in order to strengthen herself, and she is to practice herself well in the Italian and Spanish tongues," Maria Theresa added.

By this time it was May of 1767, which promised to be a significant month, as both Maria Theresa's fiftieth and Mimi's twenty-fifth birthdays fell on the thirteenth. They would not be celebrating together, however, because Maria Christina, who had conceived quickly after her marriage, was due to give birth on almost the same day. Maria Theresa had missed Mimi terribly that year; none of her other children had been able to take her place, and it was only the prospect of her daughter's approaching happiness at being a mother herself that had eased her loneliness. "I was like a silly child this afternoon," she admitted in a letter to her. "At three o'clock, I heard your sisters coming through my rooms, and, for a moment, I verily believed that I was going to see my dear Mimi again. I soon remembered that just then she was doing the honors of her own home, and rejoicing in her association with the husband who so dearly loves her."

But of course childbirth could be dangerous, and so Maria Theresa waited anxiously for updates on Mimi's condition. The news, when it came, was not good. Maria Christina had given birth on May 16 to a daughter, whom she had poignantly named Isabella, but there had been grave complications and the infant girl had died the next day. Then, in the aftermath of the delivery, Mimi herself had developed a high fever, probably due to infection, and was in a critical state. The doctors were not sure that she would pull through.

It was with this fearful report in mind that Maria Theresa was further informed that Joseph's unhappy second wife, Empress Maria Josepha, was complaining of illness, and her mother-in-law felt it was her duty to check on her. Maria Theresa arrived at her rooms and sat with the empress until the physician came to bleed his patient; she remained while the sick woman's sleeve was pulled back for the bloodletting; and that was when she, as well as everyone else in the room, saw the distinctive spots.

Maria Theresa seems to have been aware in that moment, as Empress Maria Josepha looked down at her arm in horror, that she had not perhaps been as kind and welcoming to her son's second wife as she could have been. To help quiet her and give her confidence, she stayed through the bloodletting, and when she finally left, she made a point of kissing the distraught young woman goodbye. Albert would later report that, "anxious to hide how little special fondness she had for her daughter-in-law, [Maria Theresa] made the effort, not without repugnance, to embrace her when they parted."

That was all it took. Smallpox works quickly. Joseph's second wife died less than two weeks later, on May 28, 1767. By that time, Maria Theresa, too, had contracted the deadly disease, and was not expected to live. She was given last rites.

FROM MARIA CHRISTINA'S BEDSIDE in Pressburg, Albert monitored events in Vienna closely. From the first, Maria Theresa had given strict orders that Mimi not be told that her mother had come down with smallpox. She feared that her daughter would worry so intensely that it would inhibit her recovery; she did not want Mimi to try to struggle out of her own sickbed to get to her side.

But by the end of May, Maria Christina, although still weak, was out of danger. Albert knew his wife would never forgive him if one of them were not present to ease her mother's mind at her death and to demonstrate their love and gratitude. So without telling Mimi the real reason for his visit, he hurried to Vienna.

He found his mother-in-law still conscious but sinking fast. The crisis was upon her. He entered the sickroom and joined Joseph, who, having already had the disease, was immune from it. The two men maintained a vigil by her side. No one expected Maria Theresa to live through the night.

Daylight dawned and she was still with breath, but again her aged physician, Gerard van Swieten, shook his head; she was hourly expected to succumb. And yet she did not. At fifty years old, having brought to term sixteen children, Maria Theresa fought through the most virulent disease of her age. Her beautiful hair turned white and her face was forever afterward horribly scarred, but she survived. By June 5 she was strong enough to write to her beloved Mimi. "I demand of you as a proof of your boundless love and obedience that you do not get upset when you hear that I had smallpox. Instead, Thank God that He has extended my days," she reassured her daughter.

It was well that Maria Christina received this comforting communication, as Albert did not return to Pressburg as quickly as he had planned. That's the thing about communicable diseases: they're catching. Within two weeks, Albert had come down with smallpox as well. He was fortunate to have a mild case. He recovered quickly, and the pockmarks faded with time. All at court breathed a sigh of relief. The epidemic had passed; by the end of June, the newlyweds were reunited.

It would only come out later, when Mimi failed to conceive a second time, that this seemingly inconsequential bout with the pox had likely left Albert sterile.

By August of 1767, life at court had resumed a semblance of normality. Preparations for Maria Josepha's upcoming journey to Naples, set to take place in the fall, were already underway. The bride's magnificent trousseau—over a hundred gowns in embroidered silks and velvets, many trimmed in delicate handmade lace—which had been ordered from Paris at great expense, arrived and was put out on public display (much to the disgruntlement of the local vendors, who had been shut out of this lucrative bit of business by their foreign rivals). Joseph, eager to see Italy, had volunteered to escort his sister to her new home. Maria Theresa, who had spent the summer recovering in Pressburg with Mimi and Albert, could assure herself that she had done all she could to lend majesty to Maria Josepha by sending her off sheathed as befitted her position as queen of a prominent kingdom. It now behooved her, as a mother, to move on to the next daughter in line.

And so, for the first time in her life, Maria Carolina suddenly came to Maria Theresa's attention. As Charlotte displayed many of the traits common to teenaged girls, such as hormonal mood swings and an irresistible inclination toward gossip and secrecy (not to mention general irritability), this was not necessarily a welcome development. "I do not intend to treat you as a child," Maria Theresa wrote sternly to her tenth daughter on August 19, 1767. "You are fifteen years old, and if you make proper use of the talents with which God has so richly endowed you, and follow the good advice which is required by everybody of whatever age, you will earn the approbation of your family and of the public... To my great astonishment I hear... that you say your prayers very carelessly, without reverence, without attention, and still more, without fervor," she scolded. "Do not be surprised if, after such a beginning of the day, nothing goes well... Besides this, you have lately got into the habit of treating your ladies in a manner that... has brought great discredit on you. While dressing you are just as ill-humored; on this point there is neither forgetfulness nor the least excuse... Your voice and manner of speaking are also displeasing," Maria Theresa noted bluntly. "You must take more trouble than others to amend this... You must work diligently at your music, drawing, history, geography, Latin, and other studies. Never be idle, for idleness is dangerous for every one, and especially for you, whose head must always be occupied to keep you from playing childish tricks, making improper observations, and longing for unsuitable and unreasonable amusements. As I shall now treat you as a grown-up person, I tell you that you will be entirely separated from your sister [Marie Antoinette]. I forbid you all secrets, confidences, and conversations with her; if the little one tries to begin again you have only to pay no attention or to tell your ladies. All this mischief-making will then be put an end to at once; for all these secret confidences consist of nothing but speaking against your neighbor, your family, or your ladies. I warn you that you will be strictly watched... Attach yourself to your sister Amalie, leave off the childish curiosity which annoys everybody, attend to your own business instead of other people's... Next year you will be as old as your sister Josepha is now... you take rank after Amalie," she reminded her severely. And she replaced Charlotte's old governess with Maria Josepha's, thereby making good on her threat to separate her from Marie Antoinette, who was forced to remain with their former nanny.

It seems likely from this letter, and especially the change in governesses, that Maria Theresa had settled upon Charlotte as the future bride of the duke of Parma. Charlotte was the right age for Isabella's brother, and her new governess was already practiced in Italian and Spanish, the two languages necessary for the position. A match between Charlotte and the duke of Parma made sense, especially as during this period the matrimonial alliances of her older sisters were nearing completion. Negotiations were proceeding with Sardinia for Maria Elisabeth's hand (Catherine the Great, informed of the king of Poland's suit, had registered her strong disapproval of her former lover's taking a young and pretty archduchess as a wife, so *that* union was off the table). And at twenty-one, Maria Amalia was obviously too old, and frankly too sophisticated, for the sixteen-year-old duke of Parma.★

Central Italy was only important to Maria Theresa because it had originally belonged to her family. Parma itself was an insignificant duchy, neither wealthy nor prestigious. It had been cobbled together as a face-saving domicile for a cadet branch of the Spanish dynasty, but no one *wanted* to live there. So even if Charlotte did not improve her manners and voice, as her mother had instructed, there would be no need to worry—it would not much matter in a backwater like Parma.

It is not known how the young recipient of all of this helpful maternal advice felt upon reading so chiding a letter, but in any event, Charlotte had a small reprieve from her mother's attention, as upon her return from Pressburg, Maria Theresa once again focused on the Neapolitan alliance. On September 8, 1767, at a ceremony at the Hofburg palace, ambassadors representing King Ferdinand entered a formal request for Maria Josepha's hand. Their suit was graciously accepted, the couple were officially betrothed, and it was arranged that the bridal party would depart for Naples the very next month. On October 4, in preparation for the journey, Maria Theresa decided that Maria Josepha should visit the family vault one last time, to pray at the tomb of her deceased father.

★ Maria Theresa was evidently still weighing the possibility that Maria Amalia might marry for love, as Mimi had done: no decision had yet been rendered on the attractive, if politically and financially unimpressive, prince of Zweibrücken.

The imperial vault was located in a basement beneath the Capu-chin Church, not far from the Hofburg palace. As might be expected, given its placement and function, the atmosphere surrounding the crypt was notoriously cold and gloomy. "I have visited this place more than once, not without sensations of a solemn and melancholy kind," observed an English chronicler who visited Vienna around this time. "The vault, or rather subterranean chamber, is of consid-erable size; the light being admitted into it though in parts very imperfectly. All the Emperors, Empresses, and their male as well as female issue, for more than a century past, are there ranged side by side," the traveler confirmed.

Maria Theresa went annually to the crypt to pray for Francis's soul, but this time she insisted that Maria Josepha accompany her in order to "perform her devotions for the last time among the tomb of her relations," as the English chronicler, who had the story from numerous members of the court and the local population, reported. Maria Josepha "expressed great repugnance to the melancholy cere-mony; but the Empress persisted in obliging her to submit to it. In vain the Princess implored to be excused, alleging a terror and dread that she could not surmount [but] Maria Theresa, inflexible, rejected all of her entreaties."★ Given no choice, the sixteen-year-old future queen of Naples at length submitted, although "it is generally asserted that she burst into tears when she entered the coach that was to conduct her to the church; and that while in the vault, engaged at prayer, she was seized with a shivering," the account continued. "Whether there be any exaggeration in these circumstances or not, it is certain that she sickened almost immediately on her return home to the palace. The small-pox made its appearance soon afterwards... and notwithstanding every medical assistance, she expired on the fifteenth of October 1767, the precise day destined for her departure to Naples," the chronicler reported sorrowfully.

Stunningly, the broad outline of this story is true. Maria Theresa

---

★ I'm afraid this does sound like Maria Theresa.

did insist that her daughter visit the crypt, and Maria Josepha did fall ill with smallpox almost immediately upon her return, dying less than two weeks later. All of Vienna believed that she had caught the pestilence from exposure to the decaying remains of her sister-in-law, Joseph's second wife. "It was recollected that scarcely four months had elapsed, and those months the hottest of the whole year, since the Empress Maria Josepha, second wife of the present Emperor, had been buried in the same vault," the chronicler noted. "The fact was well known, that the smallpox of which the Empress died, was of a nature so extremely malignant as to render it impossible to embalm her body. Many persons did not hesitate to declare that, notwithstanding all the precautions taken, the smell of her corpse was perceptible," he added. Certainly Maria Theresa thought so, and blamed herself for her daughter's death for the rest of her life. "It is four years today since Josepha went with me to the vault and caught smallpox," she mourned to Mimi on October 4, 1771.★

Nor did this tragic death mark the end of the heartbreak. The court was still reeling with shock when twenty-four-year-old Maria Elisabeth fell ill after attending a requiem service for her sister. It was reported that when the first of the hideous spots broke out and she knew what she was facing, Maria Elisabeth cast one last look in the mirror, "taking leave of those features she had so often heard praised, and which she believed would be greatly changed before she should see them again." She was only too prescient. Although she managed to survive the ordeal, Maria Elisabeth emerged from the sickroom so viciously scarred that when word got out of the blighting of her

---

★ It is difficult to believe that Maria Josepha actually caught the disease at the crypt, as the incubation period for smallpox is usually at least a week. She was most likely already sick when she entered. (There had been outbreaks of the infection in Vienna all through the summer and early fall; the illness had never really left the city.) This would explain her fit of shivering in the tomb—certainly the cold, clammy air in the place didn't do her any good. Moreover, the stench reported to be emanating from the crypt (no wonder she begged not to go!) would indicate that everything wasn't perhaps as hygienic as could have been hoped for, which also might have contributed to the spread of the virus to the general population.

looks, the Sardinian court abruptly backed out of the marriage negotiations.

An agonizing grief descended on the imperial court in the wake of these twin blows—but this did not prevent the government, and particularly Count Kaunitz, from aggressively pursuing Austrian marital interests in Italy. If anything, the death of Maria Josepha and the disfiguring of Maria Elisabeth only underscored the need for urgency in this area—the surplus of unmarried archduchesses, once so bountiful, had now been decimated. Substitute brides must be agreed upon and dispatched to Naples and Parma with all speed, lest another sicken before the contract was signed and the match consummated.

Maria Theresa, weakened by smallpox and age, bowed to this logic. Within days of Maria Josepha's passing, she instructed her ambassador to Spain to inform Charles III of the sad demise of the promised Austrian daughter-in-law and to raise secretly the possibility of his accepting one of the dead girl's sisters in her place. She herself wrote to the king that, "As I certainly have no less anxiety to ally my house to that of your Majesty than that which your Majesty is good enough to display to me, I grant with great pleasure one of the daughters remaining to me to repair the loss of her we regret. I have now two who might be suitable, the Archduchess Amalie, who is considered pretty, and whose health appears to promise a numerous succession [Maria Theresa was clearly pushing him toward this choice as she considered Maria Amalia, who was sophisticated and mature, to be far more suited to sit on a prestigious throne like Naples than gauche Maria Carolina]; the other is the Archduchess Charlotte, who has also very good health and is about a year and seven months younger than the King of Naples. I leave your Majesty at liberty to choose," she concluded. Charles III didn't care, but his son did; Ferdinand, discovering that Maria Amalia was an old woman of twenty-two, declined to marry a princess so advanced in years, and petitioned his father to give him the younger archduchess instead.★

Charlotte might have been unpolished, but she wasn't stupid. The 100 splendid dresses notwithstanding—no use wasting a perfectly good trousseau—she wanted no part of the king of Naples. (And she didn't even hear the bit about the mock funeral procession.) "The young Princess, little more than fifteen years of age, terrified at the recent death of her two sisters, expressed the greatest repugnance to espouse a Prince whose alliance seemed to be fatal to the Austrian family," the English chronicler, who clearly thought she had a point, revealed. But although Charlotte pleaded to be allowed to remain, she was without power or resources—what can the daughter of a great prince expect?—and her fate was sealed. "The Empress her mother's firmness, sustained by Prince Kaunitz's reasons and exhortations, surmounted, however, her opposition," the chronicler noted.

On April 17, 1768, just six months after the shocking death of her sister Maria Josepha, a frightened and forlorn Charlotte was married by proxy to the king of Naples and bundled off for Italy that very day. She did not even have the solace of the company of her older brother Joseph on the journey, although he promised to come visit her the following year. The one benefit to come out of the smallpox devastation was that Maria Theresa was finally convinced to give inoculation a try, and Joseph was set on remaining in Vienna to witness the experiment. A Dutch physician known to be an expert in the field had been invited to Vienna, and Charlotte's younger brothers, Ferdinand and Maximilian, as well as the emperor's own six-year-old daughter, Little Theresa, were going to receive the treatment.

★ It was later reported that, when news of Maria Josepha's death was broken in Naples, Ferdinand was upset, not because he had lost his bride, but because the court went into mourning and he was not allowed to go out hunting that day. To put their sovereign in a better humor, his servants organized a diversion: one of them, a good-looking, delicate young man, spotted his face with chocolate (to look like smallpox), donned a bridal gown, and lay down on a funeral bier; the others then raised him up and pantomimed a burial procession, parading around Ferdinand's favorite palace of Portici, with the young king, now appropriately amused, leading the way as the chief mourner.

Joseph did not wish to be away from his child until she was safely through it.*

So Charlotte was sent off with a suitable entourage, a long letter of advice from her mother, and a lady-in-waiting as a companion. The fifteen-year-old's distress was palpable. Maria Carolina had been brought up as strictly and chastely as though in a convent; the only boys she knew were her brothers. She, who just the previous year had spent her time playing with her twelve-year-old sister, would now be obliged to engage in bewilderingly adult acts of intimacy in order to please a husband she had never met.

Unfathomable that Maria Theresa, who had herself held out for love, would allow this. It demonstrates just how completely her office, the wars, and perhaps even her own disappointment with her marriage had hardened her. No doubt she told herself that it was all for the best; that by elevating Charlotte to the Neapolitan throne she was providing her daughter with a brilliant career. But on some level she must have had misgivings about consigning Maria Carolina to the care of so feckless a husband, because she furnished her, not with an escape clause—there was no escape—but with what might be considered a lifeline. In a gesture that was totally out of character, Maria Theresa had it written into the marriage contract that if Charlotte provided the king of Naples with a male heir, she would be given a seat on his council.

But this must have been of small consolation to her weeping daughter, who clung to her family, and particularly to her little sister, Marie Antoinette, as though to life, until at last she was pried away with a final embrace and ushered into the stately carriage that would ferry her out into the narrow streets of Vienna and, from there, south to Italy.

---

* The inoculations proved to be such a success that Maria Theresa was completely won over. She kept the specialist on to train the local physicians and paid for sixty-five children of poor parents to be vaccinated, to promote the remedy among the citizenry. Little Theresa wrote to her great-grandfather, Louis XV, "Knowing that you love me, dear grandpapa, I assure you that I am astonishingly well. I had only fifty pocks, which give me great pleasure."

11

Queen of Naples

~⊱~

Leave your husband alone as little as possible. For the small constraint or boredom that you will feel at first, you will be rewarded by the peace that you will enjoy for all the rest of your life.

—Maria Theresa to Maria Carolina

IT WAS A LONG JOURNEY, but the bridal procession made excellent progress. On April 29, 1768, less than two weeks after leaving Vienna, Charlotte reached Florence, home to her brother Leopold, grand duke of Tuscany, and his family.

Leopold was by this time an experienced married man of twenty-one. He and his wife, Maria Luisa (older sister of Maria Carolina's intended, Ferdinand), had not yet been wedded three years, but they had already produced two children, including, just a short time earlier, on February 12, a son whom the couple had named Francis. Word of the successful delivery of a prince in Florence had come to Vienna late in the evening, and Maria Theresa had been so excited to hear of the birth of a grandson, the first in the family, that she ran out of her bedroom in her dressing gown to the palace theater, where she interrupted the performance in progress to announce the news. "Poldel [the family nickname for Leopold] has a boy!" she hollered at the audience, leaning out over the railing of the imperial box. "And, just as a token of remembrance, on my wedding-day; isn't he gallant?" she crowed.

After so many days away from home, Charlotte was very relieved to see a familiar face. Although they had not been particularly close while growing up, she loved and admired this good-looking older brother, who radiated confidence. With Vienna so far away, Leopold would from now on be her nearest relation by some 300 miles. She needed him.

Leopold, to his credit, recognized this, and took his little sister under his wing. He and Maria Luisa kept her for a few days in Florence to show her around, and then escorted her personally to her husband. During this time, Leopold did his best to prepare her for rule. "She is extremely young, and if I may say so, has not been educated to be Queen of Naples," he wrote severely to his mother. "She was never intended for it, and her upbringing was not by any means the best. Frau von Brandis [Charlotte's first governess]... neither gave nor knew how to give all the instruction necessary for her entrance into the world. I can assure you that the Queen [Charlotte] sees all this for herself, and if only she could have remained a year longer with Frau von Lerchenfeld [the new governess] the difference would soon have been apparent."

And so, with his sister clearly in need of counsel, Leopold took it upon himself to school Charlotte on the finer points of sovereignty. As they did not have much time together, it was rather a crash course. Like his elder brother Joseph, with whom he was in regular contact, the grand duke of Tuscany embraced the new, enlightened philosophy promulgated by Denis Diderot and the encyclopedists. He spoke to Maria Carolina of bringing improvements to her subjects' lives through the application of reason and science. He recommended books for her to read and encouraged her to write both to him and to Joseph for advice.

Thus began a correspondence that would last a lifetime. Much later, Charlotte would attest to the value of this tutelage. "I learned many languages, including Greek and Latin; I studied literature and philosophy with my German siblings, Joseph and Leopold; and I became open-minded, strong spirited, and desired like my brothers those reforms that...increased the power of the principality," she wrote simply.

But of course, there was only so much Leopold could do on the short journey before delivering the young bride to her husband, particularly as the closer they came to Naples, the more anxious Charlotte became. "She is often so agitated that she scarcely knows what she says," Leopold reported back worriedly to Vienna. "She is dreadfully impatient and quick tempered, but it is over directly...Her behavior in public, except a little childishness, is good...everything depends upon the hands into which she falls." Charlotte's mounting distress was palpable in her letters home to Countess von Lerchenfeld, now in charge of Marie Antoinette. "I am well, but my heart is sad, for I am so near the place of my destination," she confessed despondently. "In three days, we shall be at Terracina, where the separation [with her entourage] will take place, and from there it is only nineteen or twenty hours to Caserta. More than ever I long to go back to my fatherland, and see my family and my dear countrymen again. Please tell my sister [Marie Antoinette] that I love her dearly." And again to the governess, "Write to me the smallest details of my sister Antoinette, what she says, what she does, almost what she thinks," Charlotte pleaded. "I beg and entreat you to love her very much, for I am terribly interested for her. All the kindness you show her will be done for me. Believe me, you will work on a ground that will do you credit and increase and augment the reputation you already have."

But time has no pity; it marches forward relentlessly. The three days passed and Maria Carolina, almost in hysterics, was made to say goodbye to her lady-in-waiting and the rest of her suite, as they would not be following her into Naples. Only Leopold (who feared she would collapse) and Maria Luisa continued on with her into her new realm.

The three of them arrived at the town of Portella, just across the border, on May 12, 1768, and found the king of Naples waiting for them. Less than two years older than Charlotte, Ferdinand was a gawky teenager, skinny and lanky; Joseph (who, as promised, visited early the following year) reported him as standing about five foot seven inches tall, with a large nose, dirty hands, and a great deal of dark, unkempt hair. Charlotte barely had time to be introduced — protocol demanded that she drop into a low curtsy and kiss the king's hand, after which he raised her up — before Ferdinand bundled her into yet another carriage and jumped in beside her for the long drive to the royal palace of Caserta, the court's official residence. The grand duke and duchess of Tuscany, who had been invited to attend the wedding and spend a few days, followed in a separate coach. Maria Carolina thus had the opportunity to become acquainted with her future lord and master while jostling along in the privacy of a confined space over a prolonged period of time. The experience does not seem to have relieved her mind.

Some twelve hours later, the bridal party arrived at Caserta and was met by a small group of high-ranking Neapolitan officials, courtiers, and foreign dignitaries. Ferdinand and Maria Carolina were wed that very evening by candlelight at a midnight ceremony in the palace chapel. The bride was pale but composed. She knew her duty.

The marriage was apparently consummated immediately. It is clear that Charlotte, too young for the act, felt shamed and violated. "I tell you plainly that I would rather die than suffer what I suffered at first," the new queen of Naples would later observe of her honeymoon in a letter home to her governess. "Now it is all right, therefore I can say, and it is no exaggeration, if Religion had not said to me, 'Think of God,' I should have killed myself, and that to live a week seemed to me like hell, and I wanted to die."

The groom's reaction to his wedding night was somewhat less emotional. "She sleeps like a corpse and sweats like a sow," Ferdinand apprised his household the next morning.★

And so began Maria Carolina's new life in Naples.

★ Poor Charlotte. I'd have feigned sleep too.

*   *   *

THE REALM THAT CHARLOTTE had married into, which encompassed everything south of Rome plus the island of Sicily and for this reason was also referred to as the Kingdom of the Two Sicilies, was one of the most desirable in Europe. As queen, Maria Carolina now reigned over more than 4 million subjects, representing a quarter of the entire population of Italy. The capital city of Naples alone boasted more than 400,000 citizens, which made it the third-largest metropolis in Europe, right behind London and Paris. By contrast, Tuscany, where her brother Leopold exercised his authority, could claim just over a million inhabitants, with Florence home to a mere 80,000 people.

But it wasn't its size that set the kingdom apart; it was its exotic locale and undeniable exuberance. Famous for its still-active volcano, Vesuvius, as well as for its archaeological ruins (not to mention its sunny beaches and ubiquitous ice cream parlors), the capital city of Naples was considered a must-see, along with Paris and Rome, by the flood of wealthy European culture-seekers who gadded about on what was known as the Grand Tour. Even the celebrated Goethe, a sophisticated observer, was seduced by the charms of this southern realm. "Naples at first sight leaves a free, cheerful, and lively impression," he wrote. "Numberless beings are passing and repassing each other...Let man talk, describe, and paint as he may—to be here is more than all. The shore, the creeks, and the bay, Vesuvius, the city, the suburbs, the castles, the atmosphere!...Naples is a paradise: in it every one lives in a sort of intoxicated self-forgetfulness. It is so even with me: I scarcely know myself," he confessed in awe.

So illustrious a realm naturally demanded the luxury of a suitably impressive royal residence, preferably one out of range of both Mount Vesuvius's deadly eruptions and cannon fire from any hostile gunship that might wander into the capital's harbor. For these reasons, the grand palace of Caserta, still under construction when Charlotte was married, had been chosen as the seat of the monarchy. Caserta was located on a plain 16 miles inland from the city of

Naples. There had been nothing much there when Ferdinand's father had purchased the property a decade earlier, but this had not stopped the king from sending to Rome for the most renowned architect in Italy; supplying him with the finest materials and an army of artisans, carpenters, craftsmen, and laborers; and charging him with the task of building a new royal estate based upon a single, overriding aesthetic concept: to outdo Versailles.

The architect took his sovereign's directive to heart and produced blueprints for a palatial mansion whose dimensions swelled beyond those of the Sun King's at every possible corner and in all directions. The château of Caserta contained more rooms than Versailles; its salons were larger; its five-story elevation higher; it boasted more columns, arches, and statues per square foot; even the grand marble staircase was wider and more imposing than its French counterpart (making it a somewhat daunting climb for all but the most athletic). True, there was no hall of mirrors—the blazing sun of Naples needed no magnification—but there was a riot of ornamentation: "The interior of this palace contains precious marbles, statues, and pictures by the most celebrated sculptors and painters of the age; inlaid woods, works in stucco, crystals, frescoes, and pavements of marble and mosaic, besides rare stones," raved a chronicler of the period. "It is surrounded on three sides by squares or enclosures, and facing the fourth, stretches an extensive garden, nobly adorned with obelisks, statues, marble steps, and copious fountains ornamented with figures; a stream falling suddenly from a height, and then more gradually until it spreads out into a lake."

The position of that dazzling stream was no accident. Caserta lacked a sufficient natural water supply to support a royal residence, so one had to be created. In what was undoubtedly the architect's most remarkable achievement, a monumental stone conduit based on a Roman model, set high in the mountains and spanning over 20 miles of terrain, was erected to collect and transfer water from the upper elevations to the lowlands. It had taken almost twelve years, but the project was finally nearing completion by the time Charlotte arrived, and the benefit to the surrounding acreage was undeniable. Goethe, arriving some years later, testified to the lushness of the palace of Caserta's grounds: "The site is uncommonly fine, on one of the most fertile plains in the world, and yet the gardens trench on the mountains," he wrote in wonder. "From these an aqueduct brings down an entire river to supply water to the palace and the district; and the whole can, on occasion, be thrown on some artificially arranged rocks, to form a glorious cascade. The gardens are beautifully laid out, and suit well with a district which itself is thought a garden."

This was the view to which Charlotte awoke each morning; this the palace of which she was mistress. There was nothing in Vienna to compare to the opulence of her current situation. The Hofburg palace appeared dark and cramped next to the vast majesty of Caserta's ornate rooms, with their soaring ceilings painted in brilliant jewel-like colors, their mosaic and patterned marble floors, their many oversized doors thrown open to let in the light. Even the beloved gardens of Schönbrunn, where she had so recently spent her summers, could not compete with the magnificent waterfall and charming panoramic vistas. "Placed at the extremity of Italy, and enjoying a delicious climate, upon shores to which the Romans retired when conquerors of the world, to partake of luxuries not to be attained in any other quarter, and which still are covered with the remains of Roman magnificence or Grecian splendor—Ferdinand had such means of happiness as rarely fall to the lot of mortals," a visiting English baroness commented thoughtfully. And what was Ferdinand's was now Charlotte's.

IT DID NOT TAKE the new queen of Naples long to penetrate the flaws in her husband's education and character. "He is very ugly but one gets used to that," she noted soon after her marriage. "What irritates me most is that he thinks he is handsome and clever, and he is neither the one nor the other."

What he was was infantile. At seventeen, he still played with puppets and toy soldiers. He deposited marmalade in his guests' hats and laughed when they put them on and the jam slid down their faces or got stuck in their hair. Nothing made him happier than to roughhouse with his servants; they knew to fall down in a dramatic manner at his slightest touch. When he went hunting he put the dead birds in his pockets. He kept rats and mice in cages in the palace and let them out to torment people, running after any women present and throwing the rodents at them. He needed to be constantly amused, even to go to the bathroom. Joseph, who visited in the spring of 1769 when Ferdinand was eighteen, reported this memorable anecdote in a letter home to Vienna: "He begged...to keep him company while he was sitting on the close-stool. I found him on this throne with lowered breeches, surrounded by five or six valets, chamberlains, and others. We made conversation for more than half an hour, and I believe he would be there still if a terrible stench had not convinced us that all was over...he even wished to show them to us; and without more ado, his breeches down, he ran with the smelly pot in one hand after two of his gentlemen, who took to their heels. I retired quietly."

It wasn't a lack of intelligence. It was arrested development, brought about by an absence of parental oversight and the sycophantic nature of his court. "He is now what many school-boys are in England at ten years old," reported an English envoy bluntly. Charlotte was not so much a wife as an imported au pair.

But the problems went deeper than just her husband's immaturity. Ferdinand hated to read and wanted nothing to do with ruling. His only administrative responsibility was to write to his father once a week, a task that generally took him less than fifteen minutes, as the letter typically consisted of a few lines boasting about the number of animals he had shot on the prior day's hunt. As a result, his chief minister, Tanucci, ran the government, ostensibly on orders from Charles III in Madrid, but mostly according to his own inclinations. On those rare occasions when the king of Naples was forced to attend a council meeting, he took his cues from Tanucci, agreeing to anything he wanted. Charlotte's husband did not even sign his own government's proclamations; rather, Tanucci had a stamp of the monarch's signature made up and kept it in his office. And the minister's power was not limited to the public sphere. He controlled the king's private life as well. If she and Ferdinand wanted so much as to have dinner in the garden, her husband had to apply for permission from Tanucci in advance.

This state of affairs was quite outside Charlotte's experience. None of *her* brothers would have been allowed to behave like Ferdinand. And as for one of her mother's councillors running the kingdom unsupervised (let alone invading his monarch's private life to the point of telling her where and how she might take her meals), this was unthinkable. The situation obviously required a complete overhaul.

As young as she was, Maria Carolina was nonetheless astute enough to understand that she had to move slowly, that her first task must be to win her husband's love and trust, as nothing could be accomplished if he set himself against her. Luckily, the method by which this might be achieved was clear. Everyone at court knew that Ferdinand responded well to fawning approval. So Charlotte did what countless women before her in similar circumstances have done: she pretended. "I must tell you and confess that I don't love him except from duty but I do all I can to make him think I have a passion for him," Charlotte revealed, again in a letter to her governess. It was clearly tough going in the beginning, especially in the bedroom. "One suffers a martyrdom which is all the worse because one has to always appear pleased," she admitted frankly.

And the dissembling did not end with the sunrise. Maria Theresa, in the voluminous letter she had handed Maria Carolina when she left Vienna, had instructed her daughter to "follow him everywhere, so long as he wishes to have you with him." This meant that Charlotte had to spend nearly every day sitting outside for hours on end tediously admiring the king of Naples as he hunted, rather as a devoted parent would encouragingly cheer on a young child at interminable soccer practices. (Joseph, when he came to visit, observed in disbelief that the deer were enclosed in such a small area that it was an easy matter for the dogs to chase them down, and that larger game, such as boars, were roped by servants and brought to Ferdinand, who then emptied his gun into them. "The King shoots very recklessly, and I believe he would not be too scrupulous about shooting those in his way," the emperor added, making sure to remain at a distance.) In the evenings, to amuse her husband before he went to bed, the queen and other members of the court played games like blindman's buff and hide-and-seek. Joseph, also treated to this favorite entertainment, reported that "Throughout these the King distributes blows and smacks the ladies' behinds without distinction... There is a continuous tussle with the ladies, who are inured to it and throw themselves sprawling on the floor. This never fails to amuse the King, who bursts with uproarious laughter. As he seldom speaks without shouting and has a piercing voice like a shrill falsetto, one can distinguish it among a thousand," the emperor concluded wearily.

There was more: like an annoying little brother, Ferdinand would snatch something Charlotte wanted—an article of clothing, say—and make her hunt for it, only to have her discover later that he had destroyed it. He hated decorum and if pressed into it would sometimes rebel by kicking or shoving those around him who got in his way, even ambassadors and ministers—not with the intention of hurting them (although of course he sometimes did) but merely out of pique. Observing this, Joseph asked Charlotte if Ferdinand beat her, and she admitted that she had received her fair share of blows of this sort but that it wasn't serious. By that time, she was not the least bit intimidated by her spouse. The king, she assured her brother, was neither brutal nor wicked. He simply didn't know better. "He is a right good fool," was the way she characterized her husband.

In fact, she had already secured Ferdinand's ardor and admiration, and knew how to handle him. "He fondled her in my presence very tenderly, even voluptuously," Joseph noted. The king of Naples was proud to be married to such a comely young consort, which lofty sentiment was evidenced by his attempts to get her to wear lower-cut gowns to show off her breasts. He did not view Charlotte's intelligence and strength as a threat, because she had succeeded in convincing him that they were entirely in his service. As a result, he felt that her quick wit, good manners, and superior education reflected well on him. "My wife knows everything," he boasted to the court.

No, the problem was not with her husband but with his minister. Tanucci, used to being able to manipulate Ferdinand by threatening to tattle on him to his father if he did not comply with his policies, regarded Maria Carolina as a potential rival. "He is a Tartuffe," Joseph warned her bluntly after interviewing the Neapolitan official at length. "Outwardly humble and punctilious in unimportant matters that might rouse comment, but otherwise a scoundrel...making trouble between father and son, flattering both and muffling them in the ignorance which serves his ends."

Considering the distance he had come, Joseph's visit was quite short—it lasted only nine days—but this was more than enough for the emperor, who couldn't wait to get away from his brother-in-law. Maria Carolina (who couldn't escape so easily) cried copiously at his departure, causing Ferdinand, ever the irksome juvenile, to taunt her by parodying her sobs, so Joseph's final act before leaving was to scold the king of Naples and remind him to be more sensitive to his wife's feelings.

Still, the emperor had seen enough to know that Charlotte had recovered her sense of balance, and with it her strength and purpose. In less than a year, his sister had demonstrated her resourcefulness and was doing what she could to take control of her situation. "The King...even if he had not been neglected in the past, could never have reached distinction...But I do not foresee that he will deteriorate and my sister is satisfied," Joseph wrote reassuringly to Maria Theresa soon after he left. "She [Maria Carolina], dazzled by the grandeur of the Court, the honors paid her, the beauty of the country and the freedom she enjoys, will become ever more accustomed to it, and I am quite at ease about her fate," he predicted confidently.

★　　★　　★

JOSEPH'S ASSESSMENT PROVED to be accurate. Her husband's short-comings notwithstanding, within two years, Charlotte blossomed from an unhappy, homesick adolescent into a vibrant, self-assured young woman, easily inhabiting her role as gracious sovereign of a magnificent court.

It helped enormously that, at least in the beginning, her duties were for the most part ceremonial. Naples was a party town. Her subjects, from the highest-born nobleman to the fishmonger, expected to be regaled regularly with brilliance and spectacle, and the queen, young, high-spirited, and eager to experience the sort of nightlife and grand fêtes she had begged to see but had been generally excluded from attending at home in Vienna, was happy to oblige. Whereas her mother had deemed Maria Carolina too immature to attend even her siblings' weddings, as queen Charlotte now hosted lavish masked balls that lasted until dawn; frequented all the most fashionable houses; added royal glamour to concerts and theatrical performances; and received and charmed the many foreign scholars, statesmen, and socialites who flocked to her southern Italian king-dom (tourism from Great Britain alone accounted for an influx of some £50,000 annually to Naples). One of these visitors, an En-glishwoman who was introduced to the queen on January 25, 1771, when Maria Carolina was eighteen, penned a vivid description of her in a letter to a friend that demonstrates just how far Charlotte had come from the sobbing fifteen-year-old who had spent her first weeks of marriage dramatically contemplating suicide. "Her Maj-esty is a beautiful woman, she has the finest and most transparent complexion I ever saw," the traveler declared. "Her hair is of that glossy light chestnut I so much admire...her eyes are large, brilliant, and of a dark blue, her eyebrows exact, and darker than her hair, her nose inching to the aquiline, her mouth small, her lips very red... her teeth beautifully white and even, and when she smiles she dis-covers two dimples, which throw a finishing sweetness over her whole countenance; her shape is perfect," she continued, enthralled.

221

"She is a beauty so much to my taste that I must say no more of her person...lest that should fill up too much of my paper." The English lady was rather less impressed with Ferdinand. "Do not expect a description of the King's person," she advised her correspondent. "Suffice it to say, he is not *so handsome* as his Queen."

That evening's festivity was a dress ball in the palace theater, to which the visitor was gratified to discover she was also invited. "None but such as the Queen esteems proper to receive and converse with...are ever admitted; and there are many of the Neapolitan nobility, even to the ranks of dukes, who can only see the ball from the upper boxes," she gossiped. Charlotte led the dancing, and chose her own partners; then, "At twelve, the Queen unmasks, as do all the company in the same moment...all the courtiers crowd about her on their knees to kiss her hands, which she lends on each side in the most gracious manner." Dinner was served; the feast began with "macaroni, cheese, and butter...the rest of the supper consisted of various dishes of fish, ragouts, game, fried and baked meats, perigord pies, boars-heads, etc. The dessert was formed into pyramids...of sweetmeats, biscuits, iced-chocolate, and a great variety of iced-fruits, creams, etc. The Queen ate of two things only, which were prepared particularly for her by her German cooks." Afterward, the crowd repaired to yet another of the palace's grand salons for after-dinner drinks: "This room is furnished like the coffee-houses of Paris precisely," the Englishwoman marveled. "The walls covered with shelves, on which are placed all kinds of liqueurs and Greek wines. Here are tables, behind which stand young men in white waistcoats and caps, who make and serve the coffee and other refreshments, of which there is a profusion."

And the gaiety wasn't limited to the confines of the royal palace of Caserta. All of Naples was invited to gawk at the stunning parade of luxury horse-drawn carriages, the queen's included, that rolled regularly down one of the capital's main thoroughfares, known as the Corso. "Here the Neapolitans display a magnificence that amazes strangers," the Englishwoman confided to her friend. "The coaches are painted, gilt, and varnished so admirably, as to exceed by many degrees in beauty the finest in Paris: they are lined with velvet or satin, fringed with gold or silver. The Neapolitan horses are the most beautiful I ever saw...their harness is as brilliant as it is possible to make it," she reported. "I shall only mention one set, by which you may judge of others: the whole was made of blue silk and silver...on their heads, [the horses] bore white ostrich feathers and artificial flowers...I could not but reflect on the infinite pains and labor the dressing such a number of horses requires...we have frequently seen on the Corso from four to six hundred carriages...Need I add, that the ladies who are conveyed in these superb coaches are covered with jewels and the finest cloths."

But the highlight of the Neapolitan social scene was undoubtedly its virtuoso musical productions. Italian opera was, quite simply, the envy of Europe. In recognition of this, before he had left to become king of Spain, Charles III had built a stupendous new theater, the Teatro di San Carlo, right in the heart of the capital. Its state-of-the-art interior design, combined with a brilliant company, which numbered some ninety musicians, instantly vaulted the performances at the San Carlo to the rank of the transcendent. The visiting English-woman could not praise the experience enough to her friend. "The theater is amazingly vast," she wrote. "There are six ranges of boxes...hung with silk, agreeable to the taste of their owners... The front of each range is faced with looking glass...the glasses being uncovered, produce an effect, which at first view persuades you that all is enchantment. The lights, the company, the stage, are reflected from side to side, and consequently so often multiplied, that it confounds a spectator," she thrilled. "The royal box makes a superb appearance, particularly when the Queen is present, at which time the ladies belonging to the court, and others, are full dressed, and covered with a profusion of jewels, but the Queen outshines them all, not only in magnificence of dress...but in a style of beauty, and gracefulness of air, peculiar to herself...For the first time in my life, I was sensible, that it is possible for a number of musicians to fill each his part with such precision and accuracy, that the whole harmony shall produce one perfect sound, as if one soul or mind guided all. Music here is the highest perfection," she concluded passionately.

Small wonder, then, that between the hordes of bowing, adoring courtiers, the rich clothes, the plentiful jewels (as was customary, at the time of her marriage, Ferdinand had presented her with a strong-box stuffed with precious gems), the fast carriages, and the magical theatrical evenings, Charlotte had warmed to her new realm! It helped that Ferdinand, too, seems to have become somewhat more tractable under her watchful influence. She now routinely referred to him as her "dear husband" in all of her correspondence. It is even possible that Maria Carolina had come to believe that she loved him, as she evinced jealousy whenever the king was unfaithful (which was regularly). Casanova, whose profession as lackluster gambler and seducer of inappropriate conquests forced him to move around a great deal, happened also to be in Naples at this time and so was present when one of his friends, the Chevalier Gondar, a confidence man who had married a beautiful young Irishwoman (formerly a barmaid) and introduced her into Neapolitan high society as a great lady, was suddenly exiled from the kingdom by royal decree.★ "This stroke came from the Queen, who found out that the King met Madame Gondar secretly," Casanova reported in his memoirs. "She [Charlotte] found her royal husband laughing heartily at a letter which he would not show her. The Queen's curiosity was excited, and at last the King gave in, and her Majesty read the following: *I will wait for you in the same place, at the same hour, and with the same impatience as a cow desiring the bull's approach.* 'What infamy!' cried the Queen, and Her Majesty gave the cow's husband to understand that

---

★ Gondar had gotten into Maria Carolina's good graces in the first place by pretending that his wife, Sara, was a Protestant whom he then claimed to have convinced to become a disciple of Rome. The queen was so pleased that she stood sponsor to Madame Gondar at her conversion ceremony. "The amusing part in all this was that Sara, being an Irishwoman, had been born a Catholic, and had never ceased to be one," Casanova noted.

in three days he would have to leave Naples, and look for bulls in other countries," Casanova observed.

But Neapolitan high society wasn't simply about soirees and swindlers (although it did seem to have had more than its fair share of these). There was also a small but vibrant intellectual community of accomplished scholars, scientists, economists, and naturalists to whose company Charlotte gravitated, chiefly through the influence of one man: the British ambassador to the court of Naples, Sir William Hamilton.

Hamilton embodied much that was admirable in the British character. A fellow of the Royal Society, a trustee of the British Museum, and an enthusiastic sponsor of artists, scientists, and explorers, he was a gifted archaeologist and antiquarian in his own right. Endlessly curious, he spent his free time trekking up Mount Vesuvius, taking close atmospheric and geological measurements, sometimes to his own peril; uncovering and excavating ancient ruins; composing treatises on Greek and Roman pottery; and collecting fine porcelain. His energy and breadth of interests were prodigious; he was unique among the diplomatic circle surrounding the court. People were drawn to him, and the queen was one of them. "Mr. Hamilton was a genius," Casanova reported simply.

It helped that both Joseph and Leopold knew and approved of Sir William, but Charlotte would likely have sought him out anyway — she had a serious side to her nature to which the erudite ambassador appealed. By the time she was eighteen, Maria Carolina had found a way to wriggle out of the endless hours she had formerly felt compelled to spend watching Ferdinand hunt, and she devoted much of her newfound leisure time to more intellectual pursuits. Toward this end, she had the palatine library at Caserta — a fine collection of volumes for which her husband patently had no use — moved to a spacious apartment attached to her rooms, which was then organized under her supervision. It was thus that she developed the custom of reading daily (barring illness or trauma), a habit that she kept up for the rest of her life.

Never was an envoy more successful at promoting his country's influence simply by being who he was than Sir William Hamilton. He was a walking advertisement for England. Through the ambassador, Maria Carolina became familiar with many of his countrymen, and gained an appreciation for the British that her mother had never developed.* She began to host salons to which she invited both visiting dignitaries of Hamilton's acquaintance and prominent Neapolitan legal scholars, philosophers, and poets, to further the interchange of culture and ideas and to foster cooperation. She identified Hamilton and England as effective counterpoints to the stifling Spanish influence as represented by Tanucci, and in an attempt to chip away at the minister's power, praised the English ambassador to her husband and encouraged social interaction between the two. This of course meant hunting, and since Hamilton was himself an enthusiastic sportsman willing to spend whole days shooting and spearing with Ferdinand, he soon took primacy with the king over all other envoys. "No foreign Minister, not even the *family* ambassadors of France and Spain resident there, enjoyed in so eminent a degree the favor or affection of His Sicilian Majesty," affirmed a visiting chronicler.

Tanucci, confident of his hold over Ferdinand and his value to Madrid, paid little attention to Maria Carolina. Contemptuous of females in general—"Women at Court are the very devil," he opined, "envious, irascible, and intolerant"—he made only the most unctuous attempts to disarm her and, when these failed, ignored her outright. To Tanucci, the queen's suggestions and criticisms were as inconsequential as she was, an attitude that was exacerbated by Charlotte's frustrating slowness to conceive. A year went by, then two, then three, and still the royal couple remained childless. Ferdinand fretted openly about his wife's puzzling infertility, and Maria Theresa in Vienna was no less worried: she knew that her daughter's inability

---

* Not everyone was pleased by the invasion of British tourists into the capital. "The English are like a flock of sheep," Casanova grumbled. "They follow each other about, always go to the same place, and never care to show any originality."

to produce an heir undermined her legitimacy as queen. Tanucci perceived it, too, and throughout this period remained smugly in control.

It took until she was nearly nineteen, but finally, on June 6, 1772, Maria Carolina was delivered of her first child—a daughter whom the couple named Maria Theresa after the queen's mother (because clearly there weren't enough Maria Theresas in the imperial family already). And then, as though to cement this triumph, a mere thirteen months later, on July 27, came yet another delivery. Although disappointingly, this infant, too, was a girl—Maria Luisa—the fact that Charlotte had given birth to two healthy children in a row at least settled the question of whether she was capable of reproduction.

At last, on January 6, 1775, at the age of twenty-two, to great rejoicing, Maria Carolina was successfully brought to bed of a son and heir, whom she and her husband named Carlos, after Ferdinand's father. The queen of Naples wasted no time: she was barely back on her feet before she claimed the seat on the royal council that had been stipulated to her as a condition of her marriage contract.

And that's when everything changed.

Marie Antoinette

...at the age of twelve

12

The Little One

You are the luckiest of all your sisters and of all princesses.
—Maria Theresa to Marie Antoinette

MARIE ANTOINETTE WAS BORN on November 2, 1755. Just a year earlier, an overeager American colonial had exceeded his orders and opened fire on a sleeping French reconnaissance unit, rekindling hostilities between England and France. The crisis had driven Maria Theresa into a treaty with Louis XV, arranged surreptitiously through Madame de Pompadour. Thus, it could be argued that, since both her youngest daughter and the Austrian-French alliance came into being at more or less the same moment in history, it was George Washington who put Marie Antoinette on the throne of France.

Toinette, as she was nicknamed (although she was also often referred to simply as "the little one"), was her mother's fifteenth child and youngest daughter.* She was exceptionally pretty, all big blue eyes, blond curls, and merry disposition, not unlike Maria Theresa herself as a young girl. Marie Antoinette was her father's favorite: Francis loved the sweet smiles and adorable prattle of this last baby girl, and indulged her affectionately. Of all his children, she

---

* She was christened Maria Antonia. As this was subsequently changed to the much more familiar "Marie Antoinette" when she moved to France, rather than change her name midway through the chapter and risk confusion, I have elected to call her by her French name throughout.

most resembled him, not so much in looks as in nature—she was highly social and at her best in company (and, like him, somewhat less successful in the schoolroom). There is a charming account of a gathering at Schönbrunn on October 13, 1762, just three weeks before Marie Antoinette's seventh birthday, when a pint-sized musical prodigy by the name of Wolfgang Amadeus Mozart was invited to entertain the imperial family. As the visiting musician was himself just six years old, all of Maria Theresa's children, even those in the younger group, were allowed to attend the performance. Mozart immediately won the heart of the empress by leaping onto her lap and giving her a kiss. Francis was similarly captivated, calling the boy "the little sorcerer" when he responded to a teasing dare of the emperor's by effortlessly playing the harpsichord with all the keys covered. But it was Marie Antoinette who made the most vivid impression on the small savant who would grow up to become one of the most brilliant composers in history. Unused to the polished floors of the palace, at one point during his audience (which lasted three hours), Mozart slipped and fell. Before he could right himself, winsome little Marie Antoinette ran to him and picked him up. "You *are* good," he exclaimed with a mixture of gratitude and obvious admiration. "I shall marry you!"

She was too young to know it, but this lighthearted encounter was one of her mother's few intervals of levity that fateful year. At the same time that the diminutive Mozart was enthralling Marie Antoinette and her family with his musical parlor tricks, Frederick the Great, having been saved from a crushing defeat by the fortuitous death of Empress Elizabeth, was busy retaking Silesia and Dresden, and a shattered Maria Theresa understood that the war into which she had poured all her hopes, and the horrors of which she had inflicted on her loyal subjects for the past six years, was irretrievably lost. Small wonder, then, that the emperor and empress sought to divert themselves with children whose innocent antics made for such a refreshing contrast to the cares of adult life. It was soon after the Mozart recital that Maria Christina painted the portrait of her parents at the holiday breakfast table, and there is seven-year-old Marie Antoinette, proudly holding up her new doll, significantly the only younger daughter present, secure in her position as treasured pet of the family.

This she remained through the heartache of the next few years, which included the loss of first her sister Maria Johanna, nearly twelve to Marie Antoinette's seven, and then her brother Joseph's first wife, Isabella, both to smallpox, when she was eight. In those dark days, Marie Antoinette's ready laugh, bright little face, and affectionate demeanor gladdened her parents' hearts. She was a darling, uncomplicated child, existing entirely on the surface, and these qualities were rewarded with adult approval.

Her mother, it is true, intimidated her—Maria Theresa was the disciplinarian in the family—but her easygoing father softened the rigor imposed by the empress, and Marie Antoinette worshipped him. On the hot July morning in 1765 that her parents and older siblings left Vienna to travel to Innsbruck in preparation for her brother Leopold's wedding—the younger children, as usual, being left behind—with everyone already ensconced in their carriages ready to go, Francis, much to Maria Theresa's irritation, insisted on holding up the entire procession until nine-year-old Marie Antoinette could be brought out to him for a last tender embrace. "I longed to kiss that child," Francis explained, by way of excuse for the delay. His daughter never saw him again. Her mother returned from that fateful journey a broken, black-clad widow, but the little one would remember this final testament of her father's love for the rest of her life.

FOR THE NEXT TWO YEARS, like her next-eldest sister, Maria Carolina, with whom she spent most of her time, Marie Antoinette floated just outside the periphery of her mother's attention and so was allowed the freedom of a relatively carefree childhood. These were the days of the lax first governess, whose directives were so effortlessly evaded; of hours spent giggling and pretending with Charlotte; of picnics and playing in the garden. Unlike her clever sister, however, who liked to read and found her lessons tedious because they were too simplistic, Marie Antoinette had neither the discipline nor the aptitude for scholarship. Her attention span was extremely limited; she disliked reading; she had not the focus even to learn to form her letters properly. As her mother demanded to see all of her written schoolwork, this presented a problem until her governess settled upon the happy expedient of first composing Marie Antoinette's papers for her in pencil, after which her disinterested pupil would dutifully trace over the markings in ink.

Then came the fateful autumn of 1767, and with it the death of Maria Josepha and the hurried substitution of Maria Carolina as the sacrificial bride of the puerile king of Naples. By the summer of 1768, Marianne having already gone into the Church, there were only three unmarried archduchesses left in Vienna: twenty-five-year-old Maria Elisabeth (whose Sardinian suitor had backed out due to the rumors of the ravishment of her face), twenty-two-year-old Maria Amalia (still in love with the penniless prince of Zweibrücken), and twelve-year-old Marie Antoinette. And for these three potential brides there were two realms that Maria Theresa was absolutely determined to marry into: Parma, to return the duchy to Austrian interest and thereby recover her inheritance in Italy; and France, to secure the alliance that was the great work of her reign and ensure a lasting peace with what had for centuries been the empire's foremost antagonist.

But as much as she—urged on by Joseph and especially her principal minister, Count Kaunitz (upon whom she relied even more heavily, if that was possible, after Francis's death)—pressed the French for a firm marriage commitment between the dauphin and Marie Antoinette, Louis XV, while not opposing the idea in principle, nonetheless did nothing to promote it, either. Since the death of Madame de Pompadour in 1764, the king of France had become even more indolent, preferring to occupy himself with his new mistress, Madame du Barry, a former streetwalker-turned-courtesan, rather than apply himself to the business of government or foreign policy.

Then, on June 24, 1768, the queen of France, Louis's long-suffering wife of forty-three years, died. She left behind four adult daughters, all of whom deeply resented Madame du Barry. These princesses, having never been espoused, resided at Versailles. Determined to prevent the humiliation of having their father's vulgar, déclassé mistress replace their mother at court, they came up with the happy solution that fifty-eight-year-old Louis XV honor his marital commitment to Austria not by wedding his thirteen-year-old grandson, the dauphin, to Marie Antoinette but rather by taking one of her older sisters as a new wife for himself. When Louis pronounced himself amenable to this option (his one stipulation being that the bride in question be young and beautiful), they suggested Maria Elisabeth, whom they clearly knew only by her pre-smallpox reputation.

If this dubious last-minute gambit had succeeded, there is a slim chance (although still very unlikely) that Marie Antoinette might have sidestepped destiny and gone to Parma, where she was exactly the right age and temperament for the duke, and where she could have lived as she liked and been happy, and that Maria Amalia would then have been able to marry for love, as had her sister Maria Christina. But Louis was suspicious and sent a portrait painter to Vienna; the artist confirmed the rumors of Maria Elisabeth's ruined complexion. In a clear win for Madame du Barry, he gave up on the idea of remarriage altogether and instead officially agreed to a wedding between Marie Antoinette and the dauphin. On June 4, 1769, the king of France affirmed the glad tidings to Maria Theresa by means of a personal letter: "Madame my Sister and Cousin," Louis wrote. "I can not delay much longer...the satisfaction which I feel about the forthcoming union which we are going to form by the marriage of the Archduchess to the Dauphin, my grandson...This new tie will more and more unite our two houses. If your Majesty approves, I think that the marriage [by proxy] should take place in Vienna soon after next Easter...I shall do here what I can, and so will the Dauphin, to make the Archduchess Antoinette happy," he assured her graciously.

And it was at this point that the fates of Maria Theresa's two older unattached daughters were sealed. Having run out of nominees— *somebody* had to marry the duke of Parma—Maria Amalia, much against her will, was volunteered for the position.* To ensure that there was no backsliding, Joseph himself escorted his sister south to Italy, where, on July 19, 1769, she married Isabella of Parma's eighteen-year-old brother, whose maturity was on par with that of his cousin the king of Naples, and who subsequently proceeded to be overshadowed in every way by his unhappy, resentful bride. Maria Elisabeth, sentenced by the rejection of the French king to spinsterhood and ultimately, like Marianne, the Church, was even more distraught than Maria Amalia when the news was broken to her. "She began to sob...[saying] that all [the others] were established and she alone was left behind and destined to remain alone with the Emperor [Joseph], which is what she will never do," Maria Theresa confided in consternation to a friend. "We had great difficulty in silencing her."

But maternal distress over her older daughters' wretchedness was offset by Maria Theresa's satisfaction with her youngest's good fortune. The kingdom of France, home to some 20 million subjects, was considered the apex of eighteenth-century civilization. True, England's navy was the envy of the world, and London might excel at finance and trade, but Paris was universally acknowledged to be the cultural and intellectual center of Europe, and Versailles was still the model for sovereign splendor. Any woman who ascended the throne of France would be responsible for maintaining the exalted prestige of a monarchy that traced its venerable roots to

---

* It has been postulated that Maria Theresa forced this marriage on Maria Amalia because she was her least favorite daughter, but there is no evidence of this. It was simply a matter, as with Maria Carolina, of restoring Austrian interests in Italy. Poor Maria Elisabeth, who in addition to her scars was pushing twenty-six, was spurned as being too old for the bridegroom.

Charlemagne; she would be an object of envy whose deportment would be emulated both at home and abroad. It therefore came as something of a shock to Maria Theresa when, having removed Marie Antoinette from the care of her old governess and assigned her instead, after the departure of Charlotte, to the more accomplished Countess von Lerchenfeld, it was speedily revealed that not only was the thirteen-year-old future dauphine incapable of communicating gracefully in French, but she struggled even to read and write.

There seemed no choice but to cram as much education into her as possible in the short time remaining before her departure for France. Toward this end, Maria Theresa had her daughter sequestered at Schönbrunn Palace along with a gaggle of instructors, including Viennese experts in music and art, as well as a specially imported Parisian ballet master, for Marie Antoinette required coaching in elegant posture, the mechanics of making an entrance and gliding gracefully across a room, and state-of-the-art curtsying. However, even this wasn't considered good enough for the future wife of the dauphin, so Versailles also sent its own tutor, the abbé Vermond, to ensure that the archduchess was properly educated in French history, language, and literature.

Any middle school teacher will sympathize with the abbé's predicament. He wasn't there two days before he realized that his pupil, while undeniably charming and well-intentioned, was so far behind, and had so many other demands upon her time, that it was going to be impossible to get her to read anything on her own; whatever information she absorbed was going to have to be spoon-fed to her. "After devoting my first instructions to the object of acquainting myself with the turn of mind and the degree of H.R.H.'s [Marie Antoinette's] knowledge, I arranged...the method of learning I considered most useful to Madame the Archduchess," he reported home in his initial communication of June 21, 1769, from Vienna. "In order to diminish the wearisome nature of the studies, I keep them as much as possible to the forms of conversation," he continued tactfully. "I cannot speak highly enough of the docility and good-will of H.R.H., but her liveliness and the frequent distractions militate insensibly against her desire to learn."

Six weeks later he was still gamely pursuing the same strategy, albeit with slightly more desperation. "The Archduchess will say the most obliging things to everyone," he reassured his superiors. "She is cleverer than she was long thought to be. Unfortunately, that ability was subjected to no direction up to the age of twelve. A little idleness and much frivolity rendered my task more difficult...I could not accustom her to get at the root of a subject, although I felt she was very capable of doing so. I fancied I could only get her to fix her attention by amusing her," he admitted. By October 14, 1769, two weeks before Marie Antoinette's fourteenth birthday, he was able to report with evident relief that at least her pronunciation had improved, so that she now "talks French with ease, and fairly well." His optimism in other areas, however, clearly had been worn down in the face of his student's fundamental inability to focus. "She would rarely make mistakes in spelling if she could only give her undivided attention," he burst out in a rare moment of candor. "What is most vexing is that partly through idleness and inattention...she has acquired the habit of writing inconceivably slowly... I often occupy myself with this...but I own that on this point I have made the least progress," he lamented.

But of course the true victim in all this was the prospective bride herself. As yet, Marie Antoinette demonstrated no inclination to rebel against parental authority; her demeanor and temperament remained sweetly obedient; her sole desire was to please the adults surrounding her. It was just that (with the invention of Ritalin still being some 200 years in the future) the effort required was outside her capabilities. Granted, it was unlikely that even under the best of circumstances Marie Antoinette would have developed a taste for serious reading or critical contemplation, but if she had been allowed to continue to receive instruction at home until her later teens she might at least have learned not to shun these occupations so thoroughly. As it was, the principal lesson she came away with from this intensive, months-long course in academics was to regard any time spent on books and intellectual pursuits as a punishment.

While the bride was thus occupied with her studies, preparations for the marriage ceremony and the journey for France progressed diligently. On January 21, 1770, the bejeweled ring sent by the dauphin to formalize the engagement was ceremonially slipped onto Marie Antionette's finger; this milestone was followed three months later, on April 16, by the arrival of the embassy charged with representing the groom's interests at the upcoming festivities. The French ambassador's impressive retinue and equipage included a magnificent, elaborately ornamented carriage, boasting much glass on the outside and satin on the inside, that had been expressly constructed to convey the dauphine to her new home.

Three days of solemn rites and extravagant celebrations followed. There was an evening of theater, with a new ballet written and choreographed by the renowned French master in honor of his student. The next day, Joseph hosted a formal state dinner for 1,500, complete with gold and silver plate, with a gorgeous masked ball and fireworks afterward. Not to be outdone, the French ambassador presided over a similarly brilliant gathering, dazzlingly illuminated by an even showier display of bursting colored rockets and night sparklers. The proxy ceremony itself took place on the evening of April 19, 1770, at the Church of the Augustinian Friars. Marie Antoinette, radiant in a cloth-of-silver gown with a flowing train, was led down the aisle by her mother; her brother Ferdinand, at a year older almost exactly the same age as the dauphin, stood in for the bridegroom. Maria Theresa and Joseph, seated side by side on thrones, presided over the ceremony in their capacity as co-regents. The bride and her brother the surrogate knelt before them; a papal nuncio led the service; the *Te Deum* was sung. And, just like that, the youngest archduchess was married.

It was all so sublime and stirring that Marie Antoinette, who was after all only fourteen, may be forgiven for believing that she had accomplished something wonderful. As dauphine, the little one now outranked all of her sisters, not only the unmarried abbess Marianne and (soon-to-be abbess) Maria Elisabeth but also wealthy Maria Christina and Maria Amalia, both of whom could only claim titles of duchess. Even Maria Carolina, who had achieved royalty, was beneath Marie Antoinette in terms of prestige, as sunny, pleasant Naples could not compete with powerful France. By marrying the heir to the French throne, Marie Antoinette's social position had so vaulted her into the stratosphere that after her wedding day, her only true peers within her own family were Joseph and Maria Theresa herself. With obvious reluctance, her mother acknowledged that Charlotte's standing was sufficient to permit Marie Antoinette to communicate with her closest sister if she so desired. "The Queen of Naples will wish you to write to her. I do not see any objection," was Maria Theresa's grudging concession.

Fourteen is a dangerous age at which to be exposed to adulation. Marie Antoinette was old enough to grasp the mood of seductive glamour, to soak in the exhilaration, but not sufficiently experienced to put it into context, or in this case to see through to its core. She was still highly impressionable, her character far from formed. Her august mother's dictates, reinforced by the splendid parties at which she had been the center of attention, infused her with the sense that she was a superior being, embodying the greatness of France. There is little question that she no sooner walked down that aisle than she believed the hard work was over. She had no idea the job was just beginning.

She left Vienna two days later, on April 21, stepping into her grand new carriage at 9:30 in the morning. The entire town turned out to see her go. "A truly afflicting scene took place," reported an eyewitness. "The people all flew to the way she was to take; and at first their grief was dumb. She appeared; and was seen, her cheeks bathed in tears...now and then putting her head out of the carriage...and making signs of regret and acknowledgement to the truly worthy people, who were pressing in crowds to bid her adieu.

They now no longer answered with silent tears...The avenues as well as the streets of Vienna resounded with their cries; nor did they return home till the last horseman in her suite was out of sight," he concluded sorrowfully.

But what the daughter lacked in acumen, her mother more than made up for in statecraft. Although she had professed herself much pleased by Marie Antoinette's progress under the abbé Vermond's tutelage, Maria Theresa was under no illusions about how unprepared her child was for the pressures and responsibilities she would face as dauphine of France. And she had a further worry: as with the king of Naples, she had had an advance report on the character of Marie Antoinette's new husband, and it was not encouraging. "Nature itself seems to have denied everything to the Dauphin," her spy reported bluntly from Versailles. "This prince, by his expression of countenance and his remarks, exhibits very restricted intelligence, much ungracefulness, and no evidences of feeling...It seemed necessary to inform Y. H. [Your Highness] of details which I shall expose to no one else," he rushed to assure her.

And so, although she had waved goodbye to her daughter that very morning, in a real sense Maria Theresa had no intention of letting her go. She would see to it that Marie Antoinette kept to her studies and behaved with the dignity, decorum, and common sense that her mother expected of her. It was simply a matter of arranging for some long-distance parenting.

Along these lines, she had already planted one of her oldest and most loyal diplomats, the comte de Mercy-Argenteau, as her surrogate at Versailles. A protégé of Count Kaunitz, at forty-eight the comte was practiced in the politics of court life, having formerly served as the Austrian ambassador to both Sardinia and Russia. Transferred to Paris ahead of Marie Antoinette's arrival, he was assigned the task of observing her every move and reporting back by secret messenger to her mother. With the comte de Mercy's highly detailed bulletins in hand, Maria Theresa could then keep herself abreast of everything that was happening at the French court, and so would be in a position to send instructions and recommendations back to him by the same clandestine route. The comte was also empowered to take it upon himself to advise the dauphine if a problem required immediate attention, or if her everyday behavior necessitated improvement or modification. If Marie Antoinette failed to adopt his counsel, Maria Theresa would then take up the matter directly in her personal correspondence with her daughter, and that would be an end to it.

Thus did the dowager empress console herself for having hurried her daughter into a marriage for which she knew she was unprepared. The dauphine, she reasoned, would yet have the benefit of her mother's long years of experience, exactly as if she lived at home. It was perhaps not optimal to have to do this by letter and intermediary, but Marie Antoinette was clearly an obedient girl with a good heart. And with so much combined wisdom to help her, how much trouble could she really get into?

13

Dauphine of France

I cannot understand his [the dauphin's] conduct to his wife;
is it the result of bad principles?
> —Maria Theresa to the comte de Mercy

AS HAD BEEN THE CASE with her sister Maria Carolina, it had been
agreed that Marie Antoinette would bid farewell to her Austrian
entourage at the boundary of her new kingdom and continue alone
to her new life at Versailles. Louis XV's negotiators had been very
specific about this part of the ceremony, emphasizing that the dauphine must rid herself entirely of the trappings of her old life before
being allowed to set foot on French soil; this was the reason they had
provided the carriage in which she traveled. To effect the handoff, a
small edifice consisting of an entrance salon and two smaller rooms
had been hastily constructed in Strasbourg, on the eastern border.
As much of the interior decoration for this temporary structure came
from Paris, it piqued the interest of the local citizenry. By sheer coincidence, Goethe happened to be studying in Strasbourg at exactly
the moment Marie Antoinette was expected; like many others, he
paid a bit of silver to tour the cottage, of which he observed admiringly, "had it been more durably built, it might have answered very
well as a pleasure-house for persons of rank." He found the two side
chambers charming: "Here, for the first time, I saw the specimen of

those tapestries worked after Raphael's cartoons, and this sight was for me of very decided influence, as I became acquainted with the true and the perfect on a large scale, though only in copies," he marveled. (This was before his visit to Naples on the Grand Tour.)

But the learned Goethe was stunned at the reprehensible choice of motif for the main hall. There, the wall hangings, although "larger, more brilliant, and richer," chronicled the story of Jason and Medea, "the most horrible marriage that perhaps was ever consummated," admittedly not the optimum narrative, as the vivid images included a tableau of a bride in the act of being viciously murdered. "It is just the same as if they had sent the most ghastly spectre to meet this beauteous and pleasure-loving lady at the very frontiers!" Goethe sputtered. He was so upset that he made a scene and his friends had to hurry him out of the room. "They then assured me that it was not everybody's concern to look for the significance in pictures; that to themselves, at least, nothing of the sort would have occurred, while the whole population of Strasbourg and the vicinity which was to throng thither, would no more take such crotchets [perverse fancies] into their heads than the queen herself and her court," he recorded, astounded.

In the event, the décor of the salon would prove to be the least of Marie Antoinette's problems that day. Although she had certainly been informed of the specifics of the arrangement with the French, she exhibited no apprehension in advance of the ritual; she seems not to have fully comprehended the indignity to which she was about to be subjected. The immense train of the bridal procession—the dauphine was accompanied by dozens of carriages cumulatively pulled by hundreds of horses—rattled into Strasbourg at noon on May 7, 1770, and, as had happened when she had left Vienna two weeks earlier, the whole town came out to have a look. "I yet remember well the beauteous and lofty mien, as cheerful as it was imposing of this youthful lady," rhapsodized Goethe, whose fascination with celebrity had clearly overcome his artistic reservations. "Perfectly visible to us all in her glass carriage, she seemed to be jesting with her female attendants, in familiar conversation, about the throng that poured forth to meet her train."

Marie Antoinette's fine carriage had no sooner made it through the crowds to the designated site than she was ushered out of the vehicle together with her traveling companions and hurried into one of the smaller rooms of the makeshift way station. This chamber represented the Austrian side of the border; the French entourage that would accompany her to Versailles was waiting for the hand-over in the room opposite, separated by the barrier of the grand salon with its gruesome wall treatments.

There is no question that Marie Antoinette's experience at the border of France was much worse than her sister's had been crossing into Naples. A hysterical Maria Carolina had been made to say goodbye to her lady-in-waiting and the other members of her inner circle, but at least she had been able to do so fully clothed. Marie Antoinette was forced to remove every stitch of her apparel with painstaking slowness as if engaged in a humiliating high-end strip-tease. Only after she was completely naked was she then re-dressed just as deliberately in the garments supplied by the French escort.

It was a stratagem intended to establish social superiority by wounding, and it did its job with admirable efficiency. The shame of the protocol provoked tears, as it would have in brides far older and less trusting than Marie Antoinette. She was still sobbing when her little dog was wrenched from her arms and she was made to bid fare-well to all who represented home and love.

The handover having been successfully accomplished, her French entourage entered the salon and took over. Far from resenting these representatives of her adopted kingdom for subjecting her to such mortification, Marie Antoinette looked to them as her saviors. She flung herself at her first lady-in-waiting, Madame de Noailles, as she would have pressed against her governess in Vienna for comfort. The comtesse, whose task it was to make a future queen out of this weeping mess of a child, narrowed her eyes and began at once. Shrugging off her charge, she curtsied formally and coldly indicated that such familiar behavior was unacceptable in a dauphine. Her tone and action reinforced the idea, so recently brought home by the shame of the undressing, that to be a princess of France was so exquisite, so select an honor, that any trial necessary to secure this transformation was worth the distress.

Maria Carolina had been under no illusions, when she left Vienna, about the sacrifice she was making by marrying Ferdinand. Charlotte had regarded her husband as a burden imposed on her by her mother, Joseph, and Count Kaunitz. She had a strong sense of herself and her heritage and was neither intimidated by nor looking forward to the idea of being queen of Naples. If anything, she dreaded it. "They might as well have thrown [me] into the sea," she had observed bitterly while en route to her new kingdom.

But Marie Antoinette believed everything her mother had told her. She thought she was special and that she was going to the most desirable place on earth, where she would lead a wonderful, charmed existence. Brought up short by Madame de Noailles, she abruptly remembered her good fortune and it helped her to conquer her tears. Her reply demonstrated that, for all of her struggles with her studies, here at least was one lesson in which she would need no further instruction. "Pardon me," she excused herself with all the dignity she could manage. "These are for the family and the fatherland I am leaving; for the future I shall not forget that I am French."

She was as good as her word, and was rewarded for her effort by the obvious adoration of the throngs jostling in the streets for a glimpse of her as she made her way through France. Everywhere she went there were fêtes and fireworks in her honor; adorable children presented her with nosegays; poems were recited, and plays performed for her entertainment; the streets twinkled with lanterns and even the trees were dressed up with ribbons of gold and silver thread so that they might make a good impression. Marie Antoinette's sweet smiles and endearing manner were everywhere applauded, and indeed they were genuine, for who would not be effervescent under such circumstances? It was all exactly as she had been promised.

"Long live the King!" came the cheers wherever she passed. "Long live Madame the Dauphine!"

At last, on May 14, a week after her metamorphosis into French royalty at Strasbourg, she arrived in the forest outside Compiègne, where the dauphin and his grandfather, Louis XV, were waiting to escort her to her new home at Versailles. The results of the months spent training with the renowned French ballet master were instantly and gratifyingly visible. With her head held high, Marie Antoinette, every inch a princess, floated over to the king of France and swept into a curtsy so graceful that even the persnickety comtesse de Noailles could not perceive a single flaw in it. Louis XV, who had long been publicly noted for his enthusiastic championship of desirable young women, was only too pleased to lift her up and kiss her on both cheeks.

And it was at this point that the king of France turned and presented her to his grandson the dauphin, and Marie Antoinette met her husband for the first time.

THE YOUNG MAN DESTINED to inherit the French throne at perhaps the most complex and critical moment in the history of recorded events was born on August 23, 1754, which made him just over fourteen months older than his bride. Christened Louis-Auguste, he was his parents' second surviving son. His father, commonly referred to as "Louis the Fat," was Louis XV's only legitimate male heir, and therefore dauphin of France at the time of his son's birth. Louis-Auguste's mother, the dauphine, was Maria Josepha of Saxony, one of Mimi's husband Albert's older sisters. Maria Josepha would go on to deliver three more surviving children, two boys and a girl. All of the royal progeny were known not by their names but by their titles. Louis-Auguste's elder brother, born in 1751, was called duke of Burgundy; the brother born the year after Louis-Auguste, on November 17, 1755 (which made him almost exactly the same age as Marie Antoinette), was the count of Provence; a second younger brother, who came along in 1757, was referred to as the count of Artois; and the youngest, a girl, Élisabeth, born on May 3, 1764, was known as Madame. Louis-Auguste himself was called the duke of Berry, or, within the family, simply Berry.

Berry had been so sickly as an infant that it was feared he would not live. In one of the few cases where a doctor at Versailles actually prescribed something beneficial, he was sent to live in the quiet of the country, where he could get plenty of fresh air. The remedy worked; by the time he was a toddler, Berry had sufficiently recovered his strength to return to court. But it soon became apparent that, although he remained physically healthy, his development in other ways was impeded. There was no missing the difference between Berry's behavior and that of his siblings.

He didn't speak, he didn't look at anyone, he didn't show emotion, he stayed away from other people as much as he could. He didn't even play with his brothers; they seemed to intimidate him. Instead, he went up on the roof all by himself and ran around trying to catch stray cats. Flummoxed by the boy's reticence and kindly wishing to intervene, one of his aunts brought him alone into her chambers. "Go ahead, my poor Berry, you are at home here; go ahead, talk, make a noise, yell your head off, break things, do anything!" she urged him. But he did nothing.

It only got worse as he grew older. He was a very slow learner; both his elder brother, Burgundy, and his younger, Provence, were far quicker at their studies; even Artois, three years behind him and described by his father as "spirited" rather than intellectual, was clearly more versatile. Berry was overweight, but this was not of itself an impediment—the count of Provence, too, was rotund— but Louis-Auguste was universally described as excessively ungraceful and clumsy. He didn't seem to be able to judge the relationship between his body and the outside world, a condition that plagued him into adulthood. "The Dauphin is very awkwardly made, and uncouth in his motions," noted a startled British visitor to the court at Versailles when Louis-Auguste was twenty years old.

It is a sad fact that no matter what the century, children who are perceived as being different are often bullied and humiliated by their fellows, and Louis-Auguste was no exception. His brothers treated him with outright contempt. Burgundy, the eldest (and as such the heir to the throne after his father), would make him stand in front of him while he scornfully enumerated all of his younger sibling's failings. "Please, that fault, I think I have corrected it," a bewildered Berry would stammer through the shame of tears. So beaten down was Louis-Auguste that when he was thirteen years old he titled a page in his copybook "Concerning My Faults," and underneath this he wrote: "My greatest fault is a sluggishness of mind which makes all my mental efforts wearisome and painful: I want absolutely to conquer this defect; and after I have done so, as I hope to, I shall apply myself without respite to uprooting all the others which have been pointed out to me."

Attitudes acquired in childhood, particularly within families, are not easily altered. Even after his elder brother, the duke of Burgundy, died suddenly in 1761, and Louis-Auguste became his father's heir, his remaining brothers still considered themselves his superiors. Berry himself acknowledged their adroitness. "It's not I who am clever, but my brother Provence," he noted.

Then, on December 20, 1765, tragedy struck the court. Louis the Fat, who had been coughing up blood for months, succumbed to tuberculosis at the age of thirty-six. As his eldest surviving son, the eleven-year-old duke of Berry took his father's place as dauphin of France. His mother fainted when she heard the news.

For the next two years, before her own death from the same disease that killed her husband, Albert's sister did her best to prepare Louis-Auguste for rule. Her efforts were not without a measure of success. The new dauphin, although deliberate in his mental process, was not unintelligent; in fact, and especially in the sciences, quite the opposite. He loved maps and gravitated toward geography. He also read history, particularly English history, which was then in vogue. But his learning was entirely fact- and memory-based. Nuance was beyond him. "This Forest has 32,000 acres of which 5,000 are clearings," ran one of his typical school papers when he was twelve. "It contains Avenues, Large Paths, Large Roads, Squares, Pits, Bridges, Rounds, Wards, Fences, Patches, Hills, Pools, Fish-Ponds, Moats, and Boats." To help him to organize his thoughts and keep a record of his experiences in the hopes that this information would be useful to him in the future, his mother suggested he keep a private journal. The dauphin would dutifully (if sporadically) post entries in this curious document, at the rate of about a dozen pages a year, for the rest of his life. The vast majority of his memoranda were either lists of his expenses or shorthand summaries of the day's hunting, a sport that, once discovered, would consume most of his time and attention. ("Rien," a frequent notation, meant "shot nothing today.") Occasionally he would record an activity—"I went horse-riding today" (August 21, 1766)—or jot down the advent of a cold or some other ailment. In the entire journal, which encompassed some of the most momentous events of his reign, there would be no entry that did not constitute a bland declaration of fact. It was more notable for what it did *not* say.

If his mother had lived she might have offered him some protection—might have saved him from a too-early marriage, or helped him to understand the workings of government. But when she died, her twelve-year-old son was left to his own resources. ("Death of my mother at eight in the evening," was the dauphin's journal entry for March 13, 1767.) His tutor was a small-minded man who had him copy out homilies into his notebook and called it learning, and Louis XV, who never interfered in the lives of his children or grandchildren, and who was in any event occupied with his new mistress, Madame du Barry, couldn't be bothered with him. The result was that Louis-Auguste retreated even further into himself. He spent his time either alone in his room working on some bit of carpentry, or outdoors riding and shooting until he exhausted himself. He often ate until he was ill, so that he became even more ungainly and overweight.

There was no protocol in the eighteenth century for dealing with this sort of disorder.* The dauphin faced the same prejudices that people whose behavior does not conform to the standards of polite society always face. Madame du Barry witheringly referred to him as "the fat, ill-bred boy." The Neapolitan ambassador reported in dismay that "he seems to have been born and raised in the forest." Even Louis XV's principal minister bluntly told the king that his grandson was "the horror of the nation."

The court was clearly in a quandary as to how to improve the situation when Maria Theresa began pressing for a marriage alliance, and the happy thought arose that perhaps the solution was to provide the dauphin with a wife. Might not the uncouth young man respond more readily to the gentle urgings of a tender young bride than to tutors and servants? A wife could take him in hand, soften his rough edges, influence his manners. He might mature faster under her loving guidance. Even if he didn't, he could be no worse off than he was before; and either way the court would benefit, as, once wed, the dauphin would become the dauphine's problem.

And so the match was made, and the day came when Louis-Auguste drove out with his grandfather to the woods of Compiègne to meet his wife. His servants had dressed him up in fine silks and did the best they could with his hair. He stood silently beside the king, a corpulent, round-faced, fifteen-year-old about five foot six. After Marie Antoinette's curtsy, he, his grandfather, and the dauphine all climbed into a carriage. The bride sat beside the king; her

---

* I do not use this term lightly. Had he lived in the present century, Louis-Auguste would certainly have been diagnosed with Autism Spectrum Disorder (ASD). According to the Mayo Clinic, symptoms of ASD include "Resists cuddling and holding, and seems to prefer playing alone, retreating into his or her own world"; "Has poor eye contact and lacks facial expression"; "Can't start a conversation or keep one going, or only starts one to make requests or label items"; "Repeats words or phrases verbatim but doesn't understand how to use them"; "Doesn't express emotions or feelings and appears unaware of others' feelings"; "Develops routines or rituals and becomes disturbed at the slightest change"; "Has problems with coordination or has odd movement patterns, such as clumsiness or walking on toes, and has odd, stiff or exaggerated body language." "The child you describe checks every box for Autism Spectrum Disorder," confirmed Dr. Linda Gray, a noted developmental pediatrician with three decades' worth of experience at Yale New Haven Hospital, when I contacted her about Louis's behavior without identifying him.

Louis XVI as a young man

husband, the dauphin, faced her. During the subsequent drive to the local castle, where the other members of his family were waiting to be presented, Louis-Auguste said not one word. That evening he did, however, record the day's momentous events in his journal. "Interview with Madame the Dauphine," he wrote.

IF MARIE ANTOINETTE WAS DISAPPOINTED with her husband's appearance, or thought his behavior odd (which would certainly have been a natural reaction), she knew better than to show it. It's even possible that, in her fervent desire to make a good impression on the French court, she focused so much on her own deportment and on not making any glaring errors that she barely noticed the dauphin's conduct. There were, after all, so many people to meet, remember, and hopefully charm, and so many rules of etiquette to be obeyed, that it must have taken all of her concentration to get through the next few days. That first afternoon, after the initial greeting in the forest, she had been swept off to the castle at Compiègne, where her husband's aunts (Louis XV's adult daughters), as well as other prominent cousins like the duc d'Orléans, were waiting to meet her. She stayed overnight in Compiègne and the next day, May 15, set off first thing in the morning for the convent of Saint-Denis to meet yet another aunt, who had taken refuge there as a Carmelite nun; after that it was on to the royal residence of La Muette in the Bois de Boulogne, where a dinner had been arranged with her husband's younger brothers, the counts of Provence and Artois, among others. The king's special friend, Madame du Barry, was included in this company, and it became clear at this point that Maria Theresa had kept her daughter in ignorance about this regrettable idiosyncrasy of Louis XV's, as Marie Antoinette asked innocently of her dining companions what this unfamiliar woman did at court. Even after she was informed with a barely concealed snicker that Madame du Barry's role was "to amuse the king," the dauphine clearly did not understand, as she responded, "Well, then I shall be her rival!"

But this faux pas, if it could even be labeled that, was her only misstep. At a mere fourteen years old, Marie Antoinette performed brilliantly under the pressure of an exacting court, and this was no small accomplishment. "The king, Mesdames [the aunts], and, above all, Monseigneur the Dauphin, seemed enchanted with her, and vied with one another in repeating, 'She is incomparable!'" recounted one of the nuns who observed the audience at Saint-Denis. The comte de Mercy, a much harsher critic, was no doubt thrilled to be able to report home to Vienna that "Our Archduchess Dauphine...surpassed all my hopes as much by the suitability of her expressions as by her demeanor in general...It would be impossible to appear under more happy auspices than our Dauphine has done."

A second formal wedding service was scheduled to take place the next day, May 16, 1770, at Versailles. The duplicate marriage ceremony was held that afternoon in the royal chapel in front of a packed audience, the archbishop of Reims presiding. Again the bride, as she made her way down the aisle in a magnificent diamond-studded cloth-of-silver wedding gown (made only slightly less magnificent by an embarrassing gap in the material in the back through which the dauphine's somewhat less impressive undergarments could clearly be seen, the dress having been cut too small to close properly), was forced to navigate with precision the myriad hierarchical trivialities that constituted the bedrock of the French court. "As soon as she had taken the first few steps in the long gallery, she discerned, all the way to its extremity, those persons whom she ought to salute with the consideration due their rank; those on whom she should bestow an inclination of the head; and lastly those who were to be satisfied with a smile, while they read in her eyes a feeling of benevolence, calculated to console them for not being entitled to honors," confirmed an observer well versed in these subtle distinctions. Once more Marie Antoinette, to her significant credit, delivered a nearly flawless performance, betraying the nervousness she must have felt only when she let a blot of ink spoil her signature on the marriage contract. But this was nothing as compared to the undisguised agitation of the groom, who, according to one of the wedding guests, shuddered visibly throughout the service, and "colored up to his hair when he gave her the ring."

Afterward, a ballet and opera were performed at the brand-new theater specially constructed to host the wedding reception, followed by a great state dinner, with gold service for the entire extended royal family. Like her sister Maria Carolina, Marie Antoinette received a bejeweled strongbox stuffed with diamonds, emeralds, and other rare gems, including an extravagant necklace of oversized pearls that had formerly belonged to Louis-Auguste's mother. But these delights were, of course, only the prelude to the evening's crowning event, its raison d'être: *le coucher,* the bedding ceremony.

Marie Antoinette was even younger than Charlotte had been on her wedding night, and she had the same innocent upbringing; underneath the grand French princess pose she had so bravely adopted, she must have been just as terrified. It was reported that she sat bolt upright and ate very little during the hours-long banquet.

The dauphin, too, was uncharacteristically sparing in partaking of this repast; it is likely that in his uncertainty as to what was supposed to occur, and the discomfort he clearly experienced in the close presence of others, his dread surpassed hers.

But of course, as with Maria Carolina, there was no stopping the merciless passage of time. The revelers having feasted, Marie Antoinette was accompanied to her apartments by a privileged throng of duchesses and countesses, who removed the too-small wedding dress and replaced it with an embroidered negligee; afterward she was led to the bridal chamber, where Louis-Auguste, having undergone a similar ceremony with the women's princely counterparts, waited in his nightshirt. All the same people with whom she had so recently dined, including Louis XV and the rest of the royal family, as well as all of their highest-ranking servants and friends, crowded into the room. The bride, visibly upset at being paraded before so many spectators in such a mortifying state of undress, had to wait for the archbishop of Reims to bless the bed before diving under the covers. The dauphin, his face and attitude impassive, silently got in beside her. At last the bed curtains were drawn and the boisterous company departed. Husband and wife were alone.

This was the moment that Maria Carolina had most feared for her sister. She knew Marie Antoinette would be unprepared for the act of consummation, as Charlotte herself had been. "When I reflect that her fate will, perhaps, be like mine, I wish I could write volumes to her about it," she had warned her younger sister's governess urgently by letter. "I desire greatly that she may have someone with her like me at the beginning, otherwise I frankly own that it is desperation."

As it turned out, however, Charlotte's heartfelt worry for her sister's welfare proved unnecessary. Despite the humiliating buildup, Marie Antoinette had a much easier time of it that first night than had the queen of Naples. For in the darkness of the bedroom, the groom made no move to touch his bride. Instead both teenagers confounded the adults and simply fell asleep.

*   *   *

FOR A PERSON LIKE LOUIS-AUGUSTE, who had great difficulty func-
tioning in even the most mundane social situations, having to break
his routine to endure a public marriage ceremony to an unfamiliar
young woman, and then get into bed with her, was hardly calculated
to yield favorable results. It came as something of a letdown to the
French court, who seem to have convinced themselves that the dauphin was initially so taken with his bride that his behavior already
showed signs of improvement, to discover that, not only had nothing of significance taken place on the wedding night (the Spanish
ambassador having bribed the servants to report on the condition of
the sheets) but that, once the festivities were over, Louis-Auguste
demonstrated no further interest in his wife. Immediately upon
waking that first morning he went out hunting, as was his custom,
and when he returned, he stayed in his own quarters and resumed
his former routine, which, except for dining next to Marie Antoinette at public meals, did not include her. He certainly made no
move to share her bed again. When admonished a few days into his
honeymoon to pay some attention to the dauphine, he made a great
effort and actually visited her in her apartment to inquire in one
short sentence if she had slept.* When she replied that she had, he
turned and left the room. He did not speak to her again that day, or
indeed most days. The comte de Mercy, reporting to Vienna on
May 26, voiced the frustration that he and Marie Antoinette's household felt at this unhappy turn of events. "It would be impossible to
be more interesting than this Princess by reason of the qualities she
displays," he exclaimed. "But these very qualities constitute a striking indictment of those of her husband, who at the time of the wedding appeared to be on the point of some development, but who has
now relapsed into the disagreeable state to which he is inclined by
nature. Since their first interview he has not shown the slightest sign

---

* Again, people diagnosed with Autism Spectrum Disorder can find initiating
even the simplest conversation to be extremely stressful.

of predilection for the Dauphine, or anxiety to please her—in public or private," he noted gloomily.

Having no inkling of the true nature of the problem, and at a loss as to how to remedy the situation, the comte de Mercy asked Madame de Noailles to inform Louis XV of his grandson's disinterest, perhaps in the hope that the sovereign would order the dauphin to sleep with his wife. But Louis XV declined to intervene. "At present it is necessary to let him [the dauphin] go his own way," the king of France instructed the lady-in-waiting. "He is extremely timid and shy—in short, he is not like other men."

Happily, Marie Antoinette, who was still of an age where she had to be reminded to brush her teeth, was not anxious either to rush into this mysterious act of adult intimacy with a complete stranger. So, rather than take offense at her husband's coldness, or complain about it, she instead did what came naturally to her and gently set about making friends with him. To do this, she tried quietly to enter his world. She went to his rooms in the afternoon, where he would be concentrating on some bit of woodworking—Louis-Auguste enjoyed the precision of shop craft and kept tools in his study—and asked him to show her how his lathe worked. She spoke kindly to him and did not press him for a response. None of this was an affectation on her part. Marie Antoinette was a genuinely sweet and caring young woman. Now, she instinctively relied on these qualities, to which others had always responded so well in the past, in her efforts to draw her husband into an affectionate relationship. The comte de Mercy was able to write with relief to Vienna that "Fortunately, his [Louis-Auguste's] indifference and incivility do not appear to intimidate the young Princess...her behavior is such in experience and address far beyond what her age might prescribe."

She couldn't have known it, of course, but this was exactly the right approach to adopt. Slowly, very slowly—it would take years—the dauphin began to get used to her. On February 25, 1771, nine months into the marriage, she coaxed him to attend a ball given by Madame de Noailles, at which, to the astonishment of the court, he walked in arm in arm with his wife and addressed a single statement, obviously rehearsed, to his hostess, thanking her for inviting him. "This conduct has raised hopes for which we have never before had justification," marveled the comte de Mercy to Maria Theresa. When, on New Year's Day 1772, the dauphine, under pressure from Louis XV and much long-distance berating by her mother, finally recognized the king's mistress publicly (addressing the famous statement "There are very many people at Versailles today" to Madame du Barry in company), she afterward sought out Mercy to inform him of her acquiescence. "I have done what you told me!" Marie Antoinette exclaimed. "There is the Dauphin who will bear me witness!" The comte in turn reported dutifully to Maria Theresa: "I perceived that the Dauphin understood what I was saying; he seemed to approve by certain gestures and movements of the head, but he did not utter a single word." A year later, the ambassador was slightly more optimistic, relaying the information that under his wife's influence, "I notice that the Dauphin is attaining more order in his ideas and expresses them more coherently. He even has a little shrewdness sometimes, as for instance on Monday last." Mercy had also to admit, however, that, "unfortunately, his conversations are so disconnected that I find it very hard to enunciate a few useful sentences."

The progress in the bedroom was, if anything, even slower. Although by 1771, Louis-Auguste had begun to visit his wife at night—on June 21, Marie Antoinette wrote to Maria Theresa that the dauphin had been sick but that he was improving "and promises me that it will not be long before he returns to my room"—the couple had yet to consummate the marriage. Three months later, the young wife was still optimistic. "I live always in hope, and the growing tenderness of the Dauphin does not permit me to doubt," she again assured her mother. "Though I should like it better that all were settled," she added uneasily.*

---

* The chief theory as to why Louis-Auguste was unable to perform sexually during the first years of his marriage was that he had a physical condition called phimosis, which required an operation. This would explain the dauphin's complaint that it hurt

But teenaged girls are not generally known for their patience, and Marie Antoinette was no exception to this rule. Behavior that she accepted from her husband and tried to make the best of at fourteen, when she was new to Versailles and uncertain of her surroundings, became frustrating by the time she was sixteen. By seventeen she was openly resentful. In fairness, she had no more idea than anyone else at court about the reasons for his conduct, and so could only attribute his strange habits to backwardness and obstinacy, as they did. She would request repeatedly, first sweetly, and then more insistently, that he conform his manners to generally accepted practices of civility; he would hang his head or in some other fashion wordlessly indicate his seeming assent; and then he would continue to behave precisely as he had before. Eventually, she would explode at him. "The Dauphine gave the Dauphin a lecture on his immoderate hunting, which...led him into habits of negligence and rudeness," the comte de Mercy confessed to Maria Theresa in July 1771, when Louis-Auguste was nearly seventeen years old. "The Dauphin tried to cut the reproof short by retiring into his own apartment, but the Dauphine followed him and continued forcibly to represent the annoyances caused by his manner of living. This caused the Dauphin so much emotion that he began to cry," the ambassador was compelled by candor to concede.

And her husband's inexplicable obtuseness was just one of Marie Antoinette's many disappointments with her life at court. When she first arrived, she was shackled by a schedule so restricted and monotonous that a clerk in a countinghouse would have found it tedious.

---

when he tried to have sex. But as there is no record of his ever having had this medical procedure—and there would have been, had it been undertaken—it is equally possible that the problem was simply a mixture of fear, misunderstanding, and miscommunication. Louis-Auguste apparently became unnerved whenever he developed the smallest physical complaint. For example, after a passing case of indigestion in August of 1773, Mercy commented upon "the state of apprehension and depression into which the Dauphin throws himself upon the very slightest appearance of discomfort." As will later become apparent, he was obviously perplexed by what was expected of him. It is not out of the question that, whenever he tried to consummate, he experienced the barrier presented by Marie Antoinette's virginity, identified the impact as pain, and suspended the attempt.

"I rise about nine or half-past, dress, and say my morning prayers," Marie Antoinette informed her mother. "Then I breakfast and go see my aunts, where I usually find the King. This lasts until about half-past ten, then at eleven I have my hair dressed, at twelve is my reception, and all may enter who are not common people. I put on my rouge and wash my hands before them all, and then the men go and the ladies remain, and I finish my dressing before them. At midday is mass; if the King is at Versailles I go with him and my husband and my aunts; if he is not there I go alone with the Dauphin, but always at the same hour," she continued. "After mass we dine, just the two of us, before all the company, but that is over in an hour and a half, for we both eat very fast. After that I go to the Dauphin, and if he has business I come back to my own rooms...I work, for I am making a vest for the King, which does not get on a bit, but which I hope will be finished by the grace of God, after a few years," she admitted. "At three o'clock I go to call upon my aunts...at four o'clock the Abbé [Vermond] comes to me, at five every day the music master for the harpsichord, or singing till six. At half-past six I go nearly always to my aunts, when I do not go out for a walk. From seven we play [cards] until nine...At nine we sup, and when the King is not there my aunts come to sup with me, but when he is there, we go to sup with him and await the King, who usually comes about a quarter to eleven, and when waiting for him I lie down on a large couch and sleep till his arrival; but when he is not there we go to bed at eleven."

It was a court stuck in time, like the fossilized mansion of Miss Havisham in *Great Expectations,* with Marie Antoinette playing the part of Estella. A rigid code of conduct, imposed a century before by Louis XIV to exalt the throne, still governed every interaction, every movement, every detail of dress, down to the number of buttons. But the corsets and petticoats that had been viewed as grandly fashionable in the Sun King's time were considered dowdy and cumbersome by eighteenth-century standards, and the hours devoted to the minutiae of a social code that had long since outlived its usefulness were bleakly tedious, and frankly incomprehensible, to the dauphine. Marie Antoinette took to calling the officious Madame de Noailles, who tormented her for the smallest infraction of these rules, "Madame l'Étiquette," behind her back.

"Madame de Noailles," observed Madame Campan, who would eventually replace this finicky woman as Marie Antoinette's first lady-in-waiting, "abounded in virtues; I cannot pretend to deny it. Her piety, charity, and irreproachable morals rendered her worthy of praise; but etiquette was to her a sort of atmosphere [air]: at the slightest derangement of the consecrated order, one would have thought she would have been stifled, and that the principles of life would forsake her frame [i.e., she would fall down dead]. One day, I unintentionally threw this poor lady into a terrible agony," Madame Campan continued. "I perceived the eyes of Madame de Noailles fixed on mine...she raised her eyebrows to the top of her forehead, lowered them, raised them again...the agitation of the countess [Madame de Noailles] kept increasing...her Majesty [Marie Antoinette]...said to me in a whisper: 'Let down your lappets [lace flaps], or the countess will expire.' All this bustle arose from two unlucky pins, which fastened up my lappets, whilst the etiquette of costume said, 'Lappets hanging down!'" exclaimed Madame Campan.

Even a hundred years earlier, this ridiculously artificial environment had only worked because those who surrounded Louis XIV knew themselves to be in the presence of greatness. Emphatically, the same could not be said of his successor. By 1773, Louis XV was sixty-three and in the fifty-eighth year of a rule marked by a never-ending stream of debauchery, debt, and defeat, earning it the melancholy status of perhaps the most contemptible reign in the history of the kingdom. Never one to pay much attention, even in his prime, to the details of governing, the king had for some time left the administration of his realm to his ministers, and took a perverse pleasure whenever their efforts failed (which they did regularly). "They would have it so; they thought it for the best," he would observe smugly, absolving himself of any responsibility for the policy.

Now in his declining years, he was already showing signs of senility. "Your Majesty commands me to say whether the King has taken to drink," the comte de Mercy wrote to Maria Theresa. "The report is not well founded, and arises from the fact that one may often observe in this monarch attacks of vacuity which resemble the effect of drunkenness. It is obvious that the mind of the King weakens daily." Rather than attend to the improvement of the kingdom and the needs of his subjects, many of whom were starving, Louis XV instead behaved like a wealthy retiree, spending his days hunting and his evenings catering to the extravagant whims of his mistress (not to mention the numerous other young women whom he also met regularly for quick overnight flings at his personal bordello, called Parc-aux-Cerfs, located conveniently on the palace grounds).

The king's obvious incompetence fostered a poisonous atmosphere of corruption and petty intrigue, at the center of which was Madame du Barry, a woman single-mindedly devoted to getting as much as she could out of her decrepit admirer before he expired.* Upon being informed with malicious delight by her husband's aunts of the true nature of the favorite's duties, a shocked Marie Antoinette, used to her mother's respectable, sensibly administered court, had taken their advice and refused to acknowledge her. In retaliation, Madame du Barry helped to orchestrate the exile of the minister responsible for the Austrian alliance and Marie Antoinette's marriage, eventually replacing him with an official more sympathetic to her own views and thus substantially weakening the dauphine's position. Her mother, who in truth did not understand the situation, and who was terrified that her youngest daughter would be repudiated and sent home (historically, dauphines who could not produce heirs were in danger of having their marriages annulled), barraged her child with letters, exhorting her to speak to the favor-

---

* Madame de Pompadour, Louis XV's previous mistress, had been an intelligent, highly educated woman capable of holding an informed opinion and directing policy. Madame du Barry patently lacked her predecessor's abilities. "Where is Poland?" she inquired pleasantly of an envoy who had solicited an audience in order to beg France to intervene in that country's defense.

ite. Eventually Marie Antoinette, although knowing herself to be in the right—"If you were in a position to judge, as I am, all that passes here, you would be convinced that this woman and her clique will never be satisfied with merely a word; there would be perpetual encroachments," she warned her mother—bowed to her parent's wishes, and addressed the notorious New Year's Day sentence to her antagonist. The dauphine was correct: Madame du Barry, having achieved her first aim, remained a continual problem, angling to have other members of her family presented at court, and even going so far as to try to bribe Marie Antoinette with diamonds to get her way, which insulting overture was firmly and coldly declined.

Madame du Barry

This, then, was the dauphine's life for the first three years of her marriage: tedious lessons in which she demonstrated neither interest nor ability ("There never existed a princess who manifested a more marked aversion for all serious study," Madame Campan admitted); incessant parental reproaches; long hours spent playing cards with three old maids (the aunts); ugly, uncomfortable clothes that took forever to put on and take off, owing to the number of people required to hand them to her; backbiting and false friendships.* She had to go to battle with her mother and Mercy for every small pleasure—to ride and hunt like the rest of the court, to amuse herself with a pet dog, even to play for an hour or so with someone else's children—like a knight fighting for survival. And looming over all of this was the knowledge that she was shackled for the rest of her life to an unattractive, overweight lout of a husband who had difficulty stringing together two coherent sentences in company, and whose fumbling failures to consummate his marriage humiliated her in front of the whole court.

And shackled to him she was, for despite her mother's fears that she would be discarded if she did not produce children—"The situation is incomprehensible, and I am amazed that things are allowed to remain as they are without anyone being occupied with them," Maria Theresa fumed in frustration to Mercy about the dauphin's seeming disinterest in impregnating his wife—Marie Antoinette knew that there was no danger her marriage would be annulled. Ironically, her original efforts had borne fruit. Her husband had become used to her. She was a part of his routine. As a result, she admirably served the purpose for which she had been initially recruited to court: he had not only come to rely on her—he could not do without her. When, in the fall of 1773, a stag accidentally killed a peasant while the king was out hunting, Marie Antoinette, coming upon the scene, leapt out of her coach, comforted the wife, saw to the body, and distributed all the money she had on her to the bereaved family and their neighbors. The dauphin, who had just stood there silently the whole time, only belatedly took out his purse as well. "Madame the Dauphine follows nature, and Monsieur the Dauphin follows the Dauphine," a courtier observed with accurate, if withering, sarcasm.

Small wonder, then, that the comte de Mercy one day surprised

---

* Madame Adélaïde, one of the aunts, while outwardly expressing motherly concern for her, spitefully referred to Marie Antoinette as "the Austrian" behind her back.

his young charge sitting in her room with tears in her eyes. The reality of her early experience at Versailles was clearly not what she had been led to believe the life of the luckiest princess on earth would be.

And then, at the beginning of June 1773, for the very first time, she went to Paris.

PARIS WAS ONLY 11 MILES from Versailles, but it might have been in Virginia for all the royal family saw of it. It was considered hostile territory, and with good reason: Louis XV was openly loathed in the celebrated metropolis. "Old Louis...grinds them down with infamous heavy taxes to support an insatiable favorite," bluntly observed a denizen of the capital, giving voice to the majority opinion. By custom, the dauphine was supposed to have made her sovereign entry into the city at the time of her marriage, to introduce herself to by far the most influential and populous community in the realm. As nobody at Versailles seemed in any hurry to do that, however, after three years she was forced to take the initiative, and in May 1773 personally solicited the king's approval to undertake the ceremony. Louis XV, who rarely said no to pretty women, gave his permission, and so a month later, on June 8, Marie Antoinette, with Louis-Auguste at her side, finally made the short journey and drove into the most storied municipality in Europe for her official state reception.

Parisians turned out in droves to see her. The governor handed over the keys to the city on a silver platter; legions of curtsying market women presented her with bouquets of flowers and baskets of produce; soldiers stood at attention. The boulevards along which the royal couple passed were bedecked with ornamental arches and strewn with blossoms, and everywhere crowds of people cheered their approach. The comte de Mercy described it all to Maria Theresa in the fervent tones of a man who had witnessed a miracle. "Nothing was wanting; the public was seized with a sort of delirium for the Dauphine," he raved in a letter of June 16. "In the garden of the Tuileries there were, without exaggeration, over fifty thousand souls...In the memory of man there has not been an entry that has made so much sensation or had so universal a success...The public shows an enthusiasm truly extraordinary...It is, positively, still the subject of talk in Paris, and all minds are as full of it as upon the first day."

Marie Antoinette was stunned. She had known, of course, that Paris was one of the world's great cities, but this seemingly endless ocean of cheering humanity was beyond anything she could have imagined. "Heavens, what a crowd!" she gasped, as she and the dauphin stood on a balcony overlooking the Tuileries for a final farewell. Six days later, she described the scene to her mother. "I had a fête last Tuesday that I shall not forget in all my life," the still-bedazzled dauphine confided in awe. "We made our entry into Paris. We received all imaginable honors, which, although very well, were not what touched me most, which was the affection and anxiety of that poor people who, although weighed down by taxes, was transported with joy at seeing us...I cannot describe to you, my dear mamma, the transports of joy and of affection that were shown to us. Before retiring we saluted the populace by waving our hands, which gave great pleasure. How happy we are to be able to gain the affection of a whole nation at so little cost!" she marveled before turning to a matter that had obviously worried her prior to the ceremony. "Another point that gave great pleasure on that happy day was the behavior of the Dauphin: who responded admirably to all the harangues [speeches], observed all that was done for him, and especially the joy and assiduities of the people, to whom he showed much good feeling," she assured her mother with evident relief.★

Husband and wife returned to Versailles that evening but were

---

★ Of course she must had been nervous about him; the dauphin, as she well knew, did not do well in new situations or crowds. In fact, she, Louis-Auguste, and Louis-Auguste's youngest brother, the count of Artois, had masked themselves and gone secretly into Paris the night before to attend the theater. It has always been assumed that she did this because she couldn't wait to have fun in the city, but it is also possible that her husband was apprehensive about the state entry—significantly, this seems to have been *his* first time in Paris as well—and so she may well have given him a practice run to give him an idea of what to expect. Notice that she makes no mention of the dauphin speaking, merely that he waved and "showed much good feeling."

invited back to Paris the following night to attend the opera, where the sweet blandishment of public adoration continued. An eyewitness observed: "A favorite actor, who had retired from the stage, played again for this night. The house was illuminated *en gala,* and the royal pair sat together in a box on the first story...Part of a song had the words in it, *Vive le Roi!* which the audience encored seven or eight times." When the actor improvised, adding the phrase "*et ses chers enfants* [and his dear children]!" to the final refrain, the audience exploded in cheers.

This introduction to the capital represented an epiphany for Marie Antoinette. At last she saw why she was the envy of other princesses. To conquer a city like Paris dwarfed anything else the world had to offer. "I feel every day more and more all that my dear mamma has done in the matter of settling me," she wrote with humble gratitude. "I was the last of all and she has treated me as the eldest."

But the dauphine had gotten it wrong. They were not cheering for her but for what she and her husband represented: the inevitable death of the despised Louis XV and with it release from over a half century of selfish, unfeeling, incompetent rule. Louis-Auguste and Marie Antoinette were young, they were unknown, they had come to Paris and shown themselves. As such, they were simply the blank slate upon which the population projected the feverish hope of a brighter future. But the outpouring of affection that so touched Marie Antoinette did not in fact come without a price, as she had naively related to her mother. If, upon the old king's death, she and her husband did not deliver the change that the people expected, they would find themselves confronting a very different environment. It is a sad truth that the higher the expectation, the easier the likelihood of failure—and the greater the sense of rage and betrayal. And judging by the epic size of the crowds and the frenzied deluge of accolades, the expectations of the citizens of Paris were very high indeed.

This shining moment, so significant in Marie Antoinette's life, might never have happened at all if she hadn't pressed to go to Paris, for the brilliant, explosive capital was about to get its wish. Ten months later, on April 22, 1774, Louis XV came down with a fever while staying with Madame du Barry at his private quarters at the Petit Trianon, on the northern edge of the gardens. By April 28 he was so ill that it was decided he should return to the main palace of Versailles, to be closer to his doctors. Although every attempt was made to keep the sick man in ignorance of the true nature of his ail-ment, within two days the dreaded spots had appeared. The king had contracted smallpox.

It was a particularly virulent strain of the disease and it quickly permeated the court. "The air of the palace was infected: more than fifty persons took smallpox in consequence of having merely crossed the gallery of Versailles; and ten died of it," Madame Campan reported. Louis's adult daughters, the aunts, to their very great credit, stayed by their father's side to nurse him throughout the course of the illness; as a result, each also in turn fell victim to the pestilence, although fortunately their cases were milder and they all eventually recovered.

By May 4, even Louis knew that he was in mortal danger. He called in Madame du Barry (who had done everything she could to shut out the priests, knowing that if the king asked for last rites it meant her exile) and told her to leave the court. "Madame, as I am contemplating receiving the sacrament, it is not proper for you to remain here," the king acknowledged publicly, although it was clear that he was loath to part with her. "You can come back if you hear I am better," he whispered on the side, instructing her to stay within a few miles of the palace.

But he did not get better. Two days later Louis XV confessed and received the sacraments. The crisis came on the evening of May 9, when the king was officially given no hope. Still, he held on through the night. The progress of the disease was horrible; his body was bloated and covered with blackened pustules; the stench in the sick-room was overpowering. The entire court was prepared to escape the palace the moment it was confirmed that the sovereign had expired, but it was difficult to tell exactly when that might be, and no one wanted to communicate directly with those who held vigil in that noxious apartment for fear of contagion. At length it was determined that a lighted candle would be placed on the windowsill of the king's room. So long as this taper remained lit, the king yet lived; upon its extinguishment the court would know that all was over. Finally, at approximately three o'clock on the afternoon of May 10, 1774, the candle was snuffed out.

Marie Antoinette was with her husband. They had spent the previous night praying for his grandfather's soul in the royal chapel and then had waited all morning for word of his death; they were exhausted. Suddenly, "a dreadful noise, absolutely like thunder, was heard in the outer apartment," Madame Campan remembered. "It was the crowd of courtiers who were deserting the dead sovereign's antechamber, to come and bow to the new power of Louis XVI. This extraordinary tumult informed Marie Antoinette and her husband that they were to reign; and by a spontaneous movement... they threw themselves on their knees; both pouring forth a flood of tears, and exclaiming, 'O God, guide us, protect us, we are too young to govern.'"

Their panic was not feigned. He was nineteen, she eighteen, and neither was in any way familiar with the workings of the government. The new monarch had never attended a council meeting, nor deciphered a dispatch, nor even so much as glanced at a treasury report, and his wife was even more ignorant of statecraft than he, if that were possible. The British ambassador reported, "They are all under inexpressible affliction and none more so than the King and Queen, who all day expressed the greatest anxiety for their Grandfather's recovery, and the utmost apprehension of the load which his Death would throw upon them and which their Youth and inexperience made them so little able to bear. One of the Dauphin's expressions was 'Il me semble que l'Univers va tomber sur moi' [I feel as though the Universe will fall on me]."

Not quite yet, perhaps, but it was coming. The reign of Louis XVI and Marie Antoinette had begun.

Maria Christina

"Mimi"

Maria Christina and Albert share portraits of Maria Theresa's Italian grandchildren with the rest of the family. Consigned to the background (as they were in life) are Mimi's unmarried sisters, Marianne and Maria Elisabeth, and her youngest brother, Maximilian. An obviously disinterested Joseph leans over his mother's shoulder with barely concealed impatience.

14

An Imperial Divide

*Nothing in the world has cost me as much as the loss of our
reputation. Unhappily, I must own to you that we deserve it.*
— Maria Theresa to the comte de Mercy

ALL THIS TIME, while her younger sisters were struggling with various degrees of success to accustom themselves to the novelty of their surroundings in faraway France and Italy, Maria Christina was living quietly with Albert in next-door Pressburg, only a day's journey from Vienna. By 1768, the year Charlotte was dispatched to Naples, Mimi had recovered from the cruel infection that had taken the life of her newborn child, and from which she herself had almost died, and had resumed her duties as the wife of the governor of Hungary.

These were extensive. Hungary was a vital component of her mother's realm. Although the dowager empress and the kingdom had had their ups and downs over the decades — she was still unable to impose a tax on the nobility there, for example — Maria Theresa had never forgotten the way that the Hungarians had so chivalrously come to her rescue in the early days of her reign, when it seemed as if the whole world was against her. Consequently, she had made a point of familiarizing herself with the tastes and habits of its inhabitants, particularly in the capital. This simple approach had proved to be an extremely effective means of promoting harmony with these otherwise often touchy subjects. Relations between Austria and

273

Hungary under Maria Theresa's rule were more peaceful and prosperous than at any other time in the history of the monarchy. It turned out that a little courtesy and respect went a long way.

As Maria Christina was now charged with continuing this happy trend, her mother had supplied her with a detailed letter outlining her responsibilities. It was the written equivalent of a graduate course in diplomacy. "Feast-days...or festivals of the country, you will observe by going out in the morning to church *in publico* without a sermon," the dowager empress instructed. "Make continual changes of church to give pleasure to all...On these days, the ladies of the *Zutritt* [higher nobility] may come in the morning in indoor dress... At dinner the gentlemen and even persons of lesser importance may be present. You will try to take notice of them and to be gracious to them, even to say a few words to them...Have consideration for the secondary nobility here," her mother reminded her, "for it is different from that of other countries; there are more among them of account than among the magnates, and many more devoted and more zealous. At the beginning you could make a round of all these councillors of state, chamberlains, lawyers and their wives, invite them to a meal, and the captain of the guard alone might have that honor," Marie Theresa suggested before continuing, "in general, all the bishops will dine with you, all the prelates and canons, if they are of quality or character, as well as all strangers known and present...Give one day in the week for audiences, or more, if necessary, see passers-by at all times and show them all possible courtesy, it is the one method of attracting them." The list went on and on.

Such meticulous guidance was enormously helpful. Both Maria Christina, who had watched her mother govern and had witnessed the success of her methods, and Albert, who took his obligation to the Crown seriously, adopted her approach. Their presence added glamour and prestige to the city, boosting its allure. Albert's first-hand knowledge of the kingdom's problems was impressive. In 1768, he accompanied Joseph on a two-month fact-finding tour of the countryside that took them nearly to the border with the Ottoman

Empire, the first time any member of the Austrian royal family had ever bothered to venture so far into the interior when not forced to do so en route to a battle.

Although no doubt Maria Christina found the numerous social functions she was required to attend or host tedious—these official and semiofficial engagements were the Hungarian version of Marie Antoinette's detested "etiquette"—she clearly understood their importance and seems for the most part to have successfully managed to project both imperial dignity and personal warmth, the twin trademarks of her mother's rule. "Naturally distant and haughty, she can nevertheless, when such is her pleasure, temper her demeanor with the most gracious and winning condescension," noted a visiting Englishman who spent time at the royal court in Hungary. "It is difficult to imagine a Princess more formed to represent the Majesty of the Throne," he added thoughtfully. Happily, Mimi's obligations were not so onerous that they did not leave her time to pursue her love of art. "She dedicates her leisure to the occupations of the pencil," this same Englishman reported. "She particularly excels in painting, as various apartments in the castle of Pressburg sufficiently testify; where I have seen portraits of her performance, executed in a masterly manner."

The one cloud overhanging the couple was Maria Christina's frustrating inability to conceive a second time, but in these first years they likely did not give up hope. By 1770, the year of Marie Antoinette's marriage, Mimi was still only twenty-eight, not yet past the age of childbearing, especially judging by her mother's experience. So even this was not a real worry.

She was happy and confident, and it showed. "The Archduchess Christine...is unquestionably a very superior woman," the same visitor confessed. "Her eyes are full of vivacity, her features noble, as well as regular...Over all her limbs and motions is diffused an air of grandeur, which seems to announce high birth."

Adding greatly to Mimi's sense of well-being were the enormous resources at her disposal. The couple had enough money to buy more or less anything they wanted. As Albert shared his wife's appreciation for important paintings and other fine objets d'art—his grandfather had been a noted connoisseur, and the ancestral castle in Dresden had been famous for its collection until Frederick had come along and stolen it away to Berlin—Maria Theresa made the young couple a gift of some 294 paintings that she had inherited from her father, including significant works by Dürer, Brueghel, and Titian, which were just gathering dust in Vienna anyway.

But although she was officially stationed in Hungary, Maria Christina's primary responsibility was in fact to act as best friend and confidante to her mother. Despite having two adult daughters still living at home, it was Mimi whose company Maria Theresa craved.★ Consequently, Maria Christina and Albert were given their own suite of rooms at the Hofburg and spent at least half their time in Vienna. For Mimi, this was no hardship. She was conscious that her mother relied on her and knew that she could lift her spirits as no one else in the family could. For her part, Maria Theresa trusted this favored daughter, so discerning and accomplished, to give her compassionate, sensible advice. "With such personal and intellectual endowments, it cannot, or it ought not to excite surprise...that she [Maria Christina] possesses no inconsiderable ascendance over her mother's political, as well as private conduct," the English visitor commented.

If anything, Mimi was aware that Maria Theresa needed her more now, in her declining years, than at any time in the past. A new danger had arisen, one that threatened to destroy the peace and upset the fragile equilibrium the dowager empress had fought so hard to achieve with her neighbors. In Maria Theresa's opinion, the very

---

★ Poor Marianne and Maria Elisabeth! It was no fun being stay-at-home abbesses. The English traveler observed that "they lead a gloomy, tedious life...Immured in the Imperial Palace, almost destitute of society, obliged to attend their mother wherever she moves, and compelled to assist at ceremonies or exercises of devotion, as if they were nuns [which technically they were], rather than Princesses; scarcely are they known to exist by any of the foreign nations of Europe, and never were any persons less objects of envy."

existence of the monarchy, and everything she stood for, was at stake.

Maria Christina agreed. There was no question but that they were going to have to do something about Joseph.

It is DIFFICULT not to feel sorry for Maria Theresa's eldest son. He lost the love of his life while still in his early twenties. He was still in mourning for her when he was forced to wed a woman he detested. The experience so repulsed him that when a few years later smallpox conveniently relieved him of this second, unwanted spouse, he vowed never again to marry. Instead, Joseph lavished all the pent-up tenderness he had accumulated after Isabella's death on his daughter, Little Theresa, who, as the last remnant of her cherished mother, made her more precious to her father than anyone else in the world. As she grew older, the emperor kept his daughter to himself as much as possible, supervising her education and selecting a highly cultured noblewoman from Brussels to serve as her governess. Increasingly, the rest of the family, but especially his mother, with whose intolerant views of religion he strongly disagreed, were kept at arm's length from the little girl. "The child scarcely knows me...my son loves everything which belongs to him only, unshared," Maria Theresa complained.

Then, in January of 1770, while Marie Antoinette was still in Vienna absorbed in learning how to curtsy, Little Theresa fell ill— not from smallpox, as she had been inoculated, but with a cough and a high fever. It seems to have been a bacterial infection, most likely pleurisy. A frantic Joseph insisted on nursing her himself. But there was nothing he could do. On January 23, two days after the ring ceremony signifying his youngest sister's formal engagement to the heir to the throne of France, Little Theresa died in her devastated father's arms, just as her mother had. She was only seven years old.

This cruel loss, heaped on top of the other, broke Joseph. "To be no longer a father seems more than I can bear...I shall miss my daughter all the remaining days of my life," he grieved inconsolably to her governess, asking her to gather together Little Theresa's few childish writings as well as her favorite small white nightgown embroidered with flowers for him to put away as keepsakes. Already given to an arrogant aloofness, the emperor became even more isolated, acerbic, and self-pitying in the wake of his daughter's death. He told Leopold, who by this time had already sired three children, two of whom were boys, that he would leave the perpetuation of the imperial succession to him. He was happy, Joseph assured his brother mordantly, to make do without a wife. "What would such a poor creature do with a sour recluse [Joseph meant himself] and I with a family?" he scoffed. From this time on, the emperor contented himself with prostitutes and generally unsuccessful flirtations with married women.

To further ease the pain, he threw himself into his work, but this was hardly a source of consolation. At his father's death five years earlier, he had assumed his place by his mother's side filled with energy and ideas. Since adolescence, Joseph had never lost his admiration for Frederick the Great, whom (much to Maria Theresa's horror) he viewed as an exemplary specimen of enlightened-warrior-king.★ Now a monarch himself—or, rather, a co-regent, which in the event turned out to be not *quite* the same thing—the emperor modeled himself after his hero. Like Frederick, Joseph eschewed ceremony and ostentation. He stripped the royal court of the opulent clothing that had characterized his mother's and grandfather's reigns, and cut back drastically on the number of religious holidays and feast days celebrated in Vienna. He gleefully adopted Frederick's habit of traveling incognito, pretending to be an ordinary citizen, and using a fake name. He drew up a radical platform to reform his mother's entire government, clearly based on the Prussian system of uniformity and consolidation as a means of maximizing control and efficiency.

★ Frederick, not being pious himself—in fact, he sneered at piety—was noted for his tolerance of all faiths, including Judaism, and so was commended as enlightened. In Prussia, the king did not bother his subjects about their beliefs so long as they paid their taxes and followed his orders.

But over the course of those five years, Joseph's ambitious program had been thwarted at every turn by his more moderate mother, who viewed the scope of his multitude of proposals with alarm. To change so much all at once would be disruptive. She let him eliminate most of the frippery at court—she was in mourning anyway and had lost her taste for society—but refused to act on his other recommendations, and he could do nothing without her approval. Joseph soon realized that he was not in fact a co-ruler, as his title implied, but only an adviser, on par with Count Kaunitz, whose opinion Maria Theresa still valued above all others. He referred to his position sardonically as "the empty title of Co-Regent." His resentment of his mother, particularly after the death of Little Theresa, when he was so miserable, was unmistakable. "From the time of his daughter's illness he began to separate himself from me, and this has continued more and more, so that we are now reduced, solely in order to preserve appearances, never to seeing each other except at dinner...judge the suffering of my heart, which lived only for this adored son," Maria Theresa grieved.

The one area of government where the dowager empress allowed Joseph something of a free hand was the military. As she had conceded this department to her husband when he was alive, so Maria Theresa now did the same for her eldest son. She would live to regret this decision.

THERE IS NO QUESTION that Catherine the Great started it. When she nominated her former lover as king of Poland, she simultaneously sent Russian troops across the border to ensure his election. The Turks had taken offense at this blatant grab for regional power by a new and untested woman ruler, and in 1768 had declared war on Russia. Catherine was delighted to oblige them, and between 1769 and 1770 defeated first the Ottoman army and then its navy. "I require much cannon," she observed coolly in response to Frederick the Great's hearty congratulations on these victories, "for I am setting fire to the Turkish Empire from four corners."

But the king of Prussia's eager praise was feigned. He was actually none too pleased to see Catherine winning so decisively. Frederick feared the rise of Russia more than any other threat. "It is a terrible power, which in half a century will make all Europe tremble," he warned his brother Henry grimly. Already, Catherine's soldiers had crossed the Danube. True, the king was in an alliance with the tsarina, but if her progress continued at this feverish pace, Prussia could also easily find itself swallowed up by this voracious (if supposedly friendly) neighbor.

It is surely one of history's most satisfying ironies that Frederick the Great, who from the outset of his career had deliberately targeted Maria Theresa and done everything he could to weaken her and her realm beyond recovery, now belatedly realized how much he needed a strong Austria to help fend off Russia. Although the Prussian king was aware that he was the last person on earth the dowager empress would be willing to trust, he nonetheless had to find a way to coax her into an alliance and help her to stay viable. The obvious answer was to go through her eldest son. Joseph, chafing at the restrictions placed on him by his mother, and desperate to make a name for himself among his fellow sovereigns, played right into Prussian hands.

The emperor, approaching thirty, was only too conscious that, at his age, Frederick had already stunned the world by seizing Silesia and that Maria Theresa had been even younger when she valiantly held her own against the combined forces of France, Bavaria, and Prussia. And now Catherine the Great, another mere female, had come along and on her very first time out was raining destruction down on the Turks and sweeping up cities and fortresses in her wake as though they were carved pieces on a chessboard.

So, slowly, cautiously, Joseph dipped his toe into the dangerous current of foreign conquest. After his fact-finding tour with Albert, the emperor claimed to have uncovered documents that proved that two estates just across the Polish border actually belonged to Hungary, which made them part of his mother's domain. Although upon

examination of the evidence, Maria Theresa expressed reservations—
"I have a very poor opinion of our titles," she observed unhappily to
Kaunitz—she nonetheless did not stop her son from sending troops
into Poland in 1770 to occupy these two small properties.

Joseph no doubt believed that he was in the right, and that in any
event the incursion was so insignificant as to slip by undetected. But
he was incorrect. Both Frederick and Catherine the Great noticed.
In fact, very soon thereafter, Frederick's brother Henry, who happened to be in Russia negotiating with the tsarina, reported that
Catherine specifically mentioned Joseph's recent Polish land grab to
him, and by way of floating the idea of a concerted response had
genially joked, "Why should not everyone take some also?"

She didn't have to ask Frederick twice. As usual, when it came to
usurping someone else's property, the king of Prussia was already
three steps ahead. He had understood from the outset of her reign
that it was Catherine's intention to annex eastern Poland and that, to
avoid having to fight him for it, she would allow him to take over
the part of northern Poland adjacent to Prussia. In the past, he would
have just gone ahead and made the deal and left Vienna to find out
about it after the fact. Maria Theresa would have protested, of
course, but he knew that the dowager empress was in no position to
oppose it militarily—the previous war had proven that Austria
could not take on both Prussia *and* Russia.

But if he did it that way, the usual way, then later, if Russia decided
to keep moving west, and began to threaten *his* borders, Maria Theresa would never step in to help. And then whom could he turn to
for additional soldiers? There would be no one. So he had to find a
way to get Austria to participate in the scheme to divide Poland.
That way, if Russia turned on him, he'd have an ally.

It was with this tactic in mind that Frederick made his play for
Joseph, arranging a diplomatic meeting with him and the omnipresent Count Kaunitz on September 3, 1770, in Moravia, near the border with Silesia. The Prussian king had clearly taken the measure of
his disciple; he laid it on so thick it was a wonder he could keep a

straight face. "It is impossible for me to be the enemy of a great man!" Frederick boomed admiringly upon greeting Joseph. "As for myself, when I was young I was ambitious, but I am so no longer... You think me full of bad faith: I know it, I deserved it a little; circumstances compelled it, but all that is changed," the Prussian king assured the emperor with flattering earnestness. He even pretended to pay attention when Kaunitz self-importantly took time away from the discussion to read aloud from a long political memorandum that he had composed especially for the occasion. "Your minister has the wisest head in Europe!" Frederick raved, obviously agog at this performance. He begged Kaunitz to leave the document with him so that he could "have it always under my eyes, for I sincerely wish to conform my conduct to it."

The upshot of this fawning interview, and the subsequent follow-up correspondence, was that both Joseph and Kaunitz strongly recommended that Austria join the agreement with Prussia and Russia to divide up Poland between the three powers.

Maria Theresa was appalled. Poland was an independent kingdom! The Poles had done nothing to provoke an attack! Frederick and Catherine were simply taking advantage of a neighbor's weakness to help themselves to property that by every treaty and international right belonged to someone else. This was precisely what Frederick had tried to do to her at the start of her reign, when he had ganged up on her with France and Bavaria. She, who had spent so many years fighting him—was she now to turn around and *emulate* his behavior? It was unthinkable. "I am too much oppressed by our critical situation to refrain from bringing it once again into the light of day, and trying to find a remedy, if not good, at least the least evil," she wrote passionately to her son on January 25, 1772. "We wish to adopt the Prussian attitude, yet, at the same time, to preserve the appearance of honesty... It may be that I am wrong, and that these events are more favorable than I am able to see them, but... I should always consider them as too dearly bought, since they are so at the expense of honor, the glory of the Monarchy, and of our own good faith and religion!" she burst out. "Since the beginning of my ill-fated reign, we have attempted, at least, to observe in everything a true and equitable conduct, with good faith, moderation, and fidelity in our undertakings. That won for us the confidence, I might almost say the admiration, of Europe, and the respect and reverence of our enemies; that all has been lost, in the space of the last year," she mourned.

But by this time she was in her midfifties and tired. Since the death of her husband and her bout with smallpox, she had neither her old energy nor her will to struggle. Joseph's disaffection tore at her. She did not wish to give her son a new grievance against her by undercutting his military authority, nor did she have the strength to resist both him and her chief minister. Very reluctantly, she agreed to join in the partition of Poland, authorizing Count Kaunitz to carve out a substantial chunk of Polish territory on the border with Hungary for annexation. ("Permit me to say, you have a good appetite," Frederick snorted when the Austrian minister revealed the extent of the appropriation, which measured some 90 miles north to Krakow and 200 miles east to Lemberg [Lviv].) But neither the king nor the tsarina protested, and an official treaty was signed in Saint Petersburg on August 2, 1772, that split Poland three ways along these lines. "How often did I strive to dissociate myself from an action which sullies the whole of my reign!" Maria Theresa, still unreconciled to the transgression, repented bitterly the following month. "God grant that I shall not be held responsible for it in another world. It weighs on my heart, tortures my brain, and embitters my days, which are sad enough in any case."

Her son celebrated his achievement while her nemesis gloated, knowing that, after all this time, he had won decisively at last. "The Empress Catherine and I were brigands," Frederick drawled, to the amusement of his court. "But that pious empress queen, how did she arrange the matter with her confessor?"

★ ★ ★

MARIA CHRISTINA, A FIRSTHAND WITNESS to these events, watched with increasing consternation as her mother aged visibly under her brother's and Count Kaunitz's combined efforts to pressure the dowager empress to surrender her principles and approve the dismantling of Poland. As usual, she took Maria Theresa's part, and it is at this point that she began to emerge as Joseph's foremost political opponent at court. The situation was obvious even to outsiders; Mimi's sharp defense of her mother's moderate policies "may...explain the cause of the Emperor her brother's little attachment, not to say alienation towards her," observed the visiting Englishman. "It is well known that he [Joseph] considers her as a powerful rival, capable of frustrating his views; and of impeding, if not totally overturning, his best matured plans of ambition or policy, by awakening the Empress's scruples."

There is no surer indication of Maria Christina's emerging political power than the rumor that began to circulate at the very moment when the Polish question was nearing its crisis, and the pressure on her mother was the most intense, that Mimi was having an affair with Prince Charles Liechtenstein, the Austrian military commander assigned to Pressburg. The source of this gossip was none other than Charles Liechtenstein's wife, Eleonore, who claimed that her husband had voluntarily confessed to the liaison, and that Maria Christina had been so indiscreet that Maria Theresa herself had become aware of the infidelity. Eleonore felt honor bound to share this titillating story with the emperor and a few of her other close friends, who by sheer coincidence formed the faction most allied to Joseph at court.

There are several troubling aspects to this allegation. The first and most important was that Eleonore Liechtenstein was hardly a disinterested informant. For the past two years, her name had been romantically linked with Joseph's, the emperor having very publicly fallen in love with her. Eleonore, who seems not to have reciprocated her imperial suitor's passion, consequently had a very fine line to walk between resisting Joseph's advances (which were so pronounced that her husband, Charles, complained) and not alienating the most powerful man in Vienna. It's a little too convenient that she and her husband should be the sole authorities for the gossip concerning Joseph's sister. Second, Charles had recently been passed over for promotion and had only agreed to take the appointment in Pressburg, which he considered beneath him, under protest. He was clearly a man with a grudge, and while of course he might have been telling the truth, it is also possible that this was his way of settling scores with his wife, who then used the information to her advantage, knowing that it would please Joseph to have something on Maria Christina. As for Maria Theresa's knowledge of the affair, that is hardly likely; the dowager empress was the last person to accept a married daughter's infidelity and would certainly have demoted Charles and dashed off a letter strongly reprimanding Mimi. Neither of these outcomes occurred; rather, soon thereafter Joseph promoted Charles.

Also telling against the Liechtensteins' version of events is the lack of a noticeable rift between Maria Christina and her husband during this period. If anything, Mimi and Albert had drawn even closer together, having just agreed to embark on an undertaking to which they would dedicate their considerable resources for the rest of their lives: the acquisition of a collection of masterworks intended to define the progress of art through the ages.

A new year's gift of a book of prints of her favorite paintings from Maria Christina to Albert seems to have been the catalyst for this idea, which obviously also owed a great deal to the enduring influence of the encyclopedists. What if, Mimi and Albert asked themselves, they amassed the pictorial equivalent of a comprehensive treatise on the history of fine art, acquiring exquisite prints of paintings and drawings and then putting them into context by displaying them according to chronology, countries of origin, schools of thought, and the major aesthetic movements? "It pleased His Grace the Prince [Albert] to remark that the prints of Old Masters had the capacity to combine visual pleasure with the enlightenment of the mind most advantageously," reported the ecstatic Venetian art dealer the couple hired in 1773 to bring their grandiose concept to fruition. "This was the insight that gave rise to the plan to create a collection which, being aimed at higher purposes, would stand apart from all other collections," he beamed approvingly.

This ambitious project was given an extra boost two years later when Maria Theresa, casting around for someone she could trust to check up on Maria Amalia in Parma and Maria Carolina in Naples, offered Mimi and Albert the opportunity to embark on an extended tour of Italy. The couple leapt at the chance and departed Vienna on December 28, 1775, for what would evolve into a seven-month family visit that doubled as a world-class seminar in art appreciation.

It was the first time thirty-three-year-old Maria Christina had ever traveled abroad. Prior to this, her farthest excursion from Vienna had been to Innsbruck for her brother Leopold's wedding. Albert's previous journeys, too, had been confined to his recent survey of Hungary and his army service in Germany, neither of which could by any measure be classified as pleasure trips. Now the pair advanced leisurely, as members of the imperial family and honored visitors, through perhaps the most beautiful country in Europe.

They were fêted in Venice by the doge, and rode in gondolas, marveling at the splendor around them like all the other first-time tourists. From Venice they traveled to Bologna, where they met Farinelli, once the most famous singer in Europe, now an old man in retirement. After Bologna they journeyed to Leopold and his family for a two-month stay at the elegant Pitti Palace, with its charming gardens and sublime statues. Their time in Florence was followed quickly by a month in Rome, where they were put up in the magnificent Villa Medici and the pope bestowed a golden rose on Mimi. Afterward, it was on to Maria Carolina in Naples. It was May before they made their way back through Rome and Tuscany to Maria Amalia in Parma and finally to Milan (where Mimi's second-youngest brother, Ferdinand, was governor). In each of these cities the couple made a point of seeking out the works of Raphael, Michelangelo, Leonardo, Titian, and other great masters. Like so many art lovers before them, Maria Christina and Albert stood open-mouthed before the originals of frescoes and paintings that they had previously known only by reputation. Aesthetically, the trip was a revelation.

But of course Mimi had not been sent simply to gawk. She was there to report back to Maria Theresa, which she did regularly throughout the trip. (Albert took so many notes that he eventually published a memoir of these travels.) Leopold and his family were thriving, Maria Christina informed her mother—his eighth surviving child and *sixth* son was born on March 9, 1776, while she and Albert were in Rome—her brother was certainly doing his part to ensure the succession of the monarchy. Additionally, Leopold had instituted a number of reforms aimed at improving the lives of his subjects, including taxing the Church and the nobility, streamlining government and the military, and eliminating the Inquisition. Charlotte's court was very grand, and she had improved the manners of her husband, Ferdinand, but he still spent all of his time hunting or fishing, depending on the season. The queen of Naples adored her children—by this time, three girls and a boy—and spent most of her day with them. Although Mimi never mentioned it, seeing so many nieces and nephews must have been bittersweet for a woman whose own hopes of motherhood were dwindling fast. At the close of each visit, her brothers and sisters provided recent portraits of their large families to take back to Vienna so that Maria Theresa could see her grandchildren.

The only potential discord in this otherwise idyllic holiday emanated from Parma, where Maria Amalia was deeply unhappy with both her husband and her reduced circumstances. Unlike her younger sisters, whose prestigious kingdoms and opulent lifestyles represented a step up from Vienna, Maria Amalia's rank and general standard of living had actually been degraded by her marriage.* She quarreled incessantly with her spouse and begged to be allowed to come home to Austria without him; when her petition was denied, she took over the administration of the government from his chief minister, who complained to Louis XV. Worse, from Maria Theresa's point of view, came the news that her daughter had dismissed her ladies-in-waiting, and instead spent all of her time hunting with a group of male servants. It had gotten so contentious that the dowager empress had stopped writing to the duchess of Parma altogether. "So much consolation as I have found in Naples, Versailles, Florence, and Milan," Maria Theresa observed, referring to her children in each of these cities, "equal grief has been caused me by that daughter from the moment of her departure."†

However, as Maria Amalia had recently fulfilled her wifely duty by delivering a son and heir, her mother was considering patching up their quarrel. Mimi's visit was by way of an olive branch, the first step toward the resumption of amicable relations. Mimi, who had not seen Maria Amalia in six years, was shocked by how much, in her disappointment and dissatisfaction, her sister's appearance had deteriorated. Missing was all "trace of the glamour, the beauty" of her youth, Mimi mourned. "Her beautiful figure was changed, her dress and carriage have changed even more," she told her mother. "She is less gay, less discriminating."

If anything, her sister's plight only underscored Maria Christina's

---

* The same Englishwoman who had swooned over the opera house in Naples described the theater of Parma as having "a parcel of old brown planks ill joined together, and much damaged by smoke and damp," making up a ceiling and a stage "so ill-floored that you cannot easily walk over it without tumbling." Owing to the modest income provided to its duke, the château of Parma ("unworthy of observation," the visiting Englishwoman sniffed) was in a similar state of decay. Although originally famous for its "vast collection...of bronzes, pictures, medals, and a library of books," by the time of Maria Amalia's arrival, these treasures had all been shipped to Naples on Don Carlos's orders and now adorned Maria Carolina's palace.

† Maria Amalia, angry and hurt, reciprocated her mother's animosity, so much so that when her first daughter was born, in 1770, the duchess of Parma defied tradition and alone among her siblings refused to name the child Maria Theresa, christening her Maria Carolina instead.

own good fortune. She might not have children, but she had a husband whom she loved and respected, and who shared her values. By this time Mimi and Albert had decided that upon their return to Pressburg they would expand their palace by building a gallery to exhibit their collection, which (in keeping with the new, modern age of enlightenment) they would open to the general population. Thus would Hungary for a short time become the beneficiary of one of the first public art museums in Europe.

The couple spent the last precious days of their trip huddling with their dealer in Venice. He had been busily purchasing the prints they had requested and had succeeded in amassing hundreds of them, which he now handed over to his pleased patrons; he had also gone to the trouble of composing an eleven-page catalogue that set out the goals and purpose of the collection.

Although they did not yet know it, on the very day that Maria Christina and Albert were exclaiming over their new acquisitions in the dealer's sumptuous Venetian apartments, and commending him for summarizing their intentions so fluently—July 4, 1776, as it turned out—a similarly eloquent document, also the product of the Enlightenment, had just been produced in Philadelphia, a dinky little outpost over 4,000 miles away that was so remote and inconsiderable that neither they, nor the art dealer, nor indeed anyone in Italy had ever heard of it. Penned by an educated, articulate (if disgruntled) colonist by the name of Thomas Jefferson, who referred to his handiwork as a "Declaration of Independence," it dealt not with art but with politics. This seismic treatise was about to catapult the movement for rational thought made popular by the encyclopedists into an entirely new and far-reaching arena. It was a catalogue, not of Old Master prints, but of the rights of individuals to choose their own rulers and form their own governments.

It would be some time before Mimi and Albert (who were back home in Vienna with Maria Theresa just ten days later, *oohing* and *aahing* with her over the portraits of her Italian-born grandchildren) would become aware of this development. Even then, they likely did not give it much thought. That Britain was having trouble with its American colonies was well known. What difference did it make which rationale the troublemakers used to dress up their grievances? The real worry was that the rebellion in the New World would draw the rest of Europe into the conflict with them, as it had the last time. Everybody knew it would only take one opportunist to start the whole Seven Years' War over again.

Everybody but Joseph and Count Kaunitz, that is.

UNLIKE HIS MOTHER, Joseph had taken pride in (and credit for) having added a large swathe of Polish territory to his family's Hungarian holdings. It made for a nice first step toward compensating the monarchy for the loss of Silesia and encouraged him to try in other, similarly ambitious ways to expand the borders of his mother's—and by extension, after her death, *his*—property. To this end, prodded by Kaunitz, he had for some time had his eye on Bavaria.

Bavaria, of course, was owned by that part of the family—the Wilhelmine side—who upon Maria Theresa's ascension those long years ago had allied with Prussia and France against her. It was the elector of Bavaria who had invaded Austria and gotten himself crowned emperor before Maria Theresa had turned the tables on him and occupied his home capital of Munich.* It was his teenaged son whom, after his disgraced father had died, she had graciously forgiven, returning his lands and allowing him to rule unmolested for the past thirty-odd years. It was this same relative who had been the brother of Joseph's despised second wife, Maria Josepha. The elector of Bavaria was now fifty years old and childless. The question was, who should inherit his property after his death?

This was obviously a prime example of the kind of substantial holding that Joseph was looking to add to his portfolio. As he had

---

* This episode was later immortalized in a poem: "The bold Bavarian, in a luckless hour, / Tries the dread summit of Cæsarean power; / With unexpected legions bursts away, / And sees defenseless realms accept his sway. / Short sway! Fair Austria spreads her mournful charms, / The Queen, the Beauty, sets the world in arms."

with Poland, the emperor had an underling scrounge around through the archives for whatever centuries-old documents might be found that could help provide even the most tenuous legal claim to the territory (in addition, of course, to his rights as the deceased Maria Josepha's husband; turns out she was good for something after all). With these in hand, he was all ready to go when on January 1, 1778, he received notice that his former brother-in-law of Bavaria had died the preceding day. All Joseph needed now was his mother's approval to send in troops to secure the duchy for Austria.

By sheer coincidence, the same English tourist who had been so taken with Mimi had been invited to celebrate New Year's Day with the royal court in Vienna and so was available to record Maria Theresa's reaction to her son's proposal to invade Bavaria, which it is clear he sprang on her without a scintilla of prior notice. "All the nobility and persons of condition in Vienna were then about to assemble in the great drawing room of the palace, where the Empress Queen, the Emperor, and the Archduchesses, her daughters [Marianne, Maria Elisabeth, and Mimi, who was visiting] were present," the traveler related. "Maria Theresa sat down to play; while the Emperor, who never touches cards, stood near her, engaged in conversation. I was present at an inconsiderable distance from them," he noted, by way of cementing his testimony as an eyewitness. At this point a messenger arrived, clearly with the news of the death of the elector of Bavaria. The emperor "withdrew, but returned in a few minutes and, leaning over the table at which his mother was playing, he whispered some words in her ear. She instantly let fall the cards, and rising up with evident marks of emotion, quitted the apartment...the Archduchesses, her daughters...likewise threw down their cards and followed her. We all looked at each other in astonishment," he remembered vividly. "I know however, from good authority, that...after the Empress Queen retired to her own apartments, a secret council was there held, consisting of herself, the Emperor, and Prince Kaunitz. Much difference of opinion, relative to the extent of territory to be claimed and occupied by the Austrian troops, then manifested itself. Maria Theresa betrayed great agitation, often repeating with earnestness in German, 'In God's name, only take what we have a right to demand! I foresee that it will end in war!'"

Of course, they had no clear right to any of it, but this did not stop Joseph and Kaunitz from insisting that the army must be sent in right away. They were only able to get a distraught Maria Theresa to agree by promising that they would occupy the smallest amount of territory possible, and that even this was merely a cautionary measure pending negotiations. Upon her extremely reluctant assent, Joseph instantly sent in a large force, which naturally spread out over far more of Bavaria than he had indicated to his mother.

It was a move stunning in its provocation; the work of a vainglorious older man—Kaunitz was in his midsixties, still steeped in the luster of the past—and an overweening younger one, aching to show off his prowess to the world; it almost begged for a counterattack. "Will the Elector of Saxony [Albert's nephew], whose mother is sister to the deceased Prince...take no interest in the affair?" the English traveler wondered. "Can Prussia look on unconcerned, while his most formidable enemy aggrandizes himself, and extends his territories?"

No, actually, Prussia couldn't. Frederick rolled his eyes when he heard that Austria had occupied Bavaria. After all the trouble he'd gone to at the time of the division of Poland to school the callow emperor on the etiquette of foreign policy! When a stronger power wanted to partake of a weaker one, the gentlemanly thing to do was to invite all the other strong powers in the region to the table and serve up a slice to each. Now here was Joseph trying to hog all of Bavaria for himself. "These people must think I am dead," Frederick snorted in disbelief. And he allied Prussia with Saxony, which also had a claim to Bavaria, and prepared to put a large army into the field.*

---

* Saxony, having experienced Prussian occupation once, had no desire to risk further hostilities with Frederick and so sided with him this time. "No advantages which the court of Vienna can hold out or offer to Saxony, will ever compensate for the

Maria Theresa, approaching her sixty-first birthday, was beside herself. This was exactly what she had feared would happen. She tried everything she could think of to get Joseph and Kaunitz to back down and recall the troops from Bavaria. She offered to take on herself all the blame and ignominy for having capitulated to Prussian and Saxon demands. "I will gladly commit myself to anything, even if it tarnishes my reputation," she begged in a written memorandum dated March 14, 1778. "People can accuse me of senility, weakness, pusillanimity. Nothing will stop me rescuing Europe from this dangerous situation." But Joseph was adamant, and marshaled his forces for war. He *wanted* to fight. "The Emperor alone appears unaffectedly gay, constantly in action, on horseback before the sun is risen, and ready to receive with alacrity the various bodies of troops at their arrival," the English visitor reported on March 19.

It was at this point that Maria Christina, appalled, entered the fray. What! Joseph and Kaunitz had provoked a war in which Albert, who by his marriage to her would command an army on the Austrian side, was now to risk his life fighting against his own countrymen of Saxony? "It may be his [Albert's] lot to enter Dresden, and to desolate the dominions of the family from which he springs," the Englishman pointed out. "Such a conflict of principles and obligations, cannot fail to be deeply painful to a mind of sensibility. The Archduchess, his wife, is known to be affected by it in the liveliest manner. She deprecates the prospect of a rupture...and has more than once thrown herself at her mother's feet, conjuring her with tears, while there is still time...to stop the effusion of human blood. The Emperor...may one day...punish her opposition to his favorite measures," the visitor mused.

But Maria Theresa had not the political will to emasculate her son by overruling him in so public a manner, particularly when Count

---

misfortunes almost necessarily resulting from a rupture with Prussia," the English traveler explained. "This is a truth of which the present wise Elector, instructed by his grandfather's experience and calamities, seems to have the fullest conviction."

Kaunitz, who had served her so loyally and ably for so many years, assured her that it was the right thing to do and that all would be well. "He [Kaunitz] is for the war," Maria Christina fumed to Albert, "since, according to him, it is disgraceful to give in, even if one has committed a folly...he is getting stiffer by the day, and those are the hands in which lies the welfare of the monarchy!" The best Mimi could do was to get her husband assigned to that wing of the Austrian army stationed as far away from Saxony as possible. Albert left to take command of this force on April 9, Maria Christina riding out beside him for some distance before being compelled to say goodbye, "a separation which did not take place without violent emotions on her part," the Englishman noted sympathetically. An excited Joseph, brimming with confidence and ready to make his mark on the world as the victorious general of a great army, left two days later for Prague, where the main body of his soldiers was deployed.

This rosy outlook on the part of the glorious commander lasted exactly three months, specifically until July 5, 1778, at which point Frederick, to teach Austria a lesson, invaded Bohemia, and Joseph discovered to his acute distress (not to mention that of the 160,000 Austrian troops relying on him) that he much preferred to play at war than to be a part of one. Fighting, it turned out, was unpleasant. It caused destruction. More than this, it could be dangerous. "The evils that it leads to are frightful, and...much worse than I had visualized," he quaked in an alarming letter home to his mother, in which he simultaneously despaired of all hope of success and begged for 40,000 additional soldiers, at the very least, to repel the Prussians. This despite the fact that he already commanded the largest force that in all her years of war the dowager empress had ever put into the field. "Now see what a state we are in!" Maria Theresa exclaimed in a note to the comte de Mercy after receiving this disquieting communication from her thirty-seven-year-old son. "For they [Joseph and his field marshals] think of nothing less than abandoning Prague, and the whole of Bohemia . . . And all this before we have received the slightest repulse!"*

The emperor's panicked cry for help—for that is what his letter was—gave Maria Theresa the ammunition she needed to act in what she considered to be his best interests. To Joseph's eternal humiliation, the very first thing she did was dash off a secret message to Frederick in which she promised him the key provinces of Ansbach and Bayreuth in northern Bavaria if he would please call off his soldiers and spare the life of her son.

This was of course exactly the overture Frederick had been looking for, and he made the most of his opportunity. He immediately devoted himself to the sort of double-dealing in which he excelled, increasing his demands and those of Saxony while conducting clandestine negotiations with England and Russia to bring these two powerful interests into the conflict on his side. He was assisted enormously in this regard by the French government's refusal to honor their commitments under the terms of the Austrian alliance, citing a previous obligation to aid the American colonists, but what really helped Frederick was Joseph's extreme reluctance to engage in anything approximating a battle. "Certainly no campaign in the course of the present century has more disappointed expectation, produced fewer events, or been attended with so inconsiderable an effusion of blood," the English tourist noted. "The Emperor's determination to bear all insults, even to see his provinces ravaged and ransomed, rather than hazard an engagement, was systematic and insuperable," he deplored.

Consequently, it was all over in less than a year. On Maria Theresa's sixty-second birthday, May 13, 1779, the question of who would control Bavaria was settled, not by combat, but by treaty.

---

* Joseph was so clearly unsuited to the military that his mother could not help but compare him to her former commanders. "That," she added wearily in her letter to Mercy, "restores the credit of Charles [of Lorraine]." You know you are in trouble when Charles of Lorraine seems the more competent option.

Prussia received Ansbach and Bayreuth, along with some estates in Bohemia. Saxony was granted 6 million florins as compensation for its rights. Austria, which had once again bankrupted itself, spending 100 million florins in a matter of months in pursuit of this ultimately elusive prize, gained only a small slice of eastern Bavaria. There is almost no question that Joseph and Kaunitz would have acquired far more territory if they had chosen *not* to invade and simply negotiated for a share of the inheritance with Saxony and Prussia. To Mimi's intense relief, Albert returned home unscathed, the only real casualties of her brother's misplaced militarism being the poor people of Bohemia whose homes and fields had been at the mercy of Frederick's soldiers.

THE PROSECUTION OF THIS ILL-CONSIDERED, aborted little war, which had cost so much in treasure and prestige, came with an additional, if concealed, price tag: it exhausted Maria Theresa. The anxiety she experienced from the moment Joseph had proposed the scheme until she saw him, his younger brother Maximilian (who had also been enlisted in the effort), and Albert safely back in Vienna was profound. For over a year she had spent hours on her knees in the royal chapel praying for guidance and protection. She complained of being "weary with the march of life." From this point on, her physical condition deteriorated rapidly. Mimi observed worriedly that her mother now became as short of breath merely crossing a room as formerly she would have ascending a staircase. Even writing became a painful experience. "My hands will no longer serve me," the dowager empress revealed unhappily. "I am afraid of losing the use of them. It would be particularly awkward on account of my weight. No one would be able to move me." The English visitor noted sadly that "Maria Theresa's person now retains no trace of the charms which she once possessed; and it is even difficult to conceive from her present aspect and appearance that she was ever handsome...the Empress Queen is now grown corpulent, unwieldy, and infirm."

She was in fact so overweight that the only way she could visit Francis's tomb to pray for his soul, which she insisted on doing without fail every month, was to be lowered into the vault in a large armchair. The dowager empress was unfazed when, on October 15, 1780, one of the ropes securing this contraption broke as she was being hauled back up out of the crypt. "He [Francis] wants to keep me with him," she sighed wistfully. "I shall come soon."

She was right. A month later she caught cold after being soaked by an unexpected cloudburst while traveling in an unclosed coach. She insisted on working through her illness and remained at her desk the next day. By November 25 it was clear she was dangerously ill. Mimi, Albert, and Joseph, as well as Marianne and Maria Elisabeth, were all with her on November 28 when her doctors officially gave up hope and she received last rites. Joseph urged her to try to get some rest, but his mother refused. "I do not want to fall asleep and be taken unawares," she said simply. "These fifteen years I have been getting ready for Death. I will meet him awake."

Maria Theresa, Holy Roman Empress, queen of Hungary and Bohemia, and archduchess of Austria, the only female member of the Habsburg family, for centuries the predominant dynasty in Europe, ever to rule in her own right, died the following evening, November 29, 1780, at a quarter to nine. She was sixty-three years old. Deeply flawed as both ruler and parent, blindly intolerant of all but practicing Catholics, petty in her attempts to legislate the morality of her subjects, she had nonetheless demonstrated astonishing strength, courage, intelligence, determination, and foresight during the course of her decades-long reign. Ever on the side of the common people, she was at her death working to liberate the serfs from the excesses of the privileged classes in Hungary. For nearly forty years she had held together, often by sheer will, her far-flung, disparate subjects with an energy and diligence born of her compassion for humanity, her desire for fairness and moderation, and her deep-rooted sense of responsibility.

"Maria Theresa is no more," Frederick, five years her senior and pleased to have outlived her, exulted at the news. "And now a new order begins."

But the prediction of the abbé Galiani, the Neapolitan envoy to the court of France under Louis XV, was perhaps more insightful. The dowager empress's death, he warned, would be like "an ink-bottle spilt over the map of Europe."

Maria Theresa with her
many crowns

Francis as Holy
Roman Emperor

Frederick the Great at the close of the
Seven Years' War

Maria Theresa riding up the hill brandishing the sword of Saint Stephen as part of her Hungarian coronation ceremony.

The Ladies' Carousel in Vienna celebrating the retaking of Prague from the French during the War of the Austrian Succession.

The imperial family in 1754. In the foreground, from left to right: Francis of Lorraine, Holy Roman Emperor; Marianne; Maria Christina; Joseph; Maria Elisabeth; Leopold; Empress Maria Theresa; Charles. In the background: Maria Amalia, standing; Maria Johanna and Maria Josepha, seated at the little table, with Maria Carolina and the baby, Ferdinand, in his crib in front of them. Missing are the still-to-be-born Marie Antoinette and Maximilian.

Joseph and Leopold in Rome. This portrait was painted just after Joseph's quick visit to check up on Charlotte and Ferdinand in Naples in 1769.

Mimi's self-portrait, painted the year before her marriage to Albert

Albert after his first visit to
Vienna in 1760, where he fell in
love with Maria Christina

Isabella of Parma

Mimi's painting *The Imperial Family Celebrating Saint Nicholas*. From left to right:
Ferdinand crying; Maria Christina trying to shush him; Marie Antoinette,
oblivious to her brother's distress, proudly holding up her new doll; a patient
Maria Theresa getting ready to pour out the coffee; Francis, still in his nightcap,
peering blearily at his noisy son; Maximilian taking advantage of his parents'
distraction to gobble up sweets under the table.

Maria Carolina by Élisabeth
Vigée Le Brun

Ferdinand, king of Naples,
four years into his marriage

The royal family of Naples in 1783. From left to right: At the harp, Maria Teresa (married later to Leopold's eldest son, Francis, who succeeded his father as emperor); crown prince Francesco; Ferdinand, king of Naples; Maria Carolina, queen of Naples; Maria Christina (married later to the brother of the king of Sardinia); Gennaro; Maria Luisa (married later to Leopold's second son, the grand duke of Tuscany); on Maria Luisa's lap, Maria Amalia (later the wife of the son of the duc d'Orléans and consequently a future queen of France). Charlotte would go on to have eight more children of whom only Maria Antonietta and Leopold would survive childhood.

Sir William
Hamilton

Admiral Nelson

Emma as Circe by
George Romney

Marie Antoinette by Élisabeth
Vigée Le Brun

Louis XVI

Count Axel Fersen

Maria Carolina

"Charlotte"

‿❦‿

Lady Emma Hamilton

15

The Queen Takes Control

※

Of all my daughters, she [Charlotte] is the one who resembles me the most.

—Maria Theresa

ON JANUARY 6, 1775, while her mother was yet alive and her younger sister, Marie Antoinette, had only recently been promoted from dauphine to the august throne of France, Maria Carolina, after nearly seven years of marriage to Ferdinand of Naples, finally brought forth, to the delirious joy of her husband and his subjects, a son and heir, her third child. The twenty-two-year-old queen was barely out of the birthing bed after fulfilling this key requirement of her nuptial contract before she assumed her rightful place on the royal council, a role that for the first time put her on an equal footing with the kingdom's longtime first minister, Bernardo Tanucci.

Tanucci was by this time in his seventies. He had been in power for over thirty years, having started his political career under Ferdinand's father, Don Carlos. Even though Don Carlos was now Charles III, king of Spain, Tanucci still considered him to be the true ruler of Naples; he saw the southern boot of Italy and the island of Sicily not as an independent kingdom but rather as a subsidiary of the powerful Spanish empire. Consequently, the minister took his orders from Madrid, not from the regional government at Caserta.

This system had been in place for years, mostly because Ferdinand, who had been brought up to be an obedient son, and who in any event had neither the desire nor the ability to rule, acquiesced to whatever Tanucci and his father wanted. On those rare occasions when the king of Naples seemed inclined to object to a policy, the minister knew he had only to invoke parental disapproval, or threaten to resign, to frighten Ferdinand into submission.

Then Maria Carolina came along. She was far more educated than her husband, and wished to ally Naples with Austria, as well as institute the enlightened reforms of her two brothers, Joseph and Leopold. It had not taken her long to determine that Ferdinand was unsuited to government, and this recognition put her into direct conflict with Tanucci. "I wish to God my husband was diligent, I would have preferred him to do everything by himself," Charlotte sighed in a letter to Leopold. "But his distracting life [hunting, fishing, etc.] makes it impossible for him to do his duties...So rather than see him killed by his ministers or by a bad person or led by his confessor I am forced to act."

Tanucci was aware, of course, that the queen of Naples thought he had too much influence, and that she believed that she and Ferdinand should be the ones giving the orders, not the king of Spain. But he was so secure in his position that he did not take her seriously. Rather, to put her in her place, he decided to pick a fight with her. This turned out to be a big mistake.

The fight was over government suppression of the Society of Freemasons, a laughably nonthreatening clique. Freemasonry, which was on the rise, was strongly associated with the encyclopedists and Enlightenment philosophy. The roster of great men identifying as Masons reads like a Who's Who of the eighteenth century: Voltaire was a Mason, as were John Locke, Haydn, Mozart, George Washington, and Benjamin Franklin. Maria Carolina's father, Francis, had been a Freemason, and consequently her brothers Joseph and Leopold were also Masons. Many of the Englishmen who swarmed to Naples on the Grand Tour or to visit the British ambassador, Sir

William Hamilton, were Freemasons. As it was known that the queen was a warm supporter of the order, lodges had sprung up openly in the capital city. Although the pope regarded this fraternal organization as dangerously heretical, their principal occupation, at least in Italy, seems to have been to host jolly parties.

Tanucci had no pressing reason to go after the Society of Freemasons; in fact, he had to dust off an old Spanish prohibition from 1751, before Maria Carolina was even born, as his legal justification for shutting down their lodges. But the Freemasons added to the queen's popularity, and their members were among her greatest enthusiasts, so in the spring of 1776, with the king of Spain's approval, the Neapolitan minister had Ferdinand sign a formal proclamation outlawing the society and threatening its members with prosecution if they persisted in their activities. When this failed to intimidate the lodges, Tanucci followed it up by having the royal guard break into one of their meetings and throw the participants in jail, pending trial for criminal acts against the state.

His timing could not have been worse. Maria Christina and Albert (both Masons themselves) were visiting, so Charlotte had the benefit of her sister and brother-in-law's assistance and counsel. At the queen's urging, the prison was overrun with high-ranking well-wishers bearing gifts of groceries and other luxuries for the comfort of the captive Masons, and the best legal minds in the kingdom offered their services. The judges assigned to the case were bombarded by petitions attesting to the unblemished character of the accused and the fraudulent nature of the charges. A steady stream of dukes, duchesses, and other dignitaries made their appearance at court, deploring the government's action.

The prosecution caved under the pressure; the accused were acquitted on all charges; the lodges stayed open. The king of Spain remonstrated by letter with his son but even this usually reliable expedient failed to achieve the desired effect, as Ferdinand, who hated scenes and wanted to be left alone to do his hunting, had far more to fear from his wife's unhappiness than his father's. "Until now I did not like to mention it, but since Your Majesty is acquainted with my woes, I may tell you that it is my wife who has played the devil in order to have them [the Masonic meetings] . . . and I for the sake of peace had to allow it," he whined in his response to his father. "Your Majesty wrote that I paid more attention to others' advice than your own," he continued. "I showed her [Charlotte] the letter and she replied: 'So this is why you are upset? What difference can it make? He is a stubborn old blockhead who will not listen to reason and has got this bee in his bonnet. Cheer up and do as I tell you,'" Ferdinand reported to his parent, still clearly in shock.

He wasn't the only one. Tanucci had a surprise coming as well. On October 26, 1776, after a carefully planned offensive composed in equal parts of histrionics and the withholding of bedroom privileges, followed by relenting and the rapturous resumption of loving relations, the queen of Naples brought her husband around to her point of view sufficiently to prevail upon him to sign a decree relieving his first minister of his duties. This document, which was worded in such a manner as to imply that it was simply a matter of a well-earned retirement after a long and honorable career, was delivered to Tanucci so early in the morning that the royal messenger caught him in his nightgown. "But the Catholic King [of Spain] has written me nothing about this!" Tanucci sputtered from his pillows. To which the courier, coached by Charlotte for just this contingency, countered smoothly, "Your Excellency has requested it often and the King [of Naples] has just granted your wish."

And that was how Maria Carolina, eight years into her marriage, deftly outmaneuvered a seasoned politician three times her age, overthrew Spanish authority, and took over the monarchy. From this time on, she chaired her husband's council, planned his policies, and administered his government, while he amused himself with sports and other, frequently less wholesome recreational activities. His wife's assumption of these tedious official duties suited the king of Naples. "Do you [make decisions] and then tell me," Ferdinand entrusted her.

And that is what she did.

★   ★   ★

OVER THE COURSE OF the next decade, against the languid Neapolitan backdrop of old-world glamour, spectacle, and revelry that masked the very real poverty, ignorance, and superstition of the vast majority of its inhabitants, Maria Carolina labored to improve the lives of her subjects and bolster the power and prestige of her state. Like her mother before her, she paid close attention to detail. She read every report, letter, inventory, and dossier that crossed her desk. She sought out information and expert advice. She kept to a rigorous schedule. She awoke at seven, dressed, and had her hair done in time to attend early Mass. She would check up on her children, and then the rest of the day would be given over to business: meetings with ministers, correspondence, private audiences, and petitions. She would see Ferdinand, if he were not away hunting, for lunch or dinner; after dinner she would attend the council and then go to bed. Nor did she (again in emulation of her mother) allow her many pregnancies to slow her down. Between 1777 and 1786, Charlotte maintained this formidable work agenda despite giving birth eight times, to nine additional children—three sons and six daughters, including a set of twins.

Such diligence and energy had not been witnessed in Naples since the reign of Don Carlos, and it yielded striking results. The queen stressed education, particularly for women (despite her myriad duties, Charlotte made time every day for reading), and within a few years she had broken the Jesuit hold on teaching, modernized the curriculum, and established new schools, as well as a Royal Academy of Science and Letters, the first in the history of the kingdom. In 1777, when an outbreak of smallpox threatened to turn into an epidemic, she appealed to Leopold, who recommended Dr. Angelo Gatti, the leading specialist in inoculation at the University of Pisa. She brought the physician to Naples and, although terrified to take the risk, nonetheless had him try out the method on her own children first. "No Neapolitan thought of sending for Gatti," observed the former ambassador to France, the abbé Galiani, now an adviser to

Maria Carolina, "but since he is here they get themselves inoculated." She built up grain supplies against the possibility of a future famine, abolished torture and the Inquisition, and repaired the roads. But there is no question that the reform closest to her heart, the project into which she poured a disproportionate share of her time and ardor, was the development of a navy.

It may be difficult to believe that, prior to Charlotte, no monarch or member of the government of Naples had thought that it might be a good idea (seeing that the realm, which included the island of Sicily, was after all located on a peninsula) to put together a maritime fleet for defense, but this was in fact the case. Officially, of course, the kingdom was under the protection of Ferdinand's father and so theoretically had access to Spanish warships, but unless these happened to be in the neighborhood (which they never were), this remedy was of little practical use in case of an attack. Consequently, Naples was vulnerable to occupation by any opportunistic neighbor equipped with a flotilla. Even more worrying, sea power in general was on the rise, particularly among the major European states. Catherine the Great had made building a navy the top priority of the first years of her reign, and she didn't even have a year-round port until she conquered one from the Turks.

When a survey of military officers from within the kingdom yielded no one with sufficient experience to take on a project of this magnitude, Maria Carolina asked around and identified an expatriate English captain, currently in Leopold's employ, who came highly recommended. Careful as always to maintain the fiction that everything she did was at the command of her spouse, she wrote to her brother and entreated in Ferdinand's name that the officer in question be released from his service to Tuscany and loaned to her husband's court instead. Leopold graciously granted her request, and on August 4, 1778, Captain John Acton arrived in Naples.

He was forty-two to Charlotte's twenty-six, intelligent, industrious, and knowledgeable. Although not classically handsome, he was a romantic figure, lean and commanding; he spoke his mind, and his arguments, based on actual combat experience, were persuasive. After Maria Carolina's years of dealing with a dogmatic geriatric (Tanucci) and an overgrown juvenile (Ferdinand), Acton's professionalism and can-do attitude hit her with the brisk, refreshing force of a waterfall. "If you should find anyone, be it a minister or a lady, whom you consider worthy of your trust," her mother had advised her at the time of her marriage, "then give them your full confidence...they are rare. If one...is found, that is...the best gift of God, which should be sought with zeal, and preserved with care." Within a week of his arrival in Naples, Charlotte knew that in Acton she had found her version of Maria Theresa's Count Kaunitz. He was immediately promoted to general and appointed minister of the marine.

The queen of Naples's faith in her new hire was not misplaced. Acton set to work at once. He not only built warships, he also cut graft and reorganized the kingdom's finances, saving the Crown 500,000 ducats in the process. He established new shipyards and renovated the old ones based on modern methods of production; imported specialists in nautical engineering and mechanics from abroad; and founded naval academies for the instruction of Neapolitan officers. Within two years, he had been raised to minister of war, and within five Maria Carolina had her fleet: three-masters, frigates, gunboats, galleys—in all, an impressive 150 vessels of varying sizes and capacities, complete with trained captains and crews to man them.

Such competence and productivity on the part of a foreigner, accompanied as they were by a commensurate rise in power and unprecedented access to the throne, quite naturally aroused jealousy among the native courtiers; apparently, it also aroused Maria Carolina. She saw Acton daily, sometimes for hours at a time, and by her own admission wrote him a number of incriminating letters, although it is unclear how the minister responded. The fact that he remained in her service for decades without a rupture would indicate that Acton was clever enough to declare affectionate devotion while prudently staying clear of the bedroom.

Charlotte's infatuation with her war minister, and her willingness to act upon her desires, were a reflection of the morality of the society in which she lived. Infidelity was not merely tolerated among the fashionable set in Naples; it was embraced as a way of life. (Ferdinand cheated on her regularly, and was caught just as often.) It was one of the many allures of the city, part of what made it so attractive to visitors on the Grand Tour. Naples was a place where people went on holiday and engaged in behaviors that might have been frowned upon at home. Persons of high birth regularly mingled at aristocratic parties and soirees with less respectable (if more entertaining) individuals whom they would not have acknowledged, even just to nod at, in the streets of London.

Adding to the general carousing and lack of decorum was the behavior of the monarch. Ferdinand had never outgrown his contempt for knowledge, his fondness for bawdy humor, or his coarseness. He was known as the "hooligan king." Every Christmas Eve, designated in Naples as a fast day broken with a meatless supper, he donned the cap and apron of a tradesman and went down to the stalls in the main market to play the part of fishmonger, selling calamari and scampi like a common peddler, shouting at the crowds, insulting the women, and joking obscenely with his customers, to the great delight of the underclasses. Similarly, on the evening before Lent, he would have pots of steaming macaroni brought to the elegant San Carlo theater. Leaning over the railing of the upper tier while his wife withdrew in embarrassment to the back of the royal box, the king of Naples would toss the still-hot pasta by the handful into the pits where the common people stood to watch the performances, laughing uproariously as they scrambled to grab the free food. His lowborn subjects did not resent him for this sloppy largesse; on the contrary, they considered him one of their own. While this sort of conduct might have charmed the proletariat, from a romantic point of view it didn't stand a chance against the magnetism of a mature, sophisticated, battle-hardened naval commander. It would have been odd had Maria Carolina *not* fallen for Acton.

"Ferdinand is a good sort of man, because nature has not supplied him with the faculties necessary to make a bad one," the war minister observed of his adopted sovereign.

Whether Charlotte's passion was ever consummated is impossible to determine, but rumors of her attachment were numerous enough to reach the court of the king of Spain. Ferdinand's father, having lost his influence in Naples with the fall of Tanucci, and fearing the kingdom would ally with Austria or England against him, saw the gossip as a means of reestablishing parental authority. He penned his son a lengthy missive accusing Maria Carolina and Acton of infidelity, and demanding that the minister be exiled. "Open your eyes, my son," he scolded. "Having turned you into a pasteboard king, they have now made you lose your honor...you must get rid of Acton at once...Unless you do this I shall not believe that you are a good son." Fear of parental disapproval worked as usual: no sooner had he read the letter than Ferdinand barged into Charlotte's room, waved the paper at her, and shouted, "I am trying to surprise you together. I will kill you both, and have your bodies thrown out of the windows of the palace!"

But Maria Carolina was more than a match for her husband. She locked the door behind him, and for the next twenty-four hours, with ever-increasing righteous indignation, she pitched into him for believing such filth and falling for his father's obvious ploy to reassert control over Naples. Did he wish to become a puppet of Spain again, just when she had freed him of Madrid? How dare he suspect her of such baseness, she who had already given him a dozen children, including four male heirs? Who was he to talk about adultery anyway, when it was common knowledge that he humiliated her regularly by propositioning every pretty woman in the kingdom? On and on it went. Ferdinand was only too glad to have the minister of war stay on (and to get out of that room) by the time she was through with him.

And in truth, the king of Naples admired Acton and respected his abilities. Although Ferdinand did not much see the point of trying to reform the old ways—asked once by Leopold what he had done to improve his subjects' lives, the king of Naples had thought for a moment and then famously replied "nothing"—he nonetheless could not help but appreciate that under his wife's and her minister's regime, his kingdom seemed to be thriving. Even when tragedy struck, as it did in 1783 when a horrifying earthquake leveled over 100 cities and villages in Calabria in less than two minutes, killing 32,000 people outright and an additional 30,000 over the next ten months from aftershocks and disease, the Crown rallied, sending immediate aid in the form of doctors, food, and supplies and diverting tax revenues to the affected area to help rebuild.

In fact, with garrulous, roguish Ferdinand out hunting and roving among the citizenry as the beloved public face of the monarchy, and Maria Carolina and Acton behind the scenes making all the decisions, this improbable three-way partnership succeeded so well that for nearly two decades their reign was internationally recognized as the Golden Age of Naples.

So stable was the government, and so popular the royal family, that by 1785 Charlotte felt secure enough to leave the kingdom and take Ferdinand on an extended tour of Italy. The purpose of this journey was twofold: first, to burnish her husband's image by showing off the new Neapolitan navy (the queen intended to travel by sea); second, to visit Leopold. Maria Carolina missed her siblings. She had long since forgiven Maria Theresa for marrying her to Ferdinand and had grieved deeply at her mother's death; they had communicated by courier every month since Charlotte had first come to Naples, and she felt the loss of this tie. Joseph, whom she loved and admired, had come for a short stay the previous year, and this had inspired her to do some traveling of her own. It had taken a while to convince her husband, but he finally agreed, and on April 30, 1785, the couple boarded one of their new ships—the largest and most luxurious—and, surrounded by an imposing retinue of 12 gunboats, sailed out of the harbor.

The trip took four months. They stopped first in Livorno and were met by Leopold, who took them on a tour of Pisa and Florence and spoke to them of the many improvements he had made to the tax and criminal codes, and of his desire to encourage landowner-ship among the peasantry to promote agriculture. (Ferdinand pre-tended not to be impressed, but when he returned to Naples he started a small colony clearly inspired by Leopold's reforms.) From Florence they sailed to Milan, Turin, and Genoa, traveling so grandly that Ferdinand acquired a new nickname, "the Golden King." On their way home, they ran into a number of friendly English and Dutch warships and invited them along, so by the time they put into harbor at Naples they were accompanied by a fleet of over 20 vessels. Everyone in the capital poured into the streets as they disembarked, and they were greeted with wild enthusiasm and days of rejoicing. The successful journey, the brave new ships, and the royal family's triumphant return in many ways cemented the kingdom of Naples's independence from Spain and reflected its heightened prestige throughout Europe.

Drawn by the glamour and the good times, more and more visi-tors flooded the capital. One of these was a young English courtesan of extraordinary beauty and equally exceptional notoriety. She turned up in Naples just eight months after the king and queen had returned home from their auspicious Italian tour, arriving in the city on April 26, 1786, her twenty-first birthday.

She traveled under the unassuming name of Mrs. Hart. But the world would soon come to know her as the sublime, the seductive, the incomparable Lady Emma Hamilton.

THE WOMAN WHO WOULD BECOME the world-famous Lady Hamil-ton was born into brutal poverty in northern England in 1765, which made her thirteen years younger than Maria Carolina. Her real name was Amy Lyon. She was just two months old when her father, a blacksmith who worked in a mine, died suddenly, leaving her mother a penniless widow.

To grow up destitute amid the harsh landscape of rural coal country in the eighteenth century was to face a struggle for existence that was Dickensian in its ferocity. Amy was raised by her grandmother (her own mother having decamped for London, where the prospect for work was greater) in a two-room hovel that appears to have housed at least six other members of the family on and off. She was given no formal schooling, and there was very little food and no ready money for necessities like fuel and warm clothes—even candles were considered an extravagance. By her own admission, Amy was a spirited child—she later described herself as "wild and thoughtless... when she was a little girl; so you may guess how that is." This youthful willfulness may have helped steel her to survive, although this achievement Lady Hamilton would later credit to her grandmother, to whom she sent money yearly as soon as she was able, in recognition of the many times this overburdened surrogate parent had spent her last penny to nourish her.

Wild she might have been, but she was also graceful and vivacious, with a charming singing voice even as a child, and these qualities did not go unnoticed. But what Amy really was, was pretty—very, very pretty. So pretty that by the time she reached adolescence, people would turn around to look at her as she walked down the street.

That sort of beauty is its own currency, one that is best spent in an urban environment, so at the age of thirteen she was sent to join her mother and look for work in London. Upon her arrival, she was initially hired as a housemaid, scrubbing floors and emptying chamber pots. She lasted just long enough at this drudgery to meet an aspiring actress, in employ at the same house as a servant, who introduced her to the siren song of the theater. When Amy was subsequently fired for staying out too late on one of her rare nights off, she set her sights on the stage. She got a foot in the door by taking a job as a menial to a wardrobe mistress, but this did not last and she was forced back onto the streets. Unable to find another position and with nowhere else to go, this time she stayed there.

Prostitution was the inevitable last resort for thirteen-year-old girls in vulnerable circumstances, even if they could not boast of

Amy's good looks. "I own through distress my virtue was vanquished," she later admitted defiantly, "but my sense of virtue was not overcome." But Amy was lucky—her beauty was such that, in a year or so, she caught the eye of the head of the Royal Academy of Arts, who had her sit for a painting of Venus in a state of undress. The exhibition of this portrait caused something of a sensation, which allowed Amy to move into modeling, and from modeling to a gimmicky stage extravaganza that was all the rage called the "Temple of Health," in which she portrayed a goddess in a sheer white dress who danced and sang with a number of other goddesses around a bed that the theater owner would rent out at high rates to well-heeled audience members. When this closed, it was only a matter of time before fourteen-year-old Amy, now celebrated in the press as a glamorous temptress, wound up at Madame Kelly's, the most expensive and elite brothel in London. It was the same work as on the streets, only in a nicer house with better clothes and more job security. In fact, a young woman who worked for Madame Kelly could not *stop* working for her unless she found a man who was willing to pay to get her out.

Again, Amy was lucky. At fifteen her contract at the brothel was purchased by a high-flying aristocrat who set her up as his mistress at his sprawling country estate, where in addition to her private duties, she sang and danced for the many male visitors who partook of her lover's hospitality during the hunting season.

One of these houseguests was Charles Greville, who happened to be the nephew of Sir William Hamilton, the British ambassador to the court of Naples. Greville, a staid, unmarried thirty-two-year-old member of Parliament, had a connoisseur's eye for rarities. Although he lacked the income to afford serious art or antiques, and had to settle for a collection of minerals, he knew a masterpiece when he saw it, and he fell in love with Amy. She thus had someone to appeal to when her dashing lord of the manor turned out to be a complete cad, deserting her after getting her pregnant. "What shall I dow [*sic*]? Good God what shall I dow...I have not a farthing to bless myself with . . . O for God's sake tell me what is to become of me," the now sixteen-year-old Amy wrote to Greville in a panic, imploring him to help her.

Greville knew what to dow. For him, this was the equivalent of scooping up a pre-owned Raphael, which would otherwise be unavailable to him, and at a bargain-basement price to boot. He sent her money and instructed her to have the child (which he was willing to support provided she left it with her grandmother) and afterward come to live with him on the outskirts of London. As a precaution against recognition, she was to change her name, and agree to live quietly, devoting herself to him and his domestic needs. She agreed instantly to all of it, humbly acknowledging the benevolence of this rescue—"Oh! Greville, when I think on your goodness, your tender kindness, my heart is so full of gratitude that I want words to express it." And so, a scant three weeks after giving birth, Amy Lyon traveled to a small suburban village and became Mrs. Emma Hart, housekeeper and mistress to a man twice her age.

She was true to her word. For the next five years, although it meant giving up all previous ties (except her mother, who was allowed to live with them as a servant) and all social life and other amusements, she followed his dictates and strove to please him. Theirs was a Henry Higgins–Eliza Doolittle relationship. Under his influence, she stayed at home, read, and took lessons in voice and music; dressed tastefully but modestly; and kept to a strict diet and even stricter budget. She saw to it that his rooms were cleaned and his floors polished to admiration, praised his mineral collection, sang to him, and brought him his slippers. She was a wife in every sense but the legal one. For his part, every morning and evening he had the exclusive company, and soon the genuine affection (for Emma grew to love Greville as Eliza had grown to love Professor Higgins), of perhaps the most alluring, playful, and talented goddess in England.

The one outside activity he allowed her was modeling, as this brought in money, and Greville was frequently in want of money, being the beneficiary of only a modest income by Members of Parliament standards. She began sitting for a local artist named George Romney almost as soon as she arrived in the village. Romney, in his fifties, talented but stale, needed inspiration and found it in Emma. He could hardly believe his good fortune. To have someone so young and so beautiful, and yet also so intuitive, such an actress, so near at hand! She could do anything, *be* anyone. He painted her as Circe, as Cassandra, as Medea, as Nature, as a domestic in front of a spinning wheel. She inhabited whatever character she played, classical or modern, highborn or low, with a passion and intelligence that revealed itself on the canvas. Emma sat for Romney literally hundreds of times during the five years she lived with Greville, and by the end of that period he had become the most sought-after artist in the kingdom. Foreign princes and peers of the realm vied to purchase his portraits, and soon copies were ubiquitous throughout Europe. By 1785, the year Sir William Hamilton's wife died and he came back to England on a visit from Naples to bury her, Emma's was one of the most famous faces in the world.

Sir William naturally took the opportunity while he was in London to call upon his relative, and so had a chance to meet the charming young woman whose portraits were causing such a stir. When it became clear that the Neapolitan ambassador was taken with her, his nephew had an idea. Sir William was wealthy and childless, and for years Greville had wanted to become his legal heir. He needed money—he was in debt over his mineral collection—and the best way out, he felt, was to land a rich wife. This he could not do while living with a woman who had become as well known as Emma. Much as he loved her, and he seems to have done so, he loved money more, and he knew that he would have a much better chance at a successful courtship if Sir William officially acknowledged him as his heir. So Greville came up with a plan brilliant in its reciprocity. He offered his uncle Emma if Sir William would but name him in his will. This seemed a reasonable trade-off to the fifty-five-year-old ambassador to Naples, and he took the deal.

The problem was how to explain this perfectly logical, aboveboard business transaction to Emma. Greville knew that Emma loved him and was convinced he intended to marry her. He feared a scene or, worse, that she would refuse to accept the already-agreed-upon terms if he told her of the arrangement outright. So Greville did what any self-respecting, chivalrous man of the world would do. He tricked her. He had Sir William return to Italy alone and then proposed that Emma and her mother visit the ambassador in Naples the following spring to get a little culture while he, Greville, went to Scotland on business. This would allow him to close up the house in suburban London while they were all away and save some money, he explained. When he had finished his work, which would most likely be sometime in early fall, Greville promised to come to Naples to collect Emma and her mother, and then they would all return home together.

Of course Emma believed him. She was even pleased to be able to help him economize, not wishing him to have to spend money on her account if she could live rent-free with his uncle while Greville was traveling. So she and her mother set off for Italy, arriving in Naples at the end of April 1786. Sir William Hamilton seemed extremely pleased to see her, and put up his shapely guest (with her mother still acting as her servant) in the best rooms of the sumptuous palace in which he resided, with an unparalleled view of the sea.

Emma wasn't there twenty-four hours before she understood what the ambassador wanted, but she was used to men desiring her and simply assumed that Sir William did not realize how strong her feelings were for his nephew. "Dear, dear Greville," she wrote forcefully on the very first day of her visit, "try all you can to come hear [*sic*] as soon as possible...he loves me, Greville. But he can never be anything nearer to me than your uncle and my sincere friend. He never can be my lover. You do not know how good Sir William is to me. He is doing everything he can to make me happy."

But Greville did not come, nor did he write. Sir William tried, in the gentlest way possible, to break the news to her, but she refused to believe it. "I have had a conversation this morning with Sir William that has made me mad," she wrote to Greville in May. "He speaks—no, I do not know what to make of it."

Such was the degree of her incredulity, the magnitude of the betrayal, that it took a full three months—until July—when she still hadn't received a single letter from her lover, that Emma began to consider that the heinous handover that Sir William had hinted at might be true. "I am now onely writing to beg of you for God's sake to send me one letter, if it is onely a farewell," she pleaded. "Greville, you never will meet with anybody that has a truer affection for you than I have...I have lived with you 5 years, and you have sent me to a strange place, and no one prospect but thinking you was coming to me. Instead of which I was told...No, I respect him but no, never... What is to become of me?" she urged, in unconscious emulation of the cry of her very first letter as a sixteen-year-old pregnant castoff.

At this appeal, the implored letter at length arrived in August. "Oblige Sir William," Greville wrote curtly, by which he meant "sleep with him."

Emma's anguish at this brutal confirmation of her former lover's treachery—he who had preached goodness, decorum, and integrity to her—is visceral and immediate even now, over two centuries later: "Greville, to advise me!—you that used to envy my smiles! How with cool indifference to advise me!...Oh! that is the worst of all!"

Throughout this entire drama, Sir William behaved impeccably. No man ever played his cards so well. He never forced her. He never showed resentment. He let her cry, and sympathized with her. But mostly, he did everything in his power to spoil and amuse her. He took her with him everywhere—to grand parties, to the theater in the best box, to holidays to Pompeii and Capri. He showered her with gifts: chic, gorgeous evening gowns, the sort that Greville had never allowed (and wouldn't have sprung for anyway), expensive jewelry, and even her own opulent carriage complete with liveried staff with which to parade up and down the Corso.

Slowly, Emma began to recover from the heartache and shock.

She could not help but be grateful to Sir William for his sensitivity, kindness, and generosity. And in truth she had very few options. She had no money of her own, and a mother and daughter to support. If she returned to England, it would only be to find another man to keep her, as the pay she could expect as an artist's model would not be enough to live on. And what were the chances that she would find anyone more distinguished than this doting grandfather, whose rank was so high above her own poor station, who was nonetheless (and in obvious contrast to Greville) proud to be seen publicly with her, and who sought only to please her? The life the ambassador opened up to her was one of wealth and glamour but also of acceptance, which she craved. Naples was not like England. In Italy she was applauded for her talents, not shamed for her past. And this time around, she was no helpless teenager in thrall to a savior but a strong, confident woman who knew what she wanted and how to get it. By Christmas she had moved into Sir William's bedroom. "You don't know the power I have hear [sic]," she wrote to Greville in the aftermath of the breakup. "I will make him marry me."

And so began Emma's new life in Naples. She was the toast of the capital. Her looks and bearing, set off to perfection by the sumptuous new wardrobe Sir William was only too happy to purchase for her, captivated the population.* Duchesses showered her with invitations. She was as much a marvel to visitors on the Grand Tour as Mount Vesuvius. The ambassador was so proud of his new young consort that he staged nightly performances, called "Attitudes," in his own residence that showcased Emma, spotlighted and attired in various costumes, pantomiming famous classical figures, like an actress in a silent film.†

---

* In England, people had stopped in the street to stare at her. In Naples, they dropped to their knees and *prayed* at the sight of her. When she asked her maid why they did this, the woman answered that the population could see for themselves, from the numerous statues and paintings that adorned the churches in the city, that God Himself had blessed her with the face of the Madonna.

† The omnipresent Goethe, who witnessed Emma's "Attitudes" and enjoyed them so much that he went two nights in a row, described her performance as follows: "Sir William Hamilton...has at length, after his long love of art, and long study, discov-

With so much exposure, it was inevitable that she would come to the attention of the royal court. Maria Carolina would have seen this enchanting newcomer promenading along the Corso or in the ambassador's box at the theater, but could not officially acknowledge or receive her, as protocol prohibited a paramour, however fascinating, from enjoying that honor. Ferdinand, however, exhibited no such inhibition. Emma admitted that she was "closely besieged by the King in a roundabout manner, but...never give him any encouragement." There is a story that she turned over an amorous letter Ferdinand had addressed to her to the queen as a gesture of solidarity between one wronged woman and another, thus giving Charlotte more documentary evidence to use to control her husband. Although it is impossible to determine if this actually happened, the queen of Naples did make a point of advising Sir William to marry his mistress, and indicated that she would receive her if he did so. This encouragement meant a great deal to Emma, for without the approbation of Maria Carolina, upon whom the ambassador's access and influence depended, it is unlikely that he would have taken the risk of wedding her. Profoundly flattered and grateful, Emma gave the queen her undying support and loyalty from that moment on.

And Charlotte was about to need all the help she could get. For suddenly, just when everything seemed to be going so well, when she had established her government and was on the path to a long and fruitful reign, refugees from France began to pour into Naples in increasingly large numbers, bringing with them the oddest stories of chaos at the court of Louis XVI and Marie Antoinette.

---

ered the most perfect of admirers of nature and art in a beautiful young woman...The old knight [Sir William] has had made for her a Greek costume, which becomes her extremely. Dressed in this, and letting her hair loose, and taking a couple of shawls, she exhibits every possible variety of posture, expression, and look, so that at last the spectator almost fancies it is a dream...The old knight holds the light for her, and enters into the exhibition with his whole soul...This much at any rate is certain — the entertainment is unique."

Marie Antoinette

...as a young queen

16

Queen of France

⁓

I am cut to the heart. What a style! What a manner of thought! It confirms my dread; she is rushing, by great steps, to her ruin, and she will be fortunate if, in her fall, she retains even the virtues of her rank.

—Maria Theresa to the comte de Mercy

MARIE ANTOINETTE WAS SIX MONTHS SHY of her nineteenth birthday, the equivalent of a senior in high school, when Louis XV succumbed in black agony to smallpox on May 10, 1774, and his eldest grandson, Louis-Auguste, who took the title Louis XVI, inherited his throne. Her twenty-one-year-old sister, Maria Carolina, was only just pregnant with the son and heir whose birth the following year she would so artfully use to displace Tanucci and take over the Neapolitan government. Thirty-two-year-old Maria Christina, who had emerged as the principal counterweight to her brother Joseph in the wake of the division of Poland, was governing Hungary alongside Albert; the couple were in the planning stages of their art collection, having recently hired their dealer but not yet visited Italy. Most importantly, Maria Theresa was still alive and attempting—from more than 750 miles away in Vienna—to manage her youngest daughter's transition from dauphine to queen of what was generally acknowledged to be the preeminent throne in Europe.

The first days of the new reign were disorienting. Because of the risk of infection, within hours of Louis XV's demise the entire court (with the exception of those who had nursed the decrepit patient through his illness, and who were consequently consigned to quarantine) fled Versailles for the royal hunting lodge at Choisy, about ten miles south of Paris. Even then, it was deemed safest for the new king to avoid all personal contact with the ministry and instead communicate with his government in writing for at least a week and a half, just to be on the safe side. Upon his arrival at Choisy, Louis XVI was, however, presented with his grandfather's private papers, as well as a memorandum left by his father, Louis the Fat, at the time of his death nearly a decade earlier. It was titled: "List of the various persons recommended...to that one of his children who shall succeed Louis XV."

There will never be a sadder story than that of Louis XVI. Although highly intelligent—he could absorb and retain a multitude of facts, and follow a complex argument—and motivated by a sincere desire to apply himself and improve the lives of his subjects, in every other respect he was wholly unsuited to leadership. He could not react quickly to events. He could not confront other people. He appeared wrapped in a straightjacket of physical and social dysfunction. Basic civilities, commonplace gestures, even seemingly instinctive human processes eluded Louis. As a result, far from rendering an inspiring image of majesty, he cut a pathetic figure. "If you only saw what horrid grimaces he makes, I am sure all my power of description would not reconcile you to him," wrote a startled English visitor to the court. When not making strange faces, he stood silently or looked away from people when they spoke to him. When he did converse it was to ill effect; although well-meaning and kindly at heart, he was often abrupt and rude in person, while his voice, an eyewitness observed, "possessed nothing agreeable; if he grew warm in speaking, he often got above his natural pitch, and uttered shrill sounds." Louis's love of hunting and manual labor kept him strong, but he nonetheless continued to put on weight, and later, as he grew older, he frequently ate so much that he had to be carried half comatose to bed; his own servants called him "the fat pig."

The new king's idiosyncrasies were well known at court. When Louis went through his grandfather's files, he discovered secret letters to Louis XV from his younger siblings, the comte de Provence and the comte d'Artois, entreating for the good of the monarchy that their eldest brother be written out of the succession and the crown passed instead to one of them. Historians have treated them harshly for what appeared to be selfish ambition, but in fact they were most likely only voicing a sentiment that everyone with access to the royal family shared. "She [Marie Antoinette] should at once assume the authority that the Dauphin will never exercise except with vacillation," the comte de Mercy wrote bluntly to Maria Theresa. "It would be the greatest danger to the State, and also to the whole system of government, if the power were assumed by the Dauphin." The British ambassador agreed with this assessment of Louis's capabilities. "The Throne He fills, far from raising him above Intrigue, places Him in the Center of it," he reported on June 8, at the end of the first month of the new king's reign. "Great and Eminent Superiority of Talents might, indeed, crush these Cabals, but...there is no Reason to believe Him possessed of that Superiority," he observed flatly.

What makes this story so heartbreaking is how hard Louis worked to overcome these perceived shortcomings, and indeed his very nature, and do what was expected of him. That first evening at Choisy, he locked himself in his room and pored over his father's long-out-of-date list of suitable candidates for chief minister as though searching through a ciphered text for the secret of the philosopher's stone. But even here, with his very first decision, as Mercy had predicted, the new king proved waffling: he had no sooner settled on one of the recommended names than his aunt got wind of it and bullied him into choosing another; and that is how the comte de Maurepas, who had been in exile since the time of Madame de Pompadour, and was already seventy-three years old, came to power.

But to Marie Antoinette, the death of the old king meant not the burden of toil and responsibility but the promise of freedom, sweet freedom! Freedom from the claustrophobic atmosphere of Versailles, with its interminable rituals and tedious courtiers! Freedom to wear what she wanted and see whom she wanted, freedom from having to pretend to read dreary books on English history! In the beginning, especially during the period of mourning when there was nothing much to do anyway, she spent a good deal of time with Louis, who, overwhelmed by the task ahead of him, clung to her as a lifeline; Mercy reported to Maria Theresa on June 7, 1774, that the king "goes every hour to see the Queen." But even at this point, less than a month into her reign, she was already clearly planning her escape, as in the same letter Mercy added that Marie Antoinette had asked her husband if he would give her the small château on the palace grounds known as the Petit Trianon, "to do just what I would like in it," and that he had agreed.

The formative years that the new queen of France had spent at the court of Louis XV, perhaps the most corrupt in Europe, had taken their toll. So insidious an environment would have been difficult for even a self-possessed adult to resist, let alone a vulnerable teenager keen to conform. Marie Antoinette might not have been much of a student, but she did understand that she was supposed to become French. Not really sure of what that meant, and feeling her way as a newcomer in a foreign culture, she had naturally absorbed the values of those around her. And the most powerful female influence at court during the dauphine's apprenticeship at Versailles, the person who made all the rules and to whom everyone catered, was the king's mistress. Madame du Barry, not being highborn herself, had no interest in the responsibilities of sovereignty; she held to the com-moner's view that to be royal meant reveling in the privileges and trappings of wealth. So, even though Marie Antoinette deplored Louis XV's mistress as a woman of easy virtue and made sure that one of her husband's first acts upon becoming king was to "send that creature to the convent," as she had written triumphantly to her mother, ironically, she also unconsciously emulated her. Marie Antoinette would develop her own style, of course, but her preoccupation with frivolity, luxury, and appearance emanated from a mistaken belief that it was these qualities, and not statecraft, that most became a queen of France. "I feel myself a Frenchwoman to the finger-tips," she proclaimed confidently soon after her ascension.*

But her most profound reason for wishing to carve out a life separate from the rest of the royal court at Versailles was almost certainly to limit the time she spent with her husband. Unattractive Louis, with his peculiar ungainly ways and strict routine, did not make for an enjoyable companion. Humiliatingly, at the time of her ascension to the throne, it was well known at court that her marriage had still not been consummated. At nineteen, Marie Antoinette was no longer an unformed adolescent but a vibrant young woman in full possession of all the appropriate hormones; she knew what she was missing. Here she was, the beautiful queen of a realm that more than any other nation in the world glorified the concept of romantic passion—where *L'amour! L'amour!* pulsed through every opera, play, poem, indeed every conversation, like an undercurrent of the sweetest, most delicate music—and she was without hope of ever experiencing it. She was aware that her mother and the comte de Mercy, among others, feared that she would be repudiated and her marriage annulled if she did not soon produce an heir, but Marie Antoinette knew better. Louis—get another wife? He did not know what to do with the one he had!

And so, after enduring four long years as dauphine at Versailles without complaint, with the acquisition of the Petit Trianon, the queen of France contrived her release from the many royal obligations that she found constricting. "I will enjoy the comforts of a private life, which exist not for us, unless we have the resolution to

---

* The similarities between Marie Antoinette's attitude toward rule and Madame du Barry's was not lost on her brother-in-law, the comte de Provence. By her focus on fun, fashion, and jewels, he noted, the queen of France was "held in much the same estimation as were formerly the mistresses of Louis XV."

secure them for ourselves," she declared. There was no one to stop her; her rank was such that there was only one person in the entire kingdom legally entitled to say no to her. That person was her husband, and Louis was patently no match for his wife. "Everything she does is becoming to her," he marveled. This truth was brought home to the overbearing Madame de Noailles, stickler for etiquette, within days of the court's arrival at Choisy. Upon observing Marie Antoinette in casual conversation with a commoner while out for a walk, she complained sharply to Louis XVI, as she would have to his grandfather, about this breach of protocol. To which the new king, obviously rehearsed by Marie Antoinette for just such a contingency, utterly vanquished his wife's former tormentor with a few curt words. "Let the Queen be left alone, Madame, to do as she wishes, and talk to whom she pleases," he told her coldly.* Since whatever the king willed was received as law, with this single pronouncement, Marie Antoinette was set free.

So COMMENCED, AT THE beginning of 1775, when the official period of mourning for Louis XV gave way to the carnival days of the new year, the well-known excesses of the queen's early reign. This was the era of the towering hairstyles, so fantastically bouffant that the only way for a woman of fashion to travel was to kneel on the floor of her carriage as it drove from fête to fête. This, too, was the interval when Marie Antoinette's love of diamonds became widely known; the years of her gambling at cards and horse racing (a British import); of her regular attendance at the opera, followed by dancing until dawn at masked balls; and of the queen's notorious sleigh rides into Paris, where Marie Antoinette and her set, wrapped warmly in furs, convoyed in a merry stream over the snow toward the capital, their horses' harness bells tinkling gaily in the wind,

---

* Note the similarity in style between the king's retort to Madame de Noailles and Mercy's letter to Maria Theresa—that the queen wanted the Petit Trianon "to do just what I would like in it." This seems to have been a common refrain of Marie Antoinette's that she impressed upon Louis.

while the vast majority of the city's inhabitants shivered and starved in the bitter cold.

Every age has its social media; in Marie Antoinette's time it was represented by the society magazines, broadsheets, and cheap satirical pamphlets that spread freely across boundaries throughout Europe, and for these publications, the glamorous queen of France represented an unlooked-for bonanza. Nothing sells like high-end celebrity, and the more flagrantly grandiose Marie Antoinette's style, the more she became an object of public fascination. "All wished instantly to have the same dress as the Queen, and to wear the feathers and flowers to which her beauty, then in its brilliancy, lent an indescribable charm," Madame Campan reported. "The expenditure of the younger ladies was necessarily much increased; mothers and husbands murmured at it, some few giddy women contracted debts; unpleasant domestic scenes occurred...and the general report was— that the Queen would be the ruin of all the French ladies."*

Unfortunately for Marie Antoinette, one of the mothers murmuring against her newfound fashion sense was her own. "I must mention a subject upon which all the *Gazettes* enlarge, and that is your dress," an appalled Maria Theresa sputtered from Vienna in a letter dated March 5, 1775. "They speak of hair-dressing, a *coiffure*, of thirty-six inches high from the roots of the hair with feathers and ribbons above that again! You know my opinion, to follow fashion in moderation, never to excess. A young and pretty queen has no need of follies." But by this time Marie Antoinette had received five years' worth of hectoring letters from her mother, so this latest scolding had little effect. "It is true I am rather taken up with dress; but as to feathers, everyone wears them, and it would seem extraordinary if I did not," Marie Antoinette assured her smoothly, deftly employing the standard everybody-does-it excuse favored by teenagers through the ages.

---

* Not just the French ladies. At Madame Kelly's brothel in London, where Emma Lyon worked when she was fourteen, management required that the girls wear ridiculously tall headdresses in imitation of Marie Antoinette in order to cater to the tastes of a highbrow male clientele.

The comte de Mercy, who understood all too clearly just how destructive this sort of behavior was to his charge's reputation, had the unhappy task of relaying precise descriptions to her mother of how the young woman spent her time. "Lately her Majesty went to see a horse-race that has been held near Paris," he was forced to admit on March 18, 1775. "Crowds of people flocked to this poor spectacle; but the Queen was not welcomed with the customary signs of joy and applause...The public sees that the Queen is only thinking of amusements." Six months later, he was similarly compelled to report that Marie Antoinette left the palace alone at eleven every evening (when Louis went to bed) to attend private dinners with her friends at which she stayed up all night gambling or dancing—"this time is the most critical of the day," he observed glumly. "The Queen now plays very high; she no longer enjoys games where the stakes are limited...Her ladies and courtiers are alarmed, and dread the losses to which they are exposed in order to pay their court to the Queen."

The next year brought more of the same, including the purchase of some bejeweled bracelets, which, Mercy acknowledged, she wheedled Louis into buying for her, as the price far exceeded her allowance. "The monarch received this demand with his customary gentleness, only saying mildly he was not astonished to find the Queen penniless, considering her taste for diamonds." Both Mercy and her tutor, the abbé Vermond, did their level best to get her to stop, but they were hampered in their efforts by the fact that, as a result of her preeminent rank, Marie Antoinette not only did not have to listen to them, but she did not even have to grant them an audience. "We have seen, in this time of great effervescence, that the Queen was irritated by our remonstrances; that she tried to evade them. Last week, when her projects were being executed, she avoided, adroitly, giving me any opportunity of speaking to her. Our efforts only result in rendering us hated by all those who surround and lead the Queen astray," the comte de Mercy confessed in frustration. As a result, "I observe that the amusements of the Queen are multiplying; less by variety of the objects than by the greater time taken up in pure dissipation, which consumes three parts of the day," he concluded miserably.

While Marie Antoinette bought diamonds and dresses, flitted from opera house to racecourse, and danced and gambled her nights away, her husband struggled alone with the burden of government. It did not take Louis's chief minister long to figure out how to master his sovereign. Noting that in person the king was uncertain and strangely uncommunicative, the comte de Maurepas learned to frame questions in such a manner that silence would be construed as consent. At his very first audience with Louis, he asked if the king wished to designate him prime minister, or if Louis intended to run the government himself. When Louis was unable to indicate a preference, Maurepas smoothly took control. "I shall then teach Your Majesty how not to need a prime minister," he announced.

And so Louis in effect went to school. Maurepas and two other officials, the ministers for finance and foreign affairs, playing to the king's affinity for facts, bombarded him with written materials, which the twenty-year-old studied assiduously. Louis was then able to take the information and arguments fed to him by his ministers and repeat it in his own written correspondence.* When he had to give his first speech to his council, he rehearsed in front of Maurepas until the minister was satisfied that Louis had memorized the full text and was able to deliver the words with the appropriate intonation and pauses.

But in fact the king was not making the decisions—his ministers were. Louis was "a silent spectator," in the words of one courtier. He never overruled or confronted them, even when it was clear from the notes he made in the margins of the documents they piled on him that he doubted the course they advocated. But as Maurepas

---

* Louis's surviving papers are very impressive. Taken alone, they would seem to indicate that the king was the determining force in policy-making. That is why it is so important to incorporate also the reports of those who observed his behavior, in order to understand the disparity between his considerable intelligence and his social and emotional development.

also realized that the king was easily intimidated in person, or could be coaxed into a decision in private, access to the sovereign was strictly limited. Louis almost never saw a supplicant or government official, or attended a council meeting, without his chief minister by his side. (Marie Antoinette, as his wife, was the only one who could meet with him without having to go through Maurepas first.) The king's day was defined by strict routine: up at six, an enormous breakfast, hunting if conditions permitted, back in time for Mass and the public meal at 1:00 p.m., with the afternoon and early evening hours devoted to studying official reports in his private chambers or in meetings with Maurepas, followed by dinner at nine and bed at eleven. But for his coronation on June 11, 1775, at Reims, Louis's subjects hardly ever saw their king.★ Thus the public face of the monarchy, by default, became that of the queen.

And this is what the public saw: a childless young woman who avoided her husband and treated him, the established French aristocracy, and even her own subjects with contempt. Unlike her sister Maria Christina, who endured the tedium of countless dinners and other social obligations with the ranking Hungarian nobility in order to ensure that no one attached to the court or government felt slighted, Marie Antoinette dispensed with as many of the century-old traditions of Versailles as she could get away with and instead spent her time tucked away at the Petit Trianon, an inviolable retreat that not even the king could enter without an express invitation. Where her sister Maria Carolina sought out and patronized scholars, economists, and philosophers, and established schools, Marie Antoinette focused all of her attention on her two best friends, both in their early twenties: the princesse de Lamballe (who had had the good fortune to marry a rich man who died almost immediately) and the comtesse de Polignac, a pretty nobody to whom Marie

---

★ Queens had not been crowned in France for centuries, so Marie Antoinette attended but did not participate in her husband's coronation. Madame Campan reported that the affair was arranged with "all the accustomed pomp," and that "the people's love for him burst forth," but at the moment the crown was placed on Louis's head he exclaimed, "It pinches me."

Antoinette was attracted, according to Madame Campan, because "her disposition was just what the Queen liked; she had...no presumption, no affectation of knowledge." (The comte de Mercy was compelled to admit to Maria Theresa that the queen of France engaged in "long and certainly very idle conversations" with this new favorite.) The comtesse de Polignac had not the princesse's financial resources but this was not a problem as Marie Antoinette soon remedied the potential hindrance to their friendship by lavishing lucrative royal appointments on both the comtesse and her husband. It was in the company of these two lively young women and a small circle of their relatives and friends, or with the king's brothers and their wives (but almost never with her own husband), that the citizens of Paris saw their queen.

As a result, within months of her ascension to the throne, the satirical pamphlets began to run ugly rhymes and pornographic cartoons promoting the idea that Marie Antoinette was unfaithful to the king. She was in no way the first queen to have to deal with these sorts of accusations. Slandering a powerful woman as a whore was a time-honored approach by those seeking to bring down a female political rival. (Still is.)

What was different in this case was the scale and sophistication of the attack. Pamphlets, because they were short, easy to read, and cheap to produce, caught fire and proliferated during this period to a degree not experienced previously, particularly in France. They were unregulated and could say anything they pleased, the more sensational the better. The only way to stop them was to buy up all the copies and destroy them before they were distributed or take the author to court, a remedy that only drew more attention to the embarrassing accusations. Madame Campan asserted that they were the work of the queen's enemies, "the anti-Austrian party" at court, which included, among many others, one of Louis's aunts, his younger brothers, and his cousin the duc d'Orléans. What can be stated with certainty is that this concerted propaganda attack against Marie Antoinette anticipated modern populist campaigns by employing repetition, character assassination, and fearmongering to devastating effect. Staying remarkably on message, the pamphlets hammered home the dual threat that the queen was both a dangerous foreigner who promoted Austrian interests over those of France and a depraved nymphomaniac and lesbian who cuckolded and dominated her weak husband. "Their aim was, beyond all doubt, to have her sent back to Germany," Madame Campan stated bluntly.

Marie Antoinette was of course aware of these scurrilous tabloids—the material was so ubiquitous that the cruel cartoons and verses found their way even into the public rooms at Versailles—but knowing herself to be innocent of the charges, chose to ignore them rather than fight back or change her behavior. It's unclear whether in fact there was anything she could have done, after those first eighteen months or so, to undo the damage. Possibly the renunciation of all entertainment in favor of excessive piety and charitable good works, sustained over many years, might have saved her, but as it was she ignored all the warnings and persisted in her amusements, and in doing so played right into her enemies' hands.

Underlying all of this was the queen's inability to conceive, generally attributed to indifference on the part of her husband. Within two years of Louis XVI's accession, it was well known at court that, due to the incompatibility of their schedules, the king rarely graced his wife's bed, as he complained that she disturbed his rest by coming home so late at night.

And this was where matters stood in the spring of 1777 when Marie Antoinette's eldest brother, Joseph, the emperor, decided to come for a visit.

Joseph arrived just as the attention of all of Paris was taken up with a new and inspiring development: the determination of the plucky American colonies to win their independence from the behemoth that was Great Britain.

It had taken some time for news of the revolutionaries' Fourth of July declaration of the previous year to make its way to France. But the written document, with its eloquent arguments and soaring idealism—as though phrases such as "the pursuit of Happiness" and "the consent of the governed" were actual inalienable rights and truths and not simply the untested blathering of a handful of presumptuous philosophers—touched a nerve with the general Parisian population, and with one extremely wealthy nineteen-year-old aristocrat, the marquis de Lafayette, in particular. "Such a glorious cause had never before attracted the attention of mankind; it was the last struggle of Liberty," he rhapsodized. "The great work was to be accomplished, or the rights of humanity were to fall beneath its ruin."

Desperate for military aid, to capitalize on this enthusiasm, the Americans had sent Benjamin Franklin to Paris to try to coax the French government into an alliance. The seventy-one-year-old Franklin was an inspired choice. Witty and charming, he soon took the measure of his audience, playing to the fashionable set's taste for novelty by parading around the capital in a quaint fur hat, rough-hewn walking stick, and steel-rimmed eyeglasses. "All the prettiest ladies of the Court and of the town go to solicit the favor of embracing him; and he lends himself very gallantly to their desire," a French official observed. Franklin reported home to Philadelphia that "The cry of this nation is for us, but the Court views an approaching war with reluctance." The ambassador's efforts were further overshadowed by accounts of the Americans' poor showing in the fight against Britain. "Very bad tidings arrived," Lafayette acknowledged. "New York, Long Island, White Plains, Fort Washington, and the Jerseys, had seen the American forces successively destroyed...Three thousand Americans alone remained in arms, and these were closely pursued by General Howe. From that moment all the credit of the insurgents vanished."

This was not quite true. In fact, the French government had been funneling money and arms to the Americans secretly for over a year. Louis's foreign minister feared that if British naval supremacy remained unchecked, France would lose what was left of its colonial possessions. "Two or three millions may save us our sugar islands worth three hundred million," the minister noted to Louis. As, however, France was currently at peace with Britain, the guns and ammunition could not look like they were coming from the government. An elaborate farce was thereby arranged, for which, in an appropriately absurd bit of casting, the French playwright Pierre-Augustin Beaumarchais, author of such comic masterpieces as *The Barber of Seville* and *The Marriage of Figaro,* was recruited. "We will secretly give you one million," the French foreign minister explained to his literary operative. "We will try to obtain an equal sum from Spain... with these two millions you will establish a big commercial house, and at your risk and peril you will supply the Americans with arms, munitions, equipment, and all the other things that they will need to maintain the war." This ruse did not escape the notice of the British ambassador, who cornered the French foreign minister and accused him of subterfuge. "In the history of the world there is no example of aid given to the rebels of a country one professes to be friendly with," the British envoy exclaimed. "We cannot stop smugglers," the French minister returned mildly. "Do smugglers go in fleets, Sir?" the ambassador shot back sharply.

It was to protect this deception that the king forbade Lafayette, who was an officer in the French army, from sailing to America to fight on the side of the colonists. But the marquis ignored the order. He procured a ship bound for the Carolinas from Marseilles and slipped away within a week of Joseph's arrival at Versailles.

The emperor's was not entirely a pleasure visit. He had also come to find out, and report back to his mother, the cause of his sister's persistent childlessness. All of Vienna, too, had seen the satirical pamphlets. Joseph could not take the risk that Marie Antoinette would be repudiated over the lack of an heir; he was preparing to invade Bavaria, and needed to ensure that the French alliance with Austria remained intact.

The comte de Mercy, who foresaw only too clearly what Joseph's reaction to firsthand observation of the queen of France's lifestyle would be, had done his best to warn Maria Theresa. "With regard to the Emperor Joseph's visit," he had written delicately, "I fear that His Majesty's penetration will strip bare all the faults of this nation, especially those of the present Government, and that he will conceive a disgust whose effects may be incalculable. I am also afraid that His Majesty will find too much blame in the conduct of his sister; and coldness may ensue, possibly quarrels," he cautioned her.

It therefore seems likely that Joseph had been told to watch himself, as at least in the beginning, he made an effort to control his criticism. He arrived on the morning of April 19, 1777, coming in through the public gate dressed as the ordinary citizen Count Falkenstein (his favorite disguise, which fooled no one), then slipped into the palace through a private door and up a secret staircase to the queen's apartment. There he found his sister, whom he had not seen since she was fourteen, and afterward soon met her husband and the rest of the royal family.

Mercy was right; it did not take Joseph long to identify the source of the problem. "Her situation with the King is singular," he reported to his brother Leopold. "This man is weak-minded, but not an idiot. He has some ideas and some judgment, but his apathy of body and of mind are equal. He can hold a rational conversation; [but] he has neither desire for instruction nor any curiosity." As for Marie Antoinette, "The queen is a very beautiful and charming woman, but she thinks only of her pleasures, has no love for the king...she does not fulfill either the duties of a wife or a queen," the emperor wrote. However, "she is perfectly virtuous," Joseph pronounced flatly. "A sweet-natured and straightforward woman, rather young, rather thoughtless, but with a basis of uprightness and honesty truly wonderful in her situation."

Joseph stayed six weeks, during which time he saw more of Paris and its inhabitants, institutions, and culture than either Louis or Marie Antoinette had seen in all their years at Versailles. As Mercy had predicted, after a while he did have trouble holding his tongue, belittling Marie Antoinette for wearing too much rouge, and for her gambling, overspending, and general frivolity, until she had to angrily remind him that she was queen of France. But there was an instance where he was extremely helpful. One day, after Louis had gotten to know the emperor a little, Joseph took his brother-in-law for a long walk, just the two of them, and asked him what seemed to be the problem in the bedroom.

There were very few people in the world whose rank entitled them to bring up such a subject with the king of France. His brothers might have inquired, but Louis knew that if he confided in them they would only make fun of him, or use his words against him. Joseph, however, was the emperor, the highest station in Germany, in addition to being family. Moreover, he did it just right. Like Marie Antoinette when she had first arrived at court, Joseph tried to enter Louis's world. The emperor, too, had a factual, scientific mind, and he seems to have approached the topic by kindly asking the sort of step-by-step questions that Louis could answer.

Joseph later summarized this conversation with the king of France in a letter to Leopold. "Here is the mystery of the conjugal bed," he wrote. "There are strong erections...he introduces his penis, leaves it there for maybe two minutes without agitating it, takes it out, still hard, without ever ejaculating, and says goodnight...This is incomprehensible since he has spontaneous emissions alone...He says frankly that he is satisfied and that he only does it out of duty and takes no pleasure in it."*

Evidently the emperor, before he said goodbye, enlightened his brother-in-law as to the biology of conception, because the king and queen of France seem to have worked together on the business of agitating until Louis had mastered it, an effort that took about three months. But on August 30, 1777, Marie Antoinette was finally able to write to her mother: "This is the happiest moment of my life. It is eight days now since my marriage has been consummated; the test has been repeated yesterday even more completely than the first

---

* That a healthy, intelligent, twenty-three-year-old male had to have the mechanics of intercourse explained to him would again seem to indicate some form of autism.

time." That same week, the Spanish ambassador reported to Madrid, "The king [Louis] told his aunts that if he had known how much he would enjoy the act, he would have done it sooner." When, a year after Joseph's visit, the queen of France was officially confirmed to be pregnant, Louis wrote gratefully to the emperor with news of this long-hoped-for event. "It is to you that we owe this happiness," he said.

THE BOMBSHELL ANNOUNCEMENT of Marie Antoinette's pregnancy coincided with another, equally electrifying development: the decision of the French government to officially recognize and support the American colonies in their struggle for independence from Britain.

The resolution to move from covert to open warfare with England was a direct result of the underdog colonial army's sudden, out-of-nowhere success against their formidable British opponent. On December 4, 1777, a messenger arrived in Paris with the startling news that the English general John Burgoyne, who had landed in Quebec over the summer with an invasion force of approximately 9,000 professional soldiers, 130 cannon, and a baggage train the length of Vermont, had been beaten and forced to surrender to the ragtag rebel army on October 17. Even Benjamin Franklin, who had been daily expecting to hear that the colonists had been driven out of Philadelphia (which in fact they were), appeared dumbfounded by the news.*

This upset victory convinced Louis's foreign minister that the once seemingly invincible British army was beatable, and he immediately began pushing to capitalize on English military reversals by openly allying with the colonists. His reasoning had nothing to do with the revolutionaries' lofty manifesto trumpeting the principles of liberty

---

* To help put the loss of Philadelphia into perspective, Lafayette, who by this time was with George Washington's forces at Valley Forge, wrote home to his wife: "They will say to you... 'Philadelphia is taken, the capital of America, the rampart of liberty!' You must politely answer, 'You are all great fools! Philadelphia is a poor, forlorn town, exposed on every side, whose harbor was already closed.'"

and fairness that had so resonated with Lafayette. Rather, the minister saw the colonies as a rich source of raw materials for export, and an equally lucrative import market for finished goods. If France entered the war, the appreciative colonists would no doubt switch their commercial allegiance, currently monopolized by the English, to the French, and this would more than make up for the humiliating loss of the kingdom's Canadian territory to England at the close of the Seven Years' War. Maurepas having agreed with this assessment, on February 8, 1778, the French government officially recognized the Americans as independent of Britain, and signed two treaties with them: one for the promotion of commerce between the two nations, and one promising mutual defense. The British countered by recalling their ambassador from Versailles and firing on French ships—and just like that, France was again at war with England.

The struggle for American independence was hugely popular in Paris. In emulation of Lafayette, many young aristocrats clamored for military appointments, eager to fight for so just a cause, and at first Marie Antoinette, too, supported the war. After the signing of the treaty with the Americans, she invited Benjamin Franklin to one of her card parties and even allowed him to stand behind her chair, a signal honor. She hosted a magnificent ball in February 1778 where, to celebrate the realm's new allies, she presented dancers dressed up as Native Americans. She took the trouble of ordering her hairdresser to construct a replica of a French naval vessel, and then had him hoist the large, unwieldy model atop her coiffure as evidence of her patriotism.

But she soon came to regret her initial response. By April it had become clear that Frederick the Great was mobilizing an army and preparing to invade Bohemia in response to Joseph's heavy-handed attempt to annex Bavaria. Maria Theresa, terrified for her eldest son's safety, bombarded Mercy and Marie Antoinette with letters begging her daughter to use her influence with the king to convince the French government to honor the terms of their long-standing alliance with Austria and send money and troops to Joseph's aid.

Marie Antoinette, as anxious for her homeland and family as her mother, flew to her husband and entreated him to come to her brother's defense.

Alas, Maurepas, who had been ousted two decades earlier by Madame de Pompadour, and who consequently had opposed the Austrian alliance from the very beginning, had anticipated this scenario and outmaneuvered Marie Antoinette. He had warned Louis that she would try to influence him but sternly admonished the king that the queen had no place in formal policy-making; and Louis believed him. Marie Antoinette was astonished and chagrined to discover that after distancing herself from government for four years, she could not just waltz back in and control her husband's behavior as she could on more personal matters (like getting him to appoint the comtesse de Polignac's husband as head of her stables). "I had a very touching scene with the King this morning," she wrote to Maria Theresa on July 15, 1778. "My dear mother knows that I have never blamed his kind heart; all that happens is due to his extreme weakness and to his lack of confidence in himself. Today, when he came to see me, he found me so sad and so frightened [about the Prussian invasion of Bohemia] that he was deeply touched, and he cried." But she was forced to admit that she had been unable to convince Louis to overrule Maurepas, even though it was clear he wanted to for her sake. "You see I have so many faults that I cannot answer a word," he stammered finally, falling back on the excuse he had repeated so often as a child.

And now, for the first time, Marie Antoinette saw the danger that had been apparent to her sister Charlotte from the beginning.* For all her gaiety, Marie Antoinette was a bright woman, and after this conversation with Louis she understood that the Austrian defensive alliance with France, the cornerstone of her family's foreign policy, which she had been sent to Versailles specifically to nurture and

---

* Remember that Charlotte had noted very early into her marriage that rather than see Ferdinand "killed by his ministers or by a bad person or led by his confessor I am forced to act."

protect, was over in everything but name, and that its repudiation was a direct result of her having shunned her formal responsibilities in favor of more entertaining diversions. Two days after confronting this uncomfortable truth, Mercy reported to Maria Theresa that "I have never seen the Queen so depressed; and in an outpouring of confidence she said she wished to make a general confession; she spoke of her amusements, her society, and all the details of her private life…she added that her deep trouble [being unable to convince Louis to help Joseph] had led her to think seriously of the life that lay before her."

But while for the moment she could not affect policy, she at least had the intense satisfaction that summer of announcing her pregnancy and watching the rest of the court squirm. The comtes de Provence and d'Artois especially, who after eight years of delighting in their eldest brother's and his wife's childlessness had been fully expecting to take over the succession, had difficulty masking their disappointment. "You have heard the change in my fortunes," the comte de Provence wrote glumly to a friend after Marie Antoinette's condition became known publicly. "I soon mastered myself—at least outwardly…showing no joy (for that would have been too obvious hypocrisy and you can be sure that I felt none at all), nor depression—that might have been construed into weakness of spirit. But the inner man is more difficult to conquer," he admitted sourly. Even after the baby (born on December 20, 1778, in an apartment so crowded with suspicious courtiers and members of the interested public that the new mother fainted and Louis had to break open a window to get some air into the room) was discovered to be only a girl, just the fact that the queen was now capable of producing children gave Marie Antoinette a power that she had lacked before, quieting for the time being the hateful drumbeat of "send her back" that had dogged her since her ascension.

And it was at this pivotal juncture, just when she had gained some security and had resolved to mend her ways, that the queen of France fell in love.

17

Diamonds and Debt

What is Truth to-day may be a Lie to-morrow.
—Beaumarchais, *The Marriage of Figaro,* Act 4

HIS NAME WAS COUNT AXEL FERSEN. Born in Sweden to a high-ranking and well-connected family, Fersen was the same age as Marie Antoinette; he was tall, slender, handsome, athletic, and charming; an eighteenth-century Nordic dreamboat. Although a captain in the Swedish cavalry, Fersen, inspired like Lafayette by the stirring ideals espoused by the Americans, had asked for and received permission to volunteer his services to the French army so as to be able to fight on the side of the struggling colonists. He arrived in Paris in the summer of 1778 looking for a commission, and on August 26 was formally presented at court to the king and queen.

He'd actually met them four years earlier while on the Grand Tour. Marie Antoinette had been only a dauphine then, but the dashing young Swedish count had clearly made a lasting impression, as Fersen recorded that she exclaimed, "Ah! Here is an old acquaintance," as soon as she saw him again. "The rest of the family did not say a word to me," he noted.

It took some time for the count to secure a posting, as preparations for the war effort had by no means been completed. The navy had been sadly neglected in the years before Louis's ascension, and the king, who had maintained an interest in the sea since childhood, had authorized the building of numerous ships. None of these were ready that fall, however, so Fersen settled down in Paris to await his orders. Marie Antoinette, officially pregnant with her first child and getting bigger every day, could therefore see him as often as she liked without provoking comment, and she did. Fersen's letters home are filled with her. "The queen, who is the prettiest and most amiable princess that I know, has had the kindness to inquire about me often," he boasted in September. "The queen treats me with great kindness; I often pay her my court at her card-games, and each time she makes to me little speeches that are full of good-will," he further enthused in November. "I am to go Thursday…not to Court, but to the queen's apartments. She is the most amiable princess that I know," he repeated jubilantly, in the days before she went into labor.

This situation changed, however, after Marie Antoinette had her daughter (whom she named Marie-Thérèse Charlotte after her mother and favorite sister but who by tradition was called Madame Royale). What had been an innocent friendship for a woman in the final trimester of pregnancy transformed into something significantly more suspicious once the new mother was back on her feet. The court noted with malicious glee that Fersen continued to enjoy Marie Antoinette's favor even after her figure was restored. He was invited to the little intimate dinners the Polignacs hosted for the queen and her special friends. He made up one of the anointed circle allowed access to Marie Antoinette's private sanctuary of the Petit Trianon.

The gossip was even more damaging for being obviously supported by the queen's deportment. *L'amour,* when it strikes a young woman of twenty-three for the first time, hits hard. By February, Marie Antoinette was unable to control her emotions when Fersen was in the room. She blushed when she saw him but could not stop looking at him. She trembled when he was near. Her infatuation was so pronounced that the Swedish ambassador felt obliged to inform his sovereign of this unfortunate complication. "I ought to confide to Your Majesty that the young Count Fersen has been so well received by the queen that this has given umbrage to several persons," the ambassador pointed out cautiously to the Swedish king. "I own that I cannot help thinking that she has a liking for him; I have seen too many indications to doubt it."

This crisis was dodged by the timely intervention of the French army. In April, the commander of the first troops to be dispatched to America was finally named, and Fersen was appointed aide-de-camp; the count left Paris immediately to join his regiment. The Swedish ambassador heaved a huge sigh of relief. "By thus departing he avoided all dangers," he was able to reassure Stockholm. "The queen's eyes could not leave him, during the last days, and they often filled with tears. I entreat Your Majesty to keep this secret, for her sake," he urged before continuing, "When the courtiers heard of Count Fersen's departure they were delighted. The Duchess de Fitz-James said to him, 'Why! monsieur, is this the way you abandon your conquest?'"

Thus began a period during which Marie Antoinette relied even more heavily upon the Polignacs (who were clearly in on the secret of her passion for Fersen) for emotional support and diversion. All her good intentions, such as her desire to give up gambling, were abandoned in the wake of Fersen's abrupt withdrawal. Worse, she left herself vulnerable to extortion. Mercy wrote worriedly to Maria Theresa on December 17, 1779, "I notice that the Comtesse [de Polignac] seems now extraordinarily keen to make the fortunes of her whole family; and she will be content with nothing less than obtaining, as a free gift from the King, an estate worth 100,000 livres a year...Even the Queen was rather frightened at this unreasonable demand; but finally adopted the idea, and only thought of ways of carrying it out...in the last four years the members of the family of de Polignac, without any services to the State, and wholly as favors, have received nearly 500,000 livres a year in appointments and similar benefits," he concluded gloomily.

To help fill the time, by the spring of 1780, this small clique had struck on a new amusement: amateur theatricals. Needing an agreeable place to perform, Marie Antoinette, who had already made substantial improvements to the Petit Trianon, including an English garden, ordered the construction of a small private theater on the property. It was a jewel box of a playhouse, wholly feminine like everything else at the château, all gold leaf and pale blue walls, with a soaring frescoed ceiling. The best Mercy could say to Maria Theresa about this new diversion was that at least "the time necessary to learn their parts, and the rehearsals, will keep them all out of mischief in gambling; and when they are performing in the evening they cannot be walking out on the terrace."★

But by this time Maria Theresa was in too weakened a state to object; she knew she was failing. Marie Antoinette appears not to have been informed of her mother's final illness, as she took the news of her death on November 29, 1780, very hard. Louis was so afraid of her reaction that he ducked the job of telling her and had the abbé Vermond break the loss of her mother to the queen instead. Madame Campan reported that when Louis thanked the abbé afterward for performing this service, it "was the only time during nineteen years that the King spoke to him."

Entertainments were canceled; the queen wore mourning and saw no one outside the royal family but the princesse de Lamballe and the duchesse de Polignac for days. Her grief was no doubt genuine, but it must surely have been a relief to be freed from the endless maternal criticism as well. Mercy stayed on in Paris, but with Maria Theresa's passing, he no longer informed Vienna of his charge's every move. Still, the following April there was one piece of news Marie Antoinette would dearly have liked to report to her mother: against the background of the quickly escalating war in America, the queen of France was pregnant again.

★ The grounds of Versailles were open to the public, so when Marie Antoinette and her friends walked out on the terrace they made themselves too accessible to the general population, once again giving rise to suspicions of illicit behavior.

★   ★   ★

BY THE BEGINNING OF 1781, the shipyards of France, through diligent effort, had managed to produce a fleet of some 60 seaworthy gunboats for use in the war against England, with approximately 10,000 French soldiers either already stationed in America or ready for deployment. And not a moment too soon: Count Fersen, who was among the first of these to reach the colonies, wrote urgently from Newport, Rhode Island, warning that "this country is... ruined; no money, no men; if France does not succor it vigorously, it must make peace."

But ships and soldiers cost money, lots of it; Louis had by this time already spent a crushing 400 million livres without a single victory, or even a battle, to show for it. Taxes alone could not cover this sort of outlay, and in any event Maurepas had ruled out an increase in tithes, knowing the unrest it would cause. That left the Crown no choice but to borrow, a thankless duty that fell to the director general of finances, Jacques Necker.

Luckily Necker, a wealthy Swiss banker who had married a Frenchwoman with serious social ambitions, was more than up to the task. An international money broker himself, he knew just the sort of transparency potential lenders look for when considering an investment. So he provided it, using a tried-and-true approach often employed in his line of business. In February of 1781, he published a treatise entitled *Compte rendu au Roi,* in which he made public the accounts of the monarchy. Although in actuality the royal treasury was running at a deficit of 70 million livres annually, in his pamphlet Necker managed through judicious editing to make it appear as if the Crown had an annual surplus of 10.2 million livres, more than enough to service any additional debt. Members of the financial community call Necker's method "off-balance-sheet financing" or "massaging the numbers." Ordinary people call it "fraud."

Whatever the name for it, the strategy worked: money poured in, mostly from foreign lenders, and Necker was proclaimed a financial genius. The soldiers were deployed, the ships sailed. As a result, eight months later, on October 19, 1781, came the payoff to this high-stakes gamble: the surrender of the British general Charles Cornwallis and all of his men to the allied American and French forces at Yorktown.

This battle, in which 8,000 French troops participated (equaling the number of American soldiers under General Washington), using artillery and ammunition—some 41 cannon—*also* provided by France, *plus* a French fleet in the harbor to further isolate and blockade the English, marked the turning point in the war. At the moment that Cornwallis raised the flag of truce indicating his surrender, all those intoxicating phrases about liberty and equality, formerly just words, mutated into living, breathing, tangible inalienable rights, rights that had been bravely fought for and won. The world changed that day, and Lafayette, one of two major generals who commanded the American forces in combat, knew it. "The play, sir," he crowed home to Maurepas in a letter of October 20, 1781, "is over."

And yet by the time word of this victory for American independence and the consent of the governed (which most certainly would not have been possible without France) reached Versailles eighteen days later, it had already been overshadowed by an even greater triumph. For on October 22, 1781, almost simultaneously with the defeat of Cornwallis, Marie Antoinette at long last delivered a son.

THE BIRTH OF A DAUPHIN after eleven formerly fruitless years of marriage was so stunning a development that Madame Campan reported that the room fell into a profound silence "the moment the child first saw light." Once the realization set in, however, Louis in particular could barely contain himself. This boy represented his achievement as much as the queen's. Bullied and ridiculed by his brothers and the court for most of his life for being backward and different, the king had fulfilled his responsibilities and produced an heir just like other men. Louis's "joy was boundless; tears streamed from his eyes; he gave his hand to everyone present without distinction; and his happiness raised him quite above his habitual disposition," Madame Campan remembered.

As for Marie Antoinette, there was no mistaking the boost the birth of this all-important son gave to her prestige and power in France. "That event decided all the courtiers, and they hastened with precipitation to the standard of [her] favor; whilst those who before had constituted Her Majesty's intimate and circumscribed society, were soon consolidated into a formidable party in the State," the British ambassador observed shrewdly in a report home to London. This political stampede toward the queen was intensified when, the following month, the king's chief minister, the aged Maurepas, died suddenly. "Nothing [referring to hunting]. Death of M. de Maurepas at eleven thirty in the evening," Louis wrote in his diary on November 21, 1781, of the man who had effectively run the French government for the past seven years.

As gratifying as her newfound legitimacy and influence must have been, there was another matter much closer to Marie Antoinette's heart upon which she was focused. In the aftermath of the battle of Yorktown, negotiations began for the end of hostilities in America, which culminated in the signing of the Peace of Paris on September 3, 1783. With this treaty, in which Britain conceded the fact of American independence and lost all of its colonies, came the close of the war. With the close of the war came the return of the troops. And with the return of the troops came...Count Fersen.

This time around there were no schoolgirl sighs or blushing glances. Marie Antoinette was nearly twenty-eight, with two children. She knew what she was about. Fersen, too, was more mature. He had been away for four long years, during which time he had endured privation and boredom; he had fought valiantly at Yorktown, for which he was honored with medals by both the French and American governments; he had the bearing and confidence that come with trial by fire. He would not have returned to Paris so quickly if he did not want her. As it was, he was there in September for the signing of the treaty, and he saw her at once. More than this, he had already petitioned the king of Sweden to be allowed to stay in France. The Swedish king even wrote a letter to the French court asking that Fersen be given a position of importance in the military, which request Louis granted. Marie Antoinette warmly acknowledged her support for this plan in a letter of September 19, 1783. She assured her fellow sovereign, "I shall not fail to second the views of Your Majesty in everything," by which she meant that the king of Sweden could count on her friendship and influence at the French court.

From this point on, the count divided his time between Versailles and the army base in northern France where his regiment was located. Fersen was also naturally attached to the Swedish king's entourage when, on June 7, 1784, that ruler arrived at the French court as part of a larger diplomatic tour. On June 21, Marie Antoinette made a point of entertaining the visiting monarch at the Petit Trianon. Her party made a definite impression. It was a large affair, held outdoors with music and dancing; she made sure to invite the most beautiful and fashionable women in Paris, all of whom were instructed to wear white. (The towering coiffures and glittering court dress that had characterized the queen's early reign were by this time out; Marie Antoinette was in a new phase, all flowing pale muslin and soft curls; a sort of upscale shepherdess look championed by her favorite painter, Élisabeth Vigée Le Brun.) The Swedish king was overwhelmed by the glamour of the surroundings; he called it "fairy-land." He was also struck by the queen's generous hospitality to foreigners. "She conversed of preference with the Swedes, and gave them a marked welcome," he noted with pleasure.

On March 27, 1785, nine months after this brilliant fête, Marie Antoinette gave birth to her third child, a boy, whom she and the king named Louis-Charles.* It was during this period also that the

---

* There is no evidence that Louis was ever invited to sleep over at the Petit Trianon. In fact, the purpose of the retreat was for Marie Antoinette to be alone with her friends and away from the king. Fersen, who would remain the queen's lover until her death, and who stayed with her many nights, both at the Petit Trianon and Versailles, was almost certainly the father of this child.

circle around the Polignacs began noticeably to expand their demands for riches and appointments. These friends of the queen's, the British ambassador observed candidly to his government on October 25, 1786, "are become the intimate participators of her secrets, and, having once got possession of them, they may, in fact, be said to be masters of their own mistress, and to have secured by that means to themselves the permanence of that power."

But for the moment this was not a problem. The atmosphere at court in the aftermath of the peace was expansive. The war was over and France had won! It had been a very long time since the kingdom could claim a victory, especially over Britain. True, the French had not gained much territory, but unlike their opponents they had held on to their sugar islands and improved their fishing rights in the Americas. More importantly, they had broken the English stranglehold on colonial trade and could expect to reap the commercial benefits of having helped the newly formed United States of America win its freedom.

Flush with exuberance (if not yet actual hard cash), the court went on a spending spree. Marie Antoinette further indulged her love of the simple life by building a small-scale working farm, complete with her own chickens, cows, and peasants, on the grounds of the Petit Trianon. The effect was so charming that she coaxed Louis into giving her an additional 6 million livres to purchase her very own country estate, the Château of Saint-Cloud, conveniently located some six miles from Versailles, where she could entertain in even greater privacy. She was not the only member of the family to splurge: the king had also been convinced to buy a palace for his aunts and a Parisian mansion for his sister; completely renovate the deteriorated royal residence at Fontainebleau; pay the interest on his youngest brother's debts (the comte d'Artois had managed, in the course of a few years, to accrue liabilities of some 14 million livres); and arrange for 7 million livres from the royal treasury to be given to his other brother, the comte de Provence, to purchase a second country estate (he already had one), with the understanding that, as the comte had no heirs, this château would eventually devolve upon Marie Antoinette's second son, Louis-Charles. There were other big-ticket items as well, such as the construction of a mighty new port at Cherbourg, on the English Channel, at a cost of 28 million livres. (The design was faulty and the project was eventually abandoned.) The royal family all also added to their stables and staffs, and the queen succeeded in appointing the comtesse de Polignac (now promoted to duchesse) as governess to her children, a position that carried with it a hefty salary of 400,000 livres annually.*

But all this was nothing when compared to what the treasury had spent to help the colonies achieve their independence. The French cost of the war for American liberty was 1.3 billion livres. Those extra zeros tacked on at the end of sums that distinguish the concept of "billion" from "million" make a big difference. Just the annual debt service on a figure like this, estimated at 107 million livres, was significantly more than the cost of all the family projects combined. In fact, Marie Antoinette could have worn sackcloth and reduced her entire household to a diet of bread and water and it wouldn't have made a dent in the royal deficit.

But that's not what it looked like to the public, from whom information as to the enormity of the gulf between the treasury's receipts and its payables was carefully kept. And what something *looks* like, however erroneous, can be as powerful a force as the truth, a painful political axiom the Crown was about to come face-to-face with when a deliciously titillating scandal, centered on an outsized and exorbitant piece of diamond jewelry, barreled down suddenly on an

---

* To be fair, the queen's best friend did not solicit this position. It was not she who was looking for riches but the people around her. The British ambassador reported that "the Duke and Duchess of Polignac can neither of them be supposed, from the narrowness of their capacities, to have laid, of themselves, any concerted plan whatever for the purpose of securing to themselves the duration of that favor which accidentally shone upon them." (In other words, they weren't smart enough to have insinuated themselves to this degree.) The ambassador instead named two of their circle, "M. de Vaudreuil and M. d'Adhemar, consummately ambitious and intriguing, and both attached...to the Duchess...who have had the chief direction of her conduct."

incredulous monarchy. "The case of the Necklace," the comte de Mirabeau (soon to become a rising force in French politics) would later observe succinctly, "was the prelude of the revolution."

IT BEGAN WITH THE arrival to Versailles in 1783 of Jeanne, comtesse de la Motte, a pretty woman almost exactly the same age as Marie Antoinette, who turned out to be one of the most adroit and enthusiastic con artists in the history of that lucrative profession. Although Jeanne's title was fake—her husband was really Monsieur de la Motte, a man of unassuming birth and nonexistent fortune—she did have royalty in her family tree: she was a direct descendant of Henri II, one of the Valois kings who had ruled France two centuries earlier.★ Knowledge of this princely lineage had literally been beaten into her as a child by her cruelly impoverished mother, who with each blow trained little Jeanne to beg for the family sustenance by crying out, "Pity a poor orphan of the blood of the Valois!" to the aristocratic carriages that flew past her in the street.

This harsh maternal indoctrination would be the saving of her; one day, one of those fine coaches stopped, and a tenderhearted marchioness took pity on the bruised and starving eight-year-old. She paid for Jeanne's education, had the girl's genealogy authenticated by the court, and even arranged for her to receive a small annual income of 800 livres from the royal treasury in recognition of her lineage. In that moment Jeanne, formerly a member of the disdained and forgotten French underclass, became Jeanne de Valois, a name that opened doors.

One of the doors it opened was to the magnificent château of the cardinal de Rohan. The Rohan family was one of the most prestigious and ancient in France. The cardinal was older, wealthy, and fatuous. Jeanne, now twenty-five, with extremely expensive tastes,

---

★ Two years before his death, Henri II sired an illegitimate son with a twenty-two-year-old paramour, much to the unhappiness of both his long-term mistress, fifty-eight-year-old Diane de Poitiers, and his wife, thirty-eight-year-old Catherine de' Medici. It was this son, later recognized, whose descendants eventually produced Jeanne.

recognized him instantly, in the universal language of grifters, as a mark.

At first, she just played him for small gifts of money. She would later claim that she had been his lover but he always denied it, and it didn't seem to have been necessary, as she managed to string him along nicely without recourse to this expedient. But more than money, he gave her credibility. Soon, she had established herself and her husband, a man of similar integrity and love of high living, in a small apartment at Versailles. There, she took a lover named Rétaux de Villette, who, in addition to his other upstanding qualities, had a flair for penmanship. She then began boasting discreetly of a grow- ing secret friendship between herself and Marie Antoinette, which she buttressed by the surprising revelation of a number of personal letters, written on high-quality paper adorned with baby blue fleur-de-lis, symbol of the throne, signed by the queen.

This caught the cardinal's attention, as she had known it would. Rohan was pining to gain entry to Marie Antoinette's inner circle. The cardinal's fortune was not what it once had been—a perplexing rash of bankruptcics had recently run through the aristocracy, even ensnaring some of Rohan's relations—and it was becoming more and more difficult to live up to the grand standards of the past. Everyone knew that the surest way to riches was through the queen; those previously worthless Polignacs had proven *that*. Nobody could figure out what she saw in them and yet there they were, dripping with favors and treasure. But Marie Antoinette wouldn't have any- thing to do with the cardinal de Rohan. He had once been ambas- sador to Vienna, and Maria Theresa had seen through him in an instant as a worthless flatterer and libertine, and had warned her daughter against him. Marie Antoinette shared her mother's opinion of the cardinal. Up until now, he had been frozen out at court.

The cardinal was not, however, the only quarry that Jeanne caught with her stories of cozy little tête-à-têtes with the queen. A jeweler by the name of Böhmer was also deeply in need of a friendly go-between to approach Marie Antoinette. For years, Böhmer had been trying to sell an over-the-top necklace, made of approximately 650 large, flawless diamonds that the jeweler had painstakingly collected from all over Europe.* He had originally envisioned it for Madame du Barry, but Louis XV had gone and died before Böhmer could close the sale. Given its price tag of over 1 million livres, there were very few women in the world who could afford this massive accessory, but Marie Antoinette was one of them. Problem was, she'd moved past that sort of thing and didn't want it. No amount of groveling could convince her. The last time Böhmer had tried, she had completely lost her patience. "Get up, Böhmer!" she'd exclaimed, exasperated. "Honest people do not find it necessary to supplicate on their knees. I have refused the necklace. The King wished to give it me, and I refused it again. Don't say anything more about it. Try to break it up and sell it, and don't drown yourself about it."

It was all very well for Marie Antoinette to advise him not to panic, but the fact was that the jeweler had gone into significant debt to assemble the necklace, and he was very close to declaring bankruptcy. And then a friend mentioned that he "knew a comtesse who had access to the queen," and Böhmer reached out to Jeanne.

After that, it was only a matter of putting all the pieces together. Böhmer showed Jeanne the necklace for the first time on December 29, 1784. On January 23, 1785, she informed him that she had found a buyer, "a very great nobleman." (The cardinal de Rohan had been traveling; this is what had caused the month's delay.) The very next day, January 24, Rohan turned up at the jeweler's to negotiate the terms of the sale—not for himself, mind you, but for the queen. Jeanne had explained to the mark—excuse me, the cardinal—that she had discussed the matter at length with Marie Antoinette, and that the queen wanted the necklace after all but was hesitating because she was short of funds at the moment. Jeanne, knowing of

---

* It was certainly the ugliest, clunkiest necklace ever to bring down a monarchy— just a bunch of heavy tassels hanging down around the neck. (In a pinch, it could have served as a means of tying back the drapes.) If this was a representative sample of his work, Böhmer would have been much better off in construction.

Rohan's desire to be of service to the queen, had proposed that he act as her secret intermediary in this transaction. It would be his job to work out all those pesky details of financing with which Marie Antoinette couldn't be bothered. Jeanne even provided a gracious note from the queen outlining the plan and thanking the cardinal for undertaking this tiresome task for her.

Overjoyed at this unexpected sign of royal favor, the cardinal relayed Marie Antoinette's instructions to Böhmer, pledging the jeweler to secrecy, as Jeanne had also cautioned that the queen, fearing her husband's displeasure at the large price tag, wished to keep the matter from the king for a little while. Between them, the two men worked out a timetable whereby Marie Antoinette would purchase the necklace for a total of 1.6 million livres, payable by quarterly installments over two years, with the first payment due on August 1, 1785. By the terms of this contract, the queen would take delivery of the necklace, through Jeanne, two days hence, on February 1, as she had need of it immediately. Böhmer, a stickler for form, insisted that Her Majesty personally approve these conditions, so the cardinal passed the contract to Jeanne, who passed it to the queen, who in turn returned it on January 29 signed "Marie Antoinette de France," which might have been suspicious if anyone had been really paying attention, as her official signature read simply "Marie Antoinette." As it was, however, in the two men's mutual elation, neither noticed.

It was a perfect scheme, and it worked brilliantly. On February 1, 1785, right on schedule, the cardinal brought the necklace to Jeanne's apartment at Versailles. No sooner had he arrived than there was a knock at the door and her co-conspirator, Villette, dressed up in stolen livery as a royal page, entered. Jeanne handed Villette the case with the necklace in it and solemnly instructed him to deliver it secretly to the queen. Rohan watched in gratitude as 1.6 million livres walked out the door.

Within a week, working so clumsily that they spoiled some of the gems, Jeanne and Villette had relieved the diamonds of their cumbersome setting. They at first tried to sell them in Paris, but the local jewelers found it odd that a man was walking around the city with his pockets bulging with loose diamonds and called the police. (As nothing had been reported stolen, however, they had to let him go.) After that, Jeanne wised up and sent the bulk of the stones to England with her husband, for sale to London jewelers. Although in his rush to get rid of the jewels he did not realize anywhere near their true value, there were so many of them that the comte de la Motte was able to return home that summer with a sizable fortune, which he and his wife immediately put to use purchasing carriages, furniture, bric-a-brac, and other necessities, including, for the amusement of visitors, "an automatic bird which flapped its wings and crowed."

During this period, both Rohan and Böhmer were of course disappointed by the failure of Marie Antoinette either to wear the necklace or to call them into favor by thanking them personally, but Jeanne was able to explain all that away with the excuse of the queen's continuing need to keep her purchase a secret from her husband. To appease the cardinal, she even paid a young woman who worked as a milliner in a shop in Paris, and who from a distance resembled Marie Antoinette, to meet Rohan one dark night in a public park the queen had been known to frequent. Dressed in a knockoff muslin gown similar to those in the omnipresent Élisabeth Vigée Le Brun portraits, the fake Marie Antoinette, with her face averted, just had time to hand the cardinal a rose and to murmur "You know what this means," before a warning of approaching pedestrians forced her to duck back into the shadows. That this gimmick worked gives a strong sense of the relative abilities of the various players in this high-stakes transaction.

At length, the time for the first payment drew near. Jeanne tried to put it off by claiming the queen had decided the price was too high, at which point Böhmer became suspicious and showed the cardinal a note he wished to send to Marie Antoinette, confirming receipt of the necklace. Rohan approved the idea but rewrote the letter to make it more obviously obsequious—"We have genuine satisfaction in thinking that the most beautiful set of diamonds which exists will be of service to the greatest and best of queens," he enthused—which unfortunately rendered the content of the message so incomprehensible to its recipient that Marie Antoinette concluded the jeweler was "an idiot" and burned it.

And now, at last, with 400,000 livres coming due, Jeanne played her trump card. Understanding that the cardinal would do anything rather than have it be revealed to Marie Antoinette that he had allowed her name to be mixed up in a deal as shady as this one, Jeanne insulated herself from punishment by cornering Böhmer on the sly and coolly setting up Rohan to be both blackmailed and fleeced. "You have been deceived," she admonished the astonished jeweler. "The written guarantee which the cardinal possesses bears a forged signature; but the prince is sufficiently rich, and he will be able to pay," she assured him.

It was her only mistake. Böhmer, *who still believed the queen had the necklace,* needed the money immediately to pay off his debts and knew the cardinal did not have 400,000 livres (let alone 1.6 million) lying around, as Jeanne had implied. So the jeweler went straight to Marie Antoinette to recover his property. The queen was otherwise engaged but in explaining to her lady-in-waiting why he needed to see her, Böhmer broke down and alerted Madame Campan to the whole outlandish, incredible plot. As it seemed impossible to the jeweler that a man of such high birth, standing, and education as Rohan could have allowed himself to be deceived so utterly by a trifling woman like the comtesse de la Motte, he naturally assumed the cardinal to have been the mastermind behind the operation and so didn't even bother to mention Jeanne's name. A shocked Madame Campan, in turn, relayed the story of the missing necklace and Böhmer's accusations to her mistress.

Marie Antoinette was incensed. The queen, who loathed the cardinal, was quite as ready to believe that Rohan had used her name to steal the diamonds as the cardinal had been willing to believe that

Marie Antoinette would use a go-between like Jeanne to buy an extravagant necklace on credit behind the king's back. It was a farce worthy of Beaumarchais and the Comédie-Française, the Paris opera house. Except that it would be acted out instead on the most public stage in France, the Parlement de Paris, the highest court of law in the land, with Marie Antoinette all too convincingly playing the role of the spoiled, self-indulgent, high-handed queen.*

She made every politically naive, poor choice. She did not bother to investigate further but went instantly to Louis insisting that her name be cleared. She wanted the cardinal to be not simply punished but publicly humiliated. With no Maurepas to guide him (the king had not replaced the chief minister after his death), Louis followed her lead. To heighten the shame quotient, the queen convinced the king to wait a few days, until August 15, 1785, when Rohan was scheduled to officiate in front of a packed audience in the royal chapel, before having him arrested. "Everything has been concerted between the king and me; the ministers knew nothing of it until the moment when the king sent for the cardinal," Marie Antoinette exulted to Joseph in a letter of August 22. (By which she meant, of course, that she had planned and orchestrated the arrest.) The entire court was therefore treated to the spectacle of a ranking member of the ancient and powerful Rohan family, in full ecclesiastical attire, no less, being led away by armed guards to the Bastille.

Giving in to spite in this way was the move of an amateur, and Marie Antoinette would pay dearly for it. Although one or two of his ministers did in fact try to caution Louis about the risks of trying the case publicly, on the whole the royal council was only too pleased to simply get out of the way and allow the queen to destroy herself.

The prosecution of the cardinal de Rohan in Paris for criminal theft of a 1.6 million-livre diamond necklace during a period when the

---

* In France, a "*parlement*" was not a representative legislative body like the Parliament of England. Rather, *parlements* formed the judiciary branch of the government. There were regional *parlements* all over the kingdom. The most influential was the Parlement de Paris; think of it as somewhat the equivalent of the Supreme Court.

vast preponderance of the population of France were on the brink of starvation caused a sensation. Like other watershed trials, the case gripped the public imagination and laid bare the larger implications of the underlying conflict, and with it the prejudices and grievances of the society at large. The optics were not good for the royal family. As one by one the various conspirators were caught after having fled the kingdom and dragged back to Paris to testify (only Jeanne's husband managed to avoid extradition), it became clear that the cardinal, who had maintained from the first that he had been duped, had really believed he was purchasing the ruinous diamonds secretly for Marie Antoinette. The trial therefore quickly devolved into a public referendum, not on the conduct of the accused but on that of the queen. And since everyone knew that Marie Antoinette had engaged in behavior of this kind in the past—buying diamonds she couldn't afford and keeping the purchase a secret from the king, choosing a suspect young woman like the duchesse de Polignac as her confidential playmate and promoting her over more respectable and deserving candidates—sympathy was strongly with the defendant. When on July 30, 1786, Rohan was declared innocent of all charges, it was widely viewed as a triumph of fairness over absolute power and corruption, an attitude that was only reinforced when, at Marie Antoinette's urging, Louis punished the cardinal anyway by banishing him for the crime of lèse-majesté (essentially, disrespecting the sovereign). Crowds lined the streets and cheered Rohan as a hero as he journeyed through France on his way to exile.

Jeanne de Valois was declared guilty of theft and was punished by branding and imprisonment; she escaped two years later to England, where she published a memoir proclaiming her innocence, further tarnishing the queen.

If Marie Antoinette remembered that her mother, brother, and the comte de Mercy had all warned her repeatedly during the first years of her reign that her frivolity could lead to exactly this sort of comeuppance, she gave no sign of it. "The Queen's grief was extreme," Madame Campan remembered. "I went to her, and found her alone in her closet; she was weeping. 'Come,' said her Majesty to me, 'come and lament for your Queen, insulted, and sacrificed by cabal and injustice.'"

And as if this situation were not bad enough, at that very moment, just when the Parlement de Paris had dealt the monarchy a stinging defeat and left its credibility shaken, the foreign loans made during the war for American independence came due and the kingdom of France faced a mammoth, full-on, Great Depression–sized financial crash.

DISAPPOINTINGLY, IMPROVED TRADE with the fledgling United States, which the French government had more or less been counting on to help close the deficit, had failed to materialize. The newly liberated colonists, many of whom toiled under extremely rustic conditions, had not demonstrated a strong inclination to spend what little money they had on fine Sèvres porcelain or the other luxury goods that formed the staple exports of France. Those products they did buy were the ones they were used to, and of course these came from England. As Americans, they might have reviled the British monarchy, but as consumers they remained confirmed loyalists. "No less than a hundred and twenty bankruptcies have happened at [the French port of] Bordeaux since the war, and Shipping is fallen there 50 per cent," the English ambassador gloated. "Since the month of November last not one American vessel has been seen in the harbor, nor have there been any demands whatever for exportation to the West Indies."

Faced with the prospect of the royal treasury's imminent bankruptcy, Louis's minister of finance—there was a new one by this time, Charles-Alexandre de Calonne, who understood exactly what was at stake—came up with a radical plan for fiscal reform that would ensure the kingdom's solvency over the long term. To reduce the government's future dependence on foreign loans, which were expensive and unreliable, he instead proposed to increase revenues by taxing the nobility and the clergy equally with commoners through the imposition of a land tax payable by *all* property owners. It was exactly the sort of sweeping structural change—neither the aristocracy nor the Church had ever been taxed in the history of the kingdom—of which progressives dream no matter what century they happen to live in. Calonne submitted an extensive written report outlining his program to Louis, and since this was obviously the fairest and most sensible approach to the predicament, the king approved it.

The problem was that the Parlement de Paris had to agree to register any new taxes, and based on the recent adverse judgment in the diamond necklace case, the monarchy's outlook for getting something as unprecedented as Calonne's program through was not favorable. The government couldn't even help its own case by revealing the severity of the coming financial crisis; the solution had to be in place before international bankers got wind of the true size of the deficit or there would be a panic. So Calonne suggested that Louis end-run the Parlement de Paris by calling for an Assembly of Notables, basically a group of handpicked regional officials, who would rubber-stamp the program and see to it that it was implemented generally throughout the kingdom. When Maria Theresa had tried to tax the nobility for the first time after the War of the Austrian Succession, it had taken her years of negotiation and steady persuasion. Calonne assured Louis it could be done in three months.

The Assembly of Notables was convened at Versailles on February 22, 1787, with predictable results. Once again, the visuals were not on the side of the monarchy. The regional officials, all members of the landed nobility or clergy themselves, could not help but notice how grandly the royal family lived, how many houses and horses they each possessed. It's difficult to sell the notion of an imminent financial collapse and the need for increased taxes when the people asking for the money are engaged in a suspicious number of home improvement projects. Opposition to the government's proposals was so fierce that the king was forced to repudiate Calonne's policies and sack him in less than two months.

The chaos surrounding these events—the angry voices, the quickly changing emotions, the lack of agreement on how to proceed—unsettled Louis. These were not the conditions under which the king functioned well. There was no single minister to guide him, no leftover instructions from his dead father. In his uncertainty, Louis turned to Marie Antoinette as he had during the first days of his ascension, before the appointment of Maurepas. The comte de Mercy, still at Versailles attempting to guide the queen, wrote to Vienna in May 1787 that the king came in tears to his wife every day.

This time, Marie Antoinette, thirty-two years old, the mother of three children, rose to the occasion.* She did not hand her husband off to a minister while she retired to the Petit Trianon to play with her friends, as she had when she was nineteen. Seeing that he was incapacitated—she told Mercy that Louis was "in no fit state for this"—she did exactly what she was supposed to do. She acted as both queen and wife, staying by his side and taking as much control of the situation as she could. It was absolutely what Maria Theresa, Maria Christina, or Maria Carolina would have done, and what many of the women who had sat on the throne of France before her had been forced to do as well.

But Marie Antoinette was limited in what she could accomplish by both her ignorance of finance and the sheer scope of the crisis. She brought in a friend of long standing whom she trusted to lead the government; two of Louis's other ministers quit in protest. She arranged and sat in on policy meetings both with the king and in his place; she tried to understand the issues; she did her best to advise her husband. But no amount of effort on her part could increase the flow of wealth into the system. Even the weather worked against her: severe storms followed by a drought and then excessive cold ruined the crops and forced the price of bread, the main source of sustenance for the population, to record highs. On August 16, 1788,

---

* Her fourth child, a daughter, born the year before, died around this time, on June 19, 1787, which only added to her and Louis's sorrow. (Also Fersen's, as this child, too, was likely his—certainly he believed so.)

the inevitable occurred. The royal treasury ran out of money and was forced to suspend payments on all sorts of securities. The economy collapsed. Companies went bankrupt. Many French subjects, as well as the foreign bankers, lost their life savings and incomes.

It is an unfortunate political axiom that in times of economic disaster, people tend to look for a villain. As Marie Antoinette was visibly influential in the government during the period that culminated in the official bankruptcy of France, like an eighteenth-century Herbert Hoover she got all the blame. "Her ostensible interference drew upon her, from all parties and all classes of society, an unpopularity, the rapid progress of which alarmed all those who were sincerely attached to her," Madame Campan worried. They called her "Madame Deficit."★

In this case, however, the citizens of France identified not only the heinous culprit who was clearly responsible for the dire situation within which the kingdom now found itself, but also its obvious savior. There was a great public outcry that the financial wizard Jacques Necker, the banker who had found all that money the last time, be recalled to the ministry. Louis, who by this time knew Necker to be one of the reasons they were in this mess in the first place, resisted the idea, but Marie Antoinette, understanding that at this point they didn't really have a choice, convinced him to give the financier a try. On August 25, 1788, Necker triumphantly returned to Versailles to work his magic as the king's most influential minister. Not even he could pretend to have a surplus in the royal treasury without at least *some* money coming in, however, so he advised Louis to call a meeting of the Estates General to ask for emergency financial relief.

The Estates General was the French version of a national assembly. It consisted of representatives from the first estate (the clergy),

---

★ Although Marie Antoinette's name is today synonymous with the famous line "Let them eat cake," there is absolutely no evidence from any credible source that she uttered these words. In fact, the phrase sounds nothing like her. That the saying was falsely attributed to her is simply another manifestation of her unpopularity at the time of the financial crisis.

the second estate (the aristocracy), and the third estate (everybody else). It was called exclusively at the sovereign's pleasure, which effectively meant only during periods of national crisis. To get money out of the Estates, every king knew he would be required to make concessions that limited his authority, so much effort went into getting by without having to resort to this unappealing alternative. The last time the Estates General had been summoned, for example, had been nearly two centuries earlier, in 1614.

Unfortunately for the Crown, this was an especially fraught period in which to call for a national representative assembly. News had recently arrived in France from America of yet *another* irresistibly provocative document, penned by a small group of statesmen in just four months during a conclave in Philadelphia and voted on by the rest of the country, that outlined the structure, rights, and responsibilities of a brand-new system of government. Incorporating democratic principles, the authors of this treatise had cleverly formulated a series of checks and balances, including the elimination of hereditary monarchy in favor of a chief executive elected for a specific term of office, as prevention against future tyranny. The Americans called their handiwork a constitution.

It is difficult to overestimate the degree of excitement that word of this development generated in France, coming as it did at exactly the moment when, for the first time in 175 years, the Estates General would meet and the citizenry would have a say in their government. "Nobody speaks of anything but the constitution," Fersen wrote to his father in December 1788. "It's a delirium." Expectations were raised even higher when it was announced that the number of representatives invited from the third estate (mostly lawyers, tradesmen, and other members of the bourgeois) would be doubled to reflect their majority in the general population. Necker had advised this, and since after the disastrous Assembly of Notables neither Louis nor Marie Antoinette trusted the first two estates, the king had agreed. It made sense that the realm's ordinary subjects would be far more likely to side with their sovereign in his desire to tax the nobility and clergy than would the delegates of these two formerly exempt classes themselves.

But the chosen delegates for the third estate had a far more ambitious agenda than the throne realized. This was their moment and they knew it. True, commoners had been prohibited from taking an active role in the French campaign for American independence — ironically in a struggle for equality, only the sons of aristocrats had been allowed to fight — but they were now being asked to pay for it, and it seemed only fair that they should share in the rights and ideals championed by their victorious allies. The calling of the Estates General and their expanded role just at this pivotal period seemed to them prophetic; they knew they would never have a better chance than this. Like the Americans, they must seize the initiative and drive home their demands if France was ever to secure representative government. It was entirely up to them.

With this mood upon them, they filed into the opening procession at Versailles on May 4, 1789, their plain black hats and somber coats a stark contrast to the second estate's jeweled plumes and magnificent finery, and the clergy's rich robes. In the past, these aristocratic trappings, the mark of centuries of social superiority, would have inspired respect and intimidation among the lower class. But that was before the American revolution. Now the representatives from the third estate merely narrowed their eyes and went to work. A number of important noblemen, who also embraced the ideas of liberty and equality, led by Louis's cousin the duc d'Orléans, joined them. On June 20, 1789, this group met on a tennis court and swore a solemn oath not to disband until they had forced the monarchy to accept a constitution based on the principles of representative government. Like three-foot-tall coiffures and crudely ostentatious diamond necklaces, inherited privilege in France had abruptly gone out of style.

It was a worrisome situation for the Crown, made even more oppressive by family tragedy. The seven-year-old dauphin, the first-born son upon whom Louis especially doted, had been ailing for some time; he died at one o'clock in the morning on June 4, just a month after the opening of the Estates General. Both Louis and Marie Antoinette were devastated at the loss of the boy. Yet even at this moment of the most intense grief, politics intruded. A delegation appeared that very day insisting on an immediate audience with the king to address their demands, and Louis was forced to receive them. "Are there no fathers in the Assembly of the Third Estate?" he cried piteously.

The atmosphere, in Paris especially, was ugly. It was feared that the king would dismiss the Estates rather than accept a constitution. "The Duc d'Orléans forever!" echoed through the capital. To keep order, the army was called in, which only aggravated the fear that Louis was intending to use force to subvert the public will. On July 14, 1789, the citizenry took matters into their own hands. A mob broke into the government armory and looted the weapons. Gaining strength, it rushed at the Bastille, despised symbol of torment and despotism. The governor of that underdefended fortress surrendered. For his trouble, he and his few officers were massacred in a frenzy that ended with the governor's head being paraded through the streets on the end of a pike like a grisly scepter.

It had begun.

PART III

In the Shadow of the Empress

Storming the Bastille

Maria Christina

"Mimi"

. . . as governor-general of Brussels

18

Betrayal in Brussels

❦

The Emperor Joseph possesses intellect; he might accom-
plish much. Unluckily for himself, he will always take the
second step before he has taken the first.

—Frederick the Great

MARIA CHRISTINA WAS THIRTY-EIGHT and had been married to
Albert for fourteen childless years when her mother died on November 29, 1780, and Joseph inherited all of the dowager empress's lands,
titles, and authority. Mimi's profound grief over the loss of her
parent—for Maria Theresa had been her daughter's closest friend
and supporter, just as Mimi had been her mother's—was only
amplified by the uncertainty that attended her older brother's rise to
power. Neither Maria Christina nor Albert was under any illusions
as to Joseph's character and ambitions. Although the emperor was
sincere to the point of fanaticism in his determination to make
reforms and improve his subjects' lives, he was equally resolved to
have his own way no matter what the cost. Joseph's need to demonstrate his superiority in even the most trivial of matters was only too
transparent to his sister, as were his bitterness and lack of compassion, which had a tendency to manifest themselves as vindictiveness.
Mimi knew she had fallen afoul of her brother by her outspoken
opposition to his recent ill-conceived and ultimately failed war for
Bavaria, and that she and her husband were likely to be punished for

it, even though Albert had done his duty and participated loyally in a campaign directed against his own family.

She wasn't wrong to be suspicious. Joseph barely waited until the first weeks of mourning were over before making drastic changes to the court at Vienna. He'd made no secret of the fact that he found the presence of his two unmarried sisters annoying, so almost as soon as the funeral was over he packed each of these reluctant abbesses, who had never lived anywhere but at the Hofburg palace, off to their respective convents.★ Within a month, he had stripped the court of all ceremony, abolished formal dress (which he hated wearing), and cut back significantly on the feast days, religious holidays, and other generous entertainments for which his mother's capital had previously been known. By February of 1781, having reviewed the terms of Maria Theresa's will, he negated several of her gifts to his siblings, including two houses in Hungary and the 200 or so paintings she had conferred upon Maria Christina (who was now forced to return them to Joseph), before finally turning his attention to the inherited position of governors-general of the Austrian Netherlands, a bequest that his mother had specifically assigned to Mimi and her husband in their marriage contract.

The governor-generalship of the Austrian Netherlands (basically present-day Belgium) was a plum appointment. Brussels and its adjoining provinces—Flanders and Hainaut, among others—were prosperous and peaceful. The population was overwhelmingly Catholic and long used to Habsburg rule. Governors-general lived pleasantly in a palace and their duties were largely ceremonial. It is a

---

★ Forty-two-year-old Marianne, who had rejected the nunnery in Prague during her mother's lifetime, was instead made abbess of one in Klagenfurt, on the Austrian border, about 200 miles south of Vienna; thirty-seven-year-old Maria Elisabeth was bundled off to a convent in Innsbruck, nearly 300 miles from the capital. To give a sense of her life afterward, a few years later she developed an infection on her face that ulcerated, and the English ambassador dropped by to commiserate. "Believe me, for an unmarried forty-year-old archduchess, a hole in the cheek is fun," the once-beautiful Maria Elisabeth informed her shocked visitor. "No event which breaks the monotony and *ennui* of my life can be looked upon as a misfortune." She would live this way, as abbess of Innsbruck, for the next twenty-seven years.

measure of just how desirable this appointment was that in 1744 Maria Theresa had bestowed it upon her younger sister Maria Anna and Charles of Lorraine as a wedding present. When Maria Anna died in childbirth later that same year, Charles had retained the position, although it was understood that he would also act as commander general of the Austrian army. He would remain governor-general of Brussels for the next thirty-six years.*

Charles might not have been much of a military commander, but he had made an excellent governor-general. During his tenure, not only did the Austrian Netherlands never give Maria Theresa a single moment's worry, but they also contributed some 72 million florins to her treasury. True, the various regional authorities with which he had to negotiate had their own customs and prejudices, but Charles found the inhabitants generally charming and only bemoaned the fact that Brussels was too far away for his sister-in-law to visit. "For my part," he observed to Maria Theresa, "I dare to say that these provinces are very easily governed, and with the least degree of gentleness and goodness your Majesty can do whatever you wish in them, and to my way of thinking there is nothing more flattering for a sovereign than to reign in the hearts of the subjects," he concluded wisely.

Joseph hadn't wanted to honor this bequest to his sister either, but upon being informed that the legacy was legally binding, he grudgingly acceded to it. Still, he would not allow Maria Christina and Albert to settle in Brussels until he had toured the area himself. This he did in the early summer of 1781, arriving at the end of May, at which time he spoke to dozens of local officials; reviewed all aspects of trade, finance, administration, and education associated with the region; and received thousands of petitions from ordinary people asking for help or justice in one form or another. Maria Christina and Albert were finally allowed to take up residence in July, but not before Joseph had cut back significantly on their expected salary and

---

* He died in 1779, a few months before Maria Theresa.

forced them to refuse the grand château traditionally gifted to the governor-general by the regional officials.*

But these were minor matters to Maria Christina. What she and Albert were really worried about were her brother's sweeping plans for reform. They found many of his ideas to be extreme and feared the disruption that might result from his policies. By long tradition, the Austrian Netherlands, like the kingdom of Hungary, required its monarchs to swear to uphold certain rights of the citizenry as a condition of sovereignty. In Brussels, this oath was known as the Joyeuse Entrée or Joyous Entry. Joseph, while he was visiting, had neatly sidestepped this obligation by explaining that his sister and her husband, as governors-general, would pledge their word and swear to uphold the Joyous Entry in his place.

Maria Christina had no wish to behave dishonorably and deceive her future subjects. So she and Albert went to Kaunitz, who was staying on as principal minister, and asked him point-blank if Joseph intended to violate the conditions of the Joyous Entry by imposing reforms that conflicted with the terms of the oath. If so, Mimi told Kaunitz, she and Albert would voluntarily decline the promotion to governors-general and with it the ease and grandeur of the office, and her husband would accept a much less privileged position in the army instead.

The minister admitted that the emperor did indeed have large plans, but made haste to assure the couple that these did not include the Austrian Netherlands. Count Kaunitz was not sincere in this statement, as he and Joseph had been cooking up a scheme to try to exchange Brussels for Bavaria for some time, but of course Mimi could not know this, as she had been left out of the intrigue. She took the minister at his word.

---

* In fairness, as part of his financial reforms, Joseph severely reduced expenditures throughout his lands, so much so that there was a running joke in Vienna that "the emperor has [decided] that Jesus Christ...having given useful service to the House of Austria for many centuries, deserved, in accordance with the guidelines laid down, to have his salary reduced." But it is also clear that he took particular satisfaction in stripping Mimi of these endowments. "She will have to give them up [and] will be furious about it," he told Count Kaunitz smugly.

Consequently, Maria Christina and Albert accepted the posting and on July 10, 1781, made their formal entrance into Brussels, where they were greeted warmly by cheering crowds and with feasts and fireworks. Three weeks later, before a distinguished company representing the Church and aristocracy of the region, Albert solemnly took the oath to "maintain the privileges, franchises, usages, customs, lands and property" of his subjects in an inspiring service at the cathedral in Ghent. (Maria Christina was present but for ceremonial purposes her husband represented both of them. Everyone knew that the power flowed through her by virtue of her lineage anyway; the couple was generally referred to as "the Princess Maria Christina, sister of the Emperor, and her husband.") The new governors-general settled in Brussels, where they immediately endeared themselves to the community and added to the beauty of the city by building the elegant Palace of Laeken at their own expense. As they had during their years in Hungary, Mimi and Albert promoted the arts and culture and provided a welcome glamour to their surroundings. "The virtues of these Princes, by which they adorned the Court of Brussels, and set a fair example of conjugal love, their courtesy and affability, and that affection which they had always expressed for the Flemings, with whose character they were well acquainted, had gained to them the entire esteem and confidence of the nation," reported a chronicler of the period. "No apprehension was entertained that the Councils of these Princes had suggested measures that tended to invade the rights of the people."

The chronicler's report was accurate. No one in Brussels suspected their new governors-general of duplicity, and for good reason. From the beginning, Joseph deliberately kept the couple in ignorance of his plans. Like their subjects, Maria Christina and Albert were being set up.

THE REIGN OF JOSEPH II should be thoroughly studied by every progressive politician of the twenty-first century as an object lesson in how *not* to go about improving government and society. Never did a ruler undertake to execute a more enlightened program. The very first thing Joseph did, in October of 1771, was to issue a blanket edict of toleration throughout his realm (including the Austrian Netherlands) that allowed freedom of worship to Protestants and Jews, and that even secured to these formerly excluded minorities the right to build religious schools and churches, and to hold positions in the imperial government. It was the bravest, fairest, most sweeping, liberal, and just mandate ever to have been handed down by a Catholic monarch, and if he had stopped there, and spent the rest of his career simply ensuring that this decree was followed, he would have been forever esteemed as one of the most laudable sovereigns in history.

But Joseph did not stop there. He was only just getting started. The emperor believed he could resolve every problem, streamline every inefficiency, by imposing a top-down solution, rather like a chief executive at a large corporation. So, in addition to the toleration act, he freed the serfs in Austria, Hungary, and Transylvania (much to the consternation of their aristocratic owners). He then took those slivers of land they had been working away from the nobility and gave it to these former servants; he also bestowed upon them the right to travel, marry, and pursue a trade. He abolished a large percentage of the monasteries, which he considered to be filled with lazy, superstitious monks and nuns, and forced the members of the dissolved orders to vacate the premises within five months. In the interests of uniformity—uniformity was Joseph's mantra—he decreed that from this point on, all governmental business was to be transacted in German, a language unfamiliar to the Hungarians, Transylvanians, and Bohemians.* He moved the capital of Hungary from Pressburg to the more centrally located Buda, a popular move, but then refused to summon the Diet, the national representative assembly, to the general indignation of the citizenry. Worse, even

---

* Depending upon region, ethnicity, and education, the languages spoken by the general population in Hungary and Transylvania, for example, included, variously, Magyar, Serbian, Slovak, Croatian, Romanian, and Latin—but no German.

though he himself had declined to participate in the traditional coronation ceremony, Joseph nonetheless impounded the Hungarian crown, scepter, and precious moth-eaten robe that his mother had worn, and which were so symbolic to the native population, and had them stowed away in a museum in Vienna (ostensibly for safekeeping but also likely to prevent the Diet from deposing him and enthroning someone else in his place). He redrew all of the administrative districts within each kingdom without regard for custom or antiquity and had them report directly to him in Austria. No detail of life—or death—escaped Joseph's monolithic treatment; even burials were subject to corrective regulations that mandated plain wooden coffins and identical unmarked plots for all, no matter how high their rank or notable their accomplishments. As a result, Mozart, perhaps the greatest musical genius the world has ever known, who had the misfortune to die while these dictates were still in force, was interred anonymously, denied the presence of even a mourner at his gravesite, as per Joseph's directives.

Many of these initiatives were commendable and long overdue (well, maybe not the one about the no-frills funerals). But the scope and number of the changes were unsettling; they touched on long-held beliefs and practices; and Joseph did not allow time for the inevitable confusion and upheaval that followed such dramatic realignments. Edict followed edict at an alarming pace. "I admire the inexhaustible imagination of the Emperor," murmured Frederick the Great, still alive and watching with amusement from Berlin as Joseph barraged his subjects with proclamations. "If he had gone in for poetry, he would have surpassed Homer, Virgil and Milton," he noted.

It should perhaps come as no surprise that Joseph's innovations prompted widespread revolt.* In Transylvania, the serfs rioted because they thought the new laws meant that the emperor had allocated to them *all* the nobles' land and the aristocrats weren't giving it

---

* And I didn't even get a chance to talk about his insistence on the aristocracy's paying a hefty land tax for the first time—the same proposal that went over so well in France at the Assembly of Notables.

up fast enough. Joseph had to send the army in and make an example by publicly executing the leaders of the rebellion on the wheel, a barbaric punishment that did not endear him to the very people he had hoped to help. The Hungarians engaged in endless delaying tactics, refusing even to let the emperor's officials in to conduct a general census. They held back taxes, and their statesmen resigned rather than ratify Joseph's policies. Leading members of the Hungarian nobility prepared for armed revolt and secretly made overtures to Prussia, offering to switch national allegiance in return for military support.

But Joseph just kept going. His foreign policy was as ambitious (and disruptive) as his domestic programs. Still fixated on annexing Bavaria, he entered into an alliance with Catherine the Great whereby he promised to aid Russia in a war against the Turks in exchange for her helping him acquire this much-desired province. In this way he got the tsarina to send an envoy at the beginning of 1785 into Germany to demand that the elector of Bavaria cede all of his property to Joseph and take the Austrian Netherlands instead. This so upset the balance of power in the region that the rapidly aging Frederick the Great, much to his disgust, had to come out of retirement to deal with it. "I, who am already more than half beyond this world am forced to double my wisdom and activity, and continually keep in my head the detestable plans this cursed Joseph begets afresh with every fresh day," he grumbled.

As it happened, the emperor was by this time so loathed by his fellow heads of state, who feared that Joseph would use his Russian ally to try to intimidate them into handing over their property as well, that Frederick did not even have to mount his horse to block him. All it took was a little diplomacy. On July 23, 1785, the emperor faced a united front of opposition in the form of the newly created League of German Princes, headed up by the king of Prussia, whose strenuous objections to the proposed Bavarian swap were vigorously seconded by the ministers of both France and Great Britain, two kingdoms not previously known for having agreed on foreign policy. Faced with overwhelming European condemnation, Catherine the Great, too, withdrew her support, after which there was nothing for Joseph to do but retract his demands and give up on the dream of expanding his boundaries beyond those that his mother had claimed. Frederick had won again.

It was to be the king of Prussia's last victory. He died the following year, on August 17, 1786, at the age of seventy-four. He left his nephew, the new sovereign, a fully stocked treasury, as his father had before him, and a realm ballooned by some 28,000 square miles of territory captured in battle, an extraordinary outcome his parent could not have conceived of. His people rejoiced when he was dead, for the nephew was far less demanding, but the siren song of the triumphant Frederick the Great long outlived the histories of his contemporaries. It would shape the fate not simply of Germany, but of the whole world, for centuries to come.

FROM LAEKEN, THEIR ELEGANT HOME in Brussels, Maria Christina and Albert watched in increasing dismay as opposition to Joseph's seemingly never-ending string of reforms grew ever more violent in Hungary and Bohemia. They had been blindsided by his edict of toleration, but had managed to handle the initiative as diplomatically as possible by supporting religious inclusion while simultaneously reassuring their subjects of their own and the emperor's sincere piety. It had been a tricky tightrope to walk, but on the whole they had succeeded; there were grumblings, but the atmosphere had remained peaceful. No sooner had they calmed this storm, however, than Joseph delivered another, in the form of the proposed trade of Bavaria for the Austrian Netherlands. And when this did not work out he threatened to start a war with the next-door Dutch over navigation rights, from which he had to be rescued by the French government.*

---

* To save face, in November 1785 Joseph agreed to give up his waterway demands in exchange for 10 million florins. The Dutch being unwilling to pay so much, Marie Antoinette, under intense pressure from her brother, convinced Louis to provide

The worst part of all of this was the puzzling way Mimi and Albert were being shut out of Joseph's decision-making process. As the local representatives of the imperial government, they were there to provide firsthand information on regional conditions and attitudes, so that any changes in policy could be implemented as smoothly as possible. And yet not only did Joseph fail to solicit their opinion or consult with them in any way, but he did not even bother to notify them when he was intending to act. "What afflicts us most is that we see he has no confidence in us," Mimi worried in a letter to her brother Leopold in Florence.

The grand duke of Tuscany, who was having his own problems with the emperor, understood exactly what she was talking about. Joseph had already demanded that Leopold's eldest son, seventeen-year-old Francis, because he was in line for the imperial succession (after Leopold himself), be brought to Vienna for training and married off to a sister-in-law of Catherine the Great's son in order to cement the Russian alliance.★ At the same time, the emperor decreed that Tuscany was no longer to be ruled independently of Austria, although out of respect for his brother he agreed to wait until Leopold died before claiming the duchy for himself. Still, this meant that the grand duke could no longer will his property and sovereignty to his second son, as he had intended. Leopold was so upset by this, and by the emperor's high-handed manner of governing, that he took to writing to Maria Christina in invisible ink, to prevent the suspicious Joseph (who routinely intercepted his brother's letters) from reading his private correspondence. An alliance sprang up naturally between

---

nearly half the amount. This was during the period when the queen's party was ascendant in the government; the British ambassador noted in his report home that the duc de Polignac was appointed "Intendant General of the Post...[a] very considerable trust and emolument" at exactly the same time the sum was promised to Joseph and an Austrian war with the Dutch averted. Consequently, when the royal treasury went bankrupt three years later, her subjects remembered with bitterness that their queen had funneled this money to her brother, and it contributed greatly to the accusations of her favoring Austria over France.

★ Francis was the child whose birth had so thrilled Maria Theresa that she had burst into the opera house in Vienna shouting from the balcony that Poldel had had a boy!

the two siblings, as a similarly appalled Mimi provided a remedy for Leopold's second son by making him the heir to *her* fortune.

Determined to do what they could to improve their working relationship with her difficult older brother, Maria Christina and Albert braved the snow and ice of a winter's journey to travel to Vienna to meet personally with Joseph. They arrived on January 11, 1786, and stayed for more than two months. During the whole time they were there, there was never a hint that anything was wrong. On the contrary, the emperor treated them with great courtesy, like visiting royalty. Joseph personally conducted them on a tour of all the improvements he had made to the city, including the new school and hospital he had established. He held a grand fête at Schönbrunn Palace in their honor, at which he relaxed the new regulations sufficiently to allow formal court dress as well as the purchase of costly orange and palm trees as decorations for the ballroom, a luxury he generally frowned upon as a frivolous expense. He encouraged them to visit friends and even to see their old home in Pressburg (which had fallen into disrepair, another victim of Joseph's budget cuts). "How much I regret the deterioration of that beautiful palace," Mimi mourned to Eleonore Liechtenstein. "But reasons of state come first," she made haste to add loyally.*

It wasn't until March 20, 1786, the very last day of their visit, that Joseph hit them with it.

Mimi and Albert were all packed and ready to go when they were suddenly handed a memorandum on the future of the Austrian Netherlands. A quick perusal of this document told them that since Joseph had been forced to keep Brussels and its environs rather than exchange them for Bavaria, this province, like Tuscany, would no longer be allowed an independent government. But unlike with Leopold, he had no intention of waiting for Maria Christina and Albert to die before taking over. Rather, Joseph was intending

---

* Ironically, even Eleonore, who had once accused Maria Christina of sleeping with her husband, so disapproved of Joseph's policies and methods that she took Mimi's side and became close friends with her from this point on.

sometime in the near future to appoint new bureaucrats charged with enforcing numerous reforms on the native population. Mimi and Albert could still live in their fine house in Brussels, but they were to be stripped of all authority. When they tried to protest that these changes would be contested and could even threaten Austrian rule in the long run, Joseph closed off all possibility of further discussion by responding curtly that it was his job to act in the interest of the general good and that he alone knew what was best for his subjects.

To believe that a population as educated, prosperous, and proud as the Belgians would allow the overthrow of a native system of government that had developed organically and held for centuries was an act of hubris and political naivete so mind-boggling that it would be difficult to credit the initiative if it were not so well documented.* Joseph might just as well have proposed sending Austrian officials to Versailles to impose his ambitious new improvement program on France.

Maria Christina knew it. But she had also spent too much time under her mother's tutelage not to recognize where her duty lay. It was her job to weather Joseph's reign and keep the Austrian Netherlands in the family for his successors. She was as determined not to lose Brussels as the emperor was to remold it. So she and Albert returned home resolved to do everything in their power to moderate the transition. This, she understood, was what Maria Theresa would have wanted her to do.

There was something else she knew her mother would have asked of her, and that was to check up on Marie Antoinette. Mimi had sought to visit France for years, but her youngest sister had always come up with one excuse or another to postpone a meeting. Now Maria Christina, anxious that she and Albert had only a short grace period before Joseph's new policies went into effect, tried again. The intelligence out of Versailles in the spring of 1786 had been

---

* Even Count Kaunitz was aghast at this plan.

particularly disturbing. The Parlement de Paris had recently handed down its decision against the queen in the affair of the necklace, further tarnishing her reputation.

The difficult delivery of Marie Antoinette's fourth child, a daughter, on July 9 robbed her of the excuse that she did not have the time to see a nearby member of her family. The trapped queen, confined to her rooms for the protracted recuperative process necessitated by the birth, at length extended the long-desired invitation. At the end of August 1786, Maria Christina and Albert arrived in Paris.

THERE WERE MANY REASONS why Marie Antoinette was reluctant to host her sister that summer. The humiliating verdict in the affair of the necklace had revealed the depth of public sentiment against her; this was certainly not the way the queen wished to present herself to the woman who was, in effect, a stand-in for her ever-disapproving (if deceased) mother. Nor, in the aftermath of the Dutch payoff to Joseph, was this the optimum time to emphasize Marie Antoinette's close ties to her Austrian relations.

But surely the most important consideration was the need to hide the queen's intimacy with her longtime lover from this perceptive sibling. To this end, Count Fersen, prudently absenting himself at the time of the birth of the daughter who was almost certainly his (although he did linger near the outskirts of the kingdom long enough to confirm the health of both mother and infant), suddenly remembered that he had not seen his father in some time and arrived unannounced in Sweden for a surprise visit.*

Maria Christina, of course, had no notion of this. She and Albert

---

* This is not to say that Fersen left only because of Maria Christina's visit but to defray suspicion in general. This final pregnancy seems to have come as a surprise to Marie Antoinette. (Joseph observed that, when she wrote to tell him that she was with child again, "she displayed her annoyance at it.") The queen was well aware that she could not afford another scandal in the wake of the affair of the necklace. She might even have tried to give up Fersen for good—the count would remain in Sweden for ten months, during which time he had an affair with another woman—but it seems he could not stay away and in the end broke off the Swedish relationship to return to Marie Antoinette in the spring of 1787.

had never been to France, so in addition to the family reunion, they were excited to experience Paris, to marvel at the art and architecture of this illustrious realm, and to tour the countryside. Although of course Mimi was aware of the scurrilous pamphlets and knew the stories of the queen's wild behavior, she had come not to scold but to be useful, and to embrace once more the sister she had not seen in sixteen years. The last time they were together, Marie Antoinette had been a scrawny child of fourteen, while Mimi herself had been an elegant great lady of nearly thirty. Now, Maria Christina was a childless middle-aged woman of forty-four and Marie Antoinette was a glamorous thirty-one and the mother of four. It was quite a reversal.

And since by this time the queen's mania for gambling and masked balls, like her thirst for love, had been quenched, what Mimi and Albert encountered was a charming woman, seemingly content in her role as devoted wife and mother. The evening they arrived in Paris, they were immediately invited to Versailles; Marie Antoinette saw them first for an hour in her apartments before introducing them to Louis. "The Queen is beautiful, amiable, and natural; I am not praising her because she is my sister, but you know I am telling the truth," Mimi wrote to Eleonore Liechtenstein soon after this meeting. "The King was kindhearted and cordial; he has a solid, righteous character and makes his wife very happy," she added innocently. Albert was a little more discerning. "There is nothing particularly distinguished about his appearance," he would report later of Louis. "He possesses intellect and knowledge, but he deployed them only when he felt entirely at ease and he was at home; to those who did not get to know him more closely, these magnificent gifts remained hidden."

The couple stayed in Paris for a month, during which time this first impression of contented domesticity and family unity was carefully reinforced. Maria Christina and Albert were introduced to Louis's brothers and his twenty-two-year-old sister, Madame Élisabeth. The comte de Mercy showed them around the city and introduced them to government ministers and foreign ambassadors; they played cards with the Polignacs. They attended the theater, toured churches and galleries, and visited the villa at Saint-Cloud, recently purchased by Marie Antoinette as a means of ensuring further privacy from the prying eyes at Versailles.★ Clever Mimi proved herself to be an asset at court. "The Archduchess has much more success here than people imagined she would," admitted a member of the French diplomatic corps. "She makes an effort to please, and one cannot deny that she has a great deal of wit."

But nothing could disguise the resentment toward the government, and particularly Marie Antoinette, that simmered within the capital. The first scarcities precipitated by a poor harvest and the looming financial crisis were just beginning to make their effects known to an already suffering citizenry. "I like Paris very much," Mimi observed to Eleonore in a letter dated August 25, 1786, just before they left the city, loaded down with expensive gifts of fine French porcelain and prints heaped upon them by the royal family. "But live there, not for anything in the world—not even as queen."

Maria Christina and Albert took the long way home in order to tour the naval installments along the western coast of France, arriving in Brussels at the end of September. No instructions awaited them; as usual, they were kept in the dark. And then, on January 1, 1787, as though graciously bestowing upon his Belgian subjects a cheerful holiday gift, the emperor issued his new directives.

JOSEPH'S PLAN, WHICH AMOUNTED to a sweeping overhaul of nearly every aspect of government, law, education, and religion in the region, was perhaps the most extreme initiative of his aggressively progressive reign. It was as though he augmented and refined everything he had already decreed for Hungary, Transylvania, and

---

★ Significantly, however, the queen declined to host them at the Petit Trianon, even though Mimi and Albert had asked specifically to see the gardens there, an indication that Marie Antoinette considered this visit to be an imposition.

Bohemia, stitched it all together, and lobbed it at Brussels. Even Mimi, who was well aware of her older brother's ability to ignore the feelings of others, couldn't believe it.

Under the new imperial system of 1787, the various representative assemblies (known as "the States") were abolished and replaced by nine equal-sized districts, each governed by an administrator (called an intendant) appointed by Joseph. This meant that every city, town, and village in the Austrian Netherlands, whose inhabitants were used to relative autonomy and each of whom had different economic needs and traditions, were suddenly at the mercy of an unknown bureaucrat. Overseeing the intendants was a single minister in Brussels, also appointed by Joseph. "No just bounds were set to the power of the Intendant, he was placed above the reach of the laws, and was accountable only to the Minister for his conduct," a scandalized observer reported of these developments. The minister, in turn, answered directly to Joseph.*

As if it were not enough to dispense with a centuries-old representative government, the emperor, remembering that there had been many complaints during his one visit to the Netherlands about the length of time it took to settle lawsuits, had decided to upend the legal system as well. The Conseil de Justice (the Belgians' version of a Supreme Court) and all the subordinate local courts of law were eliminated. Instead, in the interest of efficiency, Joseph decreed the establishment of sixty-four new courts, whose verdicts were to be overseen by a single judge in Brussels, *also* appointed and responsible only to Joseph.

And, of course, while he was at it, to combat ignorance and superstition and so bring his subjects' religious practices more in line with the emperor's own enlightened approach to worship, he closed a large number of monasteries and prohibited the public celebration of

---

* To understand what this must have felt like, think of the Canadian prime minister coming in, abolishing Congress and all of the state and local governments, and reorganizing the United States into nine equal-sized administrative districts, each run by an official from Toronto.

many holy days and feasts, including the ancient and very popular festival known as kermesse, which in the Netherlands was akin to outlawing Christmas. Satisfied with his work, Joseph then went off to meet Catherine the Great for an extended tour of the Crimea to help her celebrate her latest victory against the Turks, a destination so remote that it effectively put him out of communication with his government for weeks at a time.

THE OUTCRY AGAINST the emperor's directives was immediate and profound. Rich and poor, educated and ignorant, bourgeois, noble, peasant, churchman—Joseph had managed, with this one New Year's Day act, to unite *all* of the citizenry against him. It was actually quite an accomplishment.

And this time, the population did not limit itself to grumbling. "The entire country has taken up arms," a traveler who happened to be passing through reported flatly. Violent resistance broke out. An official remonstrance was drawn up and presented to Maria Christina and Albert, protesting that the new measures were in clear violation of the conditions of the Joyous Entry and so were not lawful.★ Unaware that Joseph had stripped his sister and her husband of all authority, the delegation demanded that they act immediately to uphold the binding vow they had taken at their inauguration. "The public heats in no wise abating, the States...at length declared to the Princes, the Governors-General, that unless measures were speedily taken to satisfy the just demands and allay the fears of the people, the States must make use of that authority which belonged to them [to disavow Joseph's rule]," observed the chronicler.

It was do something or lose the Netherlands, and not even Joseph,

---

★ The saddest part about all of this was that Joseph's reform mandating religious toleration, imposed at the beginning of his reign, might have taken hold if he hadn't done this. As it was, freedom of worship was lumped in with the other imperial transgressions. "While the new edicts excited such violent heats, other unpopular acts of government during the present reign now underwent a severe review, and added to the discontent that was spread through the provinces," noted an eyewitness. "Among these, the alterations in religious matters held the first place."

Mimi reasoned, would be so pigheaded as to risk the considerable tax revenues that flowed into the imperial treasury year after year from the province. So she and Albert, with the full support of Count Kaunitz, intervened. On May 30, 1787, the couple issued a formal decree scrapping imperial policy and unilaterally suspending "all changes relating to the offenses and upheavals." They assured the public that "moreover the offenses made...will be...very shortly redressed and [the people] returned to the same state they have been for the past two hundred years." Mindful of Joseph's perceived assault on religion, they ended the declaration with the pious inscription "May God in His Holiness protect you" and their joint signatures, "MARIE and ALBERT."

This timely expedient, undertaken reasonably and with obvious sincerity, worked. There was music and dancing in the streets following the announcement, and when the governors-general attended the theater the next evening, "they were received with loud acclamations and verses composed in their praise were recited on the stage." The violence died down. The States agreed to pay their taxes. The representatives were even open to discussions of moderate reform with the emperor.

But there is no saving some people from themselves. A furious Joseph, pulled away from his sojourn in the Crimea by the rebellion in Brussels (no one dared countermand Catherine the Great's orders while *she* was away), returned to Austria in July with a suspicious cough and the brusque demand that his sister and her husband meet him in Vienna to explain themselves. "With tears in her eyes," Maria Christina promised her subjects that she would go to battle for them with her brother, "that she would do anything for the Belgian provinces, for which she was ready to shed her blood and give her life." But once arrived in Austria there was nothing she or Albert could do; Joseph absolutely refused to back down. "We have never been able to get him to listen to us," she stormed in frustration to Leopold. "He seems to want to find us guilty...in his heart, I believe he accuses us of weakness at the very least."

Having ruled out compromise, Joseph's options were limited, but somehow he still managed to choose the most provocative: escalation. In December he sent Austrian troops to Brussels under the direction of one of his most notorious generals, who was well known for having brutally suppressed a recent insurgency in Hungary. Joseph is on record as having specifically instructed this commander to treat the Netherlands as a conquered province.

The general arrived at his new assignment in January 1788 under orders to ensure that the regional officials and representative assemblies registered and acknowledged the emperor's edicts and authority. He achieved this goal swiftly by surrounding the city hall and firing into the crowd that had gathered to protest the imperial agenda. Joseph sent a new civil minister, ostensibly to head the government, but as in reality this official was subordinate to the general, the city basically functioned under martial law.

A public once roused, however, is not so easily pacified. Joseph's timing could not have been worse. The Americans were in the process of voting to ratify their new Constitution, which limited the powers of the executive. The excitement this had sparked in France had spread quickly to next-door Belgium. The same pamphlets that flooded Paris could be found in Brussels, as well as many more generated locally. The emperor did his best to suppress them, even going so far as to have them burned publicly in the center of the city, but there was no stopping the revolutionary fever.

Maria Christina and Albert, who had been allowed to return on the strict condition that they were to obey both the general's and the minister's orders, could only watch in dismay as their formerly nonpartisan, easygoing friends and neighbors were radicalized by Joseph's hard-line positions. Austrian soldiers patrolled the streets, and the general's spies lurked in the corners of cafés. Those suspected of leading an underground insurgency movement were rounded up and arrested. The city seethed. The turning point came on June 6, 1789, when Joseph, impatient to crush all hope of opposition, threw down the gauntlet and issued an edict mandating that "from this day...the entire contents of the Joyous Entry are revoked, broken, and annulled."

That did it.

Aided by French revolutionaries and inspired a month later by the fall of the Bastille, the Belgians organized a civilian army. On October 26, 1789, this homegrown militia attacked the Austrian soldiers stationed at Turnhout, about 60 miles northeast of Brussels, and forced them to retreat.

The rebels' success caught Joseph's general by surprise and alarmed the Austrian minister. He asked for more troops. On the evening of November 16, he abruptly appeared at Maria Christina and Albert's door and told them that he was sending his wife away the next day. To Mimi's disgust, he commanded her to leave as well. "I was shocked by this speech," Maria Christina later told Leopold. "Imagine my feelings, dear brother, when [the minister] gave us orders as if he were the Emperor." She bristled and replied that she was not the sort of woman to take a cowardly way out, that to flee in the dark like that was dishonorable. She and her husband would only abandon the city if the Austrian army were forced to evacuate. "We were determined to leave only with the government and the troops," she emphasized to Leopold.

But the minister insisted. He produced a letter from Joseph commanding them to go. The next morning he added to the pressure: "At 10 a.m. comes my doctor, whom the minister had sent to tell us all was lost; that we should not waste a moment; that perhaps in an hour Brussels would be invaded," Maria Christina reported. "Such haste, I admit, was impossible. We sent...to the minister and the commander of the army, to give us in writing the need for this departure...Before witnesses the general gave us 36 hours."

They felt they had no choice but to obey. "As we had never seen any official bulletin, letter, or document whatsoever in this affair, we had to believe everything that these gentlemen told us," she observed bitterly. Both the minister and the general insisted that they take "the awful and tiring road to Luxembourg...on the pretext that we could be kidnapped" if they took a different route. "How will I make such an exhausting trip now, when I am ill?" Mimi, who had been sick for weeks, asked the minister, who "muttered...that we were forced to do so by order of His Majesty [Joseph]." They left the next morning at four, "in truth so as not to see the affliction of our people at our departure," she admitted bleakly.

It took them four days, but they managed to reach the safety of Koblenz, in next-door Germany, where they stayed with friends. Only after their arrival did they discover that right after they left, the general had come out with an official declaration that everything was under control and there was no need for alarm. Infuriatingly, their flight was leaked by the minister to the local gazettes, who gleefully ran stories implying that the emperor's worthless, faint-hearted sister and her husband had panicked at nothing. "Judge the pain of the role we were made to play, and if we should not believe the thing done on purpose!" railed a tormented Maria Christina to Leopold. "The least malicious construction to make of it is that the two gentlemen lost their heads for fear of carrying out His Majesty's orders too late for us, and this only because I do not wish to suspect them of wickedness." But the damage to her and Albert's reputation in Brussels was unmistakable. "Think of the discouragement this [their flight] has spread among the loyal servants of His Majesty; the alarm of all of our people who also wanted to get away . . . the impression of cowardice on our part, that also reflects on the Emperor," she mourned.

Mimi needn't have felt so bad. She and Albert wouldn't have lasted much longer anyway. The general's assessment that all was well turned out to be somewhat optimistic. By the beginning of December, there was fighting in the streets of Brussels. The citizenry turned on the Austrian garrison and launched an attack, mobbing the soldiers and assaulting them with whatever came to hand. Taking a cue from their French abettors, they donned cockades (little bunches of ribbons pinned to hats as a symbol of revolution) and began pelting the outnumbered troops with heavy stones dug out of the pavement and bombarded from the roofs. By December 12, 1789, Joseph's army had fled the city. The next week, the people of the former Austrian Netherlands officially declared themselves independent.

From Vienna, a failing Joseph fought for breath and tried frantically to negotiate. The persistent cough caught two years before in the Crimea had by this time revealed itself to be advanced tuberculosis. Fearing he had not much time left, and desolate at the thought that, rather than the aggrandizement of his property, his legacy would be one of haplessly *losing* a rich province, he capitulated on every front, agreeing to reinstate the Joyous Entry, return the judges and courts of law to their original condition, and allow the public celebration of holy days and festivals—if only the Belgians would recognize him once more as their sovereign overlord. But the time for that was long past. No one in Brussels wanted anything to do with him.

Emperor Joseph II died two months later, just before dawn on February 20, 1790, a few weeks shy of his forty-ninth birthday. The man who had faithfully nursed and soothed the last hours of his father, mother, daughter, and two wives perished without a single member of his family present to comfort him in his extremity. Marianne had passed away the previous November, and Maria Elisabeth remained unmoved at her convent in Innsbruck. Neither Mimi nor Albert, in Bonn with her youngest brother, Maximilian, all of whom knew Joseph was seriously ill, undertook the journey to Vienna to sit beside him. Leopold, it is true, was on his way from Florence, but as inheritor of his dying brother's lands and titles, he had to come to Vienna anyway—and still, he did not make it in time.

Ironically, the emperor who had championed himself as a model of the Enlightenment had failed to grasp that the movement toward reason and scientific method over superstition that had begun with the encyclopedists had mysteriously transmuted into something more probing and profound. Freedom of intellect had opened pathways, and one of those pathways had led to the questioning of established authority and centuries-old forms of rule. In the process, the desire for liberty had been unleashed. No leader who claimed the mantle of enlightenment could in the future afford to ignore this powerful force.

Joseph had learned this lesson the hard way. One of his last audiences was with a Belgian-born lord. "Your country has killed me!" the foreign prince reported the dying emperor as exclaiming. "Ghent taken was my agony, and Brussels abandoned, my death!"

Maria Carolina

"Charlotte"

...as queen of Naples

19

The Queen Takes a Stand

~∕∕∕∕∕~

A pretty woman is not always a fool.

—Lady Emma Hamilton

MARIA CAROLINA WAS thirty-seven years old and had ruled Naples for twenty-two years when Joseph died and her favorite brother, Leopold, inherited his throne. In that time, she had liberated her kingdom from Spanish influence; instituted gradual but steady reforms, particularly in education, to improve the lives of her subjects; and significantly shored up the national defense through the construction of a navy. The stability and competence of her reign had encouraged tourism, enhancing the realm's wealth and prestige. And like her mother, she had done it all while presiding over an impressively large family: she was pregnant with her fifteenth child when she received the news of Joseph's death.*

This event came on the heels of a particularly traumatic period for Charlotte. Just the year before, an outbreak of smallpox had claimed the life of her eight-year-old son, Gennaro. The tragedy was followed a few weeks later by the sickening of her youngest boy, six-month-old Carlo, who in her terror she had inoculated too early. When this infant also succumbed to the relentless disease, Maria

---

* Distressingly, due to illness, many of her offspring did not survive childhood. Including the birth of this fifteenth infant, a son, in July 1790, the Neapolitan royal family numbered seven girls and two boys.

Carolina had gone almost mad with grief. "I am a mother above all; the loss of my two sons put me outside of myself," she would later write of this torment.

Also contributing greatly to her anguish was the brutal behavior of her husband. Ferdinand, by his frequent philandering, had managed to pick up a venereal disease. The festering, telltale symptoms, most likely of gonorrhea, that Charlotte noted on his body—"You know that for a long time I have suspected that my dear husband is not entirely healthy," she had confided to Leopold as early as 1788—had begun to attack her as well.

"Our poor sister in Naples suddenly, in addition to all the other inconveniences of pregnancy, has such a discomfort in her eyes that we fear she will lose her sight," Leopold worried to Maria Christina in a letter of February 12, 1790. "Meanwhile, the king is hunting... in the company of ladies unpleasant to the queen. He did not even come back to see her, this is very consoling," he added caustically. It was probably better that Ferdinand stayed away, as he blamed his wife for his condition and on several occasions had forced himself on Maria Carolina in order to relieve his anger.

Leopold's concern for his sister's health was rooted in more than ordinary compassion. The imperial family needed Charlotte. Her brothers and sisters were well aware that, without her, they could not expect to hold Naples. Ferdinand's father had by this time died, and his older brother had inherited the throne of Spain. In an effort to bring southern Italy back under Spanish control, the brother had already reached out to Ferdinand, dangling as a lure the offer of a marriage between one of his own daughters and the king of Naples's eldest son. The ever-alert Maria Carolina had intervened quickly to convince her husband to turn down this flattering proposal. But it was clear that something had to be done, and done soon, to shore up the imperial alliance.

And so, in one of his first acts after taking over the government in Vienna, Leopold arranged to have Charlotte's two eldest daughters marry his two eldest sons, and to have one of his daughters wed her oldest boy.* It was a clean sweep; with this one stroke they protected everything—Austria, Hungary, Bohemia, the Netherlands (assuming Leopold could get it back), Tuscany (now, with Joseph gone, reestablished as an independent province), and Naples. As there was no time to waste, all three nuptials would be held in Vienna in September, as soon as Maria Carolina had recovered from her latest delivery. "And so everything is already arranged for the transfer to the next generation," Leopold observed with satisfaction to Mimi in a letter of June 12, 1790.

The proposed trip to Vienna could not have come at a more opportune moment for the queen of Naples. Since the fall of the Bastille, there had been a steady flow of French refugees into Italy, many of them to her kingdom. They were aristocrats fleeing the revolution, and the stories they told were horrifying. One of the latest émigrés was the celebrated painter Élisabeth Vigée Le Brun, who had been so close to Marie Antoinette. Maria Carolina, anxious to hear all she could of her sister, took Madame Vigée Le Brun under her protection, and commissioned portraits of her daughters and of herself. "The Queen of Naples, without being as pretty as her younger sister, the Queen of France, reminded me strongly of her," the artist mused. "Her face was worn but one readily judged that she had been handsome...This Princess had an affectionate nature and simple ways at home. Her magnanimity was truly royal."

But the picture Madame Vigée Le Brun painted of conditions in France, and of her harrowing escape from Paris, must have chilled Charlotte to the core. "I was frightened beyond measure, and thought of nothing but leaving," the internationally known portraitist attested movingly. "I had my carriage loaded, and my passport ready, so that I might leave the next day with my daughter... when a crowd of national guardsmen burst into my room with their muskets. Most of them were drunk and shabby, and had terrible

---

* Leopold's eldest son and heir, Francis, lost his first wife (Catherine the Great's relative) in childbirth just three days before Joseph himself passed away, causing a vacancy that Maria Carolina was quick to turn to her daughter's advantage.

faces. A few of them came up to me and told me in the coarsest language that I must remain." She had no sooner managed to get the threatening men out of her apartment than her neighbors, risking their own lives, crept in. Bluntly, they told her that she wasn't safe and needed to escape immediately but warned her against using her own carriage, as this was what had given her away to the guard. She took their advice and with her six-year-old daughter in tow slipped out quietly by way of the public stagecoach. Their fellow passengers on this rattling conveyance were two men, "very filthy...who stunk like the plague," and who "made violent speeches of the most fearful kind," until Madame Vigée Le Brun had to beg them to stop speaking of killing people; they were frightening her child. Nor did the danger subside once they had left the capital. "At all of the towns a crowd of people stopped the coach to learn the news from Paris...I had the gravest apprehensions concerning Their Majesties, for all along the route, nearly to Lyons, men on horseback rode up to the coach to tell us that the King and Queen had been killed and that Paris was on fire," she remembered vividly.

And this was the problem: in the midst of the chaos, communication with France had broken down. It was public knowledge that the mail could not be trusted, that letters going to and coming out of Paris and Versailles were opened by spies of the revolutionary government. The dissemination of deliberately false or misleading information, designed to inflame partisan passions, was rampant; the most sensational rumors circulated wildly. It was impossible for an anxious Maria Carolina to verify from one minute to the next what was happening to her beloved Marie Antoinette.

But now, after over two decades away, she was finally going home to Vienna. There she would see Leopold and the rest of the family, and together they could come up with a plan to rescue their youngest sister and her husband and children from these vile, lawless revolutionaries, who butchered people in the streets and paraded the severed heads of their victims on pikes. With this in mind, on August 21, 1790, Charlotte packed up Ferdinand and her two eldest daughters, boarded the ships that would carry them north, and, waving to the hordes of well-wishers who had gathered to see them off and who begged them to return as soon as possible, sailed for Austria.

MARIA CAROLINA'S TIME IN VIENNA was everything she hoped it would be. Leopold went out of his way to extol and celebrate this important family connection. He did not wait for her to come to him but journeyed nearly 300 miles south to meet the Neapolitan ships so he could welcome his sister and her family with an impressive cannon salute and personally escort them to the capital. Maria Elisabeth abandoned her convent with pleasure to embrace this resourceful sibling who had come so far, and to meet her brother-in-law the king and her excited nieces. They all made a cheerful entrance into Vienna on September 14, their long line of carriages rolling in procession through streets lined with eager spectators. The weddings took place within a week, the festivities as satisfyingly opulent and splendid as in their mother's day. "I settled with great satisfaction two marriages for my daughters," Charlotte would later report with pride.

But the nuptial feasts were only the beginning. In just seven months, chiefly by overturning as many of Joseph's initiatives as possible, Leopold had managed to restore the family reputation and stabilize the political situation. He got out of the war with the Turks by coaxing Britain and Prussia to help him negotiate a truce; he restored the Joyous Entry to the Netherlands; and he summoned the Hungarian Diet. One of the few of Joseph's policies that Leopold did *not* rescind was the edict of toleration—he not only kept that one but strengthened it for the protection of Jews. In none of this did he work against his own principles, for Leopold believed that his subjects had rights, and that it was a sovereign's responsibility to respect those rights. In fact, he thought having a constitution that limited the powers of the executive and outlined the exact relationship between a ruler and those he governed was such a good idea that during his reign in Tuscany he had written one himself.

As soon as it became clear that Joseph's successor did not intend to pursue his older brother's aggressive agenda, the relief throughout Germany was so palpable that on September 30, 1790, a mere two weeks after the Austrian marriages were performed, Leopold was unanimously elected emperor. The whole family (including Mimi and Albert, who had been handling negotiations with Brussels and so had missed the weddings) trooped over to Frankfurt to witness the coronation, which was celebrated on October 9, 1790. Maria Carolina, who had been deemed too young at eleven to attend Joseph's inauguration, had the great pleasure as an adult and sovereign herself of seeing Leopold don the antiquated robe and gloves, and raise the scepter and orb as her father had done during her mother's reign.

But there was yet one last solemn rite to observe. The Hungarians, wary of the new emperor, were still in revolt. So Maria Carolina and the rest of the family, including Mimi and Albert, who knew the kingdom well, hurried back to Vienna after the imperial coronation and prepared to go to Hungary. Leopold liberated the crown, sword, and old moth-eaten robe of Saint Stephen that Joseph had consigned to a museum, and they all set out for Pressburg wearing traditional Hungarian dress, just as Maria Theresa had done nearly fifty years before.

On November 10, 1790, Leopold made his official entry into the city surrounded by his siblings. The king and queen of Naples made an especially favorable impression on the city; foreign royalty did not often grace Hungary with a visit. In an eerie replication of his mother's long-ago supplication for support, the new emperor stood before the Diet and swore to uphold the laws and customs of the realm. Then, turning to his eldest son, the newly married Francis, to whom he had assigned Albert's old position as governor, "I offer you my son," Leopold proclaimed dramatically to the assembled Hungarian nobility, "as a pledge of my sincere regard...to promote our mutual affection."

That was all it took. Less than a week later, on November 15,

1790, Leopold was crowned king. He did it just right: he, too, mounted a stallion, charged up the same small hill Maria Theresa had, and gamely waved the sword of Saint Stephen in four directions. Hungary returned to Austrian rule.

Having successfully overcome the immediate challenges to the family's inheritance caused by Joseph's reign, Maria Carolina and her siblings were finally able to turn their attention to the plight of their youngest sister and her husband, who were by this time confined to the palace of the Tuileries in Paris. And not a moment too soon. The imperial family barely had time to change out of their quaint Hungarian costumes before word arrived that the French, not content with simply attacking their own monarchy, were now actively fomenting revolution abroad and had even launched a new campaign designed to undermine the priesthood in France.

The situation obviously called for a response, but the issue was complicated by the fact that the French royal family was being held hostage by the citizenry. Was it better to try to get them out, or to leave them there and instead help Louis regain his throne through outside pressure? The siblings were of divided opinion. Maria Carolina, appalled, wanted to send in an army to put down the revolution and forcibly return her sister and her husband to their rightful thrones. Leopold agreed that an army should be raised and an invasion threatened but only as a charade; his idea was that the beleaguered king of France could then rally the French army to an assured victory against this perceived danger and thereby regain the respect and affection of his countrymen. (It is significant that neither Charlotte nor Leopold had ever met Louis.) Both Mimi, who *had* visited her French brother-in-law, and Marie Antoinette, who was in sporadic clandestine communication with Vienna through the comte de Mercy and Count Fersen (a Swedish nobleman whom nobody in the family had ever heard of but who, seemingly through sheer chivalry, was gallantly taking an interest in their youngest sister), argued in favor of escape.

In the end, unable to come to an agreement, they decided to

proceed on all fronts. Leopold and Maria Carolina would get their kingdoms and armies ready for war, in case it became necessary, while Maria Christina would oversee the flight strategy. Having settled on a course of action, Charlotte said a reluctant goodbye to Vienna in March 1791, and she and Ferdinand began the journey home to Naples.

THE MOOD OF THE KINGDOM Maria Carolina returned to had changed in the eight months she was gone. She had an inkling of this even before she arrived; she and Ferdinand had stopped first in Rome to demonstrate support for the papacy and discuss a concerted response to the French attack on the priesthood. There, they had run into Louis's aunts, who had managed—just—to get out of Paris. The two spinsters were each nearly sixty years old by this time, and they gave Charlotte an earful. It was even worse than she had thought. The most radical elements had taken over the government. The king had been forced to accept the new policies—the aunts witheringly called them "persecutions"—under duress; the royal family had no freedom of movement and were watched constantly. The aunts themselves, ancient and respectable though they were, had had a near brush with the mob: their carriage had been stopped on the way out of Paris, and they had had to wait for hours while the National Assembly debated whether to let them go.

And the madness was clearly spreading. The queen of Naples did not need the testimony of Louis's aunts to see that the numbers of French émigrés had increased dramatically while she was away. But they were of a different character now. A significant number were only pretending to be refugees in order to disguise their true mission. They were agents of the revolution, intent on exporting violence by stirring up the general population with promises of French aid in the struggle for liberty and equality. With sharp clarity, Charlotte realized that the cataclysm that had engulfed Marie Antoinette at Versailles, and forced Maria Christina to flee Brussels, was coming for her.

There is no overestimating the dread that must have accompanied this insight. France was a world power—perhaps *the* world power. Its military, even in times of turmoil, dwarfed Maria Carolina's. The French fleet, thanks to Louis's years-long focus on shipbuilding, was far superior to hers. The king of France had also established a premier war academy, so French officers were significantly better trained, and certainly more experienced, than those of Naples. And the population of France was such that their army could call on tens of thousands more soldiers than she could ever hope to muster. Charlotte knew that this was not a fight Naples could take on alone.

The question was, where best to seek aid? She couldn't ask Leopold. The emperor was already overwhelmed by threats to his own realm. Mimi was back in Brussels, it was true, but the political situation in the Austrian Netherlands was still unstable. Leopold had had to send troops in to maintain control. Besides, Charlotte had seen for herself what the months of travel, ceremony, and worry had done to Leopold's health; he was often ill. She knew he could not take on the defense of Naples as well. And her husband was useless: Ferdinand refused even to pay attention to the news coming out of France, claiming that it had nothing to do with him. Whatever was to be done, she was going to have to do it herself.

Her first thought was to ward off France by presenting it with the barrier of a united Italy. To this end, she wrote to the two major powers in the north, Sardinia and Venice, and urged them to join her in a defensive pact. She offered to send her fleet to their aid if they were attacked first and promised that, if they banded together with her, the papacy would join them. "The hope of escaping singly," she reminded them presciently, "has ever been the ruin of Italy." The king of Sardinia, right next door to France and as worried as she, accepted eagerly, but Venice turned her down, and without Venetian ships she was no better off than before. The vision of a united Italy faded.

This left her with no choice but to look elsewhere. Her options were limited. To take on a world power, she would need a world power, preferably one with a friendly ambassador, a first-rate navy, and a history of opposition to France. All indicators pointed to England—and Sir William Hamilton.

As IT HAPPENED, Sir William was not present to receive the queen of Naples when she returned from Vienna in the spring of 1791. After much reflection, the sixty-one-year-old widower had decided to take Charlotte's advice and wed his dazzling twenty-six-year-old mistress, Emma (still going by the name "Mrs. Hart"). As the ambassador was related to the king of England, this involved return-ing to London to acquire his sovereign's approval. Élisabeth Vigée Le Brun, who painted Emma while she was in Naples, was with Sir William when he revealed that, despite the vehement opposition of his family in England, he was determined to go through with the match. "She shall be my wife in spite of them all," he burst out to the artist. "After all, I marry her for myself!"

Impossible to fathom the magnitude of the advancement in status that an offer of marriage from a man of Sir William's lineage repre-sented for a woman like Emma. With her background, she might just as well have aspired to live on the moon as to be the wife of a British ambassador. She knew it, and could not resist a note of tri-umph when announcing her and her fiancé's return visit to London: "We come for a short time... to take our last leave... Sir William will let you know on what a footing we are here," she wrote airily to her former lover, Greville, who had so callously given her away, and who was now to be her social inferior.

The couple was in England from May to September, and Emma had as brilliant a time in London as Charlotte had had in Vienna. She was once more the toast of the city; she modeled again for her old friend George Romney; she went to intimate parties with the cream of British society. "On Saturday evening, I was with... a small company, and there was Sir William Hamilton and Mrs. Hart who... previous to their departure is to be *Mme l'Envoyée à Naples* [Ambassadress to Naples], the Neapolitan Queen having promised to receive her in that quality," reported an earl who was also a member of Parliament. Although the queen of England refused to acknowledge Emma even after she was married, the king was more amused than otherwise by the affair and gave his permission for his older cousin to wed. Emma and her doting lover were duly joined in holy matrimony in London on September 6, 1791. "A propos, Sir William Hamilton has actually married his gallery of statues, and they are set out on their return to Naples," the earl quipped the following week.

But it was Emma who had the last laugh. Over the summer, word had come to Charlotte of the French royal family's failed attempt at escape, a terrible disappointment made even worse by the fact that the first tidings had mistakenly reported the flight to have been a success. "I am tormented by continual fears for the unhappy fate of my sister in France," the queen of Naples agonized. To help ease her mind, Sir William and his new wife had stopped in Paris on their way back from London in order to give a firsthand account of the political situation; while they were there, Emma had made use of her role as ambassadress to secure a private interview with Marie Antoinette, and even to smuggle a letter from the French queen out to her sister. Maria Carolina's gratitude for this service was touching. She kept Emma with her for hours going over every aspect of her conversation with Marie Antoinette, probing for details as to the health and spirits of the king and queen, as well as those of their children. From this point on, Charlotte valued the new Lady Hamilton almost as a member of her family. "I have been presented to the Queen of Naples by her own desire, and she has shown me all sorts of kind and affectionate attentions," Emma observed contentedly in a letter of December 20, 1791. The young woman with the face of an angel who at thirteen had been forced to solicit to keep from starving now counted Maria Carolina, sister to the emperor and daughter of the great Maria Theresa, as one of her closest friends.

And Charlotte needed all the support she could get. Since her return from Vienna, she and her chief minister, General Acton, had begun to do what they could to arm Naples for a possible war with France. They boosted military recruitment, acquired additional vessels to augment the fleet, and scrounged around for the guns and artillery that would be necessary to equip a decent-sized fighting force. It was slow going. Naples had not faced a hostile power in half a century. Its inhabitants were not used to soldiering.

But it was not enough, in this time of revolutionary fever, simply to defend against a foreign attack. What was so insidious about this threat was that, through promises and propaganda, the enemy infiltrated from within, turning the native population itself into a weapon of war. With bitter irony, Maria Carolina recognized that the mania for liberty and self-government, currently being expressed through the violent overthrow of authority, was somehow rooted in the enlightened teachings of the encyclopedists, *a philosophy whose adherents she herself had nurtured in Naples.* This was not a pleasant reflection. It meant that she could no longer trust those who for twenty years had benefited from her educational policies and favor.

And so, to ensure that she was not caught unawares by her own subjects as Marie Antoinette and Mimi had been, Charlotte took the decisive step of organizing a clandestine intelligence agency charged with domestic surveillance. As head of this division she chose a high-ranking nobleman who made for an effective, if ambitious, chief of secret police. His spies fanned out over the city, listening in at cafés and gelato shops, and insinuating themselves into classrooms and political clubs. Adding to the cloak-and-dagger nature of the enterprise, Maria Carolina herself debriefed these agents at midnight in a special room of the palace, which the population fearfully labeled the *sala oscura,* or dark salon.

And this was where matters stood on March 1, 1792, when Leopold, not yet forty-five but worn out by exhaustion, fell prey to an aggressive infection and died so quickly that he did not even have time for last rites. Charlotte's son-in-law, twenty-four-year-old Francis, inherited his many titles; her daughter was now empress. The new emperor, trained by Joseph, was in favor of a far more militaristic approach to France; to get the jump on him, a month later, on April 20, 1792, the French declared war on Austria. Both sides began actively marshaling troops for the conflict.

And in Naples, a grieving Maria Carolina trembled for her daughter and monitored this precarious course of events while giving birth to her sixteenth child, a son, on May 2. "The moment of dénouement approaches," she wrote.

Marie Antoinette

...and her children, portrait by Élisabeth Vigée Le Brun

20

A Desperate Gamble

❦

I at present govern Paris; but it is reigning over an infuri-
ated people, urged on by the most abominable cabals; on the
other hand, a thousand infamous tricks have been played
them, of which they have full right to complain.

—The marquis de Lafayette

In the provinces the people are intoxicated with the idea, long
spread by philosophers in their writing, that all men are equal.

—Count Axel Fersen

The majority [of the council] were for the King to stay;
time will show whether the right choice had been made.

—Marie Antoinette

ON JULY 15, 1789, the day after a frenzied mob in Paris breached the
gates of the formerly invincible Bastille, hacking off the head of its
governor and parading this questionable trophy through the streets
of the capital, Louis called a council meeting in Versailles to determine what, if anything, he ought to do about it.

Although the storming of the famous prison so captured the popular imagination that its celebration has today become synonymous
with the end of the monarchy, the fall of the Bastille was not, in
fact, the pivot on which the revolution turned. The real threat to

Versailles had occurred several hours earlier, when the same mob forced its way into the main armory for the French Guard (the troops responsible for protecting the king and keeping the public order) and redistributed all of the weapons and ammunition stored there, including cannon, to the civilian population. The stockpile of guns had been so abundant that they had to enlist volunteers to get rid of them all—the British ambassador reported to London in astonishment that two of his servants who happened to be out on the street when this occurred "were compelled to go [to the armory] where they received two very good muskets which they brought away with them." He estimated the number of insurgent citizens (he called them the "armed *Bourgeoisie*") rampaging through the streets of Paris to be "at least 50,000."

Fifty thousand angry, musket-and-artillery-wielding rioters are not a mob capable of being backed down by ordinary police; it's an opposing army. Certainly they recognized themselves as such, as one of the rebels' first actions after successfully storming the Bastille was to enlist the aid of a competent, experienced general. "You must have learnt what happened to me yesterday," the marquis de Lafayette wrote to a friend on July 16. "A word had scarcely been said to me about commanding the Parisian militia, when that idea took immediate possession of every one; my acceptance became necessary; it is become also necessary that I should remain, as the people, in the delirium of their enthusiasm, can only be restrained by me."

This, then, was the problem debated by Louis's council on that fateful evening—how best to confront this substantial and potentially deadly host. Because the question concerned the family's future, both of the king's brothers as well as his wife were included in the discussions. The principal danger, as they perceived it, was not the overthrow of the monarchy itself—it was too early for that—but rather of a coup. Already Louis's cousin, the duc d'Orléans, the wealthiest man in the kingdom and the decided favorite of the Parisians, had allied himself with Lafayette's militia (now renamed the National Guard) and was spreading his riches around, buying soldiers and support. As a result, there were more and more defections from the king's French Guard to Lafayette's National one every day. "Secret agents distribute money; these men are known nearly everywhere... The Duc d'Orléans is strongly suspected of being the leader and motive-power in all this," Count Fersen, a captain in the French army himself, complained bitterly in a letter home to his father.

Although the Crown had had the foresight to bring in additional troops to help keep order, these were not considered sufficient in the present crisis to guarantee victory in a head-on clash. Thus, the decision was whether to fall back to Metz, near the border with Germany (reassuringly close to the queen's relations), with that part of the French army who remained loyal, in the hopes that a decisive force could be raised and brought back to defeat Lafayette, or to stay while the former Estates General (now the National Assembly) continued its work, make some reasonable concessions to show goodwill, and rely upon the love and respect the French had always displayed for their king to defuse the crisis.

Neither Marie Antoinette nor the king's youngest brother, the comte d'Artois, both of whom were loathed in Paris and consequently at greatest risk, had any doubt as to which of these two strategies they preferred. Each argued strenuously to retreat with the army, call for all loyal Frenchmen to meet them in Metz, and return with an overwhelming force; the queen had in fact already packed up her jewels in anticipation of flight. But the middle brother, the comte de Provence, was just as vehement that to escape with the army was to surrender to the coup: the duc d'Orléans would instantly take over the government and, once installed with all of the resources of the kingdom to draw upon, be nearly impossible to dislodge. The comte de Provence's position was supported by the commander of Louis's army, who did not exhibit a great deal of faith in his sovereign's ability to inspire the populace. "Yes, we can go to Metz; but what do we do when we get there?" he asked wearily.

Eventually Louis grew tired of the talk and stood up from the council table to signal that the meeting was over and that he expected a decision. "Am I to go or to stay? I am ready to do either," he asked obediently, as though consulting an appointment diary.*

In the end, it was the comte de Provence, and not the queen, who was able to sway a majority of the council, and the decision was made to stay and try to hold the throne through accommodation. The insurgents had a number of demands, chief among them that Louis send the army away and that he himself go to Paris to reassure his subjects that he supported the revolution. It was settled that the king would accede to anything that was required of him, including these two terms, in order to placate the populace. Marie Antoinette was beside herself and continued to plead, especially against her husband's journey to the capital: "They never will let him return!" she exclaimed. But she could not alter the council's resolution.

Understanding that with the departure of the army, Versailles was no longer safe, she did what she could to protect those she loved. As soon as the decision was made for Louis to remain, the queen called the duc and duchesse de Polignac to her rooms. "The king goes to Paris to-morrow...I fear the worst," she revealed. "There is yet time to rescue you from the fury of my enemies; if they attack you it will be much more because of hatred for me than for you. Do not be a victim to your affection and to my friendship." Unwilling to desert her in her time of need, the couple at first resisted her entreaties; she had to use the power of the king's word to get them to obey.

They left at midnight. What this act of selflessness cost the queen is evident from the note she sent with them. "Adieu, tenderest of friends," she wrote to the woman who for a decade had been her closest confidante. "How frightful is this word! But it must be spoken. Adieu. I have only just strength enough to embrace you." There is no question that Marie Antoinette saved their lives that night.

---

* Louis is often portrayed as having made the decision to stay because he did not wish to provoke a civil war. While it is true that on later occasions he did say that he refused to fight against his countrymen, it is clear from the reports of this meeting that he would have done so had the council voted in favor of this approach. He had, in fact, used force against the citizenry on Maurepas's advice when they had rioted over the price of bread at the beginning of his reign.

The Polignacs were not the only courtiers to take advantage of the darkness to flee. As soon as it became generally known that the king was determined to give in to the Parisians and was sending the army away in accordance with their demands, there was a panicked exodus from Versailles. (The comte d'Artois and his family also escaped that night.) Marie Antoinette did not even know which of her servants had left until she called for them the next morning and was told that their rooms were empty and the doors locked—"Terror had driven them away," Madame Campan reported.

The queen, too, was afraid, but she did not abandon Louis. She knew he could not survive without her. Nor did she send the children away with the army. If she had, and news of their departure had leaked out, it could easily have been interpreted as an attempt to subvert the revolution. With the council advising that Louis go alone to Paris, she could not take this risk. (The dauphin, as the legitimate successor to the throne, would always be a threat to return with an army; to send him away would have undermined the king's credibility.) Louis's sister, twenty-five-year-old Madame Élisabeth, also stayed behind to demonstrate support for her brother, as did his aunts and the comte de Provence, author of this soothing strategy.

And so, the next day, July 17, 1789, Louis, accompanied only by a very small entourage, set off for the capital. His carriage was met at the outskirts of the city by the National Guard, who then proceeded to escort "my prisoner"—as Lafayette, who rode at the head of this force, openly called the formerly inviolate sovereign of France—to the city hall, where he was to meet with the mayor and 300 members of the National Assembly. "The entrance of the King into Paris was certainly one of the most humiliating steps that he could possibly take," the British ambassador reported, appalled. "He was actually led in triumph like a tame bear by the Deputies and the City Militia." All along the way, the streets were crowded with a double line of citizens brandishing weapons. "I think I can venture to say that there were not fewer than 150,000 men bearing arms this day in Paris," the diplomat added.

Once inside, "with a sad and anxious look," Louis read from a prepared statement indicating "his readiness to do everything in His power to quiet their minds and restore tranquility to the City," after which the mayor of Paris, in a particularly demeaning gesture, handed the king a blue-and-red cockade, symbol of the revolution, which Louis silently pinned to his hat. He then dutifully showed himself publicly wearing these colors by stepping out onto the balcony, for which act he was rewarded with the customary cries of "Vive le roi!" that until that moment had been actively stifled by the National Guard.

By all accounts, these cheers worked like a tonic on Louis. "The King breathed again at that moment, and, with tears in his eyes, exclaimed that his heart stood in need of such shouts from the people," Madame Campan reported. He evidently took the approbation as a sign that his council had chosen the correct course; certainly, he returned from this eventful day in much better spirits. His family, who had feared they would never see him again, were so happy to have him home that he didn't even have time to climb the stairs before they all came rushing down to embrace him at once. "He congratulated himself that no accident had happened; and it was then that he repeated several times, 'Happily no blood has been shed, and I swear that never shall a drop of French blood be spilled by my order,' " Madame Campan remembered.

But Marie Antoinette knew better. She understood, far more clearly than her husband, whose ability to judge human interactions was limited, what had happened that day in Paris. There is a name for the policy that the royal council had adopted: appeasement. And appeasement has a long and storied history of ending in disaster.

IT TOOK JUST TWO MONTHS for the shortcomings of this approach to be made manifest. After so many years of subjugation, injustice, and poverty, the lower classes viewed the king's swift acceptance of the revolution with suspicion. It had come too easily; they feared a trick. Rumors abounded that the queen, who was known to have an outsized influence on the government, had appealed to her brother the emperor, and that consequently an invasion by Austria was imminent.* Fury against Marie Antoinette mounted; there were calls for an assault on Versailles to capture the king, bring him to Paris, and imprison or kill the queen. Lafayette succeeded in preventing one such attack—"Their very slight inclination has been destroyed by four words which I said to them," he boasted—but by the middle of September he nonetheless felt it prudent to warn the man in charge of Louis's bodyguard, the comte de Saint-Priest, of the attempt. "The affair is off my mind," Lafayette reassured him airily, "except as to the idea of the inexhaustible resources of the plotters of mischief."

Saint-Priest was not so sanguine. He had only 800 bodyguards under his command. Accordingly, he arranged for a 1,000-man regiment to be transferred from Flanders to Versailles. This unit arrived on September 23, 1789. Two days later, Count Fersen turned up as well.

Marie Antoinette was clearly very relieved to have him with her again. The comte de Saint-Priest noted that upon his return the Swede "continued to enjoy free access to her apartments and have frequent rendezvous with her at the Petit Trianon." For appearance's sake—everyone associated with her, she knew, was now a target—she had arranged for him to have the use of an apartment at Versailles. But, as in the past, it is likely that he spent most of his nights in her rooms. Fersen, too, knew to exercise caution. "Be prudent when speaking to me about the affairs of this country and of *Elle* [*She,* meaning Marie Antoinette]," he had warned his sister, who knew of the love affair, in a letter of August 24.

They had exactly ten days together before it all went bad. The problem began with the welcoming of the Flanders regiment, whose ranking members tradition dictated should be fêted by their counterparts

---

* She hadn't. And in any event Joseph, who was still alive at this point, already had his hands full with a war against Turkey and rebellions in both Hungary and Belgium. Even Joseph knew he couldn't take on France as well.

in the local brigade. The bodyguards under Saint-Priest consequently hosted a banquet on October 1 for some 200 officers of both units in the great theater of the palace, the only room large enough to hold everyone. They did not skimp on the wine.

There's nothing like copious quantities of alcohol consumed among like-minded co-workers to bring out underlying political loyalties. The bodyguards were all royalists; "shouts of 'Vive le Roi!' shook the roof for several minutes," Madame Campan, who observed this convivial meal from one of the overhead theater boxes, remembered. Hearing the cheers, one of the commanders urged the king and queen to reward the troops for their devotion by condescending to make an appearance. Marie Antoinette thought to bring the dauphin. The royal family's arrival caused a sensation. "On all sides were heard praises of their Majesties, exclamations of affection, expressions of regret for what they had suffered, clapping of hands, and shouts of 'Vive le Roi! Vive la Reine! Vive le Dauphin!'" It was later reported that the hated blue-and-red cockades were torn off and trampled underfoot, to be replaced by white ones, symbols of the king. Madame Campan refuted this: "The fact is, that a few young men…turned the white lining of their national cockades outwards," she said—but it didn't matter; the damage was done. By the next day, all of Paris had heard of the betrayal of the bodyguards' true sympathies and of the royal family's encouragement of this demonstration of anti-revolutionary fealty. "From that moment Paris was constantly in commotion; there were continual mobs, and the most virulent proposals were heard in all public places; the conversation was invariably about proceeding to Versailles," the lady-in-waiting despaired.

Thus it was that three days later, on the morning of October 5, the British ambassador in Paris looked out his window and was "much surprised and at first much entertained with the ludicrous sight of a female army proceeding very clamorously, but in order and determined step toward Versailles. I do not exaggerate when I assure Your Grace that there could not have been less than five thousand women who, armed with every weapon they could possibly pick up, proceeded on this expedition," he reported. But the envoy's levity faded quickly "when we perceived they were followed by numerous inhabitants...besides many detachments of the Milice Bourgeoise [the armed bourgeoise]," he added grimly.

Saint-Priest received intelligence of the approach of this ominous swarm almost eight hours before its arrival. He alerted Louis, who was out shooting, and urged the king to return to the palace. Louis did so, and the inevitable council meeting was convened. As the senior military officer present, Saint-Priest recommended that the queen and the children be sent immediately to the royal estate at Rambouillet, about 40 miles southwest of Paris, where they could be better protected, but that Louis himself, accompanied by his bodyguards, should stay behind and ride out to meet the mob. With his soldiers arrayed in battle formation behind him, the king could then "order the Parisian band to retire, and, in case they should disobey...make a few charges of the cavalry to endeavor to disperse them...if this should be unsuccessful, the King would have time to regain Versailles at the head of his troops, and march immediately to Rambouillet," Saint-Priest elucidated.

As usual, this sensible plan was immediately opposed by exactly half the council, who advocated staying put, as the women's purpose "was, probably, only to present some petition to the King" (although Saint-Priest did point out that the throng's being heavily armed rather belied this interpretation). Louis, with no clear majority to advise him, of course could not make the decision himself, so he went off to find Marie Antoinette, who had been recalled hastily from the Petit Trianon.

There is conflicting evidence about what she said. Saint-Priest, who was not party to this discussion, reported in frustration that the queen "declared that she would not, upon any consideration whatever, separate herself from him [the king] and her children." But this did not mean that Marie Antoinette did not wish to leave, only that she refused to go without her husband. In fact, she seems to have been trying to convince Louis to fall back on Rambouillet with the rest of the family. She must have initially gained her objective, because that afternoon she sent a note to her household commanding them to "pack your effects; we are to leave in half an hour; make haste." But in the end she could not persuade the king to take so decisive a step on such short notice. A second note to her staff followed the first. "All is changed," the queen wrote briefly. "We are to remain here."

And so they sat at Versailles while the trudging, seething column of starving women brandishing weapons, buttressed by several better-armed, far more sinister male divisions, made their slow but deliberate way from Paris. It was the political equivalent of standing on a beach waiting for a tidal wave to hit. A member of the National Assembly, who was at the palace that critical evening of October 5, reported of the queen that "everyone except herself seemed terrified. 'I know that the people have come from Paris to demand my head,'" Marie Antoinette observed to him simply. "'But I learned from my mother not to fear death; I shall await it with resolution.'"

THE FIRST OF THE AGITATORS made their cold, wet appearance (it had rained heavily all day) at about seven that evening. They announced their presence by shouting, "We shall bring back the queen, dead or alive!" Luckily, hard on their heels followed a messenger bearing a note from Lafayette. The general wrote that he was aware of the problem and was at that very moment en route to Versailles with the National Guard to protect the royal family. All that was required was that they hold out until he got there. This they managed to do by locking the gates to the palace and by the strategic deployment of the bodyguards and the Flanders regiment.

Lafayette and the National Guard arrived at midnight as promised, at which time the general personally assured the king of his and his troops' loyalty. Trusting to this guarantee, the royal family retired for the evening, each to their separate bedrooms. Lafayette then stayed awake all night posting sentries and making arrangements to house his forces. Not until five o'clock, just before daylight, did he himself lie down to rest.

But in spite of all of his precautions, the sleeping general did not, in fact, have control of the situation. Within an hour of his retiring, clearly by prearrangement, the mob had reassembled, and as dawn broke, the soldiers whom Lafayette had assigned to guard the palace defied their orders and opened the gates. At once, "a frenzied multitude of banditti, armed with pikes and bludgeons, and some of them with sabres and muskets, rushed in...and ran with the utmost speed to the courtyard of the princes, wherein the staircase leading to the apartments of their Majesties was situated," a horrified comte de Saint-Priest, who witnessed the entire episode from his bedroom window, recounted. The majority made straight for the queen's chambers. They broke through the doors of the outer guard post and massacred two of her bodyguards. "Kill, kill! no quarter! To the queen's apartments!" they screamed.

There were four ladies-in-waiting on duty that morning; Madame Campan's sister was one of them. Upon hearing the cries, "my sister flew to the place from which the tumult seemed to proceed; she opened the door...and beheld one of the bodyguards holding his musket across the door, and attacked by a mob, who were striking at him; his face was covered with blood. He turned round and exclaimed, 'Save the Queen, madame; they are come to assassinate her!'"

Madame Campan's sister did not have to be told twice. She ducked back through the door through which she had just come, slammed it shut, and drew the great bolt to lock it fast from the inside; then she did the same with the inner door to the queen's rooms. Racing to Marie Antoinette's side, she awakened the queen with the urgent cry "Get up, madame; don't dress yourself; fly to the King's apartment!"

It is almost certain that Marie Antoinette was not alone in her bed that morning. Three days later, Fersen would write to his father, "All the public papers have told you...what happened at Versailles on Monday, 5th, and Tuesday, 6th...I was witness of it all." Like everyone else in the palace, Fersen would have seen the vicious mob arrive the night before and heard the threats to the queen's life; it is difficult to believe that the man who had once written to his sister that he would never marry because "I cannot belong to the only person I want to belong to, the only one who truly loves me, and so I don't want to belong to anyone" would have left the woman whom he considered to be his wife to face mortal danger alone.*

They had only moments to react. A terrified—Madame Campan's word—Marie Antoinette "threw herself out of bed; they put a petticoat upon her without tying it," the sister reported. A secret passageway, almost never used, led from the queen's apartments to the king's; Marie Antoinette and two of her ladies now took off down this corridor, with Fersen staying behind in her rooms to ensure the queen's escape. It is likely that each believed this to be the last time they would ever see the other.

Through the darkness the three women ran, only to discover the entrance to the king's bedroom locked from the outside on the other end. Louis, concerned for his family's safety, had gone to investigate. They hammered on the door and called out for it to be opened, expecting at any second to be discovered and butchered by their pursuers. After ten minutes of anguished commotion, one of the king's gentlemen finally heard the pounding and let them into the room. The queen's hair went white at the roots that morning. She was not yet thirty-four.

The children's governess had already shepherded her charges to the safety of Louis's rooms, and the king returned unharmed soon afterward. "The Queen saw her children again," Madame Campan reported. "The reader must imagine this scene of tenderness and despair."

---

* Two years after these events, a visiting English lord asserted that, through a third party, Madame Campan had confessed that the Swedish count had been in bed with the queen that morning, and that he had had to don a disguise, which the lady-in-waiting had provided, in order to escape. This, of course, is hearsay and so does not qualify as historical evidence. But, especially in light of Fersen's later behavior, it would have been out of character for him *not* to have been there.

Lafayette had by this time awakened—no one could sleep through that riot—and had managed, with the aid of some well-trained soldiers, to back down the mob and prevent further massacre of the bodyguards. He then went immediately to Louis's rooms to protect the royal family. Saint-Priest, who knew the back way into the king's apartments, wrapped himself up in a greatcoat to avoid detection and so also successfully gained access to the royal suite. Once inside, he found Louis "in a state of stupefaction, which is difficult to describe, or even to imagine." The crush of people outside demanded the appearance of first the king and then the queen; Lafayette went out on the balcony to try to calm them but was unable to do so; "all his speeches could not stop their shouts of 'To Paris! To Paris!' There were even a few musket-shots fired from the courtyard, which, fortunately, struck nobody," Saint-Priest attested. "I...represented to him [Louis] that delay in yielding to the wishes of the mob was useless and dangerous; that it was necessary he should promise to go to Paris...that this was the only way of getting rid of these savages, who might the very next moment proceed to the utmost extremities...To all this the King did not answer a word."

Saint-Priest was right, they had no choice; the royal defenses had been breached and the dangerous throng in the courtyard knew it. Still, it took some four hours to get Louis to agree. The royal carriages were prepared, and the family set off for Paris in the early afternoon. The journey was a ghastly one. The severed heads of the two bodyguards who had been slaughtered that morning were mounted on pikes and carried at the head of the procession, just outside the windows of the king and queen's carriage, in which also traveled their daughter, ten-year-old Marie-Thérèse; the four-year-old dauphin; and the king's sister, Madame Élisabeth. The royal entourage was accompanied all the way to Paris by the triumphant mob, whose members gloated malevolently: "We are bringing back the baker, the bakeress, and the little baker boy!" Marie Antoinette was reported as making a point of speaking calmly to her tormentors throughout this ordeal: "The king has never desired anything but the happiness of his people," she reassured those who crowded menacingly near the window of her carriage. "Many evil things have been told you about us; they were said by those who wish you harm." Louis, by contrast, did not utter a sound during the entire six-and-a-half-hour journey.

Transports carrying the king's aunts and his brother, the comte de Provence, as well as other members of the royal household, formed the train of that melancholy parade, and in one of these rode Fersen. As the Swedish count had no official position at Versailles, it may be presumed that he was following the court simply to be near the queen. "I returned to Paris in one of the carriages of the King's suite," he wrote to his father. "God keep me from ever again seeing so afflicting a sight as that of those two days."

As for Marie Antoinette, the lessons of those terrifying forty-eight hours only solidified her determination to pursue the strategy that she had advocated from the very beginning of the unrest: to withdraw to a place of safety, raise an army, and return with sufficient force to reestablish her husband on his throne. "Ah! Monsieur de Saint-Priest, why did we not go away last night!" she had cried upon seeing the commander of the royal bodyguard in the king's apartments that morning. "It was no fault of mine," Saint-Priest had answered sadly. "I know that well," she had replied.

THE ROYAL FAMILY WAS INSTALLED in Paris at the palace of the Tuileries, which had not been used in half a century; furniture had to be hauled in from Versailles to make it habitable.* The first weeks were especially trying, as the novelty of having the royal family in residence resulted in people from all over the city flocking to the gardens under their windows and demanding that the king, and particularly the queen, show themselves, like animals at a zoo. "The whole day

---

* "Everything is very ugly here, mamma," said the dauphin of his new home. "My son, Louis XIV lodged here, and liked it; we should not be more fastidious than he," his mother answered brightly. Then, "You know that I did not expect to come here," Marie Antoinette murmured in an aside to the members of her household.

was passed in that fatiguing but necessary Ceremony," the British ambassador reported. "Those very People who the day before vowed her death...now shouted *Vive La Reine,*" he added wryly. The mayor of Paris and the head of the National Assembly, which had followed the court to the capital, tried to make it appear as though the royal family's decision to relocate was voluntary, and so sent fawning delegations to welcome them. "Madame," said the mayor on one such occasion, "I come to convey to your Majesty the homage of the city of Paris with a testimony of the respect and love of its inhabitants. The city glories in seeing you in the palace of our kings; it desires that the king and your Majesty grant it the favor of making this your habitual residence." Under the watchful eyes and constant constraint of Lafayette's National Guard, who kept the royal family in as much as it kept the marauders out, Marie Antoinette had no choice but to go along with this charade. "I receive with pleasure the homage of the city of Paris; I will follow the king gladly wherever he goes, especially here," the queen answered graciously.

Still, the outbursts of violence and hatred continued. People screamed terrible threats in the garden under their windows at night; on one occasion shots were even fired at their balcony. "One cannot tell how far the malcontents may go," Marie Antoinette worried. "The danger grows from day to day." In an effort to reassure both the revolutionary government and the volatile Parisian populace that the royal policy of abject surrender was still firmly in place, on February 4, 1790, Louis made a special visit to the National Assembly. Once again reading from a prepared speech, the king promised to "defend and uphold constitutional liberty, the establishment of which has been sanctioned by the general wish of the people, as well as by my own; I will do more: I will, in concert with the queen, who shares all my opinions, early prepare the mind and heart of my son for the new order of things."

Despite her husband's statement, it is clear that, even at this early date, Marie Antoinette was already laying the groundwork for action. Just the month before, Count Fersen (who visited the queen at the Tuileries so often that Lafayette would later threaten to have her divorced for adultery) wrote to his father that "nothing but a civil or foreign war can restore France and the royal authority; but how is that to be brought about, with the king a prisoner in Paris? It was a false step to allow himself to be brought there. Now it becomes necessary to try to get him out of it," he announced flatly. "Once out of Paris, the king ought to be able to give birth to a new order of things," the count added, voicing a sentiment with which Marie Antoinette was wholly in agreement.

She wasn't the only one. In fact, the necessity of liberating Louis from the capital and reestablishing at least some of his authority as a counterweight against the violent extremism that threatened to send the country into chaos was by the summer of 1790 so obvious that even the comte de Mirabeau, one of the most outspoken leaders of the revolution, had come around to this point of view.* Mirabeau viewed the power of the mob as the greatest peril to liberty and saw the monarchy as the only institution capable of reining in this threat. "Society would soon be destroyed if the multitude, grown accustomed to bloodshed and disorder, placed itself above the magistrates and defied the authority of the law," he argued. "For it too often happens that public danger rallies men to despotism, and in the midst of anarchy even a tyrant seems a savior" (thus accurately predicting the rise of Napoleon).

Mirabeau's idea was to smuggle the royal family out to Normandy, from which safe location the king could then marshal his loyal countrymen to rise up against the worst elements in Paris (which included his overblown rival Lafayette, in Mirabeau's opinion). The

---

* Previous to this epiphany, Mirabeau had been a lacerating critic of the monarchy. Among his more pointed assertions were that "the right of sovereignty rests solely and indefeasibly with the people," and that "the time has come when men are to be estimated by what they carry in the little space under their foreheads between their two eyebrows." Similarly, it was Mirabeau who had thundered in the National Assembly that aristocrats were "egoists who think these convulsions of despair and misery will pass...are you quite sure that so many men without bread will leave you to the tranquil enjoyment of the rich repasts which you refuse to reduce in quantity or in delicacy? Nay, you will perish."

revolutionary solicited the comte de Provence's support for this daring rescue only to have Louis's brother scoff at the notion of his elder sibling's adopting so energetic a proposal. "The king's weakness and indecision are beyond all description," the comte de Provence informed Louis's would-be savior. "To give you an idea of his character, imagine oiled ivory balls, which you vainly endeavor to hold together."

But Mirabeau persisted. Shrewdly, he saw an understanding with the queen as his best chance for success and wrangled a secret audience with her. "The king has only one man near him, and that is his wife," he declared.

It's a testament to how much Marie Antoinette wanted to escape Paris that she agreed to see him at all. To her, Mirabeau was one of the villains who had inflamed the populace to march on Versailles; she held him and the duc d'Orléans equally responsible for the attack on her life. In fact, when through an intermediary Mirabeau first broached the idea of their joining forces in order to extricate her husband from his predicament, the queen had laughed. "We shall scarcely be so unfortunate, I think, as to be driven to the painful extremity of having recourse to Mirabeau," she had demurred.

But anxiety for her family's safety—the celebration of the first anniversary of the fall of the Bastille was coming up, and who knew what horrors might be unleashed by that event—convinced her to grant an interview to even this most unlikely of allies. A clandestine rendezvous was set for July 3, 1790. Marie Antoinette was at her estate at Saint-Cloud that day.* The audience took place early in the morning, Mirabeau having managed to avoid detection by slipping in through an entrance to the public park attached to the château. It was the first time the great orator had ever had a private conversation

---

* To foster the illusion that the royal family was free to leave Paris if they chose, they were allowed to spend some time that summer at the queen's residence of Saint-Cloud, the royal property nearest to the city. Every other venue, including Versailles, was dismissed by the National Assembly as being too far from the capital for comfortable surveillance. As it was, the family had to return to Paris for a day or so nearly every week to demonstrate their support for the revolution.

with the queen, and she made a tremendous impression on him. "She is very great, very noble, and very unhappy," he told his nephew immediately after this interview. "But I will save her," he prophesied grandly.

Mirabeau's escape plan was an open secret among the family that summer. Only the children were unaware that the king was considering taking the comte's advice and fleeing Paris. Louis's sister, Madame Élisabeth, could hardly contain her impatience to be free of her captors. On August 29, she wrote obliquely to a friend that "I still have torpor in my legs. Still... I fancy the cure is at hand."

But of course Louis requested that Mirabeau detail his recommendations in writing, as this was the way that the king was used to absorbing information. The resulting memorandum was unlike any government paper either Marie Antoinette or her husband had ever seen before. Louis's ministers, long accustomed to their sovereign's passive temperament, knew to couch their advice in reassuringly soothing terms. Mirabeau, the fire-eating orator, had let fly. "Four enemies are approaching with rapid strides—taxation, bankruptcy, the army, winter," he catalogued harshly. "We must prepare ourselves for events by directing them... civil war is certain and perhaps necessary," he insisted.

Start a civil war! If he had instructed them to drive around and personally set fire to Paris, his royal patrons could not have been more scandalized. Marie Antoinette immediately remembered that Mirabeau was a dangerous radical who was not to be trusted. She distanced herself from both him and his proposal. Without his wife's full support, there was no hope that Louis would agree to so aggressive a stratagem. The anniversary of the fall of the Bastille had passed without incident; the king had been cheered for his participation; the appeasement policy appeared to be working, and so remained in place. Mirabeau died early the next year believing that he had failed to be of service to the queen he had admired as being "so gifted by nature."

But Mirabeau was wrong. By presenting his solution in such

unpalatable (if accurate) terms, and thus reminding Marie Antoinette that she ought never to have confidence in a revolutionary, he paved the way for the adoption of *almost exactly the same plan,* this time couched in significantly more uplifting adjectives, by someone the queen trusted implicitly: Count Fersen.

FERSEN'S PROPOSAL, WHICH RELIED HEAVILY on the support and goodwill of Marie Antoinette's family, particularly her brother Leopold and her older sister Maria Christina, grew out of extended secret discussions between a small coterie of loyal friends and advisers. As it obviously took some time after his ascension for Leopold to stabilize the situation left to him by Joseph, the Swedish count had to wait several months before presenting the details of his rival escape plan to the king. But by early 1791, Fersen was able to write to his father that "to all the many kindnesses with which they [Louis and Marie Antoinette] have loaded me, they have now added a flattering distinction—that of *confidence;* and it is all the more flattering because it is limited to four persons," he revealed. "If we can serve them, what pleasure I shall have...what sweet enjoyment to my heart if I am able to contribute to their welfare!"

The four conspirators were Fersen; the marquis de Bouillé (commander of the French fortress of Metz); the baron de Breteuil (one of the Polignacs' original circle, who had fled with them the night after the storming of the Bastille, and who now discreetly represented the king and queen's interests at the imperial court); and the comte de Mercy, who had been transferred by Leopold from Paris to The Hague to assist Maria Christina and Albert in reclaiming the Austrian Netherlands. The consensus among this group was to follow Mirabeau's essential outline—have the royal family retreat to a safe location from which the king could summon his loyal countrymen, raise an army, and then use this force to return Louis to his throne—but to substitute the town of Montmédy, on the border with Germany and conveniently near Metz, for Normandy. This way, the advisers reasoned, should the king's loyal French soldiers turn out to be too few (an unfortunate possibility), they could be augmented by paid imperial ones.

When Louis once again asked that the strategy be detailed in a written report, Fersen, well aware of the objections to Mirabeau's scheme, made sure to underplay the inevitable bloodshed and havoc that would result from the use of foreign mercenary troops against French subjects.* Instead, he masterfully framed his argument as a heroic feat of valor by a benevolent king. "There seems no doubt that it is necessary to act, and to act vigorously, if order and prosperity are to be restored, the kingdom saved from total ruin, its dismemberment prevented [a nice touch, as Lorraine was threatening to secede], the king replaced upon the throne, and his authority returned to him," he began, in the paper he delivered to the monarch on March 27, 1791. Fersen went on to point out that Louis could of course wait until he was perfectly satisfied that he had secured all the money and foreign aid that he would require by written treaties (clearly, the approach favored by the king), but that this was destined to take a very long time, and already Louis's brother, the comte d'Artois, and the other princes who had emigrated were scheming to invade from abroad; if their efforts were successful, might not they "then be masters of the kingdom and of Their Majesties?"

But fortunately the sovereign had another choice: "to leave Paris, waiting only to be assured of the good-will of the foreign Powers and to obtain the necessary money to pay the troops for two or three months... Such a course would have something grand, noble, imposing, and audacious, the effect of which, both on the kingdom and in Europe would be incalculable," the Swedish count enthused. "It might bring back the army and prevent its total decomposition; it would fix the Constitution, and prevent the factions from making such changes in it as would consolidate the revolution, and... [it would] make the movement of the princes useful to the king."

---

* Not to mention how easily the presence of these imported warriors could be interpreted as the first wave of an Austrian offensive.

Grand, noble, audacious, inspiring—now *that* was an agenda a proud daughter of the great Maria Theresa could embrace with enthusiasm. The queen had evidently agreed to this strategy at least four months earlier, as she had placed an order the previous December for a berline, the same sort of oversized luxury carriage the duchesse de Polignac's family had used in *their* escape. There was still the problem of convincing Louis, of course, but in this effort the conspirators were aided enormously by a disturbing episode that occurred right after Fersen turned in his written recommendation to the king.

It was April 18, 1791, just before Easter, and the royal family was intending to spend a few days at Saint-Cloud before returning to celebrate the holiday in Paris. It was a period of even more unrest in the capital than usual; the National Assembly had recently begun to attack religion by requiring priests to take an oath of loyalty to the still-unfinished constitution that put them in direct conflict with the papal authority and the teachings of the Church. For the king's aunts, this had been the last straw; appalled at the assault on Catholicism, the pair had fled to Rome, where it was generally believed they were actively engaged in an intrigue with the pope to subvert the revolution.

So it was that when word leaked out that the king's coach was leaving for Saint-Cloud that day, the populace suspected that, following in the aunts' footsteps, the royal family, too, was attempting to escape, and rushed to stop them. Despite Lafayette's best efforts, the National Guardsmen assigned to protect the monarch sided instead with the vast crowd and refused to open the gates to let the carriage pass. A standoff ensued. Fersen, as ever an eyewitness, described the scene: "Detachments of grenadiers as they arrived swore that the king should not leave Paris; several showed balls, saying that they would put them in their muskets and fire upon the king if he made the slightest motion to go," the count attested. "They used the most insulting terms, calling the king...a fat pig, incapable of reigning; that he ought to be deposed and the Duc d'Orléans put in his place; that he was only a public functionary to whom they paid 25,000,000, which was a great deal too much, and he would have to do as they chose," Fersen continued. "At last, after two hours and a quarter of vain attempts and useless efforts on the part of M. de Lafayette, the king ordered the carriage to be turned around." Nor was this the end of the incident. Later that night, in the garden under their windows, "a man read aloud...a paper full of horrors about the king, exhorting the people to force the palace, fling everything out of the windows, and above all not to miss the opportunity they had lost at Versailles on the 5th of October," the count added grimly.

That settled it. Louis agreed to go.

ALTHOUGH MADAME CAMPAN, whose aid was solicited in the preparations for the escape, would later attribute the two-month delay in the royal family's departure to Marie Antoinette's determined overpacking—"It was with uneasiness that I saw her thus occupied with cares, which seemed to me useless, and even dangerous, and I remarked to her that the Queen of France would find linen and gowns everywhere," the lady-in-waiting frowned—in fact, the postponement was due to logistical complications. Fersen's strategy relied on a precise alignment of foreign regiments and allies, and, especially, the procurement of sufficient funds to ensure the loyalty of the king's forces. "We must absolutely obtain that the king may have seven or eight thousand men in his pay," the marquis de Bouillé, the military commander in charge of the operation, communicated in cipher to Fersen on May 9. "This reinforcement is necessary to restrain the troops we assemble, for though they are nearly all German, they are liable to be bribed [by the revolutionaries]; whereas with this reinforcement they will think all is possible, and their fidelity will be secured. Concern yourself above all in obtaining money," he urged strongly.

It took until the first week in June to put together the funding required to support an operation of this size, but even this was not enough, as Leopold had yet to send the soldiers he'd promised and Bouillé refused to budge until these combatants had materialized.

"If it is desired that the king should maintain himself with his own troops in his kingdom, he absolutely must wait until the Austrians arrive," the commander insisted. "I propose to wait until the 15th or 20th [of June], at which date the Austrians will surely have arrived at the line indicated."

They thus had plenty of time to devise the safest route. It was decided that the family would leave under cover of darkness and travel northeast by way of Meaux and Reims to Montmédy, a distance of 180 miles.* Louis, anxious about the journey, asked that Bouillé leave small parties of soldiers along the road to protect and guide their carriage, although Fersen did not consider this necessary. "There are no precautions to take between here and Chalons," he observed to the general. "The best precaution of all is to take none. All will depend on celerity and secrecy, and if you are not perfectly sure of your detachments it would be better to place none; or at least, place none this side of Varennes, so as not to excite attention in the country," he warned. Judging by Madame Campan's observation that the queen was "determined to have a complete wardrobe with her at Brussels, as well for her children as herself," it seems that, upon their safe arrival at Montmédy, Marie Antoinette then intended to leave her husband with his army and take the rest of the family to live with Maria Christina and Albert, who had by this time returned to Belgium.

Eventually, they received a letter from Leopold reassuring them that he had indeed ordered the required massing of Austrian troops on the border near Luxembourg; the pieces then fell into place; and the date of their departure was set for the evening of June 19. A suspicious maid attached to the dauphin's suite required them to put off their escape by twenty-four hours, but Fersen was able to report to Bouillé by ciphered message that "they start without fail Monday, the 20th, at midnight; they will be at the bridge of Sommevesle

---

* The plan also called for the comte de Provence to flee to Brussels at the same time, but in a much smaller vehicle and by a different path.

[outside of Reims, about 125 miles east of Paris] by Tuesday at half-past two at the latest; you may count on this."

And so at last came the longed-for evening of June 20, 1791. Everyone played his or her part with aplomb. The day was passed in customary activities; dinner was served at the usual time; the court retired for the night without the guards entertaining the least notion that the entire family was about to slip out of the palace through a series of secret passageways linking their rooms, whose entrances had been discreetly cut through the walls and made to look like wainscoting. The midnight flight was clearly modeled on the Polignacs' successful escape, which had involved switching identities and dressing up like characters in one of the queen's amateur performances. The children's governess, in rich attire, took the lead role of Madame Korff, a Russian baroness; Madame Élisabeth was Madame Korff's highborn companion; the dauphin, disguised as a little girl, along with his older sister, Marie-Thérèse, in calico, played the parts of the baroness's offspring; Marie Antoinette, her face and hair hidden under a drab hat and wearing a severe black cape, inhabited the role of governess; and Louis, in a wig and a plain brown coat, was the baroness's manservant. Their baggage was already stowed, Fersen having smuggled it out of the queen's apartments four days earlier. The Swedish count was there that evening as well; to ensure that they made it safely out of Paris, considered to be by far the most dangerous leg of the trip, Fersen had resolved to drive them to the outskirts of the city himself, and so was waiting in a carriage in the courtyard below, costumed as a coachman.

Lafayette was on patrol that night; it does not say much for his surveillance skills that Fersen was able to drive out and then back in again right in front of him in order to allow the various participants in the escape time to dress. "At ten and a quarter the children came out, brought without difficulty," Fersen attested. "At eleven and three quarters Madame Élisabeth, then the king, then the queen… Lafayette passed twice," he noted. Once everyone was inside, the count drove to a separate rendezvous point at which the already loaded berline, manned by one of Fersen's servants, was waiting. The count brought the smaller carriage that had carried the royal family away from the Tuileries (so crowded that the king had nearly stepped on the dauphin when he got in) alongside the berline, and his passengers gratefully transferred to the roomier conveyance. Then Fersen, hopping up into the coachman's box beside his servant, ordered him to get started. It was past midnight; they were already behind schedule. "Now quick, drive fast!" he urged.

By one thirty they had reached the northeastern suburb of Bondy, about seven miles from the center of Paris. Here the berline changed horses and Fersen left his charges. It seems that, for appearance's sake, the Swedish count was not to arrive with them at Montmédy; rather, he would follow the route the comte de Provence was taking to the Austrian Netherlands and then rejoin the royal party later, once everyone was safely under the marquis de Bouillé's protection. If the king felt any awkwardness at having relied so heavily upon the aid of the queen's close companion in his escape, he did not show it. "Whatever may happen to me, I shall never forget what you have done for me," Louis told Fersen gratefully right before he left.

To Marie Antoinette, the count made his final farewell in code, as was the couple's habit. Together they had chosen the name under whose passport the make-believe Russian baroness was traveling. It was a private joke: Madame Korff was in fact a real person, a friend of Fersen's. Now, to deceive the sentries and remind the queen again of his fealty, he saluted Marie Antoinette one last time. "Goodbye, Madame Korff," he called out chivalrously as he turned back toward Paris and rode away into the night.

THE BERLINE TOOK OFF in the darkness, the rested horses trotting smartly. The children slept; the adults were watchful. There was always the possibility that they were being followed. But however attentively the travelers listened, they could hear no sound of hoofbeats pounding in the distance, no cries of "Halt!" Instead, all was quiet. Soon, the sun came up and they could see the peaceful countryside through the berline's windows, its just-waking inhabitants still obviously oblivious to their presence.

But the real test, they knew, would be at their next stop, Meaux, some 35 miles east of Paris. They approached the town with trepidation. It was by now midmorning, and if even one member of the royal family was recognized, they might all be stopped and handed over to Lafayette's National Guard. But again, nothing out of the ordinary happened. All went exactly as planned. The fresh horses that had been ordered were waiting for them; no one questioned their papers or paid them any undue attention. The berline rolled as easily out of Meaux in broad daylight as it had out of Bondy under cover of night after Fersen had left them.

And that's when they knew they had done it. They had escaped Paris—they were free! The mood inside the carriage lifted instantly. Hampers of food were brought out and the relieved company partook of a jovial breakfast. The journey now took on the aspect of a pleasure jaunt. Their pace slowed; they stopped to take the children for a walk. Since the initial stage of the flight had worked, Louis now also embraced the idea that, once away from the capital, his presence would rally his countrymen to his side. "Here I am, outside of that city of Paris where such bitter humiliations have been heaped upon me," he declared to Marie Antoinette. "Be assured that I shall be very different from what you have seen me," he added, echoing his childhood pledge that he would do better. And as if to prove it, at the next town, when they stopped to change horses, rather than sit back silently as was his habit, he got out of the carriage and made an effort to engage with his subjects, "talking to the passers-by about the crops," as an eyewitness reported. When the coachman intervened, imploring him to keep hidden, the king was surprised. "I do not think that is necessary any longer," Louis observed kindly to the worried servant. "My journey seems to me now to be safe from all accidents."

And that certainly did appear to be the case. When they reached Chaintrix, about 90 miles east of Paris, at two thirty that afternoon (the exact time Fersen had sworn to Bouillé that they would be at

Sommevesle, some 35 miles distant, where there were soldiers waiting to escort them), and Louis again got out of the carriage to min-
gle with the townspeople, he was recognized. But, gratifyingly,
rather than being accosted by an irate mob, as he would have been in
Paris, he was instead surrounded by a crowd of awed well-wishers
who were charmed by the novelty of having the king among them,
just as the plan had predicted. It was thus with a note of unmistakable
complacency that Louis climbed back into the berline and remarked
to his wife that "M. de Lafayette, at this moment, does not know
what to do with himself."

THIS WAS AN ERRONEOUS ASSUMPTION on the part of the king; M. de
Lafayette unfortunately knew all too well what to do. Upon being
informed earlier that morning of the royal family's flight, the general had immediately taken control of the situation by mobilizing a
squadron of couriers and dashing off a proclamation intended for
wide distribution. "The King having been removed by the enemies
of the revolution," he had dictated briskly to his secretary, "the
bearer is instructed to impart the fact to all good citizens, who are
commanded in the name of their endangered country to take him
out of their hands and to bring him back to the keeping of the
National Assembly... This order extends to all the royal family," he
emphasized. Messengers on fast horses carried word of the directive
out to the provinces, and the members of the National Assembly,
too, not to be outdone, sent emissaries to track down the fugitives.

Meanwhile, word had radiated quickly out of Chaintrix that the
king was in the vicinity. At almost the same moment came a report
of the sighting of a company of German soldiers loitering suspi-
ciously at nearby Sommevesle. The people in the countryside between
these two locations did not need a proclamation from Lafayette to
understand that these phenomena were related. Just as Fersen had
cautioned, it was feared that the foreign troops were but the first wave
of an imperial invasion force intended to murder French patriots,
overthrow the revolution, and return the kingdom to absolute

monarchy. By the time the royal family rolled into their next stop, Châlons, an hour and a half later, the mood of the local population had darkened considerably. The arrival of the berline was greeted with stares and whispers. When Louis got off to supervise the changing of the horses, a French officer brushed by him warning the king in an undertone "that he was betrayed."

Alarmed, the royal family now made for Sommevesle in earnest. But by this time, they were nearly eight hours behind schedule. The German regiment, noting that an ever-increasing crowd of armed citizens had been alerted to their presence, had long since scattered, their French commanding officer off fruitlessly searching the woods at dusk for the missing sovereign. When the berline finally arrived at the appointed meeting place at nearly eleven o'clock at night, there were no soldiers to be found. The travelers had little choice but to push on to the nearest town, Varennes, in the hopes of finding fresh horses to exchange for those they had, which were exhausted. But no sooner did the heavy carriage trundle into the main square than it was surrounded. "Halt! Stand, or we fire!" shouted the guards.

What followed was a bitter lesson in political realities. The governess, in her best affronted-baroness voice, demanded that her vehicle be allowed to pass; she was overruled by brandished muskets and other makeshift weaponry. The royal family was obliged to exit the berline. They were conducted to the nearby home of the local grocer, standing in for the mayor, who was out of town that day. The grocer, never having seen the king himself, prudently sent for one of his neighbors, who had been to the court at Versailles; the neighbor no sooner entered the room than he immediately dropped to his knees and said "Sire," thus confirming the identity of the prisoner. "Yes I am your King; this is the queen and the royal family," Louis admitted frankly. Then, "I am come to seek, among my faithful subjects of the provinces, the liberty and peace which they all enjoy...I come to live in the midst of you, my children, whom I will not abandon," he announced graciously, as per the strategy outlined in Fersen's report.

The grocer and his neighbor, who in truth were both inclined to support the monarchy, were sympathetic to their sovereign's plight, but the situation was out of their control. Even the arrival of a contingent of paid German soldiers under the command of the French officer who had been out searching for the berline, and who had finally tracked the carriage to its present position at Varennes, could not help.* "Harness the horses to take them to Paris!" roared the swirling mass of townspeople who continued to pour into the main square. "To Paris, or we will shoot him in his carriage!"

The royal family's fate was sealed a few hours later when two representatives from the National Assembly, armed with Lafayette's proclamation, appeared. Marie Antoinette cast the demeaning paper on the floor in disgust, but its import was unmistakable. In desperation, still holding out the hope of rescue by the main body of troops under Bouillé, the king and queen begged for time, beseeching the grocer that he held their lives and those of their children in his hands. "If they had not left Paris they would have been murdered by the Orléans party. What then was to become of them?" Louis fretted. Marie Antoinette, "who shared his anxieties, expressed them by extreme agitation," and threw herself at the grocer's wife. "*Bon Dieu,* Madame!" the poor woman exclaimed. "They would kill Monsieur Sauce [the grocer]! I love my king sincerely but listen, I love my husband sincerely also. He is responsible, you see." Eventually, to expedite the process, the National Assemblymen resorted to the familiar ploy of manipulating the crowds outside the grocer's rooms, a populist move that the king, who was incapable of impassioned extemporaneous address before large groups of people, could not parry. "They will not go back!" the assemblymen shouted from the window. "Bouillé is coming, and they are waiting for him!" Fear of an attack by this superior royalist force now mingled with the rebirth of revolutionary fever. "They must go! They must be forced to go!"

---

* As Bouillé had feared, no sooner had the French commanding officer left his troops to consult with the king than the foreign regiment, noting the size and zeal of the opposition, switched sides and began drinking with the local citizenry.

the throng chanted back. "We will drag them by the feet to the carriage!"

And so, with Bouillé and the warriors they had paid for nowhere in sight—the marquis, judging the situation lost, was in fact already in the process of fleeing across the border into Germany—the king surrendered. The royal family filed silently back into the berline, the two deputies from the National Assembly climbing in beside them to ensure that the prisoners did not try to escape again on the long journey back. "Evidently we have been deceived as to the real state of public sentiment in France," a stone-faced Marie Antoinette noted. They spent two ghastly days in the heat and dust of roads lined by threatening spectators and gloating National Guardsmen sent by Lafayette to escort them. By the time they arrived at the Tuileries, Louis had shut down completely. The king "was as unmoved and composed as if nothing unusual were happening...He acted as if he were returning from a hunting expedition," one of the deputies who had ridden with them from Varennes observed in bewilderment.

FERSEN, WHO, AFTER LEAVING HIS CHARGES at Bondy, had ridden hard and crossed the border into the Austrian Netherlands the next day, did not hear the report of the royal family's capture until June 23, when they were already on their way back to Paris. The count was unprepared for this disastrous turn of events, particularly as he had already confirmed the safety of the comte de Provence (who, unlike Louis and Marie Antoinette, had emphasized speed and anonymity during his flight, and so had also successfully reached Belgium). With horror Fersen realized that, as a result of the aborted attempt that he had orchestrated, the woman he loved was now in even greater danger than before. His anguish was palpable. "All is lost, my dear father," he wrote despondently upon hearing the news. "I am in despair."

As for Marie Antoinette, the fear and humiliation she suffered at being captured and brought back to the capital like an escaped convict was significantly intensified by the wrenching realization that if only her lover had been allowed to shepherd the family all the way to Montmédy, they likely would have made it. The queen had just enough strength left upon her return to the Tuileries to scribble a single letter before giving in to grief and exhaustion: it was to Fersen. "I can tell you I love you, and I don't even have time for that," she wrote sorrowfully. "I am well. Do not worry about me . . . Adieu, most loved and loving of men. I kiss you with all my heart."

The doors of the palace were locked; the guards were doubled; the royal family was isolated. The end was near.

21

Terror and Tragedy

Let the sword of the laws move horizontally to strike at all the heads of great conspirators.

—Robespierre

THERE IS NO QUESTION THAT the monarchy's chances of survival fell precipitously in the wake of the botched flight. As Fersen had noted, success breeds allies. To have failed so ignominiously had the opposite effect. Where the king and queen had hoped to present themselves both at home and abroad as brave, determined, and competent, they now merely appeared hopelessly inept. This image did not augur well for the future. Ironically, both the aristocratic émigré party, comprised of some 100,000 of the wealthiest families in France (currently forced, much to their dissatisfaction, to live in exile) and its polar opposite, the radical Jacobin faction (representing the most extreme members of the revolutionary movement)* now viewed Louis and Marie Antoinette in more or less the same way: as obstacles to the triumphant fulfillment of their goals. The émigrés, noting that the comte de Provence had managed to escape without difficulty, thought they had a much better chance of recovering their

---

* "A club has been formed in Paris in the convent of the Jacobins; this is the meeting point where all the supporters of the revolution prepare the materials which are then agitated at the [National] Assembly," the comte de Mercy reported to Vienna. "This explains the expression 'the Jacobins.'"

rights and property if he, rather than his older brother, ran the kingdom. The Jacobins, intent on reinventing France as a republic, needed to eliminate the monarchy before this could be accomplished.

Even Leopold, while unquestionably concerned for his sister's security, was unsure of how best to proceed. When he had first believed her flight to have been successful—initial reports had the royal family safely across the border—he had dashed off a letter to Marie Antoinette assuring her that "all that I have is yours,—money, troops...everything. My sister [Maria Christina] and the comte de Mercy have all necessary orders to issue any manifesto or proclamation, or effect any movement or disposition of troops which you may command." But once the French king and queen had proved themselves to be such bunglers, the situation became far more complex. They would have to be extricated from their predicament, of course, but how, exactly, was this to be accomplished when they were being held as hostages in Paris, so far from the border? They might easily be slaughtered before a rescue party could get to them.

Faced with an increasingly fraught environment and limited options, the queen, upon whom the burden of the monarchy's continuance again rested (Louis having retreated into silence, sometimes for days on end, in the aftermath of the fiasco at Varennes), instituted the pragmatic policy of doing whatever she could to buy time, in the hopes of liberation by some form of foreign intervention. She was aided greatly in this endeavor by the completion, on September 3, 1791, of France's first written constitution. Two years in the making, this comprehensive work abolished all aristocratic privileges, including titles; established civil rights like freedom of speech and assembly; mandated elections; taxed rich and poor according to their means; and created a national legislative body and an independent judiciary. It did maintain the monarchy, but with significantly reduced authority. Having no real choice—his wife understood that they would likely be attacked again if he resisted—Louis publicly pledged to uphold and defend this watershed document. "To refuse would have been nobler," Marie Antoinette admitted to

Count Fersen, with whom she had managed to reestablish a secure line of communication. "But that was impossible under the existing circumstances."

The joy and relief in France at the king's acceptance of the constitution cannot be overstated. The majority of the nation believed that Louis's concurrence signified that the revolution was over, and that they had won! There were celebrations everywhere; fireworks illuminated the capital; the royal family attended a series of theatrical performances and was cheered for the first time in months. The king's sister, Madame Élisabeth, thrilled to have a break from the bleak confinement of the Tuileries, confided in a letter to a friend on September 25, 1791, "We have been to the opera. Tomorrow we go to the Comédie. Mon Dieu! What pleasures! I am quite enraptured by them."★

But the queen's acquiescence was merely a pose. "These people will have no sovereigns...they are demolishing the monarchy stone by stone," she told Madame Campan presciently. She was soon proved correct: breaking with centuries of protocol, the delegates to the National Assembly refused to stand in the presence of the king on the day Louis took the oath to protect and obey the constitution, an act of contempt that so mortified him that he later sobbed, "All is lost! Ah!...and you are witness to this humiliation!" to Madame Campan. At her husband's breakdown, Marie Antoinette "threw herself upon her knees before him and pressed him in her arms." "Oh! Go, go!" the queen cried to the lady-in-waiting, "with an accent which expressed, 'Do not remain to see the dejection and despair of your sovereign!'"

But that was in private. In public, and especially in conversations with the leaders of the National Assembly (whom Marie Antoinette contemptuously referred to behind their backs as the *enragés,* "the rabid"), the king and queen feigned unqualified support for the

---

★ It was during this brief period of euphoria that Lady Emma Hamilton, on her way back to Naples after her marriage, was able to secure a private interview with Marie Antoinette, a service of immense personal value to Maria Carolina.

constitutional government, so much so that Fersen demanded an explanation and Marie Antoinette had to rush to placate him. "Do you intend to place yourself sincerely on the side of the revolution; and do you believe there is no other resource?" the count wrote, horrified, from Brussels. "Do not be alarmed...I shall never go over to the *enragés*," she answered soothingly. "I am obliged to make use of them to prevent greater evils; but as for good, I know that they are incapable of doing it."★

Unfortunately, Louis's avowed acceptance of the constitution, despite having been obviously coerced, lent credibility to the revolutionary government, which in turn infuriated his siblings' émigré party. The exasperated exiles understood that they could not afford to let a democratic experiment take root in France if they ever hoped to get their titles, property, and influence back. The king's brothers appealed strenuously to Leopold and the other great powers for a military solution, arguing that what was happening in France posed a threat to every sovereign in Europe. The Jacobins, for their part, played right into this fear by sending agents into the Austrian Netherlands, Germany, and Italy, charged with inciting the violent overthrow of the ruling classes.

Leopold, who had only just succeeded in regaining control of the Netherlands and returning Maria Christina and Albert to Brussels, and who now in addition to everything else had to deal with a barrage of French spies, soldiers, and revolutionary propaganda pouring across the border seeking to undermine his authority, was not about to lose that province a second time. It speaks volumes as to the seriousness with which he took the threat that on February 7, 1792, the emperor announced that he had signed a formal treaty of alliance with none other than Austria's longtime archenemy, Prussia. The Jacobins had thus managed to accomplish in six months what fifty

---

★ She also found an oblique way to reassure her lover that her feelings for him remained unchanged. "When I am very sad I take my little boy [the dauphin] in my arms, embrace him with all my heart, and in a moment this consoles me for everything," she wrote. She did not mention her daughter.

years and even a vicious attack on a sitting monarch had so far failed to attain: unified by a mutual loathing of the extremists, the son of Maria Theresa and the nephew of Frederick the Great agreed to work together to restore the French king to his throne, by force if necessary.

Three weeks after this seminal event, on March 1, 1792, Leopold died and his eldest son, Francis, inherited his thrones—and with them, war.

MARIE ANTOINETTE WAS SHOCKED by the news of her brother's sudden demise. He had collapsed so quickly that she was convinced he had been poisoned. But the emperor's death did nothing to change her policy. The queen wanted the Austrians to invade. "There is no cause for being uneasy about our safety," she assured the comte de Mercy in cipher. "This country [France] is provoking the war; the Assembly desires it; the constitutional course taken by the king protects him on the one hand, and, on the other, his existence and that of his son are so necessary to these scoundrels about us that this guarantees our safety," she concluded firmly, if somewhat naively.

She was encouraged in her hopes of imperial intervention by Fersen, who since the failed escape had redoubled his attempts to free the royal family, shuttling between Vienna and Brussels on the queen's behalf. Two weeks before Leopold died, the count had even risked capture and imprisonment to visit her. He had slipped into Paris on February 13, 1792, disguised under a wig and carrying a false passport, and gone directly to the Tuileries.* He stayed overnight with Marie Antoinette, spent Valentine's Day with her, and paid his respects to her husband only as the time for his departure approached. "I found the king and queen firmly determined to bear anything rather than their present position," Fersen reported to the king of Sweden of this interview. "And from a conversation which I

---

* "Went to see *Elle*, passed through my usual way," he recorded in his diary that day. "Afraid of the [National] Guard. Marvelous relief." For more on Fersen's relationship with the queen, see endnote.

had with their Majesties, I believe that I can assure you, Sire, that they feel strongly persuaded that...there is no way of re-establishing their authority except by foreign troops and foreign assistance."

In fact, the queen and the count had used this stolen time together to rough out the framework of a daring new plan. When the war began, the emperor would launch an offensive spearheaded by Austrian troops congregated on the border with Belgium. At the same time the Prussians, using the quick-strike tactics pioneered by Frederick the Great, would take advantage of this diversion to speed toward Paris (likely left unguarded, the bulk of the French army being required to fend off the invasion in the north) to liberate the royal family. Louis would thus need to hold out only for a short period in the capital once the fighting began before he was rescued and restored to his throne.

The conditions necessary for this bold intrigue were soon fulfilled. The new emperor, Francis (Maria Carolina's son-in-law), trained by Joseph to expand his territory at every opportunity, was eager to invade, particularly as both he and the king of Prussia believed that France had been so weakened by internal discord and the defections of large numbers of their officer corps to the émigré party that they could be defeated handily and the kingdom carved up for spoils. For their part, the French National Assembly was also primed to fight—emulating the Americans, they viewed the coming conflict as their own war of independence. "The emperor! I repeat, the emperor is your true enemy!" trumpeted one of the leaders of the assembly. "Him you must combat; him you must either conquer or force to renounce the confederacy he has formed against you...you must realize what you have a hundred times sworn, The Constitution or Death!" On April 20, an obviously reluctant Louis, bowing once again to public sentiment, was forced to formally declare war on his nephew Francis in a perfunctory address delivered in a low, halting voice to the National Assembly.

Just as Vienna had predicted, the French army performed miserably in the opening weeks of combat. On April 28 a regiment from

France tried to invade Flanders and was routed in such a humiliating fashion that the retreating soldiers turned on their own commander and butchered him. Even the storied Lafayette, schooled in military tactics by George Washington and the master class of Yorktown, proved to be ineffectual against imperial warriors.

And France had yet to face the worst of the enemy. Prussia and Austria were still in the process of assembling the massive invasion force they intended to use to overrun French defenses and free the royal family in Paris. To aid her deliverers in this objective, Marie Antoinette treasonously sent confidential intelligence reports gleaned from Louis's council meetings on the movement of French troops and artillery by cipher to Fersen, who in turn ensured that this critical information was passed along to the duke of Brunswick, commander general of the Prussian army. By June, the queen had reason for cautious optimism: she had word that the offensive would begin sometime the next month. But it had taken far longer for her allies to organize than she had anticipated, and in the interim, antipathy to the royal family had increased significantly. Egged on by the dismal showing of the French army—nobody likes to lose—suspicions were raised of Louis and Marie Antoinette's complicity with the enemy. On May 1, a visitor to the city began a letter home with the words: "Do not be astonished if I write you in a few days to inform you of the murder of the unfortunate king and of his wife."

As if all of this weren't enough, the tension caused by the pending invasion created a new problem for Marie Antoinette: her husband, overcome by distress at the thought of war and the dishonor of his situation, gave up. "The King fell into a state of despondence, which amounted almost to physical helplessness," Madame Campan reported. "He passed ten successive days without uttering a single word, even in the bosom of his family; except, indeed, in playing at backgammon...with Madame Élisabeth, when he was obliged to pronounce the words belonging to that game. The Queen roused him from this state, so fatal at a critical period...by throwing herself at his feet, urging every idea calculated to excite alarm, and employing every affectionate expression," the lady-in-waiting continued. "She represented, also, what he owed to his family, and went so far as to tell him that if they were doomed to fall, they ought to fall honorably, and not to wait to be smothered upon the floor of the apartment."

She succeeded in rousing him, it's true, but not as she had intended; he did become resolved, but it was to die. Louis clearly believed that the noblest way to save his family and France was to sacrifice himself, and the National Assembly had conveniently provided a way to do this. On May 26 they passed a decree exiling all priests who had refused to swear to put their responsibilities to the state over those of the Church. Louis was extremely devout; he viewed his tolerance of this law, however feigned, as a black mark on his soul. While the constitution permitted the king a veto power over legislation, to use it in the present environment was tantamount to inviting a public execution. Louis was warned repeatedly that the mob would rise up against him if he resisted the law; his response would seem to indicate that this was exactly the outcome he sought. "I expect death, and I pardon them in advance," he replied serenely. On June 19 he vetoed the decree. Immediately afterward, he called for his confessor. "Come and see me," he wrote. "I have done with men; my eyes are turned toward heaven."

His advisers had been correct; the veto was just the excuse the Jacobins had been looking for to unleash the fury of the populace and destroy the monarchy. They didn't even have to overexert themselves. They already had a demonstration planned for the next day, which happened to be the anniversary of the royal family's flight from Paris the year before. It was simply a matter of taking the existing crush of angry protesters, already lined up and ready to go, inciting them to riot over the veto, and then pointing this deadly mass at the desired target.

The Tuileries was attacked on the afternoon of June 20, 1792, by a horde of some 30,000 raging Parisians, many of whom had spent the day drinking heavily, almost all of whom were wielding pikes, axes, and other assorted homemade weaponry. The 16,000 National Guardsmen assigned to protect the gates of the palace did nothing to stop them.* The murderous column was therefore free to charge up the front steps and into the château, breaking through to the main staircase. "The waves of an angry sea have never seemed to me so dangerous," reported a terrified bystander.

The royal family was together in the king's apartments when a member of Louis's loyal personal guard entered and advised the sovereign to show himself to the invaders in an attempt to quiet them. Marie Antoinette tried to accompany her husband—"Let me go," she entreated. "My place is with the king. I will go and die at his feet"—but he directed her to stay with the children. Madame Élisabeth went with her brother instead. "Messieurs, save the king!" cried Marie Antoinette to his attendants as he left.

What followed was a remarkable two-hour standoff between Louis and his subjects. The confrontation took place in a large room on the upper floor of the palace. The grenadiers put the king in a window alcove to prevent his being attacked from behind. They then took up their positions in a semicircle around him while their sovereign, to make himself visible to the crowd, climbed up onto a bench behind them. The door to the room was already being hacked to pieces by those on the outside, so at a signal from the guards, the entrance was unlocked and flung open. At once, hordes of armed, angry rioters rushed in. "Citizens!" shouted the captain of the grenadiers in his most terrible voice. "Recognize your king; respect him! The law orders you to do so. We shall all of us perish rather than suffer the slightest harm to be done to him."

The first line of ruffians made an attempt to get at the king; they were driven back by Louis's better-armed defenders and took their

---

* "What madness!" exclaimed a young French army officer by the name of Napoleon Bonaparte, who happened to be visiting Paris that day, and who was among a crowd of onlookers gaping at this spectacle. "How could they allow that rabble to enter? Why do they not sweep away four or five hundred of them with cannon? Then the rest would take themselves off quickly."

fury out on the furniture instead.★ After that, the invaders brandished their axes and shouted insults but kept their distance. Throughout, Louis stood stoically on his bench and faced his tormentors with
an otherworldly dignity that contrasted sharply with the turmoil
around him. He did what was asked of him, even donning a *bonnet
rouge*—a red hat, symbol of the Jacobins—handed to him by one of
the agitators (prudently attached to the end of a pike so as not to get
too close to the grenadiers' swords). Madame Élisabeth, tucked into
another window alcove, was even braver: mistaking her for the
queen, a man held a bayonet to her throat. "Be careful, Monsieur,"
the king's sister cautioned her attacker, calmly brushing the blade
away, and smiling as if the threat had been made in jest. "You might
wound someone, and I am sure you would be sorry to do that."

Meanwhile, those of the insurgents who could not fit into the
room with the king had gone off in search of the queen. To protect
her and the children, some 200 members of the guard took the family to a back room. As with Louis and his sister, they herded Marie
Antoinette and her daughter into an alcove, shoved the large conference table used for council meetings in front of them as a barricade,
and then plopped the dauphin on top of it like an ornamental candelabra, so that he could be seen from a distance. Surrounding this
tableau, they let the howling mob in. "Make way, that the people
may see the queen!" announced a senior officer, moving people
along briskly, like a docent at a museum. "Look!" he continued,
gesturing to an icily rigid Marie Antoinette and her terrified son,
"this is the queen; that is the prince royal." His audience took its cue
and filed by, screaming insults as they passed. "This is too much; it
exceeds all human patience," Marie Antoinette said under her
breath. But she refused to show fear, and this saved them. "If one of
those rascals had dared strike the queen...everyone would have followed his example, and all those who were in the room would have

---

★ Thus lending credibility to Napoleon's assertion that a small show of force would
have sufficed to break up the mob.

been massacred," reported an observer. "Happily, the queen's majesty...her air of assurance, overawed the mob."

Eventually, the mayor of Paris, who had bided his time hoping for the king's assassination, realized that the attempt had failed and made his way over to the Tuileries. Commending the crowd for its activities that day, he addressed his compatriots: "Citizens, you are come to present lawfully your good wishes to the hereditary representative of the nation [the king]," he boomed out. "You have done it with dignity, with the majesty of a free people! Return to your firesides!" And to speed up the withdrawal, the main gallery to the royal family's apartments was opened to allow those who had participated in this stirring special event to have a last glimpse of the exhibit, and perhaps steal an extra trinket or two to take home as a souvenir.

It took until nearly ten o'clock for the last of these uninvited guests to straggle out of the ruined palace and into the night. The royal family could hardly believe they had survived. "I still exist; but it is a miracle," a shaken Marie Antoinette wrote to Fersen. The queen understood now that she had been mistaken. The safety net she had been counting on—that the government needed the legitimacy provided by the king and the dauphin and so would protect them—had been an illusion. The Prussian army was their only hope. She admitted as much to the comte de Mercy in a letter of July 4. "You are already acquainted with the events of June 20. Our position becomes daily more critical," she told him. "All is lost if the malcontents are not arrested by the fear of near punishment...they wish the republic at any price. To obtain it they have determined to assassinate the king."

And so, recognizing that it was once again up to her to protect her husband and children until the rescue party arrived, Marie Antoinette took matters into her own hands. Through Mercy, the queen enjoined her deliverers to issue a declaration with the intent of so frightening the Jacobins that they refrained from any further violence against the monarchy. "A manifesto should render the National

Assembly and France answerable for his [the king's] life and the lives of his family," she urged. To give weight to these instructions, she invoked the one person she knew Mercy would not wish to fail: Maria Theresa. "I count on your devotion," the daughter of the great empress beseeched her former servant. "I flatter myself that I share the sentiments which attached you to my mother. This is the moment to give me proof of it, in saving me and mine."

She knew him well: these were words that the comte de Mercy could not refuse. He passed along the request, and the urgency of the royal family's situation, to the duke of Brunswick, head of the Prussian forces.

The queen had asked for a manifesto — and she got one.

BY THE TIME Marie Antoinette's appeal reached the duke of Brunswick at his headquarters in Koblenz, the prospect of a quick imperial victory over France seemed assured. By the middle of July, the Prussians had amassed an army of some 80,000 soldiers, to which were added 22,000 Austrian combatants and 12,000 émigré warriors, under the nominal command of the comtes de Provence and d'Artois. The emperor had also provided another 18,000 Austrians, led by his uncle Albert, on the Belgian border.

The commander had only been awaiting the arrival of the king of Prussia to review the troops before launching the invasion. His sovereign turned up on July 25, 1792, so this seemed the appropriate day to issue the manifesto that the queen of France had solicited. The duke of Brunswick was not a man to mince words. "The city of Paris and all of its inhabitants without distinction shall be required to submit at once and without delay to the king [of France]," he demanded haughtily. "If the château of the Tuileries is entered by force or attacked, if the least violence be offered to their Majesties the king, queen, and royal family," he threatened, "[we] will inflict an ever memorable vengeance by delivering over the city of Paris to military execution and complete destruction, and the rebels guilty of the said outrages to the punishment they merit." Then, having accomplished this last feat of chivalry, he got on his horse and began leading his massive army across the Rhine and into France.

If he had painted the word TRAITORS across their backs in the blood of dying French soldiers, he could not have done more damage to Louis and Marie Antoinette. Publication of this insulting proclamation and news of the enemy's simultaneous penetration of the French border reached Paris the first week of August and caused almost universal panic and outrage. Up until this point, the royal family still had its internal supporters; their courageous behavior on June 20 in particular had won them sympathy. But the duke of Brunswick's manifesto changed all that. With this single paragraph, which managed both to reveal the treachery of the king and queen and to remind the citizens of Paris of the arrogance and inhumanity of the aristocracy, the enemy commander did more to establish France as a republic than the most impassioned speech in the National Assembly ever could. The Jacobins really should have sent him a thank-you note.

On August 10, 1792, barely a week after the contents of this inflammatory ultimatum had reached a general audience, the Tuileries was attacked again, and this time no amount of stoicism could save the royal family. The Prussians had thrown down a gauntlet, basically daring the Jacobins to disobey them, and, since many Parisians believed they were all going to die anyway, they did it with relish. Louis's subjects no longer contented themselves with insults, pikes, and axes: they now brought soldiers and cannon. At the head of the avenging host was a much-feared battalion, recently transferred from Marseilles to help protect the city from imperial assault. The royal family was advised to flee the palace and throw themselves on the mercy of the National Assembly, which met in the riding school adjacent to the Tuileries. Marie Antoinette was incredulous; they still had a regiment of 800 loyal Swiss Guards; she wanted to stay and fight. "You can nail me to these walls before I shall consent to leave them," she burst out defiantly. "Madame, all Paris is in motion," came the reply. "Action is useless, resistance impossible. Do you wish to render yourself responsible for the murder of the king, of your children, of yourself...of the faithful servants who surround you?" "God forbid," she conceded, and agreed to go.

A delegation of municipal representatives and National Guardsmen helped lead them safely out of the palace and across the garden to the National Assembly, where they found temporary sanctuary. Their household attendants were not so fortunate. The Swiss Guard was massacred. The mob broke in and began murdering everyone in sight—footmen, valets, secretaries, chambermaids—anyone associated with the royal family. Madame Campan barely escaped with her life. She was on a narrow staircase, running away from a group of thugs who had just butchered one of the queen's manservants, when "I felt a horrid hand thrust down my back to seize me by my clothes," she remembered vividly. Luckily, "Someone called out from the bottom of the staircase, 'What are you doing above there?' The terrible Marseillais, who was going to massacre me, answered by a 'hem!' the sound of which will never escape my memory. The other voice replied... 'We don't kill women.' I was on my knees: my executioner quitted his hold of me, and said, 'Get up, you jade [worthless nag]; the nation pardons you.'"

Providence was even more on Madame Campan's side than she realized—she not only lived but also managed to avoid imprisonment. Almost all of the other courtiers who survived that day were eventually rounded up and arrested, including the princesse de Lamballe, whose pretty face and chic furs had caught Marie Antoinette's eye on a sleigh ride during that first playful year of her reign, and who was second only to the duchesse de Polignac in the queen's affections. The princesse had actually left France just before the flight to Varennes, only to return in order to carry Marie Antoinette a letter from Count Fersen. Afterward, she had stayed loyally in Paris to help support the queen. Now she and others, including the royal governess who had impersonated Madame Korff during their failed escape, were confined in a prison named La Force.

The royal family fared little better than their courtiers. For three days they waited in suspense as the members of the National Assembly debated what to do with them. Finally, it was decided to strip the king of his authority and place Louis, Marie Antoinette, their children, and Madame Élisabeth under arrest pending an investigation and eventual trial for alleged crimes against the nation. On August 13, 1792, they were all stuffed into a carriage and driven to a medieval tower-turned-prison called the Temple.

It was the end of the monarchy and the beginning of the Terror.

As the attack on the Tuileries had done nothing to alleviate the real threat to the city—which was that the Prussians were within weeks of marching into Paris and slaughtering every man, woman, and child in sight—the violence of August 10 in no way appeased the bloodlust of the populace. And news from the front lines was anything but comforting. On August 19 came reports that the enemy army, richly supplied with artillery, had been spotted near the French stronghold of Longwy, some 200 miles from the capital. This fortress fell to the invaders on August 23. There now remained only the citadel at Verdun, 160 miles to the east, guarding the road to Paris. After that, the countryside could offer no real resistance to the offensive. The Prussians could besiege the capital or bombard the walls with artillery and roll into it at will.

A toxic mix of fear and hatred gripped Paris. The inhabitants were packed in, waiting to die—it was like growing a lethal virus in a petri dish. It wasn't enough to incarcerate the king. Anyone suspected of monarchical loyalty was equally to blame and deserved punishment. The city turned on itself. Hundreds of people were arrested, many of them priests, for Louis was known to have used his veto in their favor. There was no need for evidence—an accusation, any accusation, sufficed to send the denounced to prison. Thus were new traitors discovered each day, which in turn only confirmed the conviction that there were more of them out there, feeding the vicious cycle of hysteria.

In a particularly troubling development, in support of those who argued that only through mass execution of these vermin could the revolution be protected, science now came to the rescue. "With the aid of my machine I will make your head spring off in the twinkling of an eye, and you will suffer nothing," Dr. Joseph-Ignace Guillotin assured the National Assembly. The curiosity surrounding this new toy was too powerful not to give in to temptation, and the contraption was set up in the square of Louis XV, which had been renamed the Place de la Révolution,* where everyone was eager to see if it worked. It did. And just in time, too. For on September 2 came word that the fortress of Verdun had also capitulated to the enemy. The invading army was now within a week's march of the city.

The next day, September 3, 1792, the citizens of Paris rose up and in the name of liberty and equality began a slaughter so grisly that it is to be doubted whether the Prussians could have improved upon it. The number of innocent victims is horrifying. In the days that followed, some 200 priests, whose only crime had been to hold true to their religious beliefs, were massacred. Fully one half of those arrested in the period following the August 10 attack on the Tuileries were executed. And this time they did not spare the women. A gang of patriots wielding axes who could not be bothered with waiting for the guillotine to do its good work broke into the prison of La Force and butchered the princesse de Lamballe, hacking off her head the old-fashioned way and then mounting it on a pike so as to be able to parade it around the Temple in hopes that the queen would see it. "At three in the afternoon we heard dreadful outcries," thirteen-year-old Marie-Thérèse, imprisoned with the rest of her family, later remembered of that day. "My father, having asked what was happening, a young officer replied: 'Well, if you want to know, it is the head of Mme. de Lamballe they wish to show you.'" Marie Antoinette gave a cry and collapsed. "That was the sole moment when her firmness abandoned her," reported her daughter sorrowfully.

---

* Today, the Place de la Concorde.

But of course, killing large numbers of helpless priests and courtiers, satisfying though it might be, again did nothing to alleviate the true threat. The Prussians were still coming, and it seemed there was nothing the capital could do about it. The people of Paris waited on a knife-edge for news of the enemy's progress, and with it, their impending doom.

And then suddenly, out of nowhere, came word that the French army had swooped in at the last moment and flung themselves up as a barrier at Valmy, some 30 miles west of Verdun, forcing a battle on September 20—which they had won! The capital was saved.

It is impossible to exaggerate how important this victory was to the preservation of the revolution. It was to France what Yorktown had been to the American colonies. With this one blow, the French army seized the momentum, and with it the outcome of the war. The Prussian king, no Frederick the Great, extrapolating from the injury inflicted on his men at Valmy that occupying Paris wasn't going to be nearly as simple or pain-free as he had been led to believe, ordered a retreat. The French remembered in that instant their glorious history, how much stronger they were than their opponents, particularly now with the third estate in control of its own destiny. What was an army of 100,000 led by aristocrats when compared to the power of the "three millions of men under arms in France," as Maximilien Robespierre, unofficial leader of the most radical faction of the revolution, soon to be the architect of some of the worst excesses of the Terror, pointed out in a speech to the Jacobins.

In Paris, the National Assembly jubilantly declared France a republic. The victorious French army made plans to invade Brussels. But the change in the country's military fortunes did nothing to abate the fury in the capital at the king and his perceived collaborators. Rather, stoked by the Jacobins, who organized tribunals to mete out the swift punishment of the guillotine to their political rivals, it transmuted into something far more dangerous: officially sanctioned vengeance. And the government of the newly announced republic had no more obvious target than the monarchy.

The trial of Louis XVI, formerly king of France, began on December 11, 1792. It was held in the National Assembly, now renamed the Convention. Louis found out about it when two guards came to the Temple and abruptly separated him from the dauphin, to whom he was giving a lesson in geography. Before this, the king, who needed the uniformity of routine, had seen his wife, children, and sister every day at the same allotted times for meals, schooling, backgammon, and, if weather permitted, the exercise of walking in the garden or climbing up to the top of the tower to take the air. But once the legal proceedings against him started, even this solace was denied him. Except for the two occasions when Louis was called to appear in person before the Convention, he was kept isolated in his rooms.

It took six weeks for the Convention to deliberate and come to its fatal conclusion. On January 14, 1793, the former king of France was convicted by a vote of 691 to 0 (with 27 abstentions) "of conspiring against liberty and an attempt against the safety of the state." Six days later, by the razor-thin margin of a single vote—361 to 360, an outcome especially notable in that the duc d'Orléans sided with the majority, in effect sealing his cousin's fate—Louis was condemned to die.

Only then, on January 20, 1793, was the king allowed to see his family one last time. It was 8:30 at night. The four of them rushed into his arms sobbing, Marie Antoinette and the dauphin on one side, Marie-Thérèse and Madame Élisabeth on the other. "He wept from grief for us, and not from fear of death," his daughter mourned. They stayed in this posture, leaning against him, trying to stifle their sobs, surrounding him with every gesture of affection, for forty-five minutes. Marie Antoinette begged that they be allowed to stay the night with him, but Louis demurred; he only convinced his family to leave by pledging to see them the next morning. "You promise us?" "Yes, I promise you...at seven o'clock. Adieu!" he called, his voice breaking. "Adieu! Adieu!" But as soon as they had left, "he told the guards not to allow us to come down again, because our presence was too painful to him," Marie-Thérèse reported poignantly. He needed to remain strong for what was to come. "Ah! Why must I love and be so tenderly loved?" the condemned king cried out to his confessor.

Louis XVI was executed the next day, January 21, 1793, at 10:30 in the morning. He was thirty-eight years old and had ruled France for eighteen years. Although his subjects did not know it, they had never had a king who had struggled so valiantly to acquit himself honorably and serve his people, one who had likely contended every day with the mysteries of human behavior simply in order to be able to function in the manner that was expected of him. To the very end, he tried: Louis, who could not speak before large crowds, reached within himself and made a last final effort to address the throngs who pushed below, eager to watch the guillotine enact its brutal justice. "I die innocent of all the crimes of which I have been charged..." he began, but his voice was drowned out by a drumroll. Without further resistance he allowed himself to be secured to the machine. The blade came down. The boy who had been born different was no more.

Some days earlier, Louis had written a will commending the welfare of his children to the queen. "I beg my wife to forgive me for all the evils she is suffering for me, and all the chagrins I may have caused her during the course of our union," it read. "May she be sure that I hold nothing against her, should she believe she has something she should reproach herself for."

MARIE ANTOINETTE WAS SHATTERED by her husband's execution. She had not loved Louis romantically, as she did Fersen, but this did not mean that she was not genuinely attached to him. Over the course of the past five years, as the crisis had intensified and the king and queen had faced it together in a way they had not done previously, a strong bond had developed between them. United in adversity, they had found strength and comfort in each other. Guilt, too, undoubtedly played a role in Marie Antoinette's despondency. She knew that it had been her task to protect the king. She had tried, but all her efforts had failed; worse, she was aware that her recent intrigues, by backfiring so badly, had contributed to, and might even have hastened, his death. "Nothing was able to calm the anguish of my mother," her daughter grieved. "We could make no hope of any sort enter her heart; she was indifferent whether she lived or died. She looked at us sometimes with a pity that made us shudder."

The queen's despair was also informed by the certainty that her husband's demise would not satisfy the Jacobins. This had become obvious even to Louis, who had once believed that the only way to save the rest of his family was by sacrificing himself. "The malcontents show this relentlessness in decrying and traducing the queen only in order to prepare the people for her destruction," the king had observed soon after his trial began. "Her death is resolved upon. They would fear, if they allowed her to live, that she might revenge me," he reflected.

His words proved prescient. Over the course of the next six months, the members of the Convention began laying the groundwork for the indictment and prosecution of the queen. At first, their campaign took the form of petty harassment of the royal family. The prisoners were deprived of everyday necessities, including clean linens; they were aroused from their beds in the middle of the night so their rooms could be tossed for evidence of treasonous activity (none was found); small items that had no significance beyond their sentimental value, such as the king's hat, which Madame Élisabeth had kept as a memento of her brother, were confiscated. Through it all, the queen wrapped herself in an aura of cold condescension and betrayed not the slightest fear of her tormentors. They could take away what they wished, her attitude seemed to suggest; it mattered not to her.

Until July 3, 1793, when they took away the dauphin.

The raid came at night, as it always did when the members of the Convention desired to be particularly brutal. Marie-Thérèse was awakened and observed it all. "They read us a decree...ordering that my brother be separated from us and lodged in a more secure room in the Tower," she later recounted. "Hardly had he heard it when he flung himself into his mother's arms uttering loud cries, and imploring not to be parted from her. My mother, on her side... would not give up her son, and defended, against the municipals, the bed on which she placed him. They, absolutely determined to have him, threatened to employ violence and to call up the guard. My mother told them they would have to kill her before they could tear her child from her. An hour passed in resistance on her part... at last they threatened my mother so positively to kill him and us also that she had to yield for the love of us," Marie-Thérèse revealed.

They wrenched the screaming dauphin from the queen's embrace and assigned responsibility for the eight-year-old's future care and education to a sadistic brute, formerly a shoemaker, who saw it as his patriotic duty to take out his loathing of the monarchy on his small charge. Even so, it took many days and a regular regimen of beatings before the cobbler was able to instill sufficient terror in the boy to stop him from crying for, or begging to be returned to, his mother. Marie Antoinette was beside herself; after this, the only way she could see her son was through a small crack in one of the walls of her apartment that afforded a view of the staircase leading up to the top of the Temple, where the dauphin was sometimes allowed to take the air. "She stayed there for hours, watching for the instant when she could see the child; it was her sole hope, her sole occupation," her daughter reported.

After all of this, it must almost have come as a relief when a month later they came to take the queen away in preparation for her trial. Once again, the delegation arrived at the Temple in the fearsome blackness after midnight to rouse the family, read the solemn decree ordering Marie Antoinette to be confined to a notorious prison called the Conciergerie, and pried her harshly away from her daughter and sister-in-law. The queen was already seriously ill by this time from the conditions of her incarceration; she hemorrhaged so heavily in the carriage on the way to her new jail that her skirts and the seat were stained with blood. They threw her into a filthy cell at three in the morning with two National Guardsmen, who kept her under constant surveillance. It was August 2, 1793.

Two months later, on October 14, the former queen of France went to trial. The proceedings were distinguished not by the verdict—Marie Antoinette's fate had already been decided—but by the unusual charges brought against her. The prosecution had evidently determined that it was not enough simply to accuse the prisoner of treason, although this crime was, of course, the main focus of the indictment against her. But the queen was too useful a propaganda tool to confine her transgressions to the complicated and ultimately sterile realm of politics. She had to stand in on a visceral level for the corruption and depravity of the monarchy in general, so as to prevent the citizenry from ever again embracing any king, and in particular her son, who had the best claim to the throne, in the future. This was done by building on the image presented of Marie Antoinette in the early satirical cartoons and pamphlets as a woman so disgustingly lascivious that she had infected even her children with her promiscuity. To this end, the dauphin's governor, through intimidation and by forcing the boy to drink until he was intoxicated, induced his pupil to admit that his mother had slept with him and had coerced him into masturbating.* Prior to the introduction of this accusation, the queen had been resigned in her attitude to the prosecution, but now she involuntarily rose up in horror and indignation from her chair. "Nature refuses to reply to such a charge against a mother," she exclaimed. "I appeal to all those who are here!"

Louis's trial had taken two months; his wife's took two days. Marie Antoinette was declared guilty on October 15 and sentenced to go to the guillotine the next morning. She was two weeks shy of her thirty-eighth birthday. The queen had not been able to write to Fersen since the attack on the Tuileries the year before; her last letter, penned just before dawn a few hours before her execution, was to

---

* Actually, it was the shoemaker who compelled the eight-year-old to masturbate. No French king was ever as vile to a child as the Jacobins were to the dauphin.

her sister-in-law. "I have to speak to you of a thing very painful to my heart," she appealed to Madame Élisabeth, referring to the dauphin's testimony against her. "Pardon him, my dear sister; think at his age how easy it is to make a child say what one wishes, and even what he does not understand...I pardon all my enemies for the evil which they have done me," she continued resolutely. "I say adieu to my aunts and to all my brothers and sisters...Adieu, my good and tender sister; may this letter reach you! I embrace you with all my heart, and also those poor dear children. *Mon Dieu!* how heartbreaking it is to leave them forever! Adieu! adieu!"

She was brought out of the Conciergerie that morning, October 16, 1793, at eleven o'clock. But for her upright bearing, the woman who got into the open cart for transport to the Place de la Révolution—aged, haggard, ill—was unrecognizable as the formerly glamorous queen of France. Alert to the entertainment value of the event, the authorities drew out her death as long as possible. The crude wagon in which she had been placed, meant to maximize her humiliation as though Marie Antoinette were a stack of firewood or a mound of cabbages, rolled slowly and heavily through the crammed streets for a full hour, the crowds jeering as she passed as they might have done in an earlier epoch at a witch or a heretic.

She withstood it all, even to having her arms tied behind her back, with dignity. She did not break even as she mounted the steps to the guillotine. She, who had come to France a sweet-natured, innocent bride of fourteen, had welded herself into a queen of iron determination. She had made her mistakes, it's true, but these were not for lack of courage. At noon, the cruel edge dropped, and Marie Antoinette passed into legend. She died every inch the daughter of Maria Theresa.

Maria Christina

"Mimi"

❧

Archduke Charles

22

A Death in Vienna

✧

You can never answer for what a nation in delirium is capable of.

—Maria Christina

DURING THE THREE YEARS that preceded Marie Antoinette's execution, her older sister had worked tirelessly to return the Netherlands to Austrian rule, not simply to secure her family's influence over this valuable province but also as a necessary first step to extricating the queen of France and her family from their dangerous predicament. Of all Maria Theresa's widespread inheritance, the Netherlands, which shared a border with France, was nearest to Paris, and so offered the swiftest and most direct means of clandestine communication with the captives. To this end, in one of his first acts in the aftermath of Joseph's death, Leopold had pulled the comte de Mercy, who after twenty years of watching over Marie Antoinette knew more about the French than anybody else in imperial service, out of Paris and sent him in the summer of 1790 to help Maria Christina and Albert negotiate their return to Brussels as governors-general.

Leopold's ascension must have come as an enormous relief to Mimi. Of all Maria Theresa's children, it was she and Leopold who had been forced to bear the worst of the blows inflicted by Joseph's hubris. A strong mutual aversion to their older brother's actions, as well as sympathy for each other's plights, had forged an indelible bond between Maria Christina and her younger brother, and now that Leopold was emperor this warm relationship blossomed into one of his regime's greatest strengths.

And their alliance was not simply political. When she and Albert were reunited in Frankfurt with the rest of the family to celebrate Leopold's coronation as emperor in October 1790, Mimi broached a subject near to her heart—the adoption of her brother's third son as her heir. It was the same gesture she had originally made to Leopold's second son when Joseph had tried to deprive him of Florence, but now that Tuscany had been returned and the young man married to one of Maria Carolina's daughters, he had no need of another legacy. So Maria Christina extended her kind offer to the next male in line, nineteen-year-old Archduke Charles. A grateful Leopold, who had sired ten surviving sons during the course of his marriage (so much for the Habsburg curse of only producing girls; Maria Theresa would have been so proud) and needed to find occupations and livings for all of them, accepted with alacrity. It was arranged that as soon as Maria Christina and Albert were reestablished in Brussels, Charles would come to live with them and get to know the country that he would one day govern.

But of course none of these well-meaning ambitions could move forward until the Netherlands was returned to Austrian rule. Even though Leopold had already assured the Belgians that he would abide by the Joyous Entry, and that everything would go back to the way it was before Joseph assumed power, the comte de Mercy's negotiations with the province dragged on, it being human nature to always ask for more. This situation the new emperor could not allow—every moment spent haggling with his rebellious subjects worked to the advantage of the Jacobins, who were flooding the Netherlands with revolutionary propaganda. It was France that was the real worry; their agents were destabilizing the entire region. So after his coronation, Leopold took matters into his own hands and sent an army of 30,000 soldiers into Belgium. This time, the Austrian troops met with little resistance. The leaders of the rebellion, plagued by political squabbling—it turned out to be not so easy to govern after all—had revealed themselves to be incompetent, and the majority of the citizenry were ready to return to the old ways. On November 25, 1790, Leopold's forces seized Namur. Two weeks later, they occupied Brussels, where they were for the most part welcomed. By the beginning of January 1791, the comte de Mercy had been appointed interim minister, pending the arrival of Maria Christina and Albert.

It was this brisk action on Leopold's part that had made possible the French royal family's aborted escape from the Tuileries that summer. The emperor, who embarked for Italy in the spring of 1791 to install his second son as grand duke of Tuscany, was too removed to oversee the plans for the escape himself, so he left this to Mimi and the comte de Mercy.* Although she would not return to Brussels until June—Albert had been ill and needed to recover, and she had also to make arrangements for an inaugural ceremony whereby the couple would vow to uphold the Joyous Entry a second time— Maria Christina was nonetheless kept fully informed of the logistics of her sister's clandestine flight from Paris. And, although Louis and those around him would later testify that the king had never considered leaving the country, and was only going to a place of safety within France, the letters between Mimi and Leopold clearly indicate that Marie Antoinette and her family were expected in Brussels. "All the news agrees that our affairs in the Netherlands are getting better, and that your arrival will have the greatest effect," Leopold wrote to Maria Christina on June 9, 1791, as the day of her and Albert's official entry approached. "The news from France continues

---

* Ironically, before he left for Florence, Leopold, who was clearly ignorant of the nature of the relationship between Fersen and Marie Antoinette, cautioned Maria Christina strongly against having anything to do with the Swedish count. "I warn you to beware of them [the French] but above all Count Fersen, whose falsity and animosity against us and me and even the queen is known to me," he wrote severely to Mimi on February 24, 1791. His sister and Mercy, better informed than the emperor, soon changed his mind. "Count Fersen arrived [and] delivered your letter to me...I spoke with him with the greatest pleasure," Leopold admitted to Maria Christina later. "He could not be more attached to the queen," he added innocently.

to be terrible. I wish you happy visits," he continued obliquely. "We dare not say more." And then later, in the immediate aftermath of the flight, when he had been informed erroneously that Marie Antoinette and her children were safely across the border, he told Mimi in a letter of July 5 sent from Padua, "As to the queen and the royal family, I authorize and charge you to procure them, as well as their retinue, all possible goods and amenities possible, and to take the queen in person to Luxembourg, if she does not prefer to come to Brussels."

Maria Christina, who had arrived specifically in time to welcome her sister, was shattered when she was told of the failure of the escape attempt. She saw Fersen on June 26, just two days after news of the king of France's arrest at Varennes became widely known. "At one o'clock went to the archduchess [Mimi]; very kind to me and much touched," Fersen recorded movingly in his diary. It was all made even worse by the high hopes she had had for success; after all, the comte de Provence, who had stolen away from Paris on the same night, had journeyed without mishap. "I have not since the death of my adored father and my mother experienced any greater anguish than the news of the unfortunate fate of my poor sister," Maria Christina poured out her heart in a letter to a friend. "You probably know that she was captured barely four miles from the border; had she taken a different route, she would have been saved, like Monsieur [Louis's brother] and his wife. I am inconsolable about my unfortunate sister and her innocent children," she agonized.*

But Mimi was not the sort of person who gave up easily, and she continued to support Fersen as the individual most likely to come up with a safe plan to liberate Marie Antoinette and her family from captivity. His older sister's advocacy carried weight with Leopold. "He [Fersen] talks about things done in moderation...with agility

---

* From this evidence, it seems likely that, although Louis believed that he was going to stay in France with the army, Fersen and Marie Antoinette were counting on his taking the advice of General Bouillé, once they had arrived safely at Montmédy, that it was necessary to cross the border after all.

and prudence," the emperor admitted. "Very different from those of the princes [Louis's brothers]...who only dream of regencies and troops, and always want money and to make noise," Leopold added distastefully.

FOR MARIA CHRISTINA, the one joyful prospect in the wake of her sister's thwarted escape and the general gloom that summer was the imminent arrival of the twenty-year-old Archduke Charles. The pains she took in preparing for this event are a sign of the deep loss forty-nine-year-old Mimi must have felt at having been denied children of her own. Even so, she was very careful to respect Leopold's rights as the boy's real father. She ran every appointment to Charles's household by her brother first, to ensure that the emperor approved of the servants, tutors, and companions who would be surrounding his son in Brussels, and informed him in advance of the sort of training Charles would receive, both political and military. For his part, Leopold, recognizing her need, mentioned his son in every letter he sent her from Italy that summer. "Charles had a couple of days of fever with a sore throat, but it is passing," he wrote reassuringly. "Charles is healed but still weak," he notified her a little later. "My son Charles is doing well and has recovered...I will make the necessary arrangements to send him to you the first thing on my return," he promised. "Charles especially behaves very well," he added.

This much-desired adopted heir came at last to his aunt's house in Brussels at the end of September 1791, and for the first time in her life, Maria Christina was able to experience a semblance of motherhood. Her happiness in having Charles with her is clear from her letters. "Your charming son is doing well and has just returned from riding school, from which he benefits and applies himself greatly," she reported proudly to Leopold. Albert seems to have had more difficulty adjusting to parenthood. Although he agreed to all she asked, and went to the trouble of helping to instruct Charles and direct his military career, Mimi would later coax her husband to show their young protégé more affection. "I know your goodness, your benevolence to him, but permit me to ask you in my motherly love to give him more attention... With the reservation you exercise in your delicate way, trust, which for Charles is so essential, will never arise," she prompted gently.

It was well she had this newfound source of comfort at home, because Maria Christina and Albert were under increasing pressure in their role as governors-general to keep Belgium safe from attack and loyal to Leopold. This task was made monumentally more difficult when, coincident with Charles's arrival in September 1791, Louis and Marie Antoinette, having no choice, publicly accepted the French constitution.

The king's announcement, coerced though it obviously was, infuriated his brothers and their band of exiled aristocrats, who were based in Koblenz. The city happened to fall under the jurisdiction of the elector of Trèves, a not particularly strong-minded, much imposed-upon German count. As the elector of Trèves's domain shared a border with the Austrian Netherlands, the worried landowner was always begging Maria Christina to give him some of her troops to help protect his property against a French attack on the émigrés.

At the same time, the Jacobins, who wanted to overthrow monarchy in general and spark revolution throughout Europe, aimed their sights at the Netherlands, with whom they, too, shared a border, as being the closest and easiest of their neighbors to infiltrate. Maria Christina, stuck in the middle of these two warring camps, was thus doubly threatened. Like Marie Antoinette in Paris, both parties saw her as an impediment to their objectives.

Throughout this increasingly fraught period, Mimi remained clearheaded in her observations and advice to Leopold. From the fall of 1791 into the new year, brother and sister corresponded as often as four times a week. "He [the elector] always urges us to make some demonstration of troops sent to Trèves," Mimi informed the emperor on January 7, 1792. "But our reasoning commits us to represent to you the danger of entangling us without need in this conflict... any [military] demonstration whatsoever... could have the effect of accelerating an attack [by the French] that it would be beneficial to avoid; but it is exactly this that the...Princes [Louis's brothers] wish to provoke, to attract you...to their cause," she warned shrewdly. "I would fail to fulfill the duty I owe you, which is so sacred and dear to me...if I did not repeat to you once again that...in the case of a French attack on the Electorate, we would find ourselves with the embarrassing alternative of stripping these provinces [Belgium] of their necessary defense, and run the obvious risk of sacrificing them, and being certain also that what [troops] we did send would not be enough to...maintain those of the Elector...Whatever happens," she concluded resolutely, "you may be assured at least that, as far as it is up to us, we will fight well on our side and that it will cost the French and our rebels here dearly to take this country a second time."

But the attacks on her credibility, fed by a campaign of deliberate misinformation by both parties, made it very difficult for her to govern. One evening, worn down by a severe headache — she suffered frequently from these during this period, and who can blame her — she begged off having to attend the theater as previously planned. Albert and Charles, seeing her in pain, elected to remain at home as well. No sooner had the three of them settled in for the night than they were informed that the entire city was in an uproar over a wild report that the Austrian regiment had been ordered to abandon Brussels ahead of a French attack, and that the governors-general had abruptly canceled their plans because they were in the process of packing up their belongings for a midnight flight, as they had the last time. "It dismayed everyone, and they say it even had a great effect on the members of the Council of Brabant...who do not overflow with courage and enterprise," Maria Christina observed dryly. No sooner had she and Albert quashed this rumor than another circulated that the emperor, furious that the Belgians had voted against paying the usual subsidies, intended to remove them from office. She notified Leopold that she had received a secret communication from Koblenz, which had reported that "an intimate of the Council of Princes had stated positively that you, dear brother, had told the Prince of Nassau that you were so unhappy with my behavior that you were going to recall me from here," she related in a letter of February 2, 1792. "If I didn't know you as well as I do, and if I didn't know that...on the contrary, in all of your letters you approved of our conduct, which was only settled according to your orders and for the good of your service, there would be something to alarm me," she added.

Rare to encounter this degree of understanding, appreciation, and trust between royal siblings, particularly during a period of acute adversity!★ Maria Christina and Leopold were a team; they relied on each other; they were ready to face whatever came together.

And then Leopold died without warning on March 1.

The courier bearing word of this tragedy arrived from Vienna a week later, while the governors-general were hosting a dinner party. The comte de Mercy, informed first, took Albert aside and spoke to him privately. Knowing the effect this information would have on his wife, Albert returned to the salon and excused both himself and Maria Christina from their guests; he then led her into a nearby chamber and told her as gently as possible that her brother was dead. Mimi wept so uncontrollably that her cries could be heard in the next room. "The blow is too terrible, too grievous for my heart, it strikes too many points," she wrote in anguish in a letter of March 16, 1792. "With my brother and master, we have lost a true friend. This will make his son [Charles], who is our greatest joy, even more precious to me. I myself had to thrust the dagger in his heart. Only my love of him gave me the strength to impart his misfortune to him bit by bit. He did not want to believe it...It is terrible to have to survive all one's family," she despaired.

But she knew what she had to do, and within a few hours managed somehow to pull herself together because Fersen recorded admiringly in his diary that "later in the evening the archduchess

---

★ Contrast their behavior with that of Louis and his brothers.

sent for all the generals and spoke to them very well and firmly."
Beyond her deep personal grief, Mimi recognized what the loss of
Leopold at this critical moment in history meant not simply to Belgium and Austria but to all of Europe. In his place now stood her
nephew Francis, Charles's older brother, a young, untested leader
with whom she had not yet had time to establish a working relationship, whom she did not in fact really know at all—and who had
been trained by Joseph.

FROM THIS POINT ON, Austria moved swiftly and inexorably toward
war with France. These were the months when the new emperor, in
alliance with Prussia, prepared to take advantage of the chaotic situation in Paris to swoop down and liberate the French royal family
from their captors; when Austria and Prussia built up a 100,000-
man army under the direction of the duke of Brunswick at Koblenz;
when Brunswick issued the infamous July 25 manifesto. Although
Maria Christina recommended strongly that Belgium not be drawn
into this conflict, she was overruled by Francis's advisers in Vienna,
who appointed Albert as commander of an Austrian regiment and
charged him with creating a diversionary maneuver by attacking the
French over the border near Mons, about 35 miles southwest of
Brussels.

Fersen, acting as go-between for Marie Antoinette, monitored the
progress of the war carefully, so as to be able to send the imprisoned
queen a schedule of troop movements. His diary entry for August 21
noted that the Prussians had scored a significant victory at Rochefort,
on the eastern border of France, taking General Lafayette and over a
dozen other French officers prisoner, along with "their servants, forty
horses, and a great deal of gold." But Fersen also revealed his frustration that Albert and his men had not yet entered the fray, recording
that an emissary had "talked to the archduchess [Mimi] about the
duke's inaction; he [the emissary] said it shamed him [Albert]; that he
might have acquired glory by attempting to take the places that confronted him, for which there was great probability of success." Fersen

went on to say that Maria Christina "had the air of feeling [the dishonor of] this, but nevertheless put forward fears on the internal tranquility of the Low Countries [Belgium]. She took note of what he said, however," the Swedish count added.

Mimi had reason to worry. Since Leopold's death, the French had been flooding Brussels with revolutionary broadsides. She and Albert feared that the populace would take advantage of the war to rebel a second time against Austrian rule. Fersen himself admitted as much, noting the continued presence of papers "inciting the people...to revolt, saying this was the moment to rise, they must profit by it and seduce the soldiery." But the orders coming out of Vienna to engage the French militarily were unambiguous, so despite their deep reservations, the governors-general relented. On September 25, 1792, Fersen was able to report in his journal that "Duke Albert has marched with his army."

Alas, it was already too late. A courier arrived in Brussels just one week later bearing word that the Prussians had been defeated and were falling back. "He [the messenger] says the combined army is worn out with fatigue, want of everything, and disease; seeing no arrival of their supply trains, the fear of being surrounded began to spread among them; the French made a bold front...this retreat is horrible in its consequences," an intensely disappointed Fersen revealed.

For Maria Christina, the news this courier brought was almost unendurable. The withdrawal of Prussia from France meant that the two people she loved most in the world, Albert and Archduke Charles (who had enlisted under his adoptive parent), would now face the full force of the enemy army. It was clear that the French expected to defeat her husband; the general who had replaced the captured Lafayette had already issued a proclamation in support of the struggle for independence from Austria. The soldiers of France were coming "as allies and brothers" in this conflict, he promised. Determined not to leave anything of worth behind for the detested Jacobins to plunder, Mimi spent the month of October packing up all of her family's valuables—Albert's and her world-famous art collection, the thousands of books that comprised their library, the government papers, money, and ancestral jewels the governors-general had in their possession—and by a great effort arranged to have these transported to Holland. It took three large ships to handle all the crates.

And not a moment too soon, for within a week the battle she had steeled herself to expect was joined. On November 6, 1792, Albert and Charles, at the head of 20,000 troops, buttressed by some 50 heavy guns, faced a French army of 78,000 men boasting 150 cannon at the town of Jemappes just outside Mons. Although outnumbered nearly four to one, the Austrians put up a determined fight, exchanging artillery fire with their opponents for three full hours before launching a cavalry attack directly at the center of the enemy forces, scattering their infantry. But the French soon regrouped and, taking the offensive, overwhelmed Albert's regiments until he was ultimately compelled to withdraw. It was reported that the French soldiers belted out their new national anthem, "La Marseillaise," as they chased the retreating Austrians.

Word of the defeat reached a panicked Brussels the next day. "Nothing was seen but people running about in search of means to get away," Fersen reported. "All the unhappy émigrés, without money, without resources, were in despair. Not a single hackney-coach could be found." The count sought out the comte de Mercy, and discovered the minister in the act of packing up. "Terror, astonishment, and fear were on all faces," Fersen revealed. "They [the Austrians] had fought hard...attacked several times and were repulsed; they lost heavily. The whole road from Mons was covered with war equipages and carts bearing the wounded."

A frantic Maria Christina had waited all day in suspense for the outcome of this critical battle. The news, when it came, was at least tinged with relief: it was confirmed that both Albert and Charles had survived the brutal combat. But just as she had foreseen, a large portion of the citizenry, radicalized by the propaganda that had been pouring over the border since Leopold's death, was eager to welcome the French army as liberators. With her sister's piteous example in front of her, she knew better than to remain in Brussels and take the risk of being captured and held hostage by the Jacobins, or perhaps even being tried for treason as they were threatening to do to Louis XVI in Paris. On November 9, 1792, two days after receiving word of the defeat at Jemappes, she, too, climbed into her carriage and, along with a few trusted members of her household, fled the city.

She drove east to Maastricht, about 70 miles from Brussels. She took the same road as Fersen, who also escaped that day; it was the only route still guarded by what remained of the Austrian forces. The way was clogged, as all those who feared reprisals by the French streamed pell-mell out of the city. "A lamentable spectacle was that of the unfortunate émigrés along the road," the Swedish count recorded in his diary. "Young men and old men of the Bourbon corps were left behind, scarcely able to drag themselves along with their muskets and knapsacks. There were even women of elegance with their maids or without them, going on foot, some carrying their children...I longed at the moment for a hundred carriages to pick up those unfortunates," he burst out compassionately. (Fersen was not sufficiently moved, however, to offer his own coach to any of the downtrodden.) It took the count until November 11 to reach Maastricht. "Nine thousand persons had arrived in two days," he observed. "Not a lodging to be had...some slept in the streets."

Maria Christina was more fortunate; she knew people in the city and had a place to stay. Albert and Charles found her there, and together they hurried deeper into Germany, pursued by the victorious French troops. "You will not doubt my sorrow and anguish when you read that once again I have been on an odyssey and am a fugitive," Mimi wrote sadly to a friend a week later from the safety of Bonn, near her younger brother Ferdinand. It was the same city she had fled to the last time. "The storm tide of the French has flooded our country...My husband is ill; I was not able to stay in

Maastricht...and not in Aachen, either, which is entirely filled with those terrible ideas and where revolution threatens any day now."

Even as Maria Christina was writing this, the French army, having encountered no resistance in the countryside, was entering Brussels. Their commander, savoring the historic nature of the moment, addressed the jubilant crowds that had gathered in the main square to greet him. "Let no foreigner rule you anymore, for you are not made for such a fate!" the general announced to resounding cheers.

They would soon learn to regret their enthusiasm. Within a month, all the local authorities had been removed from office, replaced by administrators deemed sufficiently radical by the Jacobins. The same violent measures adopted in Paris—including those directed at priests—were imposed on the Belgians and a guillotine set up in Brussels to ensure compliance. The French levied taxes, looted homes and monasteries, took political opponents hostage for ransom, and extorted loans and bribes from merchants who feared for their lives. When the native population, citing their rights under the Joyous Entry, protested these harsh directives, the occupying soldiers built a fire in the street and publicly tossed the revered document into it. By February 1793, the same people who had chased Maria Christina and her ministers out of town were begging the governors-general and their soldiers to come back.

THE AUSTRIANS DID COME BACK, but not Maria Christina. Albert, in his midfifties, tired and ill, was having difficulty recovering; moreover, the stigma of defeat clung to him. Both he and Mimi were aware that the new emperor did not have the same trust and confidence in them as Leopold had had. To clear the air and avoid embarrassment, Albert voluntarily tendered his resignation from command and Francis accepted it before graciously inviting this now permanently displaced aunt and uncle to return to Vienna to live.

They left Cologne, where Albert had been recuperating, toward the end of February. Along the way, Mimi received word of Louis's execution the previous month. The horrific details were brought by courier and disseminated generally throughout Germany. "Though I was prepared for it, the certainty of so awful a crime renewed all my sufferings," reported an anxious Fersen, who had followed Maria Christina to Bonn but now stayed behind in his continued quest to rescue Marie Antoinette. "Letters from Paris through the Hague tell me that the queen is very thin and changed...that the dauphin is charming; that his guards weep over him." The weather was as severe as the news from France; heavy snows impeded Mimi and Albert's progress. Maria Elisabeth abandoned her convent in Innsbruck long enough to meet the couple halfway, in Augsburg, for a tearful reunion, and together they completed the last leg of the journey, reaching Vienna on March 11, 1793.

Their arrival coincided with a moment of genuine optimism. While they had been traveling, the Austrian army had regrouped and taken back Liège, only 60 miles from Brussels. Archduke Charles, who had left his adopted parents in order to return to active duty, distinguished himself in battle. Two weeks later it was the French and their supporters who were forced to flee Brussels ahead of the triumphant Austrian troops. Maria Christina would not have been human had she not taken satisfaction in hearing that, this time, it was Charles and his men whom her former subjects took to the streets to cheer.

But her political influence, like her husband's military career, was over. The baton had been passed to the next generation. Mimi could only watch from afar as the revolution exacted its terrible toll. Although there had been hope, after the retaking of Brussels, that an agreement might be reached to exchange some of the prisoners captured by the Austrians for the remaining members of the French royal family, the negotiations for this initiative fell through, and after that Fersen was unable to rally support for another rescue attempt. "On the means of saving the queen...there were none but to push forward at once a strong body of cavalry to Paris," the count urged on August 11, 1793, after learning that Marie Antoinette had been separated from her children in preparation for trial. "I went to see Mercy about it and found him all ice to the idea...He believes the royal family lost and that nothing can be done for them," Fersen complained bitterly. "He does not think the factions would negotiate; he believes they will go to all lengths in order to so bind the whole of France to their crimes that there will be no course for individuals to take but that of victory or death with them. He ended by telling me there was no hope," the count admitted.

Mercy's assessment was as accurate as it was bleak. The news of Marie Antoinette's execution on October 16, 1793, reached Fersen four days later. "I can think only of my loss," he grieved. "It is awful to have no positive details; to think she was alone in her last moments, without consolation, without a person to whom she could speak, to whom she could give her last wishes. It is horrible. Monsters of hell!" he raged. Nor did his grief subside with time. "Her image, her sufferings, her death and my love never leave my mind, I can think of nothing else," he moaned. "Oh, my God, why did I have to lose *Her* and what will become of me?" And, months later, to his sister, who knew his secret, "Losing *Her* is the grief of my whole life, and my sorrows will leave me only when I die. Never have I felt so much the value of all I possessed and never have I loved *Her* so much...This child [the dauphin] still interests me," he added revealingly. "His fate increases my pain yet more."

For Maria Christina, too, the shock was very great, particularly when the prosecution's allegations against Marie Antoinette as having sexually abused the dauphin were made public and broadcast throughout Europe. Of all her siblings, Mimi had understood her mother the best; she knew the empress would have wanted her to watch over her youngest sister especially, to help protect and guide her. Mimi's inability to do so made the scurrilous charges and Marie Antoinette's ordeal even more difficult to bear. "Maria Theresa would never have believed that she had put children into the world who would be tortured by the vicious, oppressed by cabals, covered in ignominy and end their lives on the scaffold," a horrified Maria

Christina wrote. "I cannot get over the sorrow which the unfortunate had to suffer even in her last months, especially because of her children...death ends all grief and anguish," she tried to console herself.

BY THE SPRING OF 1794, Mimi and Albert had settled into their lives as private citizens. It was no doubt with a sense of nostalgia that Maria Christina chose as her new home in Vienna the villa previously owned by one of her mother's favorite ministers, Count Tarouca, the man whom a young, high-spirited Maria Theresa had wisely appointed to lecture her on her faults and correct her behavior during the first traumatic years of her reign. The house needed quite a bit of renovation, particularly after the crates smuggled out of Brussels began to arrive. Mimi and Albert were disappointed to learn that one of the ships bearing their possessions had sunk, but fortunately the lost cargo turned out to be mostly books. Their artwork, the focus of so much of their combined taste and effort, and which was by this time generally recognized as one of the most valuable private collections in Europe, survived intact. Maria Christina was even able to convince her nephew Francis to return the masterpieces her mother had given her as wedding presents (the same paintings Joseph had spitefully reclaimed at Maria Theresa's death) by compensating the emperor with some 500 prints that were more to his taste.

The years passed quietly, but they were not without worry. Combat continued. France launched a second offensive, crossing the border into the Austrian Netherlands yet again during the summer of 1794. This time the French army won decisively, forcing Archduke Charles and his soldiers to retreat. On October 1, 1795, the province was officially annexed to France and would remain so for the duration of the war.* The front lines moved to Germany and Italy.

---

* Napoleon would later boast that of all the palaces he appropriated to himself from their rightful owners, Laeken, Maria Christina's elegant country house in Brussels, was his favorite.

Anxiously, but also with pride, Maria Christina followed the career of her adopted son as Charles rose to become his brother Francis's most experienced and successful general.

The new year brought solace of another sort. Austria finally managed to free Marie Antoinette's daughter, Marie-Thérèse, by an exchange of prisoners on December 21, 1795. She arrived in Vienna at the beginning of January, the only surviving member of the captured royal family. Madame Élisabeth had followed her brother and sister-in-law to the guillotine on May 10, 1794, where she exhibited the same generosity of spirit with which she had once faced down the mob at the Tuileries. "She made them take her to the room of those who were to die with her; she exhorted all with a presence of mind, an elevation, an unction which strengthened them," Marie-Thérèse learned later from firsthand reports. "On the cart she showed the same calmness, encouraging the women who were with her. At the foot of the scaffold they had the cruelty to make her wait and perish last. All the women on getting out of the cart asked permission to kiss her, which she gave, encouraging each of them with her usual kindness. Her strength did not abandon her at the last moment which she bore with a resignation full of religion." She was thirty years old.

The dauphin's fate had been even more malicious. The sadistic shoemaker soon grew bored of his position and abandoned his charge, and no one was appointed in his place. "They had the cruelty to leave my poor brother alone; unheard-of barbarity which has surely no other example!" Marie-Thérèse exclaimed. "A poor child only eight years old, already ill...locked and bolted in, with no succor but a bell, which he did not ring, so afraid was he of the persons it would call...He lay in a bed which had not been made for more than six months, and he now had no strength to make it; fleas and bugs covered him, his linen and his person were full of them. His shirt and stockings had not been changed for a year; his excrement remained in the room, no one had removed them during all that time. His window, the bars of which were secured by a padlock, was never opened; it was impossible to stay in his chamber on account of the foul odor... for a long time that unhappy child was left without lights; he was dying of fear."* Thus tortured, Louis XVII, the title by which this much-loved son of Marie Antoinette and Count Fersen has since become known in history, perished of illness on June 9, 1795, at the age of ten.

Louis XVII, Marie Antoinette's son by Count Fersen

But Marie-Thérèse had somehow managed to survive. She was seventeen and had spent fully a third of her life in confinement under horrific conditions. She, too, had been left alone in her apartments after the death of Madame Élisabeth, but she was allowed firewood and candles and had been mature enough by that time to contrive to

---

* A young boy deliberately left completely alone in a small, barred room, *in the dark,* for over a year. It would have been kinder and frankly less vile to guillotine him.

keep her rooms at least somewhat clean. Her mother's family, elated to have her safe, did everything they could to make the daughter of Marie Antoinette feel welcomed and loved. She was given rooms at the Hofburg, and all of Vienna flocked to meet her. She must have been especially precious to Maria Christina, who was one of the few members of the family who had met Marie-Thérèse in happier times, when Mimi and Albert had visited Paris a decade earlier, in August of 1786. To bind this bruised young woman still further to her imperial relatives, the idea was floated that the rescued princess marry her first cousin Archduke Charles, a project that likely originated with his adopted mother.

But ironically, Marie Antoinette, who had been sneeringly labeled "the Austrian" by her subjects, had taught her daughter to be French to her core. Marie-Thérèse was only six years old when she met Maria Christina and did not remember her. The teenager was ill at ease in Vienna. These people were strangers to her. She was not accustomed to Austrian ways and longed for the comfort of a familiar face. Despite everything she had endured at the hands of her countrymen, she still believed, as her mother had, that French culture and society were superior to all others. So she declined to marry Charles and instead went to live with her father's brother, the comte de Provence, now styled Louis XVIII. Three years later, she married the eldest son of the comte d'Artois, her father's youngest brother, the uncle whose actions as leader of the émigré party had so callously worked against her parents' interests that his policies had hastened their deaths.

MARIE-THÉRÈSE'S REFUSAL to marry Archduke Charles was surely a disappointment to Maria Christina, as was her niece's departure from Austria. But at least Marie Antoinette's child was no longer suffering in prison. And life in Vienna was pleasant. The emperor was generous: Mimi and Albert continued to draw the income off the royal treasury that they would have had if they had remained as governors-general in Brussels, which in turn allowed them to maintain their standard of living. If anything, they threw themselves even more ardently into the pursuit of art, particularly Maria Christina, who bought up a major collection of paintings, including works by Michelangelo, Raphael, and Leonardo, as a gift for Albert when their previous owner, a friend from the couple's days in Belgium, fell in battle. It's possible that she knew she did not have much time left and wanted to show her husband how much he meant to her, for Mimi was often ill, wracked with stomach pain. Certainly by the summer of 1798, she knew she was failing.

It is characteristic of Maria Christina that she was more concerned with Albert's distress than her own and did her best to alleviate it. "My dear, precious husband," she wrote just before her death. "I am under no delusion regarding my health—I see and feel that it is not returning...If I deserve the world's respect and sympathy, it is through you alone. You made me what I am. You were...the force that propelled me to do good, my guiding star, the sole creature for whom I lived, to whom I belonged and of whom I wished to be worthy. How can I describe to you my gratitude for all the bliss you allowed me to enjoy for so many years...At this hour, my dear friend, my precious husband, you are hearing me for the last time... May you be happy. May the angel of consolation visit you at this hour!...Farewell a thousand times, my beloved husband!"

She died on June 24, 1798, and was buried in the royal crypt with her parents and siblings. In her honor, Albert commissioned the carving of an immense monument, complete with life-sized mourners, their heads bent in sorrow, trudging toward the door to her grave in a perpetual funeral. Sculpted by one of Italy's foremost artists, it is a poignant memorial to the strong, talented, courageous woman who defied the limitations of her time to live on her own terms.

It stands today in the Church of the Augustinian Friars in Vienna.

Mimi's tomb

Maria Carolina

"Charlotte"

Napoleon

23

The Lady, the Lord Admiral, and the Queen

~~≋~~

I will pursue my revenge to the tomb.

—Inscribed by Maria Carolina under a
portrait of Marie Antoinette

During the summer and fall of 1792, when both her sisters were still alive and the war between revolutionary France and Austria had just begun, forty-year-old Charlotte waited anxiously in Naples for news of the imperial offensive meant to liberate the French royal family. The early reports were encouraging, and her hopes ran high. In their initial encounters, the Prussians had overpowered the enemy. The duke of Brunswick's force was only a week's march away from Paris. Word of Marie Antoinette's safe deliverance was expected daily.

It was thus a crushing disappointment for Maria Carolina to learn in October of the French army's last-minute comeback and victory, and of the precipitate retreat of the Prussian soldiers before their rescue mission could be accomplished. This blow was accompanied by the announcement that her younger sister's husband had been dethroned and France declared a republic, an ominous turnaround that was followed almost immediately by the demand that Naples, along with the rest of Italy, recognize the legitimacy of the new government. Failure to do so would be considered a diplomatic insult of the highest degree, justifying the invasion of "five hundred thousand Frenchmen...[who] would leave not a single stone upon another," as the Jacobin envoy sent to Rome to encourage the pope's acquiescence helpfully put it.

Despite this threat, Charlotte could not bring herself to do it. What! *She* officially acknowledge the republic, and by extension the overthrow of the French monarchy, and thereby condone the actions of those responsible for imprisoning and tormenting her favorite sister! It wasn't possible. She and Ferdinand refused to receive, or even to speak to, the new Jacobin ambassador appointed to Naples, which of course had a detrimental effect upon that diplomat's social status and resulted in the distressing fact of his not getting invited to any of the really good parties.

The envoy, miffed, complained to his superiors. A war council was held to discuss the problem. As the French already had a fleet of some 52 ships patrolling the Mediterranean, the decision was taken to launch a naval attack against the recalcitrant kingdom. On November 20, 1792, this information was leaked to Naples.

Maria Carolina was taken aback. She had lived in Italy for nearly a quarter century, and in all that time her kingdom had never once been menaced by war. She and Ferdinand hurriedly gave an audience to the French ambassador, and she even humiliated herself by condescending to speak a few brief words to him.* But this belated recognition was deemed insufficient by the Jacobins. The order to attack was not withdrawn. Two weeks later, on December 12, the citizens of Naples woke up to find a line of nine French warships and four gunboats arrayed in combat formation in the harbor, with their cannon leveled at the heart of the city.

General Acton, still chief minister, argued for a military response. He had been preparing for this moment since he first heard that the

---

* She was also forced to receive his wife, an exercise in self-control that cost Charlotte so much effort that she broke her fan in fury as soon as the interview had terminated.

French had determined on a policy of intimidation. But he had been unable to get Ferdinand to take the danger seriously. No matter how often he urged the king to go out among the people "who cherish him, and encourage by his presence the workmen at the docks, the troops, and militia, this could not be managed...His Majesty repairs daily to the hunt as if nothing was happening," Acton despaired. Now that the French battleships had actually appeared, Ferdinand was even less disposed to fight; he was adamant against war and wanted nothing but to be left alone.

The decision was thus left to the queen. She knew that if she threw her support behind Acton, her husband would not have the strength to oppose her. But however much she loathed the French, she was not confident that her subjects would not turn on her and side *with* the enemy, rather than against them. Charlotte knew from her internal spies that Jacobin propaganda had made significant inroads in Naples. The lower classes were still passionately attached to Ferdinand, it was true, but the intellectuals and younger members of the upper classes were highly sympathetic to republican ideals. Maria Christina had just been chased out of Brussels by this sort of Jacobin influence; Marie Antoinette had been dethroned and imprisoned in the Temple by it. For the first time in her life, Maria Carolina backed away from a fight. Naples capitulated without the French having to fire a shot. "To avoid war, a detestable misfortune, but far less dire when the nation is in favor of it, we caress the serpent which will poison us," the queen observed.

Charlotte was soon given an example of just how far the republican government in Paris was prepared to go to defend their envoys when, two months later, in February 1793, a French army descended on Rome, took the pope prisoner, and occupied and ravaged the city as punishment for the assassination of one of its ambassadors, who had incited a riot. Every royalist émigré, including Louis's elderly aunts (still alive), as well as all the English sightseers who had been visiting the city on the Grand Tour, were forced to flee to Naples to escape capture. With their arrival came also the terrible news that the king of France had been guillotined, followed by the long-awaited and far more hopeful announcement that England had at last joined the war.

THE FORMAL ENTRANCE OF BRITAIN, the dominant naval power in Europe, into the conflict against the French gave Maria Carolina access to the world-class fighting force she had been looking for. On July 12, 1793, Naples secretly signed a treaty of alliance with England whereby she and Ferdinand agreed to provide a number of ships from the Neapolitan navy to be used jointly against French targets in the Mediterranean on condition that the British fleet come to their kingdom's rescue in the event of an attack. This agreement was not initially made public for fear of reprisals against Marie Antoinette and her children. Charlotte, still hoping to free her younger sister's family through negotiation, had sent an emissary to Paris; Russia, too, had offered to act as intermediary; and there were still various plans by loyalists to somehow disguise the captive queen of France and sneak her out of prison and across the border to safety. Maria Carolina wept and prayed on her knees in the palace chapel every day for her sister's deliverance.

But of course nothing worked, and the shocking news of Marie Antoinette's execution on October 16, 1793, was inevitably known in Naples a short time afterward. Maria Carolina, heavily pregnant with her seventeenth child, was so distraught at the violence of the act that it was feared she would lose the baby. "Good God!" she cried. "Did you ever think the French would have treated my sister and her husband in so horrible a way?" Her tenth daughter was born two months later, but even the successful delivery of a healthy infant did not lift the mother's spirits. "I am so excessively ill that I can barely hold my pen and spend only the briefest time out of bed," Charlotte wrote faintly in a letter to a friend on Christmas Day. "The torments I have endured have ruined my health."

To fill the emotional void created by the loss of this beloved sister, the queen of Naples embraced the glamorous Lady Hamilton. Since the day Emma had returned from her honeymoon with a letter from Marie Antoinette to Charlotte smuggled in her pocket, the British ambassadress had grown steadily in the grateful sovereign's affections. "In the evenings I go to her [Maria Carolina] and we are *tête-à-tête* 2 or 3 hours," Emma reported in a letter that summer. "Sometimes we sing. Yesterday the King and me sang duets 3 hours. It was but bad, *as he sings like a King*," she added. By the next year she was confiding, "No person can be so charming as the Queen. She is everything one can wish,—the best mother, wife, and friend in the world. I live constantly with her, and have done intimately so for 2 years, and I never have in all that time seen anything but goodness and sincerity in her...if I was her daughter, she could not be kinder to me, and I love her with my whole soul."

But Emma was more than just a good friend—she was a diplomatic back door to England. "Send me some news, political and private," she urged friends in London. "For against my will, owing to my situation here, I am got into politicks." Through her husband, who loved to show her off, Lady Hamilton was also exposed to confidential briefings and met everyone of importance in government and the military. When an up-and-coming officer of the British fleet named Horatio Nelson docked at Naples for a few days in the fall of that year, Sir William insisted on having the dynamic thirty-five-year-old commander to dinner so he could meet the ambassador's beautiful twenty-five-year-old wife, not perhaps the most well-thought-out move for a husband already well into his sixties. "The captain I am about to introduce to you is a little man, and far from handsome, but he will live to be a great man," Sir William assured Emma.

Having access to so powerful a protector as the British government was a boon to Maria Carolina, who needed all the help she could get. Although she and Ferdinand broke publicly with France after the execution of Marie Antoinette, the Jacobins sent to incite Naples against the monarchy had already infiltrated the capital and recruited malcontents to their cause. In March 1794, Charlotte's spies saved her when a well-organized plot to assassinate the king and queen on the thirtieth of the month was uncovered at the last minute. Fifty-three of the conspirators were apprehended. An investigation was launched; the chief of the secret police himself was implicated in the intrigue. Six months later, a lengthy trial was conducted at which, the evidence being overwhelming, all were convicted. The magistrates handed down a strikingly lenient punishment for the period—only three of the defendants were condemned to death. The rest were confined to prison.* (In Paris, by contrast, thousands were accused, tried, and guillotined within days for much less grave offenses.) The king and queen supported the judiciary and did not interfere in the sentencing, although it was clear that they were shaken by the incident. "I go nowhere without wondering if I shall return alive," wrote Maria Carolina.

In the midst of all this, just when it seemed that life at court could not get any grimmer, Vesuvius erupted again, necessitating the prompt coordination of a relief effort for the victims and the expense of rebuilding, all of which put a strain on the royal treasury. And this natural catastrophe was by no means the worst of the queen's problems. At the beginning of 1795, a twenty-five-year-old Corsican artillery officer in the French army was being recalled to Paris. The era of Napoleon Bonaparte was about to begin.

MARIE ANTOINETTE'S EXECUTION had by no means satisfied the bloodlust of her Parisian subjects; if anything, it only incited the infuriated citizenry to further acts of violence. It would have given the queen no small satisfaction, had she lived, to learn that less than a month after her own beheading, the duc d'Orléans, the traitor she considered most responsible for her husband's dethronement and death, followed his royal cousin to the guillotine; and that the next year, the two agents sent to bring her family back from Varennes

---

* They were released four years later. "They all deserved to be hanged long ago," fumed Emma. "These pretty gentlemen, that had planned the death of their Majesties, are to be let out on society again."

after the aborted escape attempt *also* climbed the steps to that murderous machine. In fact, in the general paroxysm of anarchy that gripped the city, almost no well-known public official who had previously worked to destroy the monarchy was spared. Georges Danton, who once held the National Assembly in thrall, lost his head on April 5, 1794. Robespierre, who more than any single individual had given voice to the Jacobins and launched the republic, tried to cheat the mob of its entertainment by committing suicide three months later; he was unsuccessful and after a night spent lying weakly on a table in city hall bleeding copiously from a bullet hole in his jaw was also paraded before the delighted throngs before being strapped in and subjected to the finality of the sharp blade, along with eighty-three of his supporters.

But while taking to the streets to brandish weapons, sing "La Marseillaise," and roar approval at the slaughter of those perceived to be insufficiently enthusiastic to revolutionary ideals was no doubt invigorating to the national spirit, it was not, in fact, of similar efficacy to the French public welfare. Rioting and terror, it turned out, did not provide as constructive an environment for business as might have been hoped. Stores closed; grain prices rose; commerce stalled; taxes went uncollected; banks failed; groceries were not restocked; food was scarce. By the fall of 1795, France was in the throes of yet another financial crisis, and more people starved in Paris than had while Louis XVI reigned.

Having been trained to believe that the solution to all of their problems was to attack the government, an armed assault against the Convention (the successor to the National Assembly), similar to the one that had brought down the royal family, was scheduled for October 4, 1795. This unsettling news was leaked to the members of the targeted congress the night before and caused a panic. It was felt (not without justification) that the revolution itself was at stake; that if the agitators prevailed—and there was no reason to believe they wouldn't, as so far this sort of mob rule had racked up an unblemished record of success—it would be interpreted as a sign that the

French could not govern themselves. There was even the possibility that the émigrés would take advantage of the ensuing chaos to re-establish the monarchy. These fears were sounded well into the night by the unnerved delegates, until in the midst of the commotion, a brash young artillery officer coolly agreed to mount a defense of the Convention against the agitators.

History is full of outrageous coincidences and serendipitous accidents that fundamentally change the course of human affairs, but surely there is no more pivotal long shot on record than that Napoleon Bonaparte, the most brilliant military strategist of his generation, should happen to be in the vicinity and available for the job on that momentous evening. He was only in Paris in the first place, and not with his army regiment where he belonged, because he had mouthed off to his superiors and been recalled to the capital for disciplinary action.

The hastily recruited champion spent the morning of October 4 (the expected marauders were not early risers) placing the few thousand troops and five cannon that he managed to scrounge up while he waited for the throngs to appear. At length, around three in the afternoon, some 30,000 insurgents gathered and began their usual menacing approach, waving their pikes in the air and shouting. Napoleon let them get in range and then fired into the crowd. He used grapeshot, which scattered on coming out of the gun barrel so as to wound as widely as possible.

His opponents, stunned, stopped in their tracks. This was not what was supposed to happen! The citizens were supposed to inflict the punishment, not the other way around! And yet the firing continued. Three hundred people fell dead. That was enough: the crowd backed up, turned, and fled. The Convention, and by extension the revolution, were saved. "This is my seal, which I have impressed upon Paris," Napoleon later wrote. He followed up this victory by reorganizing the National Guard and using this force to disarm the civilian population. The Reign of Terror was over.

The grateful delegates made Napoleon commander-in-chief of

their southern forces and at his suggestion dissolved their assembly in favor of a five-member Directory. But although he had quelled the city, the crisis was far from over. There still remained the problem of the ruined economy and the bankrupt treasury. France had no capital with which to rebuild commerce and feed the hungry; additionally, it was by this time fighting every major power in Europe and yet could not even pay its soldiers.★ Without a swift and significant influx of hard cash, it was only a matter of time before the general suffering prompted another round of civic violence.

But where was France to procure the funds necessary to continue to prosecute the war and to bring the country back from the brink of a serious and lasting depression? Their resourceful new commander-in-chief, it turned out, had a plan for that as well. Reasoning that the best way to get rich was by looting the place where they kept all the money, Napoleon turned his sights on wealthy Italy.

THE METEORIC RISE of the short-statured young general, soon to become one of the most famous leaders the world has ever known, began with this first campaign.† And no wonder: arriving in Nice on March 27, 1796, Napoleon found the approximately 48,000 soldiers under his command (designated in France as "the Army of Italy") ill-equipped and weakened by want of provisions. And these were all he had to combat an opposing army twice that size. The task seemed impossible.

★ In the aftermath of the execution of Louis XVI, the horrified monarchs of Britain, Spain, Sardinia, and Russia had all banded together with Austria and Prussia and entered the war against revolutionary France.

† By the time Napoleon took charge, the scope of the war had widened dramatically. France had approximately 1.5 million soldiers deployed variously in Germany, the Netherlands, Holland, Spain, and northern Italy. Against the French on the Continent were arrayed Austria, Prussia, the empire, Russia, and what remained of the émigré divisions; the Dutch and the English fought side by side in Holland. Additionally, the British fleet protected the Channel, aided Spain, and patrolled the Caribbean and the Mediterranean. As historically Italy came under Austrian protection, Francis had also allied with the king of Sardinia, whose property in Piedmont was next door to France and so in grave threat of invasion. Napoleon's Army of Italy faced a combined Austrian-Sardinian force of approximately 80,000 men.

But the enemy regiments, with a large area to protect, were spread out thinly across the region. Moreover, the Austrian general was a seventy-year-old veteran with a convincingly lengthy résumé of mediocrity.* But most importantly, Napoleon held the advantage in that he was not fighting to conquer and hold terrain. This was a straightforward smash-and-grab operation, an objective the new French commander made clear with his very first proclamation. "Soldiers!" Napoleon exhorted his men. "You are hungry and naked; the government owes you much, and can pay you nothing... I come to lead you into the most fertile plains the sun beholds. Rich provinces, opulent cities, will soon be at your disposal. There you will find abundant harvests, honor, and glory. Soldiers of Italy, will you fail in courage?"

They did not. Taking a leaf out of Frederick the Great's playbook, Napoleon used speed and surprise to sweep through Italy on his own version of the Grand Tour. He moved so quickly that the size of the opposing force became irrelevant; the Austrian general, two steps behind at every turn, was never able to summon enough of his soldiers together at one time to vanquish his French foe. On the contrary, it was Napoleon's troops who, picking off the enemy bit by bit, overpowered not only this army but also a second battalion sent to buttress the first. "The Austrians maneuvered admirably and failed only because they are incapable of calculating the value of minutes," Napoleon observed.

The French also had the upper hand when it came to co-opting the local population. As the Jacobins had in Brussels, Napoleon framed his invasion as a shared struggle for liberation. "People of Italy!" ran one of his well-publicized declarations. "The French army advances to break your chains. The French people are the friends of all nations... our sole quarrel is with the tyrants who enslave you!"

---

* It's important to remember that Vienna was also fighting a French offensive in Germany at this time. As in the days of Maria Theresa, Austrian interests in Italy were regarded as secondary to the defense of the homeland, so the army Napoleon faced was definitely the B team.

By the end of April 1796, the king of next-door Sardinia, who like Maria Christina and Charlotte could not trust that his subjects wouldn't turn and fight *with* the invaders rather than against them, had signed an armistice allotting all of his artillery, provisions, and military supplies to the French.

Maria Carolina, monitoring the enemy's progress closely from Naples, watched in increasing alarm as, following the fall of Sardinia, one city-state after another bribed Napoleon to leave them in peace. Her sister Maria Amalia, still in Parma with her husband and now the mother of four children, surrendered 2 million francs, 1,600 horses, and all of the duchy's corn to the conqueror. In an original twist on the usual terms of a military shakedown, Napoleon also demanded 20 of their most valuable paintings. The duke of Milan forfeited 20 million francs and another 20 masterpieces. With the surrender of Rome, the warrior-turned-cultural-connoisseur hit the jackpot: the pope handed over 34.7 million francs, 300 rare manuscripts, and 100 paintings (although statues could be substituted if necessary). Even Charlotte's son-in-law in Florence, younger brother to the emperor, shrugged, paid, and then cravenly invited his blackmailer to dinner. The French treasury was replenished. The revolution was saved a second time.

Although Naples was still bound by the defensive treaty they had signed with Great Britain, the kingdom was not prepared to take on a land war against so obviously brilliant a general. Charlotte sent an emissary at the end of May to negotiate terms; Napoleon was moving around so quickly that the envoy had to chase after him to present the offer. An agreement was reached on June 5, 1796, whereby Naples agreed to pay 8 million francs in exchange for neutrality (but fortunately no paintings; the Austrians were beginning to recover ground, and the French needed this armistice concluded quickly).*

---

* As commander of his brother's northern forces, Mimi's adopted son, Archduke Charles, two years younger than Napoleon, was giving the French soldiers in Germany the same kind of shellacking that they were giving the Austrians in Italy. Those riding lessons she gave him certainly paid off.

To strengthen her bargaining position, the queen had instructed her ambassador to point out that, although they preferred peace, if forced to fight, her realm could summon an army of 70,000 soldiers. Napoleon was not impressed. "If the court of Naples, in contempt of the armistice, again offers to enter the lists, I engage, before the face of Europe, to march against the pretended 70,000 men with 6,000 grenadiers, 4,000 cavalry, and 50 pieces of cannon," he scoffed.

Maria Carolina knew that this was no idle threat. She feared Napoleon as her mother had once feared Frederick the Great. So, although as Emma observed to a friend in London, the queen "loves England...and wishes the continuation of the war as the only means to ruin that abominable French council," Charlotte swallowed her pride, accepted the armistice, and prudently prepared to sit out the conflict from the sidelines.

And then Horatio Nelson sailed back into town.

SIR WILLIAM HAD BEEN CORRECT: the captain he had invited to dinner five years earlier had since that time distinguished himself in battle (losing an arm and the sight in one eye in the process) and risen steadily through the ranks; he was now a lord admiral, in command of a fleet. At the end of May 1798, Nelson's squadron was sent to hunt down the French navy, which had been detected patrolling the Mediterranean.

Problem was, he couldn't find it. It was a big sea, and the admiral did not know which locality Napoleon had set his sights on next. All Nelson had to go on was reliable evidence that the Corsican general had given over command of his land forces to an experienced subordinate so that he could personally direct the new naval operation. At first, it was feared that the target was southern Italy. "I hope we are in good time to save Naples or Sicily from falling into the hands of the enemy," Nelson wrote anxiously to Sir William on June 12, 1798. "I beg you will assure the King and Queen of Naples that I will not lose one moment in fighting the French fleet, and that no person can have a more ardent desire of saving them."

The large British community that had taken refuge in Naples was overjoyed when the ambassador announced this new development. "It would be vain to attempt to describe the sensation produced by this speech," reported Cornelia Knight, a young Englishwoman who had been visiting Italy when the war broke out, and who attended the dinner party at which Sir William Hamilton broke this happy news. "Week after week, month after month, had our eyes been directed towards the sea without ever discovering a friendly sail...But now we considered ourselves perfectly safe under the protecting shield of a British admiral, and that admiral a Nelson...and others [under his command] who so gallantly distinguished themselves as to be commonly called 'the fire-eaters,'" declared an obviously thrilled Cornelia.

But the English fleet did not appear for another two months, as Nelson instead dashed this way and that, searching relentlessly for the enemy. He had been "off Malta, to Alexandria in Egypt, Syria, into Asia...without success," he recounted in frustration in a letter home to his wife. "However, no person will say that it has been for want of activity. I yet live in hopes of meeting these fellows," he added resolutely.

Not until July 20 were Nelson's ships sighted off Capri. And it was here, at last, that the lord admiral received concrete intelligence that the French were headed to Alexandria, and that in fact enemy warships had passed Naples on their way there just three days earlier.

There was not a minute to lose. If Nelson got underway quickly, his fleet had an excellent chance of overtaking his adversary. But after two months at sea, his ships' holds were woefully depleted. The sailors desperately needed fresh water and provisions before setting out for Egypt. So the admiral dispatched a messenger with a note for Sir William requesting that the English fleet be allowed to dock in Naples in order to resupply. If not, Nelson warned, he would miss his chance, as he would be forced instead to go all the way to Gibraltar for these necessities, and "consequently he would be obliged to give over all further pursuit of the French."

The officer bearing this urgent appeal arrived on the mainland at six in the morning and woke up Emma and Sir William. Husband and wife both understood instantly that Nelson was in a position to surprise the French, and that this was an opportunity not to be missed. But they were also aware that this request presented Maria Carolina and Ferdinand with a dilemma. By the terms of the armistice that Naples had signed with Napoleon, the kingdom was prohibited from providing this sort of assistance to the British navy. Only two English ships were allowed to dock at a Neapolitan port at any one time.

Sir William dressed and went off at once to find General Acton, in order to bring the matter before the royal council. But Emma had her own idea of what to do. "I went to the queen, who received me in her bed," the ambassadress testified later. "I told her Majesty that now depended on her the safety of the Two Sicilies," Emma continued bluntly, using the English name for the kingdom of Naples. "I told her the Sicilies must be lost if Nelson was not supplied... nothing could exceed the alarm with which this communication inspired her," Lady Hamilton observed.

Maria Carolina had every reason to worry. It was a grave matter to break the armistice. She knew as well as Emma did that the royal council, recognizing this, would decline to aid the lord admiral. The risk was too great: there was no saying that Nelson would find the French fleet, let alone defeat them, but it was all too sure that Napoleon would detect the treaty violation and return with an army to punish Naples. She and Ferdinand could lose their kingdom, perhaps even their lives, and then what would happen to her children? Seven of the royal offspring were still living at home: her eldest son, the twenty-one-year-old crown prince, married to one of his Austrian cousins; three unwed daughters, aged nineteen, sixteen, and fourteen; and her three youngest, Leopold, age eight; six-year-old Alberto; and four-year-old Isabella. Might not they be imprisoned and abused by the radicals, as had happened to Marie Antoinette's poor little boy, the dauphin? No, the safe course was undoubtedly to refuse Nelson and stick to the terms of the armistice.

But Charlotte also hated the French and knew that if they were to be defeated, as she profoundly hoped they would be, she must give England this chance. "I pray'd and implor'd her on my knees; she could not withstand my entreaties and arguments," Emma reported. "I brought her pen, ink, and paper to bed." With her ladyship's help, the queen wrote out and signed a royal directive that allowed the British fleet to be resupplied, and then entrusted this document to the ambassadress, to be forwarded to the admiral to show as proof at the port. Because everyone in Naples understood that the queen was in control of the government, this command would outweigh whatever decision the council rendered. "In every way this order, I was well aware...would be more respected even than that of the king," revealed Lady Hamilton.

It worked. On Acton's advice, Ferdinand did reject Sir William's appeal, but when Nelson brandished Maria Carolina's decree at the docks it overruled her husband's authority. Two days later, on July 22, the admiral just had time to dash off a quick note to the Hamiltons: "My dear friends, thanks to your exertions we have victualled and watered...We shall sail with the first breeze."

The queen had rolled the dice. Now, it was a matter of waiting.

AUGUST MUST HAVE SEEMED a very long month to Charlotte that year. All of Naples knew that Nelson had gone off to engage Napoleon in battle. "Our conversation by day and our dreams by night had for their sole and only subject the expected meeting of the hostile fleets," Cornelia remembered. "The Court...had not publicly renounced its neutrality, though its dislike of the common enemy, and its wishes for the success of the allies, on which, indeed, its own safety depended, were well known to all parties. The common people generally agreed with the Court, but many of the young nobles were infected with the revolutionary spirit," she worried. Suspicions of Neapolitan betrayal had leaked to Paris, and the French were threatening retaliatory action. Maria Carolina, who knew she had only herself to blame, was so anxious that she became physically ill. "My Dear Miledy," the queen wrote despondently to Emma. "We received yesterday evening a courier of the 15th August from the modern Sodom [France]...It seems they wish to make us languish, to hold us paralyzed...it will be necessary to prepare for every contingency," she warned. "May God help us and animate our people with courage, or at least with obedience! Adieu!...Burn, I pray you, my letter...Pity your attached friend—Charlotte."

And then, on September 3, a lone ship neared the bay and was recognized as one of Nelson's. An officer disembarked with a communiqué for Sir William from the admiral. Soon, word had spread throughout the city. The British squadron had ambushed the enemy fleet on August 1. A great contest, the battle of the Nile, had ensued—and the English sailors had triumphed! The opposition had been crushed. Only four French vessels escaped; nine were captured, and the rest sunk; 2,000 of Napoleon's men were killed to 200 of Nelson's. True, the brilliant Corsican general himself had escaped, having earlier led the bulk of his forces inland into Cairo. But he and his remaining soldiers were now left stranded in Egypt.★ "Never, perhaps, was a victory more complete!" raved Cornelia. "What a deliverance for Italy! What a glory for England!"

The queen could hardly believe it. She had made the correct decision after all! "My Dear Miledy, what happiness, what glory, what consolation...how obliged and grateful I am to you!" she scribbled feverishly to Emma as soon as she heard. "I am all alive!...This news has given me life...What bravery! What courage!...My gratitude is engraven on my heart...I am wild with joy!" Charlotte marveled. "How shall I describe to you the transports of Maria

---

★ The French tried to minimize this defeat, claiming the losses were equal on both sides. "Look at these," exclaimed Sir William some time later, brandishing news accounts from Paris, "and ask how they can call it a drawn battle." "They are quite right," Nelson assured him coolly. "Only they drew the blanks and we the prizes."

Carolina, 'tis not possible," Emma wrote joyfully to Nelson. "She fainted and kissed her husband, her children, walked about the room, cried, kissed, and embraced every person near her, exclaiming '*Oh, brave Nelson, Nelson, what do we not owe to you . . . oh, that my swollen heart could now tell him personally what we owe to him!*'"

The rest of the fleet, led by the admiral's warship, the *Vanguard,* returned on September 22 to an ecstatic welcome. "The shore was lined with spectators, who rent the air with joyous acclamations . . . It would be impossible to imagine a more beautiful and animated scene than the bay of Naples then presented," Cornelia declared. "Bands of music played . . . 'See the conquering hero comes!'" Emma rushed on board and swooned into Nelson's one good arm when she saw him. "Oh, God! Is it possible?" she cried, perceiving how weak and pale he looked, for the admiral had become seriously ill on the return journey. Both she and her husband insisted that the commander come ashore to convalesce at their villa. "I hope some day to have the pleasure of introducing you to Lady Hamilton," Nelson wrote home just a tad disingenuously to his wife, as it was clear by this time that he and Emma were strongly attracted to each other. "She is one of the very best women in this world; she is an honor to her sex. Her kindness with Sir William's to me is more than I can express; I am in their house, and I may now tell you, it required all the kindness of my friends to set me up."

It took the hero almost a full month to recover, during which time he was the toast of the capital. "Nothing could be more gay than Naples at that period," Cornelia delighted. "All anxiety and fears were forgotten . . . it was impossible for him to appear in the streets without being surrounded and followed by crowds of people shouting out 'Viva Nelson!'" The discomfiture of the Jacobin faction, on the other hand, which prior to this setback had felt itself unassailable, was obvious. "The French consul, M. de Sieyès . . . did not venture to show himself on his balcony, and even Madame Sieyès and her pug were seldom visible," the young Englishwoman gloated.

But the stronger he grew, the more frustrated Nelson became. He had won an important battle, it was true, but these people were behaving as if the war was over, when what they needed to do was press home their advantage before the French had a chance to regroup. Napoleon had left only a few thousand men in Rome to hold the city while he was away; if Naples raised an army and attacked now, they could take back this critical military objective and perhaps permanently turn the tide of the conflict in Italy against the invader. But it was extremely difficult to get the court's attention with so many fatiguing celebratory dinners, attended by hundreds of well-wishers, being continually held in his honor. He had to find another way.

So he went through Emma (with whom he was increasingly intimate, a sure sign of recovering health) as a back channel to the queen, having already identified Maria Carolina as the principal power within the kingdom. Employing a strategy strikingly similar to the one that Fersen had used to persuade Louis and Marie Antoinette to escape Paris, Nelson submitted a policy paper on October 3, 1798, disguised as a letter to Lady Hamilton, knowing it would be passed along to Maria Carolina. "My dear Madam," the admiral wrote. "I cannot be an indifferent spectator to what has been and is passing in the two Sicilies, nor to the misery which...I cannot but see plainly is now ready to fall...by the worst of all policies, that of *procrastination*," he began bluntly. "Since my arrival at Naples I have found all ranks, from the highest to the lowest, eager for war with the French, who, all know, are preparing an army of Robbers to plunder these kingdoms and destroy the monarchy...His Sicilian Majesty [Ferdinand] has an army ready, I am told, to march...I am all astonishment that the army has not marched a month ago," he admonished sternly. "If they wait for an attack in the country instead of carrying the war out of it, it requires no gift of prophecy to pronounce these kingdoms will be divided, and the monarchy destroyed," Nelson warned flatly before finally delivering the message, couched deftly in flattery, that he most wanted Charlotte to hear. "I have read with admiration [the queen's] dignified and incomparable letter [thanking Nelson for his service]. May the councils of this kingdom ever be guided by such sentiments of dignity, honor, and justice. And may the words of the great Mr. Pitt be instilled into the ministry of this country—'*The Boldest measures are the safest.*'"

Dignity, honor, and justice—again were noble sentiments marshaled deliberately to sway a daughter of Maria Theresa. The queen trusted Nelson absolutely, as her younger sister had once trusted Fersen. Moreover, Maria Carolina's recent brush with danger in resupplying her ally only served to reinforce the admiral's maxim. She had followed his and Emma's advice and acted with courage, and the result had been a resounding success. It would have been a wonder if she had *not* listened to him.

Naples got ready to fight.

CHARLOTTE DID EVERYTHING she could think of to ensure victory. Aware that her soldiers were untested—Naples had not fought in a land war in almost half a century—she tried to enlist the support of her principal ally, Austria, pleading with her son-in-law to field a new army immediately as part of a joint offensive. But Francis could not muster an invasion force that quickly, and in any event he wished to coordinate his military strategy with the Russians, with whom he had just arranged an alliance.* The emperor consequently counseled his mother-in-law to wait until the spring, when Naples could be part of a broader campaign. As this went against what Nelson was telling her, a frustrated Maria Carolina rejected Francis's advice and told him tartly that in that case, the least Vienna could do was send a commander to lead her battalion, as there was no one in Naples with sufficient combat experience to take on the job. Francis, to appease her, gave in and sent her General Mack.

Mack arrived in Naples at the end of October. He was in his forties and had distinguished himself in battle in Belgium, where he

---

* Catherine the Great had died two years earlier, on November 17, 1796. Francis was negotiating with her son Paul, who had succeeded her.

had fought beside Archduke Charles, who thought highly of him. Mack was undoubtedly courageous under fire and well-meaning. But this was his first trip to Italy, and he was unfamiliar with the terrain, not to mention the language. There was also one other little problem: prior to this assignment, Mack had been a colonel in charge of a single cavalry regiment. Now he was being asked to command an entire army.

But of course no one in Naples knew that, and whatever misgivings Mack himself might have had were allayed by the sheer size of the force assembled for him. To the regular standing army of 35,000, the court had mustered an additional 40,000 warriors. This astonishing surge in recruitment had been accomplished chiefly by Charlotte's threatening to unseat Ferdinand in a coup if he did not give up hunting for a few days in order to actively encourage mobilization. ("The King is to go in a few days, never to return," Emma confided to Nelson on October 24, 1798. "The regency is to be in the name of the Prince Royal, but the Queen will direct all. Her head is worth a thousand.") The unproductive marital tiff was eventually resolved by Ferdinand's agreeing to increase the salary of each new soldier (prompting widespread volunteering), followed by his further acquiescing to personally accompany the battalion to Rome. As the king was still wildly popular among the common people, called the *lazzaroni,* this was all that was needed to fill the ranks. Charlotte rode out almost every day to encourage and inspect the troops. Mack, at his first review, was so dazzled by the row upon row of enlisted men—75,000 soldiers with which to pummel a French garrison less than a quarter that size gave him the sort of numerical superiority most commanders could only dream of—that he told the king rapturously "that he only regretted such a fine army would not have to encounter an enemy more worthy of its prowess."★

The massive force, with Ferdinand alongside in a carriage, set off

---

★ This sentiment would have been more reassuring if Nelson, observing the new general conduct a mock battle as a training exercise, had not burst out, "This fellow does not understand his business!"

for Rome on November 22, 1798, and almost immediately encountered difficulties. Mack had elected to embark during one of the worst stretches of weather in recent memory. For a week, the hastily trained soldiers, the vast majority of whom were accustomed to warm, sunny Naples, struggled with their heavy packs and equipment through a cold downpour that turned the roads into impassable mudholes. Because everything took so much longer than expected, food ran short and Mack tried to make up for this by pushing the men to march longer hours, to the point of exhaustion (which didn't take much, as they weren't used to this sort of exercise in the first place). By the time the army arrived at its destination a week later, it had lost as many of the infantry to sickness and desertion as it would have if it had fought a battle.

But even with the defections, there were still overwhelmingly more of them than the opposition—in fact, perplexingly, there were *no* French regiments to be found in Rome. It seemed that their adversaries had withdrawn voluntarily from the city at their approach. It was concluded that just the threat of the prodigious Neapolitan force had been enough to scare away the enemy. Ferdinand entered Rome in triumph on November 29, 1798, and immediately wrote to the pope that it was safe to return. "Leave then your too modest abode in the Carthusian monastery [where the pontiff had been exiled]," the king of Naples exulted. "All is prepared for your reception; and your Holiness may celebrate Divine service on the day of our Savior's birth."

Alas, there is a form of military strategy called the tactical retreat, with which apparently neither Mack nor Ferdinand was familiar. It involves withdrawing temporarily, supplementing the original force with additional regiments if necessary, and then launching a surprise offensive. Napoleon might have been stuck in Egypt, but he had left an experienced, competent commander in Italy in his place. Within a week of the Neapolitan army's arrival in Rome, the French counterattacked.

The majority of Mack's soldiers, under fire for the first time, behaved exactly as Frederick the Great had at *his* first battle—they turned and ran. Although among those who stayed, some fought bravely—there were 1,000 dead and 900 wounded over the course of the extremely short campaign—it's clear that most simply surrendered, as over 10,000 were taken prisoner, along with their horses, equipment, supplies, and 30 cannon. Ferdinand only escaped by exchanging clothes with his valet and passing himself off as a servant. He was back in Naples by December 13. Charlotte was distraught. "I could not answer you yesterday, for I was too miserable," she admitted in a letter to Emma. "If the people continue to fly like rabbits, we shall be lost." Nelson, used to a seasoned crew and British training, was dumbfounded that "the most beautiful army in Europe" could have failed so manifestly to achieve its objective. "Is not this a dream?" he asked when he heard the reports coming out of Rome. "Can it be real?"

Worse, the obvious ease of the victory encouraged the French general to press his advantage and pursue his departing opponents into their home country in the hopes of adding the glorious conquest of Naples to France's credit. Mack tried to regroup to hold off the onslaught, but the Crown did not hold out much hope, and the invaders were expected daily at the capital. "Like a dark cloud announcing a tremendous storm, the enemy kept gradually approaching," worried Cornelia. Nelson urged the court to escape while it still could, and to ensure the royal family's safety offered to sail them to Sicily aboard his own ship, the *Vanguard*. "Stupefied by this stroke," and "weeping without ceasing," but understanding that she could not allow herself and her family to be taken prisoner like Marie Antoinette had, Maria Carolina began packing up.

Everything had to be done secretly, as the *lazzaroni,* who detested the French and remained completely loyal to the monarchy, were determined to resist. "The populace had become very riotous, crowding about the king's palace, beseeching his Majesty not to leave them," reported Cornelia. "It was even unsafe for strangers to be in the streets, unless well known; for all foreigners were liable

to be mistaken for Frenchmen." Consequently, the Crown's possessions had to be smuggled out of the royal palace to the harbor
through the efforts of Lady Hamilton, once again the queen's chosen intermediary. "I venture to send you this evening all our Spanish
money, both the King's and my own," Charlotte wrote to Emma on
December 17, a mere four days after Ferdinand's return from the
fiasco in Rome. "They are sixty thousand gold ducats. It is all we
have, for we have never hoarded. The diamonds of the whole family,
both men and women, will arrive to-morrow evening." Over the
next few days, similar instructions were issued as the luggage piled
up relentlessly: "I will send you this evening some other boxes and
clothes for my numerous family and myself, for it is for life," the
queen observed bitterly.

They would have departed immediately, but it took a few days to
convince Ferdinand. The king did not wish to leave until he had
heard definitively that all was lost from General Mack, who was
expected in Naples to make a report. But on December 21, Nelson,
tracking the swift progress of the enemy troops, warned that if the
king and queen waited much longer he could not vouch for their
safety. It was arranged that the entire family would steal away in the
darkness that very night.

An elaborate charade was enacted to hide the Neapolitan monarchy's escape from its subjects. That evening, Sir William, Emma,
and Nelson all put on their party clothes and attended a grand fête
given in the admiral's honor. About an hour into the festivities, after
conspicuously making the rounds and showing himself, Nelson
slipped away. Emma waited just long enough to ascertain that he
hadn't been missed before she, too, exited quietly without saying
goodbye to the hostess. She then rendezvoused with the admiral,
who was waiting with several boats at a hidden corner of the bay
near the royal armory. Together the pair ducked into "a secret passage adjoining to the palace, got up the dark staircase that goes into
the Queen's room, and with dark lantern, cutlasses, pistols, etc.,
brought off every soul," Emma testified later.

There were ten in all in the royal party: Maria Carolina and Ferdinand; their eldest son, the crown prince, and his wife; the three teenaged older princesses; and the three younger children. All had to be shepherded safely down the steep steps and through the dankness of the concealed underground corridor before coming out into the frigid December night. There, they were met by armed sailors whom Nelson had left behind to guard the skiffs intended to ferry the frightened passengers to the *Vanguard.* The admiral led the way; comforting Emma took up a place near the rear with the children.

The intricate precautions worked. No one detected the flight. By midnight, the royal family was safely tucked away aboard Nelson's warship.

But they could not yet leave the harbor, as no sooner had they boarded than a fierce storm blew in. They sat in the Bay of Naples waiting for a break in either the weather or the war, but neither materialized. Mack arrived at the last minute in such a state of despair that he broke down in sobs in front of the king. "My heart bled for him," admitted Nelson, who observed this interview. "He is worn to a shadow."

Finally, on the morning of December 23, the admiral judged that the storm had abated sufficiently to make a run at Sicily. The *Vanguard* sailed out of the harbor into the open sea and that night ran smack into a tempest the likes of which "Lord Nelson had never seen for thirty years he has been at sea," Emma reported.

The ship rocked in the high waves; the wind blew with such ferocity that "all our sails were torn to pieces, and all the men ready with axes to cut away the masts," Lady Hamilton testified. Every passenger but she, her mother (still acting as servant), and Nelson was prostrate with seasickness, so Emma had to run here and there to take care of first Charlotte, then the children, then Sir William. All believed they were lost, and they probably would have been without a captain of Nelson's caliber. Ferdinand, ever the gallant, took this occasion to scream at his wife: "Madame, madame, this is where your madness of ambition has led us! You have made us all perish!"

The king was wrong. All survived—save one. Little Prince Alberto, only six years old, "my favorite," said Emma sorrowfully, was so ill that he became terribly dehydrated over the course of that day and into the next. At last, "taken with convulsion in the midst of the storm, at seven in the evening of Christmas day, [he] expired in my arms, not a soul to help me, as the few women her Majesty brought on board were incapable of helping her or the poor royal children," Emma wept.

The *Vanguard* limped into the harbor at Palermo in the early hours of December 26, 1798. Grieving and still terribly ill, Maria Carolina and her surviving children were ashore by 5:00 a.m. Her youngest son's "funeral was the first welcome which this noble island could give to the royal personages who now took refuge on its shores," mourned Cornelia, who, with the rest of the expatriate British community, also fled to Sicily.

"God help us," Charlotte wrote hopelessly to her daughter the empress upon her arrival in Palermo. "Saved, but ruined and dishonored."

24

The Corsican and the Queen

⁓

Tell your Queen that I am aware of her intrigues against France, and that... I will not leave her or her house as much land as will cover their tombs.

— Napoleon to the Neapolitan ambassador

OVER THE COURSE of the next week, the rest of the shaken royal court, as well as the entire expatriate British community, straggled into Palermo aboard any boat that would take them. "We were, in all, about two thousand persons who left Naples at that time," Cornelia judged. For most of these refugees, the overwhelming sensation upon landing was one of relief. It turned out that if one *had* to flee for one's life, there were worse places to escape to than Sicily. "Accustomed as I had been to the lovely and magnificent scenery of Italy, I was... delighted with the picturesque beauty of the Sicilian coast. Then, when the prospect of the city opened upon us, with the regal elegance of its marble palaces, and the fanciful singularity of its... architecture, it was like a fairy scene," the young Englishwoman marveled.

The queen alone remained unmoved by the scenery. She was desolate, and not simply because she had lost a child and been forced out of her home. In addition to all of her other problems, as a result of the flight, Charlotte now faced the greatest threat to her power since she had first arrived in Italy as a bride of fifteen. Disconcertingly, this new challenge came not from the French—but from her husband.

Ferdinand was furious about having had to leave his comfortable life on the mainland and blamed Maria Carolina (not, it must be said, unfairly) for having provoked the French to invade Naples by her insistence on attacking them first at Rome. To punish her, he publicly stripped her of all authority. From this time on, the king told the queen, *he* would make all the decisions, and General Acton would administer the government. "I am neither consulted nor even listened to, and am excessively unhappy," Charlotte lamented to Emma in a quick note written on January 1, 1799, just after this conversation took place.

And there was nothing she could do about it. At forty-seven, after so many pregnancies, she was no longer as attractive as she had once been, and the old wiles did not work. Ferdinand moved out of the house, established his own magnificent palace separate from the more dilapidated one that housed his family, discovered that the women and hunting were even better on Sicily than they had been on the mainland, and, having every confidence that his embattled subjects would remain loyal to him, proceeded to have a rip-roaring good time. "I know I shall recover the kingdom of Naples," he observed complacently.

It took some time, but he was proved right. The French army occupied the capital on January 23, 1799, but only after three days of intense combat with the *lazzaroni*. The Neapolitans may not have been particularly competent as soldiers battling on unfamiliar soil, but they made for ferocious street fighters at home. In the end, the foreign troops only managed to enter the city at all because the small proportion of the citizenry, mostly idealistic academics and younger members of the aristocracy, who believed the French commander's advance proclamations that his forces were coming in friendship to liberate the realm from tyranny, collaborated with the enemy by tricking the lower classes into surrendering the most important fortresses to their protection.*

---

* It is estimated that, out of a city of some 500,000 residents, only 20,000 identified as Jacobin.

Even then, the *lazzaroni,* who were very superstitious, only agreed to accept the new regime if the coagulated blood of San Gennaro, contained in an ancient basin at the cathedral, liquefied as a sign of the saint's approval. The occupying general, whose home country had famously persecuted priests and unceremoniously unseated and exiled the pope, having no alternative, condescended to abandon his revolutionary principles long enough to submit to this test of divine judgment. He joined the archbishop of Naples at the head of a mighty procession of the faithful who paraded down the streets to the church to consult the relic. Once inside, there was a long moment of suspense as the prelate peered uncertainly into the holy vessel and the worshippers held their breath. The French commander took this opportunity to lean in close to the archbishop. "Your miracle or your life," he advised coolly. Lo! The high priest confirmed that the blood of San Gennaro flowed, and Naples was declared a republic.

But the Jacobins were not the only faction who knew to solicit the aid of the Almighty in the struggle for power. On February 8, 1799, just two weeks after the French entered the capital, a loyal ecclesiastic named Cardinal Fabrizio Ruffo landed in Calabria, in southernmost Italy, and began a holy war. As the vast majority of those living in the countryside were both deeply religious and unshakably royalist, the populace flocked to serve in his "Army of the Faithful." Included among these volunteer warriors were many of the realm's most notorious highwaymen, thieves, and murderers (let out of prison for just this purpose). Their methods were brutal, but they were effective. By April, both Calabria and Apulia had been reclaimed for the monarchy.*

At the same time, word reached Palermo that the Austrians and Russians had begun the promised spring offensive. An army of 120,000 was on its way to combat the French in northern Italy.

---

* It should be noted that, while Cardinal Ruffo's men certainly committed horrendous atrocities during this campaign, so did the French and their Neapolitan collaborators. Despite all the appeals to divine justification, nobody gets to claim the moral high ground in this conflict.

Recognizing that Ferdinand needed help to recover his kingdom, an additional force of some 10,000 Turks was assigned to land on the east coast of Naples and fight its way inland toward the capital.

With so much at stake, Maria Carolina could not bear to sit by quietly. Although Ferdinand and Acton made all the decisions (which in reality meant that the general did all the work, as Ferdinand delegated everything to him as he had once delegated everything to his wife), Charlotte did her best to manage events and influence the war effort from the sidelines. She sent letter after letter to Cardinal Ruffo, encouraging his progress; kept in close contact with the courts of Austria and Russia; and consulted frequently with Nelson on military strategy.

And for once, it all worked. By the end of April, the Austrians had chalked up so many victories that the French commander at Naples was ordered to evacuate the city and march north with his men to help fight the imperial forces. Accordingly, he and his regiments withdrew from the capital on May 7, 1799, leaving behind a garrison of some 500 soldiers ensconced in the city's various fortresses (and not forgetting, before slipping away, to extort the equivalent of 60 million francs from the citizenry for the privilege of having been liberated). Within a month, Ruffo's holy Christian warriors in combination with the Muslim Turkish battalion—a shining example of religious toleration in pursuit of slaughter and spoils—entered Naples in triumph and claimed it in the name of the monarchy.

But there was still the problem of the small French garrison and the collaborating Neapolitan Jacobins, who had prudently taken hostages and holed up in the various strongholds sprinkled around the capital. At Palermo, it was decided to send Nelson, the Hamiltons, and a British flotilla to oversee the surrender of the remaining rebel holdouts, with the king following once the city was secured.*

---

* The Crown could not use its own fleet, as this had been destroyed just before the arrival of the French to prevent the ships from falling into enemy hands. Thus the bulk of Charlotte's legacy—the money spent, the decades of work involved in creating a navy—had gone up in flames a few days after the royal court fled to Sicily.

As Ferdinand made it clear to his wife that she would not be accompanying him on this expedition, Maria Carolina, knowing how important it was that the peace be managed properly, was forced once again to employ Emma as her surrogate. "I shall remain behind in great sadness, praying to heaven that all may end gloriously...It is at this moment especially, my dear lady, that I rely on your friendship," she wrote to the ambassadress meaningfully. Lady Hamilton understood exactly what the queen wanted. "This from my friend whom I love and adore," she scribbled on the back of the envelope containing Charlotte's appeal. "Yes, I will serve her with my heart and soul...Emma will prove to Maria Carolina that an humble-born Englishwoman can serve a Queen with zeal and true love."

The British fleet, led by Nelson and the Hamiltons in a top-of-the-line warship equipped with 80 guns, arrived in the Bay of Naples on June 24, only to discover that Ruffo had signed an armistice with the French and the collaborators. It seemed that the *lazzaroni,* who sought revenge for the cruelty inflicted upon them by those backing the republic during its short term in power, had gone on a three-day killing spree that was every bit a match for the atrocities perpetrated by their Parisian counterparts during the Reign of Terror. Revolted by the wanton barbarity, and anxious to prevent further bloodshed, the cardinal had agreed to let the 500 French soldiers and their Jacobin supporters leave the kingdom unmolested if they would surrender the castles peacefully. They were in the act of doing so when the admiral and his impressive gunboat arrived.

Unfortunately, Nelson had been sent with strict instructions to accept nothing less than unconditional surrender from the Neapolitan collaborators. This was perhaps the one policy decision in their long and bitterly contentious marriage upon which Maria Carolina and her husband agreed. "There must be no compassion for those who have clearly shown themselves rebels to God and to me," Ferdinand demanded bluntly. He went so far as to recommend that any Jacobins who did not surrender voluntarily were to be shot within twenty-four hours "without any formality of trial." Charlotte was less extreme and her reasoning was more strategic, but she agreed that there could be no treating with traitors. "The king...must not make a bargain or armistice which would have the appearance of fear," she warned. "I hope that the imposing force by sea, and their being surrounded on all sides, will be sufficient, without shedding blood, to induce them to return to their allegiance, for I would spare even my enemies," the queen wrote to Nelson.

The admiral, who knew an order when he heard one, immediately revoked the armistice and, leveling his 60 guns at the castle nearest in range, demanded that the insurgents lay down their arms and throw themselves upon the mercy of their sovereign. This proved to be an irresistible argument. The 500 French soldiers were released unharmed and were allowed to sail away, there being no need to provoke further retribution from Paris by mistreating so insignificant a force. But the same was not true of those native-born citizens who had welcomed the invaders and embraced the republic. These were subjected, with the arrival of Ferdinand on July 10, 1799, to a monthlong reckoning dubbed "the Chastisement."

Despite this ominous designation, and considering the seriousness of the treason, the Crown was actually quite lenient. In the end, of the 8,000 political prisoners captured, about 100 were executed and another 900 either jailed or deported; the rest were pardoned.* But because the rebels' hopes had been raised by the armistice, these punishments were considered excessive. As everybody knew that the queen ran the government, she, rather than Ferdinand, was blamed for the reprisals, even though she was not present at these proceedings and in fact had tried her best, through Emma, to mitigate some of the more unfair sentences. "The queen, who has been accused of so much vindictive cruelty, was, to my certain knowledge, the cause of many pardons being granted," Cornelia testified. Maria Carolina was fully aware of her reputation. She was "most

---

* By contrast, earlier that spring, Napoleon, still in Egypt, punished the city of Jaffa for rebelling against *him* by massacring approximately 3,000 people.

anxious to go to Naples," she wrote resignedly to Emma. "But I have been unable to do as I would have liked, and my reason tells me that it is for the best. Hated, though unjustly, but still hated as I am, evil motives and a spirit of vengeance would have been imputed to me in everything."

She was right: they were. With his wife so conveniently fitted for the role of scapegoat, Ferdinand remained beloved, even though it was he who insisted on and administered the Chastisement. But at least they had Naples back. He, Nelson, and the Hamiltons all returned to Sicily on August 8 to jubilant celebrations. Maria Carolina was so grateful to Emma that she gave her a trunk full of new gowns and jewels, and the king granted the admiral the title to a Neapolitan estate that brought in £3,000 a year. September brought even more encouraging news: the French had been vanquished in northern Italy; the Austrian army was approaching Rome. The royal court could make plans to go back to the capital in safety.

It was all going so well. And then, after an absence of nearly eighteen months, Napoleon returned from Egypt.

THE CELEBRATED GENERAL ARRIVED in Paris on October 16, 1799. Although ostensibly he had abandoned his men in Egypt because his country needed him to fight the Austrians, as long as he was back in the capital anyway, Napoleon decided he might as well stage a coup and take over the government; this was accomplished by November 11. In quick succession he named himself first consul of France, rewrote the constitution, and moved into Louis and Marie Antoinette's old quarters at the Tuileries. Having covered the basics, on January 7, 1800, the new head of the French government ordered the mustering of an additional 30,000 soldiers destined for Italy.

This should have been a cause for alarm in Palermo, but it was difficult to get Ferdinand, still in control of the government, to pay attention to it—or any other issue, for that matter. The king wouldn't even consider returning to Naples, even though his subjects on the mainland were clamoring for him. He was having far too good a time living in Sicily.

And he wasn't the only one. The exotic landscapes, the lush gardens heavy with the perfume of blossoms, the seductive nights, the languid pace, the relaxed social order—all worked its magic on Lady Hamilton and the lord admiral. Their attraction was palpable. For the first time, Emma, who had been passed from man to man all her life, was the one in control. She could choose whom she would love—and she chose Nelson. The admiral, for his part, walked around with the mesmerized expression of a middle-aged man who has just been introduced to sex, which, in a way, he was, as poor Mrs. Nelson, who had married young and been faithful to her husband, could not hope to compete in this area with a high-class courtesan of Lady Hamilton's experience.*

Even the fact of Sir William's living with his wife and her infatuated lover—to save on expenses, Nelson and the Hamiltons had taken a house together—did not interfere with the course of the affair. On the contrary, it rather added to it. Sir William was nearing seventy years old and was frequently ill. His days of playing the man-about-town were over. What he needed was companionship and someone to look after him, with that someone preferably being extremely pretty and charming. The ambassador was aware that at this stage of life he would never attract anyone better suited to these requirements than Emma. And by remaining close friends with Nelson, whom he genuinely liked and admired anyway, he was kept abreast of all current political and military developments, which was beneficial to his career. (Especially when the alternative meant a public scandal, with everyone telling him I-told-you-so for marrying Emma in the first place.) Consequently, Sir William ignored his

---

* This is not to say that Nelson's passion was not genuine. He had seen Emma, almost alone among the passengers on a crowded ship, keep her head in the midst of a typhoon and tend to those around her when all believed they would die; he knew her to be an amazing woman. Theirs was one of the great love affairs in history.

wife's infidelity, thus providing the lovers the cover necessary to maintain respectability.

In a place like Sicily, especially during a time of war, when British naval power was critical to the defense of the island, this arrangement was unremarkable. Emma, Nelson, and Sir William were a team — albeit with two of the members having a lot more fun than the third. "I must say that there was certainly at that time no impropriety in living under Lady Hamilton's roof," Cornelia testified. "Her house was the resort of the best company of all nations, and the attentions paid to Lord Nelson appeared perfectly natural."

But what might be acceptable in Palermo was worrisome in London. Class and social standards were far more rigid in England than they were in Sicily. Sir William's superiors did not like what they were hearing about the behavior and immoderate influence of the British ambassadress. On March 1, 1800, a stunned Sir William discovered that, after a marathon thirty-six years as ambassador to Naples, he was being summarily recalled and a new, younger envoy appointed in his place.

Maria Carolina was bereft at this development. She had already lost her authority; now she was to lose her best source of information and support as well. "Tell the Chevalier [Sir William] I have never felt until now how much I am attached to him, how much I owe him. At this moment my eyes are full of tears... Tell me what I should do, and I am ready to do it thoroughly," she beseeched Emma.

But there was nothing she could do; the decision had been made, the new ambassador was already on his way. The imminent departure of the Hamiltons, and with them the admiral — for Nelson, too, had been recalled to England — forced Charlotte to reevaluate her position. Her husband's public rejection made life miserable for the queen in Palermo. As Ferdinand still would not allow her to move back to Naples, she had to find another solution. "I am extremely unhappy... and have only two courses open to me, either to go away or die of chagrin," she confessed bitterly to Emma. "As for our affairs, I know nothing. Intrigues, cabals, and ill humor seem determined to make war upon me." Having no other option, she fell back on family and decided to take her children to see their cousins in Vienna. "My daughter [the empress] writes her earnest desire that I should visit her," the queen confided.

As they were all departing at the same time, they traveled together — Charlotte, her three unmarried daughters, Maria Christina, Maria Amalia, and Maria Antoinetta, aged twenty-one, eighteen, and fifteen, and her nine-year-old son, Leopold; Sir William and Emma (who, unbeknownst to her husband or the other passengers, was six weeks pregnant with her lover's child); Cornelia, who had also decided to return home; and Nelson.★ This illustrious company sailed from Sicily on June 8, 1800. After so much pain and humiliation, Maria Carolina was clearly looking forward to the consoling society of Vienna again. At their first stop, "her Majesty exclaimed with delight 'Leghorn! Leghorn!' [Livorno], no doubt as being on the way to her native land," Cornelia noted.

Their timing could not have been worse. Nelson had no sooner docked than word arrived that Napoleon had triumphed over the Austrian army at a decisive battle in Piedmont, and that consequently Genoa, too, had fallen to the enemy. "Our situation soon became very alarming, for the French army, under General Bonaparte, kept steadily advancing, and at last occupied Lucca, whence one night's march might have brought them [to Livorno]," Cornelia worried. It was decided after much discussion to change their plans and instead attempt the overland route east to the Adriatic coast, and from there to try to catch a ship north to Trieste. "My dismay was now great, for we had to pass within a mile of the advanced posts of the French army; and even the officers and crew . . . were shocked at the idea of the danger to which their admiral was going to expose himself," Cornelia confided.

It took two months of arduous travel bumping along in a dozen or

---

★ Charlotte's youngest daughter, Maria Isabella, age seven, was deemed too delicate for the trip and was left in Sicily; sadly, she died the following year while her mother was away.

so coaches and baggage wagons under the blazing Italian sun, but their luck held out. The royal party managed to outrun Napoleon and found a Russian captain to ferry them to Trieste. By August, the entire group had made it safely to the imperial court. The admiral's celebrity preceded him along the final stage of the route, for Nelson's exploits were as famous in Austria as they had been in Naples. "Great curiosity was expressed to behold the hero of the Nile at every place on the road," Cornelia reported. "At Vienna, whenever Lord Nelson appeared in public, a crowd was collected, and his portrait was hung up as a sign over many shops—even the milliners giving his name to particular dresses," she added in amusement.

For Charlotte, this homecoming was bittersweet. She was very happy to be out of Palermo, to have arrived safely, to see her sister (Maria Elisabeth was allowed out of her convent in Innsbruck to join in the welcoming festivities), her daughter, and her grandchildren. But she also had to say goodbye to her British friends, who were journeying on to England. "My dear Lady and tender friend," the queen wrote poignantly in her last letter before the ambassadress left Vienna at the end of September. "May I soon have the consolation of seeing you again at Naples. I repeat what I have already said, that at all times and places, and under all circumstances, Emma, dear Emma, shall be my friend and sister."

Nelson and a five months pregnant Lady Hamilton, in company with Sir William (still resolutely pretending that nothing in the least bit unusual was going on) and Cornelia, who appears to have been a tad on the naive side, continued their celebratory progress across Austria, Bohemia, and Germany. There were grand parties and fireworks all along the way—at Baden, Lady Hamilton sang for Haydn, and in Prague, Archduke Charles threw Nelson an enormous forty-second birthday party at the palace. The renowned group of expatriates, heavily in debt, finally straggled back into England on November 9, 1800, where they continued to draw the spotlight and claim the fascination of the public, especially after Nelson helpfully caused an enormous scandal by publicly leaving his wife, and Emma, still living with Sir William, discreetly gave birth to a daughter, whom she named Horatia, just in case there was any doubt as to the baby's parentage.★

And in Vienna, Maria Carolina, bereft now of her lifeline to powerful Britain, watched in mounting anxiety as Napoleon and his seemingly invincible army continued their southward sweep toward Naples.

HERE'S THE THING ABOUT world domination: the would-be conqueror doesn't always have the good manners to give advance notice to his opponents of the magnitude of his ambition. Sometimes, like Napoleon, he takes a little and then stops, then takes some more someplace else, all the while professing his ardent desire for peace, until suddenly he's got everything.

Charlotte was among those who understood the scope of the threat right from the beginning. "I believe that Bonaparte will do everything everywhere that he wishes and decides, and that the whole of Europe will be content to watch him with stupefaction," she declared in frustration. So when, soon after her arrival in Vienna, the Corsican general, having decisively beaten the imperial army in Italy, offered Francis a peace treaty that would cede Tuscany to the French but allow Austria to keep Venice, she argued vehemently against it. Napoleon, aware that Maria Carolina spent all her time working to convince her son-in-law to reject these terms and instead continue the war in Italy, referred to her as a "baneful influence."

In the end, though, the queen of Naples was unable to stop the negotiations, and in February 1801, Austria and France signed the Treaty of Lunéville, which granted Napoleon all the territory from Lucca to the outskirts of Rome. Francis's brother, the grand duke of Tuscany, was compensated for the loss of his home and subjects with the duchy of Salzburg (a much less desirable property), but

---

★ How these people have not yet had a miniseries made about them, I will never know.

Charlotte's older sister Maria Amalia was given no such consolation prize. By the terms of this agreement, the fifty-five-year-old duchess of Parma was summarily deposed and exiled. With no place to go, she appealed to her nephew the emperor to be allowed to return to her childhood home of Vienna, but Francis, who still had his mother-in-law with him, drew the line at yet another carping, distressed old lady relation and sent her to Bohemia instead. Maria Amalia died three years later in her small, gloomy quarters in the ancient castle of Prague.

Naples only managed to avoid being swallowed up by France as well because Maria Carolina had made an effort to cultivate the tsar and appealed to this ally to intervene on her husband's behalf. Still, Napoleon insisted that a garrison of 16,000 Frenchmen be stationed inside the kingdom to ensure that the Neapolitan crown did not renew its alliance with Britain, a condition that Ferdinand was forced to ratify. "That is the point [compelling Naples to accept these soldiers] destined to play the biggest part one day...in making me master of the Mediterranean, the principal and constant object of my policy," the victorious general revealed to his brother Joseph.

This was where matters stood when a year later Ferdinand finally agreed to let his wife return to Naples—not because he wanted her but because she had something he needed: their seventeen-year-old daughter, Maria Antoinetta. While Charlotte was away, her eldest son's wife had succumbed to consumption; the king had decided to use this sad event to assert himself and remarry the crown prince to someone from *his* side of the family for a change. His brother, the king of Spain, was anxious to provide one of his daughters for the Neapolitan heir to the throne, and Ferdinand thought it only fair to offer one of his own girls as a bride to the Spanish crown prince in return; Maria Antoinetta had been chosen for this honor.

Nothing bespoke Maria Carolina's fall from power more than these two marriages. For three decades she had kept Naples firmly in Austria's orbit; now a Spanish princess would inherit her throne, she would lose a daughter to Madrid, and she hadn't even been consulted. However, as there was nothing for her to do but accept this arrangement, she and the children returned to Naples to celebrate the weddings in September 1802.

If Charlotte had hoped that her subjects' opinion of her had softened in her absence, she was disabused of this possibility the moment she set foot in the capital. Ferdinand, who after three years had finally been coaxed into giving up the pleasures of Sicily in order to return to the mainland, had arrived before her at the end of June to thunderous applause. People came from all over the realm to cheer his ceremonial procession into the city; the streets were so packed with excited spectators that it took the king the whole morning just to reach the palace. Maria Carolina's reception, by contrast, was distinctly chilly. "The arrival of the Queen gave rise to some public rejoicings, followed by feasts such as are given on the occasions of weddings," the French ambassador to Naples conceded, "but there was not a single moment of joy or elation in all of this. The court was consistently downcast and somber, and the people indifferent and silent."*

Charlotte's relationship with her husband hadn't improved in the two years she had been gone, either. "The King lives in open hostility with the Queen," the French ambassador reported bluntly. "No sooner had she returned from Vienna than he left alone for Caserta . . . their antagonism is such . . . that they do not hide it, even when they appear in public."

Despite these obstacles, within a year of her return, the queen was nonetheless once again in control of the government. General Acton had retired, and Ferdinand had had enough of policy-making; council meetings took too much time away from hunting. It was easier to go back to the old ways and just leave everything to his wife. Maria

---

* The marriages did not go particularly well. Maria Antoinetta, shipped off to Spain, was so unhappy there that within a month she begged to be allowed to return to Italy. When she subsequently died in Madrid at the age of twenty-one, Maria Carolina was convinced that her daughter had been poisoned. Meanwhile, her twenty-five-year-old son's new Spanish bride arrived and was revealed to be only thirteen. Ferdinand's matchmaking skills clearly left much to be desired.

Carolina, for her part, was under no illusion as to the precariousness of their position. The presence of the French soldiers on their soil was a sure sign of Napoleon's further ambitions in southern Italy and thus a danger she could not afford to ignore. "We are on the eve of a great crisis," she predicted to Lord Nelson on December 10, 1803.

Of COURSE, AT THAT POINT, it didn't take much of a prophet to divine Napoleon's intentions. He'd already expanded the French military to record proportions and reorganized it into regional armies capable of attacking simultaneously in all directions. At the same time, he completely dropped the pretense of invading in the name of liberation from tyranny. His first target was in fact his home country, where he abolished what was left of the republic and set himself up as sole ruler instead. As the title of "king" had unfortunate connotations in Paris, Napoleon, whose aspirations were larger anyway, chose a more grandiose designation. On December 2, 1804, in a theatrical demonstration of such blatant hypocrisy that Maria Carolina could not contain herself, he had himself crowned emperor of France in a splendid ceremony at the Cathedral of Notre-Dame. "It was not worth the trouble to condemn and slaughter the best of kings [Louis XVI], dishonor and revile a woman, a daughter of Maria Theresa [Marie Antoinette], a holy princess [Madame Élisabeth], to wallow in massacres . . . kill six hundred prelates in a church, perpetuating horrors of the most barbarous ages at home and abroad, writing whole libraries on liberty, happiness, etc., and at the end of fourteen years become the abject slaves of a little Corsican whom an incredible fortune enabled to exploit all means to succeed!" the queen of Naples scoffed. "And on top of all these abominations he is acclaimed as Emperor!" she raged in disbelief.

The battle lines were drawn; it was only a question of when the hostilities would begin. Although prohibited by the treaty imposed by Napoleon from accepting any military aid from England, Charlotte nonetheless secretly turned once again to Nelson. As keeping Naples and Sicily, and thereby the Mediterranean, out of French hands was of immense strategic importance to the British navy, the admiral promised prompt aid in the event the new emperor of France contrived an excuse to invade southern Italy. "It is part of the plan of the Corsican scoundrel to conquer the kingdom of Naples," Nelson warned. "He has marched thirteen thousand men into the kingdom [the garrisoned soldiers]...and if the poor king remonstrates, or allows us to secure Sicily, he will call it war, and declare a conquest." Maria Carolina was greatly reassured by the admiral's response. "You render us the most essential service, and have another claim on our eternal gratitude," she declared fervently. Charlotte and Ferdinand even overcame their differences long enough to settle on a military strategy. In the event of an invasion, "My wife, son, and I shall divide ourselves. She will take upon herself the defense of Naples, my son of Calabria," Ferdinand announced to Nelson. "I shall go to Sicily," he added (what a surprise).★

Napoleon, correctly identifying the queen of Naples as his chief adversary in all of this, warned Maria Carolina directly to comply strictly with the terms of the treaty or face the consequences. The new emperor, it turned out, had a flair for an evocative turn of phrase. "Let your Majesty listen to this prophecy without impatience," he wrote to her helpfully soon after his coronation. "In the first war caused by you, you and your posterity will cease to reign, and your children will wander, begging in the different countries of Europe for assistance for their parents."

But this threat, with its implication that she had a choice, belied the queen's true situation. Charlotte knew that even if she rejected British aid, she and Ferdinand would keep their thrones in name only. They might become a puppet government of France for a short

---

★ This was one of the few times that the king took any interest at all in affairs of state. Usually, when he had to sign a document, Charlotte had to send someone with the paper and a quill out to wherever he was shooting. A colonel in the Neapolitan army, preparing to defend the kingdom, reported that once, when he ran into Ferdinand coming home from a day's hunting, the monarch asked the soldier where he was going, and the officer replied that he was going off to fight. "Against whom?" Ferdinand inquired. "Against the French, Your Majesty," the colonel was forced to enlighten him.

while, but the likelihood was that her husband would soon be deposed for a candidate more to the French emperor's liking, no matter how slavishly they debased themselves. Their only hope of long-term security, and of holding real authority, was to resist. And so, in addition to Nelson, Maria Carolina also reached out to the Russians, who promised to land an army of 11,000 soldiers on the Adriatic coast in November. These, in combination with the 14,000 or so Neapolitans remaining in active military service and the soldiers and fleet promised by Britain, she reasoned, might be enough to ward off the French. It was only a matter of waiting for Nelson to return.

He never did. The admiral was mortally wounded by the French at the battle of Trafalgar on October 21, 1805. "I believe they have done it at last, my backbone is shot through," he told the ship's surgeon stoically. "You can be of no use to me, go and attend those whose lives can be preserved." Despite the terrible pain, his last thoughts were of Emma; he had a lock of his hair cut off and asked that it be delivered to her. He perished that afternoon. All England grieved: "God gave us victory, but Nelson died," was the last line of the stirring poem written to commemorate the battle.

By the time Maria Carolina discovered her loss, the die had already been cast: the emperor of France had given his brother Joseph an army of 50,000 soldiers and ordered him to invade Naples. "I will finally punish that whore," Napoleon said.

She held out as long as she could, but the Russian troops, who had landed at the end of November, withdrew as soon as it became clear they would be vastly outnumbered. Ferdinand sailed for Sicily on January 23, 1806, leaving his wife and eldest son to defend his throne. Maria Carolina tried to motivate the *lazzaroni* to resist as they had during the previous occupation, but she had not the king's popularity, and of course his having already departed did not inspire confidence. On February 11, with the French army already marching through the kingdom and bearing down rapidly on the capital,

Charlotte finally gave up and for the second time in eight years fled to Sicily with her children in the midst of a terrible storm.

"The House of Naples," proclaimed Joseph Bonaparte with finality, in his first official proclamation upon entering the capital soon afterward, "has ceased to reign."

IT TOOK FIVE DAYS of tossing around on a turbulent sea for the royal family to make the short trip to Palermo, but at least this time everyone survived. Still, the intelligence the queen received upon her arrival was bitter: by order of the emperor of France, Joseph Bonaparte was declared king of Naples and charged with ejecting Ferdinand and Charlotte from their island refuge and conquering that territory as well. "I would rather a ten years' war than leave your kingdom incomplete and Sicily an unsettled question," Napoleon directed his brother.

But Maria Carolina had been here before and had no intention of surrendering her kingdom to her nemesis, the man whom she called, variously, "that ferocious beast," "that Corsican bastard," "that *parvenue*," "that dog!" Nor was she alone in her determination to keep Sicily from falling to Joseph Bonaparte. England was equally committed to this objective. "It is the intention of His Majesty that the French should not in any event be suffered to possess themselves of Sicily," the commander of the British fleet in the Mediterranean was instructed in no uncertain terms. As they had once done for her mother, the English government provided Charlotte and her husband with a hefty stipend—£300,000 a year, which the queen used entirely to foment an insurgency on the mainland, hoping to replicate the success achieved the last time by the Army of the Faithful. Britain also garrisoned soldiers in Sicily to help defend the island, and sent along a general sympathetic to her aims to help wage war against France.

But Naples represented only one front in a vast European conflict that saw victory after victory come to Napoleon. Two years after

Maria Carolina was compelled to flee, the Spanish crown, too, succumbed to the forces of the emperor of France. Since his brother had not succeeded in capturing Sicily, Napoleon, now with another throne on his hands, decided to move Joseph to Madrid and make him king of Spain instead, a promotion that allowed the emperor to install one of his best generals, Joachim Murat, conveniently married to Napoleon's sister Caroline, in Naples in his place. The new king and queen arrived in the capital in September 1808 and immediately made themselves at home in Charlotte's former palaces.* It was particularly aggravating that Napoleon's sister should share a name with her predecessor, as the new Queen Caroline was young and pretty and there were many approving reports of her charms in the papers.

Matters came to a head in the summer of 1809. War raged in Austria; Napoleon led a massive French army, 230,000 men in total, toward Vienna. Archduke Charles, in charge of the defense of the realm, launched himself and his soldiers into the path of this onslaught in a furious bid to halt, or at the very least impede, the enemy's progress, in the hopes of ensuring the survival of the monarchy. At the same time, Charlotte convinced England to launch a combined British-Sicilian attack against Murat. On June 11, a fleet of 250 ships carrying a force of some 14,000 soldiers left the port of Messina to take back the mainland.

Disappointingly, they never got closer than the small island of Ischia, off the coast of Naples. On July 6, 1809, Napoleon, after occupying Vienna, scored a decisive victory against Charles at Wagram, just outside the city, forcing Francis to sue for peace. Discouraged by this news and by their lack of progress—it took a month just to secure Ischia—the fleet in which Maria Carolina had put so much hope withdrew without even attempting an attack on the mainland and returned to Sicily. This was followed by the even

---

* To appease the population, they, too, made sure that the blood of the martyr liquefied. "It pains me to hear you have played monkey tricks in honor of S. Gennaro," Napoleon complained to Murat.

more shattering news that on October 14, 1809, as part of the terms of the peace treaty with the French, Austria had agreed to recognize Napoleon's sister Caroline and her husband as the legitimate sovereigns of Naples.

Charlotte's despair at these events was very great. But there was yet one last thunderbolt to come. After his triumph at Vienna, with all of Europe at his feet, Napoleon naturally turned his thoughts to his legacy. Although he loved his wife, Josephine, she had failed to provide him with a child, and what good was the richest, most expansive hereditary monarchy in the world to a man without a son to whom he could pass along his august name and empire? It was clearly time to divorce Josephine and get himself a new, young wife, preferably someone with an exalted pedigree, to make up for the comparative inferiority of his own lineage. And for prestigious royal ancestry and top-of-the-line breeding, Napoleon knew that he really couldn't do better than a Habsburg.

And so, on February 7, 1810, a marriage contract was signed in which Francis, who could not afford to go to war again and so had no real choice, agreed to marry his eldest daughter, eighteen-year-old Marie Louise, to forty-year-old Napoleon. In a surreal reenactment of the past, as though history had folded upon itself, Marie Louise was married by proxy in Vienna (with poor Archduke Charles having to stand in for the bridegroom) and sent off in a legion of carriages through the narrow streets jammed with admiring well-wishers. Again was she stripped completely of her clothing at the border of her new domain (now, as a result of the recent conflict, in Bavaria) and re-dressed in French fashions in a hastily completed pavilion composed of three rooms, one for the Austrians, one for the French, and one in the middle decorated with tapestries. Napoleon's sister Caroline (an unfortunate choice under the circumstances) had come all the way up from Naples to meet her new sister-in-law and play the role of Madame Etiquette, which she did to perfection, even to forcing a tearful Marie Louise to leave behind her little dog. Again was the bridal procession met with cheering crowds, illuminations, and little girls in white dresses bearing bouquets for the charming Austrian princess as she and her entourage wended their way west through the French countryside to Paris. Again were the bride and groom married in great splendor; again did they show themselves on the balcony of the Tuileries to the adoring multitudes crammed into the gardens below; and, finally, chillingly, again did Marie Louise observe, just as Marie Antoinette had when as dauphine she was first introduced to the thrill of the crowds in Paris, that "she was enabled to appreciate the French character, and to judge how easily she could accustom herself to a country where the attachment borne to a sovereign...and the affection such as the people seemed to feel for her...made her hope for many happy days."

And from her exile in Sicily, a weary and depressed Maria Carolina, informed of this nuptial alliance and with it her new family connection to Napoleon, could hardly believe it. "This was all that was missing in my misery," she exclaimed tartly. "To become the devil's grandmother!"

ALTHOUGH THIS MARRIAGE EASED the threat from the French by causing a rupture between Napoleon and his ambitious sister and her husband—Caroline and Murat were suspicious of the Austrian alliance, fearing that Marie Louise would influence the emperor in favor of the woman he now called "grandmamma, the Queen of Sicily"—this did not materially improve Maria Carolina's situation.* The queen was fifty-nine years old, worn down and frequently ill, plagued by loss and failure, desperate to recover her throne and yet overwhelmed by the enormity of the diplomatic, political, financial, and military tasks necessary to accomplish this goal. To these burdens were added the personal sorrows that came thick and fast over this period: her two eldest daughters died—both Francis's wife (mother of Marie Louise) and her second girl, the grand duchess of

---

* Murat even accused Charlotte of conspiring with Napoleon against him after a letter forged in her name surfaced appealing to her new grandson for help; Charlotte always flatly denied this charge.

Tuscany—as did her youngest, poor Maria Antoinetta; Sir William had preceded Nelson to the grave; Emma, still in England, was out of favor and impoverished. Charlotte's favorite daughter, Maria Christina, married the brother of the deposed king of Sardinia and left Sicily to be with her husband's family, while the queen's remaining daughter, Maria Amalia, was wed to none other than the son of Marie Antoinette's sworn enemy, the duc d'Orléans. So reduced were the queen's expectations by this time that it was enough for her when her French son-in-law disavowed his father's actions during the revolution. "I ought to detest you and yet I feel a liking for you," was all she said.

There are people who rise above defeat, loneliness, and frustration with grace and tact; Maria Carolina was not one of these. She had always worn her distress openly, weeping at her setbacks, complaining of her health and nerves, swearing that her troubles would be the death of her, and railing at those who opposed her plans. But now the British officials stationed on Sicily began to send alarming reports to London of the queen's unstable mental state. She refused to give up her claim to the throne and continued to push for the overthrow of Murat and her own reinstatement in Naples, they noted. She was intriguing with spies, encouraging assassination attempts on her rivals, screaming at her courtiers, and abusing her subjects by her authoritarian rule. Not surprisingly given her emotional and physical condition, she was prone to violent headaches, for which the British ambassador revealed disapprovingly that she drank six grams of opium a day (a common remedy; Nelson had similarly taken this drug, also known as laudanum, regularly for pain), and displayed "fits of passion that amounted to madness, so that even her attendants were afraid of her." At one point the queen had a paralytic seizure of such severity that she collapsed senseless; such was her unpopularity on the island that the wife of the English ambassador noted that many Sicilians expressed disappointment when after twenty-four hours she awoke and recovered.

The problem with relying on these accounts of Charlotte's behavior, however, is that they were clearly self-serving. History was in the act of folding over again on itself: as they had once done to her mother, the British had decided to brush aside the queen's interests in pursuit of their own. After Napoleon's defeat of Austria, England's objective in the Mediterranean diverged significantly from Maria Carolina's. She wanted Britain to continue to wage war on Naples so that she could reclaim her throne. England, however, had given that up as a lost cause. Instead, what the British wanted was control of Sicily. This would obviously be much easier to achieve if the meddlesome Charlotte was out of the way. Suggesting that she was drug-addicted and possibly deranged helped lay the foundation for her removal. "I think it is absolutely necessary that the Queen should cease to take the lead in public affairs," the British ambassador advised London. "The poor Sicilians have been tormented long enough, and if they were now released from their torment, things would go better, for without her [Charlotte] the King [Ferdinand] could be easily managed," his wife seconded, helpfully giving away the whole plan.

So that's what they did. In December of 1811, a new general was sent from London to Sicily. Maria Carolina, used to the erudite Sir William and the chivalrous Nelson, referred to this new officer as a "boorish corporal." He certainly could not be called subtle. Within a year, the British commander had compelled Ferdinand to abdicate in favor of the crown prince, who was much more pliable; arrested the queen in preparation for forced deportation; and taken over the Sicilian government. Charlotte, who had seen this coming and fought her dethronement tenaciously if fruitlessly every step of the way, was scathing in her final interview with this erstwhile ally. "Was it for this I escaped the axes, conspiracies and betrayals of the Neapolitan Jacobins? Was it for this that I helped Nelson to win the battle of the Nile? For this that I brought your army to Sicily? General, is this your English honor?" she demanded, outraged, just as Maria Theresa had once long before confronted Sir Thomas Robinson. Even Ferdinand, who had no use for his wife, protested this treatment. "I cannot believe there is any truth in what I hear about their insistence on my wife's removal and their threats to use coercion in case she will not go. However, should this be true, let my son realize that I shall allow no joking on the subject, and that for the slightest outrage against her he will be responsible to me, and will have to render me a strict account," he wrote.

But the general had the garrison of soldiers and thus all the power on his side, and Ferdinand was hardly the man to stand up to him. On June 14, 1813, at the age of sixty, Maria Carolina, having been deemed too dangerous to remain on the island, was deported from Sicily on a British ship. Just before she left, the queen went to pray one last time in the local church. Contrary to everything written about her by the British diplomats, after the service concluded a huge crowd of her Sicilian subjects followed her carriage as she was transported to the shoreline, weeping at her departure.

The queen herself was under no illusions as to the magnitude of the English betrayal. "I have been deprived of the government of my own country—of the dignity of my character—of the affection of my husband and children!...And then, I am accused of treason, because, forsooth, I wished to recover my just rights as an independent sovereign, a wife and mother," she summarized with brutal accuracy.

WITH NOWHERE ELSE TO GO, Maria Carolina returned once more to Vienna, even though Francis had made it clear he didn't want her, going so far as to issue orders prohibiting her from entering the city. But Charlotte was still a queen, and she had no intention of being consigned to Bohemia like some ancient, moth-eaten frock, as had her older sister Maria Amalia. "The daughter of Maria Theresa—a wanderer, an outcast!" she fretted. So she ignored her son-in-law's commands and brazened her way into the Austrian capital anyway, surmising that, once arrived, the emperor would not have the nerve to evict her.

She judged correctly. Francis, bowing to family ties, allowed her to stay. It didn't hurt that her timing was propitious. After nearly two decades of herculean success, Napoleon was finally on the run. The year before, he had led an enormous French army into Russia, with disastrous results. Capitalizing on his weakness, his numerous enemies (of which, the marriage to Marie Louise notwithstanding, Austria was one; that's what happens when you insist on taking other people's property) had banded together against him. In November 1813, just as Maria Carolina was settling into her apartments in Vienna, France was attacked simultaneously by Russia, Prussia, Austria, and Britain. Within a month, these allied forces had penetrated the kingdom, cutting it off with a line of soldiers that stretched diagonally some 300 miles from Flanders to the Rhône.

That was the end. Despite his best efforts, Napoleon's usually reliable luck deserted him. On March 30, 1814, Paris surrendered to the combined Prussian and Russian armies. On April 10, the Corsican general was stripped of his titles and thrones and sent into exile on the island of Elba. (Marie Louise and her only child, three-year-old Napoleon, escaped this fate by fleeing Paris for Vienna ahead of the occupation.) And on May 4, 1814, in a final, incredible reversion, Louis XVI's middle brother, the comte de Provence, a member of the triumphant coalition, rode into Paris and ascended the throne as Louis XVIII.

And that was not all. Italy, too, had been liberated. To save themselves, Murat and Caroline had turned on Napoleon and signed an alliance with Austria. There was to be a great congress in Vienna in September composed of all the victorious allies to negotiate the terms of the peace and divide the spoils. Charlotte was already making plans to return to Sicily.

She never made it. On the evening of September 7, 1814, Maria Carolina retired for the evening at the usual hour. Sometime during the night the sixty-two-year-old queen, the last surviving child of the great Maria Theresa, who perhaps more than any of her siblings most resembled her mother in strength, courage, and dedication, suffered some sort of seizure, most probably a stroke. She was found dead the next morning with one arm reaching out for the bellpull to call for help.

She was buried with her parents and the rest of her siblings, save Marie Antoinette, in the subterranean family vault at the Capuchin Church, which survives today. The frightened teenager who had been compelled to leave Vienna for Naples, and gone on to shoulder rule in that faraway land for forty years, had found her way home.

Epilogue

NINE MONTHS AFTER Maria Carolina's death, her husband was restored to his throne. Ferdinand made his triumphant reentry into Naples on June 7, 1815, to an ecstatic welcome. So pleased were his subjects to see him that on his first night back to the San Carlo theater, where in earlier days he had rained fistfuls of steaming macaroni down on his countrymen, Ferdinand received a half-hour standing ovation. He was already remarried—he had wed his mistress within weeks of hearing of Charlotte's demise—and, once returned, remained on the mainland to devote the final decade of his life to his chief love: hunting. "How happy I am with a wife who lets me do what I will, and a minister who leaves me nothing to do!" he was often heard to exclaim. On the evening of January 3, 1825, at the age of seventy-three, he retired to bed, and like his first spouse, died sometime in the predawn hours, most probably of a stroke. His and Maria Carolina's descendants ruled Naples in a continual line until the second half of the nineteenth century. Charlotte is still reviled in Italy, even today, as the cruel tyrant who orchestrated the Chastisement.

In Vienna, Albert, too, survived in comfort to old age. Unlike Ferdinand, he never remarried. After Mimi's death, the art collection they had begun together consumed all his time. He added to it, catalogued it, penned treatises on the subject, and exhibited it privately to scholars and other collectors. At his death—he outlived his wife by nearly a quarter century—he had amassed some 14,000 drawings and over 200,000 prints. When he finally passed away, on February 10, 1822, at the venerable age of eighty-three, he left it all to Archduke Charles, who kept this treasure chest of artwork intact and opened it to the public. Today, it stands as the Albertina Museum. To visit is to step back in time and behold the principles of the encyclopedists made manifest. And although Mimi's contribution to this impressive collection—"Perhaps the most beautiful and most exquisite in Europe," as it was known in its day—has been reduced over the past two centuries to the afterthought of a suffix (she is the "tina" of the museum's title), her presence, too, is tangible. It was she, not Albert, who, as a painter, brought art into their lives; she whose wealth and connections made the accumulation of such a vast store of masterpieces possible; she whose taste and eye informed all the major purchases. This was her gift to him: she lives and breathes in it. She even saved it for him, for without the care she took to pack it up and transport it out of Brussels, it would undoubtedly have been appropriated by Napoleon, as Laeken was, and today would have been broken up, with the majority of the prints consigned to a basement room at the Louvre.

Unlike that of her favorite daughter, there is no need for a visitor to search out Maria Theresa's spirit in Vienna: it is everywhere. Her statue dominates the prominent main square named for her; her name is on every tour guide's lips; the city is as much hers today as it was when she reigned more than 250 years ago. Although at the time of her death her subjects rejoiced (they were angry with her for having raised taxes in order to pay for Joseph's war), they soon learned to regret her loss, and nostalgia for her rule grew with time. Today, she is one of only three women rulers—Elizabeth I and Catherine the Great being the other two—who are celebrated for having left an indelible imprint on the history of Europe.

Count Fersen's life was cut short by the same forces that had vanquished his love's. He was waylaid, surrounded, and pummeled to death in Sweden by a Jacobin-inspired mob on June 20, 1810, exactly nineteen years to the day after he assisted Marie Antoinette and her family in their aborted flight from Paris. Fersen was fifty-four years old at the time of his assassination. He never married.

With the reinstatement of the French monarchy in 1814, the royal succession picked up more or less where it had left off: after the death of the childless comte de Provence came the comte d'Artois as Charles X, so both of Marie Antoinette's brothers-in-law would ultimately achieve their ambition to rule. But the comte d'Artois's reign was short-lived; history again turned back on itself when his subjects rebelled against him in 1830 and he was forced to abdicate in favor of his far more popular cousin, the duc d'Orléans. As this was the same duc d'Orléans who had married Maria Carolina's daughter Maria Amalia, she became queen of France, ascending to the throne once held by her mother's cherished sister, Marie Antoinette.

In 1815, soon after his return to Paris, the comte de Provence, intent on reestablishing the family honor (and with it his own legitimacy), commissioned funerary statues of Louis XVI and Marie Antoinette by a prestigious artist and conducted a search for their corpses so their remains could be transferred to the family crypt at Saint-Denis, for over a thousand years the traditional burial site of French sovereigns. On the testimony of one of the queen's gravediggers, the cemetery plot where they had been interred was identified. The royal couple was discovered to have been buried one on top of the other; their bones were removed and transferred to Saint-Denis, and there they have remained. The corpse of Louis's sister, Madame Élisabeth, having been thrown into a mass grave with the bodies of those who were guillotined with her, was never found, so today she lies anonymously in death with those whom she sought to comfort in life.

Despite an intensive search, the body of the dauphin, the poor child who died of neglect in prison at the age of ten, was never unearthed, leading to speculation that he was not in fact dead but instead had been smuggled secretly out of captivity to safety. This rumor caused his successors no end of inconvenience, as every now and then an impostor would emerge, claiming to be Louis XVII, the legitimate heir to the throne. But in a macabre twist, it turned out that the physician called in to attend the boy in his final hours had, upon his small charge's demise, cut out his heart and preserved it, pickled, in a jar as a souvenir. This valuable organ was subsequently stolen from the doctor and fell out of sight until 1975, when it was tracked down in Spain and returned to France. In 2004, the preserved heart was tested for DNA against Marie Antoinette's and found to be a match, thus confirming its authenticity.

In a curious omission, Louis's remains were never publicly tested for paternity.

Acknowledgments

This book would not have been possible without the aid of several key individuals. Heike Grebenstein generously volunteered to get me started with the research on Maria Christina by sitting for hours roughly translating some 150 pages of German while I frantically scribbled notes. I was extraordinarily fortunate to then find Barbara Ann Schmutzler, a professional translator, to take over the task of deciphering the German sources—my, that was a happy day for me! Not only did Barbara's skill and dedication bring Maria Christina to life, but her friendship also helped carry me through the many years of research. Barbara was as curious and committed to the duchess of Teschen as I was, and I am enormously in her debt.

I am also deeply appreciative of the help Dr. Franz Szabo, Professor Emeritus of History and Classics at the University of Alberta, gave me in navigating the twists and turns of imperial foreign policy during the years of Maria Theresa's and Joseph's reigns. I first came to Professor Szabo when I reached out and wrote him a fan letter about his book *The Seven Years War in Europe, 1756–1763* (hands down the most lucid and compelling account of that conflict available, I cannot recommend it highly enough) and he was gracious enough to take an interest in my research and to answer my questions. He even shared a letter written by Maria Carolina to her brother Leopold that he had discovered in an archive. Dr. Szabo is also the leading authority on Count Kaunitz and his insights into that statesman's career were invaluable.

Of similarly critical importance to the writing of this book was

Dr. Linda Gray's contribution on Autism Spectrum Disorder. Dr. Gray, a brilliant developmental pediatrician with decades of experience at Yale New Haven Hospital, is one of the most caring and dedicated physicians I know. She was kind enough to respond to my queries at length and I have absolute confidence in her opinion; she has worked extensively with children on the spectrum. I cannot thank her enough for sharing her expertise in this area.

I am also very grateful to Asya Muchnick at Little, Brown and Company for her enthusiasm for my work and especially for her careful edit; the book is demonstrably better for her suggestions. Evan Hansen-Bundy, also at Little, Brown, provided much needed support and encouragement, and Pat Jalbert-Levine and the rest of the production team were unfailingly patient and professional. Maddy Price and Natalie Dawkins at Weidenfeld & Nicolson tracked down images and provided valuable input. To Alan Samson, who from the first has championed my work and upon whose opinion I rely utterly, thank you thank you. And to Michael Carlisle, who has been with me from the beginning, my heartfelt appreciation. I couldn't have made this journey without you.

But the true heroes here are my family. To Lee and Tyler, whose adventurous spirits inspire me every day, and who provided any number of soothing photos of Patton happily destroying his chew toy to cheer me up when I felt overwhelmed, thank you. I love you both so much. And, finally, to my husband, Larry, who lived with a crazy woman who spoke to dead people for the past four years, and who, despite having his own books to write, dropped everything to help me when I needed it, who filled the role of editor, tech support staff, therapist, lover, and best friend—dear heart, I owe you everything.

Notes

Epigraphs

ix   "I would rather seem weak": Wolf, *Marie Christine*, v. 1, 55. Translation by Heike Grebenstein.

ix   "You do not know me": Wolf, *Leopold II und Marie Christine*, 66.

ix   "I leave my justification": *Correspondance inédite de Marie-Caroline, Reine de Naples et de Sicile*, 2.

ix   "Of all the daughters": Campan, *Memoirs of the Private Life of Marie Antoinette*, v. 2, 242.

Introduction

4   "She made me take": Campan, *Memoirs of the Private Life of Marie Antoinette*, v. 2, 59–60.

4   "The affair was decided": Ibid., 60.

4   "I fear the worst...take your family with you": Rocheterie, *The Life of Marie Antoinette*, v. 2, 19.

5   "whether the Polignacs...rid of all such bad people": Campan, *Memoirs of the Private Life of Marie Antoinette*, v. 2, 63.

6   "You are so good": *Lettres de Marie-Antoinette*, tome II, 173.

6   "My patient [Louis XVI] still has stiffness": *The Life and Letters of Madame Élisabeth de France*, 54.

7   "We are off...let us be off": Lenotre, *The Flight of Marie Antoinette*, 31.

Chapter 1. An Imperial Decree

11   "It is manifest": Voltaire, *The Philosophical Dictionary*, 128.

11   "a beauty that has been": Montagu, *The Best Letters of Lady Mary Wortley Montagu*, 80.

11   "She has a vast": Ibid., 82.

11   "monstrous and contrary": Ibid., 81.

14   20 suffocating yards of flannel: Vehse, *Memoirs of the Court and Aristocracy of Austria*, v. 2, 88.

14   imposed by the *pactum mutuae successionis*: Ingrao, *The Habsburg Monarch 1618–1815*, 129.

15   "I have heard that the Emperor": *The Letters of Madame,* v. 1, 253. For those who read *Rival Queens,* this is Liselotte.

15   "Well now, I never dreamed": Mahan, *Maria Theresa of Austria,* 18.

15   "loves his Queen so tenderly": Ibid.

15*n*   "I shall be eternally grateful": Ibid., 18–19.

16   Wilhelmine fought back: For those who read *Daughters of the Winter Queen,* Joseph's widow was none other than Wilhelmine Amalia, youngest daughter of John Frederick, duke of Hanover, by his wife, Bénédicte (herself the daughter of Edward, Prince Palatine, and Anna de Gonzaga). Wilhelmine had been brought up in France and was educated at the abbey of Maubuisson, run by her great-aunt Louise Hollandine, Princess Palatine. That is why Liselotte, duchess of Orléans, Louise Hollandine's niece, knew so much about Joseph's marriage, and why Wilhelmine was able, at least in the beginning, to draw powerful supporters from France and Hanover to her cause.

17   "right before the eyes": Mahan, *Maria Theresa of Austria,* 6.

17*n*   "Which of the ten patriarchs": Pick, *Empress Maria Theresa,* 18.

19   "the Pragmatic Sanction could only be guaranteed": Moffat, *Maria Theresa,* 21.

Chapter 2. *Archduchess of Austria*

21   "The motto": Voltaire, *Sequel of the Age of Louis XIV,* 29.

24   "Baron Pfaffenberg": Coxe, *History of the House of Austria,* v. 3, 134.

24   3 million in gold: McKay, *Prince Eugene of Savoy,* 213.

24   30,000 soldiers: Coxe, *Memoirs of the Life and Administration of Sir Robert Walpole,* v. 2, 588.

27   "neither beautiful nor ugly": Carlyle, *History of Friedrich II, of Prussia,* v. 3, 77.

27   "She sighs and pines": Moffat, *Maria Theresa,* 49–50.

28   "was a princess": Ibid., 49.

29   "No abdication, no Archduchess": Ibid., 52.

29   "What was most remarkable": Ibid., 55–56.

30   "I greatly love Lorraine": Vizetelly, *The True Story of Alsace-Lorraine,* 171.

31   "The important and singular": Coxe, *History of the House of Austria,* v. 3, 207.

33   "The whole country of Tuscany": Moffat, *Maria Theresa,* 63.

33   "Everything in this Court": Coxe, *History of the House of Austria,* v. 3, 225.

34   "Our only hope": Moffat, *Maria Theresa,* 66.

34   "Will it never be granted to me": Ibid., 66.

34   "It is my greatest comfort": Ibid., 68.

35   "A pot of mushrooms": Mahan, *Maria Theresa of Austria,* 54.

Chapter 3. *Queen of Hungary*

36   "I am going to play": Broglie, *Frederick the Great and Maria Theresa,* v. 1, 105.

36   "Though I am only a queen": Mahan, *Maria Theresa of Austria,* 55.

36   "An accession in these countries": Moffat, *Maria Theresa*, 71–72.

37   "The Turks seemed": Coxe, *History of the House of Austria*, v. 3, 242.

37   "The murmur of tumultuous voices": Broglie, *Frederick the Great and Maria Theresa*, v. 1, 51.

38   "distinguish between": Moffat, *Maria Theresa*, 72.

39   "You are aware": Crankshaw, *Maria Theresa*, 41.

39   "Really, the King [Frederick] is behaving": Broglie, *Frederick the Great and Maria Theresa*, v. 1, 80.

39   "of fulfilling his engagements": Moffat, *Maria Theresa*, 77.

39   "every letter they receive": Ibid.

40   "Your Majesty [Charles] may rest": Broglie, *Frederick the Great and Maria Theresa*, v. 1, 61.

40   "The Queen gains the hearts": Moffat, *Maria Theresa*, 76.

40   "perfect tranquility and submission": Ibid.

40   "He dropped the mask": Broglie, *Frederick the Great and Maria Theresa*, v. 1, 282.

41   "His principal occupation": *Memoirs of Frederica Sophia Wilhelmina*, v. 1, 39–40.

43   300 noblemen's sons: Carlyle, *History of Friedrich II of Prussia*, v. 2, 15.

43   "My brother was odious to him": *Memoirs of Frederica Sophia Wilhelmina*, v. 1, 41.

43   "shroud, *Sterbe-kittel,* or death-clothes": Carlyle, *History of Friedrich II of Prussia*, v. 2, 214.

43   "The poor prince": *Memoirs of Frederica Sophia Wilhelmina*, v. 1, 123.

43   crimson dressing gown: Carlyle, *History of Friedrich II of Prussia*, v. 2, 213.

43   "Thy obstinate perverse disposition": Ibid., 167.

44   "I am in the utmost despair": *Memoirs of Frederica Sophia Wilhelmina*, v. 1, 146.

44n "more beautiful than they paint": Carlyle, *History of Friedrich II of Prussia*, v. 2, 151.

45   "How wretched I am": *Memoirs of Frederica Sophia Wilhelmina*, v. 1, 244.

46   "Thank God that's over!": Blanning, *Frederick the Great*, 61.

47   "When one is in a good position": Broglie, *Frederick the Great and Maria Theresa*, v. 1, 90.

47   "a couple of millions": Ibid.

47n "Troops always ready to act": Ibid., 88.

48   "Do not be afraid; he will be just like": Ibid., 81.

48   "I am going to Silesia": Ibid., 96.

48   "I bear in one hand... rather than treat with him": Ibid., 97–98.

49   "I cannot remember": Moffat, *Maria Theresa*, 85.

50   "Her Majesty's subjects": Ibid., 86.

50   "Farewell friends": Mahan, *Maria Theresa of Austria*, 111.

51   "all covered with fame": Broglie, *Frederick the Great and Maria Theresa*, v. 1, 236.

51 "The security of Hanover": Coxe, *Memoirs of Horatio, Lord Walpole,* v. 2, 35.

51 "Not only for political reasons": Crankshaw, *Maria Theresa,* 59.

52*n* "If God Himself": Ibid., 50.

53 "the old laws": Moffat, *Maria Theresa,* 100.

54 "her long, loose, yellow locks": Ibid.

54 "The queen was all charm": Coxe, *History of the House of Austria,* v. 3, 268.

54 "Long live our Lady": Moffat, *Maria Theresa,* 101.

Chapter 4. Queen of Bohemia

55 "We shall only need": Broglie, *Frederick the Great and Maria Theresa,* v. 1, 166.

55 "Although a woman": Broglie, *Frederick the Great and Maria Theresa,* v. 2, 58–59.

56 "Nothing can equal": Broglie, *Frederick the Great and Maria Theresa,* v. 1, 243.

56 "You can understand": Ibid., 271.

56 "On hearing, beyond possibility": Carlyle, *History of Friedrich II of Prussia,* v. 5, 41.

57 "I hope very much": Broglie, *Frederick the Great and Maria Theresa,* v. 2, 12.

57 "I deceive my ministers": Ibid., 12–13.

57 "This proposal is a snare": Ibid., 15.

58 "I am at the head": Coxe, *History of the House of Austria,* v. 3, 258–59.

59 "The misfortune of our situation": Broglie, *Frederick the Great and Maria Theresa,* v. 2, 41.

60 "At the sight of him": Moffat, *Maria Theresa,* 118.

61 "Either they think me a rogue": Broglie, *Frederick the Great and Maria Theresa,* v. 2, 64.

61 "No one can be more touched": Ibid., 65.

61 "We must certainly": Ibid., 80.

62 "We want to put an end": Ibid., 75.

62 "Nothing could exceed his": Ibid., 77–78.

63 "Be fortunate [in battle]": Ibid., 94.

63 "If you have him to-day": Coxe, *History of the House of Austria,* v. 3, 263.

64 "Here is Prague lost": Broglie, *Frederick the Great and Maria Theresa,* v. 2, 107–8.

65 "her whole power and resources": Moffat, *Maria Theresa,* 133.

66*n* "What can I do about it?": Broglie, *Frederick the Great and Maria Theresa,* v. 2, 90–91.

66*n* "He comes to our aid": Ibid., 108–9.

67 *"A Statement of the Reasons":* Ibid., 197.

67 "had it emanated": Ibid.

68 "My dear heart": Ibid., 208.

68 "I am going to advance": Ibid., 212.

69 "Sire, Prince Charles": Ibid., 217.

69 "that these concessions": Ibid., 224.

70   "I will not let it be touched": Ibid., 225.

71   "I will grant no capitulation": Coxe, *History of the House of Austria*, v. 3, 283.

73   "take the command": Carlyle, *History of Friedrich II of Prussia*, v. 5, 260.

74   "Whoever thought himself": Pick, *Empress Maria Theresa*, 117.

Chapter 5. Holy Roman Empress

75   "If you want to get": Carlyle, *History of Friedrich II of Prussia*, v. 4, 128.

75   "The King of Prussia only wishes": Bright, *Maria Theresa*, 40.

75   "Her countenance is beautiful": Mahan, *Maria Theresa of Austria*, 228.

76   "this being most necessary": Crankshaw, *Maria Theresa*, 108.

76   "From now on, without intermission": Ibid.

76   "Every human being": Pick, *Empress Maria Theresa*, 168.

77   "for a Queen": Moffat, *Maria Theresa*, 123.

77   "loves pleasure": Mahan, *Maria Theresa of Austria*, 229–30.

77n   "Nothing affects him": Perkins, *France under Louis XV*, v. 1, 238.

78   "Sometimes only a few hours": Mahan, *Maria Theresa of Austria*, 230.

80   "If I am to be robbed": Perkins, *France under Louis XV*, v. 1, 259.

81   "The Queen and her sister": Moffat, *Maria Theresa*, 143.

81   "Tell me all this again": Morris, *Maria Theresa*, 121.

82   "The King has his master": Perkins, *France under Louis XV*, v. 1, 256–57.

83   "At last we are in Alsace": Ibid., 281.

84   "The victory of Dettingen": Dover, *The Life of Frederick the Second*, v. 1, 225.

84   "She detests Your Majesty": Mahan, *Maria Theresa of Austria*, 230.

85   "We must crush": Perkins, *France under Louis XV*, v. 1, 291.

85n   "The King asks for nothing": Reddaway, *Frederick the Great and the Rise of Prussia*, 137.

86   "What can I expect": Perkins, *France under Louis XV*, 293.

87   "God could have permitted": Moffat, *Maria Theresa*, 152.

88   "This was the only event": Dover, *The Life of Frederick the Second*, v. 1, 249.

89   "Everything that is harmful": Browning, *The War of the Austrian Succession*, 203–4.

90   "My determination is taken": Carlyle, *History of Friedrich II of Prussia*, v. 4, 100.

91   "There can be no God": Reddaway, *Frederick the Great and the Rise of Prussia*, 146.

91   "In war artifice": Coxe, *History of the House of Austria*, v. 3, 314.

92   "England has this year": Ibid., 316–17.

93   "The imperial dignity!": Ibid., 318.

94   "Francis, from Heidelberg": *The Autobiography of Goethe*, 161.

94   "welcomed in the city": Ibid.

94   "older persons, who were present": Ibid., 167.

95n   "Look! It's the Queen": Pick, *Empress Maria Theresa*, 146.

96   "My circumstances in Italy": Bright, *Maria Theresa*, 48.

96 "Nobody can deny": Pick, *Empress Maria Theresa*, 141–42.

97 "Henceforth it will not be advisable": Ibid., 153.

97 "However remote the thought": Ibid., 155.

98 "I hope that this event": Morris, *Maria Theresa*, 140.

99 "May the Almighty": Pick, *Empress Maria Theresa*, 185.

99 "Is it not better": Perkins, *France under Louis XV*, v. 1, 363–64.

100 "The English system": Ibid., 371–72.

100 "It is too late": Coxe, *Memoirs of the Administration of the Right Honourable Henry Pelham*, v. 1, 371.

101 "You sir, who had such": Coxe, *History of the House of Austria*, v. 3, 340.

102 "It is worthwhile": Perkins, *France under Louis XV*, v. 1, 368.

102 "The men who govern": Ibid., 369.

102 "This pacification": Ibid., 377.

103 "I forthwith turned my thoughts": Morris, *Maria Theresa*, 145.

Chapter 6. Imperial Affairs

104 "Thus were two powers": *Posthumous Works of Frederic II*, v. 2, 15.

104 "Even in the distant": Pick, *Empress Maria Theresa*, 262–63.

104 "without an army": Bright, *Maria Theresa*, 65–66.

104 "I believe that nobody": Morris, *Maria Theresa*, 155.

105 "Better to rely": Pick, *Empress Maria Theresa*, 201.

105 "By the extraordinary Providence": Moffat, *Maria Theresa*, 174.

105 "a wise man": Ibid., 175.

106 "All the ministers": Pick, *Empress Maria Theresa*, 190.

106 "the good and ancient": Moffat, *Maria Theresa*, 176.

107 "Who would believe": Macartney, *The Habsburg and Hohenzollern Dynasties*, 130–31.

107 "whose lectures surely": Pick, *Empress Maria Theresa*, 234.

108 "Nothing will be more": Ibid., 226.

108 "By these various cures": *Posthumous Works of Frederick II*, v. 2, 14.

109 "the fat one": Pick, *Empress Maria Theresa*, 257.

109 "I am no longer the same person": Ibid., 226.

110 "who had been defending": Ibid., 203.

110 "Don't mind me": Mahan, *Maria Theresa of Austria*, 265.

110 "He used to dine": Pick, *Empress Maria Theresa*, 165.

111 "glorious slavery": Moffat, *Maria Theresa*, 183.

112 "voluntary gifts": Pick, *Empress Maria Theresa*, 230.

112n "No person can possess": Voltaire, *Letters on England*, 36.

113 "I should have supposed": Perkins, *France under Louis XV*, v. 2, 31.

114 "He's coming!": Mahan, *Maria Theresa of Austria*, 193.

114 "had changed the old system": Perkins, *France under Louis XV*, v. 2, 34.

115 "She was rather": Williams, *Madame de Pompadour*, 22–23.

115n "thanks to the tears": Ibid., 22.

117   "You are the most": Perkins, *France under Louis XV,* v. 1, 457.

117   "My life is a perpetual": Ibid., 462.

117   "The more I see": Perkins, *France under Louis XV,* v. 2, 31.

119   "to the Fork of Ohio": Fowler, *Empires at War,* 37.

120   "I heard the bullets": Ibid., 42.

120   referred to Washington's action as "assassination": Ibid., 47.

121   "We have drawn": Reddaway, *Frederick the Great and the Rise of Prussia,* 156.

122   "the three petticoats": Mahan, *Maria Theresa of Austria,* 198.

122   "My dogs destroy": Campbell, *Frederick the Great,* v. 2, 324.

122   "I fear Russia": Fairburn, *Frederick the Great,* 41.

122*n*   "and you can smell": Blanning, *Frederick the Great,* 142.

123   "The King [Louis XV] disliked the King of Prussia": Du Hausset, *The Private Memoirs of Louis XV,* 168.

123   "Saxony would be": Macartney, *The Habsburg and Hohenzollern Dynasties,* 341.

123   "France...cannot suffer": Ibid.

125   "Now surely the King": Perkins, *France under Louis XV,* v. 2, 52.

125   "Never during all my reign": Ibid., 53.

Chapter 7. The Sisterhood of the Three Petticoats

126   "I have not abandoned": Coxe, *History of the House of Austria,* v. 3, 363.

126   "I am always a long time": Bain, *The Daughter of Peter the Great,* 289.

126   "I hate the King of Prussia": Goldsmith, *Maria Theresa of Austria,* 195.

128   "Why should you be surprised": Coxe, *History of the House of Austria,* v. 3, 363.

128   "You know already how": Reddaway, *Frederick the Great and the Rise of Prussia,* 198.

129   "In a fortnight's time": Ibid., 199.

129   "The critical state": Bright, *Maria Theresa,* 119.

129   "I must know whether": Ibid.

130   "not a country": Szabo, *The Seven Years War in Europe, 1756–1763,* 21. This saying is variously attributed to Montesquieu or Friedrich von Schrötter, an eighteenth-century Prussian minister.

131   "You it was": Bain, *The Daughter of Peter the Great,* 210.

131   "Good heavens": Moffat, *Maria Theresa,* 233.

131*n*   "His [Frederick's] treatment of the Saxons...bosom of their native country": Wraxall, *Memoirs of the Courts of Berlin, Dresden, Warsaw, and Vienna,* v. 1, 212–13.

133   known simply as "*la belle princesse*": Pick, *Empress Maria Theresa,* 258.

133   "I am concerned": Coxe, *History of the House of Austria,* v. 3, 376.

134   "The monarchy thanks you": Morris, *Maria Theresa,* 227.

134   "The Birthday of the Monarchy": Pick, *Empress Maria Theresa,* 303.

135   "Can you conceive": Smythe, *Madame de Pompadour,* 294.

135   "This neutrality is": *Memoirs and Papers of Sir Andrew Mitchell,* v. 1, 371–72.

135n cost 80,000 livres: See Goldsmith, *Maria Theresa of Austria*, 162.

136 "What is wanting": Shoberl, *Frederick the Great, his court and times*, v. 3, 84.

Chapter 8. The Favorite

141 "There are so many kinds of love": Voltaire, *The Philosophical Dictionary*, v. 7, 137.

142 "If the Queen": Moffat, *Maria Theresa*, 214.

142n "As for dramatic music": Ibid., 215.

142n "Joseph Haydn sang": Townsend, *Joseph Haydn*, 12.

143 To instruct her talented daughter: I am indebted for the information on Friedrich August Brand to Barbara Ann Schmutzler for her research and translation of German sources covering the art of this period.

143 "The day is always": Maria Theresa, *Letters of an Empress*, 32.

144 "A person of great distinction": Moffat, *Maria Theresa*, 214.

145 "It mattered not": Ibid., 277.

145 "As my son . . . a sensible judgment": Maria Theresa, *Letters of an Empress*, 27–31.

146 "safe in trusting France": Goldsmith, *Maria Theresa of Austria*, 183.

146 "the King, my Master": Bain, *The Daughter of Peter the Great*, 191.

147 "I know nothing so indecent": Morley, *Diderot and the Encyclopædists*, v. 1, 149.

148 "Men are on the eve": Ibid., 167.

148 "It would be easy to prove": Gooch, *Maria Theresa and Other Studies*, 24–25.

149 "care, devotion, and skill": Moffat, *Maria Theresa*, 237.

149 "I have been your debtor": Ibid.

150 "Never before did anyone": Perkins, *France under Louis XV*, v. 2, 109.

151 "The advantages of this": Ibid., 123.

152 "I shall do everything": Goldsmith, *Maria Theresa of Austria*, 200.

152 "In spite of the war": Moffat, *Maria Theresa*, 250.

153 living in a harem: Albert characterized the palace at Dresden during his enforced confinement as "the Seraglio"; see Koeppe, *Vienna circa 1780*, 10.

153 "All the princesses were beautiful": Moffat, *Maria Theresa*, 249.

154 "I am more afraid": Morris, *Maria Theresa*, 268.

155 "Her attainments would have": Moffat, *Maria Theresa*, 252.

156 "We have gained": Ibid., 253.

157 "dear other half": Goldsmith, *Maria Theresa of Austria*, 206.

157 "Bonjour, dear Sister": Bourbon-Parme, *"Je meurs d'amour pour toi . . . ,"* 88.

157 "Bonjour, adorable Sister": Ibid., 115.

157 "cruel Sister": Ibid., 116.

157 "very cruel Sister": Ibid., 118.

157 "I adore you and my love": Ibid., 120.

157 "You desire, dear Sister": Ibid., 100–102.

158 "You will comfort me": Ibid., 124.

158 "I want to kiss you": Ibid., 130.

158   "To be deprived": Ibid., 133.
160   "The close of my days": Fairburn, *Frederick the Great,* 70.
160   "Our allies show signs": Bain, *The Daughter of Peter the Great,* 294.
160   "Without wasting any more words": Ibid., 306.
161   "It seems to me": Ibid., 309–10.
161   "I have enjoyed the revenge": Campbell, *Frederick the Great,* v. 3, 87.

Chapter 9. An Archduchess in Love

163   "Never marry a man": Vehse, *Memoirs of the Court and Aristocracy of Austria,* v. 2, 206.
163   "The Tsar of Russia": Carlyle, *History of Friedrich II of Prussia,* v. 9, 190.
164   "Her Imperial Majesty": Ibid., 191–92.
164   "I wager that she is consulted": Moffat, *Maria Theresa,* 258.
164   "You don't realize": Goldsmith, *Maria Theresa of Austria,* 173.
164   "His nature is not": Moffat, *Maria Theresa,* 255.
164   "philosophy, morals, stories": Bourbon-Parme, *"Je meurs d'amour pour toi...,"* 162.
165   "I am told," she observed: Morris, *Maria Theresa,* 270.
165   "If the Archduke [Joseph] goes out": Bourbon-Parme, *"Je meurs d'amour pour toi...,"* 179.
165   "Death is a good thing": Ibid., 168.
165   "Allow me to tell you": Moffat, *Maria Theresa,* 254.
165   "God having given you": Maria Theresa, *Letters of an Empress,* 95.
165   "Pray for fine weather": Bourbon-Parme, *"Je meurs d'amour pour toi...,"* 152.
166   "So dark is the outlook": Morris, *Maria Theresa,* 253.
167   "She never caused me grief": Moffat, *Maria Theresa,* 260.
167   called "Advice to Marie": Bourbon-Parme, *"Je meurs d'amour pour toi...,"* 237.
167   "The Empress has an exceptionally": Ibid., 257.
168   "that *too ambitious*": Szabo, *The Seven Years War in Europe, 1756–1763,* 368.
169   "I wish sincerely": Perkins, *France under Louis XV,* v. 2, 172–73.
170   "My father wanted me": Catt, *Frederick the Great, the memoirs of his reader, Henri de Catt,* v. 1, 131.
171   "There is not a moment": Gooch, *Maria Theresa and Other Studies,* 12.
171   "I, who have suffered": Mahan, *Maria Theresa of Austria,* 225.
171   "It is better": Ibid.
172   "All the diamonds of the world": Pick, *Empress Maria Theresa,* 199.
173   "The Emperor is a very good-hearted": Mahan, *Maria Theresa of Austria,* 264.
174   "It's not jealousy": Bourbon-Parme, *"Je meurs d'amour pour toi...,"* 214.
174   "Believe that from now on": Ibid., 208.
174   "I hope it will be sunny": Ibid., 223.
174   "Perhaps we will be separated": Ibid., 229.
174   "Do not be afraid," she reassured Mimi: Ibid., 234–35.
175   "God is too benevolent": Ibid., 235.

175 "I have lost everything," he mourned: Moffat, *Maria Theresa,* 261.

175 "The only thing that comforts me": Ibid., 261–62.

177 "the most magnificent state-carriage": *The Autobiography of Goethe,* 159.

177 "The young King...in his monstrous": Ibid., 169.

177 "The rejoicings": Ibid., 168.

177 "On the 29th": Moffat, *Maria Theresa,* 269.

178 "I laugh with my lips": Gooch, *Maria Theresa and Other Studies,* 15.

179 "Let nothing remain hidden": Wolf, *Marie Christine,* v. 1, 36. Translation by Barbara Ann Schmutzler.

180 "You are to have": Moffat, *Maria Theresa,* 276.

180 "Her age is six-and-twenty": Ibid., 275.

180 "I find myself": Morris, *Maria Theresa,* 273.

180 "I am willing to believe": Moffat, *Maria Theresa,* 280.

181 "I believe that if I": Wolf, *Marie Christine,* v. 1, 37. Translation by Barbara Ann Schmutzler.

182 "who has long been known": Sorel, *The Eastern Question in the Eighteenth Century,* 13.

183 "not without reason": Moffat, *Maria Theresa,* 280.

183 "I need a little comforting": Ibid.

183 "The Infanta [Maria Luisa]": Ibid., 282.

184 "Never can I forget": Ibid., 284.

184 "I have lost in him": Vehse, *Memoirs of the Court and Aristocracy of Austria,* v. 2, 228.

185 "We have indeed": Ibid.

185 "I hardly know myself now": Moffat, *Maria Theresa,* 286.

186 "You sent my son back": Beales, *Joseph II: In the Shadow of Maria Theresa, 1741–1780,* 153.

186 "It was a long...and brother-in-law": Moffat, *Maria Theresa,* 299.

187 "out of tender love and motherly care": Wolf, *Marie Christine,* v. 1, 39. Translation by Barbara Ann Schmutzler. I am indebted to both Barbara Ann Schmutzler and Heike Grebenstein for the description of Maria Christina's dowry.

188 "The young archduchess": Bearne, *A Sister of Marie Antoinette,* 43.

Chapter 10. The Understudy

194 "Whenever she is tired": Vehse, *Memoirs of the Court and Aristocracy of Austria,* v. 2, 234.

194 "in four installments": Pick, *Empress Maria Theresa,* 217.

194 "It is my wish": Goldsmith, *Maria Theresa of Austria,* 149–50.

195 "As [her youngest children] must not be": Pick, *Empress Maria Theresa,* 221.

196n "You will be surprised": Moffat, *Maria Theresa,* 298.

199 "The young King shows no taste": Bearne, *A Sister of Marie Antoinette,* 42.

199 "All this that I indicate": Maria Theresa, *Letters of an Empress,* 163.

199   "Breakfast is to be changed": Ibid., 166–67.

200   "I was like a silly child": Moffat, *Maria Theresa*, 302.

200   "anxious to hide": Beales, *Joseph II: In the Shadow of Maria Theresa, 1741–1780*, 88.

201   "I demand of you": Wolf, *Marie Christine*, v. 1, 91. Translation by Heike Grebenstein.

202   "I do not intend . . . take rank after Amalie": Bearne, *A Sister of Marie Antoinette*, 54–56.

205   "I have visited": Wraxall, *Memoirs of the Courts of Berlin, Dresden, Warsaw, and Vienna*, v. 2, 317.

205   "perform her devotions": Ibid., 322.

205   "expressed great repugnance": Ibid.

205   "it is generally asserted": Ibid., 322–23.

206   "It was recollected": Ibid., 323–24.

206   "It is four years today": Moffat, *Maria Theresa*, 311.

206   "taking leave of": Ibid., 312.

207   "As I certainly": Bearne, *A Sister of Marie Antoinette*, 59.

208   "The young Princess . . . her opposition": Wraxall, *Memoirs of the Courts of Berlin, Dresden, Warsaw, and Vienna*, v. 2, 324–25.

209n "Knowing that you love me": Moffat, *Maria Theresa*, 313.

Chapter 11. Queen of Naples

210   "Leave your husband alone": Maria Theresa, *Letters of an Empress*, 102.

210   "Poldel [the family nickname for Leopold]": Vehse, *Memoirs of the Court and Aristocracy of Austria*, v. 2, 202.

211   "She is extremely young": Bearne, *A Sister of Marie Antoinette*, 70.

211   "I learned many languages": Recca, *The Diary of Queen Maria Carolina of Naples*, 3.

212   "She is often so agitated": Bearne, *A Sister of Marie Antoinette*, 69.

212   "I am well, but my heart": Ibid.

212   "Write to me": Ibid., 68.

213   "I tell you plainly": Ibid., 72.

213   "She sleeps like a corpse": Vehse, *Memoirs of the Court and Aristocracy of Austria*, v. 2, 236.

214   "Naples at first sight": *Goethe's Letters from Switzerland and Travels in Italy*, 233–34.

214   "Naples is a paradise": Ibid., 254.

215   "The interior of this palace": Colleta, *History of Naples from the Accession of Charles of Bourbon*, v. 1, 86.

216   "The site is uncommonly fine": *Goethe's Letters from Switzerland and Travels in Italy*, 253.

216   "Placed at the extremity of Italy": Craven, *Memoirs of the Margravine of Anspach*, v. 1, 296.

216 "He is very ugly": Bearne, *A Sister of Marie Antoinette*, 71.
217 "He begged...to keep him company": Acton, *The Bourbons of Naples*, 144–45.
217 "He is now what many school-boys": Ibid., 132.
218 "I must tell you and confess": Bearne, *A Sister of Marie Antoinette*, 71.
218 "One suffers a martyrdom": Ibid., 72.
218 "follow him everywhere": Maria Theresa, *Letters of an Empress*, 102.
219 "The King shoots": Acton, *The Bourbons of Naples*, 147.
219 "Throughout these the King": Ibid., 142–43.
219 "He is a right good fool": Ibid., 140.
219 "He fondled her in my presence": Ibid., 144.
220 "My wife knows everything": Bearne, *A Sister of Marie Antoinette*, 77.
220 "He is a Tartuffe": Acton, *The Bourbons of Naples*, 150.
220 "The King...even if he": Ibid., 152–53.
221 some £50,000 annually: Ibid., 174.
221 "Her Majesty is a beautiful": Miller, *Letters from Italy*, v. 2, 51–52.
222 "None but such...is a profusion": Ibid., 52–56.
222 "Here the Neapolitans": Ibid., 146–47.
223 "The theater is...the highest perfection": Ibid., 138–40.
224 referred to him as her "dear husband": Bearne, *A Sister of Marie Antoinette*, 73.
224 "This stroke came from the Queen": *The Memoirs of Jacques Casanova*, v. 6, 367–68. Translation by Michael Haggiag.
224n "The amusing part": Ibid., 338.
225 "Mr. Hamilton was a genius": Ibid., 354.
226 "No foreign Minister": Wraxall, *Historical Memoirs of My Own Time*, v. 1, 231.
226 "Women at Court": Acton, *The Bourbons of Naples*, 177.
226n "The English are like": *The Memoirs of Jacques Casanova*, v. 6, 362.

Chapter 12. The Little One

231 "You are the luckiest": Padover, *The Life and Death of Louis XVI*, 29.
232 "the little sorcerer": Breakspeare, *Mozart*, 8.
232 "You *are* good": Ibid.
233 "I longed to kiss that child": Rocheterie, *The Life of Marie Antoinette*, v. 1, 9.
235 "Madame my Sister": Padover, *The Life and Death of Louis XVI*, 28.
236 "She began to sob": Beales, *Joseph II: In the Shadow of Maria Theresa, 1741–1780*, 156.
237 "After devoting my first instructions": Younghusband, *Marie-Antoinette, Her Early Youth*, 119–20.
238 "The Archduchess will say": Ibid., 129.
238 "talks French with ease": Ibid., 131.
238 "She would rarely": Ibid.

240   "The Queen of Naples will wish you": Smythe, *The Guardian of Marie Antoinette,* v. 1, 17.

240   "A truly afflicting scene": Weber, *Memoirs of Maria Antoinetta,* v. 1, 6.

241   "Nature itself": Younghusband, *Marie-Antoinette, Her Early Youth,* 139.

Chapter 13. Dauphine of France

243   "I cannot understand": Smythe, *The Guardian of Marie Antoinette,* v. 1, 87.

243   "had it been more...and her court": *The Autobiography of Goethe,* 310–12.

244   "I yet remember": Ibid., 312.

246   "They might as well": Acton, *The Bourbons of Naples,* 132.

246   "Pardon me": Rocheterie, *The Life of Marie Antoinette,* v. 1, 16.

247   "Long live the King!" came the cheers: Ibid., 19.

248   "Go ahead, my poor Berry": Padover, *The Life and Death of Louis XVI,* 10.

248   "spirited": Ibid., 9.

248   "The Dauphin is very": Swinburne, *The Courts of Europe at the Close of the Last Century,* 10.

249   "Please, that fault": Padover, *The Life and Death of Louis XVI,* 10.

249   "Concerning My Faults": Ibid., 16.

249   "It's not I": Ibid., 11.

249   "This Forest has": Ibid., 17.

250   "Rien," a frequent notation: Ibid., 24.

250   "I went horse-riding": Ibid.

250   "Death of my mother": Hardman, *The Life of Louis XVI,* 22.

251   "the fat, ill-bred boy": Padover, *The Life and Death of Louis XVI,* 26.

251   "he seems to have been": Ibid.

251   "the horror of the nation": Ibid.

251*n*   "Resists cuddling...stiff or exaggerated body language": https://www
.mayoclinic.org/diseases-conditions/autism-spectrum-disorder/symptoms
-causes/syc-20352928.

251*n*   "The child you describe": To access the precise clinical criteria for this
disorder, please go to https://www.autismspeaks.org/autism-diagnosis
-criteria-dsm-5.

252   "Interview with Madame": Padover, *The Life and Death of Louis XVI,* 31.

253   "to amuse the King": Weber, *Queen of Fashion,* 39.

253   "Well, then I": Ibid.

253   "The king, Mesdames": Rocheterie, *The Life of Marie Antoinette,* v. 1, 22.

253   "Our Archduchess Dauphine": Younghusband, *Marie-Antoinette, Her Early Youth,* 28.

254   "As soon as she had taken": Campan, *Memoirs of the Private Life of Marie Antoinette,* v. 1, 48.

254   "colored up to his hair": Younghusband, *Marie-Antoinette, Her Early Youth,* 42.

254   *le coucher*: Ibid., 47.

255 "When I reflect": Bearne, *A Sister of Marie Antoinette,* 71.

256 "It would be impossible to be more interesting": Younghusband, *Marie-Antoinette, Her Early Youth,* 178.

257 "At present it is necessary": Ibid., 182.

257 "Fortunately, his [Louis-Auguste's] indifference": Ibid., 178.

258 "This conduct has raised hopes": Smythe, *The Guardian of Marie Antoinette,* v. 1, 84.

258 "There are very many people": Ibid., 180.

258 "I have done what you told me!": Ibid., 181.

258 "I perceived that": Ibid.

258 "I notice that the Dauphin": Ibid., 239.

258 "unfortunately, his conversations": Younghusband, *Marie-Antoinette, Her Early Youth,* 480.

258 "and promises me": Smythe, *The Guardian of Marie Antoinette,* v. 1, 109–10.

258 "I live always": Ibid., 148.

259 "The Dauphine gave the Dauphin": Ibid., 124.

259*n* "the state of apprehension": Ibid., 281.

260 "I rise about … bed at eleven": Ibid., 21–22.

261 "Madame l'Étiquette": Campan, *Memoirs of the Private Life of Marie Antoinette,* v. 1, 47.

261 "Madame de Noailles … 'Lappets hanging down!' ": Ibid., xcix–c.

261 "They would have it so": Ibid., 12.

262 "Your Majesty commands me": Smythe, *The Guardian of Marie Antoinette,* v. 1, 97.

262*n* "Where is Poland?": Ibid., 210.

263 "If you were in a position to judge": Ibid., 151.

263 "There never existed": Campan, *Memoirs of the Private Life of Marie Antoinette,* v. 1, 67.

264 "The situation is incomprehensible": Younghusband, *Marie-Antoinette, Her Early Youth,* 476.

264 "Madame the Dauphine": Smythe, *The Guardian of Marie Antoinette,* v. 1, 305.

264*n* "the Austrian": Rocheterie, *The Life of Marie Antoinette,* v. 1, 60.

265 "Old Louis … grinds them down": Younghusband, *Marie-Antoinette, Her Early Youth,* 544.

265 "Nothing was wanting": Smythe, *The Guardian of Marie Antoinette,* v. 1, 264–65.

266 "Heavens, what a crowd!": Rocheterie, *The Life of Marie Antoinette,* v. 1, 82.

266 "I had a fête": Younghusband, *Marie-Antoinette, Her Early Youth,* 540–41.

267 "A favorite actor": Ibid., 544.

267 "I feel every day": Ibid., 541.

268 "The air of the palace": Campan, *Memoirs of the Private Life of Marie Antoinette,* v. 1, 69.

268 "Madame, as I am contemplating": Rocheterie, *The Life of Marie Antoinette,* v. 1, 92.

268 "You can come back": Smythe, *The Guardian of Marie Antoinette,* v. 1, 355.

269 "a dreadful noise": Campan, *Memoirs of the Private Life of Marie Antoinette,* v. 1, 71.

269 "They are all under": Padover, *The Life and Death of Louis XVI,* 45.

Chapter 14. An Imperial Divide

273 "Nothing in the world": Younghusband, *Marie-Antoinette, Her Early Youth,* 467.

274 "Feast-days...attracting them": Maria Theresa, *Letters of an Empress,* 85–87.

275 "Naturally distant and haughty": Wraxall, *Memoirs of the Courts of Berlin, Dresden, Warsaw, and Vienna,* v. 2, 338–39.

275 "She dedicates her leisure": Ibid., 339.

275 "The Archduchess Christine": Ibid., 338.

276 "With such personal": Ibid., 339–40.

276n "they lead a gloomy": Ibid., 337.

277 "The child scarcely": Beales, *Joseph II: In the Shadow of Maria Theresa, 1741–1780,* 201.

277 "To be no longer a father": Moffat, *Maria Theresa,* 328.

278 "What would such a poor": Gates-Coon, *The Charmed Circle,* 134.

279 "the empty title": Gooch, *Maria Theresa and Other Studies,* 35.

279 "From the time": Beales, *Joseph II: In the Shadow of Maria Theresa, 1741–1780,* 204.

279 "I require much cannon": Hodgetts, *The Life of Catherine the Great of Russia,* 233.

280 "It is a terrible power": Perkins, *France under Louis XV,* v. 2, 291.

281 "I have a very poor opinion": Ibid., 301.

281 "Why should not": Ibid., 302.

282 "It is impossible for me": Ibid., 299.

282 "Your minister has": Ibid.

282 "I am too much oppressed...of the last year": Maria Theresa, *Letters of an Empress,* 8–10.

283 "Permit me to say": Perkins, *France under Louis XV,* v. 2, 307.

283 "How often did I": Gooch, *Maria Theresa and Other Studies,* 66.

283 "The Empress Catherine": Perkins, *France under Louis XV,* v. 2, 309.

284 "may...explain the cause": Wraxall, *Memoirs of the Courts of Berlin, Dresden, Warsaw, and Vienna,* v. 2, 340.

285 "It pleased His Grace": Schröder, *The Origins of the Albertina,* 14.

288 "So much consolation": Younghusband, *Marie-Antoinette, Her Early Youth,* 436.

288 "trace of the glamour": Vovk, *In Destiny's Hands,* 139.

288n "a parcel of old...library of books": Miller, *Letters from Italy,* v. 1, 273–76.

290*n*   "The bold Bavarian": Wraxall, *Memoirs of the Courts of Berlin, Dresden, Warsaw, and Vienna,* v. 1, 305.

291   "All the nobility... end in war!": Ibid., 308–11.

292   "Will the Elector of Saxony": Ibid., 312.

292   "These people must think": Blanning, *Frederick the Great,* 326.

292*n*   "No advantages which the court": Wraxall, *Memoirs of the Courts of Berlin, Dresden, Warsaw, and Vienna,* v. 2, 159.

293   "I will gladly commit": Beales, *Joseph II: In the Shadow of Maria Theresa, 1741–1780,* 398.

293   "The Emperor alone": Wraxall, *Memoirs of the Courts of Berlin, Dresden, Warsaw, and Vienna,* v. 1, 353.

293   "It may be his": Ibid., 355–56.

294   "He [Kaunitz] is for the war": Wolf, *Marie Christine,* v. 1, 154. Translation by Barbara Ann Schmutzler.

294   "a separation which did not": Wraxall, *Memoirs of the Courts of Berlin, Dresden, Warsaw, and Vienna,* v. 1, 369.

294   "The evils that it leads to": Beales, *Joseph II: In the Shadow of Maria Theresa, 1741–1780,* 406.

294   "Now see what a state": Smythe, *The Guardian of Marie Antoinette,* v. 2, 605.

295   "Certainly no campaign": Wraxall, *Memoirs of the Courts of Berlin, Dresden, Warsaw, and Vienna,* v. 2, 164.

295   "The Emperor's determination": Ibid., 169.

295*n*   "That restores the credit": Beales, *Joseph II: In the Shadow of Maria Theresa, 1741–1780,* 407.

296   "weary with the march": Moffat, *Maria Theresa,* 353.

296   "My hands will no longer": Ibid.

296   "Maria Theresa's person": Wraxall, *Memoirs of the Courts of Berlin, Dresden, Warsaw, and Vienna,* v. 2, 311–12.

297   "He [Francis] wants to keep": Vehse, *Memoirs of the Court and Aristocracy of Austria,* v. 2, 229.

297   "I do not want": Moffat, *Maria Theresa,* 357.

298   "Maria Theresa is no more": Vehse, *Memoirs of the Court and Aristocracy of Austria,* v. 2, 230. Specifically, "Maria Theresa n'est plus, voilà un nouvel ordre des choses, qui commence."

298   "an ink-bottle spilt": Tallentyre, *The Friends of Voltaire,* 81.

Chapter 15. The Queen Takes Control

301   "Of all my daughters": Bearne, *A Sister of Marie Antoinette,* 53.

302   "I wish to God": Recca, "Maria Carolina and Marie Antoinette," 22.

303   "Until now I did not like": Acton, *The Bourbons of Naples,* 178.

304   "But the Catholic King": Ibid., 181.

304   "Do you [make decisions]": Recca, *The Diary of Queen Maria Carolina of Naples,* 14, note 15.

305   "No Neapolitan thought": Acton, *The Bourbons of Naples,* 187.

307   "If you should find anyone": Maria Theresa, *Letters of an Empress,* 101.

308   the "hooligan king": Gutteridge, *Nelson and the Neapolitan Jacobins,* xii.

309   "Ferdinand is a good sort of man": Jeaffreson, *The Queen of Naples and Lord Nelson,* v. 1, 102.

309   "Open your eyes": Acton, *The Bourbons of Naples,* 199.

309   "I am trying to surprise": Bearne, *A Sister of Marie Antoinette,* 104.

310   "nothing": Colleta, *History of Naples from the Accession of Charles of Bourbon to the Death of Ferdinand I,* v. 1, 159.

311   "the Golden King": Ibid.

312   "wild and thoughtless": Sichel, *Emma Lady Hamilton,* 44.

313   "I own through distress": Ibid., 46.

313   "Temple of Health": Williams, *England's Mistress,* 55. See the opening chapters of this excellent biography also for the information on Emma's early career in London.

313   "What shall I dow": Sichel, *Emma Lady Hamilton,* 34.

314   "Oh! Greville": Ibid., 59.

316   "Dear, dear Greville": Ibid., 89.

316   "I have had a conversation": Ibid., 90.

317   "I am now onely": Ibid., 91.

317   "Oblige Sir William": Ibid., 92.

317   "Greville, to advise": Ibid.

318   "You don't know": Ibid., 93–94.

318   called "Attitudes": Ibid., 105.

318n "Sir William Hamilton": *Goethe's Letters from Switzerland and Travels in Italy,* 255–56.

319   "closely besieged by the King": Sichel, *Emma Lady Hamilton,* 112.

Chapter 16. Queen of France

323   "I am cut to the heart": Smythe, *The Guardian of Marie Antoinette,* v. 2, 426–27.

324   "List of the various": Padover, *The Life and Death of Louis XVI,* 48.

324   "If you only saw": Smythe, *The Guardian of Marie Antoinette,* v. 2, 491.

324   "possessed nothing agreeable": Campan, *Memoirs of the Private Life of Marie Antoinette,* v. 1, 112.

325   "the fat pig": Padover, *The Life and Death of Louis XVI,* 117.

325   "She [Marie Antoinette] should at once": Smythe, *The Guardian of Marie Antoinette,* v. 1, 358.

325   "The Throne He fills": Padover, *The Life and Death of Louis XVI,* 60–61.

326   "goes every hour": Smythe, *The Guardian of Marie Antoinette,* v. 2, 378.

326   "to do just what I": Ibid., 379.

326   "send that creature": Ibid., 365.

327 "I feel myself": Campan, *Memoirs of the Private Life of Marie Antoinette,* v. 1, 102, note 1.

327 "I will enjoy": Ibid., 128–29.

327*n* "held in much": Weber, *Queen of Fashion,* 119.

328 "Everything she does": Younghusband, *Marie-Antoinette, Her Early Youth,* 394.

328 "Let the Queen": Ibid., 567.

329 "All wished instantly": Campan, *Memoirs of the Private Life of Marie Antoinette,* v. 1, 87–88.

329 "I must mention": Smythe, *The Guardian of Marie Antoinette,* v. 2, 412.

329 "It is true": Ibid.

330 "Lately Her Majesty": Ibid., 413.

330 "this time is": Ibid., 431.

330 "The Queen now plays": Ibid., 447.

330 "The monarch received": Ibid., 445.

330 "We have seen": Ibid., 439.

330 "I observe that": Ibid., 450.

331 "I shall then": Padover, *The Life and Death of Louis XVI,* 57.

331 "a silent spectator": Hardman, *The Life of Louis XVI,* 57.

332*n* "all the accustomed pomp . . . It pinches me": Campan, *Memoirs of the Private Life of Marie Antoinette,* v. 1, 105.

333 "her disposition": Ibid., 128.

333 "long and certainly": Smythe, *The Guardian of Marie Antoinette,* v. 2, 520.

333 "the anti-Austrian party": Campan, *Memoirs of the Private Life of Marie Antoinette,* v. 1, 81.

334 "Their aim was": Ibid.

335 "Such a glorious cause": Lafayette, *Memoirs, Correspondence and Manuscripts,* v. 1, 5–6.

335 "All the prettiest ladies": Smythe, *The Guardian of Marie Antoinette,* v. 2, 570.

335 "The cry of this nation": Padover, *The Life and Death of Louis XVI,* 110.

335 "Very bad tidings": Lafayette, *Memoirs, Correspondence and Manuscripts,* v. 1, 9.

335 "Two or three millions": Padover, *The Life and Death of Louis XVI,* 108.

336 "We will secretly": Ibid.

336 "In the history": Ibid., 109.

336 "With regard to the": Smythe, *The Guardian of Marie Antoinette,* v. 2, 451–52.

337 "Her situation with the King": Ibid., 494.

337 "The queen is a very beautiful": Padover, *The Life and Death of Louis XVI,* 101.

337 "she is perfectly virtuous": Smythe, *The Guardian of Marie Antoinette,* v. 2, 494.

338 "Here is the mystery": Hardman, *The Life of Louis XVI,* 34.

338 "This is the happiest": Padover, *The Life and Death of Louis XVI,* 101.

339 "The King [Louis] told": Ibid.

339 "It is to you": Ibid., 102.

339n "They will say to you": Lafayette, *Memoirs, Correspondence and Manuscripts,* v. 1, 103–4.

341 "I had a very touching": Smythe, *The Guardian of Marie Antoinette,* v. 2, 592–93.

341 "You see I have so many": Ibid., 593.

342 "I have never seen": Ibid., 595.

342 "You have heard": Ibid., 584.

Chapter 17. Diamonds and Debt

343 "What is Truth": Beaumarchais, *The Marriage of Figaro,* Act 4.

343 "Ah! Here is an old": Fersen, *Diary and Correspondence,* 12.

344 "The queen, who is...princess that I know": Ibid., 12.

344 "I ought to confide": Ibid., 13.

345 "By thus departing": Ibid.

345 "I notice that the Comtesse": Smythe, *The Guardian of Marie Antoinette,* v. 2, 659.

346 "the time necessary": Ibid., 674.

346 "was the only time": Campan, *Memoirs of the Private Life of Marie Antoinette,* v. 1, 190. Louis almost certainly had not intended to hurt Vermond's feelings all those years. The king was in fact a very kind person. Ignoring those around them is just another symptom of Autism Spectrum Disorder, as is blurting out rude statements, something that Louis did all the time. For example, soon after his ascension in 1774, he told a minister who had fallen from favor, and whom he had consequently not seen for some time, "You have grown fat, Monsieur de Choiseul, you are losing your hair—you are becoming bald": Rocheterie, *The Life of Marie Antoinette,* v. 1, 101.

347 "this country is...ruined": Fersen, *Diary and Correspondence,* 41.

347 *Comte rendu au Roi:* Hardman, *The Life of Louis XVI,* 158.

348 "The play, sir": Lafayette, *Memoirs, Correspondence and Manuscripts,* v. 1, 444.

348 "the moment the child": Campan, *Memoirs of the Private Life of Marie Antoinette,* v. 1, 192.

348 "joy was boundless": Ibid., 192–93.

349 "That event decided": Sackville, *Despatches from Paris, 1784–1790,* v. 1, 145.

349 "Nothing [referring to hunting]": Hardman, *The Life of Louis XVI,* 166.

350 "I shall not fail": Ibid.

350 "fairy-land...a marked welcome": Ibid., 89.

351 "are become the intimate": Sackville, *Despatches from Paris, 1784–1790,* v. 1, 145.

352 1.3 billion livres: See Hardman, *The Life of Louis XVI,* 182, for the cost of the war and the subsequent debt.

352*n* "the Duke and Duchess...direction of her conduct": Sackville, *Despatches from Paris, 1784–1790,* v. 1, 146.

353 "The case of the Necklace": Funck-Brentano, *The Diamond Necklace,* 9.

353 "Pity a poor": Ibid., 63.

355 "Get up, Böhmer!": Ibid., 178.

355 "knew a comtesse": Ibid., 179.

355 "a very great nobleman": Ibid.

356 "Marie Antoinette de France": Ibid., 182.

357 "an automatic bird": Ibid., 191.

357 "You know what": Rocheterie, *The Life of Marie Antoinette,* v. 1, 300.

358 "We have genuine": Funck-Brentano, *The Diamond Necklace,* 222.

358 "an idiot": Campan, *Memoirs of the Private Life of Marie Antoinette,* v. 2, 27.

358 "You have been deceived": Funck-Brentano, *The Diamond Necklace,* 227.

359 "Everything has been concerted": Rocheterie, *The Life of Marie Antoinette,* v. 1, 309.

360 "The Queen's grief": Campan, *Memoirs of the Private Life of Marie Antoinette,* v. 2, 36.

361 "No less than": Sackville, *Despatches from Paris, 1784–1790,* v. 1, 15–16.

363 "in no fit state": Hardman, *The Life of Louis XVI,* 289.

363*n* Also Fersen's, as this child, too: Fersen called both this daughter and Louis-Charles "the children," and saw them privately when he stayed with Marie Antoinette. See Farr, *Marie-Antoinette and Count Fersen,* 146.

364 "Her ostensible interference": Campan, *Memoirs of the Private Life of Marie Antoinette,* v. 2, 43.

364 "Madame Deficit": Rocheterie, *The Life of Marie Antoinette,* v. 1, 328.

365 "Nobody speaks of anything": Farr, *Marie-Antoinette and Count Fersen,* 156.

367 "Are there no fathers": Rocheterie, *The Life of Marie Antoinette,* v. 2, 11.

367 "The Duc d'Orléans forever!": Campan, *Memoirs of the Private Life of Marie Antoinette,* v. 2, 47.

Chapter 18. Betrayal in Brussels

373 "The Emperor Joseph": Campbell, *Frederick the Great,* v. 4, 371–72.

374*n* "Believe me": Vehse, *Memoirs of the Court and Aristocracy of Austria,* v. 2, 237–38.

375 "For my part," he observed to Maria Theresa: Boulger, *The History of Belgium,* v. 1, 391–92.

376 known as the Joyeuse Entrée: Polasky, *Revolution in Brussels,* 17.

376*n* "the emperor has [decided]": Beales, *Joseph II: Against the World, 1780–1790,* 328.

376*n* "She will have to": Ibid., 55.

377 "maintain the privileges": Ibid., 161.

377 "the Princess Maria Christina": *A Review of the Affairs of the Austrian Netherlands in the Year 1787*, 25.

377 "The virtues of these Princes": Ibid., 25–26.

379 "I admire the inexhaustible": Beales, *Joseph II: Against the World, 1780–1790*, 419.

380 "I, who am already": Reddaway, *Frederick the Great and the Rise of Prussia*, 342.

382 "What afflicts us most": Wolf, *Leopold II und Marie Christine*, 35.

382n "Intendant General": Sackville, *Despatches from Paris, 1784–1790*, v. 1, 80.

383 "How much I regret": Wolf, *Marie Christine*, v. 2, 226. Translation by Barbara Ann Schmutzler.

385 "she displayed her annoyance": Farr, *Marie-Antoinette and Count Fersen*, 140.

386 "The Queen is beautiful": Wolf, *Marie Christine*, v. 2, 229. Translation by Barbara Ann Schmutzler.

386 "There is nothing particularly": Ibid., 228. Translation by Barbara Ann Schmutzler.

387 "The Archduchess has much more": Farr, *Marie-Antoinette and Count Fersen*, 143.

387 "I like Paris very much": Wolf, *Marie Christine*, v. 2, 230. Translation by Barbara Ann Schmutzler.

388 "No just bounds": *A Review of the Affairs of the Austrian Netherlands in the Year 1787*, 21.

389 "The entire country": Beales, *Joseph II: Against the World, 1780–1790*, 513.

389 "The public heats": *A Review of the Affairs of the Austrian Netherlands in the Year 1787*, 64.

389n "While the new edicts": Ibid., 28.

390 "all changes relating…MARIE and ALBERT": Marie Christine and Albert Casimir, *Lieuténants, Gouverneurs & Capitaines-Généraux des Pays-Bas*, 1.

390 "they were received": *A Review of the Affairs of the Austrian Netherlands in the Year 1787*, 67.

390 "With tears in her eyes": Beales, *Joseph II: Against the World, 1780–1790*, 523.

390 "We have never been able": Wolf, *Leopold II und Marie Christine*, 35.

391 "from this day": Boulger, *The History of Belgium*, v. 1, 405.

392 "I was shocked": Wolf, *Leopold II und Marie Christine*, 67.

392 "Imagine my feelings": Wolf, *Marie Christine*, v. 2, 22. Translation by Barbara Ann Schmutzler.

392 "We wcre determined": Wolf, *Leopold II und Marie Christine*, 67.

392 "At 10 a.m.": Ibid., 68

392 "Such haste, I admit": Ibid., 69.

392 "As we had never seen": Ibid., 68.

392 "the awful and tiring": Ibid., 69.

393 "How will I make": Ibid., 70.

393 "in truth so as not": Ibid., 69.

393 "Judge the pain": Ibid.

393   "The least malicious": Ibid., 70.

393   "Think of the discouragement": Ibid.

395   "Your country has killed me!": Boulger, *The History of Belgium,* v. 1, 409.

Chapter 19. The Queen Takes a Stand

399   "A pretty woman": Turquan, *A Great Adventuress,* 38.

400   "I am a mother": Bonnefons, *Marie-Caroline, Reine de Deux-Siciles,* 15.

400   "You know that for a long time": I am indebted to Franz A. J. Szabo, professor emeritus, University of Alberta, a specialist in eighteenth-century Habsburg and Imperial policy, for a copy of this letter, written by Maria Carolina to Leopold on July 22, 1788. The original appears in Vienna, Austrian State Archives/Haus-, Hof- und Staatsarchiv: Hausarchiv, Sammelbände, v. 11. Charlotte goes on to list the gruesome symptoms: "difficulty urinating, a boil on the neck that lasted for two months, periodic headaches in the evening, swelling in the lower parts... pistules, green discharge... an ulcerated abscess... fever": poor, poor woman.

400   "Our poor sister in Naples": Wolf, *Leopold II und Marie Christine,* 94.

401   "And so everything": Ibid., 157.

401   "The Queen of Naples, without being as pretty": Vigée Lebrun, *Memoirs of Madame Vigée Lebrun,* 72.

401   "I was frightened... Paris was on fire": Ibid., 52–56.

403   "I settled with great": Bearne, *A Sister of Marie Antoinette,* 120.

404   "I offer you my son": Coxe, *History of the House of Austria,* v. 3, 555.

406   "persecutions": Hardman, *The Life of Louis XVI,* 365.

407   "The hope of escaping": Jeaffreson, *The Queen of Naples and Lord Nelson,* v. 1, 235.

408   "She shall be my wife": Turquan, *A Great Adventuress,* 41.

408   "We come for a short time": Ibid., 38.

408   "On Saturday evening": Ibid., 42.

409   "A propos, Sir William": Ibid., 44.

409   "I am tormented by": *Correspondance inédite de Marie-Caroline,* 5.

409   "I have been presented": Jeaffreson, *The Queen of Naples and Lord Nelson,* v. 1, 229.

410   *sala oscura:* Colleta, *History of Naples,* v. 1, 185.

411   "The moment of dénouement": *Correspondance inédite de Marie-Caroline,* 4.

Chapter 20. A Desperate Gamble

415   "I at present govern": Lafayette, *Memoirs, Correspondence and Manuscripts,* v. 2, 303.

415   "In the provinces": *Diary and Correspondence of Count Axel Fersen,* 74.

415   "The majority [of the council]": Campan, *Memoirs of the Private Life of Marie Antoinette,* v. 2, 60.

416   "were compelled to go": Sackville, *Despatches from Paris, 1784–1790*, v. 2, 239.

416   "armed *Bourgeoisie*": Ibid., 238.

416   "at least 50,000": Ibid., 241.

416   "You must have learnt": Lafayette, *Memoirs, Correspondence and Manuscripts*, v. 2, 302.

417   "Secret agents distribute": *Diary and Correspondence of Count Axel Fersen*, 75–76.

417   "Yes, we can go": Rocheterie, *The Life of Marie Antoinette*, v. 2, 21.

418   "Am I to go": Campan, *Memoirs of the Private Life of Marie Antoinette*, v. 2, 60.

418   "They never will let": Ibid., 65.

418   "The king goes to Paris…enough to embrace you": Rocheterie, *The Life of Marie Antoinette*, v. 2, 19.

419   "Terror had driven them": Campan, *Memoirs of the Private Life of Marie Antoinette*, v. 2, 65.

419   "my prisoner": Lafayette, *Memoirs, Correspondence and Manuscripts*, v. 2, 307.

419   "The entrance of": Sackville, *Despatches from Paris, 1784–1790*, v. 2, 246–47.

419   "I think I can": Ibid., 245.

420   "with a sad": Rocheterie, *The Life of Marie Antoinette*, v. 2, 22–23.

420   "his readiness to do": Sackville, *Despatches from Paris, 1784–1790*, v. 2, 244.

420   "Vive le roi!": Rocheterie, *The Life of Marie Antoinette*, v. 2, 23.

420   "The King breathed again": Campan, *Memoirs of the Private Life of Marie Antoinette*, v. 2, 66.

420   "He congratulated himself": Ibid., 66–67.

421   "Their very slight inclination": Ibid., 363.

421   "The affair is off": Ibid.

421   "continued to enjoy": Farr, *Marie-Antoinette and Count Fersen*, 168.

421   "Be prudent when speaking": Ibid., 167.

422   "shouts of 'Vive le Roi!' ": Campan, *Memoirs of the Private Life of Marie Antoinette*, v. 2, 77.

422   "On all sides": Ibid., 78.

422   "The fact is": Ibid.

422   "From that moment Paris": Ibid., 80.

422   "much surprised": Sackville, *Despatches from Paris, 1784–1790*, v. 2, 263.

423   "order the Parisian band": Campan, *Memoirs of the Private Life of Marie Antoinette*, v. 2, 366–67.

423   "was, probably, only to": Ibid., 367.

423   "declared that she": Ibid.

424   "pack your effects": Rocheterie, *The Life of Marie Antoinette*, v. 2, 42.

424   "All is changed": Ibid.

424   "everyone except herself": Ibid., 44.

424   "We shall bring back": Ibid., 43.

425   "a frenzied multitude": Campan, *Memoirs of the Private Life of Marie Antoinette*, v. 2, 371.

425   "Kill, kill!'": Rocheterie, *The Life of Marie Antoinette,* v. 2, 48.

425   "my sister flew": Campan, *Memoirs of the Private Life of Marie Antoinette,* v. 2, 84.

425   "Get up, madame": Ibid., 84.

425   "All the public papers": *Diary and Correspondence of Count Axel Fersen,* 76.

426   "I cannot belong": Farr, *Marie-Antoinette and Count Fersen,* 113.

426   "threw herself out": Campan, *Memoirs of the Private Life of Marie Antoinette,* v. 2, 84.

426   "The Queen saw": Ibid., 85.

427   "in a state of": Ibid., 372.

427   "all his speeches...a word": Ibid.

427   "We are bringing back": Rocheterie, *The Life of Marie Antoinette,* v. 2, 52.

427   "The king has never": Ibid.

428   "I returned to Paris": *Diary and Correspondence of Count Axel Fersen,* 76.

428   "Ah! Monsieur de Saint-Priest...that well": Campan, *Memoirs of the Private Life of Marie Antoinette,* v. 2, 373.

428   "The whole day": Sackville, *Despatches from Paris, 1784–1790,* v. 2, 265.

428n "Everything is very ugly": Rocheterie, *The Life of Marie Antoinette,* v. 2, 55.

429   "Madame, I come to convey": Ibid., 57.

429   "I receive with pleasure": Ibid.

429   "One cannot tell": Ibid., 79.

429   "defend and uphold": Ibid., 75.

430   "nothing but a civil": *Diary and Correspondence of Count Axel Fersen,* 77.

430   "Society would soon": Barthou, *Mirabeau,* 189–90.

430n "the right of sovereignty": Ibid., 162.

430n "the time has come": Ibid., 183.

430n "egoists who think": Ibid., 201.

431   "The king's weakness": Rocheterie, *The Life of Marie Antoinette,* v. 2, 91.

431   "The king has only": Ibid., 93.

431   "We shall scarcely": Ibid., 91.

432   "She is very great": Ibid., 95.

432   "I still have": *The Life and Letters of Madame Élisabeth de France,* 53.

432   "Four enemies": Rocheterie, *The Life of Marie Antoinette,* v. 2, 96.

432   "so gifted by nature": Ibid., 97.

433   "to all the many": *Diary and Correspondence of Count Axel Fersen,* 85.

434   "There seems no doubt...useful to the King": Ibid., 85–88.

435   "Detachments of grenadiers...5th of October": Ibid., 93–95.

436   "It was with uneasiness": Campan, *Memoirs of the Private Life of Marie Antoinette,* v. 2, 135.

436   "We must absolutely obtain": *Diary and Correspondence of Count Axel Fersen,* 104.

437   "If it is desired": Ibid., 107–8.

437   "There are no precautions": Ibid., 109.

437 "determined to have": Campan, *Memoirs of the Private Life of Marie Antoinette*, v. 2, 135.

437 "they start without fail": *Diary and Correspondence of Count Axel Fersen*, 114.

438 "At ten and a quarter": Ibid., 117.

439 "Now quick": Rocheterie, *The Life of Marie Antoinette*, v. 2, 131.

439 "Whatever may happen": *Diary and Correspondence of Count Axel Fersen*, 116.

439 "Goodbye, Madame Korff": Lenotre, *The Flight of Marie Antoinette*, 45.

440 "Here I am": Rocheterie, *The Life of Marie Antoinette*, v. 2, 132.

440 "talking to the": Lenotre, *The Flight of Marie Antoinette*, 50.

440 "I do not think": Ibid.

441 "M. de Lafayette": Ibid., 47.

441 "The King having been removed": Ibid., 105.

442 "that he was betrayed": Ibid., 54.

442 "Halt! Stand, or we fire!": Ibid., 80.

442 "Sire," thus confirming: Ibid., 86.

442 "Yes I am your King": Rocheterie, *The Life of Marie Antoinette*, v. 2, 135.

443 "Harness the horses": Lenotre, *The Flight of Marie Antoinette*, 95.

443 "If they had not": Ibid., 141.

443 "who shared his . . . you see": Rocheterie, *The Life of Marie Antoinette*, v. 2, 136.

443 "They will not": Lenotre, *The Flight of Marie Antoinette*, 140.

444 "Evidently we have been": Rocheterie, *The Life of Marie Antoinette*, v. 2, 144.

444 "was as unmoved": Ibid., 145.

444 "All is lost": *Diary and Correspondence of Count Axel Fersen*, 115.

445 "I can tell you": Farr, *Marie-Antoinette and Count Fersen*, 203.

Chapter 21. Terror and Tragedy

446 "Let the sword": Lewes, *The Life of Maximilien Robespierre*, 235.

446n "A club has been formed": Mercy-Argenteau, *Correspondance secrète du comte de Mercy Argenteau*, v. 2, 301.

447 "all that I have": Rocheterie, *The Life of Marie Antoinette*, v. 2, 153.

447 "To refuse would have been": Ibid., 177.

448 "We have been": Campan, *Memoirs of the Private Life of Marie Antoinette*, v. 2, 180.

448 "These people will": Ibid., 160.

448 "All is lost! . . . your sovereign!": Ibid., 162.

449 "Do you intend": Rocheterie, *The Life of Marie Antoinette*, v. 2, 187.

449 "Do not be alarmed": Ibid.

449n "When I am very sad": Ibid., 218.

450 "There is no cause": Ibid., 206.

450 "I found the king and queen": Rocheterie, *The Life of Marie Antoinette*, v. 2, 210.

450n "Went to see *Elle*": Farr, *Marie-Antoinette and Count Fersen,* 219. Fersen, unable to be with Marie Antoinette, did by this time have another mistress, Eleonore Sullivan. He was, after all, a man in his midthirties; he needed companionship. Being publicly associated with another woman was also a useful blind. But his feelings for Eleonore never came close to what he felt for the queen. "It isn't the same love—that delicacy, that solicitude, that tenderness," he wrote to his sister. "Eleonore will not replace *Her* in my heart" (Farr, *Marie-Antoinette and Count Fersen,* 258–59).

451 "The emperor!": Coxe, *History of the House of Austria,* v. 3, 576.

452 "Do not be astonished": Rocheterie, *The Life of Marie Antoinette,* v. 2, 224.

452 "The King fell into": Ibid., 196.

453 "I expect death": Ibid., 229.

453 "Come and see me": Ibid., 230.

454 "The waves": Ibid., 236.

454 "Let me go": Ibid., 242–43.

454 "Messieurs, save the king!": Ibid., 237.

454 "Citizens!": Ibid., 238.

454n "What madness!": Roberts, *Napoleon: A Life,* 39.

455 "Be careful, Monsieur": Rocheterie, *The Life of Marie Antoinette,* v. 2, 240.

455 "Make way...overawed the mob": Ibid., 243–44.

456 "Citizens, you are come": Ibid., 241.

456 "I still exist": Ibid., 246.

456 "You are already...me and mine": Ibid., 249–50.

457 "The city of Paris": Robinson, *Readings in European History,* v. 2, 445.

458 "You can nail me...God forbid!": Rocheterie, *The Life of Marie Antoinette,* v. 2, 273–74.

459 "I felt...pardons you": Campan, *Memoirs of the Private Life of Marie Antoinette,* v. 2, 233.

461 "With the aid": Lewes, *The Life of Maximilien Robespierre,* 128.

461 "At three in the afternoon...abandoned her": *The Life and Letters of Madame Élisabeth de France,* 248–49.

462 "three millions of men": Lewes, *The Life of Maximilien Robespierre,* 190.

463 "of conspiring against liberty": Hardman, *The Life of Louis XVI,* 438.

463 "He wept from grief": Rocheterie, *The Life of Marie Antoinette,* v. 2, 312.

463 "You promise us...so tenderly loved?": Ibid., 313.

464 "I die innocent": Schama, *Citizens,* 669.

464 "I beg my wife": Farr, *Marie-Antoinette and Count Fersen,* 241.

465 "Nothing was able": *The Life and Letters of Madame Élisabeth de France,* 260.

465 "The malcontents show": Rocheterie, *The Life of Marie Antoinette,* v. 2, 311.

465 "They read us": *The Life and Letters of Madame Élisabeth de France,* 266–67.

466 "She stayed there": Ibid., 267.

467 "Nature refuses": Rocheterie, *The Life of Marie Antoinette,* v. 2, 360.

468 "I have to speak to you": Ibid., 369.

Chapter 22. A Death in Vienna

471 "You can never answer": Wolf, *Leopold II und Marie Christine*, 302.

473 "All the news": Ibid., 233.

473*n* "I warn you to beware": Ibid., 212.

473*n* "Count Fersen arrived": Ibid., 260–61.

474 "As to the queen": Ibid., 242.

474 "At one o'clock": *Diary and Correspondence of Count Axel Fersen*, 118.

474 "I have not": Wolf, *Marie Christine*, 106. Translation by Barbara Ann Schmutzler.

474 "He [Fersen] talks about": Wolf, *Leopold II und Marie Christine*, 261.

475 "Charles had a couple...behaves very well": Ibid., 221–29.

475 "Your charming son": Ibid., 290.

475 "I know your goodness": Wolf, *Marie Christine*, v. 2, 188. Translation by Barbara Ann Schmutzler.

476 "He [the elector] always...a second time": Wolf, *Leopold II und Marie Christine*, 288–89.

477 "It dismayed everyone": Ibid., 290.

477 "an intimate of the Council...alarm me": Ibid., 312.

478 "The blow is too terrible": Wolf, *Marie Christine*, v. 2, 127–28. Translation by Barbara Ann Schmutzler.

478 "later in the evening": *Diary and Correspondence of Count Axel Fersen*, 252.

479 "their servants, forty horses": Ibid., 265.

479 "talked to the archduchess...however": Ibid.

480 "inciting the people": Ibid., 253.

480 "Duke Albert has marched": Ibid., 270.

480 "He [the messenger] says": Ibid., 270–71.

480 "as allies and brothers": Vander Linden, *Belgium, The Making of a Nation*, 206.

481 "La Marseillaise": Sloane, "Radical Democracy in France. IV," *Political Science Quarterly* 25, no. 4 (Dec. 1910): 661.

481 "Nothing was seen...bearing the wounded": *Diary and Correspondence of Count Axel Fersen*, 279–81.

482 "A lamentable spectacle...in the streets": Ibid., 282.

482 "You will not doubt...any day now": Wolf, *Marie Christine*, v. 2, 142–43. Translation by Barbara Ann Schmutzler.

483 "Let no foreigner": Vander Linden, *Belgium, The Making of a Nation*, 206.

484 "Though I was prepared...over him": *Diary and Correspondence of Count Axel Fersen*, 284–85.

484 "On the means...not hope": Ibid., 293.

485 "I can think only": Ibid., 300.

485 "Her image, her sufferings...yet more": Farr, *Marie Antoinette and Count Fersen*, 259–60.

485 "Maria Theresa would never": Wolf, *Marie Christine*, v. 2, 148. Translation by Barbara Ann Schmutzler.

486n Napoleon would later boast: Boulger, *The History of Belgium,* v. 1, 415.

487 "She made them take her": *The Life and Letters of Madame Élisabeth de France,* 282.

487 "They had the cruelty...dying of fear": Ibid., 280–87.

490 Michelangelo, Raphael, and Leonardo: Schröder, *The Origins of the Albertina,* 20–21.

490 "My dear, precious husband": Wolf, *Marie Christine,* v. 2, 187–89. Translation by Barbara Ann Schmutzler.

Chapter 23. The Lady, the Lord Admiral, and the Queen

495 the Lord Admiral: Nelson's official title was Admiral, Lord Nelson, but he was also sometimes referred to as Lord Admiral. See Jeaffreson, *Lady Hamilton and Lord Nelson,* v. 2, 20.

495 "I will pursue": Bearne, *A Sister of Marie Antoinette,* 204. In French: Je poursuiverai ma vengeance jusqu'au tombeau.

496 "five hundred thousand": *The Autobiography of Miss Cornelia Knight,* v. 1, 101.

497 "who cherish him": Acton, *The Bourbons of Naples,* 255.

497 "To avoid war": Ibid., 260.

498 "Good God!": Bearne, *A Sister of Marie Antoinette,* 203.

498 "I am so excessively": Ibid., 201.

499 "In the evenings": Jeaffreson, *Lady Hamilton and Lord Nelson,* v. 1, 289.

499 "No person can be so charming": Ibid., 306–7.

499 "Send me some news": Ibid., 312.

499 "The captain I am about": Ibid., 294.

500 "I go nowhere": Acton, *The Bourbons of Naples,* 285.

500n "They all deserved": Jeaffreson, *Lady Hamilton and Lord Nelson,* v. 2, 8.

502 "This is my seal": Abbott, *The History of Napoleon Bonaparte,* v. 1, 69.

504 "Soldiers! You are hungry": Ibid., 82–83.

504 "The Austrians maneuvered": Ibid., 139.

504 "People of Italy!": Ibid., 89.

506 "If the court of Naples": Adlow, *Napoleon in Italy,* 140–41.

506 "loves England": Jeaffreson, *Lady Hamilton and Lord Nelson,* v. 1, 312.

506 "I hope we are in good": Jeaffreson, *Lady Hamilton and Lord Nelson,* v. 2, 12.

507 "It would be vain": *The Autobiography of Miss Cornelia Knight,* v. 1, 106.

507 "off Malta": Jeaffreson, *Lady Hamilton and Lord Nelson,* v. 2, 14.

507 "consequently he would be": Ibid., 17.

508 "I went to the queen": Ibid., 17–18.

509 "I pray'd and implor'd...than that of the king": Ibid., 18.

509 "My dear friends": Ibid., 21.

509 "Our conversation by day": *The Autobiography of Miss Cornelia Knight,* v. 1, 107.

510 "My Dear Miledy...your attached friend—Charlotte": Jeaffreson, *The Queen of Naples and Lord Nelson,* v. 2, 6.

510 "Never, perhaps": Ibid., 111.

510   "My Dear Miledy, what happiness": Jeaffreson, *The Queen of Naples and Lord Nelson*, v. 2, 7.

510   "How shall I describe": Sichel, *Emma Lady Hamilton*, 487.

510   "The shore was lined": *The Autobiography of Miss Cornelia Knight*, v. 1, 114–15.

510*n* "Look at these": Ibid., 119.

511   "Oh, God! Is it possible?": Jeaffreson, *The Queen of Naples and Lord Nelson*, v. 2, 25.

511   "I hope some day": Ibid., 29.

511   "Nothing could be": *The Autobiography of Miss Cornelia Knight*, v. 1, 119.

511   "The French consul": Ibid., 113.

512   "My dear Madam... *are the safest*": Sichel, *Emma Lady Hamilton*, 493–94.

514   "The King is to go": Ibid., 237.

514   "that he only regretted": *The Autobiography of Miss Cornelia Knight*, v. 1, 123.

514*n* "This fellow does not": Jeaffreson, *The Queen of Naples and Lord Nelson*, v. 2, 34.

515   "Leave then your too modest": Ibid., 21.

516   "I could not answer you": Ibid., 24–25.

516   "the most beautiful": Gutteridge, *Nelson and the Neapolitan Jacobins*, xxvi.

516   "Is not this a dream?": Ibid.

516   "Like a dark cloud": *The Autobiography of Miss Cornelia Knight*, v. 1, 124.

516   "Stupefied by this stroke": Sichel, *Emma Lady Hamilton*, 244.

516   "The populace had become": *The Autobiography of Miss Cornelia Knight*, v. 1, 126.

517   "I venture to send you": Jeaffreson, *Lady Hamilton and Lord Nelson*, v. 2, 39.

517   "I will send you this evening": Ibid., 41.

517   "a secret passage": Sichel, *Emma Lady Hamilton*, 253.

518   "My heart bled for him": Acton, *The Bourbons of Naples*, 330.

518   "Lord Nelson had never seen... away the masts": Sichel, *Emma Lady Hamilton*, 257.

518   "Madame, madame": Jeaffreson, *Lady Hamilton and Lord Nelson*, v. 2, 43.

519   "my favorite... royal children": Sichel, *Emma Lady Hamilton*, 257.

519   "funeral was the": *The Autobiography of Miss Cornelia Knight*, v. 1, 133.

519   "God help us": Sichel, *Emma Lady Hamilton*, 251.

Chapter 24. The Corsican and the Queen

520   "Tell your Queen": Jeaffreson, *The Queen of Naples and Lord Nelson*, v. 2, 134.

520   "We were, in all": *The Autobiography of Miss Cornelia Knight*, v. 1, 133.

520   "Accustomed as I had been": Ibid., 132.

521   "I am neither": Jeaffreson, *The Queen of Naples and Lord Nelson*, v. 2, 52.

521   "I know I shall": Ibid., 49.

522   "Your miracle": Sichel, *Emma Lady Hamilton*, 267.

522   "Army of the Faithful": Gutteridge, *Nelson and the Neapolitan Jacobins*, xxxii.

524   "I shall remain behind": Ibid., 295–96.

524   "This from my friend": Ibid., 297.

524   "There must be": Ibid., lxxxi.

524   "without any formality": Ibid., lxxx.

525   "The king…must not": Ibid., lxxxi.

525   "I hope that": Jeaffreson, *The Queen of Naples and Lord Nelson,* v. 2, 64.

525   "the Chastisement": Ibid., 86.

525   "The queen, who has been": *The Autobiography of Miss Cornelia Knight,* v. 1, 140.

525   "most anxious": Gutteridge, *Nelson and the Neapolitan Jacobins,* 299.

528   "I must say": *The Autobiography of Miss Cornelia Knight,* v. 1, 139.

528   "Tell the Chevalier": Jeaffreson, *The Queen of Naples and Lord Nelson,* v. 2, 105.

528   "I am extremely…should visit her": Ibid., 107–8.

529   "her Majesty exclaimed": *The Autobiography of Miss Cornelia Knight,* v. 1, 148.

529   "Our situation soon": Ibid., 149.

529   "My dismay was now": Ibid., 150.

530   "Great curiosity": Ibid., 151–52.

530   "My dear Lady": Sichel, *Emma Lady Hamilton,* 332.

531   "I believe that Bonaparte": Acton, *The Bourbons of Naples,* 470.

531   "baneful influence": Jeaffreson, *The Queen of Naples and Lord Nelson,* v. 2, 118.

532   "That is the point": Johnston, *The Napoleonic Empire in Southern Italy,* v. 1, 58.

533   "The arrival of the Queen": Auriol, *La France: l'Angleterre et Naples de 1803 à 1806,* v. 1, 46.

533   "The King lives in": Ibid., 49.

534   "We are on the eve": Jeaffreson, *The Queen of Naples and Lord Nelson,* v. 2, 128.

534   "It was not worth…as Emperor!": Acton, *The Bourbons of Naples,* 509–10.

535   "It is part": Jeaffreson, *The Queen of Naples and Lord Nelson,* v. 2, 129.

535   "You render us": Ibid., 127.

535   "My wife, son": Ibid., 135.

535   "Let your Majesty": Jeaffreson, *The Queen of Naples and Lord Nelson,* v. 2, 133.

535n   "Against whom?": Acton, *The Bourbons of Naples,* 541.

536   "I believe they": Clarke, *The Life and Services of Horatio Viscount Nelson,* v. 3, 156–57.

536   "God gave us": Ibid., 145.

536   "I will finally": Roberts, *Napoleon: A Life,* 394.

537   "The House of Naples": Jeaffreson, *The Queen of Naples and Lord Nelson,* v. 2, 136.

537   "I would rather": Johnston, *The Napoleonic Empire in Southern Italy,* v. 1, 118.

537   "that ferocious beast": Roberts, *Napoleon: A Life,* 394.

537 "It is the intention": Johnston, *The Napoleonic Empire in Southern Italy,* v. 1, 118.

538*n* "It pains me": Ibid., 203.

540 "she was enabled": Saint-Amand, *The Memoirs of the Empress Marie Louise,* 248.

540 "This was all": Maierhofer, "Maria Carolina, Queen of Naples: The 'Devil's Grandmother' Fights Napoleon," in *Women Against Napoleon,* 58.

540 "grandmamma, the Queen": Bearne, *A Sister of Marie Antoinette,* 409.

541 "I ought to detest you": Dyson, *The Life of Marie Amélie,* 70.

541 "fits of passion": Jeaffreson, *The Queen of Naples and Lord Nelson,* v. 2, 183.

542 "I think it is absolutely": Johnston, *The Napoleonic Empire in Southern Italy,* v. 1, 238.

542 "The poor Sicilians": Jeaffreson, *The Queen of Naples and Lord Nelson,* v. 2, 175.

542 "boorish corporal": Johnston, *The Napoleonic Empire in Southern Italy,* v. 1, 262.

542 "Was it for this": Acton, *The Bourbons of Naples,* 630.

542 "I cannot believe": Ibid., 618.

543 "I have been deprived": Jeaffreson, *The Queen of Naples and Lord Nelson,* v. 2, 246.

543 "The daughter of": Ibid., 245.

Epilogue

546 "How happy I am": Acton, *The Bourbons of Naples,* 669.

547 "Perhaps the most": Schröder, *The Origins of the Albertina,* 13.

Selected Bibliography

Acton, Harold. *The Bourbons of Naples (1734–1825)*. London: Prion Books Limited, 1998.

Anonymous. *A Review of the Affairs of the Austrian Netherlands in the Year 1787*. London: J. Murray, 1788.

Auriol, Charles, ed. *La France: l'Angleterre et Naples de 1803 à 1806: Letters de Napoléon et de la reine Marie-Caroline de Naples*. 2 volumes. Paris: Plon-Nourrit et Cie, 1904–1905.

Bain, R. Nisbet. *The Daughter of Peter the Great: A History of Russian Diplomacy and of the Russian Court under the Empress Elizabeth Petrovna, 1741–1762*. Westminster: A. Constable, 1899.

Barthou, Louis. *Mirabeau*. From the French of Louis Barthou. New York: Dodd, Mead & Company, 1913.

Beales, Derek. *Joseph II: Against the World, 1780–1790*. New York: Cambridge University Press, 2009.

———.*Joseph II: In the Shadow of Maria Theresa, 1741–1780*. Cambridge: Cambridge University Press, 1987.

Bearne, Catherine Mary. *A Sister of Marie Antoinette: The Life Story of Maria Carolina, Queen of Naples*. London: Adelphi Terrace, 1907.

Beaumarchais, Pierre-Augustin Caron de. *The Follies of a Day; or the Marriage of Figaro. A Comedy, as It Is Now Performing at the Theatre-Royal, Covent-Garden*. From the French of M. de Beaumarchais by Thomas Holcroft. London: G. G. and J. J. Robinson, 1785.

Blanning, Tim. *Frederick the Great: King of Prussia*. New York: Random House, 2016.

Bonnefons, André. *Marie-Caroline, Reine des Deux-Siciles, 1768–1814: Une ennemie de la révolution et de Napoleon*. Paris: Perrin et Cie, 1905.

Boulger, Demetrius Charles. *The History of Belgium*. 2 volumes. London: Published by the author, 1902–1909.

Bourbon-Parme, Isabelle de. *"Je meurs d'amour pour toi . . ."*: Lettres à l'archiduchesse Marie-Christine, 1760–1763*. Présentées par Élisabeth Badinter. Paris: La Lettre et La Plume, Éditions Tallandier, 2008.

Breakspeare, Eustace John. *Mozart*. London: J. M. Dent & Co., 1902.

Bright, James Franck. *Maria Theresa*. London: Macmillan and Co., Limited, 1897.

Broglie, Archile Charles Leonce Victor, duc de. *Frederick the Great and Maria Theresa from Hitherto Unpublished Documents, 1740–1742.* 2 volumes. Translated from the French by Mrs. Cashel Hoey and Mr. John Lillie. London: Sampson Low, Marston, Searle, & Rivington, 1883.

Browning, Reed. *The War of the Austrian Succession.* New York: St. Martin's Griffin, 1995.

Campan, Jeanne Louise Henriette, First Lady-in-Waiting to the Queen. *Memoirs of the Private Life of Marie Antoinette to Which Are Added Personal Recollections Illustrative of the Reigns of Louis XIV, XV, XVI.* 2 volumes. New York: Brentano's, 1917.

Campbell, Thomas, ed. *Frederick the Great, His Court and Times.* 4 volumes. London: Henry Colburn, 1842–1848.

Carlyle, Thomas. *History of Friedrich II of Prussia, Called Frederick the Great.* 10 volumes. London: Chapman and Hall, ca. 1888.

Casanova, Giacomo. *The Memoirs of Jacques Casanova: Written by Himself Now for the First Time Translated into English by Arthur Machen.* 6 volumes. London: Privately printed, 1894.

Catt, Henri de. *Frederick the Great, the memoirs of his reader, Henri de Catt.* Translated by F. S. Flint, with an introduction by Lord Rosebery. London: Constable and Company, Ltd., 1916.

Clarke, James Stanier, and John McArthur. *The Life and Services of Horatio Viscount Nelson from His Lordship's Manuscripts.* 3 volumes. London: Fisher, Son, & Co., 1840.

Colleta, Pietro. *History of Naples from the Accession of Charles of Bourbon to the Death of Ferdinand I.* 2 volumes. Edinburgh: Edmonston and Douglas, 1860.

Coxe, William. *History of the House of Austria.* 4 volumes. London: H. G. Bohn, 1864–1872.

———. *Memoirs of the Administration of the Right Honourable Henry Pelham, Collected from the Family Papers and Other Authentic Documents.* 2 volumes. London: Longman, Rees, Orme, Brown, and Green, 1829.

———. *Memoirs of Horatio, Lord Walpole, Selected from His Correspondence and Papers, and Connected with the History of the Times, from 1678 to 1757.* 2 volumes. London: Longman, Hurst, Rees and Orme, 1808.

———. *Memoirs of the Life and Administration of Sir Robert Walpole, Earl of Orford.* 3 volumes. London: Longman, Hurst, Rees, Orme & Brown, 1798.

Crankshaw, Edward. *Maria Theresa.* New York: Viking Press, 1969.

Craven, Elizabeth, Baroness. *Memoirs of the Margravine of Anspach, Written by Herself.* 2 volumes. London: Henry Colburn, 1826.

Cust, Edward, Sir. *Annals of the Wars of the Eighteenth Century, Compiled from the Most Authentic Histories of the Period.* 5 volumes. London: J. Murray, 1862–1869.

Dover, George Agar-Ellis, 1st baron. *The Life of Frederick the Second, King of Prussia.* New York: J. & J. Harper, 1836.

Du Hausset, N., Mme. *The Private Memoirs of Louis XV, Taken from the Memoirs of Madame du Hausset, Lady's Maid to Madame de Pompadour.* London: Nichols, 1895.

Dyson, C. C. *The Life of Marie Amélie, Last Queen of the French, 1782–1866. With Some Account of the Principal Personages at the Courts of Naples and France in Her Time, and of the Careers of Her Sons and Daughters.* New York: Appleton, 1910.

Élisabeth, Princess of France. *The Life and Letters of Madame Élisabeth de France; Followed by the Journal of the Temple by Cléry, and the Narrative of Marie-Thérèse de France, duchesse d'Angoulême.* Translated by Katharine Prescott Wormeley. Boston: Hardy, Pratt & Co., 1902.

Elizabeth Charlotte, duchess of Orléans. *The Letters of Madame: The Correspondence of Elizabeth-Charlotte of Bavaria, Princess Palatine, Duchess of Orleans, called "Madame" at the Court of King Louis XIV.* 2 volumes. Translated and edited by Gertrude Scott Stevenson. New York: D. Appleton, 1924.

Fairburn, William Armstrong. *Frederick the Great.* New York: The Nation Press, Inc., 1919.

Farr, Evelyn. *Marie-Antoinette and Count Fersen: The Untold Love Story.* London: Peter Owen Publishers, 2013.

Fersen, Axel von. *Diary and Correspondence of Count Axel Fersen, Grand-Marshal of Sweden, Relating to the Court of France.* Translated by Katharine Prescott Wormeley. London: Heinemann, 1902.

Fowler, William M., Jr. *Empires at War: The French and Indian War and the Struggle for North America, 1754–1763.* New York: Walker & Company, 2005.

Frederick II, King of Prussia. *Posthumous Works of Frederic II, King of Prussia.* 13 volumes. Translated by Thomas Holcroft. London: G. G. J. and J. Robinson, 1789.

Funck-Brentano, Frantz. *The Diamond Necklace: Being the True Story of Marie-Antoinette and the Cardinal de Rohan, from the New Documents Recently Discovered in Paris.* Authorized translation by H. Sutherland Edwards. Philadelphia: J. B. Lippincott, 1901.

Gates-Coon, Rebecca. *The Charmed Circle: Joseph II and the "Five Princesses," 1765–1790.* West Lafayette, IN: Purdue University Press, 2015.

Gaulot, Paul. *A Friend of the Queen: (Marie Antoinette, Count Fersen).* Translated by Mrs. Cashel Hoey. London: Heinemann, 1895.

Goethe, Johann Wolfgang von. *The Autobiography of Goethe: Truth and Poetry, from My Own Life.* Translated by John Oxenford. London: Henry G. Bohn, York Street, Covent Garden, 1848.

———. *Goethe's Letters from Switzerland and Travels in Italy from the German by Rev. A. J. W. Morrison.* Boston: S. E. Cassino and Co., 1884.

Goldsmith, Margaret. *Maria Theresa of Austria.* London: Arthur Barker Ltd., 1936.

Gooch, G. P. *Maria Theresa and Other Studies.* London: Longmans, Green and Co., 1951.

Gutteridge, H. C., ed. *Nelson and the Neapolitan Jacobins: Documents Relating to the Suppression of the Jacobin Revolution at Naples, June 1799.* London: Navy Records Society, 1903.

Hardman, John. *The Life of Louis XVI.* New Haven, CT: Yale University Press, 2016.

Hodgetts, E. A. Brayley. *The Life of Catherine the Great of Russia.* New York: Brentano's, 1914.

Ingrao, Charles. *The Habsburg Monarchy 1618–1815.* Cambridge: Cambridge University Press, 1994.

Jeaffreson, John Cordy. *Lady Hamilton and Lord Nelson.* 2 volumes. London: Grolier Society, 1890.

———. *The Queen of Naples and Lord Nelson: An Historical Biography Based on Mss. in the British Museum and on Letters and Other Documents Preserved Amongst the Morrison Mss.* 2 volumes. London: Hurst and Blackett, 1889.

Johnston, R. M. *The Napoleonic Empire in Southern Italy and the Rise of the Secret Societies.* London: Macmillan and Co., Limited, 1904.

Knight, Ellis Cornelia. *The Autobiography of Miss Cornelia Knight, Lady Companion to the Princess Charlotte of Wales, with Extracts from Her Journals and Anecdote Books.* 2 volumes. London: W. H. Allen and Co., 1861.

Koeppe, Wolfram. *Vienna circa 1780: An Imperial Silver Service Rediscovered.* The Metropolitan Museum of Art, New York. New Haven, CT: Yale University Press, 2010.

Lafayette, Marie Joseph Paul Yves Roch Gilbert Du Motier, Marquis de. *Memoirs, Correspondence and Manuscripts of General Lafayette Published by His Family.* London: Saunders, 1837.

Lenotre, G. *The Flight of Marie Antoinette, From the French of G. Lenotre [pseud.] by Mrs. Rodolph Stawell.* London: J. B. Lippincott Company, 1906.

Lewes, George Henry. *The Life of Maximilien Robespierre: With Extracts from His Unpublished Correspondence.* London: Chapman and Hall, 1849.

Lodge, Richard. "The Treaty of Worms." *The English Historical Review* 44, no. 174 (April 1929): 220–55.

Macartney, C. A., ed. *The Habsburg and Hohenzollern Dynasties in the Seventeenth and Eighteenth Centuries.* New York, Evanston, and London: Harper & Row, Publishers, 1970.

Mahan, J. Alexander. *Maria Theresa of Austria.* New York: Thomas Y. Crowell, 1932.

Maierhofer, Waltraud, Gertrud Roesch, and Caroline Bland, eds. *Women Against Napoleon: Historical and Fictional Responses to His Rise and Legacy.* Frankfurt, Germany: Campus Verlag, 2007.

Maria Carolina, Queen of Naples and Sicily. *Correspondance inédite de Marie-Caroline, Reine de Naples et de Sicile, avec le marquis de Gallo (1792–1806).* Publiée par M. le commandant Weil. Paris: Plon-Nourrit, 1911.

Maria Theresa, Empress. *Briefe der Kaiserin Maria Theresia an ihre Kinder und Freunde. Hrsg. Von Alfred Ritter von Arneth,* volume 2. Wien: W. Braumüller, 1881.

————. *Letters of an Empress: A Collection of Intimate Letters from Maria Theresia to Her Children and Friends.* Edited by G. Pusch. Translated by Eileen R. Taylor. London: Massie Publishing Co. Ltd., 1939.

Marie Antoinette, Queen of France. *Lettres de Marie-Antoinette: Recueil des lettres authentiques de la reine.* Publié pour la Société d'histoire Contemporaine par Maxime de La Rocheterie & le Marquis de Beaucourt. 2 volumes. Paris: A. Picard et fils, 1895–1896.

Marie Christine, Princesse Royale de Hongrie and de Bohême, &c., and Albert Casimir, Prince Royal de Pologne and de Lithuanie, &c. *Lieuténants, Gouverneurs & Capitaines-Généraux des Pays-Bas, &c.* Brussels, Belgium: Chez H. F. t'Serstevens Imprimeur des Seigneurs Etats de Brabant, 1787.

McKay, Derek. *Prince Eugene of Savoy.* London: Thames and Hudson, 1977.

Mercy-Argenteau, comte de. *Correspondance secrète du comte de Mercy Argenteau avec l'empereur Joseph II et le prince de Kaunitz.* 2 volumes. Edited by Alfred Arneth. Paris: Imprimerie Nationale, 1889–1891.

Miller, Anna Riggs, Lady. *Letters from Italy: Describing the Manners, Customs, Antiquities, Paintings, &c. of That Country, in the Years MDCCLXX and MDCCLXXI, to a Friend Residing in France. By an English Woman.* 2 volumes. London: Printed for Edward and Charles Dilly, 1777.

Moffat, Mary Maxwell. *Maria Theresa.* New York: E. P. Dutton and Company, 1911.

Montagu, Mary Wortley, Lady. *The Best Letters of Lady Mary Wortley Montagu.* Edited with a dedicatory letter to Lady Montagu by Octave Thanet. Chicago: McClurg, 1909.

Morley, John. *Diderot and the Encyclopædists,* volume 1. London and New York: Macmillan, 1891.

Morris, Constance Lily. *Maria Theresa: The Last Conservative.* London: Eyre & Spottiswoode, 1938.

Padover, Saul Kussiel. *The Life and Death of Louis XVI.* New York: D. Appleton-Century Company, Incorporated, 1939.

Perkins, James Breck. *France under Louis XV.* 2 volumes. Boston: Houghton, Mifflin, and Company, 1897.

Pick, Robert. *Empress Maria Theresa: The Earlier Years, 1717–1757.* New York: Harper & Row, 1966.

Polasky, Janet L. *Revolution in Brussels, 1787–1793.* Hanover, NH, and London: University Press of New England, 1987.

Recca, Cinzia. *The Diary of Queen Maria Carolina of Naples, 1781–1785: New Evidence of Queenship at Court.* New York: Palgrave Macmillan, 2017.

————. "Maria Carolina and Marie Antoinette: Sisters and Queens in the Mirror of Jacobin Public Opinion." *Royal Studies Journal* 1 (2014): 17–36.

Reddaway, William Fiddian. *Frederick the Great and the Rise of Prussia.* New York: G. P. Putnam's Sons, 1911.

Roberts, Andrew. *Napoleon: A Life.* New York: Penguin Books, 2014.

Robinson, J. H. *Readings in European History,* volume 2. Boston: Ginn, 1906.

Rocheterie, Maxime de La. *The Life of Marie Antoinette.* 2 volumes. Translated by Cora Hamilton Bell. New York: Dodd, Mead and Company, 1893.

Sackville, John Frederick, Duke of Dorset. *Despatches from Paris, 1784–1790, Selected and Edited from the Foreign Office Correspondence.* 2 volumes. Selected and edited by Oscar Browning. London: Offices of the Society, 1909–1910.

Saint-Amand, Imbert de. *The Memoirs of the Empress Marie Louise.* London: Remington & Co., 1886.

Schama, Simon. *Citizens: A Chronicle of the French Revolution.* New York: Alfred A. Knopf, 1989.

Schröder, Klaus Albrecht. *The Origins of the Albertina: 100 Masterworks from the Collection.* Vienna: Hatje Cantz, 2014.

Shoberl, Frederic. *Frederick the Great, his court and times,* volume 3. London: H. Colburn, 1843.

Sichel, Walter Sydney. *Emma Lady Hamilton: From New and Original Sources and Documents.* New York: Dodd, Mead and Company, 1907.

Sloane, W. M. "Radical Democracy in France. IV." *Political Science Quarterly* 25, no. 4 (Dec. 1910): 656–72.

Smythe, David Mynders. *Madame de Pompadour: Mistress of France.* New York: W. Funk, 1953.

Smythe, Lillian C. *The Guardian of Marie Antoinette; Letters from the Comte de Mercy-Argenteau, Austrian Ambassador to the Court of Versailles, to Marie Thérèse, Empress of Austria, 1770–1780.* 2 volumes. London: Hutchinson, 1902.

Sorel, Albert. *The Eastern Question in the Eighteenth Century: The Partition of Poland and the Treaty of Kainardji.* Translated by F. C. Bramwell, with a preface by C. R. L. Fletcher. London: Methuen, 1898.

Szabo, Franz A. J. *Kaunitz and Enlightened Absolutism, 1753–1780.* Cambridge: Cambridge University Press, 1994.

———. *The Seven Years War in Europe, 1756–1763.* London and New York: Routledge, 2013.

Tallentyre, S. G. *The Friends of Voltaire.* London: J. Murray, 1906.

Townsend, Pauline D. *Joseph Haydn.* London: S. Low, Marston, Searle & Rivington, 1884.

Turquan, Joseph, and Jules d'Auriac. *A Great Adventuress: Lady Hamilton and the Revolution in Naples (1753–1815).* Translated by Lilian Wiggins. London: H. Jenkins Ltd., 1914.

Vander Linden, H. *Belgium, The Making of a Nation.* Translated by Sybil Jane. Oxford: The Clarendon Press, 1920.

Vehse, Carl Eduard. *Memoirs of the Court and Aristocracy of Austria.* 2 volumes. Philadelphia: G. Barrie, 1900.

Vigée Lebrun, Madame. *Memoirs of Madame Vigée Lebrun.* Translated by Lionel Strachey. New York: Doubleday, Page & Company, 1903.

Vizetelly, Ernest Alfred. *The True Story of Alsace-Lorraine.* New York: Frederick A. Stokes Company, 1918.

Voltaire. *Letters on England.* London: Cassell, 1894.

———. *The Philosophical Dictionary: A New and Correct Edition, with Notes, Containing a Refutation of Such Passages as Are Any Way Exceptionable in Regard to Religion.* London: Wynne and Scholey, 45, and James Wallis, 46, Paternoster Row, 1802.

———. *Sequel of the Age of Louis XIV: To Which Is Added, a Summary of the Age of Louis XV. Translated from the last Geneva edition of M. de Voltaire, with Notes, Critical and Explanatory, by R. Griffith, Esq.,* volume 3. London: Fielding and Walker, Pasternoster Row, 1781.

———. *Voltaire's Philosophical Dictionary, Unabridged and Unexpurgated, with a Special Introduction by William F. Fleming.* 10 volumes. Translated by William F. Fleming. Paris: E. R. DuMont, 1901.

Vovk, Justin C. *In Destiny's Hands: Five Tragic Rulers, Children of Maria Theresa.* New York and Bloomington, IN: iUniverse, Inc., 2010.

Weber, Joseph. *Memoirs of Maria Antoinetta, Archduchess of Austria, Queen of France and Navarre: Including Several Important Periods of the French Revolution, from Its Origin to the 16th of October, 1793, the Day of Her Majesty's Martyrdom, with a Narrative of the Trial and Martyrdom of Madame Elizabeth, the Poisoning of Louis XVII in the Temple, the Liberation of Madame Royale, Daughter of Louis XVI, and Various Subsequent Events.* 3 volumes. Translated by R. C. Dallas, R. May, and Mrs. Ievers. London: Printed by C. Rickaby and sold by the author, 1805–1812.

Wilhelmina, Margravine of Baireuth. *Memoirs of Frederica Sophia Wilhelmina, Princess Royal of Prussia, Margravine of Baireuth, Sister of Frederick the Great.* With an Essay by William D. Howells. 2 volumes. Boston: James R. Osgood and Company, 1877.

Williams, H. Noel. *Madame de Pompadour.* New York: Scribner's, 1902.

Williams, Kate. *England's Mistress: The Infamous Life of Emma Hamilton.* New York: Ballantine Books, 2006.

Wolf, Adam. *Leopold II und Marie Christine: Ihr Briefwechsel (1781–1792).* Wien: C. Gerold's Sohn, 1867.

———. *Marie Christine, Erzherzogin von Oesterreich.* Wien: C. Gerold's Sohn, 1863.

Wraxall, Nathaniel William, Sir. *Historical Memoirs of My Own Time.* 2 volumes. London: T. Cadell and W. Davies, 1815.

———. *Memoirs of the Courts of Berlin, Dresden, Warsaw, and Vienna, in the Years 1777, 1778, and 1779.* 2 volumes. London: Printed by A. Strahan, for T. Cadell Jun. and W. Davies, 1800.

Younghusband, Helen Augusta Magniac, Lady. *Marie-Antoinette, Her Early Youth (1770–1774).* London: Macmillan, 1912.

Illustration Credits

299 Emma Hamilton in Mynell, Mrs. Esther Hallam (Moorhouse). *Nelson's Lady Hamilton, with Fifty-one Portraits*. London: Methuen & Co., 1911, 24.

321 Marie Antoinette as a young queen in Vuaflart and Bourin, *Les Portraits de Marie-Antoinette*, v. 2, 129.

369 Storming the Bastille in Abbott, John S. C. *The French Revolution of 1789, as Viewed in the Light of Republican Institutions,* with numerous engravings, v. 1. New York: Harper & Row, 1887, 274.

371 Maria Christina by Martin van Meytens circa 1765, Schönbrunn Palace, public domain, Alamy.

397 Maria Carolina in Bearne, *A Sister of Marie Antoinette,* 264.

413 Marie Antoinette and her children in Vigée-Lebrun, Louise-Elisabeth. *Vigée Le Brun: huit reproductions facsimile en couleurs.* Paris: P. Lafitte et cie, 1913, 58.

469 Victorious Archduke Charles of Austria during the Battle of Aspern-Essling by Johann Peter Krafft, circa 1809, Heeresgeschichtliches Museum, public domain, Bridgeman Images.

488 Louis XVII in Bearne, *A Sister of Marie Antoinette,* 226.

491 Tomb of Maria Christina carved by Antonio Canova in the Church of the Augustinian Friars, public domain, Alamy.

493 Napoleon in Hassall, Arthur. *The Life of Napoleon with Twenty-nine Illustrations.* Boston: Little, Brown and Company, 1911, 72.

Insert p. 1 (top): Maria Theresa by Martin van Meytens, circa 1745, National Gallery of Slovenia, Ljubljana, public domain, Alamy.

Insert p. 1 (middle): Francis of Lorraine as Holy Roman Emperor by Martin van Meytens, 1745, Kunsthistorisches Museum, public domain, Alamy.

Insert p. 1 (bottom): Frederick the Great by Johann Georg Ziesenis, 1763, public domain, Alamy.

Insert p. 2 (top): Maria Theresa as Queen of Hungary by unknown artist, circa 1750, public domain, Alamy.

Insert p. 2 (bottom): Ladies' Carousel in the Winter Riding School of Vienna to celebrate the defeat of the French army at Prague by Martin van Meytens, 1743, Schönbrunn Palace, public domain, Bridgeman Images.

Insert p. 3: The Imperial Family by Martin van Meytens, 1754, Schönbrunn Palace, public domain, Alamy.

Insert p. 4 (top): Joseph and Leopold by Pompeo Batoni, 1769, Kunsthistorisches Museum, public domain, Alamy.

Insert p. 4 (bottom): Self-portrait by Maria Christina, 1765, Schönbrunn Palace, public domain, Alamy.

Insert p. 5 (top): Albert, duke of Teschen, by unknown artist, circa 1760, public domain, Alamy.

Insert p. 5 (middle): Isabella of Parma by Jean-Marc Nattier, 1758, Kunsthistorisches Museum, public domain, Alamy.

Insert p. 5 (bottom): The Imperial Family Celebrating Saint Nicholas by Maria Christina, 1762, Schönbrunn Palace, public domain, Bridgeman Images.

Insert p. 6 (top): Maria Carolina by Élisabeth Vigée Le Brun, 1791, Condé Museum, public domain, Alamy.

Insert p. 6 (middle): Ferdinand IV, king of Naples, by Anton Raphael Mengs, circa 1772–1773, Palace of Madrid, public domain, Alamy.

Insert p. 6 (bottom): The Royal Family of Naples, by Angelica Kauffman, 1783, National Museum of Capodimonte, public domain, Alamy.

Insert p. 7 (top): Sir William Hamilton by David Allan, 1775, National Portrait Gallery, public domain, Alamy.

Insert p. 7 (middle): Admiral Nelson by John Hoppner, National Museum of the Royal Navy, public domain, Alamy.

Insert p. 7 (bottom): Lady Emma Hamilton as Circe by George Romney, circa 1782, Tate Britain, public domain, Alamy.

Insert p. 8 (top): Marie Antoinette by Élisabeth Vigée Le Brun, 1783, public domain, Alamy.

Insert p. 8 (middle): Louis XVI by Antoine-François Callet, circa 1779, Palace of Versailles, public domain, Alamy.

Insert p. 8 (bottom): Count Axel Fersen by Carl Frederik von Breda, circa 1800, Löfstad Castle, Sweden, public domain, Alamy.

Index

Note: Italic page numbers refer to illustrations.

About the Author

❦

NANCY GOLDSTONE is the author of six previous books, including *Daughters of the Winter Queen: Four Remarkable Sisters, the Crown of Bohemia, and the Enduring Legacy of Mary, Queen of Scots; The Rival Queens: Catherine de' Medici, Her Daughter Marguerite de Valois, and the Betrayal That Ignited a Kingdom; The Maid and the Queen: The Secret History of Joan of Arc; Four Queens: The Provençal Sisters Who Ruled Europe;* and *The Lady Queen: The Notorious Reign of Joanna I, Queen of Naples, Jerusalem, and Sicily.* She has also coauthored five books with her husband, Lawrence Goldstone. She lives in Del Mar, California.